BRETT C. MILLIER

Elizabeth Bishop

Life and the Memory of It

UNIVERSITY OF CALIFORNIA PRESS   BERKELEY   LOS ANGELES OXFORD

Parts of this book, in other versions,
originally appeared in the *Kenyon Review, Verse,*
and the *New England Review.*

University of California Press
Berkeley and Los Angeles, California

University of California Press, Ltd.
Oxford, England

Library of Congress Cataloging-in-Publication Data

Millier, Brett Candlish
    Elizabeth Bishop : life and the memory of it / Brett C.
Millier.
        p.   cm.
    Includes bibliographical references (p.   ) and index.
    ISBN 0-520-07978-7 (acid-free paper)
    1. Bishop, Elizabeth, 1911–1979.   2. Poets, American—20th
century—Biography.   I. Title.
    PS3503.I785Z78   1993
    811'.54—dc20
    [B]   92-8548
                                                            CIP

Printed in the United States of America
9 8 7 6 5 4 3 2 1

The paper used in the publication meets the
minimum requirements of American National
Standard for Information Sciences—Permanence
of Paper for Printed Library Materials, ANSI
Z39.48-1984. ∞

The publisher gratefully acknowledges the
contribution provided by the General Endowment
Fund of the Associates of the University of California
Press.

in memoriam

JUDSON BOYCE ALLEN

"in a universe incommensurate with this one"

CONTENTS

PREFACE

This book is technically a critical biography, which means in the
trade of literary criticism that it attempts to hold in focus two tasks:
telling the story of a poet's life and explaining and evaluating the
poems she wrote. I defined my task somewhat differently: to explain
as best I could, using the evidence I had, how Elizabeth Bishop's
poems got written and why they turned out the way they did. I did
not meet her; but from my first contact with her work in the fall of
1979, I knew that the deceptively smooth surface of these brilliantly
crafted poems would, with illumination from a few biographical
details, yield breathtaking human wisdom. They have not disappointed me, and they have not stopped being touchstones of wisdom. I am not alone is this regard; Elizabeth Bishop now receives
the critical attention due a major poet; that is, a poet who speaks
to us eloquently of deep and common human truths.

She was born in 1911 in Massachusetts and died there in 1979.
These dates and places conceal her existence as a chronically displaced person, always just removed from the wholeness, meaning,
comfort, and security that we all seek in our lives. It pains me to
remember Charles Tomlinson's remark, tossed off in an old review:
"The fact of the matter is, Miss Bishop travels because she likes it,

not because she is homeless." For though she was an intrepid, sensitive, and successful traveler, she would rather have stayed at home, "wherever that may be."

In its pattern of losses, disappointments, and elusive moments of happiness, Bishop's life resembled those of a great many other artists—in order to write, it seems, one must lose. Her reaction to those losses, her self-destructive alcoholism, we also know in many others of her generation: Robert Lowell, Theodore Roethke, John Berryman, and Louise Bogan among them. A poem may approach perfection, the critic Lawrence Lipking has written, but a life may not. Even more than with these other poets, Bishop's precocious familiarity with loss determined the way she saw her world. Mutability, deceptive surfaces, eerie absences, a wish to escape, an unwillingness to take even her own point of view for granted—these are her characteristic themes. Her habitual skepticism kept her from taking comfort in organized religion or in a systematic personal philosophy; she lived, as the man to whom this book is dedicated once said, by reinventing the wheel every day.

But the story of her life, as far as I may know it and tell it, is finally, not a story of failure and disappointment, but of survival and even triumph. Her whole life demonstrates that task, taken up by so many American poets in the twentieth century, of trying to discover how to get along spiritually and morally in a world where everything seems compromised. "The act," Wallace Stevens said, "of finding / What will suffice." Figuring out, in Robert Frost's wonderful line, "what to make of a diminished thing." Or as Bishop herself expressed the same idea, how to make the most of "the little that we get for free, / the little of our earthly trust. Not much." For all these poets, and for Elizabeth Bishop especially, the most we can make of life is poetry.

. . .

SOME NOTES ABOUT FORM

I have called Elizabeth Bishop both "Elizabeth" and "Bishop" in this book; there is a pattern to these designations. "Elizabeth" lived the life and wrote the poems; the work and the reputation, in the judgment of the world, belong to "Bishop." I have considered the particular risks involved in calling a female artist by her first name; I think it is wrong to do so in writing reviews and criticism. But in *this* biography, Bishop became Elizabeth, just as, for example, to Humphrey Carpenter in *A Serious Character,* Pound became Ezra.

I have tried as far as possible to reproduce Bishop's letters, drafts, and journal entries exactly as she left them. Misleading or confusing typographical or spelling errors (on her part) I have corrected in brackets, [ ]. She was fond of ellipses and dashes as forms of punctuation in her writing, both formal and informal. Her ellipses are indicated unspaced in this text (...); mine are spaced (. . .). Bishop's dashes are typically single (–) and are used to represent a variety of conventional marks of punctuation, much like those of Emily Dickinson.

With one exception, all of Elizabeth Bishop's unpublished poems and prose (excluding much correspondence) and her journals, notebooks, and diaries are in the Elizabeth Bishop Papers at the Vassar College Library, under the care of curator Nancy McKechnie. Where no repository is indicated, the material is from Vassar. All other sources are noted in the endnotes.

ACKNOWLEDGMENTS

One of the best things about writing a biography of a contemporary figure is that the process is cooperative, collaborative, even sociable. And when that figure is as charismatic and beloved as Elizabeth Bishop, it is even more so. A great many people helped me with this book, beginning with teachers, then foundations and grant givers, then students and colleagues, then curators and librarians, and, finally, Elizabeth Bishop's many friends, acquaintances, and admirers.

There have been teachers all along. Al Shoaf and the late Judson Allen, to whom this book is dedicated, showed me why and how to be a scholar. Albert Gelpi, Diane Wood Middlebrook, and W. S. DiPiero, my dissertation committee at Stanford, still influence my life and work. Carl Djerassi and David Long were my teachers in a different sense; their confidence in my abilities still astonishes me.

My dissertation on Bishop was supported by the Whiting Foundation, and I owe this book, in a large sense, to a wonderful year (1989–1990) as an Andrew W. Mellon Faculty Fellow in the Humanities at Harvard University. My colleagues in that program—Joseph Allen and Diane Dugaw, in particular—were inexpressibly helpful to me. Middlebury College has supported my work in every way, both by granting me leave and by giving me money under the auspices of the Faculty Professional Development Fund.

My colleagues in the Department of American Literature and Civilization here, especially Stephen Donadio and John McWilliams, contributed critical advice and encouragement, and Marsha DeBonis rescued me more than once. Middlebury has also blessed me with marvelous students: Nancy Walker and Jonathan Selwood, who served as research assistants at various stages of this project; Amy Drigotas and Katherine Stebbins, who taught me about Elizabeth Bishop as I tried to teach them about her; and my Alumni College class in 1991, especially Peg and Avery Post. My students in FS #0031 at Harvard in the fall of 1989—Steven Burt, Cary Berkeley, and Davis McCombs, in particular—significantly sharpened my thinking about Bishop, about poetry in general, and about what teaching it means.

Libraries have preserved the tremendous archives of Bishop's papers; without librarians, they would be lost to us anyway. Lisa Browar (now at the New York Public Library), Nancy McKechnie, and Melissa O'Donnell at the Vassar College Library; Kevin Ray at the Washington University Library; Timothy Murray at the University of Delaware Library; and others at Harvard's Houghton Library have been steadily helping me write this book since the fall of 1984.

To Alice Methfessel, executor of Bishop's literary estate, I owe the privilege of writing this book at all, and from her I have received the most generous encouragement and support. Lloyd Schwartz has been heroic in his devotion to the project. They are two among many of Elizabeth Bishop's close friends who have shared some of that friendship with me: Rhoda Wheeler Sheehan, Ilse Barker, Elizabeth Hardwick, and Dana Gioia, especially, as well as Frank Bidart, Carley Dawson, Barbara Chesney Kennedy, Jane Shore, Dorothee Bowie, Linda Nemer, Ashley Brown, John Malcolm Brinnin, James Merrill, Bill Alfred, Mark Strand, Cass Humble, Helen Vendler,

Octavio and Marie Jo Paz, Joaquim-Francisco Coelho, and Lilli Correia de Araújo.

Many others have been willing to talk with me about Bishop or to share information in other ways: Chester Page, who showed me Louise Crane's letters to her mother from 1937 to 1940; Frank Paddock and Elizabeth Helfman, who knew about Pittsfield, Massachusetts, 1930–1936; Phyllis Sutherland, Elizabeth's cousin in Tatamagouche, Nova Scotia, who sorted out the family names for me; David Fassler and Anna Holmboe, who helped me think more clearly about her childhood traumas; "Suzanne Bowen"; Mary Stearns Morse; and David Perkins. When I was following Bishop around Brazil, Anna Maria Parsons, Zuleika Torrealba, and Regina Prycybzian were savvy, tolerant, and generous guides.

Jim Clark and Eileen McWilliam at the University of California Press believed in this book even before I did and have been shepherding it ever since. I am grateful to them both for that belief and guidance. The errors in the book are, as they say, mine. Without Ann Cooper's help at the very end, there would have been more of them.

My mother, Elizabeth Candlish, is the spirit behind this book; and Karl, Jane, and David Lindholm both let me and helped me write it. More important, they have taught me what it means.

Thank you, and Goddess bless you.

One

Not until 1952, when she set up a stable and happy life in the household of Lota de Macedo Soares, could Elizabeth Bishop take objective account and make direct artistic use of her difficult childhood. During this time, she became deeply interested in her family's circumstances in her early years, and she wrote anxiously to her aunt and cousin asking for artifacts, family treasures, firsthand historical accounts of life in Nova Scotia in the late-nineteenth and early-twentieth centuries. Elizabeth dreamed aloud in letters of buying a house in Nova Scotia, an authentic old house "exactly like my grandmother's."[1] The accounts of her childhood that poured out of her in prose, poetry, and letters in this the only extended period of security in her adult life contrast with her earlier attempts at an autobiographical novel. They explore in frank first-person flashbacks how it felt to be a child in those circumstances, fatherless and essentially motherless, among people two generations removed, conversation and events circling ominously around unspoken tragedy concerning her.

Hard facts about Elizabeth Bishop's childhood, as about anyone's, are few. And yet, few writers have been as consistent and complete in writing about childhood. Bishop claimed a very literal sort of accuracy as her highest poetic value, and she is rarely caught in an error or a contradiction. Her own accounts, in poetry and prose both published and unpublished, are the main source of information about her earliest years.

Elizabeth Bishop was born the only child of William T. Bishop and Gertrude May Boomer Bishop on February 8, 1911, in Worcester, Massachusetts. William Bishop was born in 1872, the eldest of eight children, only four of whom survived to adulthood. His father, John W. Bishop, was a native of White Sands, Prince Edward Island, and his mother, Sarah Anne Foster Bishop, was born in Massachusetts. William at the time of his marriage was thirty-six years old. "One of the most capable estimators in the structural world," he was vice-president of his father's highly successful contracting firm, the J. W. Bishop Company, builders of such noted Boston landmarks as the Public Library, the Museum of Fine Arts, and the old Charlestown jail. Gertrude Boomer was born the second of five children of William Brown Boomer (the family name was variously spelled Boomer or Bulmer, with the *l* silent) and Elizabeth Hutchinson Boomer, of the British Hutchinson sailing family. Elizabeth liked to point out that her great-grandfather Hutchinson had been lost at sea off Cape Sable, and she once visited this "graveyard of the Atlantic," either to fulfill her destiny by drowning, she said, or to write about the place. The piece was never finished, but Elizabeth saw her temperamental origins in these adventurous ancestors: "That line of my family seems to have been fond of wandering like myself—two, perhaps three, of the sea-captain's sons, my great uncles, were Baptist missionaries in India."[2] She was three-quarters Canadian and one-quarter New Englander and claimed to have had ancestors on both sides of the Revolutionary War. The Boomers were New York State Tories given land grants in Nova Scotia by George III.

William Bishop and Gertrude Boomer met in 1907 and were married at New York's Grace Church in June of the following year. They honeymooned in Jamaica and sailed to Panama before returning to Massachusetts to set up house at 875 Main Street in Worcester. Elizabeth spent the earliest part of her life in wealthy circumstances in this house. Her father was a frank and cheerful man who wrote to the Boomers four days after Elizabeth's birth that her mother "has more milk than she knows what to do with, so we shall make butter probably. We started to have twins and when we changed our minds forgot to cut off half the milk supply."[3] His pleasure in his daughter was sadly brief; he died of Bright's disease on October 13, 1911, when Elizabeth was eight months old. He had been ill, off and on, for six years. A *Worcester Magazine* obituary described him respectfully as a "well-read" and "deep student," and "a self contained man" and lamented that "his love of home and quiet environment kept him from becoming very well known socially."[4]

Gertrude Bishop was a complex and intelligent young woman and a talented ice skater, but she was deeply disoriented by her husband's death. For the next five years, she was in and out of mental hospitals and rest homes and moved between Boston, Worcester, and her hometown of Great Village, Nova Scotia. Elizabeth described this from her childhood point of view in her autobiographical short story "In the Village": "First, she had come home, with her child. Then she had gone away again, alone, and left the child. Then she had come home. Then she had gone away again, with her sister; and now she was home again."[5]

Elizabeth left published accounts of only two memories of this period, and the first seems a condensed version of any number of disappointing or frightening episodes. In a 1952 review of Wallace Fowlie's autobiography, *Pantomime: A Journal of Rehearsals,* she criticized the unrelieved cheerfulness of Fowlie's treatment of Boston places and events she had experienced herself at about the same time. She wrote, "My own first ride on a swan boat occurred at the age of three and is chiefly memorable for the fact that one of the live swans paddling around us bit my mother's finger when she offered it a peanut. I remember the hole in the black kid glove and a drop of blood."[6] As in a Bishop poem, the unbelabored assumptions behind the detail are what make the passage moving. The glove is black because her mother still wears mourning three years after her husband's death. There is an implicit contrast between the two kinds of paddling swans: "live" and artificial. The simple interaction between mother and daughter is fragile, unexpectedly dangerous, easily intruded upon.

In the second account, the elegy "First Death in Nova Scotia," Elizabeth is given a lily of the valley by her mother to place in a dead cousin's hand. The death of little Arthur (whom she was later surprised to discover had actually been named "Frank") is confused in the child's mind with a number of Canadian national symbols: the red and white of Arthur's casket invites the confusion, for those are the colors of the royal family's velvet and ermine costumes, the Canadian flag, and the two dead creatures in the poem—the shot loon and little Arthur himself. The poem conveys child-consciousness through intense identification of memory and desire with objects—the loon's red-glass eyes, "much to be desired"; a lily of the valley from her mother's hand; the "frosted cake" of Arthur's coffin; the stuffed loon's "caressable" white breast. The confusion of images of things dead and far away speaks to the child's precocious familiarity with loss, and the poem's title not only suggests the first death among pioneers in a new country but also predicts a series of losses, ordered in memory by the years between the event and the poem.

Among Elizabeth's papers are several unfinished literary accounts of her brief time with her mother. One is a poem entitled "A Drunkard," apparently begun in 1959 or 1960 and worked on over ten years, in which she remembered being with her mother at a Bishop family summer home in Marblehead, Massachusetts, in the summer of 1914 at the time of the great Salem fire. The poem attaches the memory of the fire to Elizabeth's later alcoholism and is equally important as a tiny summary of the two poles of Elizabeth's mind, even at the age of three. On the one hand, she is amazed, not afraid, of the fire as she stands in her crib watching the red light play on the walls of her room. Her memory of the fire is a compendium of vivid details:

> People were playing hoses on the roofs
>   of the summer cottages in Marblehead . . .
> the red sky was filled with flying moats,
> cinders and coals, and bigger things, scorched black
>   burnt
> The water glowed like fire, too, but flat . . .
>
> In the morning across the bay
> the fire still went on, but in the sunlight
> we saw no more glare, just the clouds of smoke
> The beach was strewn with cinders, dark with ash –
> strange objects seemed [to] have blown across the water
> lifted by that terrible heat, through the red sky?
> Blackened boards, shiny black like black [feathers] –
> pieces of furniture, parts of boats, and clothes –

On the other hand, she is alone and in trouble. She stands in her crib terribly thirsty and cannot get the attention of her mother, whom she sees out on the lawn greeting refugees, distributing coffee. In the morning, as they walk among the refuse,

> I picked up a woman's long black cotton
> stocking. Curios[ity]. My mother said sharply
> <u>Put that down!</u>

As an adult, Elizabeth remembered this event as a profound rejection of herself, her curiosity, her observant eye, and, because the forbidden object was a piece of a woman's intimate clothing, perhaps some aspect of her sexuality as well. Combined with the neglect she had felt the night before during the fire, this rejection seemed sweeping. She identifies it as the incipient event of her alcoholism

("Since that day, that reprimand . . . I have suffered from abnormal thirst"), and in no later memory did she recall wishing for her mother's presence. She became, in the language of attachment theorists, an avoidant child.

Elizabeth began trying to tell in prose the story of her mother's unsatisfactory presence and ultimate disappearance shortly after Gertrude Bishop's death in May 1934. As a high school writer, Elizabeth had invented a semiautobiographical character named Lucius, a small boy living in Nova Scotia with his brother and his father, an intensely thoughtful child given to vivid and frightening fantasies. In 1934–1935, as Elizabeth began to plan for a novel about her childhood, she resurrected Lucius, first named "Gillespie" and then "de Brisay"—both names of families she had known in Great Village. The cover of the notebook containing these sketches quotes Gerard Manley Hopkins: "Enough: Corruption was the world's first woe."

This Lucius arrives in the village and leaves it at intervals he cannot predict in the company of his mother, whom he calls "Easter," her given name. Easter is clearly unwell. Her mental state is the constant concern of her family, especially of her sister, Grace, and her mother, and is discussed just out of Lucius's hearing but not out of his perception. Most of the Lucius stories rehearse material Elizabeth later treated in "In the Village"—the last visit of Easter and her son to the home of her parents in Nova Scotia and the events that precipitated her departure—but they are even more attentive than the published story is to how his mother's presence or absence affects Lucius. They record his dreams and fantasies as well as his childish misinterpretations of the events taking place.

In the first Lucius story, the boy and his mother arrive unannounced at her native village in Nova Scotia in the fall of 1913. Lucius's pleasure at being back in the village is tempered by his anxiety about his mother's feelings and about the reception they will get when they arrive at his grandparents' house. Other stories tell about what it is like for Lucius to be in the house with Easter, whom he identifies only once as his mother:

> We became quite stolidly a family when he [Grandfather] read the Bible. My wicked Aunt looked devout, and my poor grandmother almost a matriarch or "manager." Easter never joined in with our feeling for Grandfather's reading. . . . Almost always she lay on the sofa with an arm across her eyes, her other arm hanging down so that the white hand lay on the floor.

The family's conversations, which Lucius half-hears, are ominous to him. He is aware of constant tension in the air, of implied dangers, and he feels (indeed, is made to feel) that he is somehow responsible for it.[7]

> In the night she began to cry very gently and complainingly like a good child that has stood all it can. She made little imploring noises, asking someone for something. I sat up & pulled my boots on & took the stick from under the window & shut that, then I sat on the edge of the bed waiting for Aunt Grace. ~~She began to cry louder.~~ Suddenly the door opened & Aunt Grace, holding the little lamp, stuck her head in and said very low: "I guess you'll have to come, Lucius. Maybe she wants you." We walked along the hall – I took the lamp. Just as we got to the door Aunt Grace said, "Oh – I don't know what to do –"

Lucius's nights are haunted by his mother's needs; they are present in his dreams. He tells us that his mother never appears directly; but in one, he dreams of the large moths that inhabit Nova Scotia in the summertime. They grow frightening and then in a linguistic turn—"Easter came into it somehow"—become identified with "mother." "I woke up, horrified with all the fluttering moths, and just as I woke, so that the feeling was neither a sleeping one nor a waking one, I became certain that the enemy was she."

In the summer of 1952, a few months after she had settled herself in Petrópolis, Brazil, Elizabeth returned after nearly fifteen years to the material in the Lucius stories. "In the Village" describes a period of several weeks in the life of a five-year-old girl who lives with her grandparents on a farm in Nova Scotia. During this time, her mother returns to the farm from a stay in a mental hospital, suffers a relapse, and goes back to the hospital with a troubling air of finality. In the central event, the mother screams in fear as her dressmaker fits the first colorful dress she will wear after five years of mourning, terrifying her imaginative daughter. The story traces the scream's echoes through the child's days and nights in the weeks following, indicating its results in her fragmentary perception. The memory is framed by a brief introduction and a brief closing, both written in the adult narrator's voice.

Elizabeth told her *Paris Review* interviewer that one of the discoveries she made during a brief period of therapy in the mid-1940s was that she could "remember things that happened to me when I was two. It's very rare, but apparently writers often do." She continued:

> I think I remember learning to walk. My mother was away and
> my grandmother was trying to encourage me to walk. It was in
> Canada and she had lots of plants in the window the way all ladies
> do there. I can remember this blur of plants and my grandmother
> holding out her arms. I must have toddled. It seems to me it's a
> memory. It's very hazy. I told my grandmother years and years
> later and she said, "Yes, you did learn to walk while your mother
> was visiting someone." But you walk when you're one, don't you?[8]

These remarks explain the vivid way "In the Village" conveys the five-year-old's impressions of loss without the artificiality or self-pity an adult might add. Elizabeth's memories of her childhood, when they became conscious, were extraordinarily detailed.

The method of "In the Village" is essentially the same as in Bishop's poetry; memory, and the pain and pleasure associated with it, mixed up poignantly with touch, hearing, smell, taste, and sight. Memory and the meaning of memory inhere in objects that can be touched (or are forbidden to be touched), held, put in one's mouth, even swallowed accidently; in the sounds of a scream, a hammer and an anvil, a brook, a cow making "cow-flops," muffled front-room voices; in the smells of a broken perfume bottle, sachets, mint leaves, and burnt hay; in the taste of chocolates or tears, the feel in one's mouth of a nickel or a tiny glass button.

Bishop opens "In the Village" in an adult voice, with a preamble that speaks to the way adult consciousness has learned to live with what the story describes. But the story is very much about what the *child* "knows" and does not know, what parts of her world become refuges and what parts are imperiled by loneliness, talkative adults, or objects associated with "the scream." Told primarily in the first person, the story never identifies the hysterical "she" as "Mother," although in occasional third-person descriptions, the pair appears as "the woman" and "her child." The child's other relatives—"grandmother," "grandfather," "older aunt," "younger aunt," and intricate relations among the village residents—are all very clear to her. "She" is essentially a stranger whom the child feels she must please and in whose company she is decidedly uncomfortable. "She" also brought the child to the village and has come and gone in a confusing pattern of flight, that the child mimics in her dealings with "she." "The child vanishes" at the sound of the scream and "slide[s] out from under" a pat on the head; postcards from her mother's trunk and the illustrations in a drummer's Bible take her on imaginary trips; the daily journey through town to the cow pasture is a flight through the wonders and dangers of store windows and angry or fanatical neighbors. Once in the pasture, however, the child cannot stay "safely here . . . all day, playing in the brook and climbing on the squishy, moss-covered hummocks in the swampy part" because "an immense, sibilant, glistening loneliness suddenly faces" her. She goes back to the dangerous house.

The blacksmith's shop is the child's favorite refuge, for though it is dark, full of "night black" cooling tanks, where "things hang up in the shadows and shadows hang up in the things," and though many of the blacksmith's creations are "too hot to touch," the child is an honored guest in the shop, like the horses brought to be shod, "very much at home." This child of makeshift circumstances yearns for things of her own, to keep and hide so that nothing will ever happen to them. When she cries to the artisan blacksmith, " 'Make me a ring, Nate!' . . . instantly it is made; it is mine."

The mother's scream, as she stands draped in brilliant purple fabric while her dressmaker, with pins in her mouth, crawls around pinning up the hem "as Nebuchadnezzer had crawled eating grass," is indicated in one sentence early in the story: "The dress was all wrong. She screamed." In the Lucius stories the scene is fleshed out; Easter is even more obviously disturbed:

> Easter stood stiff and straight and happy. She waved at me. "Look, Lucius, I'm having a new dress! It will have gold on it. All around the hem & around the neck and sleeves, real gold. Come & kiss my hand."
>
> Miss O'Neil [the dressmaker] picked up a large pair of shears & took hold of the extra cloth, to cut it away. At once Easter fell to her knees and snatched the cloth away from her. "Oh, oh!" she cried. "You hurt me, you mustn't cut it. It shan't be cut. It's mine. . . . No, you take the scissors away. Grace! Make her stop—it will bleed. I shall bleed.". . .
>
> She jumped up & ran to the other end of the room, trailing the cloth in a wonderful swirl behind her. ~~She stood there and screamed. You want to take my dress away.~~ "The only dress I have in the world, you want to bare me naked. It's mine, it's mine. You can't have it. You want to make me all naked." But—Aunt Grace said to me, "Lucius, please take Miss O'Neil down stairs." We

went out together. Half-way down there was a louder scream from the bedroom.

"In the Village" takes up the story at this point, following the child through the earliest consequences of the scream as she makes her way in the usually safe and peaceful days of spring in the tiny town. But fear and suspicion subvert the earthy pastoral of the child's life in recurring images of darkness that shadow all her efforts to compensate: the sense of "something darkening over the woods and waters as well as the sky," the presence of profound darkness in the underworld workings of the cheerful blacksmith shop. (Lucius had noticed, "The darkness favored my family in some way.") When the child takes from her mother's "things" an ivory embroidery tool, "to keep it forever," she buries it "under the bleeding heart"; the mother's irrationally prolonged period of mourning ("morning" to the child) teaches her the mystery of blackness; her grandmother cries into her potato mash, which tastes "wonderful but wrong" because of the tears; loneliness invades the cow's pasture; the child is embarrassed while taking a package addressed to the sanatorium to the post office.

When the mother went away following the scream, she went away forever. Despite the best available care at great expense, Gertrude Bishop never recovered her mental health. (Elizabeth believed her mother had been hospitalized for a time at McLean's in Belmont, Massachusetts, though the hospital has no record of a stay there.) Many other frightening scenes between child and mother may be surmised from the few that Elizabeth recorded, but she recorded at length only this last one. "In the Village" is an account of the child's final experience of her mother in the spring of 1916. Because Gertrude Bishop lost her U.S. citizenship with her husband's death, she was hospitalized in a public sanatorium in Dartmouth, Nova Scotia, where she was diagnosed as permanently insane and where she died in late May 1934, without seeing her daughter again.

Among Elizabeth's unpublished poems are a very few other, more tentative attempts to write about this time when Gertrude Bishop and her daughter were together. All present a truncated mother, as she might be seen by a confused child, represented by her clothes, her "things," the "front-room voices" little Elizabeth overheard, and a few crystalline memories:

> A mother made of dress-goods
> white with black polk-dots,
> black and white "Shepherd's Plaid."
> A mother is a hat . . .

> A long black glove
> the swan bit
> in the Public Gardens

> Hair being brushed at night
> and brushed
> "Did you see the spark?"
> Yes, I saw the spark
> and the shadow of the elm
> outside the window
> and

> A naked figure standing
> in a wash-basin shivering   half [crouched]
> a little, black and white
> in the sloping-[ceilinged] bedroom.

> A voice heard still
> echoing
> far at the bottom somewhere
> of my aunt's on the telephone –
> coming out of blackness –
>   the blackness all voices come from

The snow had a crust, they said, like bread –
only white – it held me up but it would not hold
    her
she fell through it
and [said she'd] go home again for the snow-shoes –
    and I could slide in shine and glare while she
stepped wide.
on the

"Sestina," which followed "In the Village" in *Questions of Travel*
(1965), also evokes this time, perhaps shortly after Gertrude's final
departure from Great Village. The story prepares us with grandmother crying into the potato mash for the poem's intricate play
with the same elements: grandmother, child, house, stove, tears, and
the harsh and inevitable symbol of Elizabeth's lifelong anxiety about
the passage of time, an almanac. The child displaces the grandmother's tears to the rain, to drops of water on the stove, to the cup
of tea, to buttons. Here are the middle stanzas:

> *It's time for tea now;* but the child
> is watching the teakettle's small hard tears
> dance like mad on the hot black stove,
> the way the rain must dance on the house.
> Tidying up, the old grandmother
> hangs up the clever almanac
>
> on its string. Birdlike, the almanac
> hovers half open above the child,
> hovers above the old grandmother
> and her teacup full of dark brown tears.
> She shivers and says she thinks the house
> feels chilly, and puts more wood on the stove.

The child in the poem also draws a "rigid house," a pictorial version
of the tension that dominated Elizabeth's childhood.

Despite the anxiety lurking behind the pastoral of "Sestina," the Lucius stories, and "In the Village," Elizabeth Bishop's recollections of her Nova Scotia childhood were essentially positive. She described her grandparents as simple and loving people of conservative politics and Scots financial temperament. The stories and the poem show grandmother, "Gammie," carrying on her work despite the sadness in the house, crying into the potato mash she stirs on the stove, but stirring nonetheless. The Baptist and Presbyterian hymns she sang were her granddaughter's introduction to poetry and stayed with her all her life. Gammie's characteristic phrase in times of trouble— "Nobody knows"—became almost a mantra for Elizabeth, and she tried for years to write a poem about it. The grandfather, "Pa," Elizabeth described as her favorite grandparent. He was a deacon in the Baptist church and had owned the local tannery until machine tanners took over. In the short story "Gwendolyn," his presence in the house is captured in this line describing his reaction to extravagant displays of affection: " 'Oh, lallygagging, lallygagging!' said my grandfather, going on about his business." And in his response to Elizabeth's spontaneous tears: " 'Heavens, what ails the child now?' " A girlhood poem, "For C. W. B.," addresses Grandfather Bulmer in romantic terms: "Let us live in a lull of the long winter-winds / Where the shy, silver-antlered reindeer go / On dainty hoofs with their white rabbit friends / Amidst the delicate flowering snow." "Manners," a poem Elizabeth hoped would be the first in a book for children, also warmly characterizes Pa: "My grandfather said to me / as we sat on the wagon seat, / 'Be sure to remember to always / speak to everyone you meet.' "

Two of her mother's sisters—the oldest, Maud, and the second, Grace—had already left home, but Grace was a frequent visitor to the farm. Younger brother Arthur, the subject of Bishop's "Memories of Uncle Neddy," was an alcoholic ne'er-do-well tinsmith who lived out his life across the village green from his parents. His wife, called "Aunt Hat" in the story, was a fiery, red-haired object of fascination to the child. "Aunt Mary," Gertrude's youngest sister and a high school student when Elizabeth entered primer class, or kindergarten, appeared in her memories as an altogether normal teenager; she had "a great many suitors" and "wore white middy blouses with red or blue silk ties, and her brown hair in a braid down her back." She was frequently late to the one-room school that housed all twelve grades.

Elizabeth began her formal education in that schoolhouse, and later, when she wrote her memoir of her first school year, "Primer Class," she remembered sensations: the fascinating black writing slates, the smell of the rags used to clean them, her terror at seeing long columns of numbers on the chalkboard, and her passion for the large roll-down maps used to teach geography to the lucky third- and fourth-graders:

> They were on cloth, very limp, with a shiny surface, and in pale colors—tan, pink, yellow and green—surrounded by the blue that was the ocean. . . . On the world map, all of Canada was pink; on the Canadian, the provinces were different colors. I was so taken with the pull-down maps that I wanted to snap them up, and pull them down again, and touch all the countries and provinces with my own hands. Only dimly did I hear the pupils' recitations of capital cities and islands and bays.[9]

Not so dimly, however, that she would not remember them, and the catechism of questions they answered, when she went looking for an epigraph for her last book, *Geography III:* "In what direction is the Volcano? The Cape? The Bay? The Lake? The Strait? The Mountains? The Isthmus? What is in the East? In the West? In the South? In the North?"

Great Village, despite its paradoxical name, is a tiny town about twenty miles northwest from Truro, Nova Scotia, in the lowlands between the Cobequid Mountains and the Minas Basin. (Fifty years later, Elizabeth lived in the state of Minas Gerais, Brazil.) In the summer, it is green with thick grass, elm trees, and evergreens running down to the rocky shore. The sky is as blue as "In the Village" described it, "pure . . . too dark, too blue," and the houses and churches are white, or green and white, with an occasional dark brown. The village's half-dozen streets are now paved, and its residents remember the Boomers but not Elizabeth herself, except by reputation. People in Great Village now make their livings in dairy products, eggs, and cattle or in fishing and small, sweet strawberries and blueberries grown for commercial sale. There are apple orchards but not much other agriculture. The post office is still as tiny and lopsided as Bishop described it in her stories and memoirs. Great Village is a bigger place than it was in the early part of the century, but not much wealthier.

Living in Great Village put one, as perhaps it still does, in automatic relation with neighbors. The village itself was an expanding household whose familiar rooms for Elizabeth included the Baptist and Presbyterian churches, Nate's blacksmith shop, Mealy's candy store and town switchboard, various barns, Uncle Arthur's tinsmith shop and store, the Hills' store, a river, the pasture where Nelly grazed, the schoolhouse, the iron bridge, the dressmaker's house, the post office, the village green, houses named for the women who ran them (Mrs. Peppard's, Mrs. McNeil's, Mrs. Geddes's, Mrs. Captain Mahon's, Miss Spencer's), the McLeans' farm, the Chisolms' farm, Layton's store, and the shore. Not until Elizabeth established her place among the Brazilian inhabitants of Lota Soares's household in Petrópolis, Brazil, was she able to recapture this sense of broad and happy relations among neighbors and relatives, hospitality on a grand scale ordering a simpler life.

Fragments of unpublished poems among Elizabeth's papers, also dating from her first years in Brazil, attempt to memorialize this simplicity, identifying it as refuge from the rush of passing time:

We lived in a pocket of Time.
It was close, it was warm.
Along the dark seam of the river,

In the [?] of the alders & willows,
the houses, the barns, the two churches
hid like white crumbs.

The child who made her way in this landscape after her mother's disappearance at first displayed the uncanny adaptability of children and managed to make herself a secure home among the villagers. She loved her grandparents' house; its every arrangement and decoration pleased her: the modest objets d'art sent by Great-uncle William, a Baptist missionary in India; the luxurious carpet; the hooked rugs; the fascinating wallpaper. "I sat silent and made the wallpaper come off the wall. Small bouquets of red-gray roses, thin trellaces of golden wires, swayed, retreated and advanced, in space out from their background of wide white and faint silver stripes – up & down." In unpublished sketches for her Nova Scotia novel, Bishop said that as a child she had always felt "that the parlor belonged to me," in part because of the portraits that hung there and in part, perhaps, because it was the "best room," where all the family's solemn meetings took place and where "little Arthur" and the other Nova Scotia dead were laid out.

> Most important to me, though, and what I often went into the
> parlor to look at just for a minute, were three oil paintings of
> Grandmother's children. Two were of the same size, in the same
> gold frames with balls in the concave edge; these were of Easter
> and William, the son who had died. They had been painted by a
> travelling artist who came around when Easter was nine and
> William twelve. The children were painted at full length, about
> half life size, with thin dark colors; Easter leaning on the back of a
> red stuffed chair with long fringe hiding the legs, William, in his
> picture, leaning to the other side on a table covered by a long
> fringed cloth of the same red. They had looked very much alike,
> both slight with pale faces and dark straight hair and serious,
> dignified expressions. . . .

The outstanding picture in the parlor, however, was that of Aunt Grace.

Elizabeth later acquired the pair of portraits and brought them back with her to Brazil from a visit to North America in 1957. Her memory of them here is not quite accurate—it is Arthur in the picture, not William; Gertrude is in the other. Arthur leans on the chair, Gertrude on the table. "Memories of Uncle Neddy" gives us another version of these portraits, slightly fictionalized to protect the subject. But they clearly stayed with Elizabeth, objects of fascination and memory, throughout her life. That at the time she most admired Grace's portrait was testimony to the love little Elizabeth felt for her funny aunt, and the Nova Scotia notebooks are full of anecdotes in which Grace stars. Although Elizabeth changed the names of everyone else when she transferred them to Lucius's family, Lucius's favorite aunt is also named Grace.

Already the victim of weak lungs, Elizabeth spent much of her one full winter in Great Village being nursed through bouts of bronchitis and the more usual childhood diseases. Her memories of illness, too, are positive—of Grace reading to her, in bed with measles, the funny story called "Freckles" and of them laughing until they cried; of Gammie making maple-syrup taffy as a special treat; of the special games and toys conjured to amuse Elizabeth on long housebound days.

Despite her illnesses, the little girl in the village loved to be outdoors; she loved the woods, the brook, the legends of fairies and former inhabitants. Her vivid imagination gave her nightmares and caused her to see things that "could not possibly have happened"— such as Gwendolyn Appletree's coffin, "with Gwendolyn shut invisibly inside it forever, there, completely alone on the grass by the church door."[10] Imagination also allowed little Elizabeth, in the absence of real knowledge of her situation, to make up versions of her life in which she was self-sufficient and self-determining and almost always a little boy.

Elizabeth spent a few months at intervals in Great Village before 1916, sometimes with her mother and sometimes without; she was there continuously from spring 1916 until September 1917 and then spent two months of each summer there from 1918 until 1923. Just as Elizabeth was finishing up at boarding school in 1930, her grandfather Boomer died, and her grandmother thereafter left the Great Village house to live with Mary in Montreal, where she died in April 1931. Images from this period recur in Bishop's writing throughout her life, in personal letters, journals, and work for publication. The Lucius stories eventually became first-person memoirs or barely disguised autobiographical stories: "Primer Class," "Memories of Uncle Neddy," "Gwendolyn," "In the Village." Less personal stories, such as "The Baptism" and "The Farmer's Children," are also set in Nova Scotia. And because objects came to stand for places and times, Nova Scotia "things" turn up in New York or Brazil and draw connections straight back. Cows, particular kinds of colloquially named flowers, the blue-blue sky, the red bay with huge tides, snow, changing leaves, marshes, forged iron, ice-cold water, primerclass arithmetic, Protestant hymns, maple syrup, rocky shores with fishing boats and lighthouses—a handful of objects and impressions, freighted with the sensations of memory, stood in her mind and art for this lost childhood time, which grew idyllic as memory separated it from less happy adolescence and adulthood.

In the posthumously published short story "The Country Mouse," Bishop tells how the timeless stability of her Nova Scotia life was disturbed. The unpublished poem about the "pocket of time" puts the disruption in characteristic imagery: "But Time made a sudden gesture; / His nails scratched the roof / Roughly his hand reached in / and tumbled me out." Time's representative is not named in the poem fragment, but the end of her hope for a Nova Scotia childhood came when her paternal grandparents, the wealthy Bishops, arrived in Great Village by train in the fall of 1917 to take the six-year-old Elizabeth back to live with them in Worcester. They had retained their interest in Gertrude and Elizabeth after their son's death. One of the Lucius stories records a letter written to Easter from her father-in-law about her illness: "Now my dear girl I want you to be sensible about this. You are letting your imagination run away with you. If you could be a little more free with people. You are something like myself you do not do much talking. But you must not let yourself worry this way."

When Gertrude was committed to the hospital, her in-laws' interest in Elizabeth extended to a desire to raise and educate her, their only grandchild, to the family's standards. As Elizabeth writes in the story, "I had been brought back unconsulted and against my wishes to the house my father had been born in, to be saved from a life of poverty and provincialism, bare feet, suet puddings, unsanitary school slates, perhaps even from the inverted r's of my mother's family."[11]

Take back they did, in a railroad "kidnapping" that sealed little Elizabeth's sense of loss to a permanent condition. No household could have contrasted more negatively with Great Village than did the Bishop family mansion. Instead of a whole village of relatives and neighbors with houses and farms of their own, Elizabeth lived in splendid isolation, with a friend assigned to her by her grandmother. On occasion, she was required to bring a classmate home from school to play with. Her grandmother's rigid notion of what a "little girl" was and should be took no account of who Elizabeth actually was—cerebral, tomboyish, uninterested in dolls or clothes. The huge and chilly house with servants who were hired and fired exposed, rather than sheltered, the child. The aunt and uncle still living there were distant and ironic, the grandfather was frequently absent, and the grandmother remanded the child's care to the Swedish-speaking household staff, giving the orphan a renewed sense of her lack of relations. She thought of herself as "on the same terms in the house" as the neurotic family dog. Waited on by everyone, she was bored and restless, and her surroundings so oppressively reminded her of the idea of her dead father, her earliest loss, that in the American lyrics to the British anthem "God Save the King,"

"My Country 'tis of Thee," she took the reference to America as the "land where our fathers died" personally.

Elizabeth's lifelong trouble with her expatriate condition arose here as the essentially Canadian first-grader began her American education in the years of World War I. "The Country Mouse" reveals her preoccupation with patriotic songs, emblems of her personally divided home front. Loyal to the "Maple Leaf Forever" and the royal family, Elizabeth was discomfited by the super-Americanism of the war years. She wrote, "Now I felt like a traitor. I wanted us to win the War, of course, but I didn't want to be an American. When I went home to lunch, I said so. Grandma was horrified; she almost wept." To correct this deficiency, Grandma Bishop had the child learn all the verses of the "Star-Spangled Banner," "this endless poem," and recite them, sitting at her feet, every day. Five years later, under different circumstances, Elizabeth was sufficiently repatriated to win a Boston American Legion essay contest on the topic of Americanism. The prize was a five-dollar gold piece, and long after Elizabeth recalled that the essay's first sentence had begun something like "from the icy regions of the frozen north to the waving palm trees of the burning south," revealing her earliest tendency to invest abstract emotion in geographical reality.

The Bishops kept Elizabeth for only nine months, but it was as fateful a period as she ever lived through. Her Worcester existence burdened her with that "peculiar Bostonian sense of guilt," and she felt ashamed of her situation and horribly self-conscious. In "The Country Mouse" she recalls answering Emma, her assigned "best friend," who had asked about her missing parents:

> I said my father was dead; I didn't ever remember seeing him.
> What about my mother? I thought for a moment and then I said
> in a *sentimental* voice: "She went away and left me...She died,
> too." Emma was impressed and sympathetic, and I loathed
> myself. . . . My mother was not dead. She was in a sanatorium, in
> another prolonged "nervous breakdown." I didn't know then, and

still don't, whether it was from shame I lied, or from a hideous craving for sympathy, playing up my sad romantic plight. But the feeling of self-distaste, whatever it came from, was only too real.

Elizabeth made of this experience a literary lesson about the power and falsehood of sentimentality, but through her guilty haste to judge herself, we see that the precocious child had become alienated from her own experience; she had derived from it not legitimate grief but guilt and shame, as if her circumstances were somehow her own fault. She ignored the answer that is obvious to us: no "romantic plight" could be sadder than her real one. Her natural response had already been repressed. This was the beginning of her training in acting with stoicism, in distancing herself from real sadness, in avoiding complaints or expressions of pain and loss. Perhaps this was when she learned not to experience these feelings at all. In an unpublished poem fragment from the early 1950s, the speaker suffers by comparison to the plastic toys of her childhood:

Where are the dolls who loved me so
when I was young? . . .

Through their real eyes

blank crotches,
and play wrist-watches,
whose hands moved only when they wanted –

Their stoicism I never mastered
their smiling phrase for every occasion –
They went their rigid little ways

To meditate in a closet or a trunk
To let unforseen emotions
glance off their glazed complexions

She envies her dolls not only for their ability to encounter emotion unfazed but also for their immunity from the passage of time, their "wrist-watches, / whose hands moved only when they wanted."

The incident described in the poem "In the Waiting Room"—that fall into time, self-consciousness, and separateness—also occurred during this period, and the child knew she was "in for it now." A prose account of this incident closes "The Country Mouse"; there Elizabeth goes with her aunt to the dentist and is horrified by her identification with her aunt, the other patients in the waiting room, and the cannibals she reads about in *National Geographic.* The poem tells the story in similar terms while filling out its implications.

"In the Waiting Room" opens *Geography III* (1976). It is the first poem in which Bishop names herself and one of the very few that does not at least attempt to direct outward the experience it describes. Elizabeth dated many of her most important adult attitudes "from the age of 6," including a feeling of irremediable estrangement from the world and what she called her "feminism."[12] Six is, of course, the age named in "In the Waiting Room" and the age at which Elizabeth was kidnapped to Worcester. The poem illustrates the many consequences of this kidnapping, as they manifested themselves in Elizabeth's life and in her poems.

The climax of the poem (and of the prose account of the events) involves the simultaneous realization of selfhood and the awful otherness of the inevitable world:

> But I felt: you are an *I,*
> You are an *Elizabeth,*
> You are one of them.
> *Why* should you be one, too?
> I scarcely dared to look
> to see what it was I was. . . .
> Why should I be my aunt,
> or me, or anyone?

The inability to take for granted either her self-image or her relationship to the rest of the world stayed with Elizabeth for the rest of her life. In "In the Village," the child stays afloat in her sea of uncertainties because her Nova Scotia existence is unself-conscious, and the story conveys this unrestricted flow of events. But in "In the Waiting Room," the child is on the precipice, in nervous anticipation of the consequences of events. The terrible rush to adulthood, "like coasting downhill . . . only much worse," brings with it decision making and awareness of autonomy and responsibility. "The War was on," Bishop says at the end of the poem, and if one reads that conflict back through her life and her poetry, one finds it manifested in a recurring rhetoric of negotiation, a preoccupation with unhappy compromise, a desire to give up, submit, cease, resist. Her earliest image for this submission is the tiny collapse of wills that occurs each time a wave meets the shore, and its epigraph is the concession by "The Gentleman of Shalott" that "half is enough." The enemy, more often than not, is the passage of time itself.

Bishop's habitual manipulation of perspective in her observations—both poetic and personal—is another symptom of this war, and "In the Waiting Room" anticipates it as well. Her fear of uncertain perspective became a dependence on the chance to disrupt, to start over by rushing "to see the sun the other way around," to reverse the field. The poem weaves a self-other paradigm into the narrative by means of shifting inside/outside perspective. It opens:

> In Worcester, Massachusetts,
> I went with Aunt Consuelo
> to keep her dentist's appointment
> and sat and waited for her
> in the dentist's waiting room.
> It was winter. It got dark
> early. The waiting room
> was full of grown-up people,
> arctics and overcoats,

lamps and magazines.
My aunt was inside
what seemed like a long time

In the first line we are "in" Worcester but outside the waiting room. Then we are "in" the room, but right away "it got dark / early" outside. Then we are back "in," and Aunt Consuelo (Aunt Florence in real life) is even further "inside." In a magazine, Elizabeth looks at a picture of "the inside of a volcano" and other pictures until, "from inside, / came an *oh!* of pain," which plunges the child deep inside her self—forcing it lurchingly, sickeningly outward to the edge of the precipice, of "falling off / the round, turning world / into cold, blue-black space." Elizabeth grows faint under her own agonizing shifts of perspective, from inside herself outside to the people in the waiting room, the African women, her aunt; from the "family voice" to "my throat"; from "I" to "them" and back again:

The waiting room was bright
and too hot. It was sliding
beneath a big black wave,
another, and another.

Then I was back in it.
The War was on. Outside,
in Worcester, Massachusetts
were night and slush and cold,
and it was still the fifth
of February, 1918.

In her faint, the child goes outside the waiting room and then recovers and is "back in it." Far, far outside the room, in Europe, and deep inside the six-year-old Elizabeth, "the War was on." Directly "outside, / in Worcester, Massachusetts," were immediately hostile elements.

The inside/outside paradigm manifested itself in Bishop's poetic life as another aspect of the "war" and the desire for submission, the temptation to retreat. Throughout her poems and letters, Elizabeth toyed with the idea of withdrawal from the conflict, and this turned up in her writing in dialogues with herself about the merits of particular hiding places or about whether retreat was possible at all. Elizabeth's preoccupation with houses—in her life and in her poems—also grew from this childhood experience.

"In the Waiting Room" describes Elizabeth's fall into gender consciousness as well. In a major expansion from the prose account of the incident, the poem ties the child's disorientation much more closely to the contents of the magazine she reads. The photographs are of volcanos erupting; of the famous explorers Osa and Martin Johnson; of a dead man—euphemistically labeled "Long Pig"— prepared for cooking by cannibals; of

> Babies with pointed heads
> wound round and round with string;
> black, naked women with necks
> wound round and round with wire
> like the necks of lightbulbs.
> Their breasts were horrifying.

The child perceives here for the first time several truths about women that she will experience as restrictions for the rest of her life. The mutilations the women practice on themselves and their babies for purposes of sexual attractiveness to men are symptoms of enslavement for which Elizabeth later condemns both the masters and the slaves. In the prose account, Elizabeth is distressed to find that she is one with the falsely smiling woman sitting across from her, and here she is shocked to perceive her future as a woman—self-mutilator, sexual object, vain creature. This identification is the poem's central event:

Suddenly, from inside,
came an *oh!* of pain
—Aunt Consuelo's voice—
not very loud or long.
I wasn't at all surprised;
even then I knew she was
a foolish, timid woman.
I might have been embarrassed,
but wasn't. What took me
completely by surprise
was that it was *me:*
Without thinking at all
I was my foolish aunt

The aunt's cry is a squeak of pain at the dentist's, but it is also a woman's cry. David Kalstone's suggestion that it is akin to the scream of Elizabeth's mother in "In the Village" finds support in the poem's nervous contention that it "could have / got loud and worse but hadn't." Elizabeth's identification here is with womanly pain, the impossibly conflicted life a self-aware woman must lead, the prospect of a startling and inexplicable acquisition of "awful hanging breasts." Elizabeth's ambivalence about the value of femininity affected her thinking about herself and her eventual sexual orientation and her complex handling of questions of gender in her poems as well.

. . .

Arising from her guilt and shame, from her loneliness and anxiety in the Worcester house, bronchitis, then asthma and eczema, and even symptoms of St. Vitus' dance and other nervous illnesses incapacitated Elizabeth for her last months there, as she became allergic to almost everything in the house and yard. Her Worcester schoolteachers sent her home because of her eczema sores, and she was soon bedridden. "I felt myself aging, even dying," she wrote in "The Country Mouse." "I was *bored* and lonely with Grandma, my silent grandpa, the dinners alone, bored with Emma and Beppo, all of them. At night I lay blinking my flashlight off and on, and crying." These diseases, and shyness, stayed with Elizabeth off and on for the rest of her life, and it was nearly thirty-five years before she could settle herself in another home.

The ill and panicky Elizabeth was rescued in May 1918 by her Aunt Maud Boomer Shepherdson, her mother's oldest sister, when even the Bishops conceded that Elizabeth was hopelessly unhappy in their house. Maud and her husband, George, lived in the upstairs apartment of a run-down tenement in an impoverished neighborhood of Irish and Italian immigrants in Revere, Massachusetts. Later Elizabeth said emphatically that Maud, along with Grace in Great Village, had saved her life. The Shepherdsons were "poor and thrifty," and Maud was paid by the Bishop family to keep Elizabeth there and educate her. Maud "devoted herself" to nursing the child's asthma and eczema, introduced her to Victorian poets, and mercifully allowed her to spend two months of each summer in Nova Scotia. In "Mrs. Sullivan Downstairs," a draft memoir that seems to have been meant to follow in the autobiographical sequence begun with "Primer Class" and "The Country Mouse," Elizabeth describes the endless interest she took in the house and the neighborhood; her aunt's canaries and window-box gardens; the local smells and sights; the beautiful names of her Italian neighbors— Mr. Acquaviva was a favorite; "Barb'runt" (Barbara Hunt), the "bastard" who lived across the street, loved books, and sometimes played with her ("We were both orphans, that is, almost fairy princesses and living here just temporarily"); and especially the red-haired, green-eyed, and abundantly freckled Mrs. Sullivan. Elizabeth's account of the neighborhood is full of her dawning awareness of social distinctions, of racial and ethnic prejudices, and of the tyranny of alcoholism and bootlegging and the toll they took on her neighbors and their families.

We were almost all aliens, aliens, dreamers, drunkards. Everyone talked about "taking out their first papers"; few had actually reached full U S citizenship and probably many never bothered to at all. The Italians made their own wine some of them, or bought it from each other. We could look into one upper apartment and see Mr & Mrs. [blank] treading wine in a wooden bucket that almost filled their kitchen, side by side up and down. Their two smallest boys (they had six) lay [sidewise] on an old army cot and watched them, their heads almost in the bucket too –

Later the family moved to slightly better, yet less memorable, circumstances in Cliftondale.

Elizabeth said that in her years of living with relatives—her childhood years—she was "always a sort of guest," but she remained grateful for Maud's generosity and said that she and Maud, who was "small, worried, nervous shy," "loved each other and told each other everything and for many years I saw nothing in her to criticize." An unpublished poem called "Salem Willows" recalls a summer carousel ride and clearly cherishes the attention of this aunt: "Yes, through the willows glittered, / really, a glassy sea, / and Aunt Maud sat and knitted / and knitted, waiting for me." Also among Elizabeth's papers is an elegy for Maud, who died in 1940: "Yes, you are dead now and live / only there / in the tip-tilted graveyard."

In 1923—the year of her Americanism essay award and the year of her first hospitalization (an appendectomy performed on her twelfth birthday at the Phillips House of Massachusetts General Hospital)—Elizabeth began to make her way in the larger world. For the first time, she attended summer camp on Cape Cod at Camp Chequesset, or "the nautical school for girls." She was quite athletic, a tomboy despite her poor health, and she partook fully in the camp's hiking, swimming, and sailing program. Elizabeth returned to Camp Chequesset for the next five summers, as the Nova Scotia part of her life came to a close. By 1931, both Gammie and Pa were dead, and she had cause to mourn the loss of that life. An undated fragment entitled "First Syllables" says:

Whatever there was, or is, of love let it be obeyed:
– so that the grandfather mightn't have been blinded,
the river never dwindled to what it is now,
nor the leaning big willows above it been blighted,
nor its trout been fished out; . . .

The barn swallows belonged to the barns,
they went with the church's wooden steeple
& they flew as fast as they did because the air was so
    still –
That steeple – I can't remember – wasn't it struck by
    lightning?

Elizabeth said that she began writing poetry and prose at the age of eight, under the influence of Aunt Maud's bookshelves, stocked with Tennyson, Browning, Emerson, Carlyle, and other Victorians. She memorized so many of these poems in her days at home in bed with asthma or bronchitis that in 1978 she conceded that they must be "an unconscious part" of her. Having begun with a fascination for hymns and fairy tales—Anderson and Grimm—she discovered Whitman at age thirteen and at summer camp became familiar with Harriet Monroe's famous anthology of modern poets. Elizabeth's fondness for Hopkins began here, and she reported also having gone through "a Shelley phase, a Browning phase, and a brief Swinburne phase."[13]

Because of her lengthy illnesses, Elizabeth had very little formal schooling before the age of fourteen, when she attended Saugus High School for one year and then in 1926–1927, at the Bishop family's insistence, the North Shore Country Day School in Swampscott. (She had been accepted at the Walnut Hill School for that year but was behind on her immunizations and had to wait.) Until then, she relied on her aunt's books for education, entertainment, and companionship. By the time she arrived at North Shore Country Day, her literary gifts were manifest. The school's literary magazine, the *Owl*, contains no fewer than five pieces by the sixteen-year-old newcomer, including a brief Latin composition called "Commutatio Opinionis" and "The Ballad of the Subway Train," which posits a confrontation between a "young" God and a race of dragons, whom He punishes by transforming into subway cars. It ends:

> So in the earth the dragons crawl
>   In murky, human roads.
> The glory of the heavens once—
>   They carry human loads.
>
> Creatures that the gorgeous sun
>   Face to face had seen,
> Now are lighted by thin darts
>   Of limpid red and green.
>
> And when you're grinding through the dark
>   Aboard those "devilish cars,"
> They really are the dragons who
>   Licked up the swarm of stars.[14]

A short story recounts a brief moment of glory befalling Peter Murphy, a traffic cop in the town of Springdale, and there are two essays on Tennyson's "Idylls of the King," including one discussing the roles of women in the poem. ("In the time of King Arthur women did not play a particularly important part in the world.")

Elizabeth moved to boarding school the following year. The Walnut Hill School for Girls was and is a good college preparatory school in Natick, Massachusetts. The Bishop family paid for Elizabeth's education there, and though her means were perhaps somewhat less than those of her classmates, she was not conspicuously poor. She was, however, conspicuously homeless. Elizabeth spent the Christmas vacation of her first year in Great Village, her last stay of any length there; after that, her holidays became more problematic. Even in boarding school, where throughout the school year the girls' lives were for the most part contained by the academic, athletic, extracurricular, and residential programs of the school, Elizabeth had ample occasion to feel her lack of relations and lack of a place to go.

Holidays became horrible trials for her; deciding where to spend them was a weighing of obligations and impositions, rarely of desires. She felt she could no longer impose on the limited means of Maud; Great Village and, later, Quebec were usually too far to go; and she was thoroughly uncomfortable among the wealthy Bishops, who extended dutiful invitations without making Elizabeth feel welcome. She spent many lonely holidays at the school in makeshift quarters with makeshift meals got up by her sympathetic teachers. In summers, she passed among the homes of her friends, especially the Cape Cod home of Rhoda Wheeler near Westport, Massachusetts; summer cottages rented by parents and occupied by their daughters and shifting sets of friends; Boston hotels; and obligatory and miserable visits to the Bishop family estate at Harwichport, Massachusetts. The fear and hatred of holidays, especially of Christmas and Thanksgiving—the formal cessation of usual, comforting activities and the closing up of school; the disappearance of friends; the legislated retreat to the bosom of a family that just was not there—stayed with Elizabeth for the rest of her life. She also never lost her fondness for a house by the sea.

Frani Blough Muser, Elizabeth's classmate at both Walnut Hill and Vassar, remembers the entrance Elizabeth made at boarding school:

> When I arrived at the Walnut Hill School in Natick in 1927, I met a most remarkable girl. She looked remarkable, with tightly curly hair that stood straight up, while the rest of us all had straight hair that hung down. And she was remarkable in many

ways besides. She had read more widely and deeply than we had. But she carried her learning lightly. She was very funny. She had a big repertory of stories she could *tell*, not read, and of wonderful songs she could sing, like ballads and sea chanteys. And if some school occasion called for a new song, or a skit, it would appear overnight like magic in her hands. Her name was Elizabeth Bishop. We called her "Bishop," spoke of her as "the Bishop," and we all knew with no doubt whatsoever that she was a genius.[15]

Elizabeth and Frani became the favorites of Walnut Hill's English teacher and literary magazine adviser, Eleanor Prentiss. Prentiss took a lively and personal interest in all the activities of her students and instilled in them as best as earnest teaching could a passionate attachment to the literary and dramatic arts. Assigned topics for themes included "Firelight Fancies," "A Shelf of Books," and "Joys of the Circus." Most of Elizabeth's high school performances were directly or indirectly for Prentiss, who was gushily fond of her gifted student.[16] By the spring of the first year, Elizabeth had two poems and a story in the *Blue Pencil*, the literary magazine. "Thunder" is typical of her high school poems in its precocious mastery of the sonnet form, its interest in nature and fantasy, and its nod to Prentiss's fondness for extravagantly poetic diction and the sixteenth-century notion of a poetic conceit:

> And suddenly the giants tired of play.—
> With huge, rough hands they flung the god's gold balls
> And silver harps and mirrors at the walls
> Of Heaven, and trod, ashamed, where lay
> The loveliness of flowers. Frightened Day
> On white feet ran from out the temple halls,
> The blundering dark was filled with great war-calls,
> And Beauty, shamed, slunk silently away.
>
> Be quiet, little wind among the leaves
> That turn pale faces to the coming storm.
> Be quiet, little foxes in your lairs,

And birds and mice be still—a giant grieves
For his forgotten might. Hark now the warm
And heavy stumbling down the leaden stairs!

"Sonnet" is as romantic, though more introspective: "I am in need of music that would flow / Over my fretful, feeling finger-tips, / over my bitter-tainted, trembling lips, / With melody, deep, clear, and liquid-slow."

Elizabeth wrote by far the most sophisticated prose among her published schoolmates and much of the most competent poetry. Despite their self-consciously poetic syntax and subjects, her poems show the fanciful turn of mind that lingers into *North & South* (1946) and predicts the plainspoken modesty of tone and diction that marks all her later work. "The Wave" looks most forward among her youthful poems:

A shining wave
Fills all the skies.
Bright shadows float
Across the land.
See, crystal clear,
Its helmet rise!
And now the motion
Of a hand,
A tiny quickening
Of the heart,
And it will fall
And nothing more
Can keep the sea and land apart. . . .
We do not move,
We do not flee.
We see it shudder, lightning bright,
And dully double
On the sea.
We are too innocent and wise,
We laugh into each other's eyes.

Her prose, both in editorials and fiction, also predicts the concerns and values of her mature work. Her editorials are often solemn exhortations of her classmates to spend more time alone and avoid becoming "bores and dullards" or to observe more closely the natural phenomena around them.

> There is a peculiar quality about being alone, an atmosphere that no sounds or persons can ever give. It is as if being with people were the Earth of the mind, the land with its hills and valleys, scent and music; but in being alone, the mind finds its Sea, the wide quiet plane with different lights in the sky and different, more secret sounds. But it appears that we are frightened by the first breaking of its waves at our feet, and now we will never go on voyages of discovery, never feel the free winds that have blown over water, and never find the islands of the Imagination, where live who knows what curious beasts and strange peoples? Being alone can be fun; alone the mind can do what it wants to without even the velvet leash of sleep. But we can never understand this while we stand on the shore with our backs to the water and cry after our companions. Perhaps we shall never know the companion in ourselves who is with us all our lives, the nearness of our minds at all times to the rare person whose heart quickens when a bird climbs high and alone in the clear air.[17]

Although Elizabeth later grew less and less comfortable with extended periods of solitude, this editorial reveals what became life-long preoccupations: the fascination with the sea, with islands and the waves meeting their shores, with the urge to travel, with the work of Gerard Manley Hopkins, suggested in the last phrase.

In other *Blue Pencil* essays, such as "Giant Weather," Elizabeth urges her readers on to an imaginary world: "Come, let us clench our fists around their little fingers . . . and we shall walk for a while with the giants." Her book reviews are lively and opinionated, and she had precociously mastered the tone and idiom of the single paragraph blurb. Her remarks often reveal telling predilections. On Edna St. Vincent Millay's *A Buck in the Snow:*

> While other modern poets continue to deplore the death of verse form and the unreality of rhyme and rhythm, and hail a "new poetry" with coarse cheers, Miss Millay goes on writing poetry according to the ancient, honorable rules of the art. . . . There is, in the best of her work, though she condescends to no crudities or lack of punctuation, an almost touchable reality of beauty . . . [that has] the power of making us stop, with our fingers between the pages, and stare at a blank wall until it turns to nothing.[18]

On W. H. Hudson's *Green Mansions:* "I was filled with the longing to leave for South America immediately and search for those forgotten bird people."[19] The idea, and the book's rain forest imagery, stayed with her for twenty-five years.

But Elizabeth's first prose publication at Walnut Hill was a play set in Nova Scotia and featuring a grandmother and two of her grandchildren, Una (the name of a real Nova Scotia relative) and her cousin Nat, with whom Una is in love. The stage directions fix the setting in Gammie's kitchen in Great Village, even though this is a fictional, lower-class grandmother: "An Almanac and burnt pan-holders hang beside the stove and a woodbox is half behind it." The brief play culminates when Una drowns herself in a swamp because Nat leaves the village to pursue a literary career in the city. Although Elizabeth eventually eschewed such melodrama in her prose and poetry, it remains in later stories such as "The Farmer's Children" and "The Baptism," in which obsessive thinking—"mooning," as the grandmother in the play calls it—leads to madness and/or theatrical death.

Elizabeth's high school fiction develops along these lines: it features youthful speakers in circumstances similar to her own—they live with aunts or grandmothers or are orphaned and on their own in Nova Scotia, Massachusetts, or fairy territory made from elements of both. But these speakers are always creative, imaginative, solitary little boys. The change in gender probably allowed Elizabeth more latitude in her heroes' adventures and perhaps served as her largest single concession to disguising the autobiography in the stories. But her literary first person remained male until she wrote "Gwendolyn" in 1953, and one of her high school speakers, somewhat older and clearly in the throes of an adolescent sexual crisis, has a tense romantic affair with a fascinating woman whose beauty is marred by her overgrown thumb! Elizabeth's identification with male experience, especially literary experience, was very strong. She saw being female only as a liability, and even in the all-female atmosphere of Walnut Hill, she disguised her feminity when she could, identifying the masculine with objectivity and valuing it highly.

As a young writer, Elizabeth had no commitment to strict realism; her speakers' lives are taken up in imaginary adventures involving knights, fairies, and witches or Poe-esque pseudo-scientific experiments having to do with balloons or magic mushrooms. But these adventures are always set in carefully delineated, thoroughly realistic landscapes and circumstances. In "Picking Mushrooms," a curious old woman from the mountain sets the mood for the story: "And she was made even more curious by her background of the country store and the faltering orange light of the one oil lamp swinging between a bunch of bananas and an assortment of horsewhips, over a fine display of fearful penny candies."[20] This fondness for supernatural events in natural settings developed in Elizabeth's mature poems into the suggestion of surrealism in much of *North & South*.

Her high school letters (already a much preferred genre) show a fondness for apostrophe ("Lord, Frani!"), a nimble wit, and a heavy-handed defensive irony directed at targets both deserving and otherwise, especially the Bishop aunts and cousins. The veneer of sophistication, evidenced in references to drinking and smoking ("After our Chesterfields my aunt's pet Camels are very tame animals indeed") and the latest literary trends, is amusing counterpoint to Elizabeth's later modesty and self-deprecation. "Use the word menstruation in a sentence," she wrote to Frani and offered a characteristic contribution of her own: Mariners "feeding their pilot biscuits to the gulls: menstrurations all over the beach." A long account of a sailing accident at the summer house of her wealthy and eccentric friend Louise Crane in Falmouth, Massachusetts ("I have news of the greatest importance: I've tipped over a sailboat"), was an occasion for expansive use of her formidable descriptive powers:

> The water was a long, bright line all around the combing – then it poured over and the sail settled on the water. . . . I climbed upon the side and pulled [Louise] up – then dove in and captured the floorboards and oars that were floating away. Then I swam into the dock with the boat—very simple because the wind and waves were so strong they fairly pushed us along. Louise lay on top and waved our sweaters – it was so silly. I laughed so hard that I kept sinking.[21]

Elizabeth seemed to bear particular animosity for her Aunt Ruby Orr and her cousin Kay in the summer of 1929. Elizabeth left Harwichport with an attack of asthma after only three days of a projected week's stay and could not forbear expressing her contempt to Frani:

> Harwichport is not my future summer home, I'm afraid. I got the asthma so badly from poor Major that I had to leave Saturday morning. Of course my poor uncle and aunt couldn't bear to give me up – and Kay – it broke her heart. She kissed me as I crudely counted the change left from buying my ticket. . . . As we emerged, [Aunt Ruby] bumped the shutter and it fell down on her head...It made an awful thud – there she lay in a pool of blood and I snickered.[22]

On a spring 1930 visit to Worcester, Elizabeth's habitual discomfort with the Bishop relatives manifested itself in an unexplained fainting spell, "four times – in rapid succession. The last swoon was on the cook's bosom in the kitchen."[23]

This mild cruel streak, and especially her apparent physical inability to tolerate her relatives, were evidence of the psychological difficulties that marked Elizabeth's high school years. They were severe enough to prevent her from being happy or comfortable there and to burden her further with asthma and other physical and spiritual ailments. One administrator, a Miss Farwell, was concerned enough to take her to see a psychiatrist in Boston. Elizabeth said forty years later that it had been an "excellent idea. . . . Unfortunately, I clammed up and wouldn't talk at all."[24] Her teachers at Vassar later made the same suggestion, which she refused.

Elizabeth had applied to Vassar for the fall of 1929, with Frani Blough and the other students of her age (eighteen), though they were a year ahead of her in school. Literary successes and two years of Latin notwithstanding, she was judged as lacking sufficient preparation in mathematics to enter college that fall, so she returned to Walnut Hill, to be editor of Prentiss's literary magazine, to be the star of several of her theatrical productions, and to take algebra.

The anticipation of moving on to Vassar aside, Elizabeth enjoyed being in the senior class at Walnut Hill, among the most sophisticated students in the school. Frani had left her bicycle to Elizabeth, on which she made her way around the campus. Her group of like-minded friends—alternately tomboyish and romantic—concocted highbrow schoolgirl adventures, including an all-night excursion in January to the upper reaches of the school's gym, where they built a fire in a stove, roasted marshmallows and potatoes, and sang carols in the dark. "The whole place was filled with smoke, and those long arched windows were all silvered with ice. Way down below you could see a little red circle where we had taken a stove lid off. The singing echoed. . . . I felt exactly as if we were drunken cathedral builders about five hundred years ago."[25] On Easter, they stayed up all night to catch the sunrise, sitting on stumps eating hot-cross buns as the sun came up "like a pot boiling over, I'm afraid. . . .

Easter could be much better even than Christmas, don't you think?"[26]

By late spring, when it was clear that she could enter Vassar in the fall with the class of 1934, Elizabeth was ready to move on. Full of irony about the Walnut Hill commencement exercises, as she was about all the institutional rites of passage she encountered, she marched for the benefit of her Worcester relatives, then embarked on a summer job, at fifteen dollars a week.

Elizabeth disappears from view in the summer of 1930, working at a job we do not know where, living under unknown circumstances, and feeling we do not know how about her preparations for Vassar. She must have seen this transition both as a significant passage to adulthood and a comforting continuation of her high school experience. Seven of her Walnut Hill classmates went with her to Vassar, including longtime friends Rhoda Wheeler and Shirley Clark. It was a significant passage to the time and place when her personality and ambition to write came together as she made the decisions that launched her adult life.

Two

ELIZABETH BISHOP ARRIVED at Vassar with some of the same baggage she had had at Walnut Hill: just enough money to get by in an atmosphere of wealth, uncertainty about where to go for holiday and summer vacations, a simmering literary ambition with no clear path to its fulfillment, and the beginnings of the conditions under which she would live her adult life—depression, debilitating asthma, and growing desperation in her use of alcohol.

To be sure, her classmates shared some of these concerns. Entering college a year after the stock market had crashed and just as the Depression took hold, the Vassar class of 1934 was made aware, perhaps earlier than it expected, of the limitations on familial, and national, resources. Enrollment declined at Vassar, as it did at all colleges, especially the expensive, private ones. One hundred and ten women in the class of 1934 withdrew before graduation. Those students who stayed learned to take less for granted and ushered in a generation of well-educated, politically and socially conscious, and left-leaning young people who would leave a lasting mark on the political scene of the United States.

With everyone's resources somewhat limited, it was easier for Elizabeth to make her way. Her college expenses—twelve hundred dollars in tuition, plus books and personal needs—were paid by the Bishop family in her first and second years and then by the income from a legacy left her by her father, which she came into at the age of twenty-one. She had occasional gifts and subsidies from the Bishop aunts and uncles, but most of her decisions about vacation plans and travel were made first with financial considerations in mind, and she continued to dread the interruptions to her security that college vacations represented. She was on her own, in terms of family and finances, much more than any of her college friends.

Elizabeth's teachers at college remembered her as "unusual," interesting and intelligent, "small, charming looking in an interesting way," with a "pleasing low voice" and an "elusive charm." She was "egocentric – aloof – respond[ed] to beauty in any form" and "simply not interested in community affairs."[1] They all noted her reserve—"politely reticent"—but they could also be slightly censorious. Her freshman English instructor Barbara Swain offered this view:

> My acquaintance with Elizabeth Bishop was purely a classroom one, and very distant at that, since she was an enormously cagey girl who looked at authorities with a suspicious eye and was quite capable of attending to her own education anyway. And I was young; and I liked prickly intractable people, and I certainly let her strictly alone, except for our class sessions about Shakespeare. I remember her stooped walk, and her gimlet look from under her eyebrows, and her cramped handwriting, and the fact that she seemed to have lived between the north and the south. . . . Every year at mid-term the English Department at Vassar "writes up" its first year students, trying as best it can to say what it sees about them; I remember that I wrote on Bishop's card that she was evidently doomed to be a poet—because people who have looked up her card since have been amused and wondered why put it that way?[2]

In her unpublished poem "A Drunkard," Elizabeth placed the beginnings of her alcoholism at the age of "twenty or twenty-one"; if this was the case, then the burden of concealing such a problem on a small campus, and of coming to terms with it in her own mind, might account for some of her distances from teachers, counselors, and classmates. Her college letters do refer often to drinking, but perhaps no more so than the letters of any college student. Her adviser, Helen Sandison, wrote that she was aware of "personal problems" in Elizabeth's life but that "when I opened a door, she would turn the talk to her work, about which she was intelligent & resourceful."[3] Elizabeth's own memories of her time at Vassar are sketchily recorded, but they evoke an intensely intelligent and self-absorbed young woman with a highly developed romantic sense of adventure. She recalled that she once spent a night in one of the magnificent trees outside Vassar's Cushing dormitory and said that she had once walked the length of Cape Cod, from the lighthouses at Sandwich to Race Point, an overnight trip, by herself. She was watchful of the processes of her mind and constantly sought access to her unconscious, where she knew her source of creativity must lie. She had heard that strong cheese before bed would make one's dreams more vivid, so she kept for a time a pot of smelly Roquefort on the bookshelf in her dorm room and carefully recorded the results. Her most vivid memory of college, she said, were the many train trips beside the Hudson River between Poughkeepsie and New York.

Elizabeth majored in English literature at Vassar and took nearly half her courses in that field. Sixteenth- and seventeenth-century poetry, Shakespeare and other Renaissance drama, contemporary prose fiction, a two-semester literary critical theory survey, American literature (including especially Henry James's late novels), and modern poetry were highlights for her, and she was the star pupil of Rose Peebles, for whom Elizabeth did some of her best work. She also took four years of Greek in college to complement her three years of high school Latin and said much later that she wished she had studied only the classical languages, so important were they to her sense of how poetry should work. She ended her senior year of Greek by completing a verse translation of Aristophanes' *The Birds*.

She took three years of music, concentrating on piano, and said that she had gone to college intending to major in music but had such anxiety before the required recitals that she managed only one and gave up. She sang in the college choir in her junior year. She also took a year of history and single one-semester courses in religion and zoology. Her performances in these courses was termed "erratic"—she earned mostly *A*'s in her English courses but did drop to a *C* from time to time. In Greek, she was capable of alternating semester to semester between *D*—the college's lowest passing grade—and *A*.

Elizabeth's college essays are sophisticated and interesting and show her to be working almost from the beginning among ideas and authors that would fascinate her throughout her life. Two of her essays for Peebles's contemporary prose fiction course—"Time's Andromedas," about how novelists depict the passage of time, and "Dimensions for a Novel," about size, shape, and perspective in novels—were published in the *Vassar Journal of Undergraduate Studies* and show her thinking in sophisticated theoretical terms about the novelist's craft; she was clearly a writer reading. The questions of perspective, form, and the passage of time that these essays raise stayed with Elizabeth, and lines from them ("that sense of constant readjustment," for example) turn up in later poems. The opening of "Time's Andromedas," which takes its title and epigraph from Hopkins, reveals traits that marked all her later work: meticulous observation and description, a visual imagination, shifting perspective, and characteristic images such as specklike birds, lapping waves, and metaphors from music theory.

> One afternoon last fall I was studying very hard, bending over my book with my back to the light of the high double windows. Concentration was so difficult that I had dug myself a sort of little

black cave into the subject I was reading. . . . My own thoughts, conflicting with those of the book, were making such a wordy racket that I heard and saw nothing—until the page before my eyes blushed pink. I was startled, then realized that there must be a sunset at my back, and waited a minute trying to guess the color of it from the color of the little reflection. As I waited I heard a multitude of small sounds, and knew simultaneously that I had been hearing them all along—sounds high in the air, of a faintly rhythmic irregularity, yet resembling the retreat of innumerable small waves, lake-waves, rustling on sand.

Of course it was the birds going South. They were high up, a fairly large sort of bird, I couldn't tell what, but almost speck-like, paying no attention to even the highest trees or steeples. They spread across a wide swath of sky, each rather alone, and at first their wings seemed all to be beating perfectly together. But by watching one bird, then another, I saw that some flew a little slower than others, some were trying to get ahead and some flew at an individual rubato; each seemed a variation, and yet altogether my eyes were deceived into thinking them perfectly precise and regular. I watched closely the spaces between the birds. It was as if there were an invisible thread joining all the outside birds and within this fragile net-work they possessed the sky; it was down among them, of a paler color, moving with them. The interspaces moved in pulsation too, catching up and continuing the motion of the wings in wakes, carrying it on, as the rest in music does—not a blankness but a space as musical as all the sound.[4]

Despite later disparaging comments about her Vassar education, Elizabeth never strayed far from the authors, ideas, and convictions she developed there. Her studies in Renaissance lyric poetry, especially of Herbert and Crashaw, and her love of Hopkins remained. More important, she learned at Vassar that she could have a literary career despite the limitations of gender. Writers visited the campus: T. S. Eliot, André Maurois, Archibald MacLeish, Constance M.

Rourke, James Stephens. And her classmates were role models. Her generation at Vassar included Mary McCarthy, 1933; Eleanor Clark, 1934; and, briefly, Muriel Rukeyser. Margaret Miller, 1934, a painter and an art historian; Eleanor's sister Eunice, 1933; and Frani Blough, 1933, a writer and musicologist, were equally ambitious. (There was even a Marianne Moore in the class of 1933.) The poet Mary Barnard, two years older than Elizabeth, pronounced the late 1930s and early 1940s "the era of the Vassar girl"—and these, along with Elizabeth Bishop, were the women she meant.[5] Most of Elizabeth's anecdotes about her time at Vassar centered around this circle of articulate, ambitious friends. In many ways, however, her less gifted friends were as important to her.

Elizabeth spent her first two years at Vassar taking the required introductory courses, deciding on a major, finding her way at the college. Her summers were spent, as they had been in high school, in the summer homes of her friends, Barbara Chesney's at Wellfleet, Rhoda Wheeler's near Westport, Louise Crane's in Falmouth. There they swam and sailed in the daytime, getting "brown all over" on the deserted beaches. She and Rhoda once spent the night on the beach at Wellfleet, which altered some of their romantic notions about the friendliness of nature: "It was frightful," Elizabeth wrote. "Around six the sun came up – never a cloud in the sky, just this great ugly orb slipping up like a canned peach out of a slimy yellow sea."[6] In the evenings they drank and talked, often about the shortage of eligible men. When her invitations ran out, she stayed with her aunt Florence or at the Hotel Lincolnshire in Boston. To Frani, Elizabeth wrote, "stranded here alone" in a hotel room in one of those stretches, "It's these awkward in between days–like measuring your paces over and over on a diving board before the final spring. I envy you a certain security your summer must possess."[7] She had trouble spending time alone—said she could not write when she was alone and could not write when she had company. In one of these "in-between" stretches she penned an example of her genius for the impromptu comic poem and revealed a traveler's preoccupation with losing things: "Lives of great men will remind us / We can live life as we choose, / And departing leave behind us / Towels, safety pins, and shoes."[8]

Later that summer, after her sophomore year, Elizabeth and college classmate Evelyn Huntington embarked on a three-week walking tour of Newfoundland, a dream that Elizabeth had nurtured for several years. The two women left Boston for the five-day ferry trip on August 13, 1932, and landed at St. John's on Thursday, August 18. Elizabeth kept a running journal of the trip in a brisk present tense ("I walk up the hill and hang over a fence"), two weeks of which have survived among her papers. The entries are recognizably and vividly Elizabeth's in their intense observation of the landscape and its people and interest in why things are arranged as they are. But her position relative to the friendly strangers she meets on the island is the journal's major interest. Here we see her for the first time as the touring foreigner, in the place but not of it, wanting to "stay forever" but finding it impossible. She does not yet ask her "questions of travel," but she presents them.

She and "Ev" did walk through Newfoundland, getting rides as they could in gravel trucks or donkey carts, staying in inns (they made a plan to try the "Sea View" in every town first) or in bed-and-breakfast arrangements in impoverished private homes. Elizabeth notes the accents and idioms of the native speech, the religious artifacts that decorate people's walls, the tenuous ways in which they make their livings, what they eat.

> August 23rd. . . . Mr. Ambrose Williams, in a beautifully knit
> (rope pattern) turtle neck sweater, is very handsome. Long head,
> white hair, long white moustaches, bright blue eyes, and a red face
> – very Irish. He is 68 years old. "Me dear man," he said to Ev. He
> asked us – several people have – "Do ye bile yer kettle out?" –
> meaning, do we ever cook anything outdoors along the way. He
> told us how he makes codfish chowder out at sea. They had a toy
> mechanical seal that they wound up & displayed for us. They
> couldn't understand why we wanted two beds. Mrs. W. says: "I've

slept three in that one." They were very hard feather beds. There
was a little iron stove in the room, too suggestive of the human
form, which I dressed in my clothes – from underwear up.

August 29th. A dark, foggy day. We have a hard time trying to
escape from poor Mrs. G.'s breakfast and get back to the Benville –
were we tactful or not? We have wonderful <u>coffee</u> and toasted rolls
there. Make our farewells, go off over the hills past Clark's Beach,
Robert's Bay, Spaniard's Bay, to Harbor Grace. – 20 miles. It is
rather hot. The people at Spaniard's Bay were ruder than any
before – they followed us through the street. We went to sit down
on the beach – dark, flinty stones – and gathered a real mob. We
fed the children molasses candy and made friends, but the older
boys were awful, all sniggers. Everyone skipped stones and spat.

The two women swam without suits in isolated bays, ate enormous
breakfasts of eggs and Devonshire cream, doctored each other's
menstrual cramps with black Newfoundland rum, and distributed
small but wildly appreciated amounts of money to impoverished
hosts and their children. The journal breaks off at September 3,
though they were in Newfoundland until at least the tenth. But she
wrote to Frani her regret at having been stymied in their quest for
the remote village of St. Anthony, "for after all, isn't St. Anthony
the patron of lost articles?" The village was "practically inacces-
sible."[9]

Elizabeth returned to Vassar in the fall of 1932 for her junior year
with a much stronger sense of herself as a writer than she had shown
at any time before. She took up several quasi-literary campus activities, joining the staff of the school newspaper, the *Miscellany News,*
where she wrote "sparse and witty pieces" for the "Campus Chat"
column and was given the plum assignment of interviewing T. S.
Eliot on his visit there in the spring. Elizabeth remembered herself
as a "mysterious figure" in the *News* office, and one staff member
recalled her as "a quiet, gray presence" in a gray sweater and skirt,

"at a slight remove from the rest of us," "a character from Henry James."[10] In Elizabeth's senior year, she edited the yearbook, the *Vassarion*. But, she said, "that had *nothing* to do with writing."[11] It required her, however, to speak before a group of alumnae at the college, where she was introduced as "Eleanor Bishop" and listened to her audience shout, "LOUDER" to her at intervals. She would hate speaking in public for another forty years or so. Also that year, Elizabeth was named the "Class Aesthete," and she and two friends, including Margaret Miller, were caricatured in the paper as "The Higher Types." Elizabeth considered this an honor.

Fancying themselves the advocates of a socially conscious avant-garde, Elizabeth and her group of literary friends did battle with the dusty establishment at Vassar in the fall of 1932 before effectively seceding to start their own literary magazine, *Con Spirito*. Elizabeth described the venture, which they launched in the winter of her junior year:

> It was during Prohibition and we used to go downtown to a
> speakeasy and drink wine out of teacups. That was our big vice.
> Ghastly stuff! Most of us had submitted things to the *Vassar
> Review* and they'd been turned down. It was very old-fashioned
> then. We were all rather put out because *we* thought we were
> good. So we thought, well, we'll start our own magazine.[12]

Con Spirito published its contributions anonymously, and though it shows no precise political bias, the feeling is understandably liberal, "puritanically pink," Elizabeth later said. Her short story "Then Came the Poor" tells of a young man whose wealthy family packs its fancy furniture in its fancy car and flees a "Red" mob, which seeks to equalize property. The young man, who keeps an ironic distance from both his family and the mob, stays behind and eventually is anonymously granted a share of his family's estate. Elizabeth published four poems and two stories in the two issues of

Con Spirito ("Three Sonnets for the Eyes," "Hymn to the Virgin," "The Flood," "A Word with You," "Then Came the Poor," and "Seven Days Monologue"), before, as she told it, "the *Vassar Review* came around and a couple of our editors became editors on it and then they published things by us." This happened just after the "very poor" first issue of the 1933–1934 *Con Spirito* appeared.[13]

What stands out among these early college poems is their wit, recognizably Elizabeth's, but delivered with such detachment and irony that the tone can be nasty, the effect vaguely disgusting. Elizabeth was reading Hopkins with passionate attention at this stage, as the "sprung" rhythm, heavy alliteration, and crabbed compounds of her sonnets show. This is the third of "Three Sonnets for the Eyes":

> Thy senses are too different to please me—
> Touch I might touch; whole the split difference
> On twenty fingers' tips. But hearing's thence
> Long leagues of thee, where the wildernesses increase . . . See
> Flesh-forests, nerve-vined, pain-star-blossom full,
> Trackless to where trembles th'ears' eremite.
> And where from there a stranger turns to sight?
> Thine eyes nest, say, soft shining birds in the skull?
>
>
> Either above thee or thy gravestone's graven angel
> Eyes I'll stand and stare. The secret's in the forehead
> (Rather the structure's gap) once you are dead.
> They leave that way together, no more strange. I'll
> Look in lost upon those neatest nests of bone
> Where steel-coiled springs have lashed out, fly-wheels flown.

The Vassar literary circle was also reading the giants of poetry in the early 1930s: T. S. Eliot, W. H. Auden, and Wallace Stevens. Elizabeth rarely mentioned Eliot as an influence on her work, and though some of the mordant wit of her college poems owes itself to the steady diet of Auden she and her friends consumed, she said she knew Stevens's *Harmonium,* in its 1931 edition, almost by heart. After Hopkins's, Stevens's influence asserts itself most strongly in Bishop's early poems. The comic masks and rhetorical poses Stevens donned in *Harmonium* helped legitimize for Elizabeth her own tendency toward impersonality in her poems (Eliot's example no doubt helped as well), and his early devotion to an idea of "pure poetry," indeed, the uneasy domination of reality by imagination, helps account for the detachment in Bishop's early work. The tendency toward gorgeousness, the fondness for fanciful titles, and the "art for art's sake" privileges of obscurity and abstraction she learned in part from the early Stevens. She clung to these even after the pressures of "reality" in the 1930s had driven the older poet to a more referential art. Elizabeth continued to read Stevens throughout her life but rarely mentioned him in letters or formal discussions of her poetic influences.

By her junior year, Elizabeth had begun sending her poems out to little magazines and had had some success. At *Hound & Horn,* Lincoln Kirstein had given a group of Elizabeth's poems an "honorable mention" in a contest for young writers, and through this her work had come to the attention of Yvor Winters, one of the magazine's regional editors. Winters had in turn introduced her to Donald Stanford, a Harvard graduate student and poet. Elizabeth and Donald carried on a lively and passionate literary correspondence for nearly a year, exchanging poems and expostulating on the state of poetry, offering one another sharp but respectful criticism. When Stanford objected to a line in an early version of "The Reprimand," Elizabeth defended herself in terms that said a good deal about what she thought poetry could and should accomplish in the way of sensation:

> I think you are [quite] right about my poem—but perhaps I
> disagree with you about why. You tell me to watch out for

unpleasant phrases like 'meditate your own wet' – when I have watched out for them and put them in deliberately. It has a lot to do with what I am attempting to write so I guess I shall try to explain it to you. 'Meditate your own wet' is unsuccessful I see now because it has such unpleasant connotations and it's liable to carry the point rather afield. But – if you can forget all your unpleasant associations with the words, I think possibly you'll admit that the phrase does for a second give you a feeling of intense consciousness in your tongue. Perhaps even that is unpleasant but I think that momentary concentration of sensation is worth while.[14]

Elizabeth's thinking about poetry was at this time heavily indebted to her reading of Hopkins, Crashaw, Herbert, and Renaissance prose writers. Her essay "Gerard Manley Hopkins: Notes on Timing in his Poetry" was published in the *Vassar Review* in 1934 and contains the seeds of all her later thinking on rhythm in poetry and the possibility of crafting it through variation. The essay derives a great deal from Hopkins's own "Author's Preface," which Robert Bridges included in his 1918 edition of Hopkins's poems, yet Elizabeth had clearly absorbed both the poems and Hopkins's philosophy about them. She begins the essay by explaining her own theory of "time," hoping to discover "why poets differ so from each other; why using exactly the same meters and approximate vocabularies two poets produce such different effects; why some poetry seems at rest and other poetry in action." Timing, she says, usually involves "coordination," which is

the correct manipulation of the time, the little duration each phase of the action must take in order that the whole may be perfect. And the time taken for each part of an action is decided both by the time of the whole, and of the parts before and after. . . . This whole series together sets up a *rhythm,* which in turn enables the series to occur over and over again—possibly with variations once it is established.

Just so in poetry: the syllables, the words, in their actual duration and their duration according to sense-value, set up among themselves a rhythm, which continues to flow over them. And if we find all these things harmonious, if they amalgamate in some strange manner, then the *timing* has been right.[15]

This formulation echoes the theory, or impression, of time that Elizabeth had developed in "Time's Andromedas," in which birds flying overhead in formation "set up a time pattern of their own" that alters the "clock-pace" of the bird-watcher below. Elizabeth went on in the Hopkins essay to explain, very much in Hopkins's own language, his theory of sprung rhythm and how it allows the poet to apply stresses according to sense rather than to an arbitrary pattern. Elizabeth later saw her own poetry as "some kind of blank verse," far indeed from the rigid meters of some of Marianne Moore's poetry, the "free verse" of the 1960s, and the self-conscious strangeness of Hopkins's meters. As Elizabeth wrote about Hopkins in 1934:

[There] may be serious faults making for the destruction of the more important rhythmic framework of the poem, but at the same time they do break down the margins of poetry, blurr [*sic*] the edges with a kind of vibration and keep the atmosphere fresh and astir. The lines cannot sag for an instant; by these difficult devices his poetry comes up from the pages like sudden storms. A single short stanza can be as full of, aflame with, motion as one of Van Gogh's cedar trees.[16]

A sensually derived rhythm came to Bishop through her reading of the Renaissance poets as well, George Herbert in particular. Like Hopkins, Herbert practiced his art in the face of, and in the service of, a vast unknown. To live thus experientially is to live by one's senses, to make poems that are multiple sense impressions themselves—poems that we take in through the eyes and ears as well as through intellect, poems that we respond to viscerally.

Elizabeth also established a connection in this essay between "Father Hopkins," as she called him, and the seventeenth-century prose writers she was studying so closely at Vassar, saying that Hopkins, like the baroque sermonists, seriously attempted to " 'portray, not a thought, but a mind thinking,' " that is, the process of sensory perception. Her source, M. W. Croll's *The Baroque Style in Prose,* remained a touchstone, and this insight, among the pages and pages of notes she took on the book, turned up often in her writing. More than thirty years later, she recalled it in an interview, calling Hopkins a great innovator in "poetic psychology."[17] Remembering the baroque sermon's attempt to "dramatize the mind in action rather than in repose," she saw a clear example of this tendency also in stanza 28 of Hopkins's "The Wreck of the Deutschland":

> But how shall I...make me room there:
> Reach me a...Fancy, come faster —
> Strike you the sight of it? look at it loom there,
> Thing that she...There then!...

Bishop's later apparent digression and self-revision in her poems, much remarked on, are her version of Hopkins's method, the baroque preacher's psychological methods, which she admired.

Once the *Con Spirito* conspirators had vanquished the *Vassar Review*'s conservatism, Elizabeth was free to publish there and became the journal's most consistent contributor. Her prose, like the futuristic fable "The Last Animal" and the dramatic monologue "Chimney Sweepers," shows her vivid, imaginative response to classroom assignments. The lower-class British accent of the London sweeps, a device she used to enliven a research paper for a British social history course, is thoroughly convincing:

> But coming down a slant like this here chimney you don't have to
> brace so hard because you won't fall if you don't—and so you
> hustles down, sort of on your hands and knees. Then, see, if
> there's a sort of dip all of a sudden, and the chimney narrows a

bit, why before you know it, you're jammed in there, all doubled up and it's one bloody job getting loose again.[18]

In "Mr. Pope's Garden," two guides lead Nature herself around the famous grounds at Twickenham in June 1719, thinking they are showing her her own work of genius. Nature is, of course, offended by the artifice of it all, Elizabeth writes, in an essay on a major philosophical debate of the eighteenth century. Of the poems she published in the *Review*, "Valentine I" and "Valentine II" were reprinted in Ann Winslow's *Trial Balances: An Anthology of New Poetry* (1935). "Some Dreams They Forgot" was included thirty-five years later in Elizabeth's *Complete Poems* (1969). The "Valentine" poems look back toward Elizabeth's dependence on her seventeenth-century models, on the effects of Hopkins's crabbed syntax, and on a sometimes facile verbal wit. ("Miss Bishop's sparrows ['Valentine I'] are not revolting, merely disaffecting," Marianne Moore said in *Trial Balances*.) Their subject, capricious love, Elizabeth would not discard for several decades.

. . .

Elizabeth and Donald Stanford carried on a mild flirtation in their letters as well, exchanging photographs and making plans to meet. Elizabeth had at first refused to send a photograph, as she typically did throughout her life, and sent instead this remarkable description of herself: "I'm five feet four I think, rather small, with rather large grey or blue eyes and a very intelligent expression. My hair is my most extraordinary feature—it's brown and carries on an independent life of its own—a tactful admirer recently told me it looked like something to pack china in."[19]

Later she did send a picture, and the two young poets arranged a meeting. Afterward, Elizabeth wrote to Frani that the visit with Donald had ended her romantic hopes for the relationship: "I have met the poet, who is very sweet but extremely young. I think he is spending all the money he has made on poetry this winter on me and I feel rather guilty about it. If he were five years or so older he'd be very nice."[20]

Elizabeth's everyday social life at Vassar is not much documented, and there is no evidence in letters or elsewhere that she was concerned about her sexual orientation. She had boyfriends and dates—including a stay on Nantucket over Christmas break 1932 with her current beau, Bob Seaver ("This kind of thing wasn't so common then," she told an interviewer).[21] Her friend Barbara Chesney had introduced them; she and Bob had grown up together in Pittsfield, Massachusetts. He and Elizabeth carried on a fitful courtship, but she visited his home in Pittsfield several times, and his family knew and liked her. Elizabeth had fond memories of the Nantucket trip, of sipping sherry and hot grogs with the lighthouse keeper's wife, who had all but adopted them. Bob, who had been crippled by polio as a teenager, got about on crutches and often evoked in observers an awkward sort of sympathy. Once the awkwardnesses passed, however, their relations were easy and warm. When that relationship broke up, Elizabeth formed no other serious attachment to a man until the late 1940s and often made self-deprecating comments about her lack of "success" with men. "Love" itself is the subject of countless ironic notebook entries that reflect more or less the spirit of "Varick Street": "And I shall sell you sell you / sell you of course, my dear, and you'll sell me."

Elizabeth seems not to have permitted her emerging homosexuality to come to consciousness, despite being surrounded by examples of lesbian relationships among her teachers and classmates. She did not write about it; she apparently did not talk about it. We cannot know what she thought. But we can imagine that despite such examples, the pressure to conform was great, and the dream of a "normal" life died hard. And Elizabeth was so estranged from her feelings, it is possible she did not hear or could not respect the signals her mind and body sent. But judging from the doodling in her college course notebooks (whole columns of a name written backward, forward, upward, downward, and diagonally in block letters and in fancy script) and the luminous descriptive passages in her journals, the great infatuation, at least, of her senior year was with her roommate, Margaret Miller.

There were social structures in place at Vassar to provide sexually neutral "covers" for intense friendships between women. Elizabeth wrote to Frani in her senior year, enclosing a college newspaper clipping about two classmates who had graduated in the fall and so were given their degrees in a private ceremony. Elizabeth and Margaret had been invited, and Elizabeth noted the article's last phrase with verbal raised eyebrows—"The two alumnae will settle for the winter in Boston"—but made no reference to herself.[22] Elizabeth did not have a great many friends. Those she had, especially when she was young, were women, often women and their mothers: Margaret and Mrs. Miller, Louise and Mrs. Crane, Marianne and Mrs. Moore. The mothers were no longer married, and the daughters would never be. Later Elizabeth formed warm friendships with men, with Tom Wanning, Robert Lowell, James Merrill, Ashley Brown, John Malcolm Brinnin, Howard Moss, and others, most easily when she could steer safely clear of sexual involvement.

Elizabeth's relationship with Margaret is not well documented; letters from Margaret to her in the archive begin in 1935, just at the time when Margaret stopped calling her "Bishop" and started addressing her as "Elizabeth."[23] The letters are long and journal-like and show no trace of attachment beyond an obvious delight between the two women in their affinity of minds, similar senses of humor, and in the chance to share their impressions with each other. Elizabeth's actual journals, however, refer many impressions and ideas to this friend and often contemplate Margaret herself.

Elizabeth was a year behind Mary McCarthy at Vassar and so missed being included in *The Group*, McCarthy's vicious roman à clef about the class of 1933. Elizabeth was good friends with Mary, but felt unable to judge the book when it appeared in 1963: "It's like trying to remember a dream, to me."[24] She did manage to assign the members of the group their original identities and found Frani included, but not herself. The novel's lesbian character, Lakey, whom some have suggested might be a caricature of Bishop, evoked no sign of recognition in Elizabeth. She said the book brought "those days back only too well – sleeping in a single cot with Mary and her first husband in the other one – and how they worried about their clothes; endless discussions of new spring outfits & pathetic interior-decoration schemes –."[25]

. . .

When Elizabeth began to publish stories and poems in national journals ("Then Came the Poor," for which she received twenty-six dollars and eighteen cents, and "Hymn to the Virgin," in the *Magazine*), she became something of a celebrity at Vassar and began tentatively to think of herself as a writer with ambitions beyond college. This process accelerated dramatically when she discovered in February 1934 that Fannie Borden, the Vassar College librarian, had been a childhood friend of Marianne Moore and might provide an introduction to the poet. Elizabeth had been reading Moore's poems as she found them in magazines and anthologies and went in to see Borden to find out why the college library had no copy of *Observations*. Borden arranged for Elizabeth to meet Moore on the right-hand bench outside the reading room of the New York Public Library on March 16, and Elizabeth said the meeting changed her life forever. Her memoir of their friendship, "Efforts of Affection," tells a somewhat streamlined story of that meeting, and it has been told many times since. But polished as the essay is, her letters reveal better her enthusiasm for the woman who became her mentor. She had met Donald Stanford at almost the same time; she begins this description to Frani with the words "Much more important," having sensed which poet would mean more to her.

> Frani, she is simply amazing – she is poor, sick, and her work is practically unread, I guess, but she seems completely undisturbed by it and goes right on producing perhaps one poem a year and a

couple of reviews that are perfect in their way – I have never seen anyone who takes such 'pains.' She is very impersonal and she is a little like Miss Borden – speaks just above a whisper, but at least five times as fast. I wish I could tell you about her. . . . She is really worth a good deal of study. . . . I hope she will let me take her to the circus – she's very fond of them & it's in N.Y. now.[26]

Elizabeth returned from her first meeting with Moore still shy but confident that she and the older poet had agendas before them—personal agendas first, for Elizabeth waited four months before telling Moore and her mother that she was trying to be a poet. Elizabeth's first letter to Moore reveals her deference but also her enthusiasm and her pleasure at having encountered a mind so like her own:

My dear Miss Moore:

I think you said you had not read the life of Hopkins by father Lahey so I am taking the liberty of sending you my copy of it. If you have read it, or if on reading it you think it is another book one shouldn't bother to own, why don't hesitate to get rid of it. The portrait is very strange.

I can't thank you enough for talking so long to me – and for coming into New York for the purpose. I'm amazed at my good fortune. I hope that I didn't tire you and that you weren't late for your dinner. The party was as bad as I had expected but I went calmly through rehearsing our conversation, and I have been taking notes ever since.

Are you interested in tattooing? A wonderful book on it just came out and I am trying to get a copy.[27]

A couple of weeks later, Elizabeth did find the courage to ask Moore to accompany her to the circus. Somewhat to her surprise, Moore accepted, and on April 25 they went. Elizabeth credited her inspiration about the circus with ensuring that she and Moore would be friends.

. . .

Elizabeth tried to make after-graduation plans according to her image of what a writer's life should be like. She needed a good atmosphere for "working"—that painfully indefinable activity for writers—a good library, solitude, but not too much and not in the evenings. She wanted to go to Europe, but that proved impossible; she thought she might drive across the United States with her friend Hallie Tompkins, but that did not work out; she thought she might live in Boston with Frani in a twenty-dollar-a-month apartment that Don Stanford had found. While Elizabeth was making these plans and the end of the year at Vassar was closing in on her ("Getting out of college seems to be about the worst step one can take," she told Frani),[28] her mother died in the sanatorium in Dartmouth, Nova Scotia, where she had been hospitalized since 1916. This event had no effect on Elizabeth's daily, practical life; she wrote to Frani, "I guess I should tell you that mother died a week ago today. After eighteen years of course it is the happiest thing that could have happened."[29] But it must have had a psychological effect, serving to remind her once again of her homeless state, of her lack of a solid ground from which to launch her life. She had begun writing that spring what she hoped would be a novel about her Nova Scotia childhood, the beginnings of the "Lucius" stories, in which she could tell, in disguise, the story of her mother's illness as the child perceived it. Her mother's death, at the very least, halted those explorations for a time. Elizabeth left Vassar after commencement on June 11 for the Hotel Brevoort in New York City to begin looking for an apartment there, perhaps because Margaret Miller, Louise Crane, and now Marianne Moore, and their mothers, were all in the city. And New York was, even then, the place for a young writer to be.

Three

ELIZABETH BISHOP LEFT COLLEGE intending to be a writer, but she had a clear idea that her education was not complete, that to be a writer involved continued hard work and a great deal of reading. Accordingly, she bought a new composition book, with unlined pages and a mottled black-and-white cover, in which to record her reading notes and her reactions, to draft poems and stories, and to paste newspaper clippings that caught her eye. She kept such notebooks consistently for the next ten years and off and on for the rest of her life. Elizabeth found herself unable to write in her new composition book, however, until the middle of July 1934, afflicted as she was with a disorienting malaise that baffled her. She wrote to Frani that in the month since leaving Vassar, "some kind of instant degeneration seems to have set in & I've scarcely set pen to paper."[1] Her trouble is thoroughly understandable to us, if not to her; graduating from college has disoriented many a young adult with a lot less terrifying autonomy than Elizabeth had, especially since her mother's death on May 28. While her friends went home after graduation, she went to a hot and noisy room at the Hotel Brevoort in New York, where she spent two and a half weeks hunting for an apartment and contemplating the possibilities of her future, which was immediately before her and entirely her own responsibility. By the end of June, Mary McCarthy and her husband Harold Johnsrud had found Elizabeth an apartment at 16 Charles Street in New York, "on the verge of the Village, unfortunately," Elizabeth said. She conducted her first experiment at living alone and living in New York in this apartment, a large one-bedroom with a big living room and fireplace. Set to move in at the end of July, she left on the first with her Uncle Jack for the Bishop family home at Harwichport. A week later she headed to Cuttyhunk Island, Massachusetts, for eighteen days, the first few in the company of Bob Seaver. The first page of the new composition book is marked "Cuttyhunk, July 1934."

Elizabeth loved Cuttyhunk in the way she loved nearly all her temporary homes by the sea. She liked her landlord, Mr. Van Wuthenaur; she liked her makeshift room and its ocean view, spearfishing, and sailing; she thought she might like to stay forever and delved into the island's history, especially its reputed mention in Shakespeare's *The Tempest*. And she loved Cuttyhunk, as she had loved Nova Scotia, Nantucket, and Newfoundland and would love Key West and North Haven, Maine, because it was an island.

> Mr. Van Wuthenaur wanted to "simplify life" all the time – that's the fascination of an island. That is also why it is fun to be in a difficult situation for a few hours, in which you have to make clothes out of barrells [?], tie machinery together with strings, eat berries, etc. On an island you live all the time in this Robinson Crusoe atmosphere; making this do for that, and contriving and inventing. And the limitations are not so consciously inflicted as Mr. V.W.'s were. A poem should be made about making things in a pinch – & and how it looks sad when the emergency is over. Margaret is good at this. . . .
>
> The idea of making things do – of using things in unthought of ways because it's necessary – has a lot more to it. It is an island feeling certainly. "We play with paste till qualified for pearl – "
> The awful tears a man must shed when he carves his house with a

jackknife. Using oleomargarine during the War. Doing it deliberately different from accepting that it is all that way. (You aren't really denying yourself much – no matter what you deny yourself.)

The island fascinated her for all its island aspects—the "cows that come here and get island sick & have to be taken for a trip to the mainland"; how "when any Island child gets a spanking the whole island knows about it"; how "they keep a coffin always on hand here, in case they need one," how it is kept in the jail and the prisoner, "when there is one," sleeps on it; how the fog drifts across the island "in great streamers and flags. Sometimes it's like being in a tent, sometimes inside a great fish skeleton"; the "Nova Scotia way of talking" of her hosts; the fascinating job of lighthouse keeper; the remarkable sunsets. In the four notebook pages Elizabeth devoted to her contemplation of Cuttyhunk, we see the beginnings of, or the preoccupations behind, a half-dozen later poems: the making-do that Crusoe does on his foggy island in "Crusoe in England"—the poem she did write about "making things in a pinch – & how it looks sad when the emergency is over" (Cuttyhunk had friendly goats as well). We see the clumsy, sad resourcefulness of "Manuelzinho"; the flowing and drawing of the cold Atlantic in "At the Fishhouses"; all the awful, cheerful activity of "The Bight"; the "long necks, or tentacles" of the island "curled out on the water & around on itself, yet never quite touching, like a balancing act" suggesting the peninsulas of "The Map"; and the catching and cleaning of striped bass: "As they lay there you could see a glimpse of the rose colored sheaf of gills, crisp and bloody," as in "The Fish." The paraphrase of Emily Dickinson—"We play with paste"— suggests that the nation's greatest woman poet was closer to Elizabeth's writer's imagination than she ever admitted publicly.

Elizabeth reluctantly left Cuttyhunk for New York on July 25, convinced that it was time she got "to work." The money she had inherited from her father freed her for a time from the need to get a paying job, and by work she meant the elusive work of a writer—reading, observing, practicing description, writing from this point of view or that, trying on voices and tones to find one of her own, thinking hard about what a poet or novelist does. She had a few things finished to send out, and that work—of mailing pieces and receiving rejections—was especially onerous to her. As the summer closed and fall arrived, she took a trip to Poughkeepsie and the library at Vassar to develop a "bibliography" for the winter. She established a work space in the New York Public Library where she read, among other works, Coleridge's *Biographia Literaria* and Ignatius Loyola's *Spiritual Exercises,* perhaps to further her work on Hopkins. R. H. Wislenksi's *The Modern Movement in Art* was clearly a touchstone. Her notebooks show her copying out long passages from these works, with her own commentary interspersed. A typical series of entries from those first few weeks in New York shows the seriousness of her endeavor to learn to write, her affinity for surrealism, and how much she already knew about her own practice:

> The rain came down straight and hard and broke into white arrow heads at the tips—

> [A newspaper photograph of members of the United States Navy at the Vatican]: "They Startled the Pope by Giving the Navy Football Cheer and Ending With Three Long 'Holy Fathers!' " "And the story of the American girl drinking in a Munich beer garden. A Nazi Storm trooper in uniform came along and jerked the cigarette out of her mouth and dropped it into her beer. She exclaimed, in a loud voice: 'Well, can you beat that!' "

> The white cat who danced down my street all by himself at seven in the morning—prancing across from sidewalk to sidewalk because the wind blew at him from behind, bending his tail over his head, and ruffling up the backs of his legs. He was furious with it, but had to sail along before it—

It's a question of using the poet's proper materials, with which he is equipped by nature, i.e., immediate, intense physical reactions, a sense of metaphor and decoration in everything – to express something not of them – something I suppose, spiritual. But it proceeds from the material, the material eaten out with acid, pulled down from underneath, made to perform and always kept in order, in its place. Sometimes it cannot be made to indicate its spiritual goal clearly (Some of Hopkins', say, where the point seems to be missing) but even then the spiritual must be felt. Miss Moore does this – but occasionally I think, the super-material content in her poems is too easy for the material involved, – it could have meant more. The other way – of using the supposedly "spiritual" – the beautiful, the nostalgic, the ideal and poetic, to produce the material – is the way of the Romantic, I think – and a great perversity. This may be capable of being treated by a mere studying of simile and metaphor – This is why genuine religious poetry seems to be about as far as poetry can go – and as good as it can be – it also explains the dangers of love-poetry.

It came to her suddenly in the morning, just as she was pulling her mind up to the surface for the day – like a bucketful of water out of well – that part of the mind she'd use for that day – then dumped in again at the night, with the addition of whatever soluble things it had met during the day.

washing the face with snow – a saintly process. The white masked saints –

The third rail is almost worth some sort of prose poem. Running along silently, as insincere as poison –

I don't think we can stand too much virtue in our friends – at least not the kind that penetrates through and through.

the creme-de-menthe sea (for prose purposes only)

I should like to make, just for my own edification and satisfaction, the same sort of analysis or cataloguing of literature – or possibly just poetry –

"The Enigmas of Easter Island," descriptions of animals at the Aquarium and the Museum of Natural History, personal reviews of concerts and plays, descriptions worked up for tone and emphasis, pieces of conversation overheard, lists of material written and material to write, a list of objects that Dutch cleanser was advertised as being able to clean ("Bath Tubs, Sinks / Porcelain, Marble / Tiling, Mantels / Glazed Brick / Statuary, Bronze / Monuments"). Many of these fragments turn up later in her parable about the writer's craft, "The Sea and Its Shore." But Margaret Miller is the touchstone of this notebook (Bob Seaver disappears after its first page), the point outside herself that Elizabeth referred her impressions to ("Margaret tells me this morning, over the telephone, that it was very foggy all night over on the East River. The boats kept their fog horns going") and that often became the subject of them: "Margaret was as sweet as sherbet in her pink blouse today. Her face had that soft look about it, as if she had slept an extra hour or two, and her eyes a clear, original color that they blend for themselves out of several colors never in eyes before hers." Margaret's clever phrases or observations are recorded faithfully, as if for later attribution. A few weeks later, Elizabeth mused in her notebook, "The chief trouble with writing novels, etc., about homosexuals seems to be the difficulty of handling the pronouns: One always runs into things like, 'He took him in his arms & he...' etc."

. . .

In August, Elizabeth reestablished her contact with Marianne Moore and her mother, and Marianne began to assume the role of mentor that she would play in Elizabeth's life for the next six years. As much as Elizabeth had loved Moore's early poems, she was also grateful for the example of Moore's career. During the time of Elizabeth's apprenticeship, Moore gave no readings and attended few, confining her practice of poetry to the exacting critical circle formed of herself and her aged mother, a circle to which Elizabeth was gradually admitted. Later, after her mother's death, Moore returned to the active literary life of readings and lectures and became one of the most publicly recognizable poets ever. It was not until 1966, when Moore was nearly incapacitated by old age, that Elizabeth accepted her first teaching job; not until well into the 1970s, after Moore's death, did Elizabeth become a well-known poet in the American style. Forever shy of the camera, her face never became nationally familiar in the way Marianne's distinctive visage had. Although her poems are now perhaps more "popular," Elizabeth certainly learned by Moore's example that it was possible to be a poet without subjecting herself to the stresses of reading, teaching, and editing, as Moore had done and then ceased to do. By nature a slow and meticulous writer, a shy and extremely private person, Elizabeth had no inclination toward the public life. In college, she had gravitated toward the lawyer-poet Stevens over the more public Auden; as an adult, she seized Moore's example to justify her own reclusive tendencies.

Marianne Moore was without a doubt the most important single influence on Elizabeth Bishop's poetic practice and career. Although Elizabeth was a precocious young poet who wrote with a firm eye and hand even as a high school student; and although several of her early poems self-consciously addressed Moore's poems, what really changed for Elizabeth when she began reading Moore was her idea of what, among the objects and emotions in the world, was suitable for poetry. Her early (but postcollege) poems reflect some fondness for Moore's mannerisms—for instance, the unattributed quotation or the use of quotation marks, not as usual, but "as boundaries for units of association which cannot be expressed by grammar and syntax" (as in "Roosters" or "Wading at Wellfleet"), but she never showed an inclination toward syllabics or strict metrical verse, which Moore used off and on throughout her life.[2] In a 1954 letter to

Moore, Elizabeth discussed at length this issue of influence, which might have been much on her mind, paused as she was then between her first and second books, between her pre- and post-Brazil styles. Moore had written her, "I was dumbfounded & gratified to read in Les Journal des Poêtes that your work showed traces of my influence."[3] Elizabeth reacted thoughtfully, though with some irritation at the latest suggestion:

> I don't know what Les Journal des Poetes is, I'm afraid – you say it says I show your influence,…Well, naturally, I am only too delighted to. – Everyone has said that – I was going to say, all my life – and I only wish it were truer. My own feeling about it is that I don't show very much; that no one does or can at present; that you are still too new and original and unique to show in that way very much but will keep on influencing more and more during the next fifty or a hundred years. In my own case, I know however that when I began to read your poetry at college I think it immediately opened up my eyes to the possibility of the subject-matter I could use and might never have thought of using if it hadn't been for you. – (I might not have written any poems at all, I suppose.) I think my approach is much vaguer and less-defined and certainly more old-fashioned – sometimes I'm amazed at people's comparing me to you when all I'm doing is some kind of blank-verse – can't they see how different it is? But they can't, apparently.[4]

Even with the tempering influence of graciousness on both sides of this exchange, these serious thoughts on the issue of Moore's influence are unique in Elizabeth Bishop's prose. Although she talked and wrote a great deal about the friendship, her reminiscences and reflections are largely personal, the sort of affectionate portrait we find in her poem "Invitation to Miss Marianne Moore." Her long memoir of Moore, "Efforts of Affection," was published after both their deaths, and its title refers first to Moore's poem and then to the modest attempt of the essay itself. In it, Elizabeth recalls the circumstances of their meeting, allowing that it "was possibly to influence the whole course of my life," and comically illustrates the sort of moral "rules" Moore and her mother had for poetry. Elizabeth does not, however, address the influence of Moore's poetry on her own. She does say that eventually she herself "grew obstinate" against those rules. But the "atmosphere" at 260 Cumberland Street in Brooklyn, where Moore lived with her mother and where Elizabeth visited often in 1934–1935, was a tremendous influence and, Elizabeth said, exuded prescriptions for good living and writing: "I never left . . . without feeling happier: uplifted, even inspired, determined to be good, to work harder, not to worry about what other people thought, never to try to publish anything until I thought I'd done my best with it, no matter how many years it took—or never to publish at all."[5] This last might be the single most important aspect of Elizabeth's subsequent career.

Moore's work habits would have been a valuable example to any aspiring writer, but for Elizabeth they set a standard she could never quite reach. In a story she told several times, she remembered a bushel basket full of discarded versions of a short review Moore was working on and pointed to that and the drafts of her poems as exempla of "hard work" made more impressive by the fact that Moore disliked the review when it was "finished." In a 1948 essay that accompanied the "Invitation" poem in the *Quarterly Review of Literature,* Elizabeth again said (as she had suggested in her notebook) that she thought Moore strove a bit harder than necessary in developing her complicated stanza forms (whose perfection required all that "hard work"), but for honorable reasons. Here Elizabeth sounds slightly reductive of Moore the poet in favor of Moore the character:

> Sometimes I have thought that her individual verse forms, or
> "mannerisms" as they might be called, may have developed as
> much from a sense of modesty as from the demands of artistic
> expression; that actually she may be somewhat embarrassed by her

own precocity and sensibilities and that her varied verse forms and rhyme schemes and syllabic logarithms are all a form of apology, are saying, "It really isn't as easy for me as I'm afraid you may think it is." The precocious child is often embarrased [*sic*] by his own understanding and is capable of going to great lengths to act his part as a child properly; one feels that Miss Moore sometimes has to make things difficult for herself as a sort of noblesse oblige, or self-imposed taxation to keep everything "fair" in the world of poetry.[6]

Later Elizabeth said that Moore's poems demanded, "Let us be poets over and above the call of duty. Give more than is required; throw in trills and appoggiaturas for the joy of it."[7] Randall Jarrell also commented on the "difficulties undertaken for their own sake" in Moore's poetry, an excess Elizabeth never matched. Nevertheless, Elizabeth tended to play down the achievement of her own writing, in part because she never seemed to herself to be working hard enough or as hard as Moore worked. Moore, like Robert Lowell, was a tenacious reviser of her own poems, even after their publication. Elizabeth never practiced and professed to disapprove of such "derangement." That her two closest poet-friends practiced it was a matter of some discomfort for her.

Elizabeth also remembered in "Efforts of Affection" that Moore "believed that graceful behavior—and writing—as well, demands a certain reticence." Elizabeth's native sense of privacy and discretion was so great that one suspects the two had this belief in common from the start. So, too, Moore's intense interest in "the techniques of things" suggests Elizabeth's:

> how camellias are grown; how the quartz prisms work in crystal clocks; how the pangolin can close up his ear, nose, and eye apertures and walk on the outside edges of his hands "and save the claws / for digging"; how to drive a car; how the best pitchers throw a baseball; how to make a figurehead for her nephew's

sailboat. The exact way in which anything was done, or made, or functioned, was poetry to her.

Elizabeth's examples here are from both Moore's poems and her letters; one could compose a similar list to show her own equal fascination. Perhaps Moore's example did teach Elizabeth that such workings were "poetry": the design of a fish's insides and how it breathes; the carving of figureheads, *caranças,* on boats on the Rio São Francisco in Brazil; how swans turn their eggs; the desire to name things by their right names ("Job's Tear, the Chinese Alphabet, the scarce Junonia, / parti-colored pectins and Ladies' Ears"); how gemstones are cut; how to make parkins or orange marmalade.[8]

    . . .

By September 1934, Elizabeth was actively looking for a paying job in New York, feeling both that she had too much unstructured time and not enough money and that her absence from the labor force was politically incorrect in the atmosphere of the 1930s. Jobs were hard to find; the war boom had not yet begun, and a young woman who could not type with any efficiency was at a crippling disadvantage. After months of looking, Elizabeth took a position as a writing instructor for the shadiest sort of matchbook-cover correspondence school: "You Can Become a Published Author!" Elizabeth was not proud of the job and told the story only in a marvelous memoir that she chose not to publish, "The U.S.A. School of Writing." Her 1934 notebook contains an early draft of the piece, entitled "A Week at the U.S.A. School of Writing," in which she copied out letters from her "students," from Bertha Roy of Ellsworth, Kansas, and James Shea of Dorchester, Massachusetts, who wrote the letter to "Mr. Margolies" (Elizabeth's editorial pseudonym) that clearly fascinated her. It turns up here, in the U.S.A. School piece, and in "The Sea and Its Shore."

Elizabeth's self-portrait in the U.S.A. School memoir shows her to be fiercely observant of the atmosphere and detail of New York in the mid-1930s and of the nuances of working for an illegal business and thoroughly skeptical, as she would always be, about both political movements and the teaching of writing. Her colleague, "Mr. Hearn," a swarthy Communist woman actually named Rachel, is an ill-smelling caricature of the 1930s radical. Her students, with one or two exceptions, are uninspired isolatoes hoping for fame and a "shortcut to identity." "I could never quite believe," Elizabeth wrote years later, "that most of my students really thought that they too could one day write, or even that they would really have to work to do so. It was more like applying for application blanks for a lottery. After all, they might win the prize just as well as the next person, and everyone knows those things aren't always run honestly."[9] This lack of generosity in Elizabeth's comments about these hopefuls colored all her later teaching experiences as well. Accessible and helpful to the gifted student, she had little to say to the uninspired plodder. Lack of talent, of education, or of "a room of one's own" in an aspiring writer was a moral failing for Elizabeth, and she never overcame this native elitism. One suspects as well that her later thinking about the teaching of writing, poetry workshops, creative writing courses, and the like was influenced by this first look at the exploitation of talentless ambition.

But the essay also shows her thinking seriously about what she valued in art, about what distinguishes, say, the genuine "primitive" painter from the merely bad writer:

> There seemed to be one thing common to all their "primitive"
> writing, as I suppose it might be called, in contrast to primitive
> painting: its slipshoddiness and haste. Where primitive painters
> will spend months or years, if necessary, putting in every blade of
> grass and building up brick walls in low relief, the primitive writer
> seems in a hurry to get it over with. Another thing was the almost
> complete lack of detail. The primitive painter loves detail and
> lingers over it and emphasizes it at the expense of the picture as a
> whole. But if the writers put them in, the details are often

impossibly or wildly inappropriate, sometimes revealing a great deal about the writer without furthering the matter in hand at all.

Mrs. Bertha Roy from Kansas wrote real stories that "bounced along exuberantly, like a good talker, and were almost interesting, with a lot of local color and detail. They were filled with roosters, snakes, foxes, and hawks, and they had dramatic and possibly true plots woven around sick and dying cows, mortgages, stepmothers, babies, wicked blizzards, and tornadoes." And Mr. Jimmy O'Shea's ("James Shea" in the notebook) prose was the closest to "classical primitive": "He had developed a style that enabled him to make exactly a page of every sentence. . . . Goodness shown through his blue-lined pages as if they had been little paper lanterns." Mr. O'Shea might have been speaking for Elizabeth when he wrote about his fear of and ambition for writing to Mr. Margolies: "I am thinking of being able to write like all the Authors, for I believe that is more in my mind than any other kind of work. Mr. Margolies, I am thinking of how those Authors write such long stories of 60,000 or 100,000 words in those Magazines, and where do they get their imagination and the material to work upon? I know there is a big field in this art."

The moral difficulties forced on all writers by the Depression affected Elizabeth's thinking about poetry and its purposes through-out her life. Coming of age in an era when the artist's calling was especially hard to justify added to her own anxieties about vocation and about the value of her "pure poetry" in an age that demanded political commitment in its writers and didactic purpose in their poems. The suspicion that poetry, her poetry in particular, was somehow beside the point stayed with Elizabeth for a long time; her notebooks show her trying hard in her first few years out of college to think of herself as a novelist instead. And when *North & South* was finally published in 1946, she persuaded her publisher to include a note explaining that most of its poems had been written before 1942, which was why the book contained no apparent reference to World War II.

Elizabeth abandoned the U.S.A. School job after a very brief stint (perhaps only the "week" she mentioned in her notebook), escaping just before the proprietor was arrested for mail fraud for the second time. With her small inheritance income, she again faced New York and the cursed blessing of time to continue her apprenticeship to the art of writing, to "test the market," and to decide what to do. She and Margaret took a course at the New School, "Specimens of Advanced Mathematics: The Family of Curves," which she loved; but the real business of her life as she saw it, making her way in literary New York, was a constant torture. She wrote to Frani, "Every day I start out firmly to ask someone to let me review poems for them. I get so scared that I have to stay at home with diarrhea." Unable to prevent this "morbid purging" of fear, she settled in to live cheaply, read all the late Henry James novels in her accustomed seat at the public library, go to concerts and plays, and record all these activities in her notebook. She studied carefully James's method, the famous "composition in scenes" (which would come to characterize her own poetry), especially as he discussed it in his prefaces and in *A Small Boy and Others*. In *What Maisie Knew, The Golden Bowl*, and *The Wings of the Dove* she saw it at work. It was hard not to absorb this style as well: "I couldn't write a plain, ordinary letter any more. . . . No one would ever know what I was talking about unless they'd been reading 'The Wings of the Dove,' too."[10]

She went up to Vassar to hear Gertrude Stein's lecture "Portraits I have Written and What I think of Repetition, Whether it Exists or No" on November 10. She pasted into her notebook in its entirety and without comment the instructions for "Joke Specs with Shifting Eyes: Spectacle Mask with Eyes operated by Blowing." She saw the Philadelphia Orchestra under Leopold Stokowski do the Bach B-minor Mass on December 18 and Bruno Walter play the Mozart Piano Concerto in D Minor on December 21.

Elizabeth attempted to spend Christmas Day 1934 with Margaret and her mother but became so ill with asthma that she had to return to Charles Street and go to bed. Holidays never became less emotionally treacherous for her. Her doctor issued her adrenalin and syringes so that she could treat herself for acute asthma attacks, but there was no preventive element in her treatment as yet.

Elizabeth had first developed asthma in the Worcester house of the Bishop grandparents, and her treatments for the condition grew as research on the disease did. She was treated with multiple doses of injected adrenalin, sometimes three or four cubic centimeters two or three times a night. Later she experimented with nearly every other possible treatment for asthma, including large doses of oral cortisone. The condition dominated her life between 1934 and 1951. It fed her sense of homelessness and sent her away from places she would rather have stayed. A self-proclaimed poet of geography, she often traveled specifically in search of air she could breathe. And so for Elizabeth—who had the means to travel—asthma was intimately tied up with the idea of "place." She had at this time no scientific information about what caused her attacks and could learn this only by experience.

Asthma is depressing. Not getting enough oxygen in the blood-stream is chemically depressing, and the fear of an attack, anxiety about breathing, and the limitations the disease can place on the asthmatic's activities and destinations, the sleep lost to nighttime ambushes from unseen enemies, the sense of weakness and betrayal by one's body, the manipulation of one's moods by drugs—all conspire to keep the sufferer from rising above her illness.

Elizabeth developed flu as well at Christmas 1934 and spent the next two weeks more or less in bed, living on "adrenalin and cough syrup." Alone on New Year's Eve, she celebrated the coming of 1935 with a hot bath and shared the moment itself with the mechanical voice at Meridien 7–1212: "When you hear the signal the time will be 12 o'clock. Bzzz."[11] She spent most of the evening, however, sitting on the floor of her apartment, contemplating a framed and glassed map of the North Atlantic (the Canadian Maritime Provinces, Greenland, Iceland, Scandinavia), and writing a poem:

> The shadow of Newfoundland lies flat and still.
> Labrador's yellow, where the moony Eskimo
> has oiled it. We can stroke these lovely bays,
> under a glass as if they were expected to blossom,
> or as if to provide a clean cage for invisible fish.

"The Map" was a breakthrough for Elizabeth. First published alongside "Three Valentines" and "The Reprimand" in the *Trial Balances* anthology in 1935, it presents such a contrast to those mannered, imitative college poems that the reader wishes for an explanation. The example of meaning generated through contemplation of a single object, the familiar object reseen, the commitment to accuracy, the reach of simile, the wisdom of tone, the naturalness of diction—these are gifts Marianne Moore gave Elizabeth as well as infinite subjects less hackneyed than "sorrow" and "love" and the ability to trust her own instinct in handling those subjects. This is the first "Elizabeth Bishop" poem we have, and Elizabeth knew that well enough to place it first in *North & South* and first in her collected poems of 1969.

"The Map" opens in a fairly regular iambic pentameter, which Bishop varies to good effect in the seventh line, "Along the fine tan sandy shelf," producing an effect reminiscent of Hopkins. The *a b b a* rhyme scheme of the first and last stanzas gives way in the middle one to a loose and prosy blank verse that makes room for personally significant metaphors: Eskimo-oiled Labrador, clean cages for invisible fish, the printer's excitement, the peninsulas like the fingers of a woman's hand. Bishop drops her usual line of initial capitals in the poem as well, and we see that she has taken her models—chiefly Hopkins's sonnets, which she had imitated with such care in college—and transformed them suddenly to produce a poem in a thoroughly convincing original voice.

"The Map" proceeds, as many later Bishop poems do, by semirhetorical questions of perspective: "Shadows, or are they shallows," "Or does the land lean down to lift the sea from under, . . . / is the land tugging at the sea from under?" This is the first mature manifestation of her undergraduate belief that poetry should portray the mind thinking rather than reposing as well as the beginning of a lifelong concern with shifting perspective and scale. The whole business of maps is scale and perspective, of course; this is how the cartographic group of Scandinavian countries can resemble the fingers of "women feeling for the smoothness of yard-goods," women Elizabeth grew up among, perhaps. Bishop's poem asks questions the map cannot answer and is successful in part because it simultaneously holds forth both the map and the actual geography (the physical world not drawn to scale) as realities. And as the excitement of the printer enters the poet's contemplation, we realize that the map has a third meaning separate from what it represents, that it also contains "emotion" that "too far exceeds its cause."

This part of the map depicts Elizabeth's "home," or as near as she had come to it. Alone as she was on New Year's Eve, acutely uncertain about what the future would bring, nostalgia might be that emotion. And months earlier, Elizabeth had written in her notebook: "Name it friendship if you want to – like names of cities printed on maps, the word is much too big, it spreads all over the place, and tells nothing of the actual <u>place</u> it means to name."

When she first began working on the image, Elizabeth was contemplating the nature of her attachment to Margaret Miller, and that undefinable emotion is invested in the poem as well. The astonishing cool of the lines, "the printer here experiencing the same excitement / as when emotion too far exceeds its cause" disguises the fact that Elizabeth is working here at the heart of all that mattered to her personally and poetically. The printer—a writer—is also the poet.

The task of the mind devoted to accuracy is to be continually aware of perspective; no angle on a subject can be taken for granted, not even that of a map. In a 1948 letter, Elizabeth explained some of the poem's philosophical origins in terms of this awareness of point of view:

> A sentence in Auden's Airman's Journal has always seemed very profound to me – I haven't the book here so I can't quote it exactly, but something about time and space and how "geography is a thousand times more important to modern man than history" – I always like to feel exactly where I am geographically all the time, on the map, – but maybe that is something else again.[12]

Indeed, the poem's movement suggests simultaneous reality and impression the way flying over a familiar landmass does—the method exactly of cartographers, who transfer their impressions to paper.

> Mapped waters are more quiet than the land is,
> lending the land their waves' own conformation:
> and Norway's hare runs south in agitation,
> profiles investigate the sea, where land is.
> Are they assigned, or can the countries pick their colors?
> —What suits the character or the native waters best.
> Topography displays no favorites; North's as near as West.
> More delicate than the historians' are the map-makers' colors.

Elizabeth always liked to feel herself in place on the map and always preferred geography to history. Many of her poems describe the struggle to locate herself in the world. To be able to say, "I am this many miles from Rio" or "this many miles from New York," to be able always to say, whether she faced north or south, that the Atlantic Ocean lay just off one hand is to be able to name her point of view. Her need to name it again and again is a sign of her lifelong uncertainty about it.

This New Year's evening may also have produced the half-serious "Poem from 1935" that remained among her papers. It contemplates, once again, the passage of time:

FIGURE 1.   Elizabeth Bishop, at about
one year of age. Courtesy Vassar
College Library.

FIGURE 2.   Elizabeth, at eighteen
months. Courtesy Vassar College
Library.

FIGURE 3. Gertrude May Boomer
Bishop and William T. Bishop,
Elizabeth's parents, c. 1909. Courtesy
Vassar College Library.

FIGURE 4. Elizabeth's mother,
Gertrude; family friends Una and Elsie
Layton; her aunts Grace and Maud; in
Nova Scotia, 28 January 1916. Courtesy
Vassar College Library.

FIGURE 5.   Gertrude Bishop and her
daughter, Elizabeth, c. 1915. Courtesy
Vassar College Library.

FIGURE 6.   Elizabeth, at play with
Nova Scotia neighbors, c. 1915.
Courtesy Vassar College Library.

FIGURE 7.   "Primer Class," Nova
Scotia, 1916–17. Canadian Post-Card
Co. Ltd., Toronto. Courtesy Vassar
College Library.

FIGURE 8.   Elizabeth, at twelve.
Courtesy Vassar College Library.

FIGURE 9.   Elizabeth Bishop,
yearbook photograph, Walnut Hill
School. Courtesy Vassar College
Library.

FIGURE 10.   Elizabeth, in her Senior portrait, *Vassarion 1934.* Courtesy Vassar College Library.

FIGURE 11.   Marianne Moore, c. 1938. Photograph by Arthur Steiner. Courtesy Rosenbach Museum and Library.

FIGURE 12. Margaret Miller, Quai
d'Orleans, 1937. Courtesy Vassar
College Library.

FIGURE 13. Elizabeth in Key West, in
about 1940. Courtesy Vassar College
Library.

FIGURE 14. Hannah Almyda, Elizabeth's Key West house-keeper and friend. Courtesy Vassar College Library.

FIGURE 15. Gregorio Valdes's painting of Elizabeth's Key West House (624 White Street), the first of her "three loved houses." Courtesy Rosenbach Museum and Library.

The past
at least
is polite:
it keeps out of sight.

The present
is more recent,
It makes a fuss
but is unselfconscious.

The future
sinks through water
fast as a stone,
alone alone.

Later she would be less certain about the tractability of the past.

. . .

Elizabeth grew weary of the northern city winter as January 1935
moved along and said that only the "scenic attractiveness of snow"
kept her from heading for an as-yet-undesignated southern climate.
She used the dreary winter days to continue her reading and con-
certgoing, and her discoveries in this, perhaps the only extended
period of authentic contemplation she managed in her life, seem
luminously significant now in light of her later poems. On January
10, under the title "A Little Miracle," she wrote in her notebook:

> This morning I discovered I had forgotten to get any bread and I
> had only one dry crust for breakfast. I was resigning myself to
> orange juice and coffee and no more when the door-bell rang. I
> pushed the button, and up the stairs trailed a weary-looking
> woman, shouting ahead of herself: "I don't want to sell you
> anything – I want to give you something!" I welcomed her at that,
> and was presented with a small box containing three slices of
> "Wonder Bread," all fresh, a rye, a white, and whole-wheat. Also a
> miniature loaf of bread besides – The only thing I disliked about

the gift was that the woman opened the box, held it under my nose, and said "Smell how sweet!" But I breakfasted on manna—

This "miracle for breakfast," pressed by some longer, though indirect experience of Depression-era soup lines and hunger in New York and by the French surrealists as she read them intensely in Douarnenez and Paris in August and September 1935, became the sestina of that title.

She and Marianne Moore continued their shared investigations of such animal life as was to be found in New York during the winter. On January 25, Elizabeth asked Marianne to accompany her to Martin Johnson's jungle film, *Baboons.* Beginning in the mid-1920s, Johnson was every American's introduction to Africa, New Guinea, and Borneo, and Elizabeth later borrowed him, along with his wife, Osa, for the February 1918 issue of the *National Geographic,* in "In the Waiting Room." In the same letter to Moore, she indulged their shared love of and concern for accuracy:

> Do you know—I am sure you must—that medieval falcon cut
> from rock crystal, in one of the medieval rooms at the
> Metropolitan? I was admiring him on Saturday, and hoping that
> you had seen him, too. . . . Some of their inscriptions baffle me—a
> perfectly sensible crystal fish, for example, something like a perch,
> labelled "Porpoise." And a young man on a Greek vase who is
> obviously cutting the ends of his hair with his sword, called "Boy
> Washing Hair (?)"[13]

Elizabeth had taken away from her music studies at Vassar a passion for early music, and for a couple of years after her graduation she believed that her first big writing projects would be a verse play or masque modeled after Ben Jonson (strange lyrics for which are scattered throughout her early notebooks) and an opera libretto for which Frani Blough would compose music. As January wore on, Elizabeth began to think seriously again of taking up music, and an unexpected and large check from a Bishop relative permitted her to indulge a fantasy she had had for several months and buy a clavichord. Her notebook in the spring is filled with careful annotations of studies of early keyboard music, and she was reading, on the advice of a friend, Ezra Pound's essay on the Dolmetsches. By April, she had decided, on the advice of Ralph Kirkpatrick (whom she had engaged to give her lessons), to order a custom-made clavichord from Arnold Dolmetsch himself and to pick it up in Paris. She saw her studies in music as closely allied to her thinking about poetry and noted to Moore that Hopkins, in his late investigations of music theory and composition, "mentions some of the very things I've been studying."[14] To Frani, Elizabeth justified her purchase of the clavichord by quoting Ezra Pound to the effect that " 'the further poetry departs from music the more decadent it gets.' "[15] Her thinking about the relationship between music and poetry was an important part of her thinking about poetry in general, and part of her fondness for seventeenth-century verse lay in her idea that poetry and music had been more closely linked then. Elizabeth loved blues and jazz as well as classical music and drafted song lyrics in her notebooks for years. She published "Songs for a Colored Singer" in 1944, and in later years both Ned Rorem and Elliot Carter set her poems to music. During her stays in New York in the 1930s, she and her friends were drawn into the circle of listeners and admirers of Billie Holiday, who performed in clubs they frequented.

The clavichord figures in Elizabeth's life for the next forty years, more often as an object among her "things" than as a musical instrument. It became one of those possessions that is its own reason for being and that organizes and focuses the energy of the human beings around it. Elizabeth did take a few clavichord lessons with Ralph Kirkpatrick and a few more at the Schola Cantorum in Paris; and later, in Brazil, she restored the instrument in hopes of playing duets with a woman who lived in the same apartment building in Rio. But mostly the clavichord was being shipped, being picked up at the dock, making its way through customs, or being stored at Frani's or at Kirkpatrick's because the weather was too damp in Florida or too dry in Nova Scotia. Like the cats Elizabeth eventually owned, the clavichord demanded attention and consideration and was for a time the only thing in her life that drew her or tied her to one place or another. But the instrument was never enough by itself to do that, and after a couple of years she placed it permanently in storage. She moved it with her to Brazil in 1952 and back to Boston in 1974. In March 1975, citing a lack of space in her Lewis Wharf apartment, she sold the clavichord to Howard Moss for a thousand dollars.

New York was never a healthy place for Elizabeth to live, and if she did not know that in the spring of 1935, she was beginning to learn it. Her clavichord plan and the remainder of the large check "from the gods" enabled her to make firm plans to travel to France in July, and she engaged a tutor from Columbia University to help her polish her written and spoken French. Her spring was spent in musical investigations and French lessons as she fought off, and to some extent examined, the city malaise that engulfed her and dogged all her efforts at writing. On May 19, she wrote in her notebook about the unmanageability of time and history in New York:

> I think that it is in the city alone, maybe New York alone, that one gets in this country these sudden intuitions into the whole of contemporaneity. You go for days reading the newspapers every morning, feeling a certain responsibility about all over, everyone's, predicaments, making use of all inventions, ideas, etc., looking at modern pieces of art, buildings, scenery – and the sense of the present, the actual sensation of it like riding a surf board, never afflicts you. But then there are flashes, when you see all in a minute, what it is to be "modern"; when you catch it coming toward you like a ball, more compressed and acute than in any work of "modern art"; when you taste it concentrated, like a drop of acid.

Elizabeth's notebooks are full and busy between the early spring of 1935 and her departure for Europe on July 29. There are fewer reading notes and more accounts of dreams, memories, beginnings of essays, ruminations on travel and on being a poet. In one dream, she sees a small, pale boy on a yellow sled sliding down hills of snow that look like, and then become, clouds. The boy is transformed into the moon; then Elizabeth becomes the boy and then the moon itself. In the end, after waxing and waning like a snowball for a while, she is back on the sled, which lands in front of her grand-mother's house in Great Village. Her grandmother, dressed in black silk, does not notice that the moon has fallen from the sky and stands consulting a gold watch on a chain. Elizabeth noted that during these months, "a set of apparently disconnected, unchron-ological incidents out of the past have been re-appearing. I suppose there must be some string running them altogether, some spring watering them all." In another dream, she argues about meter with George Herbert. Together they compare his meter to John Donne's and to Marianne Moore's. They decide that "Miss Moore" is better than Donne but not than Herbert himself. "This may have been subconscious politeness on my part," Elizabeth noted. "He said he would be 'useful' to me. Praise God." Both dreams, of course, are also meditations on the idea of time.

In April, Elizabeth's first postcollege publication, "The Imaginary Iceberg," appeared in *Directions: A Quarterly Review of Literature* (not to be confused with James Laughlin's *New Directions* annual, which published its first issue, including three poems by Elizabeth, in 1936). There is no mention of "The Imaginary Iceberg" in Eliz-abeth's notebooks or letters; only a small note on one of the poem's drafts, "Aunt Maud's letter," gives us a clue as to its origin. The poem's initial preference for the "imaginary" iceberg suggests that she was thinking of Wallace Stevens, whose *Harmonium* Elizabeth said she had known "by heart" at college.

"The Imaginary Iceberg" is imaginary in part because Elizabeth had never seen an iceberg when she wrote the poem and had not yet begun the "travel" that she says preferring the iceberg would cause to "end." It is also imaginary because even real icebergs, being mostly submerged, call on the imagination—"behoove the soul"—to "see" their enormous size. The poem is abstract and hermetic, as many of the *North & South* poems would be. One group of Elizabeth's early poems can be linked together because of their remarkable clarity and straightforwardness: "The Map," "The Gentleman of Shalott," "Large Bad Picture," "The Man-Moth," "Cirque d'Hiver," "Florida," "Seascape," and "The Fish." Another group can be identified by their lack of apparent reference to outside, physical reality; their lack of climax or resolution; and their relative obscurity. "The Imaginary Iceberg" founds this line, which includes "Casabianca," "From the Country to the City," "The Weed," "The Unbeliever," "The Monument," "Paris, 7 A.M.," the two "Sleeping" poems, and "Anaphora."

The imaginary iceberg is an introspective work of art painfully partaking of a real iceberg's aspects, its frozen isolation, its invisible threat to the ship of the soul. The inwardness of the iceberg is both its fascination and danger:

> This iceberg cuts its facets from within.
> Like jewelry from a grave
> it saves itself perpetually and adorns
> only itself, perhaps the snows
> which so surprise us lying on the sea.

But the iceberg as poem is also a performance on a public stage, though an "artlessly rhetorical" one. Its white peaks have wits that "spar with the sun" while lying uneasily on the "shifting stage." Although we think "we'd rather have the iceberg than the ship," and though we think the iceberg would be worth an ultimate and ironic sacrifice—this is "a scene a sailor'd give his eyes for"—in the end, we choose the reality of the physical world:

Good-bye, we say, good-bye, the ship steers off
where waves give in to one another's waves
and clouds run in a warmer sky.
Icebergs behoove the soul
(both being self-made from elements least visible)
to see them so: fleshed, fair, erected indivisible.

Both icebergs and souls (and poems) cut their facets from within, are self-made and so self-consuming. To make them useful, to make them real, we give them bodies, flesh them out. The poem suggests that Elizabeth was aware of the unsatisfactory barrenness of poetry that is merely introspective, detached from a literal, sharable world. She had more experiments in introspection to make, but the unmarked shift between the "north" ("Cirque d'Hiver") and the "south" ("Florida") of *North & South* is also a shift from a hermetic inwardness to a manifest concern with people, and especially places, outside the self.

Before she left for Europe, Elizabeth took advantage of what New York could offer her, taking Marianne Moore and her mother to supper at Coney Island, going to the zoo and recording a meticulous description of the camel's skin. She attended plays with Margaret, particularly Clifford Odets's *Till the Day I Die, Waiting for Lefty,* and *Awake and Sing,* with which she said she was "much impressed," though she thought that *Awake and Sing* "got its utter tragedy, poignancy, etc., from having the <u>wrong</u> solution, which the playwright believed to be right. It is strange to think of the young Jews all over town using materialistic philosophy as an idealistic religion." On the way to the theater, the sun setting, "a globe of pale, illuminated rose" arrested her attention.

Four

ELIZABETH LEFT FOR EUROPE on July 29 aboard, accidentally, the Nazi freighter *Königstein,* with her college friend Hallie
Tompkins. At their departure, an old-style seeing off, the crowds of
well-wishers swarming the docks reminded Elizabeth of "the dead"
clamoring to be saved. On the German-speaking ship, she and Hallie were clearly outsiders, and as her shyness took over, Elizabeth
retreated to her notebook to record her impressions. She was fascinated by the other travelers, in particular a "pervert" whose
attempts to seduce young male passengers began with his running
up behind them saying, "You are a prince." As always, the water
and the sensation of being "at sea" captured her attention and her
pen:

> The horizon seems to be <u>boat</u> shaped – the shape of whatever
> you're on. . . . There were large round bodies, orbs, of
> phosphorescence in the water, whirling up from under the ship
> and slowing fading out in the smothering foam. They circled on
> themselves; they occurred in groups mostly – a few seconds
> between them. They looked removed from us, a true leap in the
> dark, like spirits – The water was perfectly black, nothing at all
> except blackness, then it showed its level and gave us our only

foothold by breaking out into hard [?] quickly spreading, quickly gone, white patches, set with the phosphorescence: clouds & moons – of the lower order.

But the ship made her uncomfortable, too. "A <u>hospital</u> is the only institution I can bear to be imposed upon by," she remarked. Like all other "institutions," like school and college, the ship's social scene was awful, "where one slips backwards into corners day after day, and the people who have a 'good time' walk over one more & more." Traveling for fun is easier if one is clear about "home" and what it is one is leaving behind, if not traveling toward. But Elizabeth was heading from the unknown to the unknown on a Nazi freighter with only fifty passengers, most of them Germans. "I twist like a button on a string, stretched between N.Y. & somewhere in Europe."

> Twice now, both times at the table (which is natural-enough) I have been overtaken by an awful, awful feeling of deathly physical and mental <u>illness</u>. – something that seems "after" me. It is as if one were whirled off from all the world & the interests of the world in a sort of cloud-dark, sulphurous [?] grey, of melancholia. When this feeling comes I can't speak, swallow, scarcely breathe. I knew I had had it once before, years ago, & last night, on its 2nd occurrence I placed it as "<u>homesickness</u>." I was homesick for 2 days once when I was nine years old; I wanted one of my aunts. Now I really have no right to homesickness at all. I suppose it is caused actually by the motion of the ship away from N.Y. – it may affect one's center of balance some way; the feeling seems to center in the middle of the chest.

The child uncertain about the security of her home is always the homesick one; the child with "no right" to homesickness suffers most. Elizabeth naturally resorted to intellectual analysis in these attacks of panic or anxiety, her most reliable means of distancing herself from strong feelings. "See how self-centered a ship at sea makes one –," she noted censoriously.

The *Königstein* docked at Antwerp on August 10 after sailing up the Westerschelde and through the locks. Elizabeth and Hallie left the ship early that morning and began their sightseeing with the Musée Plantin-Moretus in Antwerp, then moved on to Brussels, where L'Exposition (the World's Fair) was under way. Elizabeth found the exposition itself "frightful," but the two "halls of painting," ancient and modern, were the first fulfillment of her shipboard dreams of "paintings that wouldn't stay still – the colors moved inside the frames, the objects moved up closer & then further back, the whole thing changed from portrait to scenery & back again." Her travel notebooks are often vague and imprecise and are filled in long after the fact, but she never fails to name in long lists the artists and their paintings that were her strongest interest in each town she visited. In Brussels she found the modern paintings "went on endlessly" and were "very poor," but she was delighted by Pieter Brueghel, Rogier van der Weyden, and Hugo van der Goes, especially his "little Adam & Eve with the pink & blue serpent with a human face."

Hallie and Elizabeth spent a few days in Paris and visited Versailles before installing themselves on August 17 at the Hôtel de l'Europe in Douarnenez, France, a fishing village on the coast of Bretagne, near Brest. Elizabeth told Marianne Moore that the town's "picturesqueness is just like the water in Salt Lake, you simply can't sink in it, it is so strong."[1] But the odder and more idiosyncratic aspects of the town clearly delighted Elizabeth; she was fascinated by the rituals and customs of the Breton people. And everything she saw was fuel for writing. Her notebooks are suddenly lively again with plans and drafts for stories and poems, bits of description, and pithy quotations of French conversation. She took to staying in bed, reading and writing in the mornings before lunch, which she was surprised to discover was the big meal of the day. In the evenings, they went to movies. She enjoyed the life so much that when Hallie left on September 1 for Paris, Elizabeth stayed on alone until Louise Crane joined her three weeks later.

Before Elizabeth had left New York, Marianne Moore had suggested that she visit Winifred Ellerman Macpherson (better known as "Bryher") in London and that she contribute some poems to the new journal Macpherson and her friends had begun, *Life and Letters Today*. With this potential outlet in mind, and in the happy circumstances of her stay at Douarnenez, Elizabeth began translating French poetry, especially Rimbaud, as a way of disciplining her own verse. This was her first intimate acquaintance with the French surrealists, an important influence on her early poems, especially those she wrote in France. She wrote to Hallie in Paris that surrealism was much on her mind:

> A few days after you left I ordered . . . the NATURAL HISTORY
> Plates, by Max Ernst. . . . They arrived this morning, & I have
> thumbtacked 6 of them up around – they look very well. This little
> maid is awfully worried – she read the introduction to them by
> Arp and finally asked me to explain. The only thing I could think
> of to say, which was simple enough for both me and her, was that
> Ernst was making fun of Darwin – she appreciated that,
> apparently! . . .
> I also got from England this fall number of LIFE AND
> LETTERS TODAY, and in it there happened to be a translation
> of a story of (Jean Casson) called "Between the Etoile and the
> Jardin des Plantes." I read it, and like it – although it is a sort of
> mixture of Surrealism and romanticism & Hemingway. . . . I guess
> maybe he's just Surrealism popularized.[2]

Both poems would need a Paris setting, but here was the beginning of "Sleeping on the Ceiling" and "Paris, 7 A.M." and the suggestion behind "The Monument."

Elizabeth was also reading Henry James's short stories in her continuing study of his technique and was clearly listening carefully to the sound of her own words as she spread them on the page. "He leaned over to kiss her slightly before getting into bed – as a man dabbles one toe in the water before going swimming." "Last night I got up in the middle of the night to take a look at the sky. There were thousands of very sharp, fine little gilt stars; the sky, of the thinnest possible grey balloon-silk, was stretched over them like a circus tent on many gold-headed tent poles, dainty but secure."

Poems begin in the notebook: the "stain on the plaster of the ceiling looks like a cloud" becomes the central image of "Sleeping on the Ceiling." "The river took the reflections of the lighted houses in his hands, squeezed them, rinsed them, wrung them, and held them, wrinkled & limp, but clear again" suggests the river of "The Weed." Thinking about the short story that later became "The Baptism," she resolved to write to her aunts in Nova Scotia to learn more about Baptist theology and the rituals of conversion and baptism in the church there. Boredom sometimes overtook her even in this flurry of writing, and she began, as she later did again and again, to contemplate her struggle with the nature and meaning of time. "Somewhat the railroad-snowplow feeling," she ventured in her notebook, "all the time that has drifted in is to be pushed ahead. Trying to hold up your hand in the air when all the pressure from below is gone (= the non-importance of the last 2 weeks) and the weight, (the future, the arrival) is all on top."

Louise Crane did arrive in Douarnenez late in September, and she and Elizabeth traveled to Paris via Saint-Malo and Mont-Saint-Michel. The Crane family's immense wealth and Mrs. Crane's high standards for her daughter's lifestyle did wonders for Elizabeth's. Elizabeth had thought that Mrs. Crane might require Louise to stay with her at the Ritz, but instead she set the two young women up in a lovely apartment at 58 Rue de Vaugirard in Paris, owned by her friends the Comte and Comtesse de Chambrun. Hallie Tompkins later visited them there. The seven-room apartment, on the seventh floor of the building, came with a maid and cook, Simone, and was furnished with beautiful antiques. In particular, it housed the owners' collection of clocks, which figured largely in Elizabeth's first

French poem, originally titled "Paris, 7 A.M.: Two Mornings and Two Evenings," and fed her already heightened time-consciousness.

> I make a trip to each clock in the apartment:
> some hands point histrionically one way
> and some point others, from the ignorant faces.
> Time is an Etoile; the hours diverge
> so much that days are journeys round the suburbs,
> circles surrounding stars, overlapping circles.

The two women settled into the apartment for a three-month stay and bought a pair of doves at a street market to keep them company. They had an idea that they would take courses at the Sorbonne in sixteenth- and seventeenth-century French literature or art or otherwise conduct themselves as students and scholars. Elizabeth's notebook during this time is primarily literary; only her letters to Frani Blough and Marianne Moore, and Louise Crane's letters to her mother, describe their activities. Hallie Tompkins remembers a Paris routine designed to alleviate Elizabeth's asthma— sleeping late, staying indoors reading and writing until lunch, walking slowly around the *quartier*. Elizabeth noted Hallie's nonstop social life and stream of interested young men. "Simone, the maid . . . feels awfully sorry for Louise & me—we are considering sending ourselves some flowers just to make her respect us." She said she was tired: "I just realized that undoubtedly in a country where everything has to be observed, just to make sure it isn't different from what you're used to—of course you get tired."[3]

As she and Louise vowed to make better use of their time, they attended a steady series of concerts, recitals, and theatrical events, and Elizabeth went back to work on Ben Jonson's masques in an attempt to write one of her own; a couple of drafts are titled "Prince 'Winsome' Mannerly" and "The Proper Tears." She immersed herself in the poetry of D. H. Lawrence and in Wallace Stevens's *Ideas of Order,* which had just appeared. Her notebook shows her having made a start on all three of her "Sleeping" poems as well as "Paris, 7 A.M." and the parable "The Sea and Its Shore." Hallie's sociability broadened Elizabeth's literary acquaintance as well, as Hallie found Sylvia Beach's Shakespeare & Co. bookstore and took Elizabeth around to be introduced. Elizabeth's shyness kept her from taking full advantage of this connection; when Beach invited her to a party for André Gide, Tompkins said, "Bishop told me that she and Louise spent hours deciding what she should wear, eventually choosing a new blue dress. And Louise ordered a limousine to take Bishop to the party in style. But as Bishop stepped out of the car her courage failed her and she ordered the limousine to take her home."[4]

Elizabeth was nonetheless beginning to make a place in the literary world, in part because of the steady attention Marianne Moore paid to the progress of Elizabeth's work back in the United States and the gratifying productivity of her time in Douarnenez. *Trial Balances* appeared in October, featuring "The Map," "Three Valentines," and "The Reprimand." The book represented Bishop's work in something of a time lag—whereas "The Map" looked significantly forward, the other poems resembled nothing that she was currently producing and looked back to her days of rather slavish imitation of Gerard Manley Hopkins. Moore pronounced the book "a triumph," and Elizabeth said, as she almost always would, "I really expected it to be quite the reverse."[5] In November, *Life and Letters Today* accepted "The Man-Moth" for the March 1936 issue, and Elizabeth told Moore that she had six more poems finished but no typewriter on which to copy them. In the meantime, Moore had been working on Elizabeth's behalf with Edward Aswell of Harper and Brothers, who had written to Moore asking if she thought Bishop had enough poems for a book. In her reply, Moore announced herself as Elizabeth's mentor:

> She seems to have an instinct against precipitateness and I have
> not been able to persuade her to let me see more than a few pieces
> of her work; but I hope she will send you something. She is a

person of great promise I feel. . . . She is interested in mathematics and in music and there are in her shaping of a poem curbs and spurts that could be known only to a musician. Also, in her outlook on life she is unusual, and taking an interest in her progress does not amount to having assumed a gigantic burden.[6]

A month later, Moore offered to type Elizabeth's poems for her, but Elizabeth had located a typewriter to borrow and on November 20 announced that she had sent Aswell six poems. This did not end in a book publication, but "Casabianca," "The Colder the Air," and "The Gentleman of Shalott" were accepted by New Democracy and appeared in the April 1936 issue.

Elizabeth and Louise did not enroll at the Sorbonne; they decided that their inability to understand the catalog probably meant that they needed more work in the French language. Beginning in November, they studied two hours a day at the Alliance Française and settled into a Paris life among the Crane family's many expatriate acquaintances. Their lives were overseen by the animated and hypochondriacal Mrs. Hooper, who knew all the best doctors in Paris and so became important to Elizabeth. Their round of museums, bookstores, and lectures (by Gertrude Stein, on "entity vs. identity" when writing, among others) was appealing enough to make them want to stay a month beyond the January 10 expiration of the lease on their apartment. Elizabeth developed an unfortunate fondness for Pernod, which she acknowledged was "not a ladies drink," but she had grown bored with vermouth and Dubonnet. She and Louise bought a cocktail shaker and served "an excellent side-car before our excellent dinner every night," thus avoiding the expense of cafés.[7]

By mid-December, Elizabeth's clavichord had arrived from Dolmetsch, a lovely instrument four by two feet in size, pale green with black keys. Arnold Dolmetsch helped Elizabeth find a teacher in Paris, and she had barely begun to learn how to play when a seemingly innocent head cold settled in her ear and sent her to the

American Hospital to have it drained. The somewhat hysterical Mrs. Hooper took charge of Elizabeth's recovery, and the Cranes apparently helped pay the medical bills, which began to mount when she developed acute mastoiditis. Elizabeth went home from the hospital after a week (Christmas week, the first of many such holidays she spent in or near those relatively friendly institutions called hospitals) and was on heavy medication, but after a few days, pain, fever, and dizziness indicated that the infection was out of control and that the mastoid would have to be removed. Her illness was quite serious; before the 1950s mastoiditis was a leading cause of death among children. She spent three weeks in the hospital after the January 4 emergency operation, and when she had recovered her spirits, she circulated a photograph of herself with half-shaved head and turban bandage, which she said she hoped made her "resemble Pope a little." "All the physics of sound and balance, such fancy bones, and tuning forks" were fascinating to her, but she was fortunate to escape with no permanent damage to her hearing or her balance.[8]

The American Hospital in Paris had been full of people with addictions to one substance or another, and Elizabeth felt that after three weeks of talking to nurses, her voice had acquired "a coarse, low, cheerful tone." These informal musings about the nature of hospitals later became habitual. Fated as she was to spend a great deal of time in them, Elizabeth cultivated an interest in who ran them, how they were run, who their clientele was, what atmosphere existed, and how the more important issues of comfort, competence, and quality of care were handled. Among her papers and letters are animated descriptions, some with titles such as "More Hospital Notes," as if she were planning a formal essay on the subject. Her favorite hospital stay would be at the Cambridge Hospital in Massachusetts in 1976, in its somewhat "hip" days.

Elizabeth arrived "home" from the American Hospital on January 25 to the care of a nurse found for her by Mrs. Hooper, Nina Maximoff. Nina was a large Russian woman of great passion who quickly devoted herself to Elizabeth and Louise and later accompanied them, as Elizabeth's nurse, on their further travels. There were no further travels until the end of February, however, as Elizabeth was obliged to stay within her doctor's reach until then. In activities curtailed by her ill-health, Elizabeth and Louise spent their last month in Paris reading and writing. Elizabeth offered to write Frani an opera libretto—"You must tell me how you want it"— and was clearly at work on "Paris, 7 A.M." when she noted that "Paris has a really sinister winter-weather—a sort of hushed, frozen ash-heap, death-bed atmosphere, but it is very beautiful all the same."[9]

> This sky is no carrier-warrior-pigeon
> escaping endless intersecting circles.
> It is a dead one, or the sky from which a dead one
>   fell.
> The urns have caught his ashes or his feathers.

They went to the races at Vincennes with their cook, Simone, of whom they were both very fond, and Elizabeth managed to squeeze in six clavichord lessons before storing the instrument for the next phase of their travels.

Elizabeth and Louise left Paris for England on February 23, 1936, and spent four days in London during which they saw the renowned Chinese Exhibition at the Royal Academy and Eliot's *Murder in the Cathedral,* which Elizabeth said she hated. They left London by boat for Gibraltar as soon as they could, having decided that they hated England. "Yr. fondness for England has made me feel a little suspicious of you," Elizabeth wrote to Frani.[10]

Their first destination was Morocco, "chiefly because we cannot resist the temptation," Elizabeth said, to go to " 'the most improper country in the world.' "[11] They arrived at Tangier on March 4, and Elizabeth immediately came down with asthma and bronchitis, necessitating travel in a rented car and constant care to protect her health. Their tour began at Rabat then moved on to Casablanca,

Marrakech, Taroudant, and Agadir; then they went back to Marrakech and over the mountains to Meknes, where they hired a guide to show them the city. The guide, a large boy squeezed into the rumble seat of the rented car, sent them down a questionable muddy road in which they immediately became stuck. They sat for two hours, surrounded by laughing Arabs, before a few of them got together to lift the car out. Louise and Elizabeth refused to pay the guide after this disaster and had to get the police to help them leave. "Over 2000 Illustrations and a Complete Concordance" recalls other parts of Morocco vividly, though long after the visit (1948):

> And in the brothels of Marrakesh
> the little pockmarked prostitutes
> balanced their tea-trays on their heads
> and did belly-dances; flung themselves
> naked and giggling against our knees,
> asking for cigarettes. It was somewhere near there
> I saw what frightened me most of all:
> A holy grave, not looking particularly holy,
> one of a group under a keyhole-arched stone baldaquin
> open to every wind from the pink desert.
> An open, gritty, marble trough, carved solid
> with exhortation, yellowed
> as scattered cattle-teeth;
> half-filled with dust, not even the dust
> of the poor prophet paynim who once lay there.
> In a smart burnoose Khadour looked on amused.

Elizabeth and Louise said that they had loved Morocco and had stayed longer than they had intended; the country was so different from anywhere Elizabeth had been that it "eliminates comparison." She found the "night life" (meaning, usually, opportunities for social drinking) "fantastic" and the landscape "perfectly unearthly," but nothing she wrote at the time suggested that the country had moved her so deeply.[12] That the "holy" grave stripped of meaning should have been what frightened her most depends in the poem on the failure of truths presented to a child in her illustrated Bible; at the time perhaps it depended on a more general calling into question of cherished truths. Hallie Tompkins Thomas remembers an argument in Paris between Elizabeth and John Thomas, Hallie's fiancé-to-be, on the nature of beauty:

> For Bishop, Beauty was one of the eternal absolutes. John, a sophisticated lover of debate, took the stand that beauty is in the eye of the beholder and that the possessive instinct largely dictated one's ideas of beauty and value. Bishop argued with her 23-year-old [*sic*] emotions. John was enjoying being the *advocatus diaboli*. To Bishop he seemed to be a Philistine, but none of us knew the depth of her anguish till she left the table and went into the kitchen, where Louise and I found her weeping in frustration over a glass of gin.[13]

Perhaps for Elizabeth this desecrated tourist trap of a holy grave was a revelation akin to that she found in John's empty argument—the introduction of a specter of relativity into one of her "eternal absolutes."

Elizabeth and Louise arrived in Seville from Tangier and then Gibraltar on April 5. Spain had been on their itinerary all along, but they had not anticipated the inexorable approach of the Spanish Civil War, which was well begun by April 1936. The Spanish Popular Front had assumed power in February, and by April the situation had deteriorated. The U.S. Consulate in Morocco had advised them not to go, especially not as two women traveling alone. But they went ahead, and on their second day in Seville, Louise reported to her mother that they had gone out walking and returned home "unmolested," which steeled their courage for the remainder of the tour. Both women found Spain depressing after Morocco, full of unattractive people (or so they judged) and wartime destruction of the country's monuments. Elizabeth wrote to Hallie, "If you really want to see what the Communists are up to, what beautiful things they have ruined, you should come here. The prettiest Baroque chapel in Seville has just been saved from burning up – the ceiling all scorched."[14] In fact, in four months of Popular Front rule in Spain, four hundred twenty-one churches were fully or partially burned, though not necessarily by Communists. There was a wave of assassinations, and early in May, when President Alcala Zamora was deposed, more violence ensued and fascism rose in response. When the Spanish Civil War actually began on July 15, Elizabeth and Louise had been in the United States for a month, having cut their trip short.

Elizabeth's hatred of "Communists" (she did not distinguish between communists and fascists) began here and was reinforced by what she observed in Brazil but was never much more deeply examined. In 1956, in response to a request that she write a poem about the execution of Julius and Ethel Rosenberg, she said, "I believe that the Rosenbergs were a wretched pair of dupes and traitors, and that the hysterical and hypocritical excitement whipped up by the Communist party about their trial and deaths was just one more example, a particularly unsavoury one, of the aims and methods of that party."[15] Elizabeth was in no sense a doctrinaire conservative, and she spoke from Brazil, far removed from Joseph McCarthy and the work of the House Un-American Activities Committee; her dislike of "Communists" stemmed from her naive experience of the likes of burned churches, and that was all.

. . .

Waiting at the American Express office in Seville were three copies of the spring issue of *Life and Letters Today*, which contained "The Man-Moth" ("quite a packing problem," Elizabeth said). By the end of April, Marianne Moore was writing that the three poems in *New Democracy* had caught the eye of William Carlos Williams. All four of these poems show Elizabeth at her clever, competent best and share the coolness and reticence for which she was known throughout the early part of her career. None of the poems is "descriptive"; in fact, none makes reference to an objective landscape or setting. Although the fantasy creature "The Man-Moth" clearly lives in New York, it is a highly selected and symbolized city of indistinct facades and a generic subway with its third rail, "the unbroken draught of poison."

> But when the Man-Moth
> pays his rare, although occasional, visits to the surface,
> the moon looks rather different to him. He emerges
> from an opening under the edge of one of the sidewalks
> and nervously begins to scale the faces of the buildings.
> He thinks the moon is a small hole at the top of the sky,
> proving the sky quite useless for protection.
> He trembles but must investigate as high as he can climb. . . .
>
> If you catch him,
> hold up a flashlight to his eye. It's all dark pupil,
> an entire night itself, whose haired horizon tightens
> as he stares back, and closes up the eye. Then from the lids
> one tear, his only possession, like the bee's sting, slips.
> Slyly he palms it, and if you're not paying attention
> he'll swallow it. However, if you watch, he'll hand it over,
> cool as from underground springs and pure enough to drink.

This allegorical figure, neither man nor moth but partaking of a human fear of the urban environment and a mothlike compulsion to leave his cocoon to investigate its light, might stand for the poet or, more generally, for the terrible fear living in the city involves for the extrasensitive, who must nonetheless seek out and experience what she fears. The man-moth is the first of Elizabeth's "creature[s] divided"; "The Gentleman of Shalott" is the second. A comic figure, less frightened and less compulsive than the man-moth, the gentleman is no less trapped by the deceptions of his imagination. His description trips along in two-beat lines that seem to move from

left to right as our eyes would if we were checking out the gentleman's unlikely hypothesis:

> He felt in modesty
> his person was
> half looking-glass,
> for why should he
> be doubled?
> The glass must stretch
> down his middle,
> or rather down the edge.
> But he's in doubt
> as to which side's in or out
> of the mirror.
> There's little margin for error,
> but there's no proof, either.
> And if half his head's reflected,
> thought, he thinks, might be affected.

The gentleman of Shalott does not have a mirror "along the line /
of what we call the spine," but he thinks he does. The problem is
in his mind. And just so we know that he really is crazy, we are told
that he is reasonably happy with his delusion:

> The uncertainty
> he says he
> finds exhilarating. He loves
> that sense of constant re-adjustment.
> He wishes to be quoted as saying at present:
> "Half is enough."

Elizabeth keeps a safe distance from both her gentleman and man-
moth, making no appearance in either poem and affecting an air of
disinterested observation that belies her lifelong interest in the representative misfit, a figure she had not abandoned when she wrote

one of her last poems, the enigmatic "Sonnet." That poem returns to both the meter and situation of the "Gentleman."

> Caught—the bubble
> in the spirit-level,
> a creature divided;
> and the compass needle
> wobbling and wavering,
> undecided.

In the second stanza of "Sonnet" the creature is healed and "free," suggesting that Elizabeth did finally resolve her sense of dividedness. And given that the "Sonnet" creature's emblem of its freedom is "flying wherever / it feels like, gay!" perhaps that division did lie in her protracted uncertainty about her sexual orientation. Equally persuasive, however, is the idea that both the man-moth and gentleman are imaginary creatures made by a poet and that their situations express anxiety about the dangers of imagination and, it follows, anxiety about being a poet and about what kind of poetry one should write. Hermetic, introspective, fanciful poetry, wholly of the imagination, is dangerous.[16]

"Casabianca" and "The Colder the Air," the other two poems in this group that introduced Elizabeth to an international audience, are even more abstract. Elizabeth wrote in her journal that she wanted to see "The Colder the Air" printed with illustrations as the center of a target, and its conceit, deftly handled, imagines mastering the passage of time:

> We must admire her perfect aim,
> this huntress of the winter air
> whose level weapon needs no sight,
> if it were not that everywhere
> her game is sure, her shot is right.
> The least of us could do the same. . . .

Time's in her pocket, ticking loud
on one stalled second. She'll consult
not time nor circumstance. She calls
on atmosphere for her result.
(It is this clock that later falls
in wheels and chimes of leaf and cloud.)

In "Casabianca," the boy's love and fear (as he waits in vain, in the original poem, for his father to return and tell him to abandon the burning ship) stand for Elizabeth's bleak conviction that love, especially parental love, is a nonnegotiable trap. But she is not in the poem. It was a long time before she could write about love— any kind of love—without screens of rhetorical statement.

. . .

Elizabeth and Louise toured Spain—Seville, Toledo, Madrid, and Valencia, among other cities—but found the country "disappointing." Hemingway's writings had been their initial point of reference, and Elizabeth was sorry to find the country not at all Hemingway-esque. She liked the El Greco and Goya paintings she saw and one nice chapel in Seville and a palace in Valencia, but she said that otherwise there was "so little worth going to see."[17] Lingering skin and stomach troubles (seventeen trips to the bathroom one day in Seville), and a sudden conviction that they ought to stop traveling for a while and settle somewhere, took them to the island of Mallorca. Elizabeth gives no firsthand account of violence in Spain (and the country is conspicuously absent from her "Over 2,000 Illustrations" itinerary); apparently she and Louise traveled by train in safety. They arrived at Palma on May 11, then stayed at the Hotel Costa Brava in Puerto del Sollar for three weeks, enjoying the "really ravishing blue water and grey olive-trees" in the picturesque fishing village. Mallorca was apparently peaceful; at least, the spectacle of violence at the bullfights still seemed attractive to them. Elizabeth reported that the sport was "in its decadence" and had decayed even more since Hemingway had written about it. "I wish Hemingway had said more about the audience," she wrote to Frani. "I've never seen one that could express itself so well."[18] To Marianne Moore, whom Elizabeth had been entertaining with extravagantly appreciated postcards of her travels, she wrote, "I am torn between sending you the bull-fighter embroidered with silk and the bull-fighter embroidered with sequins–."[19] "You do extend experience," Moore wrote in reply.[20]

Elizabeth suffered from severe asthma on Mallorca. Such attacks often dogged her travels; some of her most luminous memories of the places she visited recalled nights when she lay awake, unable to breathe easily, contemplating her surroundings and waiting for morning so she could be driven to the nearest hospital for a shot of adrenalin. She lost several days of sightseeing to her illness. This, combined with the deteriorating political situation in Spain and Elizabeth's belief that it was time to go back to New York and begin working again, led the two travelers to head for Madrid around June 1. There they caught a train for Paris and then Havre, where they embarked for New York on the *Normandy*, arriving on June 10.

. . .

With no firm plans for where to live or what to work on when she landed in New York, the summer left Elizabeth even more at loose ends than usual. She went immediately with Louise to the family mansion at 820 Fifth Avenue and then to stay with Margaret Miller and her mother in Greenwich Village at 10 Monroe Street, while she searched for a summer home with an ocean view. After a few days at the Hotel Brevoort and a few more at the Crane summer home in Dalton, Massachusetts (still the home of the Crane Paper Company), Elizabeth did find her place, near Silver Beach in West Falmouth, Massachusetts, not far from yet another Crane family house, this one at Woods Hole. The three-bedroom cottage had everything—"You can take a hot bath, make toast, curl your hair, etc. etc"—and was almost dry enough for the clavichord, which had yet to arrive in New York.[21] (When it came, she paid eighty-nine dollars in duty and sent it to Frani for safekeeping.)

Elizabeth hoped that Margaret Miller and her mother would join her there for most of the summer. It turned out that she had Margaret alone for all of August and Louise for a couple of weeks, plus a visit from Frani and a few other high school and college friends. But she spent much of the summer rather too much alone. She found it hard to begin working. She finished her opera libretto, which began "We are God's angels, we are, we are, / we are," but found it "oh so silly," and she felt unable to begin the "more serious" writing that she always felt herself on the verge of manifesting.[22]

The summer passed in the usual way, with swimming, walking on the beach, drinking and talking among friends, sailing to Cuttyhunk with Louise. On Cuttyhunk, Elizabeth was given a two-month-old gray-and-white kitten, whom she christened "Minnow." This cat "panicked" in a storm on July 9 when the house was struck by lightning, with a "crash" and a "ripping noise" as the power went out. Thunderstorms, and the behavior of her cats in them, always interested Elizabeth; many years later Tobias, her beloved Brazilian cat, starred in "Electrical Storm":

> Dawn an unsympathetic yellow.
> *Cra-aack!*—dry and light.
> The house was really struck.
> *Crack!* A tinny sound, like a dropped tumbler.
> Tobias jumped in the window, got in bed—
> silent, his eyes bleached white, his fur on end.

Minnow also became something of a celebrity cat, figuring large as she did in Elizabeth's letters and in this convincing bit of light verse: "Darling Minnow, drop that frown, / Just cooperate, / Not a kitten shall be drowned / In the Marxist State."

Elizabeth tried to keep herself occupied during the summer so as not to grow too lonely; she considered joining a local church choir, for example. But for the most part, the best she could do was hang on until the next round of visitors arrived, bearing alcohol and food and the very great gift of their company. With Margaret there late in July, Elizabeth was almost happy. They worked during the days: "She sits in the front yard most of the day, and I sit in the back."[23] The absence of available young men in Falmouth and Woods Hole troubled Louise, who felt responsible for her friends' social lives, but Elizabeth remarked that she had thought of inviting T. C. Wilson down for a few days, "but now I can't seem to bother." None of the three women supposedly suffering for lack of male companionship during the summer of 1936 ever married.

T. C. Wilson, a young poet and sometime associate of Ezra Pound, had been commissioned by Pound to collect poems by young British and American poets for an anthology to be edited by Pound and published in an issue of *Westminster* magazine. Wilson later edited a poetry journal published at the University of Iowa. He was acquainted with Marianne Moore and so came to know Elizabeth's work and eventually Elizabeth herself. She found him interesting at first and recommended his work to at least one editor. But later she felt that his leftist politics blinded him to the real world and that his political views were "short-sighted" and "ignorant."[24]

Perhaps inviting Wilson down would have helped encourage Elizabeth about her writing, for despite her summer's effort to establish a working routine and to finish long-outstanding projects, and despite the success of the four poems she had published during the previous spring, she suffered an acute attack of self-doubt. Her progress seemed to her insufficient, but she judged it, not against that of her contemporaries (for whom she expressed a general contempt), but against a standard of excellence all her own. She always held herself to this standard but never reached it. On August 21, she wrote to Moore with an unusual display of emotion:

I cannot, cannot decide what to do – I am even considering studying medicine or bio-chemistry, and have procured all sorts of catalogues, etc. I feel that I have given myself more than a fair trial, and the accomplishment has been nothing at all. I had rather work at Science at which I was fairly good at college, or even something quite uncongenial for the rest of my days, than become like one of my contemporaries – But this is a great imposition – my only foundation is that your interest in behalf of POETRY will lead you to be very severe.[25]

She signed the letter "Elizabeth," the first time she used her first name alone as a signature in a letter to Moore. (Most of her friends still called her "Bishop," and with Moore she had always used her full name.) Elizabeth said for years that she had been on the point of applying to Cornell Medical School, though it seems unlikely that her one semester of zoology at Vassar would have qualified her for acceptance. Moore's response to this letter was perfectly pitched, neither alarmed nor dismissive of Elizabeth's real doubts:

What you say about studying medicine does not disturb me at all; for interesting as medicine is, I feel that you would not be able to give up writing, with the ability for it that you have; but it does disturb me that you should have the *feeling* that it might be well to give it up. To have produced what you have – either verse or prose is enviable.[26]

Elizabeth's crisis arose from genuine concern about the merit of her writing—particularly about its depth and "seriousness"— though these doubts were paradoxically combined with an ambition and a perfectionism that suggested she valued her work highly. In the same letter to Moore, she reported having just received from Mrs. Miller a copy of Wallace Stevens's *Ideas of Order*. Perhaps her rereading of the new work of one of her acknowledged masters struck her with the sense that she would never match that achievement. Her five poems then in print owe more to Stevens than to any of her other influences, and perhaps the invidious comparison was inevitable.

Elizabeth was somewhat reassured by Moore's answer, addressed for the first time to "if you mean to say so, Elizabeth," and suggesting that she send her work to Morton Zabel, the editor of *Poetry*. Emboldened by Moore's suggestion, Elizabeth enclosed in her next letter from West Falmouth "A Miracle for Breakfast," "The Weed," and "Paris, 7 A.M." Moore replied with suggestions and offered to help "place" the poems. From this point until October 1940, Moore directed Elizabeth's literary career. Moore took an active role in managing the younger poet's professional affairs, including introducing her and her work to editors and publishers, recommending reading and places for her to submit her writing, and offering line by line criticism of poems and stories. Moore made genuine contributions to Elizabeth's material success and poetic style (including important letters of recommendation and the like) when she needed desperately to be taken in hand by someone who knew how to get around the literary world. Elizabeth did not take Moore's every suggestion (though she always apologized for not doing so) and maintained some autonomy throughout the relationship, but it was not until 1940, in a difficult spot over Moore's complete rewriting, retyping, and retitling of "Roosters," that Elizabeth politely but firmly defended her original version and moved out from under the kind of guidance that would permit such an intrusion.

Elizabeth stayed on at Falmouth until the house was too cold to work in, then returned to New York to Louise's house on September 20. She stayed there for a couple of weeks and then moved to the Hotel Chelsea. Here, among plays, concerts, and an excursion to Coney Island with Moore and her mother, Elizabeth worked on a handful of nearly finished poems and stories, soliciting Moore's criticism and most often following her suggestions. One gets a lovely picture from the letters of Marianne and Mrs. Moore poring over Elizabeth's work, Mrs. Moore vigilant about possible vulgarities, Marianne more generally critical. Elizabeth accepted this attention, though at times she defended herself forcefully. When Moore said she disliked the word "apartment" in the first line of "Paris, 7 A.M.," Elizabeth showed that she was fully conscious of her choice of the word and its implications: "I am sorry I am being so obstinate about 'apartments.' To me that word suggests so strongly the structure of the houses, later referred to, and suggests a 'cut off' mode of existence so well—that I don't want to change it unless you feel it would mean a great improvement."[27]

Other times, she was painfully self-effacing:

> This story ["The Baptism"] is so untidy—worse than that, I am afraid it is a little CHEAP. But after reading those in L. & L.T., I felt a little encouraged. I was trying to produce an effect something like Hans Anderson, but I'm afraid I haven't succeeded in this one. If you don't care for it please don't bother to send it back but throw it out the window or down the elevator shaft.

When Roger Roughton of *Contemporary Poetry and Prose* rejected "The Weed," Elizabeth was abject: "Now I am so sorry that I ever caused you to be connected with it in any way."[28]

On December 4, Elizabeth and Margaret attended a lecture and reading by Moore and William Carlos Williams organized by *Poetry* at the Brooklyn Institute of Arts and Letters, an event Elizabeth retold in several versions. They arrived a bit late, while Moore was reading, Elizabeth wrote in "Efforts of Affection." "There was a very small audience, mostly in the front rows, and I made my way as self-effacingly as I could down the steep red-carpeted steps of the aisle. As I approached the lower rows, she spotted me out of the corner of her eye and interrupted herself in the middle of a poem to bow and say, 'Good evening!' " Her account in a letter written the next day is more vivid. After apologizing for her lateness, she said, "I enjoyed every moment except the one in which my own name struck me like a bullet, and I felt myself swelling like a balloon to fill the auditorium."[29]

Elizabeth's notebook reappears beginning in December 1936, with notes from Wallace Stevens's *Owl's Clover*. ("I dislike the way he occasionally seems to make blank verse <u>moo</u>—," she wrote to Moore.)[30] In its early pages we see her working on "Song" ("Summer is over upon the sea"), which she envisioned as a part of one of her masques; "The Unbeliever"; and "The Hanging of the Mouse." Early in the month, Zabel and *Poetry* accepted "Song," "From the Country to the City," and "A Miracle for Breakfast," and she felt somewhat encouraged about her prospects.

But she had also just completed "The Sea and Its Shore," a "fable," as she called it, about her feeling of mute confusion in the complex and competitive literary world. In the story, Edwin Boomer—whose initials and last name identify him with Elizabeth—makes a living cleaning up the printed-paper garbage on a public beach. He lives alone in a house, or, rather, in an "idea of a house," four by six feet, and does his work overnight, usually when drunk. Boomer harbors a private and inarticulate fascination for the work of the faceless and usually nameless authors of the art he collects and then burns. He lives, Bishop writes, "the most literary life possible," and for his effort has rounded shoulders and "had been forced to start wearing glasses shortly after undertaking his duties."[31] Boomer's job is to walk the beach at night, carrying a long stick with a nail in it and a potato sack and picking up discarded pieces of paper.

> Papers that did not look interesting at first glance he threw into his bag; those he wanted to study he stuffed into his pockets. Later he smoothed them out on the floor of the house.
> Because of such necessity for discrimination, he had grown to be an excellent judge.

Boomer's duties make him expert in the study of waste paper, its mindless behavior and uses (for insulation, papier-mâché, and, especially, burning), and typefaces and printing techniques. The potential for meaning in the letters on the papers fascinates him, but they remain largely mysterious.

The beach, Boomer's literary milieu, is a threatening and unpredictable place. When he is most drunk, "the sea was of gasoline, terribly dangerous, . . . brilliant, oily, and explosive." Other nights, the wind sends the papers flying and makes Boomer "more like a hunter than a collector" and also a student of "the flight of the papers."

At the end of each night of discarding and collecting, Boomer is again sober and free to retire to his house to study his papers. To order these in his mind, he divides them into categories: first and most numerous, "everything that seemed to be about himself, his occupation in life, and any instructions or warnings that referred to it"; second, "the stories about other people that caught his fancy"; and third, "the items he could not understand at all." The sad irony is, of course, that despite his earnest efforts at interpretation of these texts, the confused warnings and titillating story lines he develops from unrelated scraps of paper (most of which were first affixed in one or another of Elizabeth's notebooks) are "wrong," meant for someone else, or impossible to verify. And he makes no distinction among scraps of literary worth (he mentions having encountered "The Rime of the Ancient Mariner" several times), of sentimental value (the letter from James O'Shea to Mr. Margolies that Elizabeth received in her U.S.A. School of Writing tenure), or of commercial or pornographic intent.

After reading like this for a long time, Boomer begins to blur distinctions between what is printed and what is not, between what is literature and what is "reality":

> Either because of the insect armies of type so constantly besieging his eyes, or because it was really so, the world, the whole world he saw, came before many years to seem printed, too.
>
> Boomer held up the lantern and watched a sandpiper rushing distractedly this way and that.

It looked, to his strained eyesight, like a point of punctuation against the "rounded, rolling waves." It left fine prints with its feet. Its feathers were speckled; and especially on the narrow hems of the wings appeared marks that looked as if they might be letters, if only he could get close enough to read them.

Even the sand resembled printed paper, "ground up or chewed." This world-as-text, uninterpretable at that, mystifies him. Finally, however, "the point was that everything had to be burned at last," for "burning paper was his occupation, by which he made his living," and, most important, "he could not allow his pockets to become too full, or his house to become littered."

Edwin Boomer's plight is a fabulist version of Elizabeth's (his name gives him away), and the images in which he is cast—the sandpiper, the beach, the inflammable sea, the "proto . . . crypto" house—stayed with her forever. His anxiety about literature, figured comically in the nonsensical clippings and scraps he finds and feels responsible for, mirrors Elizabeth's, also figured in fragments in her notebooks. His strategy of using alcohol to distance himself from the flux was also hers. *Life and Letters Today* took the story and printed it in the winter 1937 issue.

Five

LATER IN HER LIFE in her most abject moments of guilt and
self-recrimination, Elizabeth told the story of the death of Bob
Seaver, the boyfriend of her college years, who committed suicide
in Pittsfield, Massachusetts, on November 21, 1936. Seaver had
wanted to marry Elizabeth, and she had told him that she felt she
would never marry. On her return from Europe, she had been called
on to make this point more emphatically. When Seaver shot himself,
perhaps in frustration at his loneliness and his physical limitations,
the only note he left was a postcard, which arrived in her mail a few
days after his death. It said, "Go to hell, Elizabeth."[1]

Primed as she was to absorb this kind of guilt, Elizabeth felt until
her own death that she had "ruined" Bob Seaver's life. Marrying
him was impossible, but his death and his unanswerable condem-
nation of her were devastating blows.

She escaped New York with Louise Crane for the Keewaydin
camp in Naples, Florida, on December 18, apologizing to Moore as
she was leaving: "It seems almost impolite of me to write to you
now – the way I'm going off and leaving my harder working and
truly deserving friends behind who should be in the South. I'm

afraid I won't stay very long, though, because I hate to leave the cat for long in a sort of foundling home."[2] Minnow was housed with Janet Mock, a mutual friend of Elizabeth's and Marianne's (Moore reported a few days later that Minnow seemed "constipated"), and later with Moore herself. Like the clavichord, Minnow came to represent for Elizabeth her tenuous ties to one place or another. As it turned out, she stayed at Keewaydin for two months, as one of only two guests, long after Louise returned to New York. Her one-hundred-dollar-a-month room and board, "aside from a little 'get-together'ness," proved "very agreeable."[3]

Elizabeth's attachment to Florida was instantaneous. Its excesses of scenery, flora, and fauna attracted her painter's eye, and its people's often tasteless attempts at decoration stirred her appreciation for the uniquely awful. Right away she met Charlotte and Red Russell, newlyweds spending their honeymoon at the camp, who remained her friends for forty years. Red Russell she described as "a sort of Tarzan" who wrestled alligators and hunted with a bow and arrows; "in spite of this he is extremely nice." Their sailboat and their homes (in Florida and later in Brevard, North Carolina) became refuges for her from time to time. She discovered her love of fishing—days after she pulled in a sixty-pound amberjack, her notebook shows lines and images that later became "The Fish." She was clearly enchanted: "All this fantasy takes place on a beautiful island half jungle and half a pure white beach with palm trees all along it. There isn't any gravel – it's all shells."[4] Her most vivid impressions of the beauty, ugliness, and awfulness of Florida went to Marianne Moore, who shared Elizabeth's fascination for the unusual object or animal. On the trip from Jacksonville to Naples, Elizabeth noted the train's travels through "swamps and turpentine camps and palm forests" and remarked how "in a beautiful pink evening it began stopping at several little stations." Her account of three pelicans fighting over a blowfish shows her excitement over tropical life forms, especially the "humorous" pelicans:

The other day I caught a blow-fish, who began to puff up as I pulled him in. Three pelicans immediately rushed over, holding up their tremendous bills, and by chance the blow-fish, who was just snagged, fell off the hook right into one's mouth. By that time he was as big as a large-sized balloon and the poor pelican was very puzzled as to what to do with him. He paddled off with the other two after him; then he dropped the fish and another snatched him. They kept at it for quite a while – it was really like a basketball game – the fish was clever enough to keep blown up all the time. Finally he chose the right moment, deflated, and disappeared like a wink – the pelicans hurried back to watch our lines again.[5]

Elizabeth so wanted to share the fascinating objects she encountered in Florida that she sent Moore gifts as well—obvious gifts such as oranges and alligator pears, an assortment of shells and snakes and reptiles preserved in formaldehyde, and coconuts ("I am afraid you probably had to get the janitor with his axe to open [it]"). She enclosed a brochure advertising Ross Allen's alligator wrestling skills and his ability to imitate the alligator calls: the "beller," the love call, the warning, and the social call. Her letters to Moore predict the ambivalent description of "Florida," which makes use of the pelicans, the turpentine camps, specimens from a flower show, and Allen himself:

> The state with the prettiest name,
> the state that floats in brackish water,
> held together by mangrove roots
> that bear while living oysters in clusters,
> and when dead strew white swamps with skeletons,
> dotted as if bombarded, with green hummocks
> like ancient cannon-balls sprouting grass. . . .
> Enormous turtles, helpless and mild,
> die and leave their barnacled shells on the beaches,
> and their large white skulls with round eye-sockets

twice the size of a man's.
The palm trees clatter in the stiff breeze
like the bills of the pelicans. . . .

Thirty or more buzzards are drifting down, down, down,
over something they have spotted in the swamp,
in circles like stirred-up flakes of sediment
sinking through water.
Smoke from wood-fires filters fine blue solvents.
On stumps and dead trees the charring is like black
    velvet.
The mosquitoes
go hunting to the tune of their ferocious obbligatos.
After dark, the fireflies map the heavens in the marsh
until the moon rises.
Cold white, not bright, the moonlight is coarse-meshed,
and the careless, corrupt state is all black specks
too far apart, and ugly whites; the poorest
post-card of itself.
After dark, the pools seem to have slipped away.
The alligator, who has five distinct calls:
friendliness, love, mating, war, and a warning—
whimpers and speaks in the throat
of the Indian Princess.

Elizabeth's Florida always consisted of this paradoxical mix of
animated and beautiful creatures, especially birds, and evidence of
death and decay. Skeletons, cannonballs, skulls, buzzards, and dead
trees are the mainstays of her description, which was criticized early
on as "pointless." In a characteristic manipulation of scale and perspective, the poem looks both close up and from the air at Florida,
as we shift from seeing single animals, flowers, and swamps to viewing "a state full"—the entire coastline in one sweep. Bishop appreciated the cartographic distinction of the state of Florida and the
rotting richness of its tropical climate. But her poem reveals, as

almost all her Florida writings do, deep moral ambivalence about the place.

Over Christmas 1936, Elizabeth sailed on a charter boat with the famous Captain Bra to Key West, "a place that had never even entered my consciousness until I got there."[6] For the next fifteen years, it scarcely left her consciousness. Key West had been on the upswing as a tourist destination in 1935, with the Flagler Railroad just completed and a vigorous cleanup of the island's numerous garbage dumps and abandoned shacks under way. On Labor Day 1935, a hurricane devastated the town and washed out the railroad, and Key West settled once again into peaceful, impoverished isolation, accessible only by boat until World War II began and the overland highway was completed. In 1937, it was still the home of Ernest Hemingway, John Dos Passos, an eclectic group of fishermen, sea captains, artists; white people, black people, and Cubans. On first sight, Elizabeth was taken: "The water is the most beautiful clear pistachio color, ice-blue in the shade. It is so pretty when you have actually caught one of these monster fish and have him all the way up to the side – to see him all silver and [iridescent] colors in that blue water."[7] The "monster fish" was the sixty-pound amberjack, the largest catch on her cruise. She left this ultimate island vowing to return.

Elizabeth's stay at Keewaydin was productive, as she worked on "A Miracle for Breakfast," "The Sea and Its Shore," and more lyrics she hoped Frani would set to music. Strong drafts of stanzas for "The Unbeliever" share space with paragraphs for a short story entitled "The Sandpiper's Revenge," which prefigures her later poem on the subject:

> The next wave, an enormous one, went far up the beach, a six-inch thick fan of rumbling foam. The sand piper first turned his back and ran, then had to take to his wings to keep ahead of it.
> "Zzzzzzz-ssss," it said, turning and backing down the sand.

The sand-piper lit in the wet, dragging grains of sand and gravel and his beak had begun its investigations before his legs had regained their balance.

By February 4, she had completed a draft of "The Hanging of the Mouse" to send to Moore. "I once hung Minnow's artificial mouse on a string to a chair back, without thinking what I was doing – it looked very sad."[8] Moore wrote back with her typically cool response to Elizabeth's fanciful prose pieces, "Your competence in THE HANGING OF THE MOUSE is almost criminal and should be requited by my asking if you knew that Minnow's left front paw had shrunk so that she now goes on three legs, or by my saying 'Louise Crane has probably told you that Minnow was as usual Saturday night but in the morning her tail had lost every hair and this seems to worry her.' "[9]

That night, Elizabeth dreamed and recorded in her notebook what she would say for forty years was her "favorite" dream:

The fish was large, about 3 ft. long, large – scaled, metallic like a goldfish only a beautiful rose color. I myself seemed slightly smaller than life-size. We met in water . . . clear, green, light (— more like the cut edge of plate glass, or birch leaves in bright sun, than emerald). He was very kind and said he would be glad to lead me to the fish, but we'd have to overtake them. He led the way through the water, glancing around at me every now and then with his big eyes to see if I was following. I was swimming easily with scarcely any motion. In his mouth he carried a new, galvanized bucket (I even think the red & blue paper label was still stuck on the front.) He was taking them a bucket of air – that's how he'd happened to meet me. I looked in – enough water had got in to make the bucket of air a bucket of large bubbles, seething and shining – hissing, I think, too. I had a vague idea they were to be used as decorations, for some sort of celebration.

This is a wonderful example of an asthma dream—frequently asthmatics dream about being underwater, being able to breathe underwater in positive dreams, drowning in nightmares. The dream's imagining of a delivery system for air, of bubbles that make noises like the air in her lungs, suggests a logical but impossible solution to Elizabeth's breathing problem, which had been bothering her enough at Keewaydin to send her to bed for several days. In addition, the dream prefigures "The Fish" with its anthropomorphized hero and with his guidance of the poet, perhaps even to the poem itself; he was "glad to lead me to the fish."

. . .

Elizabeth's Florida notebook considers works by Auden, Pascal, and Freud and proposes numerous unrealized poems and essays, including a poem about dolphins, a possible prose piece called "Grandmother's Glass EYE–an Essay on Style," and a substantially completed short story called "The Labors of Hannibal," which has not survived but which turned up in references in her notebooks for years to come. She had "A Miracle for Breakfast" ready to send out (after sparring with Moore over whether "crumb" and "sun" were too similar to use as end words in the sestina) and "The Hanging of the Mouse" done. In February, "The Weed" appeared in *Forum & Century*.

"The Weed" is an odd creation, which might begin to explain why, despite its polished competence, it was turned down by editors accustomed to publishing much less professional work. The poem features another "creature divided," this time a dreamed version of Elizabeth herself. She said she modeled the poem after George Herbert's "Love Unknown," and indeed, the two conceits are similar. Here is Herbert:

A lord I had,
And have, of whom some grounds, which may improve,
I hold for two lives, and both lives in me.

To him I brought a dish of fruit one day,
And in the middle plac'd my heart. But he
                              (I sigh to say)
Lookt on a servant, who did know his eye
Better then you know me, or (which is one)
Then I my self. The servant instantly
Quitting the fruit, seiz'd on my heart alone,
And threw it in a font, wherein did fall
A stream of bloud, which issu'd from the side
Of a great rock: I well remember all,
And have good cause: there it was dipt and dy'd,
And washt, and wrung: the very wringing yet
Enforceth tears. *Your heart was foul, I fear.*

And here is part of "The Weed":

I dreamed that dead, and meditating,
I lay upon a grave, or bed,
(at least, some cold and close-built bower).
In the cold heart, its final thought
stood frozen, drawn immense and clear,
stiff and idle as I was there;
and we remained unchanged together
for a year, a minute, an hour.
Suddenly there was a motion, . . .
I raised my head. A slight young weed
had pushed up through the heart and its
green head was nodding on the breast.
(All this was in the dark.) . . .
The rooted heart began to change
(not beat) and then it split apart
and from it broke a flood of water.
Two rivers glanced off from the sides,
one to the right, one to the left,
two rushing, half-clear streams,
(the ribs made of them two cascades)

which assuredly, smooth as glass,
went off through the fine black grains of earth. . . .
A few drops fell upon my face
and in my eyes, so I could see
(or, in that black place, thought I saw)
that each drop contained a light,
a small, illuminated scene;
the weed-deflected stream was made
itself of racing images. . . .
The weed stood in the severed heart.
"What are you doing there?" I asked.
It lifted its head all dripping wet
(with my own thoughts?)
and answered then: "I grow," it said,
"but to divide your heart again."

Herbert's "two lives" become for Elizabeth a characteristically
divided heart, and his consolation—that the trials of his heart were
engineered by his lord and master to make him "new, tender,
quick"—cannot exist for Bishop. Her *weed* is "new, tender, quick,"
but revelation comes after death, and her heart is left divided at the
end, beyond the reach of religious unification.

Next to "The Man-Moth" and "The Gentleman of Shalott," the
poem is another about the terrors of imagination, here somewhat
more explicitly identified with the poet. The poem argues that a
divided heart is necessary for creation; from the violent split flows
the stream of racing images. That it is a weed that enforces the
split—a weed being a common plant growing out of place—suggests
that the dream reveals as well Elizabeth's view of her poetic gift as
foundling or illegitimate. When she saw the poem in *Forum &
Century,* she said she was sorry she had let it appear there.[10]

In late February, James Laughlin, of the fledgling New Directions
Press, tracked Elizabeth down in Florida to ask if he might publish
a book of her poems. Elizabeth's immediate instinct was to say no—
not only because the suggestion probably was a bit premature but

also because she thought, paradoxically, that she could do better: "I somehow feel like NO. Don't you think, Miss Moore (although I hate to fire these foolish questions at you) that a publisher like Random House, if possible, would be better, if I ever had enough worth publishing, of which I have many of the blackest doubts."[11] Moore recommended that she say yes to Laughlin, but Elizabeth held out. She never said that she regretted this decision, though it was nearly ten years (six of earnest effort) before her first book appeared.

. . .

By March 1, Elizabeth was back in New York, in a room at the Murray Hill Hotel at Forty-first Street and Park Avenue, which became her New York base for the next several years. She stayed there with Minnow a month, having developed for herself a syllabus of medieval and Renaissance literature and attempting once again to set a daily reading-and-note-taking regimen. She was also working on "The Labors of Hannibal" and her first review essay, called "W. H. Auden: The Mechanics of Pretense." (She was also teaching Minnow to read, with flashcards saying "Meow" and "Milk," she wrote to Moore.) Neither piece survives. Her notebook shows her speculating about what use she might make of the murder and mayhem she read about in the *Daily News*. She also meticulously recorded her dreams, which often expressed anxiety about writing— sleeping on a giant typewriter, for example (perhaps a suggestion of the poem that eventually became "12 O'Clock News"). Extensive and painful dental work laid her up for a few days. Moore wrote, "I am writing rather than telephoning since it surely must retard your recovering to be holding up the receiver and listening with your cheek still invalided."[12] At the end of the month, Elizabeth put Minnow on the train to her relatives in Boston and followed her there for a week's visit. When she returned during the first week in April, she and Louise began to plan a second European trip, to Ireland and France, with Margaret Miller.

While Marianne Moore was shepherding Elizabeth's poems through *Poetry* editor Zabel's exacting standards (he finally accepted "Song," "From the Country to the City," "A Miracle for Breakfast," and "Paris, 7 A.M." for publication in the July 1937 issue), Elizabeth herself read up on the history of Ireland and prepared once again to leave New York. "PACKING is the most dreadful thing in the world," she said; it gave her the "sensation of being an exile."[13] She and Louise left New York harbor on the SS *Britannic* on May 29, bound for Cork, with Louise's car in the hold.

Elizabeth was more comfortable on this crossing; from this time onward she was, paradoxically, most at home when at sea. Her travel notebook, which opens with a description of the *Britannic*'s exit from a foggy New York harbor, lingers attentively over descriptions of other passengers—this time a group of nuns and priests returning from New Jersey to their homes in Ireland. "The nuns look very funny on deck with their veils blowing around them," Elizabeth notes. "The thought of them undraping in one cabin is appalling." Like Hopkins, on whom she had been working during the spring, she was fascinated by the motion of the sea and practiced describing it:

> What I like are the lines, or strings of white on the mounting wave—as if the white crest were being ravelled out by the pressure of the upward push. Sometimes when a wave rises high enough, without breaking at all, the light catches it so that the top becomes transparent for a second—green or blue—the same effect as when the head is suddenly turned and the bulge of the eyeball appears like a crystal.
>
> Watching the line of water slip up over the dining saloon portholes—up, up, settling ½ way, slips back—like a carpenter's level with its bubble.

These lines are a practice, a testing of the range of simile—later the sea is a "dance-floor, a ball-room for the mind and heart."

After a seven-day voyage, the *Britannic* arrived at Cork on the afternoon of June 5. The passengers were unloaded at six o'clock, after a four-hour delay, during which they all got "drunk" and "sang going in on the tender—just like a movie, exactly."[14] After the forty-five-minute ride on the tender up the foggy harbor, they arrived in the city at nine o'clock, which was still daylight. Elizabeth was impressed: "They had a coal fire for us in the grate, and the maid brought a supper of soup, 'joint' and vegetables, crackers and cheese, and tea. Then we each had a hot grog. I am getting to like Irish whiskey very much." The two women toured Ireland in the car—with excursions on foot, bicycle, and horseback—for fifteen days. The first day they spent at Cork; the next day they drove to Blarney and back ("We did not kiss it"). On the eighth, they took ponies over the Gap of Dunhoe, then on to Dingle Harbor, where they stayed the night at Benner's Hotel. The next day they took Connor's Pass to Fralee and Listouch, then along the Shannon River to Limerick and Ennis, where they stayed over. On the tenth, they drove to Kilker and then to Galway for the night, and the next day they toured through Connemara, Caskel, and Roundstone on their way to Cujden and the Kylmore Abbey, where they spent the night as guests of the nuns. They went on to Castleton and Sligo on the twelfth, Sligo to Dublin on the thirteenth. They spent a week in Dublin (their activities are unrecorded) before leaving on the nineteenth for Northern Ireland. On the twenty-first, they went through Londonderry and down the coast to Belfast, where they caught a night boat for Liverpool.

In London on the twenty-third, Louise and Elizabeth met Margaret Miller "almost by accident," and the three women spent a couple of days in the city visiting the Tate Gallery and witnessing an Albert Hall meeting for Spanish Civil War orphans. On the twenty-fifth, they took the ferry from Dover to Calais and drove to Paris through Beauvais. Elizabeth's journal breaks off at this point, and the three women's specific activities for the first three weeks in Paris are unknown. But on the seventeenth of July, they took

Louise's car for a drive through Burgundy to look at churches; on their way back on the nineteenth they were involved in an accident.

Louise was driving fast, at about five thirty in the afternoon, when a car passing them forced them off the road. Louise yelled, "Hold tight!" and the car rolled, throwing all three women out. "At first I thought we were all safe–," Elizabeth wrote. "Then we realized simultaneously, I think, that Margaret's right hand and forearm were completely gone."[15] Workers in nearby fields came running to help; one made a tourniquet for Margaret, and the driver of the other car took her to the doctor five miles away and then on to the hospital. Elizabeth sat by the roadside for an hour, "surrounded by the morbid crowds" waiting for the police. After four days in the local hospital, Margaret was moved to the American Hospital in Paris, where she remained for eight weeks.

Elizabeth was traumatized by Margaret's injury—the loss of the right arm of an aspiring painter—that it should happen to Margaret at all. This second disaster of the year, affecting someone Elizabeth cared about and being maybe her own fault, left her desperate for consolation. She noted with hope that Margaret had begun to practice writing with her left hand two days after the accident, but her progress was slow. In addition, it fell to Elizabeth to write to Margaret's mother, at Margaret's request, telling her that the injury was only a fracture so as not to alarm her into coming over from New York immediately. Mrs. Miller was not deterred, however, and left within a few days, arriving at Havre on August 4. Elizabeth went down to meet her and on the way to Paris told her that her daughter's arm had been severed. "I know now what it feels like to be a murderer," Elizabeth said.[16] Mrs. Miller fainted.

The next two months Elizabeth and Louise spent in Paris at the Hotel Foyot near the hospital, cheering Margaret as much as they could, especially as the reality of her injury set in. Elizabeth had recorded Margaret's good courage throughout the ordeal and felt deeply each of her struggles and setbacks. On August 9, Elizabeth wrote to Marianne Moore, "I wish . . . that I could see you for a few minutes. I can't think of anything that would be more of a consolation."[17] Moore responded, "In such distress, even to think toward consolation is embittering; love is all that can help; but human love being that it is, I think Heaven can not but be aware of and pity such sorrow."[18] Elizabeth was also somewhat aghast at Mrs. Miller's grief and solicitude for her daughter and characteristically wished for a refuge from strong feelings. " 'Mother-love' – isn't it awful. I long for an Arctic climate where no emotions of any sort can possibly grow, – always excepting disinterested 'friendship' of course–."[19] From the apartment on the Ile St. Louis near the Quai d'Orléans where they all stayed after Margaret left the hospital on September 8, Elizabeth expressed this emotion in a poem, copied into her notebook. It was only later dedicated to Margaret but surely written with her in mind:

Each barge on the river easily tows
    a mighty wake,
a giant oak-leaf of gray lights
    on duller gray;
and behind it real leaves are floating by,
    down to the sea.
Mercury-veins on the giant leaves,
    the ripples, make
for the sides of the quai, to extinguish themselves
    against the walls
as softly as falling-stars come to their ends
    at a point in the sky.
And throngs of small leaves, real leaves, trailing them,
    go drifting by
to disappear as modestly, down the sea's
    dissolving halls.
We stand as still as stones to watch
    the leaves and ripples
while light and nervous water hold
    their interview.

"If what we see could forget us half as easily,"
  I want to tell you,
"as it does itself—but for life we'll not be rid
  of the leaves' fossils."

The poem is intensely private and enigmatic, in keeping with the style of her early poems. But its pattern of opening out private meaning from apparently objective description looks forward to poems like "The Bight" and "At the Fishhouses." Here the healing progress of time and, one hopes, of memory is represented by the boats and leaves floating down the river; the wakes that "extinguish themselves / against the walls" represent a desirable oblivion. "The leaves' fossils," the fact of Margaret's lost arm, the painful memories associated with the accident and her slow recovery allow no such escape. Elizabeth's transfer of agency in the poem—not "if we could forget what we see," but "if what we see could forget us"— seems to privilege vision or to suggest that the tragic events would forever be associated with the place. Indeed, she never did return to France.

. . .

Elizabeth developed severe and prolonged asthma during the weeks of waiting and watching in Paris. A brief visit with Bryher in Paris had yielded the friendly suggestion that Elizabeth seek out psychoanalysis in hopes of curing the condition. Elizabeth had rejected the suggestion with some energy. To Moore, she wrote:

> Your reassurance and illumination . . . in the matter of
> psychoanalysis were extremely welcome. I am so afraid I may have
> been rude to Bryher in the notes in which I tried to escape
> making an immediate appointment at the Freudian clinic. . . . She
> says "Psychoanalysis makes one write better and more easily" – and
> if that were true of course one would want to reap its benefits
> whether one had asthma or whooping-cough – but everything I
> have read about it has made me think that psychologists

misinterpret and very much underestimate all the workings of ART! "Psycho-analysts do not see the poet playing a social function, but regard him as a neurotic working off his complexes at the expense of the public. Therefore in analysing a work of art, psycho-analysts seek just those symbols that are peculiarly private, *i.e.* neurotic, and hence psycho-analytical criticism of art finds its examples and material either in third-rate artistic work or in accidental features of good work." That is from ILLUSION & REALITY, by Christopher Caudwell – have you seen it?[20]

Although Elizabeth later acknowledged that her asthma might be affected by psychosomatic causes, she never tried to treat it with psychological therapy.

Elizabeth, feeling helpless and believing her wheezing and sleeplessness were unhelpful to Margaret, needed a change. On the second of October, she and Louise set out for Arles and a tour of Provence in hopes of finding some relief. The sense that something was ending between herself and Margaret hovered at the edge of Elizabeth's conscious mind while making these travel decisions, though she was not yet aware of how imminent and how final the break would be.

They arrived in Arles at midnight and were escorted down what seemed to be "Van Gogh's street of bordels" to their taxi driver's recommendation of "an 'honest, serious hotel.'" The next day they saw the last bullfight of the season at Nîmes, in which Elizabeth took an aficionada's interest. They spent the rest of the week touring the countryside, following in Van Gogh's ("V. G." in Elizabeth's shorthand) footsteps where possible, traveling first by train to Stes. Maries de la Mer, which Elizabeth said reminded her of Florida. "On the beach. The sky was very dark gray-blue, but all objects in the foreground were in thick golden sunlight coming from in <u>back</u> of us. The sea was milky jade, lighter than the sky, with peacocked streaks ('like a mackeral [*sic*]' V. G. said about the very spot)." On a later trip to Les Baux, Elizabeth was enchanted. "It is all romantic ruins," she wrote to Frani. "All the <u>troubadours</u> came here."[21]

"Provence must be the best part of France. Les Baux one of the nicest things I have ever seen—set in a rough sea, of gray rocks, very high up." At Saint Rémy, they visited the Asylum of the Mausoleum, where Van Gogh was for a year, and found it run by a noisy, boisterous family, though nuns still cared for "eighty mad women" on the premises.

Two days later, they returned to Les Baux to spend a couple of days, but Elizabeth's asthma, which had been worsening over the week, confined her to bed for most of their stay. On October 10, they traveled to Avignon and late that evening caught a train back to Paris, where Elizabeth went directly to the American Hospital to try to break the attack. She remained in the hospital until the eighteenth, and as was always the case with her hospital stays, she filled her notebook with observations, not about the care she received, but about the characters she encountered there, the impression one person makes on another in an atmosphere so paradoxically intimate and regimented as the hospital. Her nurse on this stay, "Madame Math,"

> resembles the "comic character" in a modern presentation of Shakespeare—one of the historical plays. One of those actors who has been given too much "business" that makes no one laugh, a good deal of wandering about on the stage alone and no very funny lines. So he does his best by pretending great surprise at discovering a hole in the toe of his shoe, bumping into things, etc. . . .
>
> She is just hopelessly silly. Her eyebrows have been carefully plucked, but that only makes her look blanker. Her hair is done in 3 big curls on each side, very neat, but it resembles a blond stage wig. Her uniform is clean and starched but doesn't seem to fit—it pops out above and below the wide belt; this morning she caught one of the pockets that stick out to the sides, and ripped it half off. Worst of all, she can't seem to walk correctly,—just from the knees down—a stage shuffle. She drops things, stoops to pick them up, & knocks off her cap.

Also in her notebook are Elizabeth's musings over her testimony for the upcoming trial on their automobile accident. On October 26, Margaret, Elizabeth, Louise, Mrs. Crane, and a battery of lawyers traveled to Gien for the trial, which was made doubly tense and unpleasant because for Margaret to benefit from the Crane family insurance policy, Louise had to be judged guilty (of the equivalent of reckless driving, one assumes), and it had not to appear to be so arranged. Elizabeth tells a funny story of the two parties at lunch beforehand—herself and Margaret in one and Louise, Mrs. Crane, and her lawyers in the other—being seated together by an overly solicitous maître d', which necessitated an elaborate acting job of all parties so that they would not appear to be in collusion. Her satire of the lawyers ranks among her finest notebook entries. Louise was found guilty but was not, as they had all feared, sentenced to jail. A moderate fine discharged the penalty, and she and Elizabeth were free to go.

They lingered in Paris for a couple of weeks, but Elizabeth's worsening asthma once again prompted them to seek a drier climate. Elizabeth felt that she "was getting on Margaret's nerves" and doing her failing spirits no good. On November 12, she and Louise gathered their twelve pieces of luggage, lunch, and a jug of wine and headed at six in the morning for the Gare de Lyons, where they met up with Nina Maximoff, Elizabeth's nurse and their dear friend, and started for Rome. Having left Paris, they completed their subdued and illness-wracked tour without rejoining the Millers. But Margaret's situation was never far from Elizabeth's thoughts. Her notebook shows these macabre contemplations:

> The arm lay outstretched in the soft brown grass at the side of the road and spoke quietly to itself. At first all it could think of was the possibility of being quickly reunited to its body, without any more time elapsing than was absolutely necessary.
>
> "Oh, my poor body! Oh my poor body! I cannot bear to give you up. Quick! Quick!"

Then it fell silent while a series of ideas that had never occurred to it before rapidly swept over it.

After their first view of the Alps and a stay overnight at Turin, the three women arrived in Rome at nine in the evening to the Hotel Angleterra and the next day began to see the sights. On a walk that evening from the hotel to the Piazza d'Espagna, Elizabeth recognized the house where Keats died, "without having seen the plaque. It was almost as bad as having found his body; and then I saw the wreath hanging at the side of the house." Elizabeth's asthma immediately improved, her first respite from the condition in three months, and she had considerable energy for exploring Italy. She said she was glad she had seen Paris first, as it would have been hard to choose between Paris and Rome as places to stay. Her notebook highlights walking to visit the Ponte St. Angelo and St. Peter's ("I never had so clear an idea before of the vast commerce, the tides of gold, of the church, and I never disliked it so much") on the first day, the Church of Santa Maria degli Angeli and its museum on the second. A friend of Nina's drove them down the Appian Way, which Elizabeth loved, and through the Borghese Gardens. Equally impressive to Elizabeth was "a day-old Siamese kitten – like a little white rat" they saw at the friend's house.

Once again Elizabeth and Louise found themselves in a country on the verge of war. "Every 3rd man is in uniform," Elizabeth noted. "There are so many different uniforms, some very smart, but some like the 'Soldier's Chorus,' but worse. Today a Von Sternberg officer, monocled, corseted, with a cigar as thick as my little finger, and 10 inches long."

In their travels from church to church, Elizabeth took photographs and made sketches of the scene and its details. "I took a lot of photographs on the portico of the Temple of Faustina – cluttered with feet, hands, torsos, segments of pillows, etc." In all her travels in Catholic regions—Spain, southern Florida, Italy, Mexico, Haiti, Brazil—she was fascinated by the crudely fashioned objects of faith, the ex-votos, the representational offerings to the Virgin in hopes of a remedy, the altar constructed in a wine bottle, the carved saints. They interested her as folk art but also as the earnestly offered products of a sensibility so different from her own—faithful, fatalistic, optimistic, impractical.

The museums drew Elizabeth most strongly; she found that the Roman antiquities recalled "illustrations from an old Latin grammar," but she was enchanted by the Etruscans. "I like Etruscan things because they are simple, 'free,' cheerful, and often humorous – compared to Roman pomposity. I'm glad the Roman things are in ruins to be looked at –. . . . I wish I could see the Etruscan things whole." At the Vatican Museum, she admired the tapestries in the Raphael Room, particularly " 'the miraculous draught of fishes,' " "the shallow blue water, reflections, the birds feathers–very Florida-like and calm." A few years later, these became the governing images of "Seascape." Here also she first saw and conceived her passion for the paintings of Caravaggio, which she sought out in each of the many museums they visited thereafter. (His *Peter Denying Christ* reappears in "Roosters.") They remained in Rome, keeping up a packed schedule of sightseeing, until November 27. Elizabeth noted particularly the churches of San Lorenzo in Lucina, Santa Maria della Pace, and Santa Maria del Popolo; the Catacombs; the Pantheone; and the Farnese Gardens. She loved the Villa d'Este, "my idea of heaven": "The charm of dabbling in the water. I stood under, inside, the big fountain & watched the water curving over me–the wonderful clear calm with which it came over the round lip of the fountain, then suddenly all 'shot' with holes, tattered in bits, and apparently much heavier, from the way it fell." They left Rome for Naples on the evening of November 27, carrying with them three owls they had bought in a street market (whose behavior Elizabeth recorded with the care of a zoologist in her notebook) and a painting Elizabeth had acquired, an eighteenth-century "classic or neo-romantic" view of the tomb of Cestus.

She loved Naples, "even in the rain," and toured the museum and the aquarium, where she was surprised by a shock from an "electric fish." They spent three days walking through the city, visiting restaurants and the Politeono, "a vast, dreary music-hall where Neapolitan songs are sung, & acrobats, etc. perform. It was the poorest sort of vaudeville, but the songs – Caruso-like tenors, and very fat sopranos – and the enthusiasm of the audience – were interesting." On November 30, they left for Paestum, via the poor fishing villages south of Naples, then back to Salerno, where they caught a small boat to Amalfi, then a drive to Ravello, where they spent the night. Elizabeth suffered an asthma attack there, so they rested. On December 2, they returned to Rome for a day, before leaving for Orvieto and Florence, where they spent their last week in Italy visiting the Uffizzi Gallery, the Cathedral, the Campanile.

Elizabeth was unsure whether she should return to the United States with Louise, who was leaving from Genoa on December 9. She felt an obligation to stay with Margaret if she was wanted, but she had not heard from Margaret in more than a month. At the same time, Elizabeth was anxious to get back to the States—to find an apartment, preferably in Brooklyn, and to begin serious work on a book of poems. She never did hear from Margaret and in the end decided to leave, but she vowed to return to Italy as soon as possible.

On their last night in Florence, Elizabeth, Louise, and Nina had a feast of oysters which made them all sick and made their trip to Genoa the next morning a miserable chore. At Genoa, the two Americans said a melancholy good-bye to Nina and sailed with luggage and owls on the *Exeter* for Marseilles and Boston.

Six

ELIZABETH WAS MET in freezing cold Boston by Uncle George Shepherdson, who took her home to Aunt Maud for the Christmas holiday. Her description of their long walk from the hotel where they had met (Elizabeth saw his holey shoes and worn overcoat and did not suggest a taxi) shows her tired and depressed at the prospect of the holiday and her future. "We talked over all the same old problems, and bought a piece of meat and a can of peas for supper." Her relatives and their friends, their identical houses and pathetic decorations, suffered in contrast to Italy, though she perked up on seeing Minnow and her kittens, born four months before in Aunt Maud's care. Elizabeth spent four days sleeping on her aunt's hard living room couch, making the rounds of relatives, eating a couple of Christmas dinners in a couple of houses, and noting her impressions of everyone's table manners and speech patterns. "I have been shown off to the neighbors, and have been so modest. . . . I conversed like an English teacher," she told her notebook. Her cousin Hazel, who was a teacher, told stories about Great Village that pleased Elizabeth, too. On December 26, she boarded the train for New York and a two-dollar room at the Murray Hill Hotel. On

January 12, she rejoined Aunt Maud and Uncle George, who had decided to move their household to Key West.

In the two weeks in New York, Elizabeth saw Marianne Moore and her mother and a play, movie, or concert almost every night. She had one literary lunch—with Mary McCarthy, F. W. Dupee, and Philip Rahv, a group then associated with the *Partisan Review*—which apparently sufficiently fueled her anxiety about writing to give her nightmares. In her notebook she recorded a series of transparent dreams that link the tools of her trade, particularly typewriters, with images suggesting war. In one dream, the typewriter keys are in a code she must solve. In another, she is at a cocktail party and suddenly has an idea for a short story. The room itself becomes her page, which she is afraid to turn because the story will disappear, and it does.

Elizabeth had been writing some during her travels. Her notebooks show work on "Sleeping on the Ceiling," "Sleeping Standing Up," "Quai d'Orleans," "The Monument" (with a sketch), and numerous poems that she did not finish. *Partisan Review* had accepted "Love Lies Sleeping" for its January 1938 issue, asking if she might have a group the magazine could publish. She had not, and her lack of production began to trouble her, as it would from time to time. Among her meditations on the dreariness of hotel life at Christmastime is a list of poems and stories she planned to finish during the winter. For one story, tentatively titled "Embarrassment and Tact," she was constantly collecting anecdotes—examples of embarrassing situations, some salvaged by tact (she thought of them as closely related concepts), all concerning the awkwardness of relations between people. It was never finished. Another story, called "In Prison," addressed some of the same anxieties and proved much easier to write.

"In Prison" is the first and most vivid manifestation of Elizabeth's lifelong daydream of solitary retirement (a conflict at last resolved in "The End of March" [1974]). It is the first-person narrative of a would-be writer who "can scarcely wait for the day of my imprisonment."[1] Having committed no stated crime, the speaker views prison as its own end. In yearning for enforced confinement—choosing necessity over infinite choice, as it were—the male speaker hopes to make an impression that he cannot seem to make "at large." The "prisoner's" discussion includes a survey of existing prison narratives from cummings to Dostoyevsky and dismisses all of those with traces of sentimentality or humor. He is quite taken with the seriousness of his enterprise and will tolerate no ambiguity in his situation. Those prisoners released during the day to go to work, whose wives washed their uniforms and hung them on the line (a scene Elizabeth had witnessed with pleasure in Key West), infuriate him with "the perpetual irksomeness of all half-measures." The view from the window of his cell, he insists, must be appropriately confined and suggestive, and here Elizabeth lifts a passage almost verbatim from her travel notebook account of her visit with Louise to the Asylum of the Mausoleum, to the cell where Van Gogh was confined. "I can still see as clearly as in a photograph the beautiful completeness of the view from that window: the shaven fields, the black cypress, and the group of swallows posed dipping in the gray sky—only the fields have retained their faded color." But, he says, "I do not feel that what is suited to an asylum is necessarily suited to a prison."

The prisoner hopes that his prison is without a library and that he will be given only "one very dull book to read, the duller the better." Preferably, he says, it will be the second volume of a two-volume work on a subject completely alien to him, for "then I shall be able to experience with a free conscience the pleasure, perverse I suppose, of interpreting it not at all according to its intent." And on that "important aspect of prison life," writing on the wall, the prisoner-writer addresses his terror of belatedness by confining his interest in the work of all prior artists to those represented on the walls of his cell. The passage speaks painfully to the ambition and anxiety of the young writer:

I . . . have already composed sentences and paragraphs (which I
cannot give here) I hope to be able to inscribe on the walls of my
cell. First, however, . . . I shall read very carefully (or try to read,
since they may be partly obliterated, or in a foreign language) the
inscriptions already there. Then I shall adapt my own
compositions, in order that they may not conflict with those
written by the prisoner before me. The voice of a new inmate will
be noticeable, but there will be no contradictions or criticisms of
what has already been laid down, rather a "commentary." I have
thought of attempting a short, but immortal, poem, but I am
afraid that is beyond me; I may rise to occasion, however, once I
am confronted with that stained, smeared, scribbled-on wall and
feel the stub of pencil or rusty nail between my fingers. Perhaps I
shall arrange my "works" in a series of neat inscriptions in a clear,
Roman print; perhaps I shall write them diagonally, across a
corner, or at the base of a wall and half on the floor, in an almost
illegible scrawl. They will be brief, suggestive, anguished, but full
of the lights of revelation. And no small part of the joy these
writings will give me will be to think of the person coming after
me—the legacy of thoughts I shall leave him, like an old bundle
tossed carelessly into a corner!

The desire to reduce the body of previous writing to a manageable
size, to contain the writer's responsibility in an area the size of a
wall, to create a context small enough in which to make an impression—these suggest the way the vocation of "writer" weighed on
Elizabeth as an impossible burden. Her anxious wish for a conflict-
free niche in the vocation—she will write only "commentary," not
"contradictions or criticisms"—lasted her whole life, and even
though she wrote a handful of book reviews, she was paralyzed into
a three-year silence when in 1970 the *New Yorker* hired her as its
poetry critic.

Elizabeth finished the story in late January and sent it right off
to the *Partisan Review* as an entry in a fiction-writing contest the
magazine was conducting. Having established the habit of running

her stories by Marianne Moore before submitting them, Elizabeth was apologetic. "I sent it to them and now of course regret it very much and hope they will send it back. . . . It is called 'In Prison' and is another one of these horrible 'fable' ideas that seem to obsess me."[2] Moore did not let Elizabeth off easily and replied, only half-jokingly, "It was very independent of you to submit your prize story without letting me see it. If it is returned with a printed slip, that will be why."[3] When the story won the contest's one-hundred-dollar prize and appeared in the March *Partisan Review*, Moore was impressed: "Never have I . . . seen a more insidiously innocent and artless artifice of innuendo than in your prison meditations." But she went on to deliver perhaps the most incisive criticism Elizabeth had yet to receive on her writing, both stories and poems:

> I can't help wishing you would sometime in some way, risk some
> unprotected profundity of experience; or since no one admits
> profundity of experience, some characteristic private defiance of
> the significantly detestable. Continuously fascinated as I am by the
> creativeness and uniqueness of these assemblings of yours – which
> are really poems – I feel responsibility against anything that might
> threaten you; yet fear to admit such anxiety, lest I influence you
> away from an essential necessity or particular strength. The golden
> eggs can't be dealt with theoretically, by presumptuous mass
> salvation formulae. But I do feel that tentativeness and
> interiorizing are your danger as well as your strength.[4]

This warning against too great a distance from her subjects, too theoretical a treatment of emotion, came from a curious quarter, but it may have been the most important single piece of criticism Elizabeth ever received. She took it, saying that her next story (about Key West and called "At Mrs. Pindar's" but never finished) "does attempt to be a little more 'important.' " But she felt lost about writing poems. "If only I could see half as clearly how I want to write poems. I wish sometime you would tell me quite frankly if you think there is any use – any real use – in my continuing with them."[5]

Elizabeth recognized the "tentativeness" Moore pointed out and blamed it on an unwillingness and inability to present a political position in the poems. "I'm a 'Radical,' of course," Elizabeth wrote. But to a young writer coming of age in the 1930s, to be "important" was to write about the social and political issues of the day. She had been forcefully reminded of this at her lunch with McCarthy, Dupee, and Rahv ("I really think they should announce themselves honestly as Trotskyists, because that's what they are").[6] Elizabeth was "baffled" by and feared the "short-sighted and, I think, ignorant views" of her friends, yet she could not arrive at "what stand to take" herself.

. . .

Elizabeth settled in Key West in a four-dollar-a-week room in a boarding house run by Mrs. Pindar, at 529 Whitehead Street just a few blocks from Aunt Maud and Uncle George, with whom Elizabeth ate dinner each night. One "roomer," Mr. Gay, fascinated her with his shelves full of "novelties," stored in cigar boxes. She began to write a story about him, featuring all the members of Mrs. Pindar's circle: Miss Lula and her servant Cootchie, Mrs. Pindar, and Mr. Gay. Although the story was never finished, its characters found their way into poems, notably "Cootchie" and the informal portrait of Mrs. Pindar's religiosity, "Sunday at Key West":

> The rocking-chairs
>   In rapid motion
> Approach the object
>   Of devotion.
> Rock on the porches
>   Of the tabernacle:
> With a palm-leaf fan
>   Cry Hail, all Hail!

When Mrs. Pindar moved house in mid-March, Miss Lula became the landlady.

Elizabeth went up to Miami on March 13 to meet Louise, as she arrived by train from New York, and together they traveled to the Gulf coast and spent a few days at Keewaydin, tarpon fishing and lying in the sun, before heading back to Key West. They spent a month as roomers in Miss Lula's house and grew to like the town so much that they decided to pool Louise's financial resources and Elizabeth's enthusiasm and begin looking for a house of their own to buy. Among the discoveries in their travels on the Key was the work and then the person of Gregorio Valdes, a primitive painter. Valdes's starkly realistic paintings had gained some attention by the time Elizabeth and Louise found him, but Elizabeth was most moved by the unself-consciousness of his art. As she wrote in her memoir of him, published in *Partisan Review* the next year:

> Gregorio was not a great painter at all, and although he certainly belongs to the class of painters we call "primitive," sometimes he was not even a good "primitive." . . . Gregorio himself did not see any difference between what we think of as his good pictures and his poor pictures, and his painting a good one or a bad one seems to have been entirely a matter of luck.
>
> There are some people whom we envy not because they are rich or handsome or successful, although they may be any or all of these, but because everything they are and do seems to be all of a piece, so that even if they wanted to they could not be or do otherwise.[7]

(Almost twenty years later she envied Robert Lowell's then-almost-miserable life because it was more "all of a piece" than her own.) When she and Louise found the house they wanted to buy, at 624 White Street (and now known in Key West as "The Elizabeth Bishop House," though it is in some disrepair), they commissioned Valdes to paint a picture of it, asking that he add a few details—more flowers, a traveler's palm, a neighbor's monkey, and a parrot.

Elizabeth was so taken with the accuracy of the picture that she later planted a real traveler's palm in the yard to complete the verisimilitude.

Elizabeth moved into the White Street house on May 24; Charlotte Russell was visiting from North Carolina and helped her. The house is the first of the "three loved houses" Elizabeth described nearly forty years later in "One Art" as "lost." It is a large, squarish, two-storey building with a wide porch extending its width and height, supported by three somewhat frail-looking and very tall posts. All its rooms are off a central hallway, which runs the length of the house, shotgun style. Then it stood all alone on the street, and in the yard there were four banana trees, two avocado trees, two lime trees, a mango tree, a sour sop tree, and a grape arbor. Elizabeth was enamored with the house and also with Key West itself, which soothed her nervous and self-critical northern nature and assuaged her continuing anxiety about the passage of time. "One of the reasons I like Key West so much," she wrote to Frani, "is because everything goes at such a natural pace. For example, if you buy something and haven't any money and promise, in a most New England way, to bring it around in ½ an hr., and then forget for 2 weeks, no one even comments. . . . And drunkenness is an excuse as correct as any other."[8] Elizabeth had a young girl to help her clean, charmingly named "Mizpah," and she hoped to settle in to write.

But less than two weeks after she moved into the house, Elizabeth suddenly flew North (her first flight) for the summer, which she spent in New York. She started out at Louise's, then moved to the Murray Hill, and then went to La Residencia, a Spanish hotel on West One Hundred Thirteenth Street, where she stayed with a Spanish friend, Sofia, and made a concentrated effort to learn the language. In mid-August, Elizabeth abandoned the city altogether and moved into a tiny shack on the beach at Provincetown, Massachusetts, on property owned by her married friends the painter Loren MacIver and the literary critic and scholar Lloyd Frankenberg.

Elizabeth worked fairly well over the summer; her notebooks are lively, and she often enclosed poems in her letters to Marianne Moore, whom she had begun to call "Marianne" for the first time. In July, *Partisan Review* published the "quite satisfactory" results of Elizabeth's work from the previous winter: "Quai d'Orleans," "Late Air," the first of her Key West poems, and another contemplation of the terrors of introspection, "The Unbeliever."

The three creatures in "The Unbeliever"—a gull, a cloud, and a man—are all high in the air above the sea. The gull and the cloud fly and float confidently, extrapolating from their success and their reflections the presence of pillars or towers that hold them up. The man has an actual pillar, however precarious, but refuses to look, insecure in *in*trospection, and chants a paranoid prayer: " 'I must not fall. / The spangled sea below wants me to fall. / It is hard as diamonds; it wants to destroy us all.' " What is absent from the poem is any possibility of affirmative belief. The gull and the cloud are silly but successful; the man is miserable. Elizabeth had obviously drawn on her reading of seventeenth-century English poetry for an ironic contrast to the questions of belief in Crashaw's "The Weeper," a poem she and Margaret Miller had both admired:

> But we are deceived all,
> Stars indeed they are too true,
> For they but seeme to fall
> As heav'ns other spangles doe:
> It is not for our Earth and us,
> To shine in things so pretious.

Elizabeth stayed alone in the cabin at Provincetown, though just down the beach from Loren and Lloyd and with a few visitors, notably Charlotte and Red Russell, up from North Carolina. She was for the most part comfortable and delighted to be there:

> At about 6 in the morning I turned my head to look out the screen door, right beside the head of the bed. The sun was rising, round & red. The light ran straight towards me, rapidly along the tops of the dune grass – a pure, rushing scarlet. That color lasted just a minute, then it turned gilt – like thousands of scuttling insects. . . . Perhaps it is because I haven't been on this beach for so long, I can't quite believe in the landscape. Dune, beach, sun, sky – longitudinal – there is a "flats" look about them, a long "set," or corridor. At the ends – the East is the end – or through a crack which may appear at any minute, I expect to see darkness, or twilight, full of traffic, cumbersome objects, lumber, buildings, noise, confusions.

The "longitudinal" landscape became the setting for "The Monument," and the perspective—lying down in bed and looking out across the room—recurred several times in finished poems.

Elizabeth loved the provisional, found-object furniture in the cabin; domestic arrangements in a makeshift space still charmed her. Her notebook is full of contemplations of the beach and the tides, her thinking about these phenomena representing the passage of time. ("The older you are the less time you have in a day. As a child one can accomplish the work of a lifetime in a morning or an afternoon. Later, it gets to be 12 o'clock before you know it, you pick up a book & it is dinner time – nothing gets written but a few letters.") She finished a few poems, notably the "jingle about the white horse," called "Spleen," which the *New Yorker* accepted a year later, by then retitled "Cirque d'Hiver." It contemplates an unexpected human drama in the operation of a windup circus act:

> Across the floor flits the mechanical toy,
> fit for a king of several centuries back.
> A little circus horse with real white hair.

His eyes are glossy black.
He bears a little dancer on his back. . . .

He canters three steps, then he makes a bow,
canters again, bows on one knee,
canters, then clicks and stops, and looks at me.

The dancer, by this time, has turned her back.
He is the more intelligent by far.
Facing each other rather desperately—
his eye is like a star—
we stare and say, "Well, we have come this far."

She also began some prophetic work with nursery rhymes, which she sent to Moore:

> My friend Frani Blough brought me a whole collection of little books of Provençal poetry – I had never read any except the quotations in Pound's essay – and I have been reading it a good deal, and also "Mother Goose," which I brought along, too. Between Piere [*sic*] Vidal & the "House that Jack Built" I have enclosed some rhyme-schemes that I hope will impress you, – or amaze, anyway.

Her linking of Pound with "The House that Jack Built" bore fruit twenty years later in "Visits to St. Elizabeths."

By the end of September, Elizabeth had had enough of the Northeast—"I shall be glad to get back to the South where time seems to pass more slowly."[9] She left Provincetown for a brief visit to Boston on September 28, then on to New York and the Murray Hill. She stayed in New York for three weeks, primarily to greet Margaret Miller as she returned from Europe, then left for Key West, arriving on October 24.

Elizabeth settled down in the White Street house to work. Although Louise joined her for several months, Elizabeth's first commitment was to writing. Her notebooks show her contemplating her surroundings with a writer's energy of description. She extrapolated dramatic plots based on the activities of her neighbors, whom she viewed at night through their bedroom window. (She was amazed to discover that her surmises about their lives had been correct.) The sound of wind in the palm trees, the marvelous phenomenon of water spouts at the shore, and the voices, the apparent attitude, and even the smell of the Negroes she lived among for the first time all interested her. (To Moore she had written, "The Negroes have such soft voices and such beautifully tactful manners — I suppose it is far-fetched, but their attitude keeps reminding me of the tone of George Herbert. 'Take the gentle path,' etc.")[10] She hired a housekeeper, Hannah Almyda, ostensibly to clean the house, but the two women developed such an attachment for each other that she became Elizabeth's nurse, adviser, even a mother figure on whom she depended. The notebooks contain innumerable contemplations of Mrs. Almyda's goodness, transcripts of her conversation, beginnings of at least one unfinished story and one poem about her. Elizabeth extolled her virtues so warmly to Moore that Moore wrote back asking only half-jokingly if Mrs. Almyda might be available to help her out, as she and her mother were burdened with illness.

As the winter passed at its lazy southern pace, Elizabeth began to see the results of the good work she had managed to do over the summer in the North: "Sleeping On the Ceiling" appeared in the October 1938 issue of *Life and Letters Today,* and "Sleeping Standing Up" appeared in the November issue. In January 1939, *Partisan Review* printed "Florida," and James Laughlin selected "The Monument" for his *New Directions* anthology for 1939.

"The Monument" presents Elizabeth's argument with herself and the world over what is and is not art and what art is meant to do. The poem is presented in two voices—a dramatic dialogue of sorts—with one an artist and the other a skeptic, but the voices are both Elizabeth's, for her skepticism is partly what kept her focused constantly on touchstones of truth. She must ask the skeptic's questions and do so with the disturbed incomprehension and weariness of voice that she herself sometimes felt when confronting pretentious contemporary art. But the artist in the poem argues that, despite its uncertain boundaries and intentions, undefined desires, and decrepitude, the monument is a potential source of revelation of what "after all / cannot have been intended to be seen":

> The monument's an object, yet those decorations
> carelessly nailed, looking like nothing at all,
> give it away as having life, and wishing;
> wanting to be a monument, to cherish something.
> The crudest scrollwork says "commemorate,"
> while once each day the light goes around it
> like a prowling animal,
> or the rain falls on it, or the wind blows into it.
> It may be solid, may be hollow.
> The bones of the artist-prince may be inside
> or far away on even drier soil.
> But roughly but adequately it can shelter
> what is within (which after all
> cannot have been intended to be seen).
> It is the beginning of a painting,
> a piece of sculpture, or poem, or monument,
> and all of wood. Watch it closely.

Despite the skeptic's questions, the poem affirms much more about the enterprise of the artist, particularly the modern artist, than any other Bishop work until, perhaps, "Poem" (1972). It also articulates for the first time what Elizabeth found moving in modest, unpretentious art in all media or genres, its urge to "commemorate," its "wanting to be a monument, to cherish something." Typically, when the poem appeared, Elizabeth wrote to Moore, "If you read the last NEW DIRECTIONS, please promise me to skip the pages of my poem. It is so TERRIBLE, I can't bear to think of it, really terrible."[11]

Nevertheless, on the strength of these acceptances, Elizabeth put together her small corpus of poems and sent it off to her first-choice publisher, Random House, in hopes of interesting it in issuing her first book. When the manuscript was returned without encouragement, she tried to consider the rejection "an indirect blow at my laziness rather than a judgement on the poems themselves" and asked Moore if she should tell Laughlin that she was now interested in his proposal.[12] A week later, she sent him the poems, but he did not renew his offer to publish her alone. When, the following winter, he offered to include her in a first-volume collection of five young poets (with John Berryman, Randall Jarrell, George William O'Donnell, and W. R. Moses), saying he needed a woman poet in the group, Elizabeth refused to act as "sex appeal." (Mary Barnard eventually agreed to appear there.) Moore wrote a conciliatory letter to Laughlin saying that she had advised Elizabeth to say no because "her idiosyncrasy is too special to be combined with that of other young writers."[13] Laughlin did come back with a proposal to publish Elizabeth in one of a series of monthly pamphlets featuring the work of young poets, with the work remaining free of copyright so it could be published later in book form. Elizabeth again refused. From this point on, she tried in earnest to find a publisher for her first book, dutifully reporting her failures to Moore. Late in the spring of 1939, she told Allen Tate that she could not participate in his "Chapel Hill Poets" plan because she was at that time "negotiating with a publishing house."

In February, Elizabeth invited her Key West neighbors, the philosopher John Dewey and his physicist daughter Jane, to dinner for the first time. Elizabeth always said that she understood nothing of Dewey's philosophy but had boundless admiration for the man. Dewey and Moore were, she said, the most truly "democratic" people she knew—able to talk easily with people of any social, economic, or educational class. Jane Dewey became one of Elizabeth's most loyal friends, and her farm in Havre de Grace, Maryland, was one of Elizabeth's favorite refuges. "A Cold Spring" is set there and is dedicated to Jane.

Winter became spring in Key West. Louise went back to New York for a while; Loren MacIver and Lloyd Frankenberg came down. There was a big flower show held in town, and the painter Loren and the poet Elizabeth took to sketching and describing the flowers and gardening around the White Street house. Things grew in the garden, thunderstorms crashed over the island, "an epidemic of kites" overtook the population. A baby goat was born ("It was all black—the fur felt like a kitten's, and the biggest things were the tail and ears and hooves") and died the next day of neglect. Elizabeth, ever vigilant about neglected offspring, was furious. They "could have saved it if we'd brought it home."[14] Gregorio Valdes died of pneumonia in the middle of May, and Elizabeth's memoir of him appeared in the June *Partisan Review*.

Spring became summer. Louise left Key West for good on June 17, and Elizabeth followed on July 4. She took an apartment in New York on West Twentieth Street. Her summer and fall are almost entirely undocumented. She later referred back to her "troubles in New York" and years later said that her habits had "changed drastically" in 1939. She gained twenty-five or thirty pounds over the next couple of years, which she did not lose until she got to Brazil in 1952. But there are no other available details about what befell her in the city, where she would hereafter be almost intolerably uncomfortable.

By 1939, the tentative mastery Elizabeth had achieved over the losses of her childhood had clearly started to come undone. The details of her suffering at this time are sketchy, but we do know that she was often depressed. This depression had begun in some sense in Worcester in 1917, and it lasted the whole of Elizabeth's life. It both fed and was fed by her major physical conditions, the asthma that had also first developed in Worcester and the alcoholism that, by 1939, had begun to dominate her life. Under the shock of Bob

Seaver's suicide, the terrible injury to Margaret Miller, and Elizabeth's own painful indecision about how she would live her life, these physical conditions grew beyond her ability to control them.

Elizabeth traced the origins of her alcoholism to the frightening scene at Marblehead, Massachusetts, when she and her mother witnessed the Salem fire of 1914. In the unpublished poem entitled "A Drunkard," the earliest mention of which occurred in 1960, Elizabeth remembers being amazed at the fire's glow, being "terribly thirsty," but being unable to capture the attention of her mother, a ghostly figure on the lawn giving coffee to refugees arriving on the beach in boats. When, the next morning, the curious child picks up a woman's black cotton stocking from the rubble, her mother says sharply, "Put that down!"

> I remember clearly, clearly—
> But since that day, that reprimand . . .
> I have . . . suffered from abnormal thirst—
> I swear it's true—and by the age
> of twenty or twenty-one I had begun
> to drink, & drink—I can't get enough
> and, as you must have noticed,
> I'm half-drunk now...

Elizabeth ends the poem with a half-hearted disclaimer: "And all I'm telling you may be a lie." But her description of the Salem fire corresponds perfectly with newspaper accounts of June 26, 1914, and her relationship to her mother in this scene is familiar from her descriptions in "In the Village" and in other unpublished poems and stories. If the poem does not tell "the" truth, it tells a version of it; in her own mind, her alcoholism was tied to her early losses.

Lucius, the autobiographical figure of Elizabeth's early stories about her childhood, fixes his grandfather rum toddies on winter evenings. Elizabeth began to talk about her own drinking in college, indeed, at the "age of twenty or twenty-one," when she and her friends drank wine in speakeasies just before the repeal of Prohibition and brought each other bottles of bourbon and scotch as house presents in the summer. Elizabeth drank destructively from that time onward, and her life by 1939 was dominated by her need for alcohol and by the effects of heavy drinking on her body, mind, and relationships. The guilt and shame attached to her abuse of alcohol made it impossible for her to live comfortably, and alcoholism fed her homelessness. For a person without family or real ties to any one place, an embarrassing drinking bout was cause for self-banishment. When she wrote in 1948 that she "left Wiscasset under a cloud," the cloud was alcoholic. "The Prodigal," which dates from the same period, describes a young man self-exiled in the family pigsty—"(he hid the pints behind a two-by-four)." At times, he is at home among the pigs and their excrescence; at other times, he is horrified:

> Carrying a bucket along a slimy board,
> he felt the bats' uncertain staggering flight,
> his shuddering insights, beyond his control,
> touching him. But it took him a long time
> finally to make his mind up to go home.

Elizabeth said the inspiration for this poem came from a visit to a Nova Scotia relative, a second cousin, and alcohol does figure in her sketchy recollections of her family. "Memories of Uncle Neddy" amply documents the decline of her mother's brother, Arthur, and as Elizabeth said, "Father had to stop [drinking], and his father, and three uncles. It can be done."[15] Several recent studies conducted on adopted boys (no studies have yet been done on girls) show that sons of alcoholics, even when they have been raised by nonalcoholic adoptive parents, may be as much as four times more likely to develop alcoholism than sons of nonalcoholics.[16] If alcoholism has a genetic component, Elizabeth was in line to receive it. She was also subject to the "environmental triggers" of the condition that

affected a whole generation of male American writers—Scott Fitzgerald, Ernest Hemingway, William Faulkner, and Eugene O'Neill,
among others. The romance of breaking the law during Prohibition
and the ethos of the "drinking writer" claimed victims in Elizabeth's
own generation of poets as well: Robert Lowell, Theodore Roethke,
Anne Sexton, Delmore Schwartz, and John Berryman.

Elizabeth Bishop drank destructively because she was an alcoholic, but why she drank at all is a more complex question. The
answer she posited in "A Drunkard" is comprehensive—many users
of alcohol describe drinking to fill a perceived void, and the ache at
the heart of that poem is the distance between the child in her crib
and the mother on the lawn and the harsh words that are their only
exchange. There was a void at the center of Elizabeth's life, and she
was poorly suited by temperament and training to confront it,
mourn for it, heal it. In a nature so reticent, which kept painful
memory and personal anguish even from itself, alcohol provided
license to talk, to cry, to stop being the stoical New Englander she
had been raised to be. But, of course, this opening up is false; no
constructive mourning can be done under the influence of alcohol.
Elizabeth's friends say that her most painful self-revelations often
occurred in alcohol-induced "blackouts," and she would not
remember having made them at all. In 1939, she began what became
a lifelong practice of making late-night telephone calls to friends
and even casual acquaintances, taking advantage of the cover of
drunkenness to feel her misery and finally to say how she felt.

Elizabeth's trouble with the physical sensation of the passage of
time finds its way into all her work, from letters and journals to
published poems. In her most cogent and persuasive statements
about her use of alcohol, she said she drank to lose that dizzying
sense of time rushing past. But the stepping out of time that being
very drunk seemed to allow was itself frightening. When in 1960
Robert Lowell sent her a draft of his poem "The Drinker," which
begins, "The man is killing time—there's nothing else," she
responded with empathy, identifying first with the man's need to

escape time. "The sense of time is terrifying – have hours gone by, or one awful moment? – How long have the cars been parked?" She commended the "release" of the poem's ending, "a sense . . . that only the poem, or another fifth of Bourbon, could produce."[17]

Her nature was as fearlessly observant as it was reticent, and she also drank to escape from the tyranny of that observing consciousness. Several times she complained in letters about the burden her "famous eye" placed on her, and her autobiographical Robinson Crusoe laments in "Crusoe in England" that he dreams of

> other islands
> stretching away from mine, infinities
> of islands, islands spawning islands,
> like frogs' eggs turning into polliwogs
> of islands, knowing that I had to live
> on each and every one, eventually,
> for ages, registering their flora,
> their fauna, their geography.

He then ferments his island's one kind of berry and makes home brew. Hemingway, among other writer-alcoholics, insisted that he drank to stop writing when he had done his days work. Although by middle age he was combining alcohol with work, to the detriment of both his health and his art, his point is useful. Elizabeth herself could never write productively and drink heavily at the same time, and her long fallow periods often corresponded to times when her drinking got out of control. This situation separates her from still other writers, who argue that because poets are inhibited by the world, they must drink to escape it, to free themselves so they can write.[18] She could write only when she was firmly "in" the world.

By 1939, Elizabeth may also have fallen victim to an "environmental trigger" akin to the masculine mythos of the "drinking writer." Studying the surrealists in France, she would have imbibed, along with Pernod, the highly romantic notion of the artist in touch with the darkest depths of his soul, willing to suffer degradations of various kinds to experience that depth. She never claimed a wish for a place in such a grouping, but certainly the model of the tormented and troubled artist was attractive to her and to others of her generation. Because she was an alcoholic, her experiment with such a lifestyle proved disastrous.

Elizabeth does not seem to have drunk to acquire courage for writing, though she was painfully shy as a young woman and found it useful to bolster her social fortitude. She does not seem to have drunk for "inspiration," to gain access to subconscious material, as other writers have said they do. In fact, the period of her greatest clarity about her childhood and its deprivations occurred when she settled in Brazil and stopped drinking, with the help of Antabuse, for several years. She never said that alcohol provided her with a new perspective on her world or that it endowed the ordinary with beauty and strangeness, but other writers have said so, and it is impossible to know how much of the intensely transformative descriptions and perspectives of her early poems can be attributed to the influence of alcohol. But surely a figure like the only human presence in "Love Lies Sleeping," the one for whom

> morning comes,
> whose head has fallen over the edge of his bed,
> whose face is turned
> so that the image of
>
> the city grows down into his open eyes
> inverted and distorted. No. I mean
> distorted and revealed,
> if he sees at all

is at least hung over, if not dead drunk. The sometimes dizzying, even queasy shifts from "normal" perspective ("Sleeping on the Ceiling," for example) and the ubiquity of semiconscious figures in

the poems ("Little Exercise," among others) may also stem from the
poet's experience with alcohol.

. . .

Elizabeth returned to Key West on October 26, 1939, having
shipped most of her belongings down, including her clavichord,
clearly with the intention of staying for a while. She settled in her
house with evident relief. "I got into such an awful state in N.Y.
that although I had things to say I couldn't say them, and since I've
been here . . . I'm more coherent."[19] As the Key West winter community gathered—Louise came down, Red and Charlotte Russell
arrived, Elizabeth's British friend Mrs. King took a hotel room in
town—Elizabeth began to feel comfortable. She weathered the roller
coaster of emotions over her publishing prospects with some equanimity—rejected by Viking Press in November, she sent her manuscript on to Simon and Schuster right away, which also rejected
it, "graciously." When the *New Yorker* took "Cirque d'Hiver," paying a gratifying one dollar per line and asking her to send more
poems, she said she hoped she could supply them but insisted that
she was working on several longer poems, which she hoped to sell
to the *Nation,* and a little book "or two," with Loren MacIver as
illustrator. She did not pursue her relationship with the *New Yorker*
for several years, so angry was she when, in the fall, an editor there
wrote to Moore asking for a poem and then rejected it. One of the
"longer" poems, "The Fish," appeared in *Partisan Review;* she did
not publish in the *Nation* until 1947.

The highlight of the winter of 1939–1940 in Key West was a five-
day canoe trip Elizabeth and Louise took with Charlotte and Red
through Florida's Ten Thousand Islands. They left from Coxambus
on November 30 and spent their first night (after paddling eight
miles) at Dismal Key. From the start this was a literary adventure
for Elizabeth. She kept a daily diary, which she hoped to turn into
an essay to accompany photographs taken by Louise. Whereas the
trip was a great success, the essay was not. The project dragged on

and on, giving Elizabeth several opportunities to castigate herself for her inability to finish anything, work steadily, or write for an audience. From the start she had promised to send the piece to Moore, and when she did on February 23, it was with apologies. "I know this will be very disappointing to you, after all my talking. . . . Send it back sometime, and I'll save it and hope for the right way to use it all."[20] The piece was never finished and resides among her papers, alongside an essay she intended to write about Sable Island in Canada, in a folder of unpublished prose. Memories of the trip, however, stayed with her long enough to appear as aspects of Crusoe's island in "Crusoe in England" (1972).

More successful for Elizabeth that winter was "The Fish," a finished draft of which she enclosed in a letter to Moore in January 1940. Moore sent back criticism, some of which Elizabeth heeded: "I did as you suggested about everything except 'breathing in' (if you can remember that) which I decided to leave as it was. . . . I left off the outline of capitals, too, and feel very ADVANCED."[21] "The Fish" became the most anthologized of Bishop's poems and is still most representative among the early poems of Bishop's voice. Its main character is the enormous Caribbean jewfish that Elizabeth caught at Key West, but it shares top billing with the fisher, the "I" of the poem. "I caught a tremendous fish / and held him beside the boat / half out of water, with my hook / fast in a corner of his mouth." "I caught" with "my hook." Here is no indirection or distance.

As many have said about "The Fish," the accumulation of detail forces its conclusion. But the details about the speaker who is examining the fish are as important as those of the fish itself. The "event" in the poem happens less to the fish than to the fisher; her revelation, her epiphany, spreads the rainbow around the boat and seals her covenant with the other battered creature. The person we are introduced to here, perhaps for the first time in her poems, is Elizabeth Bishop herself: the soon-to-be "famous eye" that sees not only the beautiful and not only the surface, that imagines entrails, and that extrapolates from present conditions a vivid past:

A green line, frayed at the end
where he broke it, two heavier lines,
and a fine black thread
still crimped from the strain and snap
when it broke and he got away.

The poem also reveals an independent morality carving its own way between the extremes and hypocrisies of convention. Here Elizabeth "takes a stand" of her own. As a rule, she goes fishing and keeps her catch. She judges this case independently, finding in her imperfect communication with the fish a reason to let him go. When he reviewed *North & South* in 1947, Randall Jarrell was enormously attracted to the person who spoke this poem, her sense of personal responsibility and accountability to what she saw.

She is morally so attractive, in poems like "The Fish" or "Roosters," because she understands so well that the wickedness and confusion of the age can explain and extenuate other people's wickedness and confusion, but not, for you, your own; . . . that when you see the snapped lines trailing, "five-haired beard of wisdom," from the great fish's aching jaw, it is then that victory fills "the little rented boat," that the oil on the bilgewater by the rusty engine is "rainbow, rainbow, rainbow!"—that you let the fish go.[22]

Elizabeth grew weary of the famousness of "The Fish," eventually telling an anthologist or two that they could have any *other* poem. Nevertheless, in 1940 it was a breakthrough and a triumph and launched her on a successful series of Key West poems. In March, *Partisan Review* printed "The Fish" and asked Elizabeth to write a "Florida Letter." She thought she might be able to work something up from the "10,000 Islands" pieces and in April announced to Moore that she had written it, but the essay was never printed. Elizabeth's contemplations of Florida were to be entirely poetic, with the exception of the Gregorio Valdes piece and "Mercedes Hospital," published in 1984, five years after her death.

Louise stayed in Key West for only a few weeks in December and January, having begun a job in New York, and did not return until June. Elizabeth spent time in the winter and spring with her aunt and uncle and struck up friendships with others of her neighbors. Pauline Hemingway, recently divorced from Ernest, became a good friend, as did her sister, Evelyn Pfeiffer, a few years later. (Pauline reported that Ernest had admired "The Fish," praise Elizabeth said in 1964 "meant more" to her "than any praise in the quarterlies.")[23] Elizabeth vowed to stay in Key West until July and then travel with Louise to Nova Scotia, bypassing New York as much as possible because she wished to avoid the city and its pressures and because she said she was afraid to face her friends "without a finished manuscript under my arm." As it turned out, she stayed in Key West until August and then spent two months with Charlotte and Red in Brevard, North Carolina, and then two months in New York before returning to Florida in late November. She and Louise did not travel together again.

On the first of June, Stanley Young of Harcourt Brace wrote asking Elizabeth to submit a volume of poetry, and Elizabeth shared her pleasure with Moore:

> The letter is so nice I think I'll enclose it for you to read. . . . If only the poetry were better! I sent it off last Tuesday and I hope so much that something will come of it this time. I, probably unwisely, said that I was afraid the general impression was one of slightness of subject-matter, but that I felt that in the work I am doing now I am "finding myself" and that it is more serious, etc. I also sent him the stories.[24]

Harcourt Brace wrote back a month later that they felt her manuscript was not yet complete and her poems not yet strong enough
but that they would like to publish her "some day." Elizabeth was
disappointed but, she said, not surprised. "When I think about it
really hard, I am afraid I can only number 5 or 6 poems that I think
are worth two cents, anyway."[25] The result of this exchange was that
Elizabeth and Harcourt Brace more or less waited for each other for
the next five years, and Elizabeth stopped circulating her manuscript. As this disappointment sank in, she became discouraged
about the writing of poetry, though she was still convinced that she
was "finding herself" and would eventually write the kind of "serious" poems she dreamed of writing.

> I scarcely know why I persist at all – it is really fantastic to place so
> much on the fact that I have written a half-dozen phrases that I
> can still bear to re-read without too much embarrassment. But I
> have that continuous uncomfortable feeling of "things" in the
> head, like icebergs or rocks or awkwardly-shaped pieces of
> furniture – it's as if all the nouns were there but all the verbs were
> lacking – if you know what I mean. And I can't help having the
> theory that if they are joggled around hard enough and long
> enough some kind of electricity will occur, just by friction, that
> will arrange everything – But you remember how Mallarmé said
> that poetry was made of words, not ideas – and sometimes I am
> terribly afraid I am approaching, or trying to approach it all from
> the wrong track.[26]

Elizabeth waited a long time for that electricity. By the end of
1940, she had written most of the poems that would make up *North
& South* and had reached a discouraging impasse in her prose writing
as well. The next five years were a painful period of professional
anxiety and personal turmoil, deepened by several events. The first
was the misleading communication from Harcourt Brace, which
Elizabeth interpreted as indicating that she had a publisher waiting

in the wings. The second was the death of Aunt Maud Shepherdson on a visit to Great Village in early August. Elizabeth had left Key West for North Carolina with her friend Nora Hasecher on August 6 and on her arrival there the next day found the telegram waiting for her. Her Uncle George continued to winter in Key West, but the provisional family Maud had provided for Elizabeth for much of her life was lost. She did not attend the funeral. For years she struggled to write an elegy for her aunt, unable to get beyond the first few lines, which placed Maud in the cemetery in Great Village: "Poem: For M. B. S., buried in Nova Scotia."

> Yes, you are dead now and live
> only there, in a little slightly tip-tilted graveyard
> where all of your childhood's Christmas trees are forgathered
>   with the presents they meant to give,
> and your childhood's river quietly curls at your side
> and breathes deep with each tide.

The third transformative and disorienting event of Elizabeth's fall was a major change in her relationship with Marianne Moore. Over the previous year or so, Elizabeth had come to rely increasingly on the rigorous readings Moore and her mother gave the poems and stories and on the thoughtful advice Moore could give about publishing prospects. Elizabeth had shared with Moore, and heeded her suggestions on, the group of Key West poems that had made up the previous winter's work, including "The Fish," "Cootchie," and "José's House" (later "Jerónimo's House"). Accordingly, when Elizabeth finished a draft of "Roosters" in October 1940 (begun, she said, years before at five in the morning in the backyard of the Key West house, "with the roosters carrying on just as I said"), she sent it to Moore for comment.[27] In an excess of well-meant enthusiasm, Moore and her mother rewrote, retyped, and retitled the poem and sent it back. Moore's version, called "The Cock," eliminated

Elizabeth's regimented three increasing-beat lines and one-rhyme stanza form (which Charles Sanders has pointed out Bishop learned well from Crashaw's "Wishes to his Supposed Mistress") and "purified" the poem, removing such indelicacies as "water closet." The revision shocked Elizabeth and caused her to deliver her most spirited self-defense to date, less than a month after her abject letter of September 11:

> What I'm about to say, I'm afraid, will sound like ELIZABETH KNOWS BEST...However, I have changed to small initial letters! & I have made several other of your corrections and suggestions, & left out 1 of the same stanzas that you did. But I can't seem to bring myself to give up the set form, which I'm afraid you think fills the poem with redundancies, etc. I feel that the rather rattle-trap rhythm is appropriate – maybe I can explain it.
>
> I cherish my "water closet" and the other sordidities because I want to emphasize the essential baseness of militarism. In the 1st part I was thinking of Key West, and also of those aerial views of dismal little towns in Finland & Norway, when the Germans took over, and their atmosphere of poverty. That's why, although I see what you mean, I want to keep "tin rooster" instead of "gold," and not to use "fastidious beds." And for the same reason I want to keep as the title the rather contemptuous word ROOSTERS rather than the more classical COCK; and I want to repeat the "gun metal." (I also had in mind the violent roosters Picasso did in connection with his GUERNICA picture.)

Elizabeth went on to defend her use of "glass-headed pins" (to suggest the charting of war projects on a map) and of quotation marks around "to see the end," a phrase from the Bible. "I can't bring myself to sacrifice what (I think) is a very important 'violence' of tone – which I feel to be helped by what you must feel to be just a bad case of the Threes." She defended the aspects that showed it most clearly to be her first politically relevant poem and the only one that addressed World War II at all directly. But Elizabeth broke her self-defense off here, saying she felt it sounded "decidedly cranky." She eventually mailed the letter, but carefully distanced her poem from Moore's version: "May I keep your poem? It is so interesting, what you have done."[28] From this point on, she no longer routinely sent Moore poems in draft for comment and enclosed in her letters only relatively finished work, which she announced as such. In her memoir of Moore, Elizabeth mentions the incident and remarks about having "grown obstinate" against Moore's fastidiousness. But this was a painful transition. Elizabeth sent her own version of "Roosters" to Edmund Wilson at the *New Republic,* where it was published in a special literary supplement in March 1941.

Seven

IN THE FALL OF 1940, and again in 1941, Elizabeth stopped on her way North from Key West at the mountain home of Charlotte and Red Russell in Brevard, North Carolina, south of Asheville. Rustic and distantly surrounded by Appalachian hill people, the little camp and guesthouse were about as isolated from the familiar world as they could be. Elizabeth's letters and notebooks from Brevard are filled with details of the appalling poverty of the neighbors and their bare-bones resourcefulness in "making do" with what they had. She was particularly interested in a reputedly crazy hermit woman named Cordie Heiss, whom she and Charlotte took the trouble to visit in her cabin deep in the mountains, ignoring Heiss's posted sign, which read, "PLEASE STAY OUT FROM PROWLING AROUND ON MY LAND. CORDIE." Elizabeth copied the sign and sketched the cabin with great detail in her notebook. It was "cleaner than most," and Cordie was industrious and conscientious about her labors. Elizabeth was moved by her self-sufficiency. "She kept telling us 'You're the first people I've seen today,' – when she can't see anybody for weeks on end in that lonely place."

Brevard's scenery did not interest her as much as its people did. "I am not much of a Thoreau," she wrote in her notebook. "All this leafiness is very depressing." But she was taken with the town's ingeniously improvised comforts. "We keep a large bag of lime in the privy, to shovel down the hole. Some of the huge crickets . . . got into it, and now they wander around the walls all white, like ghosts – no, clowns – and leave white hieroglyphics when they jump." She liked the place. "Brevard is a rather nice little mountain town – I like the way the 2 main streets are so steep that coming up one to where they cross under the one stop-light it looks as though it ended in mid-deep-blue air." (She admired the same phenomenon in Ouro Prêto, Brazil, twenty years later.) With Nora Hasecher in 1940, and Marjorie Stevens in 1941, she attended the town's modest festivals and shows. She enjoyed evenings with Charlotte and Red and movies at the local theater. Elizabeth left reluctantly, staying long after her announced departure date, in part because leaving Brevard meant arriving in New York to the Murray Hill Hotel, but also because the primitive life there had a deep appeal. She stayed two months in New York during the fall of 1940, just over a month in 1941. When it came time to leave Key West in the spring of 1942, she went to Mexico.

Leaving New York to return to Key West in late November 1940, Elizabeth once again alluded to the "New York troubles" she was leaving safely behind. Again, little is known about those troubles, though her worsening alcoholism seems to have been a factor. Living alone at the Murray Hill, she was unable to control her drinking. Her aunt's death and her "quarrel" with Moore may also have depressed her, and she wrote no poetry during her stay. She arrived in Key West "very happy to be back" and spent a quiet winter and spring uneasily watching the town's growing activity as war grew imminent. She wrote very little; her notebooks show her working mostly on a short story and then a poem about her beloved Hannah Almyda. The one remaining draft of the poem is promising but breaks off without reaching its conclusions:

of former birds who rested
on ice-flows, who resisted
dragons, who nested
by the streams of lava
where they lived alone,
where marks of feathers can
be seen upon the stone
or in the crumbling tufa . . .

who tore their breasts
for lining for their nests
or otherwise expressed
that love was difficult,
no trick, like balancing,
but endless worrying
at such discouraging
details with small result,

who cared for, much too long,
the one ungainly young
who couldn't learn his song,
or a stupid mate
whose only active thought
to flap his wings & fight—
quarrelling half the night
for rotting meat;

In prose, she worked toward the poem:

Mrs. Almyda as a Phoenix, a mythological bird of some sort, . . .
self-sacrificing, brooding on a nest. A phoenix that's forgotten how
to set fire to itself and just waits. No, I guess the Pelican, self-
sacrificing, tearing feathers from its breast to line its nest, is
closest. Her exclamations of "Precious Love!". . . etc. somehow
add to the mythological character. . . . Her heaviness—clumsy

hands, although she never breaks a dish. Her heavy pats of affection, are like the clumsy pelican taking off on one of her wonderful, powerful flights – once off the water she soars – Mrs. A's love is like that.

In the notebook she stuck a photograph of Hannah Almyda, broad, square, and stern looking, with large, capable hands resting on an apron covering her knees.

On February 8, 1941, Elizabeth noted her thirtieth birthday "& nothing accomplished." One day after the birthday she and Frani Blough (now Mrs. Curt Muser) shared, Frani gave birth to a daughter named Cynthia. Elizabeth noted in her letter of congratulations ("I hope to send a more accurate clue to what I consider you have done for yourself and the race soon now") that Almyda was urging her to have a child, and that although she had "pickaninnies on my knee most of the time here," "I can take white ones & especially if they have red hair, which I should think yours just possibly might."[1]

During the spring of 1941, Elizabeth met Marjorie Carr Stevens, the wife of a Navy man then living apart from her husband in a rooming house at 623 Margaret Street in Key West. Elizabeth wrote few letters during the spring and mentions nothing of their early relationship in her notebook, but on June 27 she rented out her White Street house and moved in with Marjorie. She advertised this as a way of saving enough money to travel, though she had no specific plans. As it turned out, she and Marjorie stayed in Key West all summer, watching the sleepy town become a busy military center, then spent two and a half months (until the camp closed on November 15) with the Russells at Brevard. Arriving alone to the Murray Hill Hotel, Elizabeth penned in her notebook, "Lester [Littlefield] says if I only come to N.Y. for a brief visit once a year my friends will all stop loving me and forget me, but I think on the other hand that it is the best way of perpetuating friendship & interest & curiosity, the greatest help to both." She stayed only six weeks.

"Roosters" appeared in the *New Republic* on April 21, and the Key West "tript-itch" of "Jeronymo's House" (as the title first appeared), "Cootchie," and "Seascape" was published by the *Partisan Review* in September. Otherwise, Elizabeth's 1941 literary activities were few. She had continual letters of inquiry from James Laughlin about publishing her in his pamphlet series and a serious nibble from Colt Press in San Francisco, but she continued to wait on the "chameleons" at Harcourt Brace, who continued to wait on more new poems from Elizabeth. Edmund Wilson urged her to accept the Laughlin offer right away, but she held out in the slim hope of getting some kind of advance from the better-known publishing house.

Elizabeth returned to Key West and her White Street house at mid-December, but once tenants for the house were found a couple of weeks later, she moved into Marjorie's Margaret Street house. After Pearl Harbor, the military activities in Key West were in full swing, and Elizabeth reported tiredly that the busy, crowded town was "no place to be unless one is of some use."[2] She shed possessions, leaving the clavichord in New York with Ralph Kirkpatrick, and talked of traveling to South America in March or April. Why she was thinking of South America is unclear, though Elizabeth said later she wanted to visit and write about the South American equivalent of Key West, Tierra del Fuego.

A journey to South America proved impossible, however. Wartime travel was restricted and complicated, and the trip was too long. Instead, in April 1942, she and Marjorie left for a stay of indefinite length in Mexico, ostensibly to study Spanish. They stopped in Miami, "glad to get away," on April 12; then on April 17 they flew to Havana and on to the Yucatán city of Mérida.

They spent two weeks in Mérida, the most important event of which was meeting Chilean poet Pablo Neruda, who was then on a diplomatic appointment in Mexico. Elizabeth and Marjorie were immediately taken with Neruda and his wife, Delia, though Elizabeth had her doubts about his poetry. To Moore, she wrote, "I'm afraid it is not the kind I—nor you—like—very, very loose, surrealist imagery, etc. I may be misjudging it; it is so hard to tell about foreign poetry, but I feel I recognize the type only too well."[3] Much later Elizabeth acknowledged that Neruda had been a significant influence on her work, and surely the two shared a belief in the truth of geography and the numinousness of objects. In 1948, she borrowed from his "Alberto Rojas Jiménez Viene Volando" for her tribute to Moore, "Invitation to Miss Marianne Moore." Here in Mexico, Neruda helped Elizabeth find a Spanish tutor, and he and Delia acted as hosts to the two travelers, taking them on automobile trips and inviting them to spend the month of August at their home in Cuernavaca.

Neruda escorted Marjorie and Elizabeth to Mexico City on May 5 and installed them in an apartment at 7 Calle de Paris. They planned to stay for a month or so in these inexpensive accommodations, long enough to get over the "faraway & all gone" feeling and lightheadedness resulting from high altitude. On May 14, Elizabeth said, without elaborating, that the trip had been "difficult," and she reported having lost her writing case in Mérida, notebooks and all. "Work" did not go well. When James Laughlin asked her for three poems for an anthology he was putting together for Pelican Books, Elizabeth deliberated long and then sent "The Imaginary Iceberg," "The Weed," and "Roosters" and lamented that she had done nothing further, having been thus far unable to make anything of her Mexican experiences. Moore offered consolation and advice: "I hope you aren't 'striving to write,' Elizabeth. Do be kind to yourself and take things as they come. . . . Don't feel shabby if you seem to be wasting the time. The best things need to season."[4] Elizabeth stayed in Mexico City with Marjorie—fighting asthma, studying Spanish with a tutor, and trying to write—until August, when they joined the Nerudas in Cuernavaca.

Elizabeth's notebook resurfaced in August, apparently found and returned in her writing case. She did not much like Cuernavaca but was enamored of the small surrounding mountain towns, Taxco and others. The details of decoration in the tiny churches, once again a mixture of Catholicism and Indian mysticism and superstition that Elizabeth always found attractive, compelled her. She painted in watercolors some and recorded descriptions and anecdotes in her notebooks and letters. The famous Grutas caves impressed her: the trip in, armed with lanterns and candles; the dramatic formations of stalagmites and stalactites; dripping water; bad air.

> The arched ceilings are as high and dark as if the heavens were made of stone. In fact, once in a while we'd almost forget we were in caves and feel as if we were a queer band of explorers or pioneers going through a rocky valley at night. The guides, one at the head of the group & one at the tail, wear high boots & tin helmets & carry electric lanterns. In each cave, or Sala, they wait till all the stragglers have caught up and then. . . . With complete solemnity the leader shouts: "On the right we see the King. On the left the Queen. Over our heads to the right the Spread Eagle. I am standing beside the Loaf of Bread. The shadow cast by the tall rock ahead is an exact silhouette of President Camacho," etc. etc. . . . Nothing else was given us in the way of information; it is just a system of Correspondances. But the Mexican imagination is poverty-stricken, anyway.

"Coming out, the daylight ahead looks like pale blue water, and the fresh air feels like tepid, rather tasteless water, but wonderful." Her experience in the caves served her as a metaphor of despair and hope in the darkest times of her life.

The Cuernavaca notebook records numerous interesting local characters and travelers but rarely manages a cheerful tone. Although the pace was a welcome change from New York, time in Mexico seemed chaotically slow, if that was possible. "Time in Mex: Where one sits at the instrument board of an unknown machine & the indicators on the dials spin." Mexico is "dreary dreary dreary dreary / Where time keeps falling back on itself like a snake."

Elizabeth and Marjorie spent two weeks of September back in Mexico City with new friends Mr. and Mrs. Helzel, then traveled to Puebla and Cholula, the "Rome of Mexico"—so called for its more than one hundred churches. She adored the churches in nearby San Francisco Acatapec and Santa María Tonantzintla for their beautiful facades. In the town named for the goddess Tonantzin, Elizabeth found the mix of cultures that always fascinated her:

> The outside of Santa Maria T. is one of the oddest looking churches I've ever seen – red texontle set with blue tiles just here & there. & over the doorway busts, or ¾ statues . . . with big heads & hands, very stiff, of a glowing cream-colored stone. The ghost [?] effect is beautiful, though, in a clumsy way – The inside is the one the Indians decided to repaint for themselves, quite recently, and they have done an amazing job, with all sorts of metallic paints, the most garish and iridescent possible – it is incredible, too bad in a way, & yet I thought probably it gave one quite a good idea of what the pre-conquest decorations looked like –

She found Puebla "clean and prosperous" and liked it best among the Mexican cities she had visited.

On September 16, Elizabeth and Marjorie caught a narrow-gauge Pullman train for Oaxaca, a twenty-hour trip through the mountains, along the steep sides of gorges, with derailments every once in a while. The odd scale disturbed her. "It was hot and dirty, of course – & we all looked too big for the train, like giants – a very uncomfortable feeling to have to keep up for 20 hours." Elizabeth liked Oaxaca, the landscape, the town, the people, and she ended her Mexican adventure positively. Her notebook entries are enthusiastic and eloquent for the first time, and she reports she is writing stories as well.

> The mountains around here are beautiful dark blues & greens, set with odd squares & patches of lighter green fields. The whole is

somehow translucent-looking (painted in glazes). The white clouds drift around them, it rains in places & is clear in others, & in one I saw the beginning of a rainbow – just the enormous bands of colors, broader than it was long. Some of the hills as they spread out on the valley look quilted. They are very thinly greened over; the cloud shadows & their own pattern of shadows interplay – here & there a thin line of smoke, from the charcoal burners, goes straight up.

She admired the pistachio-green stone with which most of the churches and public buildings in Oaxaca were built; the messy, dirty isolation of the town; the florid baroque of its architecture; the town's marvelous and awful cathedral: "Very solid, with extremely overanimated plaques,...etc. of the sandstone, & bright green moss & weeds growing here & there & a few cracks and disjointed pillars & moldings from the last earthquake." Her love of the unsophisticated, even awful gesture of faith or decoration would eventually attach her to Brazil.

The height of the forest of organ pipe cactus around the village of Mitla astonished Elizabeth, and she contemplated the town's primitive pottery works:

They have been making it for thousands of years the same way – not even a wheel, properly speaking, but 2 clay saucers inverted on each other that they manage to turn round & keep balanced at the same time. The clay is thick & gray, when baked it comes out a sad gun-metal color. . . . The pots are a beautiful round shape – but desperately sad – used only for water and mescal. It seemed to me to be the dreariest artistic tradition I've ever seen.

Both Elizabeth and Marjorie (who appears very little in the notebooks) caught terrible colds in Oaxaca ("name like a cough") from trying so many different clay whistles in the market, Elizabeth thought. They left Mexico for New York on September 30.

. . .

Elizabeth spent October and November 1942 in a room at the familiar Murray Hill Hotel. Once again, her activities are largely undocumented, though Marjorie Steven's letters to Elizabeth from these years have survived. They tell us that Elizabeth met e. e. cummings and his wife, Marion Morehouse, for the first time at a party in early November at the home of Dwight Macdonald and that she had several dinners, a movie, and a trip to the Metropolitan Museum with Marianne Moore. Elizabeth sat for a portrait by Loren MacIver. The letters do not tell us that at Loren's studio on Perry Street in Greenwich Village, Elizabeth was introduced to Lota de Macedo Soares, a Brazilian woman of aristocratic background who had traveled to New York with her American friend, Mary Stearns Morse. Elizabeth had known Morse slightly as a classmate of Barbara Chesney at Smith College. As they left, Morse and Soares invited Elizabeth to visit them in Rio de Janeiro should she ever actually make her South American trip.

Stevens wrote to Elizabeth every other day, worrying about her, urging her to take her sleeping medication: "Be brave," "Don't get depressed," "Don't stay in New York," "Don't drink when you're overtired." Marjorie was obviously devoted to Elizabeth, offering to get a job so Elizabeth could spend all her energy writing, imploring her to come back to Key West. Elizabeth was apparently less demonstrative in the relationship and caused Marjorie considerable anxiety. But Elizabeth flew to Miami on November 29, where Marjorie met her and drove her back to Margaret Street, Key West. She stayed there longer than she had ever stayed in one house or one place, until May 1944.

Elizabeth published no poems in 1942 or 1943, wrote few letters, and kept no notebook that survives. She had the long-distance telephone to use now, and she did so for her most immediate communications. She reappears in June 1943, saying that she kept making plans to leave Key West and kept canceling them and that she would stay "another three weeks at least." At mid-July, she apologized to Moore for being unable to write "all this dreadful time," indicating she and Moore had talked recently. "I keep dragging on with about six be-draggled old poems & a couple of stories. I find it awfully hard to work properly – everything seems to lead to everything else." The Key West life had its usual pleasures—the sun, the sea, the air, "a wonderful garden, really wonderful, for a while – I didn't know I was capable of such farming."[5] Marjorie was working, leaving Elizabeth home alone all day, and she frustrated herself again and again by being unable to make use of the time. Hannah Almyda was working in the furniture store in town; everyone had a job to do, and Elizabeth could do nothing. Time began to weigh on her, and she vowed to return North, "maybe for good" on September 1. Instead, she set out to find a wartime job for herself, securing a place grinding binocular lenses in a U.S. Navy optical shop, but she lasted only five days. "The eye-strain made me seasick, & the acids used for cleaning started to bring back eczema, so I had to give it up – & I must admit I was only too glad to because the work was so finicky & tedious that it was getting to be a torture to me & I was doing it all night long in my sleep, & getting very cranky." But the experience made a wonderful letter to Moore, if nothing else.

> But I'm glad I tried it – it was the only way of ever finding out what is going on in Key West now, seeing the inside of the Navy yard & all the ships, & learning lots of things I had no idea about before. It took three whole days of red tape to get in . . . & it is taking me at least 2 weeks to get my "honorable discharge."
>
> The water is jade green, the gray ships looked bright blue against it, & of course I could spend a lot of time – had to – watching everything through magnificent optical instruments of every kind, including periscopes.

The tattooed sailors she worked with called her "Kiddo" or "Sis," and she was astonished at their patience, "fiddling day after day with those delicate, maddening little instruments. I don't think I could do it, even if it hadn't made me sick. And their lack of imagination would get more & more depressing – not one of them had any idea of the theory of the thing, why the prisms go this way or that way." Her "honorable discharge" was granted on August 28.

Elizabeth did not go North on September 1. She stayed in Key West, though Marjorie was away for three weeks and it was "terribly lonely," as she felt herself "growing stupider & stupider & more like a hermit every day."[6] She was unable to write and unsure about why not, vowing to come North and not doing it. "I feel I must do something about my Life & Works very soon – this wastefulness is a sin – but I just can't seem to figure out what. I wish it were 1934 all over again – I'd do everything quite differently."[7]

A month later she sent Moore a version of "Large Bad Picture" and the group of "Songs for a Colored Singer." Moore returned them with gentle comments and the latest literary news—Mary McCarthy's marriage to Edmund Wilson and his new position at the *New Yorker*. Elizabeth was unable to continue the small writing rally she had managed in November, as she fell ill with flu and then asthma and spent yet another miserable Christmas. But on the back of a grocery receipt dated December 27 are the first scribbled notes about the petals of rock roses that became "Faustina," a poem she worked on over the next six years about Faustina Valdez, the colorful nurse / housekeeper / lottery ticket seller in Key West.[8] Elizabeth found time as well to secure for Moore a mosquito net to send to her brother Warren, then in the navy stationed in Honolulu. Moore was virtually housebound caring for her mother, whose health was steadily failing, and Elizabeth sent presents—oranges, alligator pears, a box of Cuban tree snail shells—to cheer them.

Elizabeth suffered from asthma almost constantly from December until July 1944, and it was this illness that finally convinced her to leave Key West for New York, ostensibly for good. Loren MacIver found her an apartment, a tiny garret at 46 King Street, where

Elizabeth headed, via doctors in Miami, early in August. Her plans were altogether uncertain. She considered getting a master's degree in Spanish, possibly at the University of Florida, and becoming a teacher; Moore earnestly recommended the Delahanty Institute for a course in mechanical drawing. In the spring, Elizabeth had sent Moore a copy of "Anaphora" and asked if she thought *North & South* would do as a title for her manuscript. Moore warmly praised the poem and the title. "Songs for a Colored Singer" appeared in the September *Partisan Review.* But the consensus seemed to be that Elizabeth should earn some money, should join the war effort and work, and should, above all, have less time on her hands.

Elizabeth did not get a job in New York, but she remained there, quite miserable most of the time, until February 1945. She struggled to lose weight, to avoid drinking excessively, to remain cheerful, to save money. Early in her stay, she found herself by accident in front of Grace Church, where her parents had been married. She told Moore the story, who wrote wisely, "I often have thought how your mother (your father never seemed so <u>present</u> to me) must hover over your health <u>and</u> your writing."[9]

Marjorie worried constantly about Elizabeth and their relationship and offered steady advice, encouragement, and money. She came to New York for a visit in October, which seemed to satisfy no one. She wanted to meet Marianne Moore but was out—by accident or by design—when Moore paid one of her very rare visits to Elizabeth's New York apartment. Elizabeth suffered so much from asthma in the city that she undertook to see an allergist. Her condition deteriorated. She was depressed about her work, uneasy and perhaps a bit paranoid in her relationship with Moore and in the literary milieu of New York City. She was drinking self-destructively and was unable to stay alone at King Street. Marjorie urged her to come back to Key West and the care of Mrs. Almyda. Elizabeth retreated instead to the home of her friend Anna B. Lindsay and began to look for a psychotherapist.

By early December, Elizabeth was seeing a psychiatrist, a Dr. Jameson, whose work seemed to help her at first, though she abandoned him a short time later. Marjorie worried that she and Key West might be "psychoanalyzed out" of Elizabeth; no small part of the tension in Elizabeth's life was her growing uncertainty about her commitment to Marjorie, and perhaps to a lesbian identity, which Marjorie saw clearly. Whether to return to Key West and to Marjorie became an important decision, and the consensus among Elizabeth's friends was that she should not go. New York hardly seemed a good alternative, however. She made plans to return to Key West in February.

Soon after, however, Elizabeth announced that she was "much, much better, . . . almost human."[10] Her improved spirits came partly from a letter she received from Jean Pedrick of Houghton Mifflin inviting her, on the strength of "Songs for a Colored Singer," to submit a manuscript for the company's first annual Poetry Prize Fellowship. The one-thousand-dollar award would be presented in the spring by a panel of judges—Ferris Greenslet, Katharine White, and Horace Gregory—and would include publication of the manuscript by Houghton Mifflin. Elizabeth hesitated at first, "still waiting" on Harcourt Brace, but she began preparing a clean manuscript to send. On Moore's advice she did apply, asking Moore, John Dewey, and Edmund Wilson to be her "sponsors." This activity of asking people to write letters of recommendation was ever a torture to Elizabeth, though she was always able to muster excellent letters. This may account in some part for her extraordinary success in competition for fellowships, awards, and the like. She mailed her manuscript, entitled *North & South* (the ampersand was intentional), to Houghton Mifflin on January 15, 1945, then left for Key West on February 20. Late in May, she got a telegram from the company announcing that hers had won the award over the manuscripts of 833 "servicemen and women and civilians of every trade and profession." By May 30, she was on her way back to New

York to have herself photographed and to see to the publication of her first book.

Elizabeth got her award money on June 1 and was warmly grateful. But her relationship with Houghton Mifflin deteriorated from that point on. For the next year, she and her editor, Ferris Greenslet, and his colleagues argued over almost all the publishing details, in particular the publication date. Elizabeth announced immediately that she wanted to add poems to the manuscript, and, much as Harcourt Brace had done, Houghton Mifflin sat back to wait for Elizabeth to send them. She "unexpectedly" returned to Key West in September and tried hard to finish the "two or three" poems she had on hand. She wanted time to publish them in magazines first; she needed the money. "Anaphora" appeared in *Partisan Review* in the fall.

"Anaphora" carried no dedication on its first publication, though Elizabeth dedicated it to Marjorie after her death in 1959. As "Quai d'Orleans" was for Margaret, "Anaphora" was for Marjorie, a monument to a shared time and place, not altogether happy. Begun in Puebla and finished in Key West, the poem anticipates the "days" and "distance" quandary of "Argument":

> Each day with so much ceremony
> begins, with birds, with bells,
> with whistles from a factory;
> such white-gold skies our eyes
> first open on, such brilliant walls
> that for a moment we wonder
> "Where is the music coming from, the energy?
> The day was meant for what ineffable creature
> we must have missed?" Oh promptly he
> appears and takes his earthly nature
> > instantly, instantly falls
> > victim of long intrigue,
> > assuming memory and mortal
> > mortal fatigue.

More slowly falling into sight
and showering into stippled faces,
darkening, condensing all his light;
in spite of all the dreaming
squandered upon him with that look,
suffers our uses and abuses,
sinks through the drift of bodies,
sinks through the drift of classes
to evening to the beggar in the park
who, weary, without lamp or book
    prepares stupendous studies:
    the fiery event
    of every day in endless
    endless assent.

The poem shares with many Bishop poems, and a dozen or so eloquent notebook entries, a description of the sensation of waking in the morning, of opening one's eyes slowly and contemplating the furniture, the room, the window, the sky, often from the sideways perspective of lying down. It shares with "Rain Towards Morning" and the unpublished "It is marvellous to wake up together"—also probably about Marjorie—the sensation of coming to consciousness in the morning in bed with a lover. The poem takes as its starting point the extraordinary light in Key West and the notion, pervasive in Elizabeth's thinking, that to awaken is to fall back into time and that to fall into time is to be subject to the sufferings of "memory and mortal / mortal fatigue." The sun rises in the first stanza, and it sets in the second, also a famous event in Key West. Current tourists there gather in huge crowds each evening in Mallory Square—"the drift of bodies, / . . . the drift of classes"—cued by signs giving the time, to watch the sun go down in an often "stupendous" display. They applaud when it finally disappears over the horizon of aquamarine water and disperse to the town's many bars and restaurants. Even to the short-term visitor this anaphora, this repetition, is amazing and benumbing and ironic: the cheer goes up when the sun goes down.

"It is marvellous to wake up together," which appears in an apparently final, though handwritten, draft in the back of one of Elizabeth's notebooks from the early 1940s, extends from another dramatic Key West climatic condition, the island's tremendous electrical storms:[11]

> It is marvellous to wake up together
> At the same minute; marvelous to hear
> The rain begin suddenly all over the roof,
> To feel the air suddenly clear
> As if electricity had passed through it
> From a black mesh of wires in the sky.
> All over the roof rain hisses,
> And below, the light falling of kisses.
>
> An electrical storm is coming or moving away;
> It is the prickling air that wakes us up.
> If lightning struck the house now, it would run
> From the four blue china balls on top
> Down the roof and down the rods all around us,
> And we imagine dreamily
> How the whole house caught in a bird-cage of lightning
> Would be quite delightful rather than frightening;
>
> And from the same simplified point of view
> Of night and lying flat on one's back
> All things might change, equally easily,
> Since always to warn us there are these black
> Electrical wires dangling. Without surprise
> The world might change to something quite different,
> As the air changes or the lightning comes without our blinking
> Change as our kisses are changing without our thinking.

Sorrow and uncertainty—a forecast end to the relationship perhaps—invade the warm opening sentiment of the poem. "It is marvellous to wake up together," yet black electrical wires "warn us"
that this may change "without our thinking." To wake is to face
change, which in Elizabeth's experience to 1945 is loss.

Through the summer, she also worked on two relatively minor
poems, "Chemin de Fer" and "Little Exercise," and the relatively
major "Large Bad Picture." All three poems were published in the
New Yorker in the spring of 1946; Elizabeth's relations with the
magazine had healed when poetry editor Katharine White helped
her win the Houghton Mifflin Prize and Edmund Wilson, also an
editor there, suggested that Elizabeth once again send poems. One
suspects that White could not see that the cry in "Chemin de Fer"
that "love should be put into action" speaks eloquently to Elizabeth's struggle to accept her homosexuality. The "echo"—a voice
like one's own—that "tried and tried to confirm it" might belong
to Marjorie Stevens or perhaps the hermit voice is Marjorie's. Elizabeth also finished "Wading at Wellfleet" for the book, another
enigmatic image of resistance and collapse. In her notebook are
apparently polished drafts of half a dozen other poems never finished
or published: "Bone Key," "Baby's Grave, Key West," "The Salesman's Evening," "Edgar Allan Poe," and "The Juke-Box."

Despite her conviction that she would have at least two of these
poems done in time to include in *North & South,* Elizabeth was
unable to provide them. Her correspondence with Houghton Mifflin shows her to have already developed her lifelong antipathy
toward publishers and her chilly and often accusatory professional-
correspondence tone. This, combined with Elizabeth's legitimate
but rather fastidious concern with the physical details of the book,
put Houghton Mifflin's editors, production managers, and designers on the defensive early on. One senses from their letters that they
felt Elizabeth should spend more time writing poems and less time
worrying about typefaces and binding techniques and demanding
last-minute corrections and changes.

Elizabeth had numerous anxieties about the book, particularly its brevity, but she also became defensive about its apparent detachment from contemporary events. Throughout the 1930s, she had apologized for her failure to take a political "stand" in a political age, and in the 1940s she was embarrassed by her failure to respond in poetry to World War II. Even though "Roosters" might be, and has been, called an antiwar poem, Elizabeth sought to defend herself against charges of indifference or naïveté. At her request, Houghton Mifflin inserted a "disclaimer" in the front of *North & South:* "Most of these poems were written, or partly-written, before 1942."

Elizabeth spent the fall of 1945 in Key West with Marjorie at Margaret Street. She had a late-November deadline for new poems from Houghton Mifflin and set out to finish the elusive two or three. Moore gave comfort by counseling her not to struggle to write more, but Greenslet felt the book would be "exceedingly thin." "Faustina, or Rock Roses," was nearing completion, and her notebook shows her approaching as well "Over 2000 Illustrations and a Complete Concordance." She claimed to Houghton Mifflin's editors that she had her next book nearly complete and was anxious for *North & South* to appear. As they argued back and forth about who was neglecting whom, Elizabeth continued to struggle.

She left Key West for New York in December, then returned in early January, only to leave again on the nineteenth. As she struggled to write, her relationship with Marjorie Stevens was ending. Marjorie's letters to her in the spring of 1946 suggest that Elizabeth was drinking heavily, that her lifelong tendency to use the long-distance telephone when she was drunk had begun to irritate the recipients of her calls, and that she was wavering painfully in her decision to leave both Marjorie and Key West. Finally Marjorie, essentially out of kindness, forbade her to come back. "I don't think you should consider it a possibility any more, for as long as you do you obviously aren't going to adjust yourself to anything else. . . . [We've been] trying to make something work that doesn't."[12] When she came North, it was for more than a year, and when she returned in the winter of 1947, she lived for a time in Pauline Hemingway's house at 907 Whitehead Street.

In the spring of 1946, Elizabeth went back to a psychiatrist, Dr. Ruth Foster. Despite her failure to cure Elizabeth of alcoholism, Dr. Foster remained an important figure in the poet's life. Elizabeth's notebooks contain many drafts of a poem called "Dear Dr. Foster," which begins "Yes, dreams are in color, / and memories are in color," and when she died in 1950, Elizabeth was deeply saddened. She never discussed the nature of her work with Dr. Foster in any detail, though she said it had helped her "very much." Years later, she told a friend that Foster had said Elizabeth was "lucky to have survived" her difficult childhood.

Out of the country, perhaps intentionally, when her book was published in August 1946, Elizabeth had left New York for Keene, New Hampshire, on June 9, apparently intending to stay for a while. We do not know whom she visited there, if anyone, but because of what she later called "miseries," she left abruptly for Halifax, Nova Scotia, and the Nova Scotian Hotel on July 1. She spent two or three weeks in Halifax (across the bay from the hospital in Dartmouth where her mother had lived and died). She visited her friend Zilpha Linkletter and the deBrisays, childhood friends from Great Village, and spent a day with John Dewey, who kept a house in Hubbards, Nova Scotia. While she was alone in Allendale, staying at the Ragged Islands Inn, advance copies of *North & South* were issued, though it took another week for Houghton Mifflin to sort out her various addresses and get her a copy. She pronounced herself generally happy with the book, though she apologized to everyone for its thinness. To Houghton Mifflin, however, she was already talking about her next volume, to be titled *Faustina and Other Poems*. Elizabeth's friends sent their compliments. Marjorie liked it but said it was a "pity" that there were not more poems. Marianne Moore, who felt she had been somewhat neglected by Elizabeth of late, was warmer, if more idiosyncratic, in her praise. Among the comments in a long, detailed, and almost indecipherable letter is this one: "This book, this book, Elizabeth, which is even beyond expectation, and I had expected the most. . . . What rhetoric; or do you dislike the word rhetoric? What diction."[13]

Elizabeth was miserable in Nova Scotia, this her first trip back since her mother's death. Marjorie's letters are full of consolation for the "dreadful time" Elizabeth was having (as well as information about the sale of the White Street house, which was under way). Elizabeth apparently wrote long and detailed letters to Marjorie, who asked to visit her (told her to ask Dr. Foster if she thought it would be a good idea), but Elizabeth asked for the letters back to destroy, and Marjorie obliged. Why she so carefully saved all Marjorie's letters to her is also a mystery; by the end of the summer Marjorie was sure that Elizabeth "hated" her.

She moved around a good deal and at short notice, ending her stay with her first visit to Aunt Grace and Great Village in almost fifteen years. From the many notebook entries of this summer, and the poems that grew from those notes, it seems clear that the trip was both deeply disturbing and deeply significant to Elizabeth in ways that it would take her years to articulate.

At Lockeport Beach on the Atlantic Ocean, she made a note to herself: "Description of the dark, icy, clear water – clear dark glass – slightly bitter (hard to define). My idea of knowledge. this cold stream, half drawn, half flowing from a great rocky breast." Earlier, in the evening sunlight at Ragged Islands, she had noticed

a million Christmas trees stand
waiting for Christmas.

I know how they feel. . . .
The seals play (their barking)
between 2 rocks
leaping out of the calm water with small splashes
you can see where they're going to come up
the water is so clear –

the sun slides over their wet fur –. . . .
Surface of water swelling slowly as if it were thinking of brimming
over.

Elizabeth had a poem in mind when she made these notes; next to
each of the ideas that eventually contributed to "At the Fishhouses,"
and some that apparently did not, is the notation "GM"—explained
once as "Geographical Mirror" and suggesting that the trip and the
later poem were part of an attempt to find herself reflected in the
land and sea. The charming details of Nova Scotia geography—
quaint names of towns like Five Islands and Five Houses—were first
marked for this poem but evolved into another when, at the end of
the trip, Elizabeth caught a bus from Great Village to Boston.

Marjorie had seen to the sale of the White Street house; Elizabeth's signature was needed on the deed. It had to be signed in the
United States and right away, and so, once again on short notice,
she left for Boston on the bus. She wrote detailed accounts of this
trip to Marjorie (who destroyed them, as Elizabeth requested) and
to Marianne Moore:

> I've always loved those big farm collies, haven't you? – the present
> generation wait along the side of the roads for the buses to stop &
> their owners to get off. There are two now at my aunt's, an old
> one named Jock, and his son. . . .
> My plan was to take a room at a near by farm so that I could
> have a little peace & privacy to work in, and stay on a few weeks.
> But the deed to the Key West house had to be signed right away
> and in the U.S., for some legal reason, so I had to leave. I came
> back by bus – a dreadful trip, but it seemed most convenient at the
> time – we hailed it with a flashlight and a lantern as it went by the
> farm late at night. Early the next morning, just as it was getting
> light, the driver had to stop suddenly for a big cow moose who
> was wandering down the road. She walked away very slowly into
> the woods, looking at us over her shoulder. The driver said that

one foggy night he had to stop while a huge bull moose came right up and smelled the engine. "Very curious beasts," he said.[14]

Both "At the Fishhouses" and the poem that eventually became "The Moose" took rough shape in Elizabeth's mind relatively quickly, though she was unable to finish the latter poem to her satisfaction until 1972, when she decided to read it as her Phi Beta Kappa address at Harvard University. When she did, it became even clearer that this trip home gave Elizabeth back her childhood as artistic material.

Elizabeth had not been back at King Street a week before reviews of *North & South* began to appear. Her introduction to the pleasures and terrors of reading the judgments of strangers about her work was unfortunate. Edward Weeks, writing in the August *Atlantic,* seemed to touch her where she was most vulnerable by suggesting that her own doubts about her work were indeed accurate:

> Her poems may be roughly divided into two categories, bizarre fantasies which can be interpreted pretty much as the reader chooses, and straight descriptive verse, much of it growing out of the author's experience in Florida, to which she has added a moral or emotional fillip. . . .
> I cannot find much satisfaction in this verse. What confounds me is the author's difficulty in finishing what she begins so well. . . . In sum, it seems to me that she is afraid to risk pure lyricism, and is rather shy of ideas.[15]

The review distressed Elizabeth, though she admitted to Greenslet only that she felt Weeks was "slightly unfair."[16] Oscar Williams in the *New Republic* disliked the book as well, and privately Elizabeth forgave neither of them. As more positive, and more typical, reviews appeared, Elizabeth clipped them and reported them to her publisher, each time asking that the book be advertised more widely and forcefully; she was extremely concerned about sales and was inclined from the start to believe that Houghton Mifflin was neglecting her.

She might have taken more comfort than she did in the reviews, so accurately did some of them identify the strengths of her method. Barbara Gibbs writing in *Poetry* said, "It is this ability to hold her art and her experience in a fast and yet living relationship, to be never in doubt where she stands with regard to the one or the other, that is the sign of Miss Bishop's almost perfect artistic acumen."[17] Her friend Lloyd Frankenberg said in the *Saturday Review*, "For once a prize committee has chosen well. . . . [In 'Quai d'Orleans'] acute observation has led beyond itself. The stream of sensation, the streaming rhythm have evoked a third correspondence: memory. Disappearing while we watch them, events produce it as if we were remembered by them."[18] Seldon Rodman in the *New York Times Book Review* commented, "If the author of the thirty-two remarkable poems in this book used paint, she would undoubtedly paint 'abstractions.' Yet so sure is her feeling for poetry that in building up her overall water-color arrangements she never strays far from the concrete and the particular."[19] Marianne Moore and Randall Jarrell also reviewed the book positively, and Jarrell's perhaps five hundred words were so deeply appreciative and so eloquent that they stayed with Bishop's work for the rest of her life and beyond.

> Instead of crying, with justice, "This is a world in which no one can get along," Miss Bishop's poems show that it is barely but perfectly possible—has been, that is, for her. Her work is unusually personal and honest in its wit, perception, and sensitivity—and in its restrictions too; all her poems have written underneath, *I have seen it.*

He went on to praise "Roosters" and "The Fish" particularly for the moral vision they display, "that morality, for the individual, is usually a small, personal, statistical, but heartbreaking or heartwarming affair of omissions and commissions the greatest of which will seem infinitesimal, ludicrously beneath notice, to those who govern, rationalize, and deplore."[20] This praise may have been sweet to Elizabeth (though it would be years before she would admit to having any respect at all for Jarrell's work), but it must also have seemed ironic, so much was her life a slippery moral struggle to "do well"— with alcohol, as she saw it; in her relationships, sexual and platonic; in the eternal dilemma of "work." That she had managed to project, at least for Jarrell and these other readers of her poems, a relatively firm moral and artistic voice must have struck her as a matter for laughter, or tears. Young Robert Lowell, who had also published his first commercial volume in 1946, reviewed *North & South* the following summer and saw the struggle a good deal less romantically:

> There are two opposing factors. The first is something in motion, weary but persisting, almost always failing and on the point of disintegrating, and yet, for the most part, stoically maintained. This is morality, memory, the weed that grows to divide, and the dawn that advances, illuminates and calls to work, the monument "that wants to be a monument," the waves rolling in on the shore, breaking, and being replaced, the echo of the hermit's voice saying, "love must be put into action"; it is the stolid little mechanical horse that carries a dancer, and all those things of memory that "cannot forget us half so easily as they can forget themselves." The second factor is a terminus: rest, sleep, fulfillment or death.[21]

Eight

ROBERT LOWELL HAD had the benefit of a conversation with Elizabeth Bishop before he wrote his review of *North & South*. The two met at a dinner party hosted by Randall Jarrell, who, based on a brief earlier meeting with Elizabeth and the strength of her poems, thought she and the young author of the just-published *Lord Weary's Castle* should meet. Elizabeth was terrified of the occasion—of dinner with Jarrell and of meeting Lowell, whom she knew only through his intimidatingly "serious" poems and his famous family name. Years later Elizabeth made notes for an essay, never finished:

> That evening, that I approached in fear and trembling, turned out to be one of the pleasantest I can remember. First I found myself feeling very much at home with Randall Jarrell and his wife, and their big black cat, and Jarrell talked a blue streak while putting Kitten through his tricks. Then Lowell arrived and I loved him at first sight. He was living in a basement room on Third Avenue, I think at the time, and he was rather untidy. He was wearing a [rumpled] dark blue suit; I remember the sad state of his shoes; he needed a hair cut, and he was very handsome and handsome in a[n] almost old-fashioned poetic way. I took to him at once; I didn't feel the least bit afraid, my shyness vanished and we started

talking at once. . . . In my taxi on the way home to . . . my
genuine G V [garret] I remember thinking that it was the first
time I had ever actually talked with some one about how one
writes poetry – and thinking that it . . . could be strangely easy
"Like exchanging recipes for making a cake."

Six years younger than Elizabeth, "Cal" Lowell was then in the
midst of his divorce from Jean Stafford. Elizabeth had yet to
acknowledge fully her homosexuality, and she initially expressed no
doubts about her sexuality to Lowell. She indeed "loved him" in
one way or another. She was clearly fascinated by Lowell as an
example of "poet" and as a charismatic, handsome, and unstable
man. When *Lord Weary's Castle* edged out *North & South* for the
1946 Pulitzer Prize and garnered Lowell the Guggenheim Fellowship
and an American Academy of Arts and Letters Award, he became a
major figure in a way Elizabeth would not be for thirty years or so.
She became aware through him of the array of possible grants and
awards that might support her and eventually won the same ones,
but as his career was university centered from the start, Lowell lived
closer to the inner circles of poetry than did Bishop. She benefited
from his meteoric rise and influence in these matters from the start.
Their friendship, which verged from time to time on romance,
developed more slowly.

The fall of 1946 is the proper beginning of Elizabeth's career as
Elizabeth Bishop the poet. With a book in print and well reviewed,
she began to make plans for her next volume as well as a volume of
prose pieces "about certain parts of South America," which she
asked Houghton Mifflin to advance. The South American continent
probably drew Elizabeth on its own merits, but she also intended
to use any advance to visit Mary Morse and Lota de Macedo Soares
in Brazil, whom she had been trying to see since meeting them in
New York in 1942.

In October, Elizabeth herself applied for a Guggenheim, asking
Marianne Moore, Ferris Greenslet, Katharine White, John Dewey,

Edmund Wilson, Horace Gregory, and Philip Rahv to recommend her. Her project was to be *Faustina,* a book "more serious than N & S . . . & more unified in style. Also the emphasis in the work I have done so far seems to be more directly on real people who have deeply interested me." In November, the *New Yorker* offered her a "first-read" contract, which asked that Bishop submit her poems first to the magazine and offered her in return 25 percent above the regular per-line rates. Elizabeth was pleased with this confidence shown by Katharine White but sounded a familiar theme in thinking about her own work: "I doubt that they would actually be interested in any of the more serious poetry I have in mind for the coming year."[1] When Lowell chose to point out the apparent "triviality" of a couple of poems in his review of *North & South,* Elizabeth felt her worst fears confirmed, and it was years before she got over this invidious comparison with Lowell—that he wrote "real" poems and that hers were "solid cuteness" or simple description. Nevertheless, Elizabeth accepted the first-read contract and published nearly all her poems after 1947 in the *New Yorker,* even while she made almost constant fun of the magazine's conservative editorial policy. In December, she received her first royalty check from Houghton Mifflin for one hundred seventy-four dollars and fifty cents. And she was awarded the Guggenheim, twenty-five hundred dollars, in April 1947.

January and February 1947 were miserable for Elizabeth as she suffered constantly from asthma and dragged herself around New York in her first northern winter in almost ten years. But the poems she had failed to finish for *North & South* began to appear in the magazines—"Faustina, or Rock Roses," in the *Nation* on February 22; "Varick Street," in the *Nation* on March 15; and "Argument," in the spring *Partisan Review.* In "Faustina," which Elizabeth had been struggling with since at least 1943, she chooses among many facts and anecdotes about the black Cuban woman, a familiar figure in Key West in the 1940s, and focuses on a single visit she made to

Faustina at work, caring for an elderly white woman in her home. The poem is unsympathetic to the relatively wealthy but helpless white woman and her dilapidated feminine trappings—faded wallpaper, chipped enamel, "white disordered sheets / like wilted roses. / / Clutter of trophies, / chamber of bleached flags!" The figure of Faustina—dark and masculine by contrast—presents both the woman and the visitor with "a cruel black / coincident conundrum." The reversal of roles—powerful white woman made helpless by age, powerless black woman given absolute sovereignty—leads to the question "Oh, is it // freedom at last, a lifelong / dream of time and silence, / dream of protection and rest? / Or is it the very worst, / the unimaginable nightmare / that never before dared last / more than a second?" "It" may be death, and "it" may be the political question raised by the reversal of roles: is it a "dream" to be so absolutely served that one's servant becomes one's master? The question splinters off into many others, "helplessly / proliferative." But "There is no way of telling. / The eyes say only either." The poem asks some of the same questions that "Cootchie" had asked less subtly—"who will shout and make [Miss Lula] understand" the meaning of her servant's life and death?

Elizabeth said that "Varick Street" came to her almost intact in a dream, with the refrain "And I shall sell you, sell you / sell you of course, my dear, and you'll sell me." The scene is her King Street (the original title of the poem) neighborhood, with its noisy factories and their activity. The mechanical moons waxing and waning and presses printing "calendars / I suppose" anticipate the intractability of time in "Argument," another problematic love poem, with a "hideous calendar / 'Compliments of Never & Forever, Inc.' ":

Days that cannot bring you near
or will not,
Distance trying to appear
something more than obstinate,

argue argue argue with me
endlessly
neither proving you less wanted nor less dear. . . .

The intimidating sound
of these voices
we must separately find
can and shall be vanquished:
Days and Distance disarrayed again
and gone
both for good and from the gentle battleground.

As testimony to the struggles in her relationship with Marjorie
Stevens, the poem speaks to the rootlessness of Elizabeth's existence
in the 1940s and to her uneasy negotiations with the passage of time.
She once said that the only birthday she had minded passing had
been her thirty-fifth, which she did in 1946. And the poem contemplates "Distance," the stretch of geography between New York and
Florida as well:

Remember all that land
beneath the plane;
that coastline
of dim beaches deep in sand
stretching indistinguishably
all the way,
all the way to where my reasons end?

Robert Lowell came and went from New York during his tri-
umphant winter and spring of 1947, and on the one occasion when
he had a chance to see Elizabeth again, she was ill and could not
hold the reciprocating dinner she had planned for Lowell and the
Jarrells. This, and the announcement of his awards, occasioned her
first letter to him, written in care of his publisher on May 12, 1947.
"Maybe if you're still in town you would come to see me sometime,

I should like to see you very much."[2] Lowell was, but Elizabeth was again ill when they tried to get together. Then Lowell was at Yaddo, the writer's colony in Saratoga Springs, New York, and after that was on his way to Washington, D.C., to be the 1947–1948 poetry consultant to the Library of Congress. They did not meet again until the following fall.

During the spring, Elizabeth began seeing Dr. Anny Baumann, a general practitioner in New York who was building something of a specialty practice treating artists and writers. German-born, efficient, and stoical even beyond the ethnic stereotypes, "Dr. B." became Elizabeth's main medical resource for her chronic depression, asthma, and alcoholism as well as a touchstone for truths about self-discipline, "character," and physical and mental resourcefulness. She spent a good part of the spring in Dr. Baumann's office as she suffered from asthma almost constantly and developed her first major eczema outbreak in many years. Dr. Baumann insisted that Elizabeth should not drink at all, and against this standard she measured her progress.

Elizabeth spent the summer of 1947 in Nova Scotia traveling with Marjorie Stevens. In six weeks at Briton Cove, Cape Breton, they stayed in a guesthouse run by a Scottish family and hiked and fished around the cape, "the most beautiful place I've ever seen," while Marjorie helped Elizabeth stay away from alcohol. This she said she did, though her asthma was so severe that in a letter she asked Dr. Baumann painfully, "Do you suppose my system is wheezing away for alcohol? Horrors."[3] The images of this stay in Cape Breton— with the asthma and the struggles with alcohol submerged—made their way into "A Summer's Dream" and "Cape Breton." In the latter poem, the landscape's beauty is sadly inconsequential and is menaced by intrusions from a faster, noisier world:

The wild road clambers along the brink of the coast.
On it stand occasional small yellow bulldozers,
but without their drivers, because today is Sunday.

The little white churches have been dropped into the
    matted hills
like lost quartz arrowheads.
The road appears to have been abandoned.
Whatever the landscape had of meaning appears to have
    been abandoned,
unless the road is holding it back, in the interior,
where we cannot see,
where deep lakes are reputed to be,
and disused trails and mountains of rock
and miles of burnt forests standing in gray scratches
like the admirable scriptures made on stones by stones—
and these regions now have little to say for themselves
except in thousands of light song-sparrow songs
    floating upward
freely, dispassionately, through the mist, and meshing
in brown-wet, fine, torn fish-nets.

"At the Fishhouses," the poem that emerged from her "Geo-graphical Mirror" notes of the previous summer, appeared in the *New Yorker* on August 9 while Elizabeth was still in Cape Breton and brought her the well-deserved congratulations of her friends, new and old. Marianne Moore, mourning the July 9 death of her mother, wrote to thank Elizabeth for the poem: " 'Melancholy stains like dried blood where the ironwork has rusted' is accurate beyond compare."[4] Lowell, at Yaddo, speculated that the poem was her best to date, though he felt that the word *breasts* in the last stanza was "too much." Her new friend Joseph Summers, a young scholar working on a book about George Herbert whom she had met in the fall of 1946 through Loren MacIver and Lloyd Frankenberg, also wrote to express admiration. (Elizabeth responded by writing to tell Summers that she felt his translations of Herbert's Latin poems were inaccurate.)[5] The poem surely was her "best." Beginning with her description of the five fishhouses and her conversation with the old fisherman, "a friend of my grandfather" (the line came to her in a "letter dream," she said), her meditation on the meaning of the sea proceeds in fits and starts, interrupted by necessary contemplations of physical reality, the objects, sensations, and smells that connect the place with memory, with knowledge:

Cold dark deep and absolutely clear,
element bearable to no mortal,
to fish and to seals...One seal particularly
I have seen here evening after evening.
He was curious about me. He was interested in music;
like me a believer in total immersion,
so I used to sing him Baptist hymns.
I also sang "A Mighty Fortress is Our God."
He stood up in the water and regarded me
steadily, moving his head a little.
Then he would disappear, then suddenly emerge
almost in the same spot, with a sort of shrug
as if it were against his better judgment.
Cold dark deep and absolutely clear,
the clear gray icy water...Back, behind us,
the dignified tall firs begin.
Bluish, associating with their shadows,
a million Christmas trees stand
waiting for Christmas. The water seems suspended
above the rounded gray and blue-gray stones.
I have seen it over and over, the same sea, the same,
slightly, indifferently swinging above the stones,
icily free above the stones,
above the stones and then the world.
If you should dip your hand in,
your wrist would ache immediately,
your bones would begin to ache and your hand would burn
as if the water were a transmutation of fire
that feeds on stones and burns with a dark gray flame.
If you tasted it, it would first taste bitter,

then briny, then surely burn your tongue.
It is like what we imagine knowledge to be:
dark, salt, clear, moving, utterly free,
drawn from the cold hard mouth
of the world, derived from the rocky breasts
forever, flowing and drawn, and since
our knowledge is historical, flowing, and flown.

The chill maternal image at the end of the poem is startling but reminds us that Elizabeth Bishop's Nova Scotia is her motherland, the scene of her disturbed and disturbing childhood. Having spent a good part of the previous two years working with Dr. Ruth Foster on the origins of her depression and alcoholism, Elizabeth must indeed have felt that her inheritance from her mother, what she "derived" from that troubled relationship—her "knowledge" of herself and her Nova Scotia past—was indeed "flowing and drawn" and hopelessly temporal and irremediable, "historical, flowing and flown."

Elizabeth stayed in Nova Scotia until the third week in September, spending the last month in Great Village visiting Aunt Grace Bowers. When Elizabeth got back to New York, she made immediate plans to return to Key West via Washington, D.C., where she would visit Robert Lowell and record readings of her poems for the Library of Congress. She and Lowell had talked in September, and by mid-month he was begging her to come, in the scrawled capital letters he wrote in: "I'll be grieved, you know, if you don't."[6] Elizabeth had recorded the previous spring for Jack Sweeney, curator of the Poetry Room Collection at Harvard University, with very poor results, but she was willing to take her place in the library's archive. She was in Washington from October 14 through 17 and enjoyed her stay chiefly because it brought her closer to Lowell. After an anxious recording session, he took her to lunch with William Carlos Williams, who was in Washington to visit his old friend and antagonist Ezra Pound at St. Elizabeths Hospital. They spent the afternoon at the National Gallery. "I had brought along a pair of flat shoes to wear for gallery going . . . and I remember Mr. Lowell politely carrying my shoes for me." She thanked him for making the trip a success, and by the time she was settled in Key West—in Pauline Pfeiffer Hemingway's house at 907 Whitehead Street—their correspondence had begun in earnest.

Elizabeth's relationship with Pauline Hemingway is not much documented, but her stay in the house (while Pauline was away) initiated a complex series of relationships with the three Pfeiffer sisters (Virginia and Evelyn as well) that would affect Elizabeth positively and negatively over the next four years. She stayed at Pauline's for two months, enjoying the luxury of a lighted swimming pool ("One's friends look like luminous frogs"). When Pauline returned, Elizabeth moved to an apartment given her by John Dewey at 630 Day Street, settling in until May.[7] Her asthma slowly improved; she managed to get some work done on the Cape Breton poems and a second poem about Faustina, which she did not finish. This bifurcation in her interests concerned her: "I . . . am beginning to worry lest I have only two poetic spigots, marked H̲ & C̲."[8] A couple of months later she was trying to finish two "not very serious" poems about Key West, "& then I hope I won't have to write about the place any more."[9] But the place kept imposing itself on her. Earlier, she had noticed that the excavations under way at Garrison Bight in Key West had created a familiar-looking disorder: "The water looks like blue gas – the harbor is always a mess, here, junky little boats all piled up, some hung with sponges and always a few half sunk or splintered up from the most recent hurricane – it reminds me a little of my desk."[10] The poem that followed, "The Bight," with its revealing subtitle, "On my birthday," retains these details:

> Some of the little white boats are still piled up
> against each other, or lie on their sides, stove in,

and not yet salvaged, if they ever will be,
        from the last bad storm,
like torn-open, unanswered letters.
The bight is littered with old correspondences.

The punning change from "my desk" in the letter to "old correspondences" in the poem universalizes (and makes more "literary") the description without eliminating its personal meaning. The "correspondence" between the seer and the scene depends on the seer's accurate perception, on her steady gaze, which eventually forces the scene to yield up its meaning, its "response." Yet the perception is idiosyncratic in ways of which Elizabeth was aware but generally refused to acknowledge. "I *always* tell the truth in my poems," she told a student once.

> With *The Fish,* that's *exactly* how it happened. It was in Key West, and I *did* catch it just as the poem says. That was in 1938. Oh, but I did change *one* thing; the poem says he had five hooks hanging from his mouth, but actually he only had three. Sometimes a poem makes its own demands. But I always *try* to stick as much as possible to what *really* happened when I describe something in a poem.[11]

"The Bight" is a wonderful example of a Bishop speaker viewing a scene, telling "what really happened," and at the same time demonstrating her individuality, even personality. The poem avoids all explicit reference to the viewer of the excavation except in its subtitle. The "objective" description of the animals and machines is charged from the outside with Bishop's personal perspective, her own "correspondences." Surely these are Baudelaire's *correspondances,* his *"forêts de symboles / qui l'observent."* Indeed, she mentions him in the poem: "If one were Baudelaire / one could probably hear it turning to marimba music." Bishop's version of Baudelaire's *profonde unité* in the world of symbols is simply the organizing force of her own perspective.

Despite its wit, the poem describes the activity of the bight as "awful" before "cheerful," and activity here is not just of dredges and bulldozers but of strangely mechanized, razorlike animals as well: oversized birds, crashing pelicans "like pickaxes," "man-of-war birds" with tails like scissors, shark tails like plowshares. The sense that the whole scene might at any moment catch fire and burn spectacularly is supported by the juxtaposition of "pilings dry as matches" and water "the color of the gas flame," which one can smell "turning to gas." Things that ought to have power are strangely ineffective: the "water . . . doesn't wet anything"; "the frowsy sponge boats" are like dogs or are stove in and unsalvaged. Despite the expression of sufficiency, "all the untidy activity continues, / awful but cheerful." Neither the speaker nor the reader can take comfort in the simple idea that things do, after all, correspond. The unnamed correspondences here are not ecstatic, Emersonian revelations of relationship; rather, they are almost wholly negative. Because the poem's method is metaphoric, it deals in correspondence to an unusual degree. The disorder and latent violence in the vehicles convey the disorder in Elizabeth's mind as she thinks about Key West and her birthday. "Thirty-seven / and far from heaven," she noted.

. . .

In Robert Lowell, Elizabeth now had a real confidant in matters of writing, and even though she labored under the weight of her invidious self-comparisons, she did not hesitate to offer him incisive criticism of the drafts he sent her. Her criticisms were often phrased like questions, with apologies attached: "I'm not being 'critical' you know, just curious or dumb."[12] She would then pick apart a poem line by line, attacking even its typographical errors. At the same time, she sought his advice on all literary matters (though she sent him drafts of poems only rarely). Should she add her new poems to the second edition of *North & South*, or should she save them for a new book? (He said no; she did not.) Should she accept an invitation to speak at Wellesley College? (He said yes; she would not.) Her letters to Lowell also gave her an outlet for her increasingly conservative and sharply defended opinions about the state of American poetry as well as her deepest anxieties about her own:

> You [are] apparently able to do the right thing for yourself and your work and don't seem to be tempted by the distractions of travelling – that rarely offers much at all in respect to work. I guess I have liked to travel as much as I have because I have always felt isolated & have known so few of my "contemporaries" and nothing of "intellectual" life in New York or anywhere. Actually it may be all to the good.[13]

She read Lowell constantly now, worried that she would "soon be accused of imitation" of Lowell's enviably vivid characterizations in "Mother Marie Therese" and "Falling Asleep Over the Aeneid." She was "very sick of sounding so quiet."[14] But Lowell's influence was stronger on her professional life than on her poetic practice. And he learned a great deal from Bishop's style—his conversion to looser forms and a more conversational tone came slowly over the next ten years, but he attributed it in part to reading Elizabeth Bishop.

Elizabeth suffered from asthma all winter, which necessitated trips to the doctor in Miami, a brief hospital stay there, and disorienting experiments with new drugs. She struggled to keep her drinking "record" as clean as possible—from her boasts about it one infers some success; when she is silent one feels her losing control. She wrote very little but did complete "Over 2000 Illustrations and a Complete Concordance," which appeared in the June 1948 *Partisan Review*. Mostly, she made and unmade plans for the future, at one point suggesting to Lowell that he come with her to live in Paris, her preference now.

Lowell's felony conviction as a conscientious objector to World War II kept him in the country until 1951. But his presence in

Washington put him in touch with Ezra Pound, then in his second year of incarceration at St. Elizabeths Hospital, and Lowell began to think of himself and his poetry in Pound's characteristically international terms. He spoke with enthusiasm to Elizabeth about Pound. She said simply that she was "pretty mystified by most of [his] message to the world."[15] Nevertheless, as she made plans to head North in late April, she scheduled a stop in Washington, and Lowell promised to take her to see him. She arrived on April 30 with baggage and a canary in a cage and stayed, at Lowell's suggestion, with his fiancée, Carley Dawson, at her elegant Georgetown home. Elizabeth and Dawson became friends—Lowell and his instabilities were the major topic of conversation between them—and Elizabeth discussed struggles with drinking relatively frankly with her in a brief but intense correspondence lasting a little over a year.

Lowell took Elizabeth to see Pound shortly after her arrival in Washington, and Elizabeth pronounced herself "really endlessly grateful" for the experience. The exaggeration and disharmony of "really endlessly" are not typical of Elizabeth's style in any genre; her anxiety is easy to detect and might arise from the makeup of the trio at St. Elizabeths that day. There were perhaps no two more ambitious poets in the English-speaking world in 1948 than Robert Lowell and Ezra Pound. Pound had all his life directed his art outward, trying to alter the course of poetry itself with his writing and fully believing that his prescriptions for form and meter had saved poetry from extinction in the modern age. His determination to alter the course of political and economic history as well had finally overtaken his poetic crusades; broadcasts of his wrongheaded and often deplorable beliefs had resulted in his being charged with treason at the end of World War II. The work of his lifetime, the *Cantos,* was eighty-four poems long with the publication of the *Pisan Cantos* in 1948 and sought in the grandest possible gesture to encompass all literary, political, and personal history. Robert Lowell had also embraced poetry in the grand style, thinking in terms of the large gesture, history, and politics.

Since her uncommitted path through the left-leaning 1930s, Elizabeth had been uncomfortable in the presence of political commitment, and she was envious of Lowell's and gleefully dismissive of Pound's. Even though she may have been looking to the end of "sounding so quiet" and thinking so small in her poems, she was still witnessing Lowell turn out stanza after stanza of "The Mills of the Kavanaughs" and watching her own slowly produced work shrink in comparison. Elizabeth had refused to do new recordings on the trip (her old ones had been lackluster, and an annoying buzz on the tape had been bad enough to make Lowell ask her to redo them), and when he asked her to do a reading at the Library of Congress on April 19, she moved her trip back to May 1. Like Pound, Lowell conceived of his work as important to the history of poetry and of poetry as important to the history of the world. He conceived of being a poet as a profession that involved reading, writing criticism and reviews as well as poems, and teaching—all activities Elizabeth found herself unable to perform.

But she enjoyed her visit in Washington, steering clear of, but observing carefully, the strange conflicts in Lowell's romantic and sexual life. Then she went North to New York to her King Street garret to see Anny Baumann and to organize her own affairs. Lowell visited Elizabeth in New York almost immediately, and together they heard Marianne Moore read. "You're so warm and friendly to me," Lowell wrote. "It's such a joy seeing you. I called up to say goodbye, but you weren't in."[16]

. . .

Elizabeth had rented a house in Wiscasset, Maine, for the summer, and she traveled there early in June. She stayed for six weeks, part of the time in the company of Tom Wanning, her friend of several years in Key West and New York and possibly her lover. Certainly they were not good for each other—their alcoholisms interacted, their depressions kept them from bolstering each other, their mutual rootlessness kept them on the move. But they had a kind of fun, and the relationship may have been serious; on June 4, 1948, Pauline Pfeiffer wrote to Elizabeth from Key West asking, "Are you engaged?"[17] But it is virtually undocumented. It seems likely that Wanning is the subject not only of "Little Exercise," published in 1946, but also of one or more of the "Four Poems" sequence of ambivalent love poems that Elizabeth began composing this summer.

When Tom was not with her in Wiscasset, Elizabeth lamented her "boring solitude" there and struggled with both asthma and the urge to drink self-destructively. Perhaps she should have gone to Yaddo, she wrote to Lowell, as she invited him to come up. Carley Dawson was already coming; Elizabeth desperately needed company. Trying to write, she foundered. At the end of June, she was upset with William Carlos Williams for using the despairing and accusatory letters from the young poet Cress in *Paterson*, seeing in Cress's situation a version of her own. "I think Williams has always had a streak of insensitivity," she wrote. "And then maybe I've felt a little too much the way the woman did at certain more hysterical moments – people who haven't experienced absolute loneliness for long stretches of time can never sympathise with it at all."[18]

Her health discouraged her, and she asked Anny Baumann if her asthma might be psychosomatic and therefore amenable to cure by psychological therapy—she had hoped that her work with Dr. Foster would help, but so far it had not. Elizabeth admitted with pain that the only time in the last "8 or 9 years" that she had been free of asthma was in New York, "which I find rather depressing, since I dislike New York."[19] Her search for a place to live was still intimately tied with her search for air that she could breathe, and she worked desultorily over the summer on a story called "Homesickness" and a poem about Tobias and the prodigal son. Wiscasset was not home.

I think almost the last straw here though is the hairdresser, a nice big hearty Maine girl who asks me questions I don't even know the answers to. She told me 1: that my hair "don't feel like hair at all." 2. I was turning gray practically "under her eyes." And when I'd said yes, I was an orphan, she said "Kind of awful, ain't it, ploughing through life alone." So now I can't walk downstairs in the morning or upstairs at night without feeling I'm ploughing. There's no place like New England.[20]

When Carley Dawson arrived on July 26, the two women went up to Stonington, Maine, for the day and liked it much better. (Elizabeth seems to have felt that she had worn out her welcome at Wiscasset; she left, she said, "under a cloud.") They decided to stay up there for the remainder of the summer and moved in on July 30 to await the arrival of Lowell a few days later. Elizabeth had written asking him to come bearing liquor because their supply was low, and he did. Only Marjorie Steven's comments on this interesting ménage survive—Lowell and Carley evidently about to part ways (Lowell had told Elizabeth early in July that he felt himself "drifting" away from his fiancée), Elizabeth and Tom Wanning and someone named "Sally" conducting dramas of their own. Marjorie wanted to know if perhaps Carley feared Lowell's interest in Elizabeth and if Elizabeth feared Tommy's interest in Sally. As it turned out, after nearly two weeks of awkwardness and unrecorded scenes, Carley Dawson left Stonington with Tom Wanning, who delivered her to the train station, leaving Elizabeth and Lowell alone for one glorious day.

Lowell's biographer says that for a few weeks after this stay at Stonington, Lowell told people that he was going to marry Elizabeth Bishop.[21] Yet Elizabeth was not one of the people he told. Years later, in 1957, he wrote to her in six closely typed pages his explanation of what had happened that August in Stonington as a way of apologizing for some inappropriately amorous behavior during Elizabeth and Lota Soares's visit to Castine in 1957.

Do you remember how at the end of that long swimming and sunning Stonington day after Carlie's [sic] removal by Tommy, we went up to, I think, the relatively removed upper Gross house and had one of those real fried New England dinners, probably awful. And we were talking about this and that about ourselves, and I was feeling the infected hollowness of the Carlie business draining out of my heart, and you said rather humourously, yet it was truly meant, "When you write my epitaph, you must say I was the loneliest person who ever lived." Probably you forget, and anyway all that is mercifully changed and all has come right since you found Lota. But at the time everything, I guess (I don't want to overdramatize) our relations seemed to have reached a new place. I assume that would be [sic] just a matter of time before I proposed and I half believed that you would accept. Yet I wanted it all to have the right build-up. Well, I didn't say anything then. . . . And then there was that poetry conference at Bard and I remmember [sic] one evening presided over by Mary McCarthy and my Elizabeth [Hardwick] was there, and going home to the Bard poets' dormitory, I was so drunk that my hands turned cold and I felt half-dying and held your hand. And nothing was said, and like a loon that needs sixty feet, I believe, to take off from the water, I wanted time and space, and went on assuming, and when I was to have joined you at Key West I was determined to ask you. . . . Then of course the Yaddo explosion came and all was over. Yet there were a few months. . . . Asking you is the might have been for me, the one towering change, the other life that might have been had.[22]

As a document from the early stages of one of Lowell's manic phases, this letter is no doubt full of evasions and misrememberings. But it seems to be essentially true from his point of view. At about the same time, and with more coherence, he recorded in a poem that the failure of the "moment" in Stonington had been there from the start:

WATER

It was a Maine lobster town—
each morning boatloads of hands
pushed off for granite
quarries on the islands,

and left dozens of bleak
white frame houses stuck
like oyster shells
on a hill of rock,

and below us, the sea lapped
the raw little match-stick
mazes of a weir,
where the fish for bait were trapped.

Remember? We sat on a slab of rock.
From this distance in time,
it seems the color
of iris, rotting and turning purpler,

but it was only
the usual gray rock
turning the usual green
when drenched by the sea.

The sea drenched the rock
at our feet all day,
and kept tearing away
flake after flake.

One night you dreamed
you were a mermaid clinging to a wharf-pile,
and trying to pull
off the barnacles with your hands.

We wished our two souls
might return like gulls
to the rock. In the end,
the water was too cold for us.[23]

When Lowell sent Elizabeth a draft of this poem, she wondered first whether the houses had looked more like clamshells than oyster shells. For her part, she remembered the swim in the icy water, and she recollected that Lowell, inadvertently posed against a tree trunk, had for a moment resembled Saint Sebastian.

Elizabeth's own feelings for Lowell were complex and frightening to her. It seems likely that she steered clear of moments when Lowell might have screwed his courage to the point of proposing to her; certainly in the face of his constant pleas that she join him at Yaddo (where he returned after his year in Washington) she made sure that when she went, it would not be when he was there.

Elizabeth stayed at Stonington until October 1948, trying to write and feeling in considerable turmoil about what she would do next. Marianne Moore was staying with friends at Ellsworth, Maine, and Elizabeth paid a visit there with Tom Wanning. Elizabeth and Marianne saw little of each other in the year following her mother's death, and Moore's letters to Elizabeth are heartbreaking confessions of helplessness and grief. "I'm trying to be peaceable about things, Elizabeth; and not aggrieved that life is nothing like what life should be. I can't see how Mother should have been trustful and grateful, always, no matter what the distress or the uncertain aspect; and I so hesitating and 'backward.' "[24] Keenly aware of her mentor's suffering, Elizabeth, asked by the *Quarterly Review of Literature* to contribute an essay for a special issue on Moore, had worked as well on a poem. It appeared in August 1948. Her "Invitation to Miss Marianne Moore" quite literally invites Moore out of grief and back into the world. Its loving request that Moore "please come flying," idiosyncrasies and all, "from Brooklyn, over the Brooklyn Bridge" to visit Elizabeth in Manhattan, "all awash with morals this fine morning," is also a gentle indication of how far she had come in her relationship with the older poet:

> Whistles, pennants and smoke are blowing. The ships
> are signaling cordially with multitudes of flags
> rising and falling like birds all over the harbor.
> Enter: two rivers, gracefully bearing
> countless little pellucid jellies
> in cut-glass epergnes dragging with silver chains.
> The flight is safe; the weather is all arranged.
> The waves are running in verses this fine morning.
>   Please come flying. . . .
>
> For whom the grim museums will behave
> like courteous male bower-birds,
> for whom the agreeable lions lie in wait
> on the steps of the Public Library,
> eager to rise and follow through the doors
> up into the reading rooms,
>   please come flying.
> We can sit down and weep; we can go shopping,
> or play at a game of constantly being wrong
> with a priceless set of vocabularies,
> or we can bravely deplore, but please
>   please come flying.

Elizabeth was troubled when a friend said she thought the poem was "mean"; surely it appreciates in Moore aspects she enjoyed in herself. Its method and message are in perfect keeping with the dialogue the two women carried on in their remarkable correspondence, and the personality Elizabeth captures here also radiates from Moore's letters. "How speak, Elizabeth, when you do so much for me—" is how she began the first of many appreciations for the poem, and in perhaps an ultimate compliment, she chided Elizabeth for a misspelling in the published version by saying, "Mackeral,

Elizabeth? If they feel the way I do about the poem, presently everybody will be spelling it with an 'a.' "[25] For the rest of Moore's life, her letters would from time to time burst into appreciative reminiscence of the poem. In 1956, when it was reprinted in *A Cold Spring,* she wrote, "Never could I deserve so lovely a thing. I shall always be trying to justify it."[26] In particular, she was honored to be associated with the New York Public Library lions and recognized Elizabeth's appreciation of her poetic devices, her use of color ("beyond compare in the small blue drums and the mackerel sky and the jelly-colored epergnes"), her exact-but-obscure metaphors. Elizabeth offers the poem as an invitation to the grieving Moore; her letters proffer similar, real invitations.

And yet the poem's gentle humor—pointed shoes and wide-brimmed black hat, the priceless vocabularies—seems to treat Moore not quite seriously. By 1948, Elizabeth had moved past her youthful terror at Marianne and her mother's moral presences and past the poetic style that relied for its effect on rigid impersonality, on the minutest details, and on the most precise metaphors. At the same time that the poem gestures in warmth and friendship to a grief-stricken friend, its gentle parody allows Elizabeth to say that she is no longer under Moore's tutelage. Her essay, which accompanied the poem, is equally flamboyant, and slightly reductive, in its praise of Moore as "The World's Greatest Living Observer."

As Elizabeth struggled through the fall with what to do next and where to go, Lowell argued that she should first come to Yaddo. Elizabeth herself acquired brochures describing freighter trips around the world and remarked that she would "settle for some form of dignified concubinage as long as it was guaranteed."[27] Her spirits were low; though Tom Wanning was in Stonington for most of September, she was often lonely and contemplating the nature of the suffering that she was "most at home with & helpless about. . . . I think it is so inevitable and unavoidable there's no use talking about it."[28] "I had a wonderful letter here from Poetry Magazine," she wrote to Lowell, with irony. "It requests a contribution

& congratulates me on my poetry's having 'perceptivity' & 'sure-ness,' etc., that 'seem often to be lacking in the output of the run-down sensibility of the forties.' I think we should make a modest fortune by working out a prescription for run-down sensibilities."[29]

Elizabeth left Stonington rather abruptly on September 30, hav-ing been persuaded in the end by her old high school teacher Eleanor Prentiss, now at Wellesley College, to read and give a brief lecture there on October 19. Elizabeth went first to her King Street flat, then left for Boston on October 13. She was terrified but sur-vived the reading. "Not too bad" was all she would say (and, to Moore, that the audience had liked the "Invitation" poem best). She stayed in Boston another week at the Hotel Vendome, finding her stay "literary beyond belief." She was invited to parties at Andrews Wanning's (Tom's brother), Richard Eberhart's, and Rich-ard Wilbur's; saw and fell in love with a Kokoschka show at the Institute of Contemporary Arts; and visited the Glass Flowers at Harvard's Museum of Natural History. She returned to New York early in November in time for the poetry symposium at Bard Col-lege, where Joe Summers and James Merrill were then teaching. She saw Lowell again, Lloyd Frankenberg and Loren MacIver were there, and so were William Carlos Williams, Richard Eberhart, Richard Wilbur, Jean Garrigue, and Kenneth Rexroth. Thanking Joe and U. T. ("University of Texas") Summers for their hospitality, Elizabeth wondered "if Cal ever did get off?" and hoped she had been "a credit to you, more or less."[30]

She remained in New York for the rest of November, then headed to Key West, stopping on her way outside Baltimore to visit Jane Dewey, who had become a physicist for the U.S. military. Together they visited "three museums" and "Poe's grave in the pouring rain."[31] Arriving in Key West on December 14, Elizabeth immedi-ately found an apartment she loved, at 611 Francis Street, which she described on a postcard of a "Caribbean Jew-Fish." (Her note begins, "These are the Fish," referring to her poem.) The apartment was large, with "a screened porch up in a tree, & a view of endless waves of tin roofs and palm trees."[32]

Despite the loveliness of this apartment, Elizabeth fell into a precipitous decline in the winter of 1949. And even though the poems she had managed to finish in Maine over the summer were appearing—notably "The Bight" on February 19—and Lowell was making efforts on her professional behalf, she struggled. In response to his constant urging that she come to Yaddo, she finally wrote:

> All right–I think I shall write to Mrs. Ames right away, as soon at least as you tell me what you think would be a good month. July? I haven't any plans at all, really. . . . I think it would be awfully nice to have one big set task. I always seem to be trying to do six or seven different poems at the same time and just hoping I can keep them all well-nurtured enough so that one of them will suddenly get strong enough to take over all by itself until it is done. . . . The "loneliness" is pretty bad here, too–in fact I'm sure in some ways it's much more boring than Yaddo.[33]

Feeling her floundering, Lowell went to work. In his capacity as a former poetry consultant to the Library of Congress, he had some influence in the search for a successor in that role to Leonie Adams. He managed to get Elizabeth placed second in line for the job behind Marianne Moore. When Moore refused to take the time off from her translations of LaFontaine's fables, Elizabeth was named to the post. This solved a huge problem for her—where to go, what to do—but she was months making up her mind whether to accept the job and was upset by the irony she saw in its coming to her:

> I've always felt that I've written poetry more by not writing it than writing it, and now this Library business makes me really feel like the 'poet by default.' At 1st I felt a little overcome and inclined to wire you a frantic 'no,' but after having thought about it for a day or two I've concluded that it is something I could do (there isn't

much, heaven knows) and that even if I haven't written nearly enough poetry to warrant it that maybe it will be all right . . . particularly if I work hard from now until then.[34]

The poetry consultant's job paid five thousand dollars (oddly, fifty-seven hundred to Lowell) to a poet for one year's work supervising the acquisition and maintenance of the Library of Congress's holdings in poetry, organizing meetings of the Society of Fellows, and serving as a clearinghouse for information about poetry in the government. (The representative wanting to quote Shakespeare correctly in a speech on the floor of the House might call the consultant, for example.) The major project of Lowell's tenure had been the completion of the library's collection of poets recording their own poems. The task lingered over into Adams's and then Elizabeth's terms, as she wrote liner notes and brochures for the series. Elizabeth felt able to handle the secretarial and administrative work, though she loathed the thought of it. But she was terrified that the job would involve "public appearances" and readings, the idea of which left her weak with fear. As she awaited an official invitation from Washington, she worried. She made tentative plans for the summer—a month at Yaddo, two months in Nova Scotia—but by her thirty-eighth birthday on February 8, she "fell into a slough" of depression that seems to have been serious. On February 19, in a desperate attempt to pull herself out of it and to get away from Key West (and, perhaps, a scheduled visit from Louise Crane), she left for Haiti with Virginia Pfeiffer—apparently on her friends' strong advice. The critic Seldon Rodman lived in Haiti part of the year and entertained a stream of writers in the late 1940s. Elizabeth said she did not much like Rodman, but it seems the decision to leave Key West was not entirely hers to make.

Elizabeth loved Haiti and was delighted by Jinny Pfeiffer, who had been visiting Pauline from her home in Italy. Elizabeth's notebooks show her contemplating the multilayered ironies of life in the dusty, impoverished city of Port-au-Prince, alive with complex religious traditions—Catholic and native voodoo curiously mixed (a combination of Mexico and Morocco, Elizabeth said)—and complex social conditions supported by racism and a rigid caste system. "Mass starts at 4 AM in the churches so that the very poor (90%) who haven't any decent clothes, can come in the dark," she reported to Lowell.[35] Her letter to Carley Dawson about the trip was effusive: "WE had a simply wonderful time – in fact I don't believe I've ever had such a good time in my life before." They swam and spearfished, snorkled, sailed, hiked, ate, and drank. "We turned out to be Amazons although we'd both considered ourselves just a pair of middle-aged hypochondriacs before." Elizabeth returned to Key West "much restored and in my right mind, etc." and made plans to visit Jinny in Rome. Elizabeth wondered if Lowell might not come, too. Her literary pursuits seemed far away: "I am merely a large stupid under-water spear-fisher-woman who hasn't read a poem for a month."

Harriet Higginson, a college friend of Elizabeth's who had been partially paralyzed in a murder attempt five years before, had been staying in Elizabeth's Key West apartment while she was in Haiti, and Elizabeth returned home to Harriet's absorbing company. "She is one of the bravest people I've ever known and very funny and a great pleasure to have around. . . . I'm delighted to have her and I'm much better off with someone around anyway – I don't suffer from the [temptation] to drink too much then at all – which afflicts me when I get lonely."[36] But when Higginson left and returned to New York, Elizabeth again stumbled.

To Marianne Moore, Elizabeth gave cheerful news of her progress in writing (she said she had finished "Cape Breton" and, significantly, "The Prodigal"), and her asthma had improved, but it seems clear that her life was spinning out of control, led by her addiction to alcohol. To her friends, she said she had been "sick" since her stay in Haiti and speculated cheerfully that perhaps she had been "zombified" by a witch doctor there. To Anny Baumann, Elizabeth was only slightly more explicit:

A day or so after I got back evrything [*sic*] just seemed to blow up. It was all aggravated by worrying about this 'job' (still uncertain) and a couple of other problems that I really can't do anything about at all. . . .

The asthma, strange to say, has been gradually going away. . . . I am hoping it is a good sign and that this last sad business I put my friends and myself through may mark the beginning of some sort of metamorphosis.

Everyone has been unbelievably kind. You know I'm sorry so I won't say that. I'm taking the pills and at least feel sane again and thank you once more for your help. I have someone staying with me at night temporarily – that's a help. . . .

PS: – if I can just keep the last line ["awful but cheerful"] in mind everything may still turn out all right.[37]

This kind of language—apologies, talk of reform—usually attached to the aftermath of a drinking binge. Dr. Baumann had arranged for Elizabeth to be seen by a Dr. Fischer in Miami, where she spent a week in the hospital. What "pills" she was taking is unknown, though it does not seem to have been Antabuse or any other aversion therapy for alcohol.

Elizabeth finally heard from Leonie Adams, confirming the appointment to the Library of Congress post, on April 22, but this did not improve her condition. By the end of the month, she was back in New York at the Hotel Earle (the King Street apartment building was being torn down) and was seeing a doctor every day, "trying to get myself straightened out again." She was worried about the job, though she felt "it would be the saving of me if I could just do it properly."[38] She was worried about Lowell, who was showing the first signs (visible to Elizabeth, anyway) of his profound insta-bility in the so-called Mrs. Ames affair at Yaddo, the subject of vicious and volatile literary gossip in the city. Elizabeth had firsthand knowledge of the event, having received three letters from Lowell's soon-to-be wife, Elizabeth Hardwick, who evidently felt that because Lowell had invoked her name in his testimony against Elizabeth Ames, she ought to know what was happening. Elizabeth also met Jean Stafford at a party and heard her version of her ex-husband's character and mental health. Lowell's ringleading in the bizarre accusations of communist sympathy against Elizabeth Ames, Yaddo's executive director, made moot forever the question of whether he and Elizabeth Bishop would ever be there at the same time. He was not invited back.[39] When Elizabeth wrote to him, inquiring gently, he responded, "I'm in grand shape. . . . The world is full of wonders."[40] The whole affair upset Elizabeth terribly, she told Carley Dawson. "We have had too much of that kind of thing in both our lives."[41]

Elizabeth had to move her belongings out of the King Street apartment on this trip to New York, and as she struggled to get control of herself, it seemed to her that "the whole thing" hinged on the next four or five months, when she must find a place to live and figure out what to do until time to head to Washington in September. The more she tried to make definite plans—to go to Washington and find an apartment there, for example—the more she could not. She did finally accept the job on May 3 and made a plan of sorts to stay in New York for at least "six weeks more." Tom Wanning was staying at the same hotel, and his company, however unreliable, was a help.

Elizabeth left on May 14 for a weekend visit with Jinny Pfeiffer, then staying with her uncle in Connecticut. Apparently alarmed at Elizabeth's condition, Pfeiffer drove her immediately to Blythewood, an expensive psychiatric hospital/rest home. She stayed there two months—though she was free to go out for her meals and for an occasional weekend. She seemed to regard the place in part as a stopgap between the terrors of New York and the unknowns of Yaddo (where she would go for August, even though she was sure that Lowell would disown her if she did) and Washington. Although she tells almost nothing about the treatment she received at the hospital—except that she liked her doctor and was allowed to drink socially—Elizabeth's letters are full of humorous anecdotes about the other patients and their social pretensions. Through the irony, it is clear that she desperately needed constant company and twenty-four-hour, disinterested care. She was embarrassed to be there, asking her friends not to reveal her whereabouts (and begging Carley Dawson not to call the hospital a "sanitarium" on the envelope of her letters, a restatement of the anxiety she had felt about her mother's "address" in the Lucius stories and "In the Village"). As would occur many times in years to come, the MacIver-Frankenberg apartment at 61 Perry Street in New York became her cover, giving her a safe address now that her King Street building was really gone and she was without a permanent home.

Elizabeth read for two months at Blythewood—*Middlemarch, To the Lighthouse,* a life of Tennyson, Michaux's *A Barbarian in Asia* ("all that kept me going")—painted watercolors, and practiced the piano. She had written no poetry since March ("Cape Breton" appeared in the June 18, 1949, *New Yorker*) and wrote virtually none until her second stay at Yaddo in the fall of 1950. When she left Blythewood on July 14, saying that the place was "on its last legs . . . & really doing more harm than good," she spent a few days in New York at the New Weston Hotel, including a lunch with an editor friend and Eudora Welty. Then Elizabeth retreated to West Hampton, Long Island (with her Key West friend Mary Pentecost), before heading to Yaddo on Saturday, July 23. "I didn't tell Cal, of course."[42] She let Dawson secure a room for her in Washington in the boardinghouse of Miss Bertha Looker ("Chez Mlle. Voyeuse," Elizabeth said).

Nine

ELIZABETH ARRIVED at Yaddo in the midst of a terrible heat
wave and languished in it for several days before getting her bearings
in the eccentric architecture and atmosphere of the "retreat." The
mansion and its surrounding buildings are set in elaborate grounds
and gardens, including the crown jewel, the rose garden. The
accommodations were luxurious (Elizabeth was given a room in the
West Tower, which she said "occupies about ½ an acre & has 34
windows & a marble bath carved with water-lilies"), and Elizabeth
Ames saw to it that the guests—painters, writers, and composers—
were given as much freedom and privacy as possible.[1] Breakfast and
dinner were served in a dining hall; guests were given a box lunch
to eat where they chose. Despite these conveniences, Elizabeth was
lonely and miserable at Yaddo for her first ten days there, as she
would be in most institutions; it was "much much worse than one's
first week at boarding school."[2] Although the other guests included
Pearl Kazin, Wallace Fowlie, and John Malcolm Brinnin, all of
whom eventually became dear friends, she found she could not
"mix." And it was Brinnin who told her he had heard that Robert
Lowell was to marry Elizabeth Hardwick; he says that Elizabeth
crumpled at the news. Certainly it upset her but probably only

added to misery she was already feeling, the same misery that had held her prisoner since early February.

Just as she was leaving Blythewood, Elizabeth had reported to Carley Dawson that a major transition seemed about to occur:

> There is just a possibility that my living plans might change very
> drastically – and a hope – but it's a slight one & I won't say any
> more now except to hint in a most unladylike way that I have
> been having fearful troubles, Carley, not unlike your own of last
> year and they have accounted to some degree for the recurrence of
> my old problems and my general unreliability. However, I guess
> its almost over now.[3]

Dawson's troubles of the previous year were with Robert Lowell; Elizabeth seems to be saying that she was at the decision point in a relationship, that either she would live with (perhaps marry) the person or the relationship would be "over." Tom Wanning's letters to Elizabeth do not survive; he had left on May 26 for Ireland, and the date of his return is uncertain. Perhaps he is the "god's gift to women" Elizabeth told Loren had driven her up to Yaddo. Her letters to MacIver are explicit in their description of her misery but are written to someone who knows the story already:

> My chief worry seems to be that Dr. B will 'give me up' – also that
> Harriet, Mary, Marjory, Margaret, you, Tom, Cal, as well as the
> pf [Pfeiffer] sisters have all come to dislike me. I really think those
> damned drs. have undermined me thoroughly and for good &
> all. . . . What about Marianne? WHAT SHOULD I DO? . . . I
> am so frantic about – I DON'T KNOW WHAT TO DO and I've
> GOT to do something – maybe it was entirely my fault I don't
> know – I did know more or less what to expect i suppose, though I
> didn't think it would be so thorough, and I wildly overestimated
> my own strength, I guess – Do you really think Dr B has given me
> up as a bad job – I don't want to be this kind of person at all but
> I'm afraid I'm [really] disintegrating just like Hart Crane only
> without his gifts to make it at all plausible –[4]

Elizabeth's problems, whatever they were—the broken relation-ship, some unexplained (perhaps imagined) difficulty with Mar-ianne, her fear that she had lost all her friends—became circular and multiple as she coped with them by drinking and then grew ashamed and guilty in consequence. She lived in constant fear that the other guests at Yaddo would "find out" about her drinking bouts (they did), and as a result she was ashamed to take any social ini-tiative. She grew lonelier and lonelier and more and more afraid of the future, of the responsibilities of being a public poet ("If I were a painter none of this would ever have happened," she wrote to MacIver).[5] As her friends reassured her—she talked to everyone on the phone, Jinny Pfeiffer was friendly and forgiving, Mary Pentecost invited her back to Westhampton, Loren wrote reassuring letters—she regained some equanimity and began to write a little. The third of the "Four Poems" sequence, "While Someone Telephones," was enclosed in a letter to MacIver on August 12, "but I guess they're all (3 now) unpublishable," she remarked.[6] An earlier draft of a poem in "this unfortunate sequence" began, "Your eyes, two darkened theatres / in which I thought I saw you – saw you! / but only played most miserably my doubled self."[7] She also passed among her friends a polished draft of a poem called "The Owl's Journey," of about the same size and shape as the sequence. This poem looks in a different direction—toward "The Armadillo," perhaps:

> Somewhere the owl rode on the rabbit's back
> down a long slope, over the long, dried grasses,
> through a half-moonlight igniting everything
> with specks of faintest green and blue.
> They made no sound, no shriek, no <u>Whoo!</u>

She struggled all summer as well to write an essay for John Ciardi, who was assembling an anthology-with-commentary called *Mid-Century American Poets*. He had asked for five thousand words, and Elizabeth was already months late with her contribution, resenting deeply that Ciardi could obligate her to a kind of writing she hated just by making his request. And Lowell urged her to write it. What she wrote reflects her state of mind on a number of pressing issues; in barely two hundred words she sounds as cornered as she was feeling at the time:

> To all but two of the questions raised here my answer is *it all depends.* It all depends on the particular poem one happens to be trying to write, and the range of possibilities is, one trusts, infinite. After all, the poet's concern is not consistency.
>
> I do not understand the question about the function of overtone, and to the question on subject matter (any predilections? any restrictions?) I shall reply that there are no restrictions. There *are,* of course, but they are not consciously restrictions.
>
> Physique, temperament, religion, politics, and immediate circumstances all play their parts in formulating one's theories on verse. And then they play them again and differently when one is writing it. No matter what theories one may have, I doubt very much that they are in one's mind at the moment of writing a poem or that there is even a physical possibility that they could be. Theories can only be based on interpretations of other poet's [*sic*] poems, or one's own in retrospect, or wishful thinking.
>
> The analysis of poetry is growing more and more pretentious and deadly. After a session with a few of the highbrow magazines one doesn't want to look at a poem for weeks, much less start writing one. The situation is reminiscent of those places along the coast where warnings are posted telling one not to walk too near the edge of the cliffs because they have been undermined by the sea and may collapse at any minute.
>
> This does not mean that I am opposed to all close analysis and criticism. But I am opposed to making poetry monstrous or boring and proceeding to talk the very life out of it.[8]

Elizabeth did eventually find a few congenial guests at Yaddo (Jim Powers and Bill Burford, among others), went to the races in Saratoga with Pearl Kazin (losing forty dollars on her first day there), and bought a bottle of soap bubble solution and sat on her private balcony blowing bubbles—before she came down with mumps and had to be quarantined in her room. At this point, she announced herself "mortified" at being such a "bad guest." She left Yaddo with trepidation—at going to Washington, at seeing Dr. Baumann again ("How on earth can I ever explain to her anything")—but with spirits somewhat improved. Nevertheless, she felt that Yaddo had not been "the right place" for her.

Elizabeth's six-month-long crisis may well have been precipitated by the end of the relationship with Tom Wanning. If it was, then the pain of its ending may also have involved the end of her hopes for a so-called normal heterosexual life. Although Elizabeth may have had brief sexual relationships with men after 1949, she was never again involved in a sustained one. Years later in the middle of another crisis with an unstable friend, Elizabeth remarked that she in the remote past had had the "sense to get out of" a relationship with a mentally ill man "after two years." This seems to have been that relationship, though it is almost entirely undocumented.

The week in New York passed, seeing friends, visiting Anny Baumann (which seems to have been easy in the end), and attending a party given by a painter she had met at Yaddo. Then she left for Jane Dewey's farm in Havre de Grace, Maryland. Dewey drove Elizabeth down to Washington on September 12, and she moved into Bertha Looker's all-female boardinghouse ("no gentlemen callers") right away. Elizabeth pronounced it okay but asked a Washington acquaintance to help her look for an apartment; there were "too many ladies" at Miss Looker's. In her first week in Washington, Elizabeth worked part time with Leonie Adams, hoping to ensure a smooth transition from one consultant to the next. In the afternoons, she visited and fell in love with the Phillips Collection, a private museum holding a wonderful group of paintings, French impressionists and others, including Renoir's *Luncheon of the Boating Party* and a couple of Daumiers that Elizabeth said later made her feel as if her entire life had been wasted. On Monday, September

19, she sat behind the consultant's desk alone for the first time. Her secretary, Phyllis Armstrong, quickly became a confidante, and together—with much more work done by Armstrong, one surmises—they kept the office running.

Elizabeth limped her way physically and emotionally through the year. Her asthma bothered her; Anny Baumann had recently started her on theoglycinate, the latest in asthma therapies, and she had a ventilator, a kind of water pipe that she said made her feel like the caterpillar in *Alice in Wonderland*. She was tired, working an eight-hour day and a forty-hour week for the first time in her life. But throughout the fall of 1949, she managed. She agreed to do the obligatory reading at the library (then canceled when she found it did not pay extra) and then agreed to read for John Malcolm Brinnin at the YMHA in New York on April 6. In an exchange of favors he saw to it that Dylan Thomas read and recorded his poems at the library as one stop on his first whirlwind tour of the United States. Elizabeth said that hearing Thomas read was a highlight of her Washington year, which had precious few of them. She was also host to Robert Frost and Robert Penn Warren, who was married to her college classmate Eleanor Clark, and she made regular visits to Ezra Pound at St. Elizabeths—an unwritten duty of poetry consultants in those years.

Pound was never one to put his guests at their ease, and as the year progressed and Elizabeth grew less and less confident of her ability to succeed in the public world of poetry, the visits took on an aspect of torture. But she did visit, bringing him gifts and pirating books from the library (forbidden to the prisoner suspected of treason). She said much later that she had had large bound volumes of maps of the Paris sewer system delivered to him at the hospital, without asking for an explanation. She endured constant harangues from Pound on the library's failure to subscribe to all the world's little magazines. In December 1949, she reported on a Christmas visit to the hospital: "I'm about to go see Pound and take him [some] eau de cologne—so far my presents have not met with much success but maybe this will." Later she took other young poets to meet him, also an unofficial consultant's duty. Her sketchy diary for the year 1950 notes on February 21:

> Took Weldon Kees with me to St. Elizabeths to call on Pound – I think I left my favorite pen there – we didn't get there until almost 3:30 because I had completely forgotten (the perfect slip) that visiting hrs. are over at four. He was very talkative – has a new blue back-chair, already broken from his throwing himself back in it, almost full-length. He said he was using my hair-lotion – I think it was eau-de-cologne, though!

Kees recalled the same visit, and his letter illuminates Elizabeth's relationship with her difficult charge:

> I looked up Elizabeth Bishop, a very nice person, and she asked me if I'd like to see Pound. She had to go over to the hospital the next afternoon to take him some books from the Library of Congress. He receives visitors from 2 to 4 every afternoon, and Mrs. Pound, who lives in Washington, goes to see him daily. I found the experience somewhat inhuman, rather like visiting a museum, but certainly not an experience to have missed. He "receives" at the end of a corridor in the hospital, which is a pretty gloomy affair, with catatonics and dementia praecox cases slithering about; but he certainly keeps up a spirit. Very lively and brisk, and his eyes go through you like knives. . . . (Pound calls [Elizabeth] "Liz Bish," which she doesn't care for; nor does she care much for Pound, regarding him as a pretty dangerous character, through his influence—particularly the anti-Semitism—on the young.) . . . But he's far from crazy, I'd say, though an egomaniac of the first water.[9]

Elizabeth felt that Pound mistrusted her motives in bringing young poets to see him: "Pound is very forgiving about my not coming oftener, although he sees right through me – tells everyone how I always 'have to bring someone else along,' etc."[10] She said she found his conversation "exhausting" and intimidating.

Elizabeth's visits to Pound in 1949–1950 also confronted her with an opposite model to her own idea of how to be a poet, an idea she had learned from Marianne Moore during a quiet time in Moore's life. These meetings with Pound were a confrontation between Elizabeth Bishop and a whole tradition of modernist poetry, a potential way of life. Pound had directed literary (and economic) world affairs largely from self-appointed positions but still conceived of himself in 1949 as a man of letters and a literary figure. Had his politics not taken an unfortunate turn (and it is said that he wished to return to the United States at the start of the war but could not), he might have been the country's leading literary spokesperson instead of the possibly mad, supposedly traitorous, incarcerated genius. Pound still held court for his subjects at St. Elizabeths but was no longer forced, or allowed, to make choices about the conduct of his life. Elizabeth faced him from about as opposite a position as she could be in and still also be a poet. They were opposite in poetic style; though Pound's days of iconoclasm were largely behind him, he must have found Bishop's poems, if he read them, woefully provincial and traditional. Elizabeth herself said that she "didn't care much for grand, all-out efforts" in art and even as a young woman had a clear idea of what her strengths and weaknesses as a poet were.[11] Next to "accuracy" (an idea she promoted at every opportunity), Elizabeth Bishop most valued modesty in art; she and Pound could hardly communicate on that issue.

Elizabeth did not write her poem about these meetings with Pound until 1956. But it is clear that in 1949–1950 she had already begun to form the complex sentiment at the heart of "Visits to St. Elizabeths." Facing Pound from an opposite point of view about the uses of poetry, and from an opposite position in political awareness, personal style, and future prospects, Elizabeth measured herself against him and found herself wanting. Seven years later, she would not.

In the spring of 1950, Elizabeth's determination to do well at the consultant's job failed her. She fell into a cycle of destructive binge drinking and missed a great deal of work. In February, she wrote to John Malcolm Brinnin canceling her scheduled April 6 reading at the YMHA, a failure of courage that embarrassed her from time to time for the rest of her life. Brinnin was "nice" about it, and Dylan Thomas came to the library anyway, on March 8 and 9, to make his now-famous recordings. In April, she reported to Anny Baumann a "bad spell" of drinking and at the same time moved from Miss Looker's boardinghouse to Slaughter's, a residential hotel, perhaps once again out of embarrassment.

Elizabeth escaped her Washington solitude on several weekends to Jane Dewey's farm in Havre de Grace, where she watched the spring unfold from week to week. Her diary for the year, in which she attempted to write on a daily basis, records its progress in the nightly appearance of fireflies ("exactly like the bubbles breaking in a glass of champagne"), the fields of wild flowers, the "rank smell" of the swamp, the new moon rising over the hills. "A Cold Spring," the poem that grew out of these observations at Jane Dewey's, may have been the major literary achievement of Elizabeth's year in Washington, but she could not finish it until the following winter at Yaddo. During the year, she worked on "View of the Capitol from the Library of Congress," first noting on June 23, "The band playing on the steps of the Capitol – 1st sounds unreal, a sort of imagined band, then in short bursts, real. There isn't any wind, & looking out one has the sensation that this effect is being caused by the great masses of the trees between the band & here." She began to draft the poem immediately.

She also contemplated, as she often did, the phenomenon of time and its passage.

> I think when one is extremely unhappy – almost hysterically
> unhappy, that is – one's time-sense breaks down. All that long
> stretch in K. W. for example, several years ago – it wasn't just a

matter of not being able to accept the present, that present, although it began that way, possibly. But the past & the present seemed confused, or contradicting each other violently and constantly, & the past wouldn't "lie down" (I've felt the same thing when I tried to paint – but this was really taught me by getting drunk, when the same thing happens, for perhaps the same reasons, for a few hours.)

A few months earlier, she had seen moss growing on the facade of the post office building in Washington. "Quite bright green. – How wonderful this place would look if all the facades were like that. (Ver-de-gris – one definition is ver de Greece) (Those green green roses in the Freer) (Time is sometimes green – I want to write a villanelle & that sounds like a possibility.)" The unpublished villanelle, called "Verdigris," alternates the lines "The catalogues will tell you that they mean" and "The time to watch for is when Time grows green" to explore the effect of aging on the patina of art objects and on us: "Left in the earth, or out, it is foreseen / we get like that; also if lost in foam." She had Dylan Thomas on her mind at this time, perhaps "Fern Hill" specifically.

Elizabeth also wrote two brief reviews—the first of her career—for the library's official organ, the *United States Quarterly Book Review*. The first was of Gwendolyn Brook's *Annie Allen*, and the other of cummings's *XAIPE: 71 Poems*. Even though she continued to hate reviewing, the cummings piece, barely a hundred words, clearly engaged her at least for a moment:

> Often Mr. Cummings' approach to poetry reminds one of a smart-alec Greenwich Village child saying to his friends: "Look! I've just made up a new game. Let's all write poems. There! I've won!" And in front of the wood-and-coal man's basement shop, on the wall of the Chinese laundry, along the curbs of the dingy but flourishing park, appear poems and ideograph-poems in hyacinth-colored chalks.[12]

On the strength of these, she accepted an invitation from the *New Republic* to review a new edition of Emily Dickinson's letters to Dr. and Mrs. Josiah Holland. The brief review took her nearly a year to write and appeared in the magazine on August 21, 1951. She also published in the May 1950 *Poetry* four translations from the French of Max Jacob's poems, "Banks," "Hell is Graduated," "Patience of an Angel," and "Rainbow," which she had worked on during the previous summer at Yaddo.

Elizabeth was sick much of May and June, away from her office with flu, bronchitis, and asthma as well as with a bad case of poison ivy and with her deepening depression, which she was beginning to correlate with the ambiguity of early spring. "A Cold Spring" manifests this ambivalence about the season:

> A cold spring:
> the violet was flawed on the lawn.
> For two weeks or more the trees hesitated;
> the little leaves waited,
> carefully indicating their characteristics.
> Finally a grave green dust
> settled over your big and aimless hills.
> One day, in a chill white blast of sunshine,
> on the side of one a calf was born.
> The mother stopped lowing
> and took a long time eating the after-birth,
> a wretched flag,
> but the calf got up promptly
> and seemed inclined to feel gay.

The great weight on her spirits was once again the question of where to go and what to do when the mixed blessing of the consultant's job ended in September. She had applied for a Fulbright but had a premonition that she would not win, and she did not. In an astonishing display of generosity, Elizabeth Hardwick wrote offering her the chance to accompany Hardwick and Cal Lowell to

Italy to stay indefinitely. Elizabeth wrote back a polite refusal, saying that she was desperate to settle down and write, having done nothing during the year, and that she would not have the money to travel until she finished and sold a few stories. Her plan was to go to Yaddo for "a few months" if possible and then go abroad, perhaps to Italy, in January 1951. Her priority was to finish the book she had promised Houghton Mifflin, already long overdue. In her notebook she drafted an ambitious and pristine daily schedule for herself at Yaddo, "if I really do go."

> 7:30 to breakfast
> quick walk around the garden
> WORK till 1:30
> lunch – & play clavichord – letters only then
> LONG walk
> bath & change
> – maybe downtown, or walk down
> Dinner
> READ till 12 – almost entirely languages – Fr., Sp.,
>   German – or clavichord
>
> Job hunt in N.Y. until Oct. 1st –

Elizabeth did manage to see Lowell before he and Hardwick sailed for Europe on September 28. Their departure had been delayed by the death of Lowell's father; otherwise Elizabeth would have missed them altogether, perhaps intentionally.

She dragged herself through the summer in Washington, hating the climate, the job, the circumstances. She had six weeks of asthma in June and July and missed work much of that time. She dutifully took visiting poets to see Pound and endured his requests for books and microfilms. She sat for an official portrait for the library and hated the results ("I came out looking exactly like one of those old cartoons of char-ladies in 'Punch' ").[13] She went up to New York to have Marion Morehouse take her photograph to accompany a brief notice in *Harper's* and was horrified by it as well. She went to the movies, visited the Phillips Collection, and spent her weekends at Jane Dewey's, biding her time until September 18, when Conrad Aiken would take over the consultant's job and she would head to New York and then to Yaddo on October 1.

Elizabeth was gratified to find herself writing well as soon as she got to Yaddo; by November 10 she was reporting that she had sold eight new poems and was finishing a "perfectly endless story," unidentified.[14] At the same time, however, her adjustment to the place was awkward and difficult. Despite guests Alfred Kazin and May Swenson, who became her friends, and Polly Hansen, Elizabeth Ames's secretary and a fine poet and eventual friend, Elizabeth again could not find her place. She suffered from asthma and drank heavily in her first month there, occasioning a five-day hospital stay and the by-now familiar cycle of shame and embarrassment. She blamed her collapse on the terrible pressure of being among other artists: "At Yaddo one must produce," she told her notebook. And she thought she might be mourning the "deaths of three people close to me." Only one of the three is identified; Dr. Ruth Foster died in mid-October, and Elizabeth was devastated. She said Dr. Foster had helped her more than anyone else had, and though she understood her grief as a common response to the death of one's former therapist, she had trouble controlling it. Years later, she said that this time at Yaddo had been "the most wretched and unpleasing stretch" of her life and that she regretted she had been "a burden" to Elizabeth Ames. It was well known around Yaddo that Elizabeth had a serious drinking problem; the small community kept track of who was absent for a stretch, out of whose room those empty bottles were carried. After an intense drinking bout ending on November 25, the night a major hurricane roared through New England and

New York ("One of my walls actually fell off"), Elizabeth swore to Anny Baumann that she had reached bottom and would drink no more:

> I'm going to writeyou a letter that I'll probably not send but maybe I'll re-read it every day as a reminder to myself. I've been having a sort of a brainstorm ever since I got here, just can't stop writing, can't sleep, and although at the time I wrote before I had managed not to drink for a stretch I've certainly made up for it since & made a damn fool of myself & got into a peck of troubles. – & made a very good [friend] of mine here very unhappy.
>
> Well, last night as the trees came crashing down all around me andI felt like death it seemed a sort of natural phenomena [*sic*] equal to the brainstorms and I suddenly made up my mind. I will not Drink. I've been stalling along now for years & it's [absolutely] absurd. Dr Foster said "Well, go ahead, then – ruin your life" – and I almost have, I also know I'll go insane if I keep it up. I cannot drink and I know it. . . .
>
> I shake so I can't sign my name.[15]

But as the strange warm fall turned to a snowy winter, she could not stop. After a binge lasting more than three weeks, she solved her problem of where to spend Christmas 1950 by checking into the Saratoga Hospital to dry out. Her notebook of the stay records her ironic observations of other patients and her fifteen-hour headache.

Despite, or perhaps because of, these troubles, the guests at Yaddo in 1950 remained among Elizabeth's dearest friends. Ilse and Kit Barker, a German writer and a British painter, respectively, arrived in early November just as Elizabeth was falling apart for the second time. May Swenson helped see her through as well. With these three, she maintained lifetime correspondences. Calvin Kentfield, Alfred Kazin, Beaufort Delaney, Polly Hansen, Wallace Fowlie, and Peggy Bennett were good friends to a different degree, but all were remarkably loyal to Elizabeth throughout her humiliations. To Anny Baumann, Elizabeth said that she had "pretty [insoluble] problems," which she did not explain, but that "the other guests here know about it, . . . [and] they have all been extremely nice to me, heaven knows why."[16] She speculated that on the verge of turning forty, exactly the age at which her father had died, she was somehow belatedly responding to her earliest loss. Despite her rapport with other people at Yaddo, Elizabeth was also uncomfortable, as she always was, in an exclusively literary or artistic environment. She so lacked self-confidence that she could not break her habit of invidious comparison, and when she compared, her own intelligence, learning, productivity, and "seriousness" always fell short. Her indecision about the future plagued her as well, and her unsettled personal life and lack of an intimate, sustaining relationship left her too much to herself. Despite the shelter that Yaddo gave her—an inexpensive and beautiful place to live away from New York City—it also threw her so forcefully back on herself and her work that she could not face it directly. As her alcoholism took hold, she was more and more in its power and less and less in her own.

Elizabeth told Marianne Moore very little about these troubles, but Moore was sensitive enough to see that Elizabeth desperately needed to settle somewhere, to belong to a place with no more than a few, not too onerous, obligations. With this in mind, she recommended Elizabeth for the first Lucy Martin Donnelly Fellowship from Bryn Mawr College, which Moore believed had a residence requirement and would provide Elizabeth with a salary and a place to live for the following year in a community less intimidating than the one she had found at Yaddo. The fellowship was awarded to her on March 7, a few days after she had left Yaddo, and in fact gave her twenty-five hundred dollars free and clear, requiring only two brief visits to the campus. At that, her vague plans for travel to Europe began to crystallize.

Despite her struggles with the atmosphere and her life there, Elizabeth was surprisingly productive while at Yaddo. Her first writing "binge" lasted until mid-November and astonished her in its intensity, coinciding for perhaps the only time in her life with an alcohol binge of equal intensity and duration. She told Edmund Wilson that she had begun work on her "third book," the second being all finished and put aside. Although the "eight poems" she said she had sold by early November do not quite tally with those she published in the following year, and although the "endless story" and an "endless poem about Key West" have disappeared (endless to Elizabeth seems to have meant, not "long," but "refusing to end"), her list of finished poems is impressive: the "modern dramatic sequence" of "Three Poems" (later "Four Poems," including "O Breath"); the "View of the Capitol from the Library of Congress," a wonderful bit of impressionism commenting indirectly on bureaucratic indirection; "Insomnia" (which Marianne Moore called "a cheap love poem"); "A Cold Spring"; and the astonishing double sonnet, "The Prodigal."

Elizabeth said that "The Prodigal" shared the method of "that spiritual exercise of the Jesuits—when they try to think in detail how the thing must have happened."[17] She had read the Ignatian spiritual exercises, but the poem sprang first, she said, from her thoughts when "one of my aunt's stepsons offered me a drink of rum, in the pig styes at about 9 in the morning," on her trip to Nova Scotia in 1946.[18] The poem also speaks painfully and eloquently to her own experience with alcoholism in 1950:

> The brown enormous odor he lived by
> was too close, with its breathing and thick hair,
> for him to judge. The floor was rotten; the sty
> was plastered halfway up with glass-smooth dung.
> Light-lashed, self-righteous, above moving snouts,
> the pigs' eyes followed him, a cheerful stare—
> even to the sow that always ate her young—
> till, sickening, he leaned to scratch her head.
> But sometimes mornings after drinking bouts
> (he hid the pints behind a two-by-four),
> the sunrise glazed the barnyard mud with red;

the burning puddles seemed to reassure.
And then he thought he almost might endure
his exile yet another year or more.

But evenings the first star came to warn.
The farmer whom he worked for came at dark
to shut the cows and horses in the barn
beneath their overhanging clouds of hay,
with pitchforks, faint forked lightnings, catching
    light,
safe and companionable as in the Ark.
The pigs stuck out their little feet and snored.
The lantern—like the sun, going away—
laid on the mud a pacing aureole.
Carrying a bucket along a slimy board,
he felt the bats' uncertain staggering flight,
his shuddering insights, beyond his control,
touching him. But it took him a long time
finally to make his mind up to go home.

When the poem appeared in the *New Yorker* on March 17, 1951, it drew universal compliments, even from the fastidious Moore, who in another time might have objected strenuously to the word "dung."

Elizabeth also wrote at Yaddo one poem to her asthma and the negotiations it demanded. She struggled with the meter and punctuation of "O Breath" to reflect the lung capacity and speaking pace of an asthma sufferer:

Beneath that loved   and celebrated breast,
silent, bored really   blindly veined,
grieves, maybe   lives and lets
live, passes   bets,
something moving   but invisibly,
and with what clamor   why restrained
I cannot fathom   even a ripple.

(See the thin flying   of nine black hairs
four around one   five the other nipple,
flying almost intolerably   on your own breath.)
Equivocal, but what we have in common's   bound to be
    there,
whatever we must own   equivalents for,
something that maybe I   could bargain with
and make a separate peace   beneath
within   if never with.

"O Breath" is the last in the group of tentative, tortured love lyrics
eventually called "Four Poems" and is read in that context as the
speaker's contemplation of her lover's chest and her seeing there
evidence of a fatal and final difference, a fundamental incompati-
bility. And yet, as the title suggests, the poem is also an apostrophe
to breathing itself, and the asthma ("with what clamor   why
restrained") becomes a symbol for the cautious, constrained relationship. The poem makes most sense if we think of both the
speaker, who speaks in the broken phrases of one running out of
air, and the subject, whose breath is "restrained," as "asthmatic,"
both unable to breathe, or love, freely. Thus, "what we have in
common's   bound to be there."

The poet David Wagoner, who was at Yaddo with Elizabeth,
memorialized the composition of the poem in his own "Poem about
Breath (*a memory of Elizabeth Bishop, 1950*)":

She was at work on a poem about breath.
She asked what punctuation might be strongest
For catching her breath, for breath catching
Halfway in her throat, between her straining breastbone
And her tongue, the bubbly catching of asthma. . . .

                              people with trouble breathing
Think about it, and breathe, and think about it.

They think too many times of clearing the air
They have to breathe, about the air already
Down there in their lungs, not going out
On time, in time, and when it's finally gone,
Not coming back to the place longing to keep it.

Each breath turns into a problem like a breath
In a poem that won't quite fit, giving the wrong
Emphasis to a feeling or breaking the rhythm
In a clumsy way, where something much more moving
Could happen to keep that poem moving and breathing.[19]

. . .

Elizabeth had planned to spend only a couple of weeks in New York after she left Yaddo on March 4, then leave for Europe right away, perhaps on March 20 and perhaps with Tom Wanning. The obligations attached to the Bryn Mawr fellowship helped change her plans, as did an award from the American Academy of Arts and Letters, which she was scheduled to receive on May 23—further incentive to stay in the country at least that long. She reported to Lowell, then living in Italy and constantly urging her to come, that Houghton Mifflin was pressuring her to complete the book before she left and that she had had a quarrel with the Internal Revenue Service serious enough, she said, that she would have been "arrested on the dock."[20] So she stayed to finish the book, sell a story or two, and, perhaps more important, be near enough to Dr. Anny Baumann to have help in trying to turn her life around.

Elizabeth spent March and April in New York hotels and at Jane Dewey's farm. Dewey worked during the day, and Elizabeth found herself each morning at half past seven in "imaginary possession" of the "huge estate," with three branches, or brooks, "to mix with her bourbon." In her return to Havre de Grace, she found the finishing touch for "A Cold Spring": "I saw a calf born on the

neighboring hillside the other day – and in ten minutes it was up
on its feet, and in an hour taking little jumps, up and down."[21]

A sublet apartment on East Sixty-ninth Street in New York was
home from May 1 until September 30, 1951, and the spring and
summer passed in fits and starts of work, travel, and socializing.
Elizabeth spent a good deal of time in Havre de Grace and in frequent visits to Anny Baumann's office for adjustments in her asthma
medication and to begin trying to conquer her chronic depression.
She struck up a friendship with a young man named David Newton
and kept up a schedule of dinners and lunches.

Her burning ambition for the summer was to visit Sable Island,
Nova Scotia, where her grandfather Hutchinson had been lost at
sea: "If I am not fulfilling my destiny and get wrecked, too, I think
I can turn it into an article or maybe a poem or two."[22] She had
high hopes for the journalistic essay she planned to write and had
spent the money she thought the *New Yorker* would pay her for it
long before she made her trip there. The Sable Island Tourist Board
welcomed her and arranged private transportation for her out to the
island, and after the trip and a few days at the Dalhousie University
archives in Halifax, she returned enthusiastic about the prospect of
the essay. But Dalhousie University stands directly across the bay
from her mother's hospital in Dartmouth, and perhaps because of
this, the essay remained unfinished. In any case, it stood as a symbol
of her inability to function in a New York world of deadlines and
attendant pressures to perform. The surviving draft is barely four
handwritten pages, a promising start but not at all worked over. At
only one point does it suggest the depth of the island's impression
on Elizabeth's imagination and its connection with the circumstances of her childhood:

> Anyone familiar with the accent of Nova Scotia will know what I
> mean when I refer to the Indrawn Yes. In all their conversations
> Nova Scotians of all ages, even children, make use of it. It consists
> of, when one is told a fact—anything, not necessarily tragic but

not of a downright comical nature,—saying "yes," or a word halfway between "yes" and "yeah," while drawing in breath at just the same time. It expresses both commiseration and an acceptance of the Worst; and it occurred to me as I walked along over those fine, fatalistic sands, that Sable Island with its mysterious engulfing powers was a sort of large scale expression of the Indrawn Yes.

The expression of the Indrawn Yes finally found its medium when she finished "The Moose," her deepest consideration of her Nova Scotia, twenty years later.

Elizabeth returned from Canada convinced that she would not settle in New York but still unclear about immediate plans. She spent a week at Dennis, Massachusetts, with Randall and Mackie Jarrell and then a final month, September, being miserable in New York. By mid-October, after another stay in Havre de Grace and in New York hotels, she had made up her mind, at Anny Baumann's insistence. On Friday, October 26, she would board a freighter for Tierra del Fuego and the Straits of Magellan and, eventually, for a trip around the world to Europe. Her first stop on this ambitious and solitary journey would be Rio de Janeiro, where she would visit Pearl Kazin, then staying in Rio with her new husband, Victor Kraft, and Mary Morse and Lota de Macedo Soares. Elizabeth did not leave on October 26—a dock strike delayed her passage—but on November 10 she boarded the SS *Bowplate* in New York harbor and headed South.

Ten

ELIZABETH MAY HAVE left New York convinced that she had no options, but she had enough of a sense of purpose to make her trip around the world a writer's trip. Her shipboard notebook is systematic in its consideration of her immediate surroundings and her intentions for the future, of the trivial ("Sidewise [as I see them lying in bed] the locks on my luggage look like John Foster Dulles. [speaking]"), and of the more serious:

> The flying-fish remind me sometimes of falling stars – falling stars, flying stars, or a procession of meteors? – I think I just read a description of such somewhere, but where was it – a sort of flock of meteors progressing together, silently, then vanishing. Something unearthly about them – flying saucer-ish – phantom skipped stones – skipped stones in dreams.

These images figure in the poem she drafted as the first entry in her trip notebook, first titled "P. P. H." (underlined three times) and then called "Crossing the Equator: P. H." The poem is a conversation, presumably with the late Pauline Pfeiffer Hemingway, who had died suddenly in California on October 1, about death, hard choices, and the reasons for the trip. Elizabeth's notebook draft is very rough, though she talked about the poem for a long time after, as if she had meant to finish it:

> You set off, sweetie, (as you said), to the stars . . .
>   like a dream of skipping stones,
> or skipping sapphires, rather. . . .
>
> Do not blame me if
> I choose geography,
> perhaps just because it's easy – . . .
>
> We imagine an horizon, and it hardens
> into faultless definition: the horizon.
> It begins to illustrate imagination.
> Dear, other things that we imagined
> were not often so obliging.
> Still the horizon is unbroken.

The draft approaches the "questions of travel" Elizabeth began to articulate over the next seven or eight years.

Elizabeth left the United States for South America contemplating, along with the reflections of "moonlight in league boots" on the waters of the Atlantic, questions of lifestyle and identity, specifically of a lesbian lifestyle as it might relate to her public and private identity. For one thing, she was trying to write a review for the *New Republic*, a kind of companion piece to the one on Emily Dickinson's letters to the Hollands, of a new book called *The Riddle of Emily Dickinson*. Interest in Dickinson was rising now that Thomas Johnson's restoration of the texts of her poems and letters was under way and well publicized. Elizabeth later said that she had little appreciation for Dickinson's poems before the Johnson edition appeared, though that statement underrepresents the number of references to Dickinson in Elizabeth's notebooks and the obvious interest that would prompt her to write these two reviews.

The example of Dickinson's self-contained artistic life, like Marianne Moore's, must have appealed to Elizabeth in her struggle to find a way to live as a poet. Rebecca Patterson's search in *The Riddle of Emily Dickinson* for the figure behind Dickinson's great outpouring of poems led her to Catherine Scott Anthon, whom she took to be the love of Dickinson's lonely and sequestered life. In Bishop's outraged review, she allowed that this thesis might be "partially true"—she apparently did not object to the notion that Dickinson might have fallen in love with another woman—but she was furious at the reductiveness of all such explanations. On the point of a great change in her own life, she found the book "finally just unpleasant": "Perhaps it is because, in order to reach a single reason for anything as singular and yet manifold as literary creation, it is necessary to limit the human personality's capacity for growth and redirection to the point of mutilation."[1] In her notebook, Elizabeth says only that she is "finishing that awful review." But her defensiveness here perhaps indicates the need for a reevaluation of her own life and choices.

By the second day of her trip, Elizabeth had also become fascinated by a passenger, Miss Breen:

> Miss Breen, with whom I share a bath, is almost 6 ft. tall—enormous, rather vague in speech, manner, & shape—large blue eyes & bluish-white waved hair. There is something very appealing about her, but I can't quite place it—something wistful, perhaps. She was "head of the Women's Jail" in Detroit for 26 years—has been retired 4, I think & has obviously had the exact day-dream of travel that I have had, down to the slightest detail of scenery, birds, etc.—This has come out gradually, but so accurately that we are both self-conscious about it now. She has a sort of muffled voice & manner—extremely kind to the rest—She confessed, after much goading by Miss Lyton (?) about people who led "interesting lives," that she <u>had</u> been "written up," "with photographs" in "<u>True Detective Stories</u>". Most of her stories hinge, in her muffled, apologetic way, on murder. She speaks a lot

to me of her "roommate," for many years, I gather – a woman lawyer named Ida, who has recently come back from setting up a Woman's Police Force in Southern Korea.

Miss Breen received her second widest bit of notoriety from Elizabeth in "Arrival at Santos": "Miss Breen is about seventy, / a retired police lieutenant, six feet tall, / with beautiful bright blue eyes and a kind expression. / Her home, when she is at home, is in Glens Fall // s, New York." (The local paper in Glens Falls noted with pleasure the poem's publication in the *New Yorker* of June 21, 1952.) But what Elizabeth got from this brief acquaintance was a vision of an accomplished and successful lesbian life, not at all secretive or ashamed, at a time when she was herself at a major transition, a moment of courageous "growth and redirection" unprecedented in her life.

This trip is a "shake-down" trip for me, all right. I know I am feeling, thinking, looking, sleeping, dreaming, eating & drinking better than in a long long time, & when I read something like "The question about time is how change is related to the changeless" – & look around – it doesn't seem so hard or far off. The nearer clouds seem to be moving quite rapidly; those in back of them are motionless – Watching the ship's wake we seem to be going fast, but watching the sky or the horizon, we are just living here with the engines pulsing, forever.

That she should so soon glimpse freedom from her anxiety about time—apparent in early poems such as "Paris, 7 A.M." and "Verdigris," or in letters and notebooks, or in the essay, recalled here, "Time's Andromedas"—to rest comfortably in the paradox of time both flying and standing still, was the first sign of how deeply a life in Brazil would agree with her. The fascination with Miss Breen suggests that Elizabeth was ready to come to some resolution about her sexuality, at least as far as it related to how and with whom she would live her life.

Elizabeth noted on November 21 that the ship had "crossed the Equator some time in the night. I sat out on deck between 3 & 4— quite rough, ½ a moon—masses of soft, oily-looking stars & a damp wind." This compelling passage, the "rush / to see the sun the other way around," is recorded in "Questions of Travel" and seems related to the positive reversal dreamed of in "Insomnia," written at Yaddo the previous winter. The poem credits the moon with the courage to remake her life:

> By the Universe deserted,
> *she*'d tell it to go to hell,
> and she'd find a body of water,
> or a mirror, on which to dwell.
> So wrap up care in a cobweb
> and drop it down the well
>
> into that world inverted
> where left is always right,
> where the shadows are really the body,
> where we stay awake all night,
> where the heavens are as shallow as the sea
> is now deep, and you love me.

The reversal was a renewal, and learning to see the sun and stars from the opposite side, though it was disorienting ("I don't know whether it's a good idea to have to change all one's names for everything so late in life!"),[2] was also liberating. To see the world from the other side may also be a privilege or task of acknowledging, at least to herself, her passion for women.

On the afternoon of the twenty-sixth, the passengers caught their first glimpse of the coast of Brazil, just south of Rio de Janeiro, on their way to their first port of call, Santos. Elizabeth and Miss Breen, by now fast friends, were the only passengers leaving the ship at Santos, and the "funny little tender" with its "nice, elderly Negro pilot" steered them through the "26 or so" other ships and dropped them on the mercy of the enormous customshouse. The first of many serendipitous events in Elizabeth's life in Brazil occurred when she and Miss Breen were met and escorted quickly through customs by Miss Breen's friends from her Detroit days, Mr. and Mrs. Brito. The Britos whisked the travelers and all their bags right to São Paulo, secured Elizabeth a hotel room, helped her get a train ticket to Rio, and got Mary Morse on the telephone for her. Thus freed of tedious details, her first walk in a Brazilian city was memorable and humorously typical:

> I went out to find a hairdresser & some lunch & got lost over & over – it's the most confusing city I've ever been in, I think, & with the worst traffic – well, maybe Mexico City is as bad that way. This idea that the people speak English is completely erroneous—even at the hotel the man who's supposed to really doesn't – One druggist almost had me on a <u>bus</u> before I could stop him – I finally just took to my heels & ran. A large dept. store <u>Mappin</u> – rather like a small Wanamakers' – has an <u>Elizabeth Arden</u> salon – it all cost about 4.00. The shampoo <u>girl</u> breathed heavily on me – I <u>can't</u> order food & fainting with hunger lunched on a tiny roast beef sandwich & coca cola. Thank goodness for coca cola even if I don't like it much.

The flowers, especially orchids, struck her, as did the coffee, the magnificent array of fruit at every meal, and the efficiency and helpfulness of the maids in the hotel. She also found herself emboldened by the new circumstances.

> I took a cab to the huge Versailles-in-yellow Museum – it was raining – the museum was closed – however I did something I wd. never have dreamed of doing in the "States." Some men were being let in, & I just walked right in & although nobody could understand anybody, someone finally started, very graciously, considering, showing me around, unlocking doors, opening window-blinds, etc. The Indian stuff was marvelous.

That evening she left São Paulo for Rio, escorted to her train by Miss Breen and the Britos.

From the window of the train, Elizabeth got her first glimpse of the landscape that would fascinate her for twenty years:

> Brilliant scenery suddenly appeared, in sunlight – a long section of huge perfectly round hills like domes of St. Peters' – grass-covered, enormous, completely impractical landscape, somehow. One had a little tile-roofed shed on top & a fence around the house, & was dotted all over with cows & horses who had eaten almost all the grass off it – it looked like some mysterious type of Noah's Ark. [A sketch in the margin, looking indeed like an ark.] But I felt from the minute I opened my eyes that if I'd been dumped there from the sky I'd know right away I could be in no place but South America.
>
> A feathery quality to the landscape – the grass has that bright but sparse look of Mexican grass – the lush banana trees, etc., – but against the sky the bamboos & flamboyants & all the Lent trees – rather pale & lacy, slightly Chinese – & this effect appears in all the old engravings, I think.

The Brazil that greeted Elizabeth in late 1951 was in the second of Getúlio Vargas's two political reigns, stalled at the end of a long period of expansion, change, and struggles to plan for the disposition of the country's tremendous natural resources. Less than half the population was literate (and half of those were under the voting age); yellow fever and malaria had only recently been eradicated from Rio. Brazilian culture, as Elizabeth was able to glimpse it early on, attracted her as Moroccan, Mexican, and Haitian culture had attracted her, not for its political progressiveness, but for its population of relatively primitive, uneducated people whose lives were governed by a dynamic, creative religion. Regulated by the powerful Catholic church, the religion actually practiced by the lower classes in Brazil was a potent mix of the Catholic, Indian, and African traditions expressed in art that was primitive and often tasteless but, at its best, earnestly put forth and strangely beautiful. The society, Elizabeth said, was essentially feudal—by which she meant that the small landowning upper class both lived off of and provided a living for the large underclass, creating households consisting of the typically large Brazilian extended family and the multiracial extended families of their servants. For the chronically lonely Elizabeth, such continually available company took her back to her warm memories of Great Village and the extended household of her grandparents. That her status as a wealthy white woman put these people in some sense under her control made the situation ideal—she liked to be waited on. The "atmosphere of uncritical affection" gave her what she had been starving for since the age of five.

Mary Morse and Pearl Kazin met Elizabeth's train in Rio on the morning of November 30, 1951, and Mary took Elizabeth up to the eleventh floor corner apartment that she and Lota de Macedo Soares shared in the Leme district, overlooking the Copacabana and the Sugar Loaf—"fantastic, improbable, & impractical scenery." After two days of touring Rio in Lota's Jaguar, the three women headed to Petrópolis, sixty miles inland from Rio in the mountains, to see the house that Lota and Mary were building on a spectacular piece of steep, rocky land. It was called "Fazenda Samambaia" (a *fazenda* is a wealthy farm or country estate; a *samambaia* is a giant fern).

Maria Carlota Costellat de Macedo Soares was a year older than Elizabeth, the daughter of a prominent and powerful Brazilian newspaperman. She had been born in Paris and educated in convents, and like most educated upper-class Brazilians, she conducted her life in at least three languages, Portuguese, English, and French. A woman of tremendous ability, Soares was unappreciated in her native country and constantly in need of something to do to occupy her enormous energy. Mary Morse had come to South America in 1941 on a ballet company tour and had met Lota in Rio. She had made a home in Brazil by 1951 and still lives there today.

Lota and Mary had turned their Rio apartment over to Elizabeth for her stay, which lasted until the next passage of her freighter line for Buenos Aires on January 26. But Elizabeth found Rio depressing, "a mess," and despite her intentions to stay there and work, she was more and more drawn to the half-finished house and fantastic scenery of Samambaia and the company of her hosts. Lota's imperious and effective supervision of the workmen, the very idea of building one's house to suit oneself on the very spot of earth where one would choose to live, could not help but compel Elizabeth. She was there on December 12 for the customary celebration when the roof was put on and heard the drunken workmen shout, "Viva Dona Lota! Viva Dona Morse! Viva la choppe [draft beer]!"

Elizabeth managed to begin "Arrival at Santos" in mid-December, gathering the prose impressions she had been recording—the "frilly" impractical scenery, Miss Breen, the tender, the port. But her thoughts kept returning to the great change taking place in her life. In her notebook, she wrote out a chant, or a prayer-poem, in her usual ambiguously affirmative manner, but more affirmative than she had ever been before:

> I believe:
> that the steamship will support me on the water,
> & that the aeroplane will conduct me over the mountain,
> that perhaps I shall not die of cancer,
> or in the poorhouse,
> that eventually I shall see things in a "better light,"
> that I shall continue to read and continue to write,
> that I shall continue to laugh until I cry with a certain few friends.
> that love will unexpectedly appear over & over again,
> that people will continue to do kind deeds that astound me.

Sometime between December 12 and Christmas Day, Elizabeth sampled the exotic fruit of the Brazilian cashew tree (*cajú*) and fell violently ill with an allergic reaction—"Quincke edema," Anny Baumann called it. Elizabeth's face swelled horribly so she could not see, and her hands swelled so she could not write. Three weeks later, after unsuccessful attempts at treatment by Brazilian doctors, the reaction had subsided into constant asthma and eczema "on my ears and hands – just the way I had it as a child but I've never had it since." Bedridden in Petrópolis, Elizabeth was astounded by the outpouring of attention and concern given her by Lota and Mary and the many servants and members of their household; she was sure that her being ill had endeared her to them. By mid-January, she had decided to stay and be taken care of for at least another month, and she put off her departure for Buenos Aires to the end of February. From her sickbed she wrote to Anny Baumann, "Aside from my swelled head and the asthma I feel fine & although it is tempting Providence to say so I suppose, happier than I have felt in ten years."[3] By February 10, she had admitted that the idea of continuing her trip, or of going back to the United States, was further and further from her mind. For her birthday on February 8, a neighbor who procured animals for zoos had given her "the dream of my life," a toucan, which she named, in a burst of Yankee pride, "Uncle Sam." Together they settled into Samambaia, the large estate (consisting primarily of undeveloped land) that had come to Lota Soares through her family. By April, Elizabeth was headed back to New York, with Lota, to make a last, obligatory visit to Bryn Mawr and to close her North American life and arrange for the shipping of her possessions to Brazil.

The life that Elizabeth was leaving in New York and the United States held little nostalgia for her. She arranged to stop over in Miami to see Marjorie Stevens in Key West, and get the books stored there. In New York, she said a difficult good-bye to an aging Marianne Moore and received assurances from Anny Baumann that she would be available for consultation and prescriptions through the international mails. Elizabeth also said good-bye to Anna B. Lindsay and Tom Wanning. Beyond those, there was no one (and nothing) she would not rather leave behind. The six years (1945–1951) in which her life had been centered on New York and its racing, competitive literary scene had offered her little personal sustenance. And her life in Brazil, having an opposite emphasis, was already taking shape. By the time the two women had left for New York, Lota Soares had offered to build Elizabeth a writing studio on the hillside behind the new house, next to the stream, and it must have seemed to her that all the practical considerations of living as a writer were about to be addressed. She would not live alone; she would not have to get a job (the income from her father's estate would keep her in Brazil as it could not in the United States); she would be out of reach of the dissipating influences (and opportunities to exercise her habit of self-denigrating comparison) of the New York literary "scene"; and in the "timeless" Brazilian world she would be free at last from the pace of New York, which had seemed to her a dizzying plunge toward loss and death. The very impracticality and inefficiency of the Brazilian way of doing things charmed her thoroughly and seemed to indicate that here, anyway, one could control the rate of one's decline. By the time they returned to Rio on June 7, she was glad to be "home." On June 21, "Arrival at Santos" appeared in the *New Yorker,* with its luminous last line, "We are driving to the interior," suggesting an agenda for her future.

Elizabeth thanked Anny Baumann numerous times over the years for encouraging her to leave New York for South America. Baumann may have seen that Elizabeth was at a critical pass in her life, that her alternatives were really very few. But even Dr. Baumann probably did not foresee the tremendous success of this experiment or the impact of Lota Soares on Elizabeth's life. Like Marjorie Stevens, Soares was prepared to provide the economic means for Elizabeth to write, and this time Elizabeth was prepared to accept them. In her notebook, she remarked dryly, "Sometimes it seems – this is probably profoundly untrue but anyway – sometimes it seems – as though only intelligent people are stupid enough to fall in love, & only stupid people are intelligent enough to let themselves be loved." Perhaps in these new circumstances she was indulging her "stupid," passive side, finding in it the "intelligence" finally to let herself be loved.

Lota Soares and Mary Morse remained friends, and if there was unease in this triangle with the compelling figure of Lota at its center, it is not apparent. Lota called Elizabeth "Cookie" and Mary "Morsey," and Cookie and Morsey figure almost equally in the few English letters of Soares's that survive. At first, Elizabeth and Lota moved into the Petrópolis house in its half-finished state, while Mary kept the apartment on the Avenida Atlántica in Rio. A few years later, however, Soares gave Morse land and helped her build a house just down the hill from her own, and Morse lived with them throughout the construction. From the time Morse adopted the first of her four daughters early in 1961, the traffic between the two households made them almost one. Elizabeth and Mary were the two heirs to Soares's estate when she died in 1967, with Morse inheriting Samambaia and the house, and Elizabeth the Rio apartment.

In August 1952, Marianne Moore closed a letter to Elizabeth by offering love to her "(and to Lota if that is permissible)."[4] In her reply, Elizabeth enclosed "The Shampoo":

The still explosions on the rocks,
the lichens, grow
by spreading, gray, concentric shocks.
They have arranged
to meet the rings around the moon, although
within our memories they have not changed.

And since the heavens will attend
as long on us,
you've been, dear friend,
precipitate and pragmatical;
and look what happens. For Time is
nothing if not amenable.

The shooting stars in your black hair
in bright formation
are flocking where,
so straight, so soon?
—Come let me wash it in this big tin basin,
battered and shiny like the moon.

"The Shampoo" made the rounds for several years before it was finally published in the *New Republic* in July 1955. The *New Yorker* turned it down, as did *Poetry,* and one wonders if the editors found themselves unable to recognize this new Bishop tone or unable to accept what is clearly a love poem between women. As a love poem, it stands in remarkable contrast to her earlier attempts in its ability to find a place to celebrate within the conflicts and potential losses of love. Its scene, the pool in the stream behind Lota's house; its ostensible subject, the two symmetrical bright streaks of gray in Lota's long black hair (an earlier draft is titled "Gray Hairs"); its real subject, Elizabeth's gentle truce with the passage of time ("Time is / nothing if not amenable"); and the easy intimacy of the final lines were all newly acquired pleasures that came to her with Brazil, along with shiny tin basins for carrying water and rocks with many-colored lichens growing on them. In a letter written in the same month, she remarked with pleasure on how much easier it was to live "exactly as one wants to" in Brazil.[5] And no small part of that ease was her ability to find a relatively still, safe sanctuary in the inevitable passage of time toward death. "Within our memories," the lichens are the same as they always were, though we know objectively that they "grow." The shooting stars of gray in Lota's hair are evidence of decline; the tender ritual of hair washing is a timeless gift. Elizabeth said that the streaks of gray made Lota look "exactly like a chickadee,"[6] and years later she recalled a hot night when "Lota woke me up in the middle of the night to go out and look at the stars because they had never looked so close before–close and warm, apparently touching our hair–and never so many–."[7]

. . .

Not surprisingly, among the tropical molds and mildews, Elizabeth suffered constantly from asthma in her first months in Brazil and did until she consented to try a complicated and expensive cortisone therapy. But her attitude toward the condition was much changed. By August 1952, she was considering her asthma a useful ballast, "like sandbags in a balloon," to keep her from floating too high on her recent happiness. But weeks of difficult breathing caused her to reconsider, and by mid-September she had decided to try the cortisone by injection and by mouth (cortisone inhalers had not yet been invented). The results were phenomenal—she could breathe—though she struggled with the powerful drug's side effects, jitters and sleeplessness during a period of "euphoria," followed by a plunge in spirits as she went off the drug. Elizabeth's early cortisone treatments were managed from afar by Anny Baumann, and knowledge of its effects and side effects was still incomplete. Indeed, even today doctors know little about how corticosteroids do their miraculous and multifaceted work. But the drug manipulated her emotions enough that Elizabeth grew afraid of it, and eventually, despite the good results, she refused to take it. In the early months, however, the sleeplessness induced by the drug combined with a period of furious creativity, and she wrote—primarily autobiographical prose—all day and all night and reported herself delighted with the cortisone's effect. The management of her asthma was her chief medical concern during her first months and years in Brazil, to be followed somewhat later by a concentrated attempt to control her drinking with aversion therapy in the form of Antabuse.

As Elizabeth settled into life in Petrópolis, she felt called on to defend her decision to stay there. Although she could not bring herself to say, "I am here because the one I love is here," Lota figures in all Elizabeth's explanations. To Joe and U. T. Summers, she said how much she liked living in Brazil, but not "because it's Brazil, particularly."[8] To Marianne Moore, who continually urged her to "come home," Elizabeth extolled "the really lofty vagueness of Brazil, where no one seems to know quite what season it is, or what day of the week, or anyone's real name." She said she had read Moore's poems to Lota in the evenings when she first arrived in Brazil, "something I should never dare to do on the other side of the Equator, I know, but here it seemed easier to."[9] To Robert Lowell, Elizabeth offered a couple of explanations:

> I started out intending to go all over the continent but I seem to have become a Brazilian home-body, and I get just as excited now over a jeep trip to buy kerosene in the next village as I did in November at the thought of my trip around the Horn. I wasn't even particularly interested in Brazil to start with, but it was my freighter's first stop – in fact I wanted to go around the world ending up about now [visiting] you only they had made some mistake about my reservations on that freighter, so I haphazardly settled on South America.[10]

Elizabeth liked to say that most of what she had "decided" to do in her life had happened by accident or chance; one suspects that there was more intention in her decision to visit Brazil that she lets on here. Later, challenged by Lowell (who was writing from his own improbable outpost, Amsterdam), she defended her decision more briskly:

> I don't feel "out of touch" or "expatriated" or anything like that, or suffer from lack of intellectual life, etc – I was always too shy to have much "intercommunication" in New York, anyway, and I was miserably lonely there most of the time – here I am extremely happy, for the first time in my life. I live in a spectacularly beautiful place; we have between us about 3,000 books now; I know, through Lota, most of the Brazilian "intellectuals" already and I find the people frank, – startlingly so, until you get used to Portuguese vocabularies – extremely affectionate – an atmosphere that I just lap up – no I guess I mean loll in – after that dismal year in Washington and that dismaler winter at Yaddo when I thought

my days were numbered and there was nothing to be done about it. – I arrived to visit Lota just at the point where she really wanted someone to stay with her in the new house she was building. We'd known each other well in New York but I hadn't seen her for five or six years [*sic*]. She wanted me to stay: she offered to build me a studio – picture enclosed – I certainly didn't really want to wander around the world in a drunken daze for the rest of my life – so it's all fine & dandy.

But Brazil is really a horror – but sometimes I must tell you more.[11]

To Anny Baumann, Elizabeth was even more frank:

The drinking seems to have dwindled to about one evening once or twice a month, and I stop before it gets really bad, I think. . . . I get to worrying about the past ten years or so and I wish I could stop doing that but . . . the drinking and the working both seem to have improved miraculously. Well no it isn't miraculous really – it is almost entirely due to Lota's good sense and kindness. I still feel I must have died and gone to heaven without deserving to, but I am getting a little more used to it.[12]

Even though within a year or so she sought help in controlling her drinking (at Lota's insistence), it is impossible to overestimate the transformation that her removal to Brazil and her alliance with Lota Soares wrought in Elizabeth. Although she was not instantly cured of her depression, her asthma, or her alcoholism, she took her boldest efforts yet in getting them under control. Those efforts brought her substantial relief for the next ten years.

Eleven

BY THE FALL OF 1952, Elizabeth was saying that she had already done "more work in this last stretch than in several years." To work was to write, and suddenly she was writing about her childhood. She found it odd that she should have "total recall" about Nova Scotia in its geographical mirror image, Brazil; but she did. And what she recalled came out in prose. After "Arrival at Santos" and "The Shampoo," she managed only "The Mountain" as a poetic exploration of Brazil in her early years there. It is perhaps her weakest published poem, and she abandoned the attempt to write about Brazil until after *Poems: North & South—A Cold Spring* had appeared in 1955. She launched several short stories about the country, none of which she ever finished, but she was writing frankly autobiographical prose "like mad." In rapid succession she completed "Gwendolyn," her marvelously evocative account of her childhood fascination with frail, dying Gwendolyn Appletree; and "In the Village," the story she had been trying to write for twenty-five years, of Gertrude Bishop's last breakdown and her own loss. Both she wrote directly on the typewriter (she had never done that before), and she said she produced "In the Village" in two nights and under the influence of "a combination of cortisone and the gin and tonic I had in the middle of the night"; she thought each story was more the product of inspiration than composition.[1] The *New Yorker* accepted them both, though Katharine White had to argue with the other editors to have "In the Village" treated as a "prose-poem" and therefore exempt from the magazine's rigorous standards of "accuracy" and verisimilitude. There were to be more stories in this fragmentary and slightly fictionalized autobiography—she eventually published "Memories of Uncle Neddy" and left fairly complete drafts of "Primer Class" and "The Country Mouse" among her papers—but in the rush of memory that accompanied her settling in Brazil, she completed only these two. In letters as well she began to reminisce, almost fondly, about her northern past. Writing to Lowell, who was staying with friends at Duxbury, Massachusetts, she recalled, "I also visited there with my mother at the age of three – we visited a Mrs. Tewksbury of Duxbury – and I had chicken-pox."[2] She thought it would be a "wonderful place to live," and twenty years later spent happy days and weeks at the home of John Malcolm Brinnin in the picturesque coastal town.

Elizabeth's difficulty with writing poetry about Brazil, combined with her enthusiasm for her recent prose, made her think that her next book would be a volume of short stories. Robert Lowell was already urging her to combine stories and poems—perhaps to help her fill out, finish, and move past the book she had waiting at Houghton Mifflin. He included his own "91 Revere Street" in *Life Studies* in 1958; "In the Village" eventually "filled out" *Questions of Travel* in 1965. Elizabeth arranged to have the stories retyped in New York by May Swenson, then working as a secretary and desperately needing money. In the end, there were only seven completed stories (Elizabeth insisted there would be a dozen), and Houghton Mifflin, with some confusion, refused the project.

Paul Brooks of Houghton Mifflin finally found her in December 1952, writing to inquire about the status of her poetry manuscript and, incidentally, to congratulate her on the eight-hundred-dollar Shelley Memorial Award she had won that fall. He had been holding eighteen poems (Elizabeth oddly insisted that there were twenty-four, though her own table of contents listed only eighteen) intended for her second book, now tentatively titled *Concordance,* for nearly four years in the face of absolute silence from Elizabeth much of the time. In three more years of negotiations, she added only "Arrival at Santos" and "The Shampoo" (and resurrected "Letter to N.Y.," which she had discarded from *North & South*) to the volume, arguing that her new work, as yet unfinished, was different in tone and content from her pre-Brazil poems. In fact, "Arrival at Santos" and especially "The Shampoo" are themselves departures—and give the volume as it was finally published a strange, forward-looking lift at the end. After tedious misunderstandings and delays on both sides, Houghton Mifflin decided there were simply too few poems; Elizabeth at one point insisted that she had *measured* them and that the new volume was as long as *North & South,* or would be as soon as she finished "After the Rain" and "Crossing the Equator," which she could not do. Houghton Mifflin solved the problem by reissuing *North & South* at the same time. The combined volume was called *Poems: North & South—A Cold Spring* and turned out to have been a happy compromise when the book won the 1956 Pulitzer Prize.

But on the way to that compromise, agreed on finally in April 1954, Elizabeth quarreled with her publisher about formats and deadlines, promised poems that she could not deliver, and finally said she would never write a poem against a deadline again. But she conceded that most of her problems with Houghton Mifflin had been her own fault and vowed to pay attention to the progress of her "career" as she never had before; her book would not be published unless she insisted that it be published and made her wishes promptly known. But she was much easier in general about the pace of her writing. Elizabeth Bishop wrote no more poems in Brazil than she had in New York; but she had the luxury of taking her long fallow periods in stride. As long as Soares's money held out (later she was land-poor and constantly short of cash), no one asked

Elizabeth what she had or had not written, what had or had not been accepted. This freedom from the pressures of expectations, deadlines, and finances was a great gift that lasted for several years and was reinforced by periodic grants and prizes, often unsolicited, as the Shelley Award had been.

Getting *A Cold Spring* out and behind her was an important milestone for Elizabeth. She felt badly about the "misbegotten little book" from the start, though she acknowledged that it contained her best poems to date in "At the Fishhouses" and "Over 2000 Illustrations and a Complete Concordance." When the book appeared in August 1955, it met general acclaim, and most critics saw a move forward in her writing between the two volumes. Richard Eberhart writing in the *New York Times Books Review* noted that the later poems had a more "confessional" tone; Howard Nemerov commended her for moving generally "away from thought and towards vision." To Donald Hall, she was "one of the best poets alive." Only Anthony Hecht found the newer poems inferior to the old ones. Edward Honig writing in *Partisan Review* disliked both volumes, and his review was negative enough that the editors wrote to warn Elizabeth, one of their best contributors, and to apologize. Honig's charge that Bishop's poems treated trivial subjects said more about him as a reader than Bishop as a poet, but she had so often criticized herself on those counts that despite the overwhelmingly positive response, she once again felt that she had not yet written "real" poems and that the Pulitzer should have gone to Randall Jarrell. She tolerated the review well enough, she thought, but despaired at what it might have done to her had it happened when she was in New York a few years before.

When "O Premio Pulitzer" was announced in May 1956, Elizabeth found herself something of a celebrity in Petrópolis; having acquired a vocation with tangible results, she was now definitively a *poeta*—a title of honor among Brazilians. She was especially relieved that Lota would no longer have to convince her friends that the *Americana* really did write poems.

As you probably knew before I did [she wrote to May Swenson in New York] – I received the Pulitzer, to my great surprise. A man from O GLOBO, a Rio paper, got me on the telephone day before yesterday, in the AM. I was all alone except for the cook at the time and I'm afraid she was not sufficiently impressed. It was rather fun, though – after lunch reporters and photographers (Lota had said NO photographers, since we're both camera shy, but they came anyway) arrived, six or seven of them, and stayed until six, and we were ready for bed when they left. It rained steadily – Lota had just had the wooden floors waxed and the marble ones washed, and yesterday they were absolutely a mess – muddy footprints, cigarette butts, old flash-bulbs, etc., everywhere. We're all – i.e., Lota, another friend, the cat, the cook's baby, etc., appearing in the Brazilian newsreel next week and will undoubtedly look horrible. Except the cat – he likes photographers.[3]

But her favorite story of the Pulitzer had an opposite message:

Lota went to market, to our regular vegetable man, and he asked her if it wasn't my photograph he'd seen in the papers. She said yes, and he said it was simply amazing what good luck his customers had. Why, just the week before, one of his customers had bought a ticket in the lottery and won a bicycle.[4]

. . .

Among the literary discoveries of Elizabeth's first few months in Brazil was *Minha Vida de Menina* (My Life as a Young Girl), the diary of one "Helena Morley" (Dona Alice Brant) between the ages of thirteen and fifteen in the Brazilian village of Diamantina in the mid-1890s. Elizabeth undertook to translate the book, which had been published to popular and critical acclaim in Brazil in 1942, first as a way of practicing her Portuguese. But as she began to read, she was taken by Helena's telling of the stories of her childhood. Life in Diamantina in 1893 bears unmistakable resemblance to life "In the Village" in Nova Scotia in 1916, though Elizabeth had hardly begun translating Helena when she wrote the story. Helena lives in an extended family of half-Brazilian, half-English diamond miners who have almost no money but maintain a resourceful gentility in the isolated town. She is not at all an Elizabeth figure; sturdy and outgoing, unscholarly and vain, she is rather a type Elizabeth admired. But Elizabeth said that when she had trouble translating some of Helena's grandmother's pithy pieces of advice, she tried to remember what her own beloved Gammie would have said. Elizabeth also said specifically that Diamantina reminded her of Great Village. The happy coincidence of her discovery of the diary and her renewed interest in childhood—her own and others'—combined to make *The Diary of Helena Morley,* as it was titled when Farrar, Straus, and Cudahy published it in 1957, a consuming labor of love for Elizabeth. For five years, she devoted her literary energy to the project to the exclusion of almost all other work.

She promoted the book with Houghton Mifflin until, once again, her inopportune silences and the publisher's lack of real interest led Elizabeth to seize the initiative as she had not before and hire an agent to see after her interests in New York. On Bernice Baumgarten's advice, Elizabeth let it be known that only the publisher of the diary would publish her next, as yet unwritten, volume of poetry. And though in the end it all soured somewhat, as she quarreled with Alice Brant and her husband over what little money there was to be made off the book, she never lost her fascination for the clever, resourceful Helena Morley and her innocent facility with language. Elizabeth's introduction to the volume, at thirty-five pages nearly her longest piece of published prose, is also her strongest and the first of her several attempts to explain Brazil to outsiders. In it, she says that her favorite entry in the diary is, not surprisingly, Helena's soliloquy on the uncertainties of time, November 5, 1893. There she tells the story of her mother's attempt to tell time when only men could wear watches, getting her daughters out of bed for four o'clock mass at midnight because the rooster had already crowed twice. Says Elizabeth in the introduction:

> I like to think of the two tall, thin girls hanging onto their mother's arms, the three figures stumbling up the steep streets of the rocky, lightless little town beneath the cold bright moon and stars; and I can hear the surprised young soldier's voice, mama's polite reply, and then three pairs of footsteps scuttling home again over the cobblestones.

The story also recalls the early morning masses Elizabeth saw on her visit to Haiti in 1949.

Elizabeth admired the diary for its accuracy and detail and for the fact that "*it really happened;* everything did take place, day by day, minute by minute, once and only once, just the way Helena says it did."[5] In her translation she took pains to render Helena's fresh, idiomatic Portuguese accurately as well, and none of that immediacy is lost. This book by a stranger, in a strange genre and a strange language, became an almost perfect expression of Elizabeth's highest literary values. At the same time, her access to the child-consciousness of Helena helped give her access to her own.

. . .

After her rush to complete and publish the two Nova Scotia stories and her launching of a daily regimen of translating the diary's pages, Elizabeth found herself able to write very little formal prose or poetry, especially about Brazil. But her letter writing flourished. Within the first two years of her arrival in Brazil, she was maintaining major correspondences with Ilse and Kit Barker, Robert Lowell, Marianne Moore, Joseph and U. T. Summers, Loren MacIver and Lloyd Frankenberg, Anny Baumann, and May Swenson, in addition to two or three dozen other more casual or professional contacts. And as the circumstances of her life changed, the character of her letters changed as well. She grew expansive; some of her letters to the Barkers are among her longest pieces of prose. She grew unself-conscious about her subject matter and unconcerned with the lit-erariness of her own letters, though she maintained a high standard of seriousness and coherence for the genre and was a great admirer of the letters of Keats and Coleridge, among others. There are warmth and humor in these letters that nearly all her correspondents remembered years later. *"Abraços e saudades"*—roughly, "Hugs and greetings from far away"—became her regular closing, as these pen-friends became her only connection to her past and to the English-speaking world.

By this time, she had also realized that her letters might one day be collected (she proposed doing it herself in 1960; she and Lota were in need of money), and how her life might strike posterity became at least an occasional concern. But the strongest difference between her "before-" and "after-Brazil" letters is how, freed from anxiety about career and circumstances, she became concerned with the processes of life itself—the births, deaths, and marriages in Lota's extended family; the birthing of cats and dogs and the hatching of eggs; the snake in the bird's nest; the domestic tragedies unfolding in the cook's kitchen. After books—she read a great deal and rec-ommended books all around—the major subjects of Elizabeth's early letters from Brazil are landscape, cats, cars, and babies. And she let herself think that whereas she had usually had to choose between writing letters and writing poems, now writing letters was "like working without really doing it."[6]

She complained often in early letters that she found herself unable to write about Brazil, but there she was, doing it, "working" in the best sense, to learn what she thought about the country, to discover what tone she would take when she did come to write formal prose and poetry. As she always did, Elizabeth waited to acquire knowl-edge about Brazil—plunged into Darwin and Burton and *A Natu-ralist in Brazil*—before she wrote. But when she did write, she described what she had felt all along; "Brazil" was always known to

Elizabeth, insofar as it could be known at all, in armadillos and lizards, in recipes for manioc root and black beans, in "the crudest wooden footwear / and, careful and finicky, / the whittled fantasies of wooden cages." The investment of meaning in objects—a political and cultural synecdoche—was both the strength and weakness of Elizabeth's understanding of Brazil, but it served her well as a poet and as a letter writer.

> I am getting dull – it is hot in Rio, and heavy, and the beach is covered with bathers and umbrellas, etc. Last night I looked out and saw just at the water's edge, where the sand was wet, what looked like a large glowing coal or the remains of a small fire – the breakers came right up to it, almost around it and it throbbed and glowed. Finally I thought it must be some kind of red-phosphorescent jelly-fish; I could stand it no longer and went down – 11 floors – in the elevator and crossed the street and waded down to the water in the sand. Someone had dug a little pit, about 18 inches deep, and at the bottom of it there was a lighted candle. We don't know whether it was just a trick for someone to watch from an apartment, like me, to see how high the tide came or something – or maybe it was some kind of "macumba," voodoo – we see them around in the outskirts of town quite often, but usually there is a bottle of wine and a dead chicken, and bits of red wool, etc. – The nicest thing I saw on a drive yesterday was a man trying to sell papayas by the side of the road. He had them hung up by strings, like a little clothesline and an old bugle to his mouth, blew a <u>bugle call</u> and pointed majestically at the line of big sagging yellow fruits. I think they all are slightly crazy sometimes – (the cliché remark about Brazilians) – We stopped to buy oranges on our trip, about 8 A.M. – and while we bought, the man put on a victrola record on an old wind-up victrola standing in the ditch –[7]

In the management of their pets—Lota's dogs; Elizabeth's beloved cat, Tobias; Mary's cocker spaniel, Phillip—Elizabeth found a way to talk about a host of Brazilian shortcomings and an elemental cycle of life and death:

But two bitches are really too much...! If I had been here when these came – one was a gift & one a stray – I would certainly have had them spayed, being rather tough on that subject, but I arrived later and it is probably too late to have it done now. I had dear Tobias "altered" at six months because you really can't keep a Tom cat – but the whole idea of fancy pets is relatively new here and people are very much inclined to laisser faire anyway. They thought I was being mean to Tobias, who is now so beautiful, and NOT fat or lethargic – hunts all the time, and is almost too good a butcher—arranges little rows of gall-bladders and other portions of the mice he doesn't care for on the kitchen floor. But I am terribly worried for fear the Airedales will kill Phillip if we don't watch out and if their owners won't keep them at home. . . . They haven't the faintest idea how to treat pets, and imported them at I hate to think what expense – and they come all the way up here covered with burrs and bites and may get killed by snakes.[8]

As her connection to Lota's family grew, as she came to know well the five children of Lota's adopted son Kylso, and as Maria Elizabeth, the cook's daughter, was born on February 7, Elizabeth's letters become even more a compendium of information about child-rearing and child development and about the shortcomings of the Brazilian lower classes in this regard.

. . .

Elizabeth's health in the first half of her stay in Brazil was a continuing saga of asthma and its treatment. The major breakthrough in the management of chronic asthma—the introduction of corticosteroids into her therapy in 1952—gave her unprecedented relief from prolonged attacks, but the Brazilian environment of exotic molds and mildews, spectacular grasses and flowers, and clouds of blowing dust in the dry season also gave her those attacks. Between 1952 and 1954, she took oral and injected cortisone over four extended periods. She was subject to most of the drug's major side effects, including weight gain and extreme nervousness and sleeplessness, but for a time these seemed a reasonable price to pay to breathe freely. Whatever else the cortisone might have done to her, it always cleared her lungs. But taking cortisone over a long period in the spring of 1954, Elizabeth found herself unable to tolerate or make use of the "jag" of sleeplessness and nervousness (as she had been able to do in 1952, writing both "Gwendolyn" and "In the Village" under the spell of sufficient oxygen and a cortisone "high"), and she began to medicate that nervousness with alcohol. Because she was an alcoholic, she could not control this drinking on her own, and in June 1954 Lota insisted that she be admitted to the Hospital Estrangeiros in Rio to "rest" and dry out. There she began a program of aversion therapy using Antabuse, which she maintained, with a few lapses, until 1964. Lota Soares concerned herself with Elizabeth's drinking throughout their years together and was known to chastise Elizabeth's friends for encouraging her to drink. Realizing the pattern of the so-called binge alcoholic, or dipsomaniac, Lota tried to limit Elizabeth's access to large amounts of liquor. After 1961, when Lota was more and more away from home in her work for the city of Rio de Janeiro and Elizabeth was more and more alone, she fell gradually back into a pattern of destructive drinking.

Elizabeth said she felt less guilty about her drinking in Brazil and that this freedom from the self-hatred and shame she had always associated with her alcoholism made it easier for her to drink moderately and, with the help of Antabuse, not to drink at all. She and Robert Lowell exchanged recipes for nonalcoholic drinks and strategies for staying sober.

. . .

Elizabeth's days in her first couple of years in Brazil were spent at Samambaia for the most part, to some extent helping Lota supervise work on the house and gardens but more often just tagging along with Lota. Elizabeth awakened most mornings to a breakfast tray at seven brought to her by Maria, the cook. She liked to read in bed and began and ended each day reading, as did Lota. Between them, Elizabeth liked to say, they had more than three thousand books in their library and got all the American and British magazines and journals regularly, if late and often in the wrong order. After her studio—the little square room of her own up behind the house in a clump of bamboo—had been built in mid-1952, she generally spent her mornings there trying to finish the elusive piece about Sable Island or put into words her complex feelings about the strange country. When she found she could not do either of these things, she spent her hours in the studio writing letters, answering business correspondence, working on the Helena Morley translation, and dreaming of the traveling she and Lota would do together. On the wall before her, Elizabeth tacked photographs of Baudelaire, Marianne Moore, and Robert Lowell.

The concerns of Lota's aristocratic, landowning life became Elizabeth's concerns, and she was able to indulge her fascination for the spirit of improvisation and "make-do" creativity she had first rediscovered (after Nova Scotia) on Cuttyhunk in 1934. The unreliability of the roads, the copper telephone wires that got stolen regularly, the operation of kerosene lamps and primus stoves in the absence of electricity, the domestication of the wild Samambaia setting into gardens for flowers and vegetables, the maintenance of cars, the raising of children, the below-stairs dramas in the lives of the servants, and the lives and deaths of puppies, toucans, and kittens all provided opportunities for creative intervention and innovation that she found exhilarating. Elizabeth's experience at giving herself adrenalin injections made her the shot-giving expert and general medical specialist at Samambaia; once she was mortified to find that she had hit Lota's sciatic nerve with an injection, giving her a sore "bum bum" for two weeks. Most of Elizabeth's other contributions to the self-sufficiency of their provincial outpost were more successful. She made marmalade from the oranges they grew and boasted that she could tell the sex of kittens at birth.

Such inefficiency and shoddiness as later soured her on the Brazilian way of doing things were now charming to observe, if not to live.

> When I knew Lota in N.Y. even, I noticed how she constantly spoke of things being "well-made", "well-finished" or "beautifully-tailored" etc. – and now after living here I see how everything is wretchedly made, unfinished, and that for so long only the rich with good taste could have anything better, and of course then it was always English – The same thing is true of looks – I think I take it for granted that my friends are handsome, their babies are pretty, etc. . . . But the general level of looks is rather low, I'm afraid – and the ugliness of the "poor people" – I don't know what to call them – is appalling – nobody seems "well-made", except some of the Negroes.[9]

Elizabeth and Lota did do some traveling together—New York trips in 1952, 1957, and 1961 notably—but not until 1964 did they make the European trip they had planned for virtually every year until then. Within Brazil they made excursions to São Paulo for the *Bienal* art exhibitions in 1952 and 1954, and in April 1953 they drove in Lota's Jaguar nearly three hundred miles to visit the exquisitely preserved eighteenth-century town of Ouro Prêto in the state of Minas Gerais. There Lota knew Lilli Correia de Araújo, the Danish widow of one of Brazil's finest painters, Pedro Correia de Araújo, and now a well-known intellectual and keeper of the Pouso do Chico Rey, an exquisite guesthouse in the town. In Elizabeth's notebook is a log of this trip—mileage and expenses in both their handwritings—and one long paragraph of notes for what Elizabeth hoped would be "a saleable piece" of semijournalistic prose about it. (She had caught the prose-writing bug in part because of the more than twenty-five hundred dollars she had received in payment for the two Nova Scotia stories, in contrast to the roughly two dollars per line she had been paid for her poetry.) But she had yet to find a way of writing about her experience of Brazil, and only the brief notes remain of a trip that was finally "too bizarre" to sell to the *New Yorker*.

. . .

Elizabeth's life in Brazil changed somewhat in 1955. *A Cold Spring* finally appeared, and she was once again a poet (she had published no poems between 1952 and July 11, 1955, when the *New Republic* printed "The Shampoo") and free to move past her old poems and on to new ones. On February 7, the Samambaia cook, Maria, delivered a daughter whom she named for Elizabeth. Maria Elizabeth, called "Bettchy," was a bright, cheerful black child (not at first, however; Elizabeth was delighted to note that her namesake, like most Negro babies, was born "looking very much like a violet" and turned "black" beginning at the extremities, ears, and fingertips).[10] Maria asked Elizabeth to be the baby's godmother, but she could not be under the rules of the church because this "believer in total immersion" and author of "The Baptism" had never been baptized herself. Elizabeth said that Bettchy resembled an Abyssinian princess (Elizabeth had been trying to write a poem about the Delacroix painting on that subject ever since she had seen it in the National Gallery in Washington) and that she liked to have the child brought to her with her breakfast tray each morning at 7:30. Elizabeth and Lota supervised the raising of Bettchy, relying heavily on Dr. Spock. They talked of adopting her or of placing her in school somewhere to "save" her from the poverty and ignorance of her parents; but in the end she left Samambaia when her parents did in 1960, and Elizabeth never saw her again.

At about the time of Bettchy's birth, Kylso's rapidly growing family became regular visitors at Samambaia. The legendary story among Lota's friends was that on an excursion to see about adopting a dog, she had been offered the polio-crippled son of the owner as well. She had taken this child and raised him, and by this time Kylso had married. In the summer, when Rio was hot and unhealthy, Elizabeth and Lota were hosts to three, four, or five small "grandchildren." At such times, the household was virtually converted to a nursery, and Elizabeth, when she was not making lunch for the children or organizing an egg-dyeing party, retreated to her study to write. Although it was forbidden, Bettchy would sometimes appear at the door, a welcome distraction. Elizabeth and Lota felt a little frustrated and helpless as they watched Kylso's family grow beyond his capacity to support it—the fifth child, Patricia, was born in August 1959 when the oldest was six. Helena, Paulinha, Roberto, and Lotinha were regular, long-term visitors and sometime residents at Samambaia between 1955 and 1960, when Lota quarreled with her son and lost contact with the family.

The birth of Patricia, lamented though it was for economic reasons, gave Elizabeth an image that she could not shake, though she never completed the poem she wanted to write about it: "I have stolen the last x-ray of [the child in utero], seated very neatly upside down, with semi-translucent bones, its little spine rather like a pearl necklace – towards the tail, at least, – perfectly beautiful–."[11] Elizabeth said that child-raising was Lota's gift, not her own, though she liked her role as "auntie" and later liked it even more with the arrival of Mary Morse's Monica in 1961. Surrounded by children and thinking often about what a child needs, at a minimum, to grow up healthy, Elizabeth could not help but evaluate her own childhood.

> Children really seem to be much easier to take care of, and to be much healthier and happier in general than they used to be. It may be just a matter of their being better fed – However, love's the main thing always – I'm sure what saved me from being a complete wreck forever was my one aunt who loved me so much. (And my miseries as a child weren't anyone's fault, anyway – most of them were due to chance.) Even before I came to Brasil I used to read all the books, just out of curiosity – and I do recommend old Spock and Gesell to you, just for fun – even if you won't agree with some of the latter, maybe. Here I've seen so much more of children than I ever had before and I do think it's something one shouldn't miss if one can help it. From six months to four years,

say – that's the age I like – after that they are more difficult. The amount of knowledge they acquire, even in the first year, is fantastic – Lotinha discovering her voice, for example, and amusing herself trilling away by the hour, all alone.[12]

Among the first poems she published after *A Cold Spring* appeared are two explicitly about her childhood. Elizabeth envisioned "Manners" as the first of a book, perhaps, of children's poems. It recalls "Pa," grandfather Boomer in Nova Scotia, and his lessons about kindness and good manners, already in 1918 becoming impractical and outdated:

> When automobiles went by,
> the dust hid the people's faces,
> but we shouted "Good day! Good day!
> Fine day!" at the top of our voices.
>
> When we came to Hustler Hill,
> he said that the mare was tired,
> so we all got down and walked,
> as our good manners required.

"Sestina," originally titled "Early Sorrow," works directly with the terms of "In the Village" and Elizabeth's childhood—grandmother, house, stove, tears, almanac—and also of her recent reading and thinking about child psychology, in Benjamin Spock, Melanie Klein, Arnold Gesell, and others. The child in the poem draws houses for her weeping grandmother. Their "rigid" form reflects the insecurity of her makeshift home and her attempts to "domesticate" it:

> *It was to be,* says the Marvel Stove.
> *I know what I know,* says the almanac.
> With crayons the child draws a rigid house
> and a winding pathway. Then the child

puts in a man with buttons like tears
and shows it proudly to the grandmother.

But secretly, while the grandmother
busies herself about the stove,
the little moons fall down like tears
from between the pages of the almanac
into the flower bed the child
has carefully placed in front of the house.

Time to plant tears, says the almanac.
The grandmother sings to the marvellous stove
and the child draws another inscrutable house.

The memory of childhood uncertainty and the losses that happened "by chance" survive into the adult. The same tenuous grasp on security is here in the flower beds and pathway, as it was in "Jerónimo's House" with its leftover Christmas decorations and in the traveler's wistful look at the nativity scene ("a family with pets") in "Over 2000 Illustrations and a Complete Concordance."

In "Squatter's Children," published first in Portuguese in March 1956, Elizabeth combines her current thinking about childhood with one of her earliest attempts to write poetry about Brazil. She said in July 1955 that she was dreaming about houses almost every night. This is a poem about poverty and the resourcefulness of children, but to read it as a lament for the impermanence of houses is not to detract from its political message. The uncertainty behind the children's play is economic, and the way their several houses grow smaller and larger in a typically Bishop manipulation of perspective speaks to this poem's place among her others about the unreliability of houses and the terrible suspense of an insecure childhood:

On the unbreathing sides of hills
they play, a specklike girl and boy,
alone, but near a specklike house.

The sun's suspended eye
blinks casually, and then they wade
gigantic waves of light and shade.
A dancing yellow spot, a pup,
attends them. Clouds are piling up;

a storm piles up behind the house.
The children play at digging holes.
The ground is hard; they try to use
one of their father's tools,
a mattock with a broken haft
the two of them can scarcely lift.
It drops and clangs. Their laughter spreads
effulgence in the thunderheads,

weak flashes of inquiry
direct as is the puppy's bark.
But to their little, soluble,
unwarrantable ark,
apparently the rain's reply
consists of echolalia,
and Mother's voice, ugly as sin,
keeps calling to them to come in.

Children, the threshold of the storm
has slid beneath your muddy shoes;
wet and beguiled, you stand among
the mansions you may choose
out of a bigger house than yours,
whose lawfulness endures.
Its soggy documents retain
your rights in rooms of falling rain.

Elizabeth was not sure about this poem, even after it appeared in
the *New Yorker* in March 1957; she felt it was "too rigid." These
children of the gardener Manuelzinho have several houses; none is

very "rigid," one would imagine. The first is "specklike," and the second is "unwarrantable." The third is religious: "In my Father's house are many mansions" (John 14:2). This should be their consolation for having to live unlawfully on barren land, too poor to buy proper tools. But Elizabeth's irony toward all religious consolation sacrifices even these happy children. They stand "wet and beguiled," cheated, and deceived, and the rooms of the only mansion they "may choose" protect them only as falling rain does. Elizabeth's undermining of the positive picture of creative, resilient childhood (as against the Mother's voice, "ugly as sin") in the first two stanzas serves her political purpose, and her attempt to say something important about Brazil. In the second half of the poem, the storm defeats the children, the "unwarrantable ark" sinks, even their small security washes away. Elizabeth's political pessimism is joined in the poem with her lifelong distrust of houses. From the "childish snow-forts" of "Paris, 7 A.M."—ready at any time to "dissolve and die"—to the miracle of Samambaia, which Elizabeth still could not quite believe, houses were, for her, always, always "soluble."

In this mood of considering childhood, Elizabeth also undertook a review for *Poetry,* extraordinary enough in itself, of Walter de la Mare's *Come Hither: A Collection of Rhymes and Poems for the Young of All Ages.* She delighted in its selection and especially in its introduction, which de la Mare wrote in the voice of an old woman. Instructing a child about poetry, the old woman counsels, "Learn the common names of everything you see . . . and especially those that please you the most to remember: then give them names also of your own making and choosing—if you can." "He loves 'little articles,'" Bishop went on, "home-made objects whose value increases with age, Robinson Crusoe's lists of his belongings, homely employments, charms and herbs." She admired his footnotes and his "transparent delight in what he is telling" and called the collection "the best anthology I know of." Perhaps to illustrate de la Mare's potential audience, she evoked her own child-filled household:

At my house as I write there is a four-month-old baby who has just discovered his voice; not his crying voice, but his speaking, singing, or poetry-voice, and he devotes stretches of the day to trying it out. He can produce long trills, loud or soft, and repeated bird-like cries, obviously with pleasure. There is also a little black girl of three who vigorously pedals a tricycle around and around in perfect time to an old Portuguese children's song. *Tere-sínha de Jesús* she goes, in mixolydian (I think), telling another story about the same Teresa as Crashaw's (who is not in *this* book).[13]

The baby is really a "she," Kylso's Lotinha.

. . .

When Elizabeth began to publish poems about Brazil, they appeared at a steady rate (for her) between 1956 and 1960. She began with "Manuelzinho"—her portrait of the endearingly unreliable gardener at Samambaia—perhaps because she felt she could make Lota the speaker in the poem and thereby suspend the question of whether she herself "knew enough" or had a right to talk about the complex Brazilian social hierarchy. "It is supposed to be Lota talking," Elizabeth said about the poem, which she saw as her "first attempt to say anything much about Brazil."[14] The fiction is necessary because the poem's message has to do with the distance between the tenant and the landowner, and Elizabeth herself owned no land. The poem delineates social distinctions carefully; we are told in the first two lines that Manuelzinho and his family are tenants, more or less, and that they are white. Lota Soares is their keeper in the paternalistic (or maternalistic, in this case) social system. The family's long tenancy ("the steep paths you have made— / or your father and grandfather made— / all over my property") gets them the landowner's tolerance, but little else. Impractical, "helpless, foolish," Manuelzinho is Lota's charge as well as her servant, and the power shifts back and forth between them in ancient ways:

Or, briskly, you come to settle
what we call our "accounts,"
with two old copybooks,
one with flowers on the cover,
the other with a camel.
Immediate confusion.
You've left out the decimal points.
Your columns stagger,
honeycombed with zeros.
You whisper conspiratorially;
the numbers mount to millions.
Account books? They are Dream Books.
In the kitchen we dream together
how the meek shall inherit the earth—
or several acres of mine.

The poem does not question deeply the paternalistic system; rather, it examines anecdotally the thinking of one of its participants. Even though Elizabeth saw the ironies of the system, her comfortable existence in Petrópolis depended on it, and within a few years of her arrival in Brazil, she was convinced that the Brazilian lower classes were uneducable. Defending herself years later against a reviewer's charge that the poem was condescending, she said simply that Brazilians had loved the poem, and when May Swenson objected to Elizabeth's saying in a letter that she and Lota were hoping that the premature baby of a servant would die, Elizabeth was firm in her self-justification:

Now I am going to scold you a bit–well, not scold–but just say that although as you say "life is cheap" here (although that's not a good expression, now that I think of it–what is true is that infant mortality is terrific) everything was done for that poor infant Maria had that could possibly be done...The parents are so ignorant, savage, suspicious, etc that now they are blaming us and it is very unpleasant, naturally, but exactly what one has to contend with (and the U S nation has to contend with, too) when dealing with backward people who are incapable of any of the more highly refined emotions. We've been through it for years with Lota's adopted son, for example. It seems to take generations of education for anyone to feel trust in anyone else – and gratitude is rare even among the most highly educated, as I'm sure you must know as well as I do by now. . . . We have been through this kind of thing so many times in the past ten years – Lota all her life. – If you say "You must eat vegetables, you know" – they leave, because they think you're forbidding them to eat meat – their luxury article – and so on. It is why one has serious doubts about the Peace Corps![15]

President John F. Kennedy had just proposed the Peace Corps when Elizabeth wrote this letter, and so convinced was she that the problem in Brazil was the lack of capacity for education and refinement in the lower classes that she called the idea "silly."

But all her life Elizabeth had had a romantic, esthetic appreciation of poor people and the ways in which they "made do" on limited resources, especially the ways they made art: Jerónimo (whose "house," his "fairy / palace, is / of perishable / clapboards"), the Catholic churches decorated by Indians in Mexico, the sad potters in Mitla, Cootchie's life and death, Cordie Heiss, the "Songs for a Colored Singer"; Cape Breton's meadow, "establish[ing] its poverty in a snowfall of daisies"; Faustina. In Elizabeth's years in Brazil, she acquired a marvelous collection of crudely carved saints, primitive furniture and art, altars-in-bottles; despite her despair about the educability of such characters as the Riverman and Micuçu, the Burglar of Babylon, they retained their esthetic interest for her.

"Questions of Travel," also published in 1956 though begun much earlier, is wholly successful because it expresses some contradictions in Brazilian culture from a modest perspective; the poem is about the limitations of one's knowledge and understanding of a foreign culture. In that sense, it opened the way for the Brazil poems that were to follow, poems that attempt to express understanding of the culture but that, at their best, are aware of their outsider's perspective and, at their most naive, participate fully in the paternalistic culture. "Questions of Travel" opens with an observation about the Brazilian climate that Elizabeth had made often in letters:

There are too many waterfalls here; the crowded streams
hurry too rapidly down to the sea,
and the pressure of so many clouds on the mountaintops
makes them spill over the sides in soft slow-motion,
turning to waterfalls under our very eyes.

After this careful depiction of the disorderly movements of time in Brazil, the poem poses its questions: "Should we have stayed at home and thought of here?" "Where should we be today?" "Oh must we dream our dreams / and have them, too?" Its tentative answers come from a wholly esthetic appreciation of the country, the landscape, and the people:

But surely it would have been a pity
not to have seen the trees along this road,
really exaggerated in their beauty,
not to have seen them gesturing
like noble pantomimists, robed in pink.
—Not to have had to stop for gas and heard
the sad, two-noted, wooden tune
of disparate wooden clogs
carelessly clacking over
a grease-stained filling-station floor.
(In another country the clogs would all be tested.
Each pair there would have identical pitch.)
—A pity not to have heard
the other, less primitive music of the fat brown bird
who sings above the broken gasoline pump
in a bamboo church of Jesuit baroque:
three towers, five silver crosses.

In the end, however, the traveler-poet throws her hands up over the question of "Where should we be today?" and writes in her "notebook":

"Continent, city, country, society:
the choice is never wide and never free.
And here, or there...No. Should we have stayed at home,
wherever that may be?"

The last among this first group of Brazil poems is "The Armadillo," published in the *New Yorker* on June 22, 1957. Elizabeth had been working with its principle elements—the fire balloons, the armadillo, the owls, the baby rabbit—for several years in her letters. She wrote to Isabella Gardener of the armadillo, or *tatú*, she saw in the road on May 13, 1956. Appropriately to Marianne Moore, the author of "The Pangolin," Elizabeth wrote:

After all this time, I've just found out we have armadillos here–I see one crossing the road in the headlights at night, with his head and tail down–very lonely and glisteny. There's also a kind of small owl that sits in the road at night–I had to get out and shoo one away from the front of the car last night. They have large eyes; when they fly off look exactly like pin-wheels–black and white.[16]

These animals appear in just these poses in the poem, though in response to another form of bright violence, fire balloons. In a letter written on St. John's Day (June 24) of the previous year, the shortest day of the year in the Southern Hemisphere and a holy day celebrated with the balloons, Elizabeth described them:

Fire balloons are supposed to be illegal but everyone sends them up anyway and we usually spend St. John's night and the nights before and after watching the balloons drift right up the mountain towards the house–there seems to be a special draught; Lota has a

sprinkling system on the roof just because of them. & They are so
pretty—one's of two minds about them.[17]

The balloons, forms of foolish religious worship subject to Elizabeth's usual irony for such things, and her usual appreciation for
their artistic resourcefulness, are a reasonably safe and pretty form
of entertainment in the first third of the poem. Although they are
"frail, illegal," they are also "like hearts," stars, or planets until,

receding, dwindling, solemnly
and steadily forsaking us,
or, in the downdraft from a peak,
suddenly turning dangerous.

Last night another big one fell.
It splattered like an egg of fire
against the cliff behind the house.
The flame ran down. We saw the pair

of owls who nest there flying up
and up, their whirling black-and-white
stained bright pink underneath, until
they shrieked up out of sight.

The ancient owls' nest must have burned.
Hastily, all alone,
a glistening armadillo left the scene,
rose-flecked, head down, tail down,

and then a baby rabbit jumped out,
short-eared, to our surprise.
So soft!—a handful of intangible ash
with fixed, ignited eyes.

This next-to-last stanza expresses delight in spite of the fleeing
animals' terror. Bishop catches herself in the fallacy that the descrip-

tion—exact, supported by apt simile, and charmingly drawn—is "accurate." It is not, and the revelation in the final stanza reinterprets the animals and their flight:

> *Too pretty, dreamlike mimicry!*
> *O falling fire and piercing cry*
> *and panic, and a weak mailed fist*
> *clenched ignorant against the sky!*

Bishop left both interpretations in the poem so that instead of a detached, impressionistic portrait of animals fleeing in strange light, we get an exchange in the running argument she had with poetry itself over seeing accurately, describing accurately, and accepting the responsibility inherent in the poet's heightened ability to see. The "too pretty, dreamlike mimicry" is both the poem's attempt to render the animals and the fire balloons' imitation of the destructiveness of war. In her developing argument about Brazil, the poem presents another image of an ignorant, victimized lower class.

   . . .

As Elizabeth found her tone and voice for writing poetry about Brazil and about her childhood, she also found the means to express her complex feelings about two other large questions in her life—about gender roles and poetic ambition—in poems enough out of character that they were not published in the *New Yorker*. In the April 1956 *New World Writing*, Elizabeth published a poem utterly anomalous in her oeuvre, "Exchanging Hats." She never reprinted the poem—in retrospect it embarrassed her in some way; but she turned against it only years after the initial publication, as if she had come to see the poem's possible meanings long after she wrote it. In "Exchanging Hats," she speculated on the limitations inherent in gender and gender stereotypes and reflected on the changes in perspective that cross-dressing might bring about. She had never done anything like this in print before.

Unfunny uncles who insist
in trying on a lady's hat,
—oh, even if the joke falls flat,
we share your slight transvestite twist

in spite of our embarrassment.
Costume and custom are complex.
The headgear of the other sex
inspires us to experiment.

Anandrous aunts, who, at the beach
with paper plates upon your laps,
keep putting on the yachtsmen's caps
with exhibitionistic screech,

the visors hanging o'er the ear
so that the golden anchors drag,
—the tides of fashion never lag.
Such caps may not be worn next year.

Or you who don the paper plate
itself, and put some grapes upon it,
or sport the Indian's feather bonnet,
—perversities may aggravate

the natural madness of the hatter.
And if the opera hats collapse
and crowns grow draughty, then, perhaps,
he thinks what might a miter matter?

Unfunny uncle, you who wore a
hat too big, or one too many,
tell us, can't you, are there any
stars inside your black fedora?

Aunt exemplary and slim,
with avernal eyes, we wonder

what slow changes they see under
their vast, shady, turned-down brim.

The poem feels like a speculation on one of those nineteenth-century paintings featuring a gay beach party of men and women (Renoir, perhaps). But *Alice in Wonderland,* the location of the mad hatter's original beach, is its truest antecedent, and the poem is both playful and serious without settling on one or the other. May Swenson, who gave the poem its first live airing at a reading in New York, said her audience responded with "respectful hilarity," an apt summary of its mixed intentions.[18] Words as strong in sexual content as "transvestite," "anandrous," and "perversities," both betray the subtext about sexual preference and prevent us from tripping lightly through the deceptively regular stanzas and taking the poem's message to be the humor of fashion trends. The nauseating shifts in perspective of Alice's journey come to mind in the middle stanzas, as the liberating effect of crossing gender lines is reflected. The poem continues the contemplation of reversals that Elizabeth had begun when she crossed the equator on her way to Brazil.

The speaker in the poem (a niece or nephew) asks the uncle and aunt—now dead, it seems—how far or how deeply they can see within the protection and limits of their own hats, in this case covering their faces for eternity. The uncle who "wore a / hat too big," were he not dead, might tell us what his gazing into his hat has taught him. And the aunt, whose "avernal eyes" (merely "anxious" in the first published version) may record "slow changes" under the brim of her own hat, speaks from the underworld. Limited as they were by stultifying custom, they died that way. The poem is a strange elegy for these aunts and uncles, and one reason the poem is one of only four that Elizabeth published and then declined to collect might be that it makes cruel fun of the aunts and uncles who raised her. Certainly they struggle under stereotypes—the aunts screeching, exemplary, slim; the uncles slow but hard-working, "unfunny," unimaginative. Frozen in those stereotypes by the beyond-the-grave perspective of the last two stanzas, the portraits may have seemed in retrospect to appropriate distorted versions of real people in a way that Elizabeth always hated. And perhaps the poem is franker than she at first realized about the persuasiveness of the "transvestite" wish to see the world from the other sexual side.

Also in 1956, the Italian poet and editor Alfredo Rizzardi asked Elizabeth (and many others) for a poem about Ezra Pound for an Italian collection of tributes to the great modernist, still incarcerated at St. Elizabeths. The "sort of a poem, not much really," that Elizabeth contributed, is "Visits to St. Elizabeths." It appeared in Rizzardi's Italian translation first and then in a special issue of the *Partisan Review* devoted to Pound in the spring of 1957.

The unnamed Pound who appears in Bishop's poem describing her year of confrontations with him in Washington, 1949–1950, "lies in the house of Bedlam." Her poem is constructed on the model of the ancient nursery rhyme "The House that Jack Built," which posits a series of mutually dependent events that all turn out to promote the marriage of "the maiden all forlorn" and the "man all tattered and torn" by the "priest all shaven and shorn." It begins, of course:

> This is the house that Jack built.
>
> This is the malt
> that lay in the house that Jack built.
>
> This is the rat
> that ate the malt
> that lay in the house that Jack built.

And so on: this is the cat that killed the rat, this is the dog that worried the cat, this is the cow with the crumpled horn that tossed the dog and is milked by the maiden all forlorn.

Jack's house gains a context from this concatenation—eventually we meet the farmer sowing his corn that kept the cock that crowed in the morn that waked the priest all shaven and shorn and so on. It is a lesson for children on the interrelatedness of events, the inevitable progress of cause to effect. Like this nursery rhyme, Bishop's description opens progressively wider as its causes grow more distant and yet more necessary to the final result. When after seven years Elizabeth finally distilled her visits to Pound into a poem, she placed him at the center of a vortex of madness on the hospital ward, surrounded by, defined by, the characters he had attempted to screen out of his literary conversations.

Elizabeth described Pound as "the sanest-seeming one on the ward" in St. Elizabeths, and, significantly, none of the adjectives she uses to describe him in the poem suggest that he is "crazy" or belongs in "Bedlam." Instead, the colorful characters around him enact the events and attitudes that led to his incarceration, while "the man" himself, his mood changing from visit to visit, ages as we might see him age in a series of still photographs taken years apart. Building her impressions in the manner of "The House that Jack Built," Bishop establishes the refrain "the man / that lies in the house of Bedlam," which she varies throughout the poem. Her subtle development of the other residents of the ward reminds us again and again of his various contexts. In the first stanzas, she places him in his time and describes him as "tragic," then "talkative," before he is joined by his fellow patients:

This is the sailor
wearing the watch
that tells the time
of the honored man
that lies in the house of Bedlam.

This is the roadstead all of board
reached by the sailor
wearing the watch
that tells the time

of the old, brave man
that lies in the house of Bedlam.

These are the years and the walls of the ward,
the winds and clouds of the sea of board
sailed by the sailor
wearing the watch
that tells the time
of the cranky man
that lies in the house of Bedlam.

This is a Jew in a newspaper hat
that dances weeping down the ward
over the creaking sea of board
beyond the sailor
winding his watch
that tells the time
of the cruel man
that lies in the house of Bedlam.

This is a world of books gone flat.
This is a Jew in a newspaper hat
that dances weeping down the ward
over the creaking sea of board
of the batty sailor
that winds his watch
that tells the time
of the busy man
that lies in the house of Bedlam.

This is a boy that pats the floor
to see if the world is there, is flat,
for the widowed Jew in the newspaper hat
that dances weeping down the ward
waltzing the length of a weaving board
by the silent sailor

that hears his watch
that ticks the time
of the tedious man
that lies in the house of Bedlam.

These are the years and the walls and the door
that shut on a boy who pats the floor
to feel if the world is there and flat.
This is a Jew in a newspaper hat
that dances joyfully down the ward
into the parting seas of board
past the staring sailor
that shakes his watch
that tells the time
of the poet, the man
that lies in the house of Bedlam.

This is the soldier home from the war.
These are the years and the walls and the door
that shut on a boy that pats the floor
to see if the world is round or flat.
This is a Jew in a newspaper hat
that dances carefully down the ward,
walking the plank of a coffin board
with the crazy sailor
that shows his watch
that tells the time
of the wretched man
that lies in the house of Bedlam.

By its accumulative method, "Visits to St. Elizabeths" takes in world events and literature from nursery rhymes to the Bible as no other Bishop poem does. Her contact with the overpowering personality of Ezra Pound inspired a poem as anomalous in its way as "Exchanging Hats" was. Elizabeth Bishop was not given to attacking living people in public forums.

Elizabeth had been living in Brazil for four years when she finished "Visits to St. Elizabeths," and the poem put to rest Pound and what the example of his career had meant to her. Having done the life of the poet her own way—living in Brazil, ignoring politics and economics, writing in her own subdued, accessible style—she had acquired a poetic voice all her own and had just won the Pulitzer Prize and a twenty-seven-hundred-dollar fellowship from *Partisan Review*. Even without placing undue emphasis on these marks of outside approval (Elizabeth certainly did not, except for the money), she could address the imprisoned Pound from a position of strength. Given her sensitivity to "confession" in poems and her usual shying away from current events, she would probably not have published the poem unless she had had an important point to make. One might be an actual dislike of Pound, a willingness to pity him in print. When, as Pound was released from St. Elizabeths in 1958, it was rumored that he might come to Brazil, she entertained the idea for a moment (she said she would have to keep Lota from arguing with him) and then said that the country already had "too many crackpots." In 1953, she had dismissed him as "a maniacal old [man]."[19] But the poem is also Elizabeth Bishop's declaration of her "freedom at last" from the pressures of poetic ambition, which had clustered so destructively for her in that miserable year in Washington, 1949–1950, "just about my worst so far," as she had written on the title page of her diary.

Twelve

"SOBRIETY & GAYETY & PATIENCE
& TOUGHNESS"
1956–1960

THE FOCUS of Elizabeth's Brazilian life in 1956 and 1957 was the completion of her translation of *Minha Vida de Menina,* which she had tentatively titled "Black Beans and Diamonds." By March 1956, she had finished a first draft of the diary itself and was carrying pages back and forth between her typists and Alice Brant, the author of the diary, and her husband, who insisted on going over every word. In April 1956, Elizabeth finally made the trip to Diamantina she had been planning for several years in order to write her introduction.

Diamantina, in the state of Minas Gerais, was an isolated provincial village in 1956; one flew in from Belo Horizonte because the roads were so unreliable. (Elizabeth had waited so long in part because she hated to fly; she revised her will before each trip.) At more than five thousand feet above sea level, Diamantina was then the highest town in Brazil and, Elizabeth said, "god-forsaken," despite its sixteen tiny churches. "Set in a vast Atlantic Ocean of rocks – steely gray rocks that all turn red at 6 P M" and "eaten up with the passion for finding diamonds in every brook," the town was "wonderful" to Elizabeth, as the comical episodes of Helena Morley's childhood took on location and context. Most of the details of her trip went into the introduction to the diary. She traveled to Diamantina with her Brazilian journalist friend Rosinha Leão, who returned to Rio after two days; Elizabeth stayed for six. She visited the mines, which in 1956 were already American owned. She was an honored guest at the town's hotel, and her stay alone in the city made her conspicuous.

> I was on my own, or on my own Portuguese – I can't really say alone, because the tiny town took such an interest in my every move and people came out of their shops to walk with me wherever I was going, and having lunch in the hotel (a brand new one, by Neimeyer, but not good architecturally – I was the only guest most of my stay) the little girls on their way to the convent would stop and stand in a row, with their noses pressed against the plate-glass, watching me eat.[1]

After a circuitous flight back to Belo Horizonte and then to Rio, Elizabeth settled in to write her introduction and to argue with the Brants over finer points of grammar and idiomatic expression. She "fussed over" the introduction, wanting to use Burton's visit to the town in 1867, Helena's details from the diary, and her own observations from 1956 to give her American and English audiences a sense of the strangeness of the place. The introduction was her first, and remains her most complete, attempt to explain primitive, isolated Brazil to herself and to a less traveled audience. By September 1956, she had finished both the translation and the introduction, and she began to plan a trip to New York to see to its publication. Her agent was sending excerpts around—the first time that Elizabeth had not had to do such humiliating work herself. Finally, Robert Giroux of Farrar, Straus, and Cudahy decided, with some reservations, to take on the book.

With that task complete, Elizabeth had found her way to write about Brazil. She went back to work on the stories she had begun— she reported five under way in October 1956—and began new poems. She launched a plan for a book of travel essays about Brazil, which she had first proposed to Houghton Mifflin in 1946 and which she worked on in fits and starts for the next fifteen years. She hoped she could sell her sketches individually before collecting them—the unfinished pieces about the Ten Thousand Islands and about Sable Island were the only works she had done in that genre, though she continued to think of it as a kind of lucrative journalism she might be able to carry off. As it turned out, she could not. "A Trip to Vigia" is the only piece of travel prose about Brazil that she finished, and it was not published until after her death. She eventually made successful excursions into journalistic writing about the country, and she traveled a good deal with writing in mind, but the "travel pieces" she was always about to write never came to be. Although she finished poems on some of the same subjects, she found herself unable to generalize from the wealth of detail she recorded in her notebooks to write prose. In the poems, the details speak for themselves.

Elizabeth also undertook a short-term, intense, and complicated Portuguese translation project working with the author, Henrique Mindlin, on his book about Brazilian architecture. The project was unique in her experience of commercial writing against a deadline; she and Mindlin worked well together many hours a day for several weeks, and they ended up liking each other more than when they had started the project. Elizabeth cherished the knowledge of architectural styles and terms that she took in with the work.

By the time *Poems: North & South—A Cold Spring* was out, reviewed, and honored with the Pulitzer Prize and the fellowship from the *Partisan Review,* Elizabeth was thinking seriously about her next book. Her tentative title was *Grandmother's Glass Eye,* which she proposed and abandoned more than once in her life. In the spell of writing she managed in 1956–1957, her most promising new poem was about a trip home to Nova Scotia, "a long one" that she promised to dedicate to Aunt Grace.[2] The earliest extant drafts of "The Moose" date from this fall, making it, even though she did not finish it until 1971, another among the outpouring of Nova

Scotia poetry and prose that came to her as she settled in Brazil.

With the Pulitzer Prize, Elizabeth acquired some American-style recognition. On February 8, 1957, she found herself listed along with Lana Turner in an American newspaper under "Today's Birthdays." ("Now that's fame," Elizabeth said.) She gained some courage about writing critical prose from her happy experience with the introduction to *The Diary*. In October 1956, she agreed to write a monthly column on U.S. writing for a new Rio magazine; Lota would translate for her. Although there is no evidence that the magazine ever appeared or that her first essay, on a new edition of Coleridge's letters, was ever used, her willingness to take on the task showed a new confidence. She used it to review William Jay Smith's translations of Jules Laforgue for her friend Bobby Evett, now an editor at the *New Republic*. The review gave her trouble because she had her doubts about translating poetry at all and about writing reviews.

> I like Laforgue so much and I do know Bill, after all, so I thought I'd try writing a short simple one. . . . At first I thought it was excellent; the more I work and re-read Laforgue the more weak bits I find. But I don't want to write a carping review, so of course my original 3 or 4 paragraphs are getting longer and more complicated by the minute. But it's almost done – and just the fact that I can do one at all pleases me – I never used to be able to. Even so, I am wrestling with hostility, I suppose it is, every minute. . . . John Crowe Ransom is one of the very few writers I know who can say someone is wrong, from beginning to end, without ever sounding angry, and without, I feel sure, hurting the person he's reviewing's feelings.[3]

As it turned out in the published review, she fussed over particulars of Smith's translations briefly, then abandoned the attempt, telling her readers that if they really wanted to read Laforgue, they should learn French. Despite her optimism here, she never got comfortable in the reviewing mode and never mastered the skill of criticizing gently.

. . .

Elizabeth and Lota spent six months in New York in 1957, arriving on March 31. The plan for the trip was to see to the publication of *The Diary of Helena Morley,* which Elizabeth rightly assumed would need more shepherding through the process than had either of her other books. She said her negotiations with Robert Giroux and Farrar, Straus, and Cudahy were the "dark side" of an otherwise pleasant stay in New York, and though Giroux eventually became a close friend, she greeted his work on *The Diary* with her habitual distrust of publishers and their motives. And her complaints—about the book jacket, about the six hundred dollars the publisher wanted for corrections—indicated that her relationship with Farrar, Straus, and Cudahy was simply a continuation of the one she had had with Houghton Mifflin.

Elizabeth said that five years was about the right length of time between visits to the New York literary scene, with its dizzying pace and crowds of poets and acquaintances to be seen. She saw them— Marianne Moore, Mary McCarthy, Anny Baumann, Randall Jarrell, Wallace Fowlie, Polly Hansen, May Swenson, Isabella Gardner, Bobby Evett, Jane Dewey, Joe and U. T. Summers, Loren MacIver and Lloyd Frankenberg, Tom Wanning, Bobby Fizdale and Arthur Gold (the piano duo, friends of Lota's), Clement Greenberg, Katharine White, Andrews Wanning, Jack Sweeney, Pearl Kazin, Marion Morehouse, and e. e. cummings (whom she visited in the hospital). Aunt Grace came down from Nova Scotia to see her; she saw Aunt Florence Bishop in Boston. She spent a week in September visiting Marjorie Stevens in Key West, and she and Lota ended their stay on October 3 by throwing a huge party in the apartment they had sublet on East Sixty-seventh Street, including many of these friends and Alexy Hiaff, Eleanor Clark and Robert Penn Warren,

Louise Bogan, Dwight Macdonald, Monroe Wheeler, Glenway Wescott, Morton Zabel, and James Merrill.

The most problematic of Elizabeth's visits to her friends were those with Robert Lowell. After their first meeting on this trip to New York, Lowell apologized for his inappropriately amorous behavior, blaming it on the martinis. Elizabeth then delayed a promised visit to Lowell and Elizabeth Hardwick in Boston, and instead she and Lota joined them at their summer home in Castine, Maine, in early August. That visit coincided unfortunately with the early, accelerating stage of one of Lowell's periodic breakdowns, and once again he wrote apologizing for making romantic claims on Elizabeth, saying that his illness made him irresponsible. During the visit, Lowell suggested that he might come to Brazil alone the following year, which prompted Elizabeth to write to Elizabeth Hardwick saying that such a visit would be a bad idea. Feeling conspired against, Lowell wrote to Elizabeth in New York those six closely typed pages of self-justification in which he traced his uncontrolled behavior to the summer of 1948, when he had thought, without sharing the thought with Elizabeth Bishop, that the two of them would marry. Saying that his failure to propose to her was "the might have been" in his life, he promised never again to overstep his bounds.[4] And he promised not to come to Brazil alone.

What these awkward partings and apologies obscure is the real friendship between Elizabeth and Lowell, which transcended both of their physical and spiritual illnesses. During Elizabeth's stay in the United States, she and Lowell found peaceful and friendly time enough to talk for hours about their lives, their poems, their mutual friends. Both recalled their talks together during these months warmly, and Elizabeth freely and unreservedly forgave Lowell his illness and the indiscretions it prompted. In her response to this particular visit, which must have been difficult for her, she offers her strongest encouragement, invoking George Herbert's translation of a "Treatise on Temperance and Sobriety":

Dear Cal, do please please take care of yourself and be an ornament to the world (you're already that) and a comfort to your friends...It seems to me in our conversations we just did the ground-work and never got on to the more constructive and hopeful parts of things. . . . —& There <u>are</u> many hopeful things, too, you know. Sobriety & gayety & patience & toughness will do the trick. Or so I hope for myself and hope & pray for you, too.[5]

After 1957, Elizabeth was a frequent eyewitness to Lowell's attacks of manic-depressive illness. According to Lowell's biographer, imagining himself "in love" often accompanied the onset of Lowell's illness—a small sorority of women in several countries were appropriated by him in this way. The frustrated energy of the attraction between Lowell and Elizabeth may have helped set off his illness when they were together; or perhaps her presence at his breakdowns was coincidental. For Elizabeth, her relationship with Lowell after this time replayed again and again dimly remembered negotiations with her equally ill and irrational mother.

During this stay in New York, Elizabeth also watched firsthand the development in Lowell's mind and on paper of the *Life Studies* poems, and Lowell himself suggested that reading and talking with Elizabeth that summer had helped him find the looser, more natural style he had been seeking to replace the old cramped, convoluted, distant (so it now seemed to him) style of *Lord Weary's Castle* and *The Mills of the Kavanaughs*. Lowell had written no poems for two years (he, too, had been writing long pieces of autobiographical prose), and the outpouring of astonishing new work that accompanied Elizabeth's visits and the escalation of Lowell's breakdown set off nothing short of a revolution in American poetry. Elizabeth left New York having seen "Skunk Hour," which Lowell said was indebted to "The Armadillo" and would be dedicated to her.

Elizabeth toyed with the idea of taking up her role as professional poet fully during this stay in New York. There were meetings with

Giroux and others at Farrar, Straus, and Cudahy about *The Diary;* there were numerous literary readings, lectures, lunches, dinners, cocktail parties, and weekend retreats. In June, a celebration held at Brandeis University in honor of William Carlos Williams drew poets from all over the country. There Elizabeth made the acquaintance of William Alfred, who later became a great friend and benefactor, and got to know better Randall Jarrell, whom she came more and more to admire. As word got around that she was in the country, she was showered with invitations to do readings and give lectures, several of which she tentatively accepted—at Vassar, at Wellesley, and for Jack Sweeney's Morris Gray Series at Harvard. She worried about them all: "I've already had a nightmare in which I was speaking to a small group, about 20, on a stony beach. I couldn't find my book, and as I groped around for it under some stones, I had the awful experience of seeing all the 20 drift away, one by one, until no one was left."[6] A month later, just back from the strained visit with Lowell in Castine, she canceled all the readings and announced that she and Lota were anxious to return to Brazil. The United States, she said, was depressing her.

> There [were] super-highways and clover-leafs in 1951, but they have ex-foliated beyond my wildest dreams since then. . . . Every time I've made a trip, a side-trip on this trip, I mean, I've come back depressed, I don't know why – I think it's mostly <u>automobiles</u> – and then decide it's just some lack of vitality in myself that makes me feel so hopeless about my own country. . . . And then I feel just as hopeless about Brazil, so I suppose I am just a born worrier, and that when the personal worries of adolescence and the years after it have more or less disappeared I promptly have to start worrying about the decline of nations...But I really can't <u>bear</u> much American life these days – surely no country has ever been so filthy rich and so hideously uncomfortable at the same time.[7]

Elizabeth and Lota left New York on October 15, a month earlier than they had planned. The freighter trip, on the SS *Mormacstar,* was to take eighteen days to Rio de Janeiro. The leisurely mode of travel had suited Elizabeth well when she was alone, but a restless and bored Lota (who dreamed in shipboard letters to Loren MacIver of nine-hour jet flights to and from New York) made "Cookie the sailor" feel guilty for insisting that they travel that way. For the first few days they slept, adjusting down from the hectic pace of the city. ("The weather is bad but the silence is admirable," Lota wrote.)[8] After stops in Charleston, South Carolina (where Elizabeth had intended to, but did not, stop off to pay a visit to Flannery O'Connor at Milledgeville, Georgia), and then-desolate Aruba (where she found the "pocket-sized volcanoes" she would place on Crusoe's island a few years later), they "finally" arrived in Rio on November 3. Lota had "nearly died of boredom," Elizabeth said.

Among the seven trunks, four wooden boxes, four large crates, three barrels, and twenty-six pieces of luggage that Elizabeth and Lota had carried with them back from New York and then, a bit at a time, up from the customs building in Rio, were the two framed portraits of little Gertrude Boomer and her brother Arthur. Grace Bowers had sent them down to New York from Great Village, and Elizabeth had the crate transferred unopened to the freighter. Back in Brazil, she opened them up.

> They are awfully nice; just as I'd remembered them, except that
> I'd had Uncle Arthur leaning on the red-plush-hung table and my
> mother leaning on the red-plush chair, [instead] of vice versa – I
> suppose because I like the chair so much. They are in huge gold
> frames, a little hard to reconcile with our modern architecture, but
> so charming we can't resist them. "Gertie" aged 8, wears little
> boots with one leg crossed over the other, and "Artie" aged 12, has
> his little boots crossed the other way. (He looks very much like
> me). And how strange to see them in Brasil.[9]

When she began "Memories of Uncle Neddy" a few months later (it was published in the *Southern Review* in 1977), she made much of the strangeness, particularly the strange presence of little Arthur of Nova Scotia in the tropics. She held on to the story, partly finished, until Arthur's widow died.

Robert Lowell's *Life Studies* poems were waiting for Elizabeth in Petrópolis when she got there on November 4. It took her some time to respond. ("POEMS LOVELY HAVENT FORGOTTEN YOU," she cabled on November 21.) And when she did, she had to work her way up to real commentary over two letters of anecdote and small criticisms and her habit of invidious comparison. Reading Lowell's poems about his relatives, she was thinking of what she might do with the portraits of her "ancestor children":

> [The poems] all also have that sure feeling, as if you'd been in a stretch (I've felt that way for very short stretches once in a long while) when everything and anything suddenly seemed material for poetry – or not material, seemed to be poetry, and all the past was illuminated in long shafts here and there, like a long-waited for sunrise. . . .
>
> But "broken down to where you've always been" – what on earth do you mean by that? I haven't got anywhere at all, I think – just to those first benches to sit down and rest on, in a side-arbor at the beginning of the maze.

She admired "Skunk Hour," most, she said, though "I suppose it's exercises compared to the other ones." And then she remarked:

> And here I must confess (and I imagine most of our contemporaries would confess the same thing) that I am green with envy of your kind of assurance. I feel that I could write in as much detail about my Uncle Artie, say – but what would be the significance? Nothing at all. He became a drunkard, fought with his wife, and spent most of his time fishing...and was ignorant as sin. It is sad; slightly more interesting than having an uncle

practising law in Schenectady maybe, but that's all. Whereas all you have to do is put down the names! And [the] fact that it seems significant, illustrative, American, etc., gives you, I think, the confidence you display about tackling any idea or theme, seriously, in both writing and conversation. In some ways you are the luckiest poet I know! – in some ways not so lucky, either, of course. But it is hell to realize one has wasted half one's talent through timidity that probably could have been overcome if anyone in one's family had had a few grains of sense or education …Well, maybe it's not too late![10]

This was an uncommonly harsh judgment of Gammie and Pa, Maud and Grace, or even of the Bishops. And soon after this, she recovered her enthusiasm for Uncle Artie and found him "illustrative" enough to share with an audience. It seems not to have occurred to her that Lowell's "assurance" might have had as much to do with the privileges of gender as of family background.

Six weeks later, after she had gotten the stereo system she had bought in New York set up (thanks to the gift of a transformer from Jane Dewey in Maryland), she had musical metaphors to add to her awe-inspired praise of Lowell's poems:

They are awfully well worked out, real, and I like the rather gentle, really, tone…more a muted trumpet this time, or even a cello. . . . They seem exactly like what I'd always wanted, vaguely, to hear and never had, and really "contemporary." That strange kind of modesty that I think one feels in almost [everything] contemporary one really likes – Kafka, say, or Marianne, or even Eliot, and Klee and Kokoschka and Schwitters…Modesty, care, space, a sort of helplessness but determination at the same time.[11]

This "modesty" was her highest poetic value, and her highest moral value as well.

. . .

The Diary of Helena Morley was published on December 3, 1957. Despite excellent, if brief, reviews and Elizabeth's high hopes, the book sold only seven thousand copies in the United States in its first five months and even fewer in the edition that appeared in England a year later. Most reviewers noted the fortuitous match of Bishop's style to the diary's spirit, and there was praise for the introduction. In all, however, Elizabeth was disappointed that her labor of love was so underappreciated. And she had been counting on a profit that, even split with the Brants, would allow her and Lota to take another trip sometime soon. As it turned out, her total income from writing in 1958 was two hundred thirty-eight dollars, a very small part of which came from royalties on *The Diary*. She was disappointed as well at how her relationship with the Brants deteriorated. She came to find them greedy and suspicious, in the stereotype of Mineiros (natives of the state of Minas Gerais).

Elizabeth and Lota settled back into their Samambaia life, in its peaceful times dominated by the presence of Kylso's children (Lotinha was born in December 1957), who spent several weeks each summer in Petrópolis to escape the heat, crowds, and water shortages in Rio. The children of Lota's sister, Marietta Nascimento, also stayed at Samambaia during the hot season. In the more difficult times, Lota began to have legal problems over the ownership of her land and quarreled with her sister over who owned what. Lota was the principal landowner in the hills above Petrópolis, and as the town became a popular summer destination, she had to conduct more and more complex negotiations for the sale and development of parts of the estate. Subject to nervous illnesses (she complained of "aching all over" from boredom on the freighter trip), Lota bore these anxieties but paid for them in poor health—tooth problems, neuralgias, and menopausal difficulties.

After a nearly two-year hiatus, Elizabeth suffered a relapse of her asthma and spent several weeks in the spring of 1958 battling lung troubles of various kinds. She had a happy relationship with her allergist, who treated her with attention and without charge, in honor of her being a poet and a friend of Lota's. In February, Elizabeth went back on cortisone but did not fully recover until the rainy season ended in May. She also found it hard to begin writing again after New York and felt discouraged about Brazil and her life there. They lived, she said, "in a state of broken down luxury."[12] She would leave if it were not for Lota. And, considering her options, she remarked sarcastically to Joe and U. T. Summers that "drabness is what characterizes all countries except the rich, gleaming, deodorized U.S.A."[13] Maria, mother of Bettchy, bore a second child, Alisette Mara, who resembled, not her husband, but one of Lota's gardeners. This marital crisis kept Maria from cooking, and Lota fired her. Both Lota and Elizabeth had grown discouraged watching Maria and her husband "ruin" Bettchy before their eyes. Feeling that trying to adopt her would be too hard, they finally let her go.

At the same time, Loren MacIver let Elizabeth know that Margaret Miller had developed a mental illness. Margaret, a staff member at the Museum of Modern Art in New York, was still a powerful figure in Elizabeth's emotional life, and she and Lota mobilized to help her if they could. Lota arranged through the art museum in Rio to get Margaret a free one-month "consulting" visit to Brazil; Elizabeth sent two hundred dollars and put aside one thousand more to send if needed. She put Margaret in touch with Anny Baumann and bore it quietly when Margaret's letters turned hostile toward her. (She sent them to a handwriting analyst.) Margaret did not come to Brazil; Elizabeth remained ready to fly to New York to help her, if only Margaret would ask. But she did not, and Elizabeth was forced to get her news of Margaret through their mutual friends. This pattern of mental illness and then hostility in those she loved would become painfully clear in Elizabeth's life.

Elizabeth accidently poisoned her toucan, Uncle Sam, in March 1958. In the continual cycle of life and death at Samambaia, this event might not have stood out, except that Elizabeth was heart-broken and guilt-ridden and returned again and again to the incident. "My darling toucan died," she wrote to Lowell.

> I still can't bear to think about it. It was all my fault – I used an insecticide the man in the store said was "inoffensive" to animals, and it killed him. There he lay, just like life only with his feet up in the air. I want to get another one – but Lota says we're having a little vacation from toucans now. I am trying to write Sammy an ode – incorporating a lot of poems I wrote about him from time to time – "Most comical of all in death."[14]

The ode for Sammy she worked on from time to time for the rest of her life and could never finish. The drafts that survive bog down in grief: "Sammy, my dear toucan . . . / I killed you! I didn't mean to, / of course, I cried & cried – / it <u>was</u> my fault, / Sammy, dear Uncle Sam."

At Christmas 1957, Elizabeth and Lota began what became a happy five-year "tradition" of spending the holidays at Cabo Frio, an as yet sparsely developed resort town on a peninsula northeast of Rio. The brother of their friend Rosinha Leão owned a house there, and a group of their mutual friends usually joined them for a week or two of fishing, walking, sunning, and eating "hundreds of dollars worth (at New York prices)" of shrimp and seafood. But the scene fascinated her as much as the vacation:

> Anyway – if you can imagine how Venice probably looked about the year 750 AD – that's the town – a line of stone buildings on a low quai, almost flush with the water, lovely colors. One reaches it over a high-arched one-way bridge, over a tidal basin below. In back are the dunes, that rise higher than the buildings, and snow, snow white – and miles and miles of different beaches. Our friend Manoel has a very nice beach house right on them – again it strikes me as Russian, Turgenev-like, somehow – pink-painted stone, big round pillars, ten or so pure white hammocks slung up – AND the

staggering [quantities] of food and sweets (four or five desserts to a meal). . . . The town and the fishing villages are awful, frankly, – such poverty and filth. – But we went off to secret beaches every day and spent hours in swimming – with only a turtle raising his head to stare at us once in a while, out in the water – and such magnificent rocks, and cascades, and those dunes – [15]

Year by year, the colors fascinated her more: "[It is] all in <u>whites</u> – dunes, salt-piles, shell-piles, churches & chapels – They make both salt & white-wash there – In the salt-pools, <u>salinas</u>, – hundreds of lovely windmills, some very <u>short</u>, stand around just like zinnias." The "fine, fine, and really snow white" sand charmed her for years. "It's white all the way out, too – so the water on that beach is absolutely glass-like, cut-glass green."[16] By 1963, she could see that "they" were spoiling the town, "just as fast as they can," even though it had not yet been "discovered" and turned into "the new St. Tropez."[17] In January and February 1964, she worked on the poem that came of these observations, "Twelfth Morning; or What You Will," struggling to find a way to express her ambivalence about the beauty of the place and its potential for exploitation.

> Like a first coat of whitewash when it's wet,
> the thin gray mist lets everything show through:
> the black boy Balthazár, a fence, a horse,
>   a foundered house,
>
> —cement and rafters sticking from a dune.
> (The Company passes off these white but shopworn
> dunes as lawns.) "Shipwreck," we say; perhaps
>   this is a housewreck.
>
> The sea's off somewhere, doing nothing. Listen.
> An expelled breath. And faint, faint, faint
> (or are you hearing things), the sandpipers'
>   heart-broken cries.

It is worth noting that Elizabeth was never at Cabo Frio on January 6 (Epiphany, or the Feast of the Magi, in the Christian calendar) of any year. Perhaps the boy Balthazár was real, and the date was suggested by his name (also the name of one of the Magi). Or perhaps she wished to invoke the world of unexpected reversals, of things not what they seem, of Shakespeare's play, which had also played off the notion of Epiphany. The irony at the expense of Christianity, of the poor boy named for a king bearing a tin-can crown, is undercut by his cheerful confidence. "The world's a pearl," he says—the figure Elizabeth found to express the overwhelming whiteness of Cabo Frio—*and I, / its highlight!*"Balthazar is dramatically foregrounded in the poem (you can hear the water in his can but not the surf—he sings "beyond the genius of the sea") but then "is perspective dozing" in this landscape of white on white?

"Twelfth Morning" was the last of Bishop's Brazil poems to be included in *Questions of Travel.* Her second wave of poems about her adopted country had begun in 1959 when, after a year of struggling to write, she again found the voice and tone in which to describe and comment. Her false starts are interesting. Bolder and more overtly political than the poems she finished and published, they show her attempts at and her frustrations with trying to speak in poetry about Brazil as a political entity. She is far more comfortable with a personal point of departure. In the unpublished fragment "Brasil, 1959," she confronts head-on the country's economic crisis and her disgust with the plans for the new capital at Brasília:

> The radio says black beans are up again.
> That means five hundred percent
> in the past year, but no one quite believes it. . . .

> And endless lines
> waiting and waiting for the busses
> with "wash me" written on their tails . . .

Send trucks. Why doesn't the army send us trucks?
And meanwhile far inland . . .
a fairy palace, small, impractical

rises upon a barren field of mud
a lovely bauble, expensive as a jewel . . .

Meanwhile, you've never seen
a country that's more beautiful.
– or this part of it, anyway –
The delicacy of the green hills
the new bamboos unfurl; the edges
are all so soft against the pink
watery skies below, the purple Lent trees.

Shall we change politicians? . . .
swap the playboy for the honest madman?

This is the sort of poem that Elizabeth could never write and that
she condemned when other poets did. "When has politics made
good poetry?" she asked in notes for a review of Denise Levertov in
1970.

"Brazil, January 1, 1502," another of these second-wave poems, is
the only one of her Brazil poems without an obvious personal angle;
it draws instead from the years of reading she had been doing on
the history of the country. It was the first of this second batch to
appear in print (in the *New Yorker* on January 2, 1960). In it, she
takes on, not the contemporary Brazil she was growing so disillu-
sioned with, but the country's colonial past. She had remarked as
early as 1956 that the mountains around Rio resembled a tapestry
("Sorry to be so unoriginal but they do, – a brand new tapestry,
maybe").[18] And in November 1959, as she was finishing the poem,
she tipped off its central image to Aunt Grace:

> Watching the lizards' love-making is one of our quiet sports here!—
> the male chases the female, bobbing his head up and down and
> puffing his throat in and out like a balloon—he is usually much
> larger and much uglier. The female runs ahead and if she is feeling
> friendly she raises her tail up over her back like a wire—it is bright
> red, almost neon-red, underneath. He hardly ever seems to catch
> up with her, though—[19]

The poem must have been well under way by the time Elizabeth
wrote this letter (two weeks later she indicated that she had sent the
poem off), but it renders in innocent terms what seems much darker
in the poem—the female lizard is equated with the female Indians
and the female land as objects both exploited and somehow inviting
that exploitation. Bishop's method in the poem, as in "The Map,"
"Large Bad Picture," and "Poem," is to move with little warning
between the reality ("Nature," the North Atlantic, Nova Scotia) and
the artistic representation (the tapestry, the map, Uncle George's
paintings), blending the two to make, of course, the poems. In this
case, the tapestry is imaginary; but the effect is the same.

> Januaries, Nature greets our eyes
> exactly as she must have greeted theirs:
> every square inch filling in with foliage—
> big leaves, little leaves, and giant leaves,
> blue, blue-green, and olive,
> with occasional lighter veins and edges,
> or a satin underleaf turned over;
> monster ferns
> in silver-gray relief,
> and flowers, too, like giant water lilies
> up in the air—up, rather, in the leaves—
> purple, yellow, two yellows, pink,

rust red and greenish white;
solid but airy; fresh as if just finished
and taken off the frame.

. . . Still in the foreground there is Sin:
five sooty dragons near some massy rocks.
The rocks are worked with lichens, gray moonbursts
splattered and overlapping,
threatened from underneath by moss
in lovely hell-green flames,
attacked above
by scaling-ladder vines, oblique and neat,
"one leaf yes and one leaf no" (in Portuguese).
The lizards scarcely breathe; all eyes
are on the smaller, female one, back-to,
her wicked tail straight up and over,
red as a red-hot wire.

Just so the Christians, hard as nails,
tiny as nails, and glinting,
in creaking armor, came and found it all,
not unfamiliar:
no lovers' walks, no bowers,
no cherries to be picked, no lute music,
but corresponding, nevertheless,
to an old dream of wealth and luxury
already out of style when they left home—
wealth, plus a brand-new pleasure.
Directly after Mass, humming perhaps
L'Homme armé or some such tune,
they ripped away into the hanging fabric,
each out to catch an Indian for himself—
those maddening little women who kept calling,
calling to each other (or had the birds waked up?)
and retreating, always retreating, behind it.

As a dramatic monologue, "The Riverman" also freed Elizabeth from the task of direct commentary on Brazilian culture. With details taken in large part from Charles Wagley's *Amazon Town,* the poem develops a character wholly imaginary—a mode in which Elizabeth worked only rarely and uncomfortably. She worried about the poem—Lota hated it. It was an Amazon poem written without seeing the Amazon, and that was "inauthentic." When Robert Lowell told her what an effective fairy tale it was, she was comforted— as if its possible interpretation as magical fiction had not occurred to her. The poem can be read as a metaphor for the poet's decision to leave the living world of everyday concerns and harness herself to the dolphin-spirit of the muse; but it evidently struck Elizabeth as a tentative anthropological study with insufficient evidence behind it. It is marvelous in its detail, testimony to Wagley's work as well as Bishop's powers of selection.

Perhaps the most effective of this last group of Brazil poems is the more personal, yet discreet, "Song for the Rainy Season." Indeed, Elizabeth told her friends to watch for the poem in the October 8, 1960, *New Yorker* (unusual for her—if she did mention an upcoming poem, she usually said something like, "Don't read it"). She said it was about the Petrópolis house and hoped it might give them an idea of what it was like—as had "Electrical Storm" (with Tobias's cameo appearance) a few months earlier. But the poem is less literal than that, though her friends would recognize the lichens, waterfalls, and "private cloud" from her letters. It is a nearly perfect expression of Bishop's most persistent theme: the loss inherent in the passage of time. As a portrait of Brazil, it is one she can comprehend and manage. Its dimeter and trimeter lines and rhyme scheme show a successful version of the meter she had been working on, with some frustration, in "The Moose." Stanzas one and four, she said, had "just happened" in 1954. Six years later she was able to finish it, though she felt she had not been able to perfect it.

Hidden, oh hidden
in the high fog
the house we live in,
beneath the magnetic rock,
rain-, rainbow-ridden,
where blood-black
bromelias, lichens,
owls, and the lint
of the waterfalls cling,
familiar, unbidden.

The damp fecundity of the rainy season breeds ferns and lichens and "fat frogs that, / shrilling for love, / clamber and mount." And, of course, insects, and asthma-causing fungi and molds abound:

House, open house
to the white dew
and the milk-white sunrise
kind to the eyes,
to membership
of silver fish, mouse,
bookworms,
big moths; with a wall
for the mildew's
ignorant map;

darkened and tarnished
by the warm touch
of the warm breath,
maculate, cherished,
rejoice!

In the inevitable reversal, the dry season, Bishop sees the ephem-erality of all amplitude and sufficiency and another example of heart-less mutability:

> For a later
> era will differ.
> (O difference that kills,
> or intimidates, much
> of all our small shadowy
> life!) Without water
>
> the great rock will stare
> unmagnetized, bare,
> no longer wearing
> rainbows or rain,
> the forgiving air
> and the high fog gone;
> the owls will move on
> and the several
> waterfalls shrivel
> in the steady sun.

Bishop "situated" this poem about place more specifically than she did any other poem. "The house we live in" is the Sitio Alcobaçinha, in the Fazenda Samambaia, in the town of Petrópolis, in Brazil, as she noted at the end of the poem.

. . .

Elizabeth had been thinking about taking a trip down the Amazon River from Manaus to Belém for several years before she finally did it in February 1960. She had been anxious to discover how "accurate" she had been in "The Riverman," and she had in mind to write both a "post-Amazon" Amazon poem and a travel essay about the trip. She went with Rosinha Leão and her sixteen-year-old nephew, Manoel, flying to Belém and then up the river to Manaus on February 17. Elizabeth kept a complete but rough journal of the first week of the trip, and she wrote at least two long, journal-like letters to Lota. Despite some pressure to publish substantial prose pieces to earn money (Lota's financial circumstances were increasingly strained), Elizabeth was never able to write formal prose about the trip, though it affected her profoundly for years afterward. "Oh it was really wonderful," she wrote to the Barkers.

> I want to go straight back and go up from Manaus now – which would be a much tougher trip but I imagine even better in some ways – the river narrows, and there are rapids, and more Indians – However – it was never wide the way one expects, because the boat keeps going up all the side-alleys – [sometimes] a half a day in one – at night branches swept the screen door off our cabin sometimes. The night stops, at little places (one named Liverpool) with only candle light or flares – absolute silence except for frogs and fish splashing – paddles dipping – to take someone sick on board. (We had a madman, a girl bitten by a snake, children – two or three doctors, though, one of them a young girl who spends most of her time rushing around in a launch and who was very interesting).[20]

For months afterward she recorded dreams about the river, felt it pulling her back. She made immediate plans to return, but they never materialized.

The boat, the *Lauro Sodré*, was a combination tourist and cargo ship, that made stops to pick up passengers, produce, and livestock in the settlements along the river and its tributaries—Itacoatiara, Urucurituba, Parintins, Juruti, Oriximiná, Óbidos, Alenquer, Santarém. Elizabeth's journal records the comings and goings of hens and turkeys, turtles as they are carried down river to be "raised," dogs and cats, alligators, the enterprising villagers greeting the riverboat with their wares on the shoreline, and the remarkable birds living along the river. "In a big gray dead tree, silver gray, quite bare, at least a 150 white herons were sitting – against a dark blue stormy sky – In that light they stood out luminous – glowed – no – weird, silver white – [floating] in their silver gray tree – unearthly." In the *caboclo* and *mamaluco* towns—more Portuguese and Indian than the south of Brazil—she, Rosinha, and Manoel got off the boat and looked around, in houses and churches and markets.

Elizabeth's journal breaks off just as the boat arrives in Santarém; her brisk and businesslike account of what she saw could not convey her impression of the town at the confluence of the Tapajós and Amazon rivers. On February 28, she wrote to Lota from Belém about how much she loved the Amazon and wanted to come back right away. "And Santarém—I'd like to go there for a rest cure or some-thing—no pavements,—just deep orange sand, beautiful houses and absolute silence."[21] With a few notes about the town and a handful of photographs to stir her memory, her poem about Santarém, begun within a year or so of the trip but not finished until 1978, escapes its author's commitment to accuracy and takes on an air of myth. In the months after the trip, Elizabeth referred often in her letters to an "endless" "post-Amazon Amazon poem"—endless here taking on Elizabeth's special significance of "refusing to come to an end." "Santarém" and an unpublished fragment called "On the Amazon" refused for a long time to cohere. "On the Amazon" tries to record the strangeness of her impressions, including, as she often noted in the journal, the precariousness of the houses:

> Down the wide river
> comes the soft rain
> dark, dark-silver
> racing forward
> on pink water—...
>
> The river, we are told, goes faster than the ship
> tilts into the sea, tilting us, spilling us out to sea—
> (—if we keep our shape that long—)
>
> (oh gentle crocodile
> "embalmed and stuffed with straw"
> with your head cruelly bent down to your breast
> to look like a dragon, I suppose
> no wonder you cry
> tears of yellow varnish, down your belly—...)

A bar on stilts, a bird on stilts
a boy on stilts—
stem the river with straws or toothpicks
stick a straw in the water for security
the neat palm thatch
the sitting hen on her individual platform—
the delicate hammocks—

"Santarém" lingers over the magical qualities of the town itself, focusing on the poet's wish to hide there and retire from the struggle—another of her lifelong preoccupations:

That golden evening I really wanted to go no farther;
more than anything else I wanted to stay awhile
in that conflux of two great rivers, Tapajós, Amazon,
grandly, silently flowing, flowing east.
Suddenly there'd been houses, people, and lots of mongrel
riverboats skittering back and forth
under a sky of gorgeous, under-lit clouds,
with everything gilded, burnished along one side,
and everything bright, cheerful, casual—or so it looked.
I liked the place; I liked the idea of the place.

The long lines linger over details—colors, zebus, river sand, houses, the church "(Cathedral, rather!)," crazy shipping, cows, damage from a lightning storm—until the poem's central confrontation:

In the blue pharmacy the pharmacist
had hung an empty wasps' nest from a shelf:
small, exquisite, clean matte white,
and hard as stucco. I admired it
so much he gave it to me.
Then—my ship's whistle blew. I couldn't stay.
Back on board, a fellow-passenger, Mr. Swan,

Dutch, the retiring head of Philips Electric,
really a very nice old man,
who wanted to see the Amazon before he died,
asked, "What's that ugly thing?"

And the dream of retreat or withdrawal is once again set aside in favor of continuing the difficult journey, misunderstood by the other passengers.

Elizabeth, Rosinha, and Manoel lingered in Belém for a few days at the end of their trip, taking in the sights of this major city on the Amazon. There Elizabeth met several poets, including a seventeen-year-old named Joaquim-Francisco Coelho, who would interview her about the state of American poetry and who would later that year immigrate to the United States to study, bearing postcards of introduction (which he never presented) from Elizabeth to her most prominent poet-friends—cummings, Lowell, Moore, Merrill, Wilbur, Frank O'Hara, and Howard Moss. Years later, Coelho, now a professor of comparative literature at Harvard University, remembered being utterly fascinated by this intense, charismatic woman who wore her white hair like a crown and chain-smoked cigarettes between sips of strong coffee. He also remembered her saying little and seeing much and being spontaneously and expansively generous.

From Belém, Elizabeth took a side trip that produced the only piece of travel prose she came close to finishing. "A Trip to Vigia" was published by Bishop's estate four years after her death; clearly she did not consider it finished. But neither is it a rough journal entry. The trip, which Elizabeth and her friend "M." took in a broken-down car with a shy poet (a friend of Coelho's) named Ruy Barata and his son, was to see the famous church at Vigia, about sixty miles toward the Atlantic from Belém. Bishop's account of the trip is her most sensitive and least judgmental description of Brazilian life and her interactions with it. The events of the trip to

Vigia, occasioned by the regular failure of the car, overshadow the more typical tourist attraction of the church itself. And the real interest of the piece is the discomfort of Elizabeth and her companion (called "M." here but presumably Rosinha Leão) in the company of the river people. She describes the magnificent landscape: "Certain varieties of glazed tropical leaves reflected the light like nickel, or white enamel, but as the car passed they returned to their actual gray-green. It was confusing, and trying to the eyes." And she remarks on the villages and their inhabitants: "A glass case offered brown toffees leaking through their papers, and old, old, old sweet buns. Some very large ants were making hay there while the sun shone." But such description is framed by comments like this: "We were the funniest things they had seen in years. They tried not to laugh in our faces, but we 'slayed' them." Or later, she wrote:

> It was one o'clock by now and we were starving. The hotel had given us lunch, a good-sized roast hen, fresh rolls, butter, oranges, a hunk of desirable white cheese. But no one would eat a bite. They *never* ate lunch—what an idea! I made a chicken sandwich and offered it to José Augusto. He looked shocked and frightened, and moved closer to his father's knee. Finally M. and I miserably gobbled up some lunch by ourselves.[22]

Her willingness to stay with the awkwardness and conflict, to restrain her urge to impose a North American, even New England, standard of judgment, makes this unfinished piece among her strongest writings about Brazil, linked, perhaps paradoxically, with "The Burglar of Babylon" in this regard.

. . .

The two surviving letters from Elizabeth to Lota, written from the Amazon back to Petrópolis, betray some anxiety about the situation at Samambaia. "All my love. be good – Don't Worry! – I'm going to make money now. Read all my mail. Give my love to Mary.

Drive carefully for the love of God," ends the first one.[23] "And oh how I hope you are all right – and WHY didn't you write to me?" closes the second.[24] In 1960, life at Samambaia began to change, both for Elizabeth and Lota. The departure of Maria and Bettchy, Lota's growing estrangement from Kylso, and continuous worries and negotiations over sales and development of the *fazenda* lands were troublesome and depressing to Lota and worrisome for Elizabeth. She had arrived back in Rio after the Amazon trip to a frantic visit from Lota's friend Alexander Calder and his wife. They were hard-drinking, hard-partying guests whose visit coincided with a show of Calder's sculptures and thus occasioned complicated negotiations over sales, which it fell to Lota and Mary Morse, the Portuguese speakers, to handle. When most of the sixteen thousand dollars in sales that they arranged fell through, Lota's spirits dropped further. Elizabeth began to plot more and more desperately to earn money so that they could travel; Lota, she said, was "exhausted," and they had to get away. She hoped to finish one of her "endless" poems—a long one that would earn a lot of money from the *New Yorker*, which paid for poems per line; "potboiler" is another of her synonyms. It was both her blessing and her curse that she was never able to write such poems and able on only two occasions to write prose primarily for money.

With the departure of the children from Samambaia, and the increasing complexity and financial strain of being a large landowner in Brazil, Lota began to lose interest in the life of an aristocrat. At the time, she was building a house for Mary Morse at Samambaia (designed by their Polish-Brazilian architect friend Maya Osser); Mary had been trying for several years to adopt a child and had chosen Samambaia as the place to raise the as-yet-unborn baby girl. But as this project moved forward and as Lota suffered through a series of minor but frustrating illnesses, the time seemed right to travel for six months or a year; but there was no money. Elizabeth confided this cash poverty, as she often did, to Robert Lowell. Lowell, as he often did, responded with the name of the Chapelbrook

Foundation and details about applying for one of its travel grants. In October 1960, she was awarded seven thousand dollars over two years, and she and Lota began to make plans for a trip to Greece and Italy in April 1961. In the meantime, they hoped to earn a bit more between them to finance the purchase of a Volkswagen, which they would pick up in Italy and use for their travels.

As she applied and then waited to hear about the Chapelbrook *bolsa* (Portuguese for purse or scholarship), Elizabeth considered how she would make use of her Amazon trip and Brazil in general. To Lowell, she wrote:

> I worry a great deal about what to do with all this accumulation of exotic or picturesque or charming detail, and I don't want to become a poet who can only write about South America, etc – it is one of my greatest worries now – how to use everything and keep on living here, most of the time, probably – and yet be a New-Englander-herring-choker-bluenoser at the same time.

She was "in fine shape," she wrote, "except for these worries about money and whether I'm going to turn into solid cuteness in my poetry if I don't watch out."[25]

She was cheerful about the poems she had finished or nearly finished: "The Riverman" appeared in April, and she was gratified that on visiting the Amazon she had found her pre-Amazon poem fairly accurate; there *were* pink and gray dolphins in the river. "Electrical Storm" appeared in May, and "Song for the Rainy Season," the poem she liked best of the group, was published in October. In April, she had insisted that she and Lowell "exchange drunkard poems," and Lowell dutifully sent a draft of "The Drinker."[26] Elizabeth hung fire with her own "A Drunkard"; it was never finished, and the earliest extant draft is from about 1972. She originally considered "From Trollope's Journal," an anti-Eisenhower poem and one of her best. Eisenhower was gone from Washington by the time the poem was published (Elizabeth said that the *New Yorker* had held it until after the 1960 elections), and it became a more general evocation of her own dismal time in the city, "As far as statues go, so far there's not / much choice." "The reason it doesn't sound like me is because it sounds like Trollope," she told Lowell.[27] She also promised the imminent appearance of a poem about Emily Dickinson and Gerard Manley Hopkins in which she would compare them to "self-caged birds," but it was never finished. "A Letter to Two Friends"—Lowell and Moore—also remained perpetually in draft. But it shows how the thoroughly domestic concerns of her Brazilian life before 1961 affected her poetic practice, her "method of composition":

> Heavens! It's raining again
> and the "view"
> is now two weeks overdue
> and the road is impassable
> after shaking all four paws—
> the cat retires in disgust
> to the highest closet shelf,
> and the dogs smell awfully like dogs,
> and I am sick of myself,
> and sometime during the night
> the poem I was trying to write
> has turned into prepositions:
> ins and aboves and upons
>
> what am I trying to do?
> Change places in a canoe?
>   method of composition—...
>
> Marianne, loan me a noun!
> Cal, please cable a verb!
> Or simply propulse through the ether
> some more powerful meter

The radio battery is dead,
for all I know, so is Dulles

"The toad as big as your hat," later to star in "Rainy Season; Sub-Tropics," makes his first appearance in the next stanza of this poem; "Heavens!" anticipates "Poem," soon to begin to take shape in her mind; and the poem also works with the trimeter line and complex rhyme scheme that had been giving her fits in "The Moose" for several years. Elizabeth penned pseudonyms for Marianne and Cal in the margin of the draft, "Carlinda" and "Paul"; perhaps the poem remained unfinished because it was too personal an appeal.

Elizabeth was alternately anxious and pleased about her writing, and she worried from time to time about the effect of her relatively happy domestic life on her work. Would she ever find reading and writing "curiously self-sufficient"? Lowell asked. "I guess I don't really like solitude," he wrote. "The fun is hammering bits of it out of a crowded life."[28] Elizabeth responded by restating her periodic wish for withdrawal from the conflict, even the conflict over what to read—the "In Prison" narrator's wish for one dull book.

> And then I've always had a day dream of being a light-house
> keeper, absolutely alone, with no one to interrupt my reading or
> just sitting—and although such dreams are sternly dismissed at 16
> or so they always haunt one a bit, I suppose—I now see a
> wonderful cold rocky shore in the Faulklands [sic], or a house in
> Nova Scotia on the bay, exactly like my grandmother's—idiotic as
> it is, and unbearable as the reality would be. . . . Perhaps it is a
> recurrent need.[29]

The international PEN conference was held in Rio in June; there for the first time Elizabeth met May Sarton, whom she quoted as having said, "I've fallen in love with solitude." This Elizabeth could not claim. Also at the conference were Elmer Rice and Robie and Anne Macauley, and Elizabeth and Lota served dinner for them one evening at Petrópolis. Technically a member of PEN (Houghton Mifflin had signed her up), Elizabeth endured a luncheon and one tedious session before giving such activity up, having fulfilled her obligation to the "friends of friends" who were there.

Life at Samambaia during the wet summer and cold winter of 1960 was complicated by the arrival of a "whole new 'staff' " of servants. Alberto and Maria, the new butler and cook, were, by Elizabeth's account, honest, hardworking, primitive people who needed much training. Maria barely knew how to boil water, she said, and Elizabeth spent a great deal of time in the kitchen herself making dinners and teaching Maria as much as she could. She had always liked cooking and had the gift—she wrote often to Aunt Grace asking for old Nova Scotia recipes and took up bread-baking in a wood-fired outdoor brick oven—and at this point she took over primary responsibility for feeding the household. Now nearly finished, the house was a popular destination for a certain kind of tourist—busloads of foreign architects, for example—and she was busy with entertaining. She and Lota dreamed about, and then planned, travels and worried all the time about how to finance them. Lota's troubles with her son and with real estate developers continued, and Elizabeth insisted that she needed a break. Elizabeth plotted a second Amazon trip—up river from Manaus into Ecuador and Peru—even in her sleep: "Last night I dreamed there was a narrow road that began at Tierra del Fuego and went straight north, and I had started to walk it, quite cheerfully. – A large primitive stone coffin was being carried on mule-back alongside of me, ready for me when I gave out – the mule driver had a toothache. (I can't understand that part.)"[30]

Together Elizabeth and Lota did travel to Ouro Prêto to see Lilli Correia in May. On the thirtieth, Elizabeth left a confident poem in the guest book of the *pouso:* "Let Shakespeare & Milton / Stay at a Hilton– / I shall stay / At Chico Rei–." In September, they visited Paratí, a small coastal village midway between Rio and São Paulo; Elizabeth was enchanted by the town, seemingly unchanged for two hundred years. But change was coming; the townspeople had already had electricity for one month when Elizabeth and Lota arrived: "Everyone was still very excited about it – at night there were circles of children under every lamp post, just like moths." "Every single house is perfectly beautiful," she said. "I'd like to buy the whole town, just to preserve it. But unfortunately the bay is too shallow, no good swimming, and I'm afraid it would be hot."[31] They went to Cabo Frio in October and spent Christmas 1960 in the Rio apartment, which Lota had decided not to rent out.

Both women were feeling positive about the future of Brazil after the elections of 1960. Although the economy continued to struggle and inflation to rage (the cost of living had tripled between 1956 and the end of 1960), new president Jânio Quadros had campaigned as a candidate of the common people and had promised curbs on inflation and reforms in government. Quadros's election (compromised somewhat by the separate election of his enemy João Goulart to the vice-presidency) was widely cheered as a revolution, a victory over the long-powerful Getúlio Vargas forces in the government. Although Quadros would almost immediately be thwarted by Vargas allies still in congress, he took office amid popular enthusiasm and optimism. Carlos Lacerda (a Petrópolis neighbor) was elected governor of the new state of Guanabara, which had been created when Brasília became the official capital of Brazil in April 1960. Over the Christmas holidays, he came to the Rio apartment to ask Lota Soares to work for him directing the development of a large piece of fill on Guanabara Bay into a public park. In celebration of all their expectations—of travel, of the job, of the future of Brazil— the two women had a party on New Year's Eve, which in Rio was celebrated traditionally with offerings for Iemanjá, goddess of the sea.

> The whole length of the beach, about 2 miles, was filled with
> people dressed all in white. They dig great trenches in the form of
> crosses, etc. in the sand and fill them with big white candles –

thousands and thousands of candles – and white flowers, mostly
white lilies. Then they march around and sing and finally all walk
into the sea up to their necks, throwing flowers out into the water –
This is all right at the edge of the breakers so the lights reflect in
the breakers and on the wet sand – then the whole ocean is littered
with lilies. The Goddess – Moon and Sea, too, I think – will bring
good fortune for next year. Maybe at midnight I'll go down (in
my nightgown) and throw in a few lilies for all of us –[32]

FIGURE 16.   Robert Lowell, c. 1950.
Courtesy Houghton Library, Harvard
University.

FIGURE 17.   Publicity photo for the
winner of the first Houghton Mifflin
Poetry Prize Fellowship Award, 1946.
Photograph by Joseph Breitenbach.
Courtesy Vassar College Library.

FIGURE 18.   View from the patio at
Samambaia, Petrópolis, Brazil,
Elizabeth's second "loved house."
Courtesy Vassar College Library.

FIGURE 19. Elizabeth's *estudio*, at Samambaia. Courtesy Vassar College Library.

FIGURE 20.   Lota de Macedo
Soares, with Uncle Sam, the
toucan, Samambaia, 1954.
© Rollie McKenna.

FIGURE 21.   Maria Elizabeth
(Bettchy), Elizabeth's Samambaia
namesake. Courtesy Vassar
College Library.

FIGURE 22.   Monica Stearns Morse,
daughter of Mary Morse and apple of
Elizabeth's eye, in 1962. Courtesy
Vassar College Library.

FIGURE 23.   Elizabeth and Tobias, on
the patio at Samambaia, 1954.
Photograph by J. L. Castel. Courtesy
Vassar College Library.

FIGURE 24.   Elizabeth at Samambaia,
1954. © Rollie McKenna.

FIGURE 25.   Elizabeth in Brazil, 1954.
Courtesy Vassar College Library.

FIGURE 26.   *(Below)* Elizabeth Bishop
in New York, 1951. © Rollie
McKenna.

FIGURE 27.   Lota, Elizabeth, and Lilli
Correia de Araújo, near Elizabeth's
Ouro Prêto renovation project, the
third of her "three loved houses."
Courtesy Vassar College Library.

FIGURE 28.   Elizabeth with Ivar Ivask,
in Norman, Oklahoma, where she
received the Neustadt Prize, April
1976. Photograph by Astrid Ivask.
Courtesy Vassar College Library.

Thirteen

THE TRANSFORMATION in Elizabeth Bishop's Brazilian life in 1961 was almost more than she could bear. Lota Soares threw herself into her job as, roughly translated, "the chief coordinatress of the fill" and into the maelstrom of Cariocan and Brazilian politics. Her commitment to Carlos Lacerda meant transferring the comfortable, spread out, rural Samambaia life she shared with Elizabeth to the Rio apartment in the hot, crowded, troubled city. Like many a woman before her, Elizabeth followed this uprooting, though it meant for the first time in their relationship that she would spend most of her time alone, while Lota worked long and hectic days, at the end of which she would arrive home exhausted.

Lota Soares's job was complex, to say the least. Placed in charge of the development of a three-mile piece of fill along the southern shore at the mouth of Guanabara Bay, she had to battle the ancient Latin resistance to taking orders from a woman to negotiate with contractors, architects, and designers of everything from bathrooms and playgrounds to public lighting, from model airplane arenas to miniature locomotives large enough to carry children around the park. Her efforts to raise money for the development ran into competition from other city projects, and her close relationship with

319

Lacerda gave rise to persistent rumors that they were having an affair. Both women were pessimistic about the chances of Lota's staying to see the end of the park project and about its being built at all. But Lota loved the work. Displaced and lonely as Elizabeth was, in the early, frantic months of the project she said she would not change their "split-level living" (Tuesday to Friday at sea level in Rio; weekends at three thousand feet in Petrópolis) because Lota was so obviously happy and fulfilled by her work, having "at last" found something to do for Brazil. "It is so wonderful for her," Elizabeth said later, "that I try just to forget my dreams of travel."[1] In fact, they suspended all travel plans, and Elizabeth banked her Chapelbrook money.

Elizabeth's life was dramatically affected from another direction by the arrival of Mary Morse's first adopted daughter, Monica Stearns Morse. Morse was living with Elizabeth and Lota while her Samambaia house was being finished; Monica arrived directly into all three of their lives. By her own account, Elizabeth "fell in love" with Monica, a tiny, cheerful baby who seemed to "accept the universe," Elizabeth said, "cunning" rather than pretty, but immediately dear. Morse's adoption of Monica was extralegal; by law in Brazil "spinsters" under the age of fifty were not allowed to adopt children. Elizabeth and Lota had gone to pick up the baby for Mary ("We knew that if she saw it first she'd take it, even if it had four arms") and so were involved from the start.

> It has turned out perfectly so far – there couldn't be a happier, brighter baby – her looks have improved a lot and it is such a pleasure to wake up and have a <u>laughing</u> baby deposited on one's bed. – The cook and her husband are crazy about her, and all the "peasantry" for miles around have been to call, thrilled by the romantic story of the "poor" baby adopted by the "rich" foreigner. In fact, when Mary moves we're going to miss her horribly–[2]

Beginning in mid-1960, Elizabeth also experienced for the first time since the early 1940s the proximity of relatives. Her cousin Elizabeth Ross, daughter of Gertrude Bishop's younger sister Mary, had married a Brazilian, and early in the year they moved to Rio. Although the two women had their names in common (both were named for Elizabeth Hutchinson), the relationship was strained from the start as Elizabeth Bishop found her cousin defensive and unfriendly. She could not make friends with her cousin's children either. Elizabeth Ross's presence in Rio did bring Aunt Mary to Brazil, the only visit Elizabeth Bishop had from a Canadian relative.

Elizabeth managed very little work in the first six months of Lota's job. Taken as she was with Monica, and powerless as she felt in the back and forth between Rio and Samambaia (Lota, she said, could not bear to be alone), it was relatively easy to avoid the *estudio* and her typewriter, except for letter writing—which she did almost constantly. Her correspondents were her company during these months, her confidants in her anxieties about Lota's new, fast, and public life and her own fears of being left behind; in her new attachment to Monica; and in her fascination with each step of the baby's development. When a sharp decline in the efficiency of the Brazilian post office caused more than the usual number of letters to go astray, she instituted an elaborate insurance system, making carbon copies of each letter and mailing them separately, so desperate was she for contact. To the Barkers, she wrote ruefully, "I have a feeling some things have been lost in both directions – but now probably we'll never get it straightened out until all things are straightened out in eternity–at least that might be one way of filling up eternity, finding lost and mislaid articles."[3]

Elizabeth said she planned to publish two books in 1961 or, at the latest, 1962. Although she was not sure who her publisher would be—Farrar, Straus, and (now) Giroux had published *The Diary,* and she was thoroughly disgusted with Houghton Mifflin, but she had no formal contract with either—she thought she had a volume of poems nearly ready, to be titled *January River.* The book of travel essays about Brazil, for which she made plans from time to time, was the other. Even though she could complete neither of these projects very soon, Elizabeth Bishop was clearly reevaluating her thinking about poetry, especially about the revolution in American poetry that had begun with Robert Lowell's *Life Studies*. That revolution threatened to leave her relatively polished, discreet, formal style behind. To Lowell, she wrote:

> I get so depressed with every number of POETRY, The New Yorker, etc. (this one I am swearing off of, except for prose, forever, I hope –) so much adequate poetry all sounding just alike and so boring – or am I growing frizzled small and stale or however you put it? There seems to be too much of everything – too much painting, too much poetry, too many novels – and much too much money, I suppose. . . . And no one really feeling anything much.[4]

May Swenson wrote her about a "poet population explosion" in New York, and Elizabeth watched from afar as the Lowell protégés and imitators—W. D. Snodgrass, Anne Sexton—began to publish and as the Beat generation reached a wide enough audience to represent one side of the infamous open form/closed form split in American poetry of the 1960s. With so much time to herself, Elizabeth became an even more thorough reader of American and British periodicals than she had been. And it was perhaps this renewed wide reading that prompted her to let go of her *New Yorker* first-reading contract. She thought that she could spread the few poems she was writing around and that the prose she planned to write about Brazil would be "unsuitable" for such a genteel audience. In the same letter to Howard Moss in which she announced her refusal to renew the contract, she enclosed the one "old poem" she had managed to finish during the spring, "A Norther-Key West," "for the winter travel season," she said. The magazine ran the poem on January 20, 1962, but Elizabeth refused to reprint it in either *Ques-*

tions of Travel or the 1969 *Complete Poems;* by then its reference to "little Negroes" may have seemed less acceptable, even (or especially) to a liberal audience. It was perhaps her last self-conscious "*New Yorker* poem."

Her decision to leave the *New Yorker* and what she perceived as its preference for witty, urbane, and superficial poems was symptomatic of an old debate she had been having with herself over whether she would ever write "real poems." Lowell's poems had once been her standard for their intellectual ambition and technical sophistication. As his poems turned sharply toward the personal, she was surprised by their continued power to affect her. When she was interviewed by *Time* magazine in 1967 and persuaded to make her now-celebrated comment about confessional poetry ("You just wish they'd keep some of these things to themselves"), she did not know the interview was for an article about Lowell. Until he began his massive sonnet production in the late 1960s, Elizabeth followed him, supporting him in his use of undisguised, often unpleasant personal experience in his poems. He was not, now or in 1967, among the "confessional" poets she disliked.

In her voluminous reading of the summer (winter in New York) of 1961, she found much to help focus her thinking about her own, at the moment almost hypothetical, poetry. As she read Lowell's interview for the *Paris Review*'s "Writers at Work" series, she questioned his assertion that the contemporary poet need not be "revolutionary":

> What you say about Marianne [Moore] is fine: "terrible, private, and strange revolutionary poetry. There isn't the motive to do that now." But I wonder–isn't there? Isn't there even more–only it's terribly hard to find the exact and right and surprising enough, or un-surprising enough, point at which to revolt now? The beats have just fallen back on an old corpse-strewn or monument-strewn battle-field–the real protest I suspect is something quite different– (If only I could find it. Klee's picture called FEAR seems close to it, I think..)[5]

Elizabeth had temporarily lost sight of her own "point at which to revolt" and felt estranged from poetry, even from "work" in general. In June, she wondered if she should have taken up teaching, as so many other poets had done; maybe she would have wasted less time.

. . .

The heady optimism that came with Quadros's inauguration in January 1961 lasted only a few months. But the same kind of enthusiasm gathered around the charismatic figures of John F. and Jacqueline Kennedy as they were installed in the White House in the United States in the same month. Although this enthusiasm faltered somewhat over the Cuban crises, it died only with the young president in November 1963. Artists joined the Kennedy bandwagon in unprecedented numbers after a decade of alienation in the McCarthy era and the Eisenhower years. Lowell wrote to Elizabeth that he felt "like a patriot" for the first time in his life,[6] and under the influence of his enthusiasm and Lota's sudden and total involvement in work (without pay) for her government, Elizabeth asked Lowell if he would mention to someone at the White House that she would like to do something for her country in Brazil. Although Arthur Schlesinger's letter to her in July 1961 asking for her suggestions about American involvement there was merely a formal gesture, her own reach out into the political arena was unprecedented.

This surprising willingness to take on the larger issues of politics and culture manifested itself when Time, Inc. Books asked her in June 1961 to write the Brazil volume for the new Life World Library series; she said yes. She had been at a loss as to what she should do now that Lota had a job and Mary had Monica. "Everyone seems to be finding her true vocation these days," she remarked wistfully.[7] Time offered ten thousand dollars, an expense account for travel within Brazil, and a trip to New York in 1961 for the "rewrite" in exchange for thirty-five thousand words of text. Elizabeth accepted the "pot-boiling" job to see if she could write journalism—that is, produce a lot of text as simply and rapidly as possible. Then she thought, "I have plenty of material and I think Lota and I can have quite a lot of fun using up our favorite jokes, putting in our favorite people, etc."[8] But two weeks later when the first *Life* photographers arrived in Petrópolis and Rio, she said she was feeling "overwhelmed." By the end of July, she was wishing aloud that she had not taken on the project; her first deadline was for one hundred pages by the end of August, and she had not yet begun to write. Her expense account for travel proved useless; she wrote so slowly that she had no time to make trips. And she and her editors were immediately on opposite sides of a debate over what should go into the book; Elizabeth's interest in flora and fauna conflicted with Time's professed interest in "people" and politics—specifically the circumstances affecting the potential for American-style democracy in the country. Likewise, its interest in "nature" extended only to exportable natural resources—Brazil's vast, untapped mineral wealth; rubber from Amazonas; the potential for large-scale cattle raising on the high plains. By September, she was "a month behind" on the book, and her scheduled early October departure for New York with the manuscript finally took place in the first week of November.

But she did write the book. She worked each morning before Monica awoke and captivated her attention. Despite their commuters' life and its disruptions, and despite a major change of course in the book when Quadros resigned the presidency on August 25, 1961, bringing the country to "the brink of civil war," she took with her to New York a nearly complete draft. It would be ravaged in tone and emphasis by Time editors dead set on promoting the United States and the democratic future of Brazil.

The five weeks that Elizabeth and Lota spent in New York, staying in Loren MacIver's empty studio at 61 Perry Street in Greenwich Village, were intense and exhausting. For the first time in her life, Elizabeth worked long days under pressure from editors. Her growing hatred of the book she felt she was being forced to write and her dislike of the people doing the forcing made the task an utterly ungratifying one. In the end, her only sense of triumph came from finishing the book and managing to preserve most of the first three chapters of her prose intact. Although she said it was worth doing the book for the money, when Time offered her the chance to revise it three years later for more money, she gleefully refused.

Elizabeth said she worked from "seven to seven" in New York, leaving little time for seeing plays, wandering through galleries, or even visiting friends. She and Lota did manage to attend a few dinner parties—with May Swenson and Jean Garrigue; with Willem de Kooning and John Stamos; with Meyer Shapiro; and with Valerie and T. S. Eliot at the home of Robert Lowell and Elizabeth Hardwick. The Lowells were making plans to come to Brazil for a month the following summer, sponsored by the Congress for Cultural Freedom. Elizabeth also saw Mary McCarthy and Anny Baumann (who, she felt in her weary overworked state, lacked the maternal instinct—the only criticism of Baumann she ever wrote down); and she reestablished contact with her best high school and college friend, Frani Blough Muser, with whom she had lost touch in 1941. She saw a very frail Marianne Moore and met at Loren MacIver's suggestion the photographer Mariette Charlton, who later became a friend and correspondent. She visited Jane Dewey in Havre de Grace for a day and made a dreary and dutiful visit to a Worcester nursing home to see that Aunt Florence Bishop was being well cared for. Her Bishop cousins, Nancy and Kay Orr and Priscilla Coe, met her there, as the four of them represented Florence's closest relatives and likely heirs. When Florence died in March 1963, she did leave her estate to her four nieces, and Elizabeth announced herself as "the only [Bishop] left"—the end of an undistinguished line.[9] Her last act in New York was to hire a new income tax accountant, Harry Blum, who advised her to leave the United States as soon as possible to avoid paying fifteen hundred dollars in taxes on her Time, Inc. salary.

Elizabeth and Lota arrived back in Rio a week before Christmas 1961. Lota returned with a vengeance to her park job, more eager than ever to see the project through now that radical leftist João Goulart had succeeded to the presidency in a provisional parliamentary government. The political situation, intimately involving her friend Carlos Lacerda, was set for several years of nervous instability and economic disaster. "I'm on the side of the Army," Elizabeth wrote ruefully as the Brazilian military ensured Goulart's succession even as the government was completely restructured to prevent his having the traditional powers of the presidency.[10] Goulart reseized those powers a year later but was unable to secure congressional support for any reform measures. The country floundered, drifting unconvincingly toward communism until the widely popular military coup of April 1, 1964, toppled the Goulart government and forced him into exile.

In this atmosphere of tension and intrigue, Lota Soares went to work on the park. By January, she was already working "fearfully hard" at a job that kept her in meetings most nights of the week. As her effectiveness became apparent, her power grew, and she became an increasingly important force in Rio politics. "We are getting too official for my taste," Elizabeth complained; more and more of their "social" life involved dinners and meetings connected with either the government or the park.[11] Left to her own devices more than she liked, Elizabeth tried to throw herself into her own work. The loose ends of the Brazil book required more cables (and more acrimony) between Rio and New York. On January 19, an exasperated Oliver E. Allen, editor of the Life World Library, wrote to her, "I have never before felt compelled to try to prove that I or my staff was honest or fair or dispassionate, and I hope I will never have to do it again."[12] Elizabeth said she would have sued Time, Inc. if she had had a slightly different temperament.

> They welcomed many of my ideas enthusiastically and then did
> nothing about them whatever. . . . Yes – Imagine a Brazil without a
> bird, beast or flower in it. And there are marvellous Indian
> pictures – their houses, costumes, dances, etc, – not a one. . . . And

now it has just dawned on me – they are afraid of nakedness –
They publish the dirtiest movie reviews in the world, etc – horrible
sexual implications all the time – yet are afraid of a naked Indian –
or – you may remember my hysteria on that subject – the word
POT. . . .

Their idea is to present their own undisturbed pre-conceptions
of a country. I insisted on at least one page of animal pictures
every day. – I wrote 2 Or 3 nice pages about NATURE – the
[effect] on the language – pets – caged birds, etc – all cut out. And
yet – the day before I left they had started in briskly on half of
AFRICA and they were all looking with rapture at color
photographs of lions, zebras etc – because they already know lions
live in Africa. – They are not interested in sloths, boa constrictors,
(one attacked a child in the city of Belém yesterday) ant-eaters,
morfo butterflies, orchids – 4,000 varieties of fish, and so
on...parasol ants, jaguars.[13]

Elizabeth fired off one of these passionate diatribes once a week
or so for a couple of months (and "corrected" gift copies of the
book in green ink). But the salutary effect of her frustration over
the waste of her labors—the sorting of notes and photographs, the
research, the gathering of her thoughts about Brazil after ten years
in the country—was her renewed conviction that she should write
that book of travel essays she had been planning for so long. She
hoped to make a stern-wheeler trip down the Rio São Francisco in
March 1962 (she did not go until 1967), and when the *New Republic*
responded to her pointed letter to the editor about a biased and
uninformed story on political events in Brazil by asking her to write
a regular "Brazil letter" for them, she considered the idea seriously
before turning it down.[14]

But her brief stay in New York convinced her that her first priority should be her next book of poems. May Swenson had suggested that she borrow the title *Questions of Travel* for the book,
and Elizabeth saw that it would accommodate the group of poems
about Nova Scotia and her childhood better than *January River*

would have. And the poems that she was able to finish, now that the Brazil book was out of the way, were not about Brazil.

In February 1962, Aunt Grace sent Elizabeth a copy of a history of Great Village in which members of the Boomer/Bulmer and Hutchinson families figured prominently. Elizabeth had been wishing for details about the village of her childhood so she could finish the "Uncle Artie" piece, and she was delighted with the gift. Already on her desk and nearly finished was her first poem about her childhood since "Sestina," the elegy "First Death in Nova Scotia." It recalls the winter funeral of "little Arthur" in Nova Scotia, probably in 1914. It also recalls directly, for the only time in a published poem, her mother. ("My mother's watch" in "One Art" is the other, indirect mention.) She initiates her small daughter into the rituals of death and loss. The child sees the ritual in terms of the icons of her British/Canadian identity and dismantles it with her confusion (which "him" did Uncle Arthur shoot?), with the "why" and "how" questions she must ask. She knows intuitively that objects, her desire for earthly things, will compensate for her loss.

> In the cold, cold parlor
> my mother laid out Arthur
> beneath the chromographs:
> Edward, Prince of Wales,
> with Princess Alexandra,
> and King George with Queen Mary.
> Below them on the table
> stood a stuffed loon
> shot and stuffed by Uncle
> Arthur, Arthur's father.
>
> Since Uncle Arthur fired
> a bullet into him,
> he hadn't said a word.
> He kept his own counsel
> on his white, frozen lake,

the marble-topped table.
His breast was deep and white,
cold and caressable;
his eyes were red glass,
much to be desired.

"Come," said my mother,
"Come and say good-bye
to your little cousin Arthur."
I was lifted up and given
one lily of the valley
to put in Arthur's hand.
Arthur's coffin was
a little frosted cake,
and the red-eyed loon eyed it
from his white, frozen lake.

Just after "First Death in Nova Scotia" appeared in the *New Yorker* on March 10, 1962, Robert Lowell enclosed in a letter "The Scream," a barren versification of "In the Village." He said he had thought the story would make a good poem (ignoring that she had already written her own version, "Sestina"). Elizabeth was at first shocked and fell into her habit of invidious comparison, with her Nova Scotia relatives again the victims.

> I don't know why I bother to write "Uncle Artie", really – I shd.
> just send you my first notes and you can turn him into a
> wonderful poem – he is even more your style than the village story
> was. The Scream really works well, doesn't it – the story is far
> enough behind me so I can see it as a poem now. The first few
> stanzas I saw only my story – then the poem took over – and the
> last stanza is wonderful. It builds up beautifully, and everything of
> importance is there. But I was very surprised.[15]

Lowell detected some displeasure in this passage, but Elizabeth denied it. A few years later she did tolerate, with some irritation, May Swenson's similar recasting into a poem of one of her letters, about a pair of birds, *bicos de lacre,* that she was keeping at Samambaia. When it was published (after a long exchange of "corrections" and suggestions), Elizabeth remarked that she ought to improve her letter-writing style. Lowell's poem, published in the *Kenyon Review,* might well have been an early symptom of what became an almost pathological compulsion to versify every aspect of his world. Elizabeth forgave Lowell this intrusion, as she forgave his every weakness and error.

She even forgave him for insisting on mentioning her sex in nearly every bit of praise he bestowed on her poetry. He compared her to Moore or Dickinson, thought of her as the best "woman poet" of their day, and praised poems he especially liked as "womanly and wise." Elizabeth did not tolerate this kind of gender-biased evaluation in other friends, but she never called Lowell on it.

Elizabeth herself had a hard time accepting her place in a tradition of women writers. Even though she supported female poets whom she liked—she rigorously edited May Swenson's *To Mix With Time* at her request and wrote a blurb for the jacket—she was deeply uncomfortable with the notion of a tradition of women's poetry, after Emily Dickinson and Marianne Moore. Presented with Anne Sexton's *To Bedlam and Partway Back* in May 1960, Elizabeth first grappled with its painful "confessional" nature. "Houghton Mifflin sent me her book, with your blurb on the jacket," she wrote to Lowell,

> and that sad photograph of her on the other side of it. She is good, in spots, – but there is all the difference in the world, I'm afraid, between her kind of simplicity and that of Life Studies, her kind of egocentricity that is simply that, and yours that has been – what would be the reverse of sublimated, I wonder – anyway, made

intensely <u>interesting</u>, and painfully applicable to every reader. I feel
I know too much about her. . . . I like some of her really mad
ones best; those that sound as [though] she'd written them all at
once. I think she must really have been in what Lota called the
other day the "Luna Bin."[16]

Later she was more willing to group Sexton, unfairly, with other
women writers she was inclined to dislike.

That Anne Sexton I think still has a bit too much romanticism
and what I think of as the "our beautiful old silver" school of
female writing which is really boasting about how "nice" <u>we</u> were.
V. Woolfe [*sic*], K. A. P., Bowen, R. West, etc. – they are all full
of it. They have to make quite sure that the reader is not going to
mis-place them socially, first – and that nervousness interferes
constantly with what they think they'd like to say. . . . I wrote a
story at Vassar that was too much admired by Miss Rose Peebles,
my teacher, who was very proud of being an old-school Southern
lady – and suddenly this fact about women's writing dawned on
me, and has haunted me ever since.[17]

From this list of offenders, it appears that Bishop might well have
located her criticism in something about the British, rather than
something about women writers, and her comment is almost nonsensical when applied to Sexton. Perhaps this passage reveals Elizabeth's fear that she had written a "precious" kind of poetry herself.
For even though Sexton's record of her suffering is sometimes
romantic, it is hardly genteel (nor was it likely to be, given Sexton's
middle-class background). Elizabeth was fond of this formula for
dismissing women writers and evoked it often. Although she said
she had been strongly feminist since the age of six, she was the sort
of feminist who believed that an individual, exceptional woman
could "make it" in any male-dominated field; she was not the sort
who found much intrinsic value in being female. Even her most
consistent praise for women—that they were more observant of

detail and nuance than men—she attributed to their having been confined to the home, where details were all they saw. She refused throughout her life to be included in all-women anthologies and journal issues and never voluntarily took her place in a tradition of women poets, arguing that art was art, no matter who created it. Her need to distance herself from other women writers arose from the emergence of feminism and the growing interest of readers and critics in reading women writers relative to one another as well as to the male critical establishment. She did not want to be a "woman poet" because she felt, perhaps rightly in her time, that to be considered a woman poet would limit her power to reach a wider audience. "Human experience," not "women's experience," was the proper subject for poetry, and she was quick to label overtly feminist poetry as "propaganda." She had admired the young Adrienne Rich but did not follow her past *Snapshots of a Daughter-in-Law*. When they met in Cambridge in 1972, it was as members of opposite camps. Elizabeth was kind to Sexton, whose illnesses she had heard about, and Sexton wrote elaborate letters of thanks and praise in return.

. . .

Elizabeth struggled with a review of *A Marianne Moore Reader* in the Brazilian summer of 1962—she liked and wanted to praise Moore's "mad and good" quirky prose, but she found many faults with the editing of the reader. (Moore herself commented, "I never protest at being diminished but had I known that I was being outwitted, I would have disrupted the peace in any language known to me.")[18] This made the review, a genre in which Elizabeth was never comfortable, especially difficult to write. As it turned out, she rightly titled her piece "A Sentimental Tribute" and mentioned her reservations about the book only briefly at the end. The piece marks the beginning of Elizabeth's serious, literary consideration of her relationship with Moore, and of the memoir, "Efforts of Affection," which she nearly finished after Moore's death in 1972 but never published. (Her estate published the piece in 1983.)

Elizabeth overcame a strangely critical notice in a *Time* magazine feature on American poets—which remarked on the "cool, eely slickness" of her poems and found them "sometimes repellent"— to finish and publish "Sandpiper."[19] The poem had been with her for several years and takes on questions about observation and vision that were often on her mind. Men, she said, tended to focus on larger issues, trends, and patterns and to miss the details. This had been her complaint about her left-leaning, reform-minded friends in the 1930s, and it remained her first-line defense against her own perceived inability to prefer the pattern over the individual case ("I'm not too good at 'ideas,'" she wrote. "It's like being tone deaf").[20] This was habitual modesty to some degree, but the poem takes on the question of big picture/small detail with the "two minds" Bishop always brought to such matters. The "student of Blake" sandpiper "takes for granted" the enormous ocean alongside and the regular transformations his "world" undergoes. His confusion is expressed in the terms of the old notebook sketch from 1937, "The Sandpiper's Revenge."

> The world is a mist. And then the world is
> minute and vast and clear. The tide
> is higher or lower. He couldn't tell you which.
> His beak is focussed; he is preoccupied,
>
> looking for something, something, something.
> Poor bird, he is obsessed!
> The millions of grains are black, white, tan, and gray,
> mixed with quartz grains, rose and amethyst.

The last two lines suggest that even though the sandpiper may not find the "something" he seeks, his magnified vision (or "look," if "vision is too serious a word") of the grains of sand somehow suffices. In 1965, Elizabeth received a pair of powerful binoculars and remarked on the effect:

> I adjusted them immediately and it is just too bad there aren't any
> interesting ships on the sea at the moment. However, I have
> examined an ancient Brazilian Navy cruiser from bow to stern,
> and a couple of Portugese [sic] fishing boats and a group of fat
> ladies playing bridge or something on the beach – all look
> wonderful, – the boats have links in every chain, meshes in every
> fish-net, and the ladies have hairs on their arms. The world has
> wonderful details if you can get it just a little closer than usual.[21]

. . .

Elizabeth had a visit from her old high school friend Barbara Chesney Kennedy and her husband in February 1962, and early in July, the Lowells arrived—Cal, Elizabeth Hardwick, and their five-year-old daughter, Harriet. Elizabeth and Lota had spent a good deal of time preparing for the visit—Elizabeth had made literal translations of Lowell's poems into Portuguese to be used at his readings; together they had double-checked all Keith Botsford's (the Congress for Cultural Freedom representative in Brazil) arrangements. The visit was exhausting for everyone involved; Elizabeth said she loved having Cal around but was good for only about four hours of literary conversation a day, not six. Their cook "ran off" during the visit, and Elizabeth prepared most of the meals. They got to the relative peace of Petrópolis for only one weekend in the two months the Lowells were in South America and made only a brief visit to Cabo Frio.

By mid-August, it was clear that once again, coincidentally or not, Elizabeth would be present at the onset of one of Lowell's manic episodes. The "going off," as Lowell called it, was severe this time, but Elizabeth saw only the early stages. After failing to convince him to give up his planned excursion to Buenos Aires in late August and go home to Boston (Hardwick had already left with Harriet), she sat back to recover and see what would happen. Her day-to-day journal of Lowell's decline she mailed to Hardwick, feeling that someone should document these events. Keith Botsford eventually left Lowell alone in Buenos Aires; Elizabeth found Botsford in Rio and insisted that he go back and collect his increasingly fragmented charge. To do so required a straitjacket and a good deal of maneuvering on Botsford's part, and Lowell spent three months at the Institute for Living in Hartford, Connecticut, on his return.

Elizabeth had got what she was afraid of when Lowell had first suggested that he come visit her in Brazil in 1957—a man with whom she had deep emotional ties declaring his love for her (and a few other South American women, including the novelist Clarice Lispector) and going absolutely mad before her eyes. Characteristically, Elizabeth criticized everyone around Lowell—Botsford, Hardwick, even Harriet—but did not blame Lowell himself for any of his behavior. Lowell was mentally ill; "blame" would have been an inappropriate response. But she so shielded him at the expense of those who had suffered much more from his illness that her bias was apparent.[22] She also shielded herself from the pressure of Lowell's love for her: "Lota and I never stop loving you for a moment," she wrote, reassuring him after he was back in the United States and in the hospital.[23]

Months later she recalled for May Swenson a memory of Lowell's visit to rival the one he had immortalized in "Water":

> I think the high points of this visit, almost, were those parrots and then the <u>boobies</u> (I think they were) at Cabo Frio–did he tell you about those? There is a very spectacular spot on the south-east tip of the coast there, jagged rocks piled very high–high surfs–at high tide it spills over into a huge wild crater, just like Inferno. It is very dangerous but beautiful. We were all sitting up on the highest edge–a drop of over 100 feet into the surf–and for a long time we watched two birds diving right into the wild seething foam–heading into a strong wind and then diving like–well bombers, I suppose–big brown birds with whitish heads–and they must have been terribly strong. . . . They were so dramatic we

stayed watching for a long time – it didn't seem possible they could fly against that wind, or see <u>anything</u> in that raging sea or dive so far from so high quick enough to catch anything – [24]

. . .

Perhaps at Lowell's suggestion, Elizabeth began in the fall of 1962 to translate five short stories by Clarice Lispector, her first extended translation since finishing *The Diary of Helena Morley.* She tried to set up a regular schedule for work in the Rio apartment, now that Monica had moved with Mary Morse back up to Petrópolis. Elizabeth would work on poems in the morning; having begun negotiations with Farrar, Straus, and Giroux to bring out *Questions of Travel,* she was "desperate" to finish more poems for the volume. In the afternoons, she would work on translations—first the Lispector stories, brief surreal and fablelike pieces that Robie Macauley would publish in the *Kenyon Review* in 1964 (certainly at Lowell's suggestion), and then poems by João Cabral de Melo Neto and Carlos Drummond de Andrade. Although she had taken Lowell almost to task in 1961 for the liberties he had taken in his "imitations" (his translations of Rimbaud and others she feared would leave him "open to charges of careless[ness] or ignorance or [willful] perversity"), she had backed off right away, questioning her own convictions. "I just *can't* decide how 'free' one has the right to be with the poet's intentions."[25] But once again, Lowell's courageous example spurred her on to translate a handful of Brazilian poems that she felt would go into English relatively easily. The first of these, excerpts from Cabral de Melo Neto's *The Death and Life of a Severino,* appeared in *Poetry* in October 1963. Stymied as she was in finishing her own poems, she chose poems to translate that took up subjects she was having trouble addressing on her own.

The Lispector stories, "The Smallest Woman in the World," "A Hen," and "Marmosets," all address in a muted, fablelike way the complex question of being a woman in a man's world. In "A Hen," a nondescript chicken destined for the supper table surprises herself with her will to live and escapes from under the cook's knife. In flight, however, she cannot triumph: "Stupid, timid, and free. Not victorious, the way a rooster in flight would have looked. What was there in her entrails that made a being of her? The hen is a being. It's true, she couldn't be counted on for anything. She herself couldn't count on herself—the way a rooster believes in his comb."²⁶

"The Smallest Woman in the World" startles a white man exploring in Africa with her frank sexuality, though she is only seventeen inches tall. Her picture in the newspaper stirs the erotic interest of men, women, and children. Asked by her "discoverer" if she liked living in a tree, she expressed another Bishop preoccupation: " 'Yes.' . . . It was very nice to have a tree of her own to live in. Because— she didn't say this but her eyes became so dark that they said it— because it is good to own, good to own, good to own."²⁷

In "The Death and Life of a Severino," Elizabeth took on the question of the Brazilian underclass, once again in a voice safely not her own. And in Carlos Drummond de Andrade's poems about the negotiations within a family, "Travelling in the Family" and "The Table," she found a way of talking about those as well and found some help with the trimeter line she was working on in "The Moose."

Lowell's example also prompted Elizabeth to accept at last an invitation to read her poems in public. In November 1962, she read at a women's club, most of whose members were the wives of British and American diplomats. "It sounded like the easiest to begin with," she wrote to Lowell, "but as it turned out I think almost any college or highbrow audience would be easier – the 200 or so ladies looked awfully blank – . . . . A singer followed – a buxom lady with a pink orchid on her bust and a [fierce] voice – and she got a much bigger hand. Then there was a tea [party]."²⁸

As Lota's life grew busier, Elizabeth sought more ways to keep herself comfortable and sober in her new solitude. By the time winter had turned to spring in September 1962, she had spent a chunk of her Chapelbrook Fellowship, still banked in hopes of imminent travel, on three air conditioners for the Rio apartment; Lota's job would keep them there for at least three more summers, and they might as well be comfortable. She returned to painting watercolors during these months, and she made a collage and an assemblage on childhood out of found objects (a child's rubber sandal), magazine cutouts, and purchased toys, in fond imitation of Joseph Cornell. She made friends with Mrs. Humel, who lived on the eighth floor of their building and played several medieval instruments. They played piano-recorder duets, and Elizabeth was moved to have her clavichord cleaned and restrung in hopes that there would be more. Missing Uncle Sam and the other exotic birds she had been able to keep at Samambaia, and missing Tobias, she began keeping canaries—tangerine-colored Zephyrino was a Christmas present in 1962, delivered just before a much-welcomed ten-day stay in Cabo Frio with Mary and Monica Morse. (He died of asthma a few months later and was replaced.)

Back in Rio after the holidays, Elizabeth began to steal a few days here and there at Samambaia, leaving Lota to work her long hours in Rio. Lota's "fearfully hard" work and commitments almost every evening caused Elizabeth to again feel left out. She tried to be useful to the cause and took up reading Lewis Mumford and others on city environments so she could talk about Lota's work and offer ideas. Lota's terrible temper intimidated her colleagues, Elizabeth said, and made life hard for her, too. She wondered facetiously whether Lota was "heroic or dotty."[29] She thought about traveling by herself to visit the Barkers in England and wondered if she could possibly leave Lota alone for that long. Her imminent departure was delayed when Mary Morse left suddenly for the United States because a relative had died and Elizabeth was called on to baby-sit with Monica for a month. Although she found herself a "NERVOUS mother"—always aware of the many potential dangers in Monica's world—her letters fairly glow with her pleasure at this "vicarious motherhood." It brought out her "worst competitiveness," she said, as she defended Monica's looks and intelligence against the disparaging comments of American acquaintances in Rio. When Mary returned and Monica went back with her to Petrópolis, Elizabeth missed the child "horribly."[30] In April 1963, Morse's second daughter, Martha Shaw Morse, arrived through the same illegal channels. Although Elizabeth was fascinated by Martinha (and watched the baby rather too closely for traces of Negro blood), her focus remained on Monica's attempts to accommodate her new little sister and her growing powers of speech and imitation. The Barkers became new parents to Thomas Crispin Barker early in 1963, and Elizabeth and Ilse found an eager audience in each other for all talk of children.

After Monica left, Elizabeth settled in to work in hopes of finishing and then selling a couple of stories for more travel money and completing as many poems as possible for *Questions of Travel*, which had been announced for 1964. Even more important, she wanted to give herself a sense of dignity and purpose in the context of Lota's busy life. She had been spinning her wheels for a long time, "reading too much" on a variety of subjects, and writing not enough. Her muse was "suffering from leukemia," she said, and she felt she could not finish her Brazil stories because she now knew too much about the country and had lost the freshness of her first impressions and her ability to focus only on the details.[31] "I sometimes wish I could be 22 again and absorbed in a poetic effect for a day at a time, <u>one little thing</u>. – these spreading ripples as one grows older – more & more, and less and less–."[32] She tried writing reviews (none of which was published), and when Elizabeth Hardwick and her colleagues started the *New York Review of Books* (its first issue appeared in February 1963), they asked her to write them a "Brazil letter." She tried but could not. The Ford Foundation offered her a grant for work in the theater—Lowell had one and was producing *The Old Glory,* his group of plays on American themes, and May Swenson had also accepted one—but after some soul-searching, she found herself without a single idea of what she would do with such a grant and turned it down.

Unable to interest herself in anything she was working on at the time, Elizabeth wrote more and more letters. Events in the poetry world of New York and the United States gave her plenty to think about, and her sense of isolation made her wish even more for information, even gossip, from her correspondents. The year 1963 saw many deaths among American writers and the beginning of several years in which the timely deaths of the generation of modernists and the early deaths of contemporaries would give those who lived on cause to mourn and a greater sense of their own responsibility for the future of American letters. The list had perhaps begun with Hemingway's suicide in 1961 and the deaths of Faulkner and e. e. cummings in 1962. Robert Frost and Sylvia Beach both died early in 1963, followed soon after by W. H. Auden, Clifford Odets, William Carlos Williams, Theodore Roethke, Louis MacNeice, and Sylvia Plath. The next few years brought many more deaths, most notably for Elizabeth, Flannery O'Connor in 1964, T. S. Eliot and Randall Jarrell in 1965, and Frank O'Hara and Delmore Schwartz in 1966.

Other literary events in 1963 affected Elizabeth even more directly. When Mary McCarthy published *The Group* that summer, Elizabeth said she was at first afraid to read it for fear she was in it. She had been reading Leon Edel's Henry James biography and she wondered what James would have thought of McCarthy's cruel use of her friends for literary gain. The book's relatively frank treatment of sex also made Elizabeth feel out of step with the times: "In fact—I am appalled, bored, sickened, etc. by all the late VULGARITY . . . well–filth–I suppose it is a defence against the great American slickness, perhaps—but it does sound dated, just the way the beat poets did, and makes me feel even more like a late late member of the post–World War I generation rather than my own–."[33]

Elizabeth was moved to begin thinking about her poems and her life in a broad literary context by an inquiry from Anne Stevenson, who had been asked by Donald Hall, general editor of the Twayne United States Authors Series, to write a book about Bishop. Impatient and uncooperative as she had always been about inquiries into her personal life and work, Elizabeth was at a point when she could enjoy the attention and had the time to respond in detail to Stevenson's questions. She dismissed Stevenson's speculation that she "despised professionalized criticism" and offered her complete cooperation. After inquiring carefully about just what the Twayne series was and who Stevenson was, Elizabeth took a personal liking to the author (whom she always referred to by her then-married name, Mrs. Mark Elvin) and was astonishingly forthcoming with information about herself, her family, and the origins of her poems. Her letters to Stevenson are remarkable documents and show that beginning in 1963, and especially throughout 1964 (when she visited Stevenson in England), she had assembled her thoughts about her childhood and about the influences on her poetry enough to write long, long letters right on the typewriter that remain her most cogent statements on those subjects. She and Stevenson corresponded intensely for three years, beginning in March 1963, and casually for three more. Elizabeth had the opportunity to approve the manuscript before it was published; she kept it for months before giving her approval. And even this did not prevent her from dismissing it as "inaccurate" a few years later.

She also read in 1963 the famous "symposium" on Lowell's "Skunk Hour"—a poem whose dedication to herself she had taken to heart. Her reaction was more typical of her response to "close readings" of poems, though it was no automatic response. She considered the limitations of each participant and expressed her belief that perhaps poems *could not* be talked about honestly.

> I brooded over the "Symposium" last night. The best poet is by so [*sic*] far the best, isn't he...Wilbur is class-room-ish. Nims – well – isn't he quoting from his (dreadful) translation of St. John of the Cross? Oh dear I do loathe explanations, explanations, etc. – and it seems to me a "symposium" should do more, or less, – something quite different, at any rate. All this explaining shd. mostly go

without saying, I think – and yet that is what people ask for – Berryman so much brighter than the other two. I don't like his [telegraphic] style – but at least it does give the impression that he's right there, reacting, and not having to rack his brain for everything he can say that will show off how much he knows – He's the only one who really seems to like the skunk! I feel undercurrents of ENVY in the other two, too. To hell with explainers – that's really why I don't want to teach. Even talking to Isa (my "pupil") or Flavio for an hour or so about poems – I find myself impressing them with all kinds of extraneous material, twisting things just a little bit here & there so they'll laugh, or like it, or recognize something familiar.[34]

She and Lowell shared a laugh over the symposium's inability to attach meaning to the "red fox stain" that "covers Blue Hill" in the poem; the red cast that hillside grass takes on in the early fall is still known to Mainers as a "fox stain." But Elizabeth's thoughts about teaching here reveal her continued anxiety about the ambiguous nature of knowledge and her almost incapacitating commitment to modesty and honesty. Her statement leaves no legitimate room for a teacher's own craft in helping her students learn.

Elizabeth published no original poems in 1963; in her letters she mentions two or three poems about Rio, one of which was probably "Pink Dog." Although it was not finished until 1979—it was the last poem Elizabeth finished—"Pink Dog" dates from the Carnival season of 1963 and expresses her growing disaffection with Brazil's poverty, finding irony even in the people's good spirits. Restating (or anticipating) a theme suggested in "In the Waiting Room," the poem expresses a good deal of ambivalence about femaleness as well. The hairless female dog who trots along the street is a sight for sore eyes.

Of course they're mortally afraid of rabies.
You are not mad; you have a case of scabies
but look intelligent. Where are your babies?

(A nursing mother, by those hanging teats.)
In what slum have you hidden them, poor bitch,
while you go begging, living by your wits? . . .

Now look, the practical, the sensible

solution is to wear a *fantasía.*
Tonight you simply can't afford to be a-
n eyesore. But no one will ever see a

dog in *máscara* this time of year.
Ash Wednesday'll come but Carnival is here.
What sambas can you dance? What will you wear?

Another Rio poem from this year is the unpublished "Apartment
in Leme," a lovely and more positive consideration of the sea as it
dominates life along the Copacabana, in images unmistakably her
own:

Off to the left, those islands, named and re-named
so many times now everyone's forgotten
their names, are sleeping.

Pale rods of light, the morning's implements,
lie in among them tarnishing already,
just like our knives and forks.

Because we live at your open mouth, oh Sea,
with your cold breath blowing warm, your warm breath
    cold,
like in a fairy tale.

The poem goes on in three more sections to describe the celebrants
of the festival for Iemanjá, the candles in the sand, the worshippers
wading into the sea.

In April 1963, she had watched idly from the balcony in Rio as police pursued a thief over the steep hills behind the building. A few days later, she sat down and wrote forty stanzas of a *faux naif* ballad about the events. She added a five-stanza refrain a little later, and "The Burglar of Babylon" was complete, if not finished. The poem's rigid structure and childish rhyme scheme gave her license to deal in political generalizations she could not make convincing in her own voice. Its bare facts, made to rhyme, and its imaginative entry into the consciousness of Micuçú, an individual product of the Brazilian economic system, seemed to her suddenly the best way to express her political message. She learned this lesson in the use of popular forms from the Rio Samba Schools, which each year made songs of current events to be sung at Carnival.

On the fair green hills of Rio
    There grows a fearful stain:
The poor who come to Rio
    And can't go home again.

On the hills a million people,
    A million sparrows, nest,
Like a confused migration
    That's had to light and rest,

Building its nests, or houses,
    Out of nothing at all, or air.
You'd think a breath would end them,
    They perch so lightly there.

But they cling and spread like lichen,
    And the people come and come.
There's one hill called the Chicken,
    And one called Catacomb;

There's the hill of Kerosene,
    And the hill of the Skeleton,
The hill of Astonishment,
    and the hill of Babylon.

Elizabeth also said that she had two poems about Darwin started and that she was rereading *The Origin of Species* and *The Voyage of the Beagle*. This, combined perhaps with her reading of Marianne Moore's 1963 *Paris Review* interview, got her thinking about what drew her to the lonely explorer and scientist. Anne Stevenson had asked her about Darwin and about the subconscious origins of poems. Moore had asked rhetorically in her interview, "Do the poet and scientist not work analogously? They are willing to waste effort. To be hard on himself is one of the greatest strengths of each. . . . Precision, economy of statement, logic employed to ends that are disinterested, drawing and identifying, liberate—at least have some bearing on—the imagination, it seems to me."[35] Elizabeth echoed these ideas in a January 1964 answer to Stevenson in which she tried to draw a connection between the act of observation and the act of creation:

> I can't believe we are wholly irrational—and I do admire Darwin!—
> But reading Darwin, one admires the beautiful solid case being
> built up out of his endless heroic <u>observations</u>, almost unconscious
> or automatic—and then comes a sudden relaxation, a forgetful
> phase, and one <u>feels</u> the strangeness of his undertaking, sees the
> lonely young man, his eyes fixed on facts and minute details,
> sinking or sliding giddily off into the unknown. What one seems
> to want in art, in experiencing it, is the same thing that is
> necessary for its creation, a self-forgetful, perfectly useless
> concentration.[36]

Elizabeth's sketchy notebooks from these years show her also considering a poem about "Monica, falling asleep," something titled "A Trip to the Interior," and an ambitious villanelle about an aviary in the rain, with these unwieldy rhymes: fiduciary, subsidiary, sumptuary, and beneficiary. Five sad lines were all she could coax from her experience of Lowell's breakdown:

> Two of my friends
> are in the madhouse, still another
>   should be there
> Too delicate, determined – what their ends
> will be, God knows. (Or for that matter, my own

Elizabeth said she felt "stuck" in her writing, unable to finish anything because she was "feeling too many things at once" to sort them out.[37] By December, she had postponed *Questions of Travel* for another year.

. . .

Elizabeth's most vivid fantasies in her letters from 1963 are about escape from the public, hectic, tension-filled life she and Lota lived in Rio. "I am going through another wave of nostalgia for the NORTH," she wrote Aunt Grace in Great Village.

> Even Lota has asked me to write about the price of a little old
> house we know of in Connecticut. This is just the wildest day-
> dreaming – but I'd STILL like to own something in or around G
> V [Great Village], I think. . . . Are Norman . . . & Hazel still
> living in the old house? I mean our – your – old house? Would
> they ever want to sell it? (But don't mention me, for heaven's sake –
> both sides of my family seem to think I'm a millionaire, I suspect! –
> when they're all richer than I am...I do live in a big house – but
> it's somebody else's!) . . . Do they have oil furnaces in N.S. now? –
> I think they must – I don't think I could cope with an old
> fashioned furnace.[38]

Six weeks later, she thanked her aunt for information about available Great Village houses: "I'd like something *old,* with one of those heavenly peaceful views…and with as much land as possible. – I'd want a cow and some ducks!–and a pig or two–Well, it may happen yet." In the same letter, she announced her pleasure at receiving a tangible piece of her Nova Scotia past:

> Mary sent me a little painting by Uncle George (I'm sure. – It isn't signed; but it must be) – tiny, a long shape – adorable. – Do you remember it? I am crazy about it – it is really awfully good – just a little sketch. I think it must be Nova Scotia – there's a brown house, the other ones white, and it looks like N S – I never saw that kind of brown house anywhere else! Do you know anything about it? I am awfully glad to have it.

At the end of the letter, she announced her return to Nova Scotia in her poetry as well. "I have three NS poems on the fire now – and a new short one about the painting – IF it turns out all right."[39] "The Moose" is one of the three, and "Poem" (which she originally titled "Small Painting") eventually found a way to connect the memorializing impulse of the poet with that of the painter.

The house fantasy grew more detailed, though not more likely.

> I was tempted to cable you – PLEASE BUY LIGHTHOUSE – but have thought better of it! I don't like the Geddes house – I want an old farmhouse – with the only improvements electricity and a good furnace – or I'd put them in myself. I hate panelling! – I want wall-paper. – I vaguely remember that house at Spencer's Point – but I think it's a bit too out of the way and I'm not that mad about the Bay of Fundy. – I love it, but I think it's better to go to, or see from a distance – not be right there with the rocks and mud. Oh well – this is all a day-dream. . . .
>
> How much land goes with that lighthouse? I want some land and some woods and a brook – and a pasture for a cow! And some old apple trees – When does it begin to get spring-like? May? (I have no heavy coat!) Shad and salmon – and clams! – and I love to go fishing, you know. –[40]

Elizabeth's urge to escape was appeased somewhat by Lota's promise that they would travel in Italy in 1964, and she transferred her desperate wish to "get away" from Rio to Lota's nephew, Flavio de Macedo Soares Regis. She had become quite fond of the bookish, asthmatic young man and was impressed by his abilities as a poet, translator, and jazz aficionado. Flavio was good company in Lota's absence, and Elizabeth grew almost fixated in her idea that he needed to be "saved" from the poverty and corruption of Brazil. In letters to her academic friends—Lowell, Joe Summers, and others— she extolled his virtues and asked for help in getting him into an American university for a year or two, with a scholarship. Both Elizabeth and Flavio were deeply discouraged when, despite her best efforts and Lowell's, Harvard would not come up with money and he could not go. "Oh God. I don't know whether anyone can 'save' anyone else," she conceded in a downcast mood.[41]

The Brazilian spring of 1963 brought Elizabeth's frustrations with the Rio life to a flashpoint. The city had endured the driest winter in seventy years; water and electricity were being rationed. The political situation was worsening, and a violent revolution seemed likely. Lota was working long hours, and Elizabeth felt like "a recluse." All winter long, she had endured the noise and clutter of workers remodeling the Rio apartment. Despite a few weeks' respite in the empty air-conditioned rooms of her American friend Betty Theorides and the diversion of a tremendous tidal wave, which deposited a good deal of Copacabana's beach sand on the doorsteps of the oceanfront apartment buildings (workers removed it, "just like snow," she told Grace), she was exhausted and frustrated.

Both she and Lota had been feeling ill for a week or so in mid-July when Lota was rushed to the hospital with an intestinal occlusion that required surgery. She was extremely ill and spent two weeks in the hospital before she could go home to recover. Elizabeth had stayed with her there, as her *accompaniante*, and was astonished at the social occasion Lota's friends and relatives made of her very serious illness once she was out from under the protection of the hospital's "no visitors" policy. Mary Morse stayed down in Rio to help Elizabeth "entertain" their guests. "It sounds crazy—and it is—they're all crazy, really," Elizabeth complained.[42] Lota refused to allow herself time to convalesce, and after only two weeks more she went back to work. As a result, she contracted typhoid fever, and Elizabeth herself retreated to the Hospital Silvestre for a "rest," which usually meant the time and attention she needed to break a destructive cycle of drinking. When they were both out of the hospital, they retreated to Samambaia, where Lota could "sleep most of the time" and be "in a fury the rest."[43]

At mid-October, they returned to Rio and to the task of entertaining Konstantinos Doxiades, the well-known Greek city planner whom Lota had invited to advise her on the progress of the park. Brazilian politics was relatively calm ("the calm of despair," Elizabeth said), and though inflation continued to rage ("When I sell my $$$ I can hardly carry them home"), both women settled in to await the European trip they were planning for the spring of 1964.[44] The assassination of John F. Kennedy hit Brazil very hard; Elizabeth said that for weeks afterward she received notes and calls of condolence, and the randomness of the event damaged what idealism was left in Brazil, serving to separate the country's vision of its future from that of the United States. Both Elizabeth and Lota caught the general depression that followed the news, and 1963 closed on a low note. Lota's park was taking shape beautifully, Elizabeth said, but at "what . . . cost in nervous energy"?[45]

Fourteen

"THERE *IS* NO RAILROAD
NAMED DELIGHT."
1964–1965

ELIZABETH AND LOTA spent ten relatively peaceful days at Samambaia over the 1963 Christmas and New Year holidays. They planned to stay until January 6 or 7, Elizabeth told May Swenson as she was finishing "Twelfth Morning." "It depends how much of a holiday the 'Day of Kings' – the 6th, our 12th Night – is – You'd think they'd *know* by now, after several hundred years of celebrating it and thousands of little boys named [Balthazár], Melchior, etc – but as Lota said, without a trace of humor – 'no [one] ever knows.' "[1] Elizabeth sent "Twelfth Morning; or What You Will" in January to Elizabeth Hardwick at the *New York Review of Books* as a favor to the new magazine, which she was already finding very much better than the *New York Times Book Review.*

When Lota and the maid, Joanna, left Petrópolis for Rio and work, on January 7 as it turned out, Elizabeth stayed behind for a few days in the quiet. "No poems of my own in sight," she wrote early in the month. The major accomplishment of her stay in the country was an extraordinary letter to Anne Stevenson, written on January 8. Elizabeth had found Stevenson "bright" and had made a decision to help her as much as possible. The letter contains the famous Darwin discussion and a host of other explanations about

Elizabeth's life and her art both in a personal context and in the larger scheme of literary history. It speculates about influences on her work, her dislike of writing criticism ("Weeding out has to be done . . . but I don't want to do it!"), the origins of her taste in art ("snobbery," she said), her pleasure at the secondhand praise by Ernest Hemingway of "The Fish," her poetic values ("Lack of observation seems to me one of the cardinal sins"), her current love of Chekhov's short stories, the "sense of loss" (as Stevenson found) in her poems, and her "contribution" to poetry, including her persistent feeling that she had been limited by the circumstances of her life to writing poetry that was less than "real":

> Because of my era, sex, situation, education, etc. I have written, so far, what I feel is a rather "precious" kind of poetry, although I am very much opposed to the precious. One wishes things were different, that one could begin all over again. One almost envies those Russian poets a bit – who feel they are so important, and perhaps are. At least the party seems afraid of them, whereas I doubt that any American poet (except poor wretched Pound) ever bothered our government much. But then I remember that in the late 16th century poetry that was even <u>published</u> was looked down on; the really good poetry was just handed around. So one probably shouldn't worry too much about one's position, and certainly never about being "contemporary."

Yes, she confessed in the dark days of early 1964 in Brazil, "my outlook is pessimistic. . . . I think we are still barbarians, barbarians who commit a hundred indecencies and cruelties every day of our lives, as just possibly future ages may be able to see. But I think we should be gay in spite of it, sometimes even giddy, – to make life endurable and to keep ourselves 'new, tender, quick.' "[2]

In her lonely solitude in Rio, Elizabeth focused all her energy on the European trip she and Lota were planning for May. After Lota's illness the previous September, Elizabeth had become unwilling to leave her alone, but she was mulling over in her mind an invitation she had just received from the University of Washington in Seattle to take over Ted Roethke's English Department chair for a term or two teaching the reading and writing of poetry. Elizabeth would ordinarily not have considered such a job, though she saw Lowell and Swenson doing it, except that she thought Lota might come along which might somehow break her of her tendency to overwork and to be profoundly depressed over the ups and downs of her country. Elizabeth had trouble deciding; she had never taught before and believed that writing really could not be taught, and Seattle was altogether a new idea. She had gotten to know the current Fulbright professor in Brazil, David Weimer, and his family, so she had an example of a teacher-scholar before her to contemplate. So in November 1964, seeing that the situation in Brazil was unlikely to improve, she wired a tentative "yes" for the winter and spring terms of 1966, still hoping that Lota would come.

The crisis that both Elizabeth and Lota had been predicting for Brazil came on April 1, 1964. In late March, Goulart had staged a massive rally asking the public to support his plans for agrarian reform and the nationalization of some industries, thereby convincing his opposition that he intended to extend his sympathy for communism into a leftist dictatorship with himself at the head. The citizens of Brazil (Lota and Elizabeth included), discouraged by a currency worth only 10 percent of what it had been worth in 1962 and a cost of living that had tripled in the same period, were ready for almost any change. When Goulart failed to intervene in a strike by enlisted men in the Brazilian navy (thereby undermining the authority of military leaders), Governor José de Magalhaes Pinto of Minas Gerais declared his state to be in revolt against the federal government; Carlos Lacerda and the state of Guanabara followed suit on April 1 – the Brazilian "Day of the Lie." Lota was very much involved – she spent the tense day of the bloodless revolution in the governor's palace in Rio, while Elizabeth relied on Mary Morse's shortwave radio communications for news. As the divided army – half defending Goulart, half supporting the new revolutionary leaders – unified itself in opposition to Goulart late in the afternoon, crowds poured out into Rio's rainy streets to celebrate, shouting slogans and proclaiming victory over communism. "The Truth Came Out on the Day of the Lie" the slogans went, and Elizabeth and Lota joined with the millions in support of the new regime under General Humberto de Alencar Castelo Branco. In her new involvement with national politics, Elizabeth felt she could judge Castelo Branco and decided that she liked him, especially as he seemed to view his ascent to power with an ironic sense of humor.

Elizabeth was furious when she began to see foreign accounts of the revolution. To U.S. observers, it looked like a military coup had established a fascist state, with McCarthy-style "witch-hunts" for known or suspected communists. In the heady days following the revolution, few people in Brazil expected that the military regime would betray its idealistic aims of restoring economic order, eliminating corruption in the government, and moving Brazil away from communism while maintaining a representative democracy. The Institutional Act of April 9, 1964, seemed necessary at the time: the government seized the power to dismiss elected officials and public servants and to disenfranchise for ten years those found guilty of subversion or corruption. Not even the three thousand arrests in the city of Rio in the few days following the revolution depressed the country's mood – "no workers or students were arrested," Elizabeth said in the army's defense. Any action of the military regime was deemed necessary to restore order before a popularly elected government could take over. Few foresaw the tremendous abuse of power that would follow, particularly after 1968: the thousands of arrests on flimsy evidence, the "disappearances," the disenfranchisement of anyone voicing opposition to the military rule. And few in Brazil guessed that it would be twenty-five years before the country would again have a popularly elected president. Lota would follow Carlos Lacerda as he considered running for president of Brazil and then capitulated to the authoritarian measures enacted by the revolutionary government. The progress of political events only increased her despair over her country's future.

But in April 1964, it seemed that Brazil's situation might change for the better. Elizabeth was happy that the new government had "the communists on the run," and Lacerda, grateful to Lota for her support and aware of her hard work over four years, immediately granted her four weeks of vacation and a travel expense account. She and Elizabeth at last made plane reservations to fly from Rio to Milan, where they would visit the Triennale exhibition of painting, design, and architecture, then pick up a car and tour Italy together. Elizabeth was giddy at the prospect of the trip—and at the sight of an elm or an oak "and grass you can sit on."[3] The *New Yorker* check for "The Burglar of Babylon" paid her airfare.

They left on May 14 and spent a month in Milan, Florence, and Venice enjoying a lovely Italian spring—green wheat and wildflowers—and tracking down every Piero della Francesca painting they could find. Elizabeth was delighted to discover that the painter's contemporaries had reported him to be "lazy," needing prodding to accomplish anything; but she was moved to tears by the window in time she saw in *The Scourging:* "It's the best-preserved—oil, on a wooden panel, rather small—and superb—As if there were an instrument like a telescope or microscope – for time – you're looking straight through dark centuries into bright sunlight, only it's all silent—."[4]

Lota and Elizabeth parted company on June 15—Lota flew back to Brazil to work, and Elizabeth headed for England and her first visit in nearly fifteen years with Ilse and Kit Barker and their son Thomas. The companionship she felt on this visit, the long sessions of talking at the local pub, both comforted her and reminded her of what she had been missing in the past few years in Brazil. She apologized to the Barkers for talking so much ("I'm so lonely I'm garrulous") and thanked them for a visit that had done her a world of good. Then she went up to the Hotel Pastoria in London for a week of theater and parties with the assembled poets of England and America. While there, she visited with Stephen Spender, Philip Larkin, William Empson, Robert Bly, Cleanth Brooks, John Wain, Gene Baro, Donald Hall, Richard Wilbur, and a Portuguese poet in exile named Alberto Lacerda. She was interviewed by the *Times*'s Edward Lucie-Smith and was photographed for the paper sitting on a bench in the rain in Leicester Square. Lucie-Smith quizzed her on her feelings about various English writers and the difference between contemporary American poetry and the British version. She was feeling "cheerful" about the interview, and her sense of humor and deep knowledge shone forth. American poetry was "more surprising," she was quoted as saying. She once again expressed her impatience with her own tendency to write descriptive poetry: "I want to avoid the picturesque, to write something more abstract." She admitted that her favorite English writer was Darwin and she confessed only a mild impatience with the British:

> They scold you a great deal. And I'm suffering from caffeine-withdrawal. I haven't had a cup of what I'd call coffee since I got here. All the same, it's nice not to have to tell my jokes in Portuguese. But then, I've only thought of one funny thing since I got here—that being in England is rather like going to the movies after you've read the book.[5]

Elizabeth had hated England on her first visit there in 1937, and privately in 1964 she was similarly critical. She loved the Barkers and their four-hundred-year-old cottage ("They live . . . exactly like Beatrix Potter," she reported); but as a nation the English made her feel "not small enough, rugged enough, polite enough," and except for the fact that they were "not as clean as we are," she found they had "too much civilisation."[6] And the poets, she said, suffered from a "deadness" or "hopelessness," "as if they've thrown off Victorianism, Georgeianism, Radicalism of the '30s – and now let's all give up together. Even Larkin's poetry is a bit too easily resigned to grimness, don't you think? – Oh I am all for grimness and horrors of every sort – but you can't have them, either, by shortcuts, by just saying it."[7] But England kept reminding her of Nova Scotia, she said, remembering all the British books of her childhood.

Elizabeth spent a couple of days with Anne Stevenson Elvin and her husband, a professor of Chinese history, at Cambridge. Although Elizabeth managed to get in a session of punting on the Cam, her stay was violently interrupted by a late-night asthma attack caused by "the ghost of a dog" who had lived in the house for twenty years until his recent death. A doctor gave her cortisone to break the attack, and she spent the rest of her trip on the "high" that was a side effect of the drug for her. As a result of her illness, she canceled an excursion through Wales and the Lake District to Scotland and instead stayed another week in the excellent company of the Barkers and then a few extra days in London. Among her side trips was a pilgrimage alone to Darwin's house in Kent, which she talked about for weeks afterward.

Elizabeth left London by the freighter SS *Brasil Star* on July 18, about two weeks ahead of her original schedule. She was "dying to see Lota," she said, but was ambivalent about returning to Brazil. But she was not at all ambivalent about the prospect of seventeen days of peace and work aboard her ship, though midway she admitted that she was unable to contemplate the ocean with as much pleasure as she had in her youth. Their first port of call was Lisbon, where Elizabeth spent a day of heady solitude on a private tour of the city conducted by a taxi driver, including all the sights, the big flea market, and his own neighborhood. She was proud of speaking serviceable Portuguese and of maintaining her composure eating lunch alone in an elegant restaurant in the city, while the waiters in tuxedos fell all over themselves to serve her. And Lisbon itself pleased her, as all Latin-Catholic countries did, with its mix of ineffable beauty and "active" bad taste:

Lisbon is awfully pretty – climbs up the hills from the Tagus very steeply, all dazzling white and pale colors like mints – particularly pale-green or orange, with white trim. . . . The little castle of Belem, as you come up the river, where so many discoverers started off, looks like a <u>postage stamp</u> – an old and rare one – I suppose it's the crumbly gray color and the crenellations that look like perforations. . . . But alas they are putting up some smallish monstrosities – and a Christ on the opposite bank of the river – worse than Rio's.

The ship also docked briefly at Tenerife on July 25, and then "never a ship – nothing, nothing, just flying fish, hundreds of them floating off to either side most of the time." Alone among sixty passengers, most of them "the wrong sort" of British, Elizabeth took her meals at the captain's table but kept to herself, writing letter after letter and getting more work done in two weeks than she had in "the whole time" in Rio. (If the ship turned around and went back, she said, she would write a novel. The long short story she said she did finish on the trip might have been "May Day," one strange draft of which is among her papers.) She found the other passengers depressing and felt that her being "single" and a writer made her too strange for their comprehension. "They don't believe in me, I can see that! – Too bad – I was getting to feel quite real again in London – back in Brazil I often have doubts, too –." Ten days into the trip she remarked, "My the world is big. – We haven't even crossed the equator yet."[8]

Lota, Mary, and Monica greeted Elizabeth's *navio* as it arrived in Rio, two days ahead of schedule. She had a couple of weeks to recover (on August 12 she was still "heaving gently" with the ship) before Anny Baumann was scheduled to arrive in Brazil for a two-week visit. Both Elizabeth and Lota wanted to be especially healthy for Baumann's arrival, as she equated good health with good moral fiber, and they wanted to be judged well. This would prove harder for a weary Lota than for Elizabeth. Baumann had treated Carlos

Lacerda when he was exiled in New York in the late 1950s, and her visit was a combined vigorous vacation and house call to three of her favorite patients. Lota and Elizabeth had a hard time keeping up with her, though Elizabeth was immensely grateful for her company. On a three-day trip to see Lilli Correia de Araújo in Ouro Prêto and the famous Aleijadinho statuary at Congonhas, they had hours of conversation, particularly about Lota. Elizabeth's letters to Baumann after this visit begin "Dear Anny" for the first time, and in a confiding tone they address the problem of Lota and the increasing effects of stress and overwork on her health. She was exhausted but could not sleep and had a temper even quicker than usual and bordering on the irrational. Baumann dispensed sleep aids, including Nembutal and Seconal, to both women.

Baumann's departure on September 11 left Elizabeth understandably let down and bereft of the prospect of intensely sympathetic and English-speaking company for the first time in several months. She felt like an exile and a recluse and pinned her hopes on travel—perhaps a long-dreamed-of trip to Tierra del Fuego, alone. If not that, then they certainly would go to Italy again in the spring. Her hopes for travel were bolstered by "another of those surprising awards"; her election to the Academy of American Poets in August 1964 awarded her five thousand dollars, and though she felt the award "undeserved," she happily banked the money against the cost of the next trip.

Flannery O'Connor's last letter to Elizabeth Bishop had introduced her friend Ashley Brown, who would be coming to Brazil as a Fulbright professor in 1964–1965. Brown arrived in August, just as O'Connor died. Perhaps because the two were associated in her mind, and because she was so sad about O'Connor's death, Elizabeth made a special effort to meet and become friends with Brown, and they took an immediate fancy to each other. Her need for English-speaking company was temporarily resolved. Brown was then a forty-year-old professor at the University of South Carolina, one of the founders of the journal *Shenandoah,* and a self-styled repository of information about contemporary American letters. He also proved to be an ideal traveling companion; for a year or so, Elizabeth had ready company whenever she wanted to travel within Brazil and an eager conversationalist with whom she could joke in English. His interview with her, the first substantial one of her career and probably still the best, was published in *Shenandoah* in the winter of 1966. They corresponded for years afterward as well.

Elizabeth Hardwick asked Elizabeth if she would write a piece about O'Connor for a memorial section of the *New York Review of Books*. She said yes, uncharacteristically; she had long admired O'Connor's work, recommending it to her friends and praising its poetic qualities. She had jokingly suggested that Bishop Tarwater in *The Violent Bear It Away* was her namesake, and she long regretted not having accepted one of O'Connor's several invitations to visit the Anadalusia Farm in Milledgeville, Georgia. Elizabeth's tiny eulogy for O'Connor is moving in its honesty; she did not know O'Connor well, but they shared a certain turn of mind and an appreciation for earnest awfulness in the expression of religious belief. And Elizabeth admired her courage. The piece remembers the letter of appreciation O'Connor wrote for a gift Elizabeth had sent: a piece of Brazilian folk art consisting of an altar and a cross made of cardboard, tinfoil, and ribbon and constructed in a wine bottle.

The major U.S. literary events of 1964 were the publication of John Berryman's *77 Dream Songs* and Lowell's *For the Union Dead*. (Perhaps it was well that she delayed *Questions of Travel* for a year; the *Dream Songs* won the Pulitzer Prize, and Roethke's *The Far Field* won the National Book Award.) She had seen most of Lowell's book quite recently and had chided him for what she perceived as inaccuracies. A felt presence throughout the book, she had contributed much to its composition. It opens with "Water," Lowell's poem about their day in Stonington in 1948, and the third poem is "The Scream," his adaptation of "In the Village." "Dropping South: Brazil" commemorates his trip there.

Berryman's *Dream Songs* confused her; once again she was confronted with poems she judged powerful, original, and "confessional." "I'm pretty much at sea about that book," she wrote in October. "Some pages I find wonderful, some baffle me completely. I am sure he is saying <u>something</u> important—perhaps sometimes too personally?"[9] To Anne Stevenson, Elizabeth showed more confidence in her evaluation:

> [Berryman] echoes: "The Wreck of the Deutschland," Stevens, Cummings, Lowell, a bit, Pound, etc etc.—but it is quite an extraordinary performance, although I think I really understand probably barely half of it. If I were a critic and had a good <u>brain</u> I think I'd like to write a study of "The School of Anguish"—Lowell (by far the best), Roethke, and Berryman and their descendents like Anne Sexton and Seidel, more and more anguish and less and less poetry. Surely never in all the ages has poetry been so personal and confessional—and I don't think it is what I like, really—although I certainly admire Lowell's.[10]

As the Second Institutional Act was dissolving existing political parties in Brazil and further suppressing the political rights of dissidents, Lota's park was receiving a name. The Parque do Flamengo was about to be lit by designer Richard Kelly, whom Lota and Elizabeth had entertained in November, and its construction phase was winding down. But the remaining details kept Lota from resting; she "needs a vacation NOW," Elizabeth reported with anxiety. Elizabeth's concern that Lota would never extricate herself from public life and overwork in Brazil brought about renewed consideration of the lucrative but terrifying University of Washington job offer and intensified Elizabeth's hope that Lota—the old, funny, energetic, loving Lota—would come with her.

. . .

After an exhausted few days at Samambaia over the Christmas holidays, Elizabeth left with Ashley Brown for a visit to Ouro Prêto and Tiradentes. She felt guilty leaving Lota in Rio, she said, but Lota was tired and fighting with everyone, and getting away seemed like a good idea; Brown's desire to see the town gave Elizabeth a reason to go. Brown stayed at Lilli Correia's *pouso* in Ouro Prêto, while Elizabeth stayed with Lilli at her own house. Brown left on the seventeenth; Elizabeth stayed five more days and would have stayed longer, she said, but the weather had turned foul, and her concern for Lota was drawing her back to the hot city. Ouro Prêto and Lilli's company became an important haven from the chaos in Rio over the next year or so, and Elizabeth returned whenever possible. Lilli, her friend Ninita, and their bohemian visitors were known among the Ouro Prêto townspeople as "the French ladies," in amused and tolerant recognition of their complex lesbian ménage.

Elizabeth arrived back to four cables from the *New York Times Magazine* asking her if she would write an article about Rio on the occasion of the city's quatercentenary. She needed the money, she said, and once again wanted to prove to herself that she could write slick, rapidly produced journalistic prose. She had just over three weeks to write the piece, which she did, she said, under the influence of dexedrine, coffee, and all the willpower she could muster. Even then, its last one thousand words were delivered by cable, and she quarreled with the editors over her opening, their choice of photographs, and the inaccurate headline they chose for the piece: "On the Railroad Named Delight." "There is no railroad named Delight," she said. (The magazine had borrowed from her translation of one of the 1965 Carnival sambas for the catchy title.) But those quarrels were nothing compared to those she conducted after the piece was published and had been read in Rio.

In the daily paper *Correio da Manha,* columnist Fernando de Castro attacked the article on every count, clearly misunderstanding Bishop's chief literary tools—irony and understatement. In writing her piece, Elizabeth had been unable, or perhaps unwilling, to suppress her current disappointment with Carlos Lacerda, the city of Rio, and the Brazilian government. Her every praise of the city is undermined by ironic disparagement; Rio is not a beautiful city, for example, but a beautiful setting for a city. The sambas were wonderful but are now being ruined by commercialization. After four hundred years, the city has grown shabby. And Castro would not, or could not, recognize the depth of this praise from Elizabeth Bishop: "All together, the city's activities were a completely Cariocan . . . mixture: Latin and African, Catholic and pagan; mildly military, with a touch of progress; a bit disorganized, but with a great deal of unexpected beauty." On only two subjects is she unequivocally positive. First, Lota's Flamengo Park represents a great gift to the people of Rio, "three year's hard work on an unpromising, hideous stretch of mud, dust, pipes and highways long known as 'the fill.' " (Elizabeth does not mention Lota by name.) Second, and "far more enduring,"

> is another compensation for those who have to put up with the
> difficulties of life in Rio. One example will make it plain. Recently
> a large advertisement showed a young Negro cook, overcome by
> her pleasure in having a new gas stove, leaning across it toward her
> white mistress, who leaned over from her side of the stove as they
> kissed each other on the cheek.
>   Granted that the situation is not utopian, socially speaking, and
> that the advertisement is silly—but could it have appeared on
> billboards or in the newspapers, in Atlanta, Ga., or even in New
> York? In Rio, it went absolutely unremarked on, one way or the
> other.[11]

Elizabeth had watched with the rest of the world the civil rights march on Washington of August 28, 1963, and had been greatly moved by the sight of a quarter million African Americans converging on the Capitol. With Lowell and others of her friends, she had applauded John F. Kennedy's and then Lyndon Johnson's prodding of Congress toward the Civil Rights Act of 1964 and had cheered Martin Luther King's Nobel Peace Prize. In the same month as this magazine piece appeared, she scolded Aunt Grace severely:

"Dr. Martin Luther King is NOT a communist!"[12] Her attitude toward race was typical of liberal, well-intentioned white Americans of her generation; she was deeply supportive of the civil rights movement, and she had spoken often of qualities in the black people she knew that she admired. She had been a casual friend of Billie Holiday's in New York in the 1930s; and she believed that black poets deserved special consideration and support. But she was also capable of hoping fervently that Mary Morse's daughter would not turn out too "Negroid," of saying when she once got poor service in a hospital, "I had thought I liked Negros, too."[13] There was a condescension in her thinking about black Americans and Brazilians that grates on contemporary ears and was apparent in her applauding of the stove advertisement; she did not see that the black servant was right where the most unregenerate racist would have wanted her to be.

When Fernando de Castro, and another columnist, Carlos Swan, attacked the anecdote as evidence of Bishop's racism, she was incensed. It was open season for newspaper attacks on Lota Soares in 1965; no doubt Elizabeth's well-known connection to Lota made her an easy target for the Rio press (which in her article she had called "wildly inaccurate and frequently libelous"). She defended herself in a furious letter, which Lota translated into Portuguese, in which she accused Castro of being unable to read or understand English figures of speech. She also could not resist a withering ad hominem attack: "I hasten to assure Sr. Castro that if I thought he was of the slightest importance as a writer, I would bring suit for libel immediately."[14]

Castro had pointed out that Bishop's admiration of the advertisement made her a racist; Swan's more subtle point was that she had shortchanged the Brazilians by suggesting that their good record in race relations was somehow "unconscious." This idea Elizabeth embraced—racial tolerance was best when it was unconscious, and it was unlikely that the United States would ever reach such a point of unconscious harmony. Elizabeth was not prepared to consider the deeper implication of the Brazilians' "unconscious" acceptance of the social status quo in their country. The servants in Brazil were (and still are) almost always black; the mistresses and masters were relatively pale, if not absolutely white. As long as black Brazilians did not object to this arrangement, a remarkable racial peace did reign. This absence of conflict was an absolute good to Elizabeth, even as she watched King lead American blacks to demonstrate for change in the United States. In her own defense in the reply to Castro, she cited the fourth of her "Songs for a Colored Singer" as "a prophecy, or a prayer, that justice will eventually triumph for the Negro in the U S A." If Castro had had trouble with figurative language in the article, it is unlikely that he would have seen the dark prediction in the poem.

> See it lying there like seeds,
> like black seeds.
> See it taking root like weeds,
> faster, faster than the weeds,
>
> all the shining seeds take root,
> conspiring root,
> and what curious flower or fruit
> will grow from that conspiring root?

Elizabeth spent an awful afternoon at Lota's birthday party on March 16 watching people cast pitying looks on her and slowly discovering that most of them had read the Castro column, of which she had not yet heard. After this, she spent more and more time away from Rio "to keep from going to pieces"; she was at Samambaia whenever possible, with Lota whenever she could get away, and eventually traveled alone to Ouro Prêto. Parque do Flamengo celebrated its grand opening on April 3, and Elizabeth pronounced it a great success and noted Lota's increasing fame. Cars would pull up alongside in the city, and their inhabitants would recognize Lota and shout, "Dona Lota, thank you for the park!" The park looked real, she wrote to Lowell, Lota did not. Elizabeth went back to Ouro Prêto for two weeks in May and spent a week in Salvador, Bahia, with Ashley Brown in July. There she encountered well-known Bahian novelist Jorge Amado and visited his *candomblé* meeting, one of the sometimes tourist-oriented celebrations of the richly developed African religions that had come to Brazil with slaves in the eighteenth and nineteenth centuries. A mixture of African, Catholic, and native traditions, the *candomblé* (*macumba* in Rio and *umbanda* in the south) appealed to Elizabeth the way all such religious amalgams did.

Between her travels, she tried to work. Anne Stevenson had sent the manuscript of the Twayne Series book for approval, and even though Elizabeth carried it with her everywhere she went, it was six months before she could bring herself to comment on it and grant her permission. Stevenson had remarked on some similarity of Bishop's philosophy to Wittgenstein's, and Elizabeth took pleasure in the idea that like M. Jourdain, who found he had been speaking prose all his life, she had "a philosophy" despite her inability to describe it. Stevenson sent her a copy of one of Wittgenstein's books, which Elizabeth read haltingly but faithfully. *Questions of Travel* was on Farrar, Straus, and Giroux's schedule for October 1965, and in March she gave up trying to finish more poems in time to be included and persuaded Robert Giroux to print "In the Village" between the "Brazil" and "Elsewhere" sections of the book. Robert Lowell had convinced her that it was a good idea, not merely "imitative" of his own inclusion of "91 Revere Street" in *Life Studies*. The story gave the book the bulk it needed; at twenty poems, including the very long "Burglar of Babylon," and the story, the volume turned out to be considerably more substantial than *A Cold Spring* had been. Two poems apparently just missed being included; one, she said, was about Rio and would be dedicated to Lowell, and the other, called "Crusoe at Home," just would not let itself be finished. The Rio poem might be the draft "Apartment in Leme" or perhaps

"Going to the Bakery"; when she could not finish it, she dedicated "The Armadillo" to Lowell, because he had admired it and said that it had influenced "Skunk Hour." "Crusoe at Home," granted new life when she visited Darwin's house in Kent, took on considerable depth of feeling in the next six years and became "Crusoe in England."

Elizabeth had come back from her February 1965 trip to Ouro Prêto inspired once again to write about the place. With that inspiration, and the renewed interest in travel within Brazil that Ashley Brown and her sense of estrangement from Lota's Rio life prompted, she seized again on the idea of completing a book of prose about the country—memoirs, places, churches, popular music, and one or two life stories, she said, to be called *Black Beans and Diamonds*. When she mentioned this idea to Lowell, he sent along to her an application for a Rockefeller Foundation grant, and by October she had completed and mailed it. She was eventually awarded twelve thousand dollars over two years, 1967–1969.

But for a while, she thought she would have to choose between the University of Washington teaching job and a Rockefeller grant, should she get one. And almost everything suggested that Seattle, teaching, leaving Lota alone, and becoming a "prize pig poet in residence" ought to be avoided at all cost. Elizabeth was terrified a year in advance of the job, certain that the students would be rude, that she would never be able to say anything about Ezra Pound's poetry, that she had never had "the slightest desire to set people right about anything" (perhaps Castro would have begged to differ).[15] In the end, she decided, she would go with fear and trepidation and do it for the money and for the chance to get away, at least for a time, from Lota and Brazil.

By June 1965, watching Lota's health and good spirits deteriorate had become Elizabeth's major activity when she was in Rio. When they got up to Samambaia for a weekend, Lota would "pass out" and sleep most of the time. She was "killing herself with work," Elizabeth said, and in August, Elizabeth summoned two doctors to the Rio apartment to watch Lota long enough to be sure she was not having a heart attack. Elizabeth responded to this strain by suffering relapses of drinking and severe attacks of asthma and bronchitis.

She found the altitude and relative peace of Ouro Prêto good for her lungs and Lilli good for her nerves and began to go there more and more often. The eighteenth-century mountain town, with its eleven baroque churches, tile-roofed houses, and steep cobbled streets, was exquisite in its way and under the protection of the Patrimonio, Brazil's agency for historical preservation. Elizabeth was completely charmed by the atmosphere and setting. In her loneliness and frustration with Lota's commitment to Rio and its carnivorous government, she turned to Lilli for love and comfort.

Lilli kept her husband's beautiful paintings of women hanging all around her house and inn. Since his death in 1955, she had had only lesbian relationships, thereby preserving his memory, she said. Lilli herself was tall, blond, and Nordic looking, and the two women shared an occasional nostalgia for northern things, especially the spring. Among the objects Elizabeth left for Lilli was a poem, framed in her own watercolor illustrations, that speaks to that common nostalgia; the different, yet reminiscent, chill of the mountain air; and the painful compromises their love involved; and the sheer joy of their intimacy.

> Dear, my compass
> still points north
> to wooden houses
> and blue eyes,
>
> fairy-tales where
> flaxen-headed
> younger sons
> bring home the goose,

love in hay-lofts,
Protestants, and
heavy drinkers...
Springs are backward,

but crab-apples
ripen to rubies,
cranberries
to drops of blood,

and swans can paddle
icy water,
so hot the blood
in those webbed feet.

—Cold as it is, we'd
go to bed, dear,
early, but never
to keep warm.[16]

Elizabeth had stayed in Lilli's house on her January and May visits to Ouro Prêto, and when she returned in August, spontaneously catching a ride with Lilli as she was driving up from Rio, Elizabeth intended to stay two weeks; she stayed two and a half months instead. She spoke with warmth and admiration of Lilli in the few letters she wrote from Ouro Prêto, but she did not discuss the nature of their relationship. Nevertheless, in May she had noted with pleasure that "there is also a small water-fall right under my bedroom window – the house sits up high on a ledge overlooking the town – and it is good water, so every passerby, every car and truck almost, stops for a drink of water, and I lean out and eavesdrop on their conversations – mostly talk of sicknesses, funerals, babies, and the cost of living."[17]

The bedroom overlooking the fountain was Lilli's own. In the dedication to "Under the Window: Ouro Prêto," which Elizabeth finished and mailed to the *New Yorker* while she was there in September, she quietly commemorated that fact. Her letters to Lilli after she left Ouro Prêto in November 1965 were frank and happy expressions of her love and apologies for the sad state her alcoholism had brought her to in Lilli's presence. The relationship was impossible; Elizabeth said she could never leave Lota. Such complexity had never been easy for Elizabeth to tolerate, and she stumbled under the pressure of her conflicting feelings.

Elizabeth said she stayed in Ouro Prêto for so long in the Brazilian spring of 1965 because she was negotiating to buy a house there, a house she said emphatically that she did not need; she would go back to Rio and live with Lota. But she bought it with the Academy of American Poets money, and it was a complicated process involving the appeasement of the twelve sons and daughters (all of whose signatures were required for the deed) of the elderly owner of the house, Seu Olimpio; the transaction took "forever." (She thought she would write a story about "buying a house in Brazil—incredible and very funny.") Why she bought the house (for three thousand dollars cash—her store of traveling money) was perhaps even more complicated. The early eighteenth-century colonial was across the street from Lilli's, uninhabitable and in a woeful state of disrepair. Elizabeth bought it to save it, she said—a wealthy mine owner wanted the house, and both she and Lilli were determined that he not get it—and perhaps also to give herself hope that she would have a Brazilian life, even with Lota, outside the frenzy of Rio. Lota drove up to see the house during the long purchase process. She "thinks I'm slightly mad," Elizabeth said, "but is <u>interested</u>."[18] Ouro Prêto's great attraction for Elizabeth was that it was "boring." Its backwardness and inefficiency charmed her, the way Brazil itself had charmed her after her struggles with New York. These qualities would have been anathema to Lota. But it is clear that Elizabeth "fell in love" with the house.

The house has the most beautiful roof in town – it is like a lobster lying [on] its stomach with its tail curled at right angles – and that's the kitchen – there is scarcely a straight wall in it, and the oldest walls (some a yard thick) are made of what I think you call mud & wattle (?) – the sticks tied together with raw-hide. This has never been used since about 1730. And I have a huge tract of land – another brook, all kinds of fruit trees, laurel, quince, peaches, guavas, the biggest avocado trees ever seen – I haven't even had the land measured yet. A long walled garden – 27 meters long – with yard-thick stone walls, covered with moss.[19]

Lilli acted as contractor for the restoration of the house because she was there in Ouro Prêto and knew a great deal about colonial architecture. And as they parted, knowing that seeing each other again would be complex and difficult, the emotions of their brief affair became invested in the careful recreation of the old house.

Lota drove the eight hours from Rio to Ouro Prêto unannounced in the first week of November to fetch Elizabeth home; she had stayed much longer that they had agreed on. "She wanted me back," Elizabeth wrote to several friends, sounding a little incredulous. Behind her, Elizabeth left a note taped to Lilli's windowpane:

Dear Lilli, I liked this view,
I also liked to visit you,
but scarcely could prolong my stay
so bought the house across the way:
number twenty-eight. Now you
must visit me, and see my view.
            /s/ Elizabeth[20]

She returned to Ouro Prêto for a week in early December to get Lilli started on the house, she said. There she had an "attack"—not asthma, but anxiety, which she medicated with alcohol. The changes she could see coming in her life required major readjustments. She would make them, but it would not be easy.

Questions of Travel appeared in November 1965, and despite her usual disparaging comments—the book was "too pretty" or "a little chi chi" and, of course, too thin—she was very pleased. In a happy coincidence, Frani Muser's oldest daughter, Cynthia, a young book designer, had worked on the book (she designed all the rest of Elizabeth's books). And it is a lovely book, the jacket teal blue with a violet rendition of a sixteenth-century map of the *Nuevo Mundo* and a drawing of Bishop by Brazilian Darcy Penteado in place of the usual photograph or series of "blurbs." Lowell's effusive statement ("When we read her, we enter the classical serenity of a new country") is on the inside jacket. She had made, as usual, few changes between the magazine publication of the poems and the book version. In "Arrival at Santos," reprinted at the beginning of *Questions of Travel,* the speaker and Miss Breen import bourbon; it had been scotch in *A Cold Spring.* This was "a change from the general to the particular," she explained to Ashley Brown.[21]

The reviews of *Questions of Travel* were overwhelmingly positive, but there were dissenters. Elizabeth had been afraid that *Time* would savage her; magazine photographers had been in Rio to take her picture in November, so she knew she was going to be reviewed, and she thought her recent quarrels with *Time* would earn her a panning. They did not, but William Jay Smith found the book "uneven" and confusing in "direction"; her "miniaturist" perspective struck him as "merely peculiar and tiresome."[22] Louis Martz found the Brazil poems "stagy" and "factitious."[23] Sheridan Baker remarked with some petulance, "It almost looks as if there were a world-wide reviewer's pact never to say anything bad about Elizabeth Bishop's poetry. I can't even initial, let alone sign such a pact." He found her descriptive poetry "no better than what any decent novelist might dash off as workaday scenery" and contended that "poem after poem fails to get anywhere." "She patronizes where she should love." "Manuelzinho" should have been titled "*Sozinho*," he said, a Portuguese word indicating "isolation and bereftness."[24]

But the praise far outweighed the negative or even lukewarm responses. And for the first time, more than a few considered deeper patterns and implications in the poems. Jean Garrigue worked on the correspondences between "In the Village" and the poems and noted that Bishop's "artfulness seems like the most pristine naturalness."[25] For Peter Davison, the book "saves the vintage" of a poor year for American poetry; she is the expatriate, writing "with clear-eyed observation, absolute and lovely simplicity, and a gentle flickering humor."[26] Robert Mazzocco noted in the *New York Review of Books* "the true tenor of her work," moving "toward measured distances, scales, steps; side-stepping the 'vulgar beauty of irridescence [*sic*],' and side-stepping, too, the intimate." "Her objects turn into subjects," he wrote. "Elizabeth Bishop is the cat curiosity did not kill. Also the cat who walks alone." She is "one of the shining, central talents of our day."[27] Nearly all the critics felt the poet's search for a "home" in the book, tipped off, of course, by the title poem; and many noted her Wordsworthian manner and tone. Richard Howard pronounced the Brazil section "perfect."[28] And Phillip Booth was the first to note the "deceptive casualness" of her poems.[29] Howard Moss's "All Praise" in the *Kenyon Review* was an especially thorough appreciation of a poet he was pleased still to publish regularly in the *New Yorker*.[30]

Fifteen

ELIZABETH SAW more of these reviews as they appeared than she had in the past; she headed to Seattle on December 27 to be the poet in residence at the University of Washington, with her name and her work very much on the minds of her colleagues. A National Book Award nomination followed. It was not easy to leave Lota, who would not come with her and did not want her to go and who insisted that Elizabeth would never make a good teacher, offering pantomimed parodies to demonstrate. Elizabeth asked Anny Baumann to urge Lota to come along, but to no avail. "Lota is against it," Elizabeth wrote, "but after a sad scene is now resigned."[1] And Elizabeth could scarcely admit, even to herself, that leaving Lilli was hard. But Lota's suspicions were aroused; the relationship was already painfully out of reach. With the travel money now in the Ouro Prêto house, Elizabeth had little hope of getting away from the chaos of Brazil unless she took the job and the money—an astounding seven thousand dollars per quarter—she said would pay to replace the lovely roof.

She had little idea of how or what she would teach; she asked David Wagoner to order an anthology for her modern poetry class, which she did not see until she got there. She asked all her academic friends—Lowell, Ashley Brown, Joe Summers—for advice on reading lists and procedures but took little comfort in their ambitious replies. Irony was her defense; "I have lots of ideas that will probably discourage them all forever," she wrote.[2] The truth was that she had never taught before, had no experience with a university, and had had none with a college since 1934. She was following in the footsteps of a very large figure at the University of Washington; Theodore Roethke was everyone's idea of a poet there, and Elizabeth Bishop could not have been more different. It is no surprise that she was very much afraid.

. . .

Elizabeth arrived at the old Meany Hotel in Seattle on December 28 after a tedious flight via Lima, Miami, and Los Angeles; classes were to begin on January 3. Although she had been offered places to live, that she could not drive made all of them unsuitable, so she started off at the hotel, then moved to the University Motel and its rows of tiny apartments with kitchenettes. Later she was moved by a group of adoring students to an apartment they had found her on Brooklyn Avenue N.E., within walking distance of her classes.

Her first week was a predictable nightmare; every first-time teacher has endured some version of it. Elizabeth had a moderate asthma attack, had trouble staying sober, and was convinced that she would be fired for incompetence. By January 6, she was already saying that to have taken the job at all was "a dreadful mistake." She felt intellectually dishonest and socially misplaced and wrote at least five letters to Lilli (and no doubt as many to Lota) in the first ten days. Struck by the absurdity of her position, she clung with secret and sometimes ironic pride to a wavering sense of her real self, which her Washington colleagues, she fancied, would never know. After an "awful" New Year's Eve party given in her honor, she wrote to Lilli:

> It's so funny—I go around so sedate and neat and <u>sober</u> (yes—absolutely), all in black last night, my new Esmerelda dress—

everyone treats me with such respect and calls me Miss B – and
every once in a while I feel a terrible laugh starting down in my
chest – also a feeling of great pride because nobody knows. – And
how different I am from what they think.[3]

How different she was indeed—a sexual person, not an "old maid,"
in love with Lilli and with Lota and painfully fresh from scenes of
intolerable alcoholic degradation, masquerading (she felt) among
intellectuals and teachers. How could she help but feel an impostor?

After that terrible first week, Elizabeth settled into some routine
of teaching and preparation for her two classes, a poetry-writing
seminar, and "Types of Modern Poetry," a reading course. She had
thirty-eight students in the first quarter, so paper grading—also a
brand-new experience—consumed much of her time. The university asked its faculty to meet with each class for five hours a week;
Elizabeth did manage to cut this back to four and then three, but
the work load was no less overwhelming for that.

There was much to get used to in Seattle: rain, rows and rows of
wet wooden houses, rain, marvelous green forests, fog (she said she
saw Mt. Rainier only once during her six months there—in early
May), rain. It had been five years since she had been in the United
States—she had yet to witness any manifestation of the 1960s—and
she had never been in the West. Beards and long hair were new to
her; the easy informality of the classroom disoriented her at first.
The "authority" of the teacher had already begun to erode, and she
found it hard to find her place.

> It might as well be China, as far as I'm concerned, everything
> strikes me as so totally foreign. First, the USA strikes me as that
> way now – every 3 [*sic*] years is not enough to keep up with our
> progress towards death & damnation. . . . Actually I haven't seen
> any of it except the one "old" (60 years) building where I do my
> teaching (– both classes in the same room, at different hours,) and
> a kind of wooden shack next door where I have a filthy little
> cubby-hole where I am tracked down by my relentless (but

affectionate) students, for "conferences" – usually just when I'm gulping down a can of Metracal for lunch, or applying make-up, or something...Times certainly have changed since dear old EB was a college girl...when I remember the respect and veneration and manners – at least to their faces – we showed our teachers. Or maybe it's just the WEST – I really don't know. They certainly are breezy, and tell me the most amazing things without turning a hair. Two of my lady-students (many more boys than girls, however) have told me they are "on the PILL..." One said she thought my eyeshadow was "nifty." And one dear dumb enthusiastic boy brought me my own book (they have all bought it, coitados, and a lot of them work all night in asylums, or wash cars, etc., to keep going) and asked me to inscribe it for his wife— "We've been separated two years, of course." Then said he'd found a misprint: "windrows" instead of "windows.." When I advised him to look up windrows in the dictionary, he just laughed – whereas it seems to me in his place in my day I would have probably committed suicide.

But as she was given to do, Elizabeth found allies immediately. Dorothee Bowie, the English Department secretary, became her chief troubleshooter, devoted helper, and willing excuse-maker when drinking interfered with her duties. The poet Henry Reed, at Washington for the year, became a close friend and soulmate—they talked on the phone in the evenings, reading each other amusing sentences from their students' papers and laughing hysterically. When they fell out of touch after this year, Elizabeth was sad. She said she preferred the "bohemians" and painters who hung about the edges of the university community to the academics who dwelt within it, but she found allies in both places.

In fact, everyone has been extremely nice to me – and if I didn't have to WORK I think I'd be having a wonderful time! I even enjoy the mad "conferences" and think my students darlings, now that I am used to their quaint western ways – but I would never give a "class" voluntarily in my life – and I was never meant for a teacher; Lota was right – although I'm not telling her so![4]

At that New Year's Eve/welcoming party given by the poet Carolyn Kizer, she had met and made friends with Suzanne Bowen, the twenty-six-year-old pregnant wife of a local painter who became her friend, care-giver, and finally lover.[5] From the start, Suzanne had a great deal in common with Lota Soares: the fierce intelligence; the gift for organization; the ability to accomplish, especially to finish, a task; the courage to face complex social situations and difficult problems; the tremendous energy, which Elizabeth always admired. Her married status and obvious pregnancy made her a "safe" companion for Elizabeth, who could not admit, even to herself, that she had fallen in love and who had no experience living as a lesbian in the United States, where all the rules seemed to have changed while she was gone. In the meantime, Lota was calling and writing frantic and accusatory letters and cables as her illness and anxiety escalated. Lilli, who virtually never wrote letters (Elizabeth teased her about being an *analfabetica*), sent one or two in response to Elizabeth's early expressions of abject misery, but by February communication between them on matters other than the house had virtually stopped. "Elizabeth always had to be in love," Correia de Araújo has said, "and she fell in love easily. She also fell out of love easily."[6] Even though Elizabeth had every intention of returning to Brazil, the prospect grew less and less inviting. In her isolated life with Lota, she said she had forgotten what it was like to have people be nice to her. Every stranger in Seattle was kinder than Lota had been over the past four years, Elizabeth told Anny Baumann.[7] She had let Lota "boss" her for too long. Suzanne's loving attention kept her from the terrible solitude she feared, and she grew bolder in her thinking about the rest of her life.

Wesley Wehr, a painter and one of Elizabeth's students in the spring of 1966, has published the notes he took in her classes and on conversations they had. The notes give an idea of the sort of teacher she was. According to Wehr, she had opened the first class meeting this way:

> I've gone through the poems which you handed in to me, and I've never seen so many haikus in my life. They're not very well written either. They're more like the sort of thing one might jot down when one is feeling vaguely "poetic."
>
> Some of your rhymes are simply *awful!* And you seem to write a lot of free verse out here. I guess that's what you call it. I was rather appalled. I just couldn't scan your "free verse"—and one *can* scan Eliot. . . . These poems of yours are splattered all over the page and I don't see any reason for it.[8]

Elizabeth was also appalled by her students' emphasis on self-expression over craft ("If anyone ever says to me again, 'But that's the way I wanted it'—over any obvious catastrophe—I'll go as mad as my predecessor in this job [Roethke], whose ghost haunts my every word") and by their insistence on writing about madness and suffering, even though, as far as she could see, they had had no experience with either.[9] Their lack of preparation and poor command of written English became her pet peeves. Her impulse, she said, was to fail everyone. Unconfident in theoretical discussions of poetry, her teaching focused on details and forms and emphasized memorization and explication. For her writing students, the best of whom was the poet Sandra McPherson, she insisted that they learn to write in rigid metrical forms first, use more concrete objects and fewer abstractions in their poems, and employ impeccable grammar across lines and through stanzas.

The first quarter passed, but in the last week of the term, Elizabeth was stricken with one of the "Asian" flus that frequently sweep through the Northwest. She thought she was having a heart attack and called an ambulance at five in the morning to take her to University Hospital, where she stayed for a week, missing her last three classes and a trip to San Francisco and Los Angeles she had planned for spring break. Suzanne Bowen cared for Elizabeth while she was ill.

She repeated her two courses, with slight variations, in the spring term and found the going much easier, though her new students were less dear to her than the first group. By the time the term was over in early June, she was thoroughly exhausted, too exhausted to fly directly back to Brazil to the terrible uncertainty of Lota's condition, indications of which she had been receiving in the mail and over the telephone. She spent a week in the San Juan Islands north of Seattle with Suzanne, whose child was due in early August, and did not leave for Rio until July 3.

Elizabeth's work during the spring consisted almost entirely of the duties surrounding her teaching job. She wrote no poems during 1966, though "Under the Window: Ouro Prêto" appeared in the fall. In February, she had managed a brief contribution to Lowell's memorial volume for Randall Jarrell, who had died after being hit by a car in October 1965. Barely two hundred words long, "An Inadequate Tribute" is characteristically honest in its assessment: "Randall Jarrell was difficult, touchy, and oversensitive to criticism. He was also a marvelous conversationalist, brilliantly funny, a fine poet, and the best and most generous critic of poetry I have known."[10] Delmore Schwartz also died in the spring and Frank O'Hara in the fall, more blows to this circle of poets and critics of which Elizabeth was marginally a member.

Elizabeth Bishop did not win the National Book Award in 1966; nonetheless, she was in the newspapers and magazines constantly as *Questions of Travel* was reviewed all over the country. The novelist Tom Robbins interviewed her for a Seattle magazine in the spring; and Frank Warnke, one of her colleagues in the English Department, wrote a warm review for the *New Republic*. She considered going back to Brazil via New York to meet with Bob Giroux and see old friends, but her friend Sylvia Marlow, the harpsichordist, had visited in Seattle, bringing lots of New York gossip, and Elizabeth felt she just could not face the city.

. . .

She went back to Brazil profoundly ambivalent, this time via the hectic Mexico City airport. She had left everything but her clothes and her writing case in Seattle; she would wire Dorothee Bowie if she wanted them sent to Brazil. The situation in Rio was as bad as she had imagined. The Third Institutional Act of February 1966 had further limited the rights of political dissidents, and the atmosphere in the country was even more hysterical than when she had left. A year ago, she been able to argue that Brazil was not under a dictatorship (and to applaud the arrest of intellectuals picketing the Organization of American States meeting in Rio, carrying signs denouncing the dictatorship and "cultural terror," because they should not have chosen "poor" Castelo Branco to pick on), but now she was less sure. "I CAN'T understand the [political] situation," she said. "Everything seems worse, that's all."[11] And Lota was much worse.

They spent July at Samambaia for the most part; Lota had finally admitted that she was too ill to work. By August, Elizabeth's nerves had begun to fail under the barrage of criticism and accusation from Lota, especially about her alcoholism and her "abandonment" of Lota to go to Seattle. Elizabeth escaped alone to Lilli and Ouro Prêto for most of August. Lota came up at the end of the month, ostensibly for a rest herself, but her problems continued to escalate. Driving in her new car with Lilli, she had an accident in which the car rolled and they were both thrown out. Neither was injured, but the shock of the accident added to the tension.

Back in Rio on September 1, Elizabeth was desperate. Lota's breakdown had become inextricably intertwined with her own alcoholism and the painful store of guilt that was a part of that condition. In addition, Lota had intercepted one of Suzanne Bowen's letters, setting off a terrible scene. Elizabeth had arranged, oddly, to route the letters through Lilli (among other friends), who would open them and read them to her over the phone, then destroy them; but one had slipped through. Elizabeth managed to keep secret her own frequent letters to Suzanne. Lota had developed an "obsession" about Elizabeth's drinking, had insisted that Elizabeth had spent six months in Seattle drunk and would leave her to drink; to that, Lota added the obvious infidelity reflected in the letter she had read. In her own defense, Elizabeth said that she missed no classes in Seattle because of drinking and that although she had "cheated" her Antabuse program in the past two or three years, she found it easier to stay sober away from Lota now than with her; Suzanne was just a particularly passionate student. When Lota physically forced Elizabeth to take a whole Antabuse pill (which Elizabeth insisted made her depressed), she appealed to Anny Baumann for help. "I can't endure the situation much longer. If you could just reassure her about me, a bit, somehow – and suggest a vacation – with me, if possible – it might help some . . . make her lay off me a bit –."[12]

Although by the end of September Elizabeth understood clearly that Lota was having a "nervous breakdown" in the old-fashioned sense, her belief that a "change" would help them both led her to invest some of her Seattle earnings in two plane tickets to Europe. Although Lota was seeing a psychiatrist five times a week in October, and Elizabeth was barely holding herself together under the strain, they flew to Amsterdam on October 23, planning to stay six weeks in Holland and England. Elizabeth hoped that "Dutch stolidity and English stoicism" would prove a cure for "Latin hysteria."[13]

The trip, which ended after only three weeks, was for the most part a waste. They toured Amsterdam and the Hague and visited the Barkers to catch the opening of Kit Barker's show of his paintings in London on November 1 (Elizabeth was in desperate need of their company and comfort). In Oxford, Elizabeth saw her friend Joe Summers at All Souls. Back in London, she saw Stephen Spender again, had tea with Irene Worth, and met with Cecil Day Lewis at Chatto and Windus about bringing out a British selected poems, to be published simultaneously with a "collected" planned by Farrar, Straus, and Giroux for 1967. Katy Carver, her editor there, later became a close friend. Elizabeth managed to get a lunch on

November 9 with Henry Reed, who had been very dear in Seattle but who seemed to have avoided her since. But the various tensions at the lunch made it impossible, and Elizabeth decided right there that her strategy of taking Lota from social occasion to social occasion had been a mistake. Her illness was not, Elizabeth realized, a "nervous breakdown" that could be cured simply by getting her out of Brazil. They left for Rio on the eleventh. Their friend Magú Leão met them at the airport and quietly took Lota home.

For another week, they pretended that things were relatively normal. The Parque do Flamengo had been turned over to a foundation for completion and maintenance, and on November 16 Lota attended its first meeting. But by the end of the month, she was in the hospital, heavily medicated and sleeping many hours a day. Elizabeth, unable to stand the strain or be alone while Lota was away, went off to Ouro Prêto and the little community she had begun to find there. Lilli and the flamboyant poet and author of *Black Orpheus,* Vinicius de Moraes, kept Elizabeth company, and she wrote often to Suzanne. Elizabeth talked to Lota twice a day on the phone, she said, but stayed away ten days longer than she had intended, unwilling to return and face the barrage of criticism and the guilt it inspired.

She returned to Rio in the second week of December to face the huge question of what she, and especially Lota, would do next. After her years of power and accomplishment, it seemed unlikely that Lota would again be satisfied as an aristocrat farmer. Elizabeth wanted to go back to their former Samambaia life, to raise pigs on the *fazenda,* and to live out their days far from the pressures of politics and government, which she was convinced had caused Lota's illness. She asked Robert Lowell about resident fellowships in the United States, one at Wesleyan University in Connecticut, perhaps—she could teach, and she and Lota could live there safe from New York and from Brazil. Elizabeth made and unmade alternative plans to live with Suzanne Bowen somewhere in the United States or Puerto Rico. In the short term, she and Lota decided to abandon the Rio apartment and move back to Petrópolis; when she returned to Rio, Elizabeth saw to the packing and moving of their belongings. On December 20, Lota was released from the hospital, and they went together to Samambaia to face a dreary Christmas holiday. On December 24, "Under the Window: Ouro Prêto" appeared in the *New Yorker*.

Exactly what happened over Christmas at Samambaia in 1966 is not known, but Elizabeth and Lota returned to Rio "almost at once." By the first of the year, Elizabeth had packed a suitcase and had moved out of the apartment and into a Rio hotel. She had had to leave on very short notice; her presence was damaging to Lota's attempts to regain her sanity, according to the doctor. She was asked to stay away for a long time—six months to two years. Out "in half an hour," "after fifteen years with a few dirty clothes in a busted suitcase, no home any more, no claim (legally) to anything here," she sat in her hotel room and tried to get her shock and grief under control.[14] Reading Auden on January 6, she copied out passages of inspiration: "DO NOT FORGET this FIRST QUOTE...MOST IMPORTANT OF ALL:

> "The drunk is unlovely to look at, intolerable to listen to, [and] his self-pity is contemptible. Nevertheless, as not merely a worldly failure, but also a [willful] failure, he is a disturbing image for the sober [citizen]. His refusal to accept the realities of this world, babyish as it may be, compels us to take another look at this world and reflect upon our motives for accepting it."

> Much more important and from now on–January 6, 1967– NEVER forget this:

> "One ceases to be a child when one realizes that telling one's troubles does not make it any better." Cesare Pavese

> (This would not seem to apply to telling it to doctors, but to friends.)

Auden adds: "Exactly. Not even telling it to oneself. [Most] of us have known shameful moments when we blubbered, beat the wall with our fists, cursed the power which made us and the world, and wished we were dead or that someone else was. But at such times, the I of the sufferer should have the tact and decency to look the other way."[15]

Elizabeth was looking for comfort in literature, as she always did, and this comfort confirmed the stoical teachings of her childhood. A less repressed nature, one that told its troubles more easily, might have weathered the traumas of this life better as well. But it would probably have written very different poems.

Unable to stay alone in her hotel and needing supervision to keep from drinking constantly, she checked herself into the Casa de Repouso, where she tried to rest and make plans for the future. She would travel for six months within Brazil, then check back to see how Lota was doing. She and Lilli would take the Rio São Francisco trip she had been planning for several years. Her two impulses—to stay and try to help Lota and to get out of the country as soon as she could—pulled at her all the time, and the idea of once again traveling because she had nowhere else to go had lost its appeal. She left the Casa de Repouso in late January and went in the company of her friend Isa Aguirre to Samambaia to pack a trunk. Alone for a few hours in her *estudio* by the waterfall, she typed out a few lines:

INVENTORY

Bed, birdcage, and a chest of drawers,
the biggest shell, the flat and foot-shaped
piece of granite I found myself,
the paddle, and the portable ink-well;
the baby-book, . . . the cloisonne
coffee spoons with blue enamel,
           the living cat
where – where can I take them next?

Oh let me not have looked
Let it somehow be that I never saw

& the cascade seems hurrying to some
climax, but really never [changes] –

Then she joined Lilli at Ouro Prêto to prepare for the São Francisco trip but broke down herself almost immediately. Lilli took her to the Clinica Botofoga in Rio, where Lota had first been taken.

The "worst attack of asthma since the age of 8"—an "attempt of the poor psyche to deal with the impossible"—resulting from a long period of uncontrolled drinking, kept her in the clinic for two weeks.[16] She realized she would have to leave Brazil, and she made plans to travel to New York in early April, promising to deliver a poem at the Phi Beta Kappa induction ceremony at Vassar in May. But Lota's condition suddenly improved; she took Elizabeth from the clinic back to the Rio apartment and then up to Petrópolis, where they attempted once again to resume their normal life. Elizabeth, to her own astonishment, was almost immediately able to write. And even though she was at this point finding her own breakdown comparable to Lota's, she was convinced that her recovery was so swift because, unlike Lota, she would "always have something to do"; she could always write or try to write.[17] Lota was bored and depressed at Samambaia, unable to take up her rural life and suddenly cut off from her city life both by her health and by a change in leadership in the Rio government. She had quarreled irretrievably with Carlos Lacerda, and the park was now out of her hands (and being ruined, she was convinced). But Elizabeth, for the first time in nearly two years, opened her notebook and began to write.

She first completed the strange prose poems grouped under the title "Rainy Season; Sub-Tropics." Her long fascination with out-of-scale things and animals culminates here. In high school she had written an essay called "Giant Weather" in which she expressed her delight in "things planned on a different scale from our own mortal feet and inches." One of the aspects that she had first found endearing in Brazil had been its people's fondness for out-of-scale vegetables (the "pumpkin 'bigger than the baby' " of "Manuelzinho," for instance) and animals.[18] She had written to James Merrill in 1955 a description of the "Rousseau jungle" outside the Petrópolis house, which had "waterfalls coming and going according to the weather" and "clouds spilling over the tops" of mountains:

> Things are very much out of scale, too, like a Rousseau – or out of our scale, that is. The "Samambaia" mentioned at the top of the page is a giant fern, big as a tree, and there are toads as big as your hat and snails as big as bread & butter plates, and during this month butterflies the color of this page [pale blue] and sometimes almost as big flopping about –[19]

Some of these animals reappear as the radical misfits of "Rainy Season; Sub-Tropics," who are painfully aware of their outsized existences. Despite their various beauties and values (which echo Bishop's poetic strengths and values), they labor under their strangeness and suffer abuse from the world. The Giant Toad moans:

> I am too big, too big by far. Pity me.
>   My eyes bulge and hurt. They are my one great beauty, even so. They see too much, above, below, and yet there is not much to see.

His neighbor the Giant Crab is literally displaced: "This is not my home. How did I get so far from water?" What he treasures—"compression, lightness, and agility"—are "all rare in this loose world." "I believe in the oblique, the indirect approach, and I keep my feelings to myself." The Giant Snail shares the Toad's handicap ("Our proportions horrify our neighbors"). "Withdrawal is always best," he offers, especially for those in his condition. "But O! I am too big. I feel it. Pity me." And the creatures cannot comfort one another.

Elizabeth Bishop had always looked on the world and its objects from an odd angle, and she knew it. The celebrated observer's accounts of her experience—whether in letters, poems, stories, or memoirs—direct their gazes from an awareness of altered or unusual perspective. This is not a rhetorical device or mannerism but a way of seeing, the only way of seeing for the perpetual outsider. Alienated from the conventional view all her life—by her homosexuality, by her alcoholism, by the trauma of her mother's illness and the "false self" she had invented to cope with it, by the fact of being a poet at all—she was forced to take nothing for granted, to look at a map and feel the tug of the tide, to look at a painting and see the paint, to see beyond the palm-lined boulevard to the heap of "skeletons" at the side. She had felt her strangeness all her life, had escaped it for a time in Brazil, but now that sense was back. "They don't believe in me," she said of the other passengers on the SS *Brasil Star* in 1964; feeling "real" had become a slippery idea in 1967 as well.

"Going to the Bakery," which she had been working on since 1960, when she had first tried to comprehend her role as a relatively rich American in the overwhelmingly impoverished city of Rio de Janeiro, was also finished in this stretch. The poem begins with a description of the moonlight's transformation of the "ordinary sights" on the Avenida Copacabana. The sense of poverty and decay in the poem is overwhelming. The "unexpected beauty" of the moon is no longer sufficient to make Rio tolerable; its light cannot transform the gray illumination of rationed electricity. Bakery goods take on human diseases, and the humans are no more animate than the loaves of bread or "milk rolls." And the poet's words, which had endowed many a depressing scene with saving dignity, are here ineffective:

> Now flour is adulterated
> with cornmeal, the loaves of bread
> lie like yellow-fever victims
> laid out in a crowded ward.

The baker, sickly too, suggests
the "milk rolls," since they still are warm
and made with milk, he says. They feel
like a baby on the arm.

Under the false-almond tree's
leathery leaves, a childish *puta*
dances, feverish as an atom:
chá-cha, chá-cha, chá-cha....

In front of my apartment house
a black man sits in a black shade,
lifting his shirt to show a bandage
on his black, invisible side.

Fumes of *cachaça* knock me over,
like gas fumes from an auto-crash.
He speaks in perfect gibberish.
The bandage glares up, white and fresh.

I give him seven cents in *my*
terrific money, say "Good night"
from force of habit. Oh, mean habit!
Not one word more apt or bright?

Elizabeth struggled with this poem for some time, sending one version to the *New Yorker* in early May, then withdrawing it and substituting another on August 14. Her tone in writing about Rio had never quite satisfied her; in this poem she could hardly control it.

She also wrote a gallery note for the paintings of Wesley Wehr. The note was never used, but for years Elizabeth said it was the finest page of prose she had written. Her interest in Wehr's small, accurate works is no surprise. The note articulates values she had held for a long time and in method recalls "The Map" and "Large

Bad Picture" and anticipates "Poem" as it moves between Wehr's
paintings and her memory of the landscape they depict:

> I have seen Mr. Wehr open his battered brief-case (with the
> broken zipper) at a table in a crowded, steamy coffee-shop, and
> deal out his latest paintings, carefully encased in plastic until they
> are framed, like a set of magic playing cards. The people at his
> table would fall silent and stare at these small, beautiful pictures,
> far off into space and coolness: the coldness of the Pacific
> Northwest coast in the winter, its different coldness in the
> summer. So much space, so much air, such distances and
> lonelinesses, on those flat little cards. One could almost make out
> the moon behind the clouds, but not quite; the snow had worn
> off the low hills almost showing last year's withered grasses; the
> white line of surf was visible but quiet, almost a mile away. Then
> Mr. Wehr would whisk all that space, silence, peace and privacy
> back into his brief-case again. He once remarked that he would
> like to be able to carry a whole exhibition in his pockets.

"It is a great relief to see a small work of art these days," she goes
on, comparing Wehr's work to Chinese scroll paintings, Klee, Bissier, and the instrumental pieces of Webern.

Elizabeth was pleased with her work in March and April 1967
and began to talk about finishing the book of Brazil essays. "Writing
a lot," she asked Howard Moss if she might renew the *New Yorker*
first-reading contract she had abandoned in 1961. She had some time
to think about poetry again, about Berryman's remarkable "Opus
Posthumous"—she thought if one had to write one's poems in baby
talk, something was probably "very seriously wrong." In the middle
of her own catastrophe, she told Lowell, "We must beware of the
easiness of the catastrophe!–the catastrophic way out of every poem
– but how can one help but be gloomy and take a gloomy
outlook?"[20]

. . .

The Samambaia experiment lasted two quiet but uneasy months; Elizabeth canceled her plans to go to New York, told Vassar that the unnamed Phi Beta Kappa poem would not be done in time, and tried to write as much as possible in the peaceful moments she had. But by the end of May, Lota had decided that she could not stay idle in Samambaia and through the intervention of friends got a federal job somewhere in the Rio bureaucracy of price setting and inflation control. She was also drawn back into work on the park. Elizabeth decided in late May that she should again get away to Ouro Prêto and finally take the Rio São Francisco trip. Lota's doctor had suggested that she go alone, without Lilli, to avoid exciting Lota's jealousy. She did go, arriving in Pirapora, Minas Gerais—the point at which the river becomes navigable—on May 29. On a "tour" with fourteen others, she spent eight days on the river, arriving in Salvador on June 6. In Bahia for three days, writing up the trip while it was fresh, she had high hopes of selling the resulting travel essay so that she could continue work on the Ouro Prêto house.

The rough draft of "A Trip on the Rio São Francisco" that survives describes the river, the life along its shores, the boat, and the other passengers in terms of what she saw and of what she had read about navigation on the river. It seems typical of what she had in mind for the Brazil book; it opens with a personal anecdote (doing her laundry after the trip and finding that her clothes retained the yellowish color of the river rinse after rinse) and proceeds to description and historical asides. It lingers especially on the boat itself, the American-built *Wenceslau Braz* (named for a president of Brazil), one of only seventeen stern-wheelers, or *gaiolas,* still in use on the river. Like Mark Twain before her, she was taken by the rhythm of the wheel.

> The chief charm of a gaiola (aside from the wood-heaving and other noises that might be considered "modern") is its quietness. As we meandered slowly downstream we went ppph...ppph...

ppph...softly, rather like a seal coming up for air. And the paddle-wheel made a soft, rhythmical splashing, but that could be heard only quite close to.

We sported a very tall smoke-stack, painted and re-painted with yellow-orange paint. At night this gave off a stream of big sparks; by day it moved along looking like a yellow wax crayon, – as if a big child were tracing the course of the Rio São Francisco for his or her geography lesson.

The draft breaks off abruptly and was never finished. She later wrote asking May Swenson for a good Swedish name for the only other non-Brazilian on the trip with her, a young man from Santos, and that name, Sven, is incorporated in this draft, so apparently she wrote more than one. Not here, but in letters she wrote about the trip are anecdotes about the indescribable "human misery" she witnessed on the riverbanks and about the cargo of animals they carried, butchering them to eat as they went along. She talked about the piece a good deal, worrying about its length and where to send it; but, like most of the pieces she tried to write about Brazil after *Questions of Travel* ("Going to the Bakery" and "Under the Window: Ouro Prêto" are the only exceptions),[21] she could not strike the right tone and could not finish it.

Throughout June 1967, Elizabeth struggled with the question of leaving for New York. Back in Rio, life was tense and uncomfortable; Lota's father had died recently, and though she had been estranged from him for years, she was once again upset. She tried to continue working and fighting off her depression and illness, but without much success. On June 19, Elizabeth said she might fly to New York soon; on June 20 she invited Ashley Brown to visit them in Rio in July. On June 30, she renewed her visa. On July 3, she visited her Rio lawyer and revised her will. She left everything to Lota, "of course," but fifteen thousand dollars left ostensibly to Anny Baumann disguised a bequest to Suzanne Bowen ("She will need it badly and I feel a heavy obligation to her").[22] Carrying only forty pounds of luggage, Elizabeth flew to New York that night. She said she had left against her own wishes and on the advice of Lota's doctors.

. . .

Elizabeth said later that Lota's doctor had told her that there was nothing she could do in Rio and that Lota would be unable to travel before September at the earliest. She would wait for Lota in New York and in the meantime would bring together the scattered pieces of the Brazil book; prepare her "collected poems" for Farrar, Straus, and Giroux; and help with a children's edition of "The Burglar of Babylon," with woodcut illustrations by Anne Grifalconi, that her publishers planned for the following year. She arrived at Loren MacIver's studio at 61 Perry Street on July 4. The studio had been vacant for two years and was dusty and depressing, and New York was its usual empty summer self; she found it "terribly lonely." Her neighbors across the street, Harold Leeds and Wheaton Galentine, were friendly and helpful; but May Swenson, Robert Lowell, and almost all her old friends were away. She also arrived with lingering dysentery from her Rio São Francisco trip and, she discovered a couple of weeks later, a concussion. She had fallen at the home of Lota's doctor in Rio, and the "bump on the head and nosebleed" were much more serious than she had suspected. Dizzy spells, black-outs, headaches, and nausea kept her spirits low as well.

Elizabeth had very specific plans for her return to Brazil with Lota in September; she wanted to finish the Ouro Prêto house and the Barkers were seriously considering a visit. She bought a *santo* in New York—a carved statue of a Catholic saint (she had begun to collect them in Brazil)—and said she would have it restored in Rio. She found a litter of Burmese kittens she was sure Lota would love. But in the meantime, she had to get comfortable in New York, which was never easy for her to do. And Greenwich Village in the summer of 1967 was not an environment with which she was famil-iar. "The Village will rejuvenate me, no doubt," she wrote to Lowell in Castine, Maine. "I never appear without earrings down to my bosom, skirts almost up to it, and a guitar over my shoulder. I am afraid I am going to start writing FREE VERSE next."[23]

At the end of July, Elizabeth finally went out to Long Island to visit the vanished New Yorkers—May Swenson, Bobby Fizdale, and Arthur Gold, among others—and then went on to Jane Dewey's farm in Havre de Grace to rest and recover from the lingering effects of the concussion and to write.

The farm was always a favorite place to work, and by August 8, she said she had written "two whole poems," one of which was probably the new version of "Going to the Bakery"; the other was "In the Waiting Room." "You are such a bright boy," she wrote to Lowell from New York on August 30.

> Perhaps you can tell me what's the matter with this poem...I really mean it, and say what you think–I'll scrap it, if necessary. I like the idea–but know there's something very wrong and can't seem to tell what it is. . . . Maybe it should be cut–maybe it should rhyme–maybe it's all the fault of the damned METER. (It is one of those I dream–woke up one morning at Jane's with almost the whole thing done.) It was funny–queer–I actually went to the Library & got out that no. of the N G [National Geographic]– and that title, The Valley of 10,000 Smokes–was right, and has been haunting me all my life, apparently.[24]

Of course, she sent it to Lowell; it was a wish (perhaps) to show him how far she had come toward him in the new, relatively "confessional" style. Lowell's reply is lost, and two and a half years passed before she solved her difficulties with the poem and finished it. But even at this point, she suspected that she would write a new kind of poetry from now on. The "You are an *I*, / You are an *Elizabeth*" of "In the Waiting Room" launched that new phase.

Elizabeth had a bit of social life in New York that summer. She saw James Merrill, and she lunched with Robert Giroux and Susan

Sontag, whose work thoroughly intimidated her. Margaret Miller visited. She had refused to speak with Elizabeth since 1957, and Elizabeth was excited and somewhat unnerved at seeing her. She had never lost the love for Margaret that had developed when they were roommates at Vassar, had been tested by the car accident in France in 1937, and had tortured her when she had felt so powerless to help Margaret from Brazil in the late 1950s. They were uneasy friends from 1967 until Elizabeth's death. Suzanne Bowen was in New York in August as well, but Elizabeth apparently did not see her.

At mid-August, Lota's doctors decided that it would be unwise for her to travel before December. Elizabeth heard this advice and heeded it, though she thought Lota sounded much better in her letters and phone calls. But Elizabeth asked Ashley Brown to bring back a few of her winter clothes when he came north and reluctantly settled in to wait. Early in September, Lota cabled Elizabeth saying she wanted to come to New York right away, and Elizabeth, lonely and unable to ignore Lota's urgent request, told her to come ahead. Elizabeth said she cabled the doctor to make sure it was safe but got no reply.

Lota arrived in New York on the afternoon of September 19. She came bearing presents of coffee and curios for her friends but looking, Elizabeth said later, tired and depressed. They spent a "peaceful and affectionate" evening together and then went to bed.[25] Sometime during the night, Lota got up and took an overdose of tranquilizers. By the time Elizabeth awoke and went to her at half past six, she was nearly comatose. With the help of Harold and Wheaton, the police, and Anny Baumann, Lota was admitted to St. Vincent's Hospital in the Village within half an hour. It seemed likely that she would survive; the hospital found only Valium in her system (though she had been clutching an empty bottle of Nembutal when Elizabeth found her), and overdoses of Valium are rarely fatal. But Lota had arteriosclerosis and a history of heart trouble, and no one seemed to know if she had had anything to drink as well. After five days in an unbroken coma, she died at the age of fifty-seven.

Elizabeth had spent the anxious week trying to keep her already frayed nerves under control. A friend of May Swenson's stayed with her nights; other friends also helped. When Lota died on the evening of the twenty-fifth, Anny Baumann came to tell Elizabeth. The awful activity of the next few days—undertakers, arrangements for transporting a body overseas, worry about what would be said in the newspapers—kept her busy and numb. But once Lota's body had been returned to Rio, the huge funeral had been concluded, and she had been laid beside her father in the Macedo Soares family tomb in São João Batista, Elizabeth was left alone with her grief and the guilt she seemed unable to avoid. She had "if only" nightmares, imagining what she had done wrong "that Sunday"—if only she had said the right thing, if only she had not fallen asleep. The consolation of their fourteen years of relative happiness helped her only occasionally; at other times she begged her friends to forgive her for "all the wrong things" she had done. Anny Baumann comforted her by saying that Lota had died because she was sick, not because of anything anyone had done. But Elizabeth played nightmares of her own failures, real and imagined, again and again in her head.

Anny Baumann advised Elizabeth not to go back to Rio with Lota's body to face the strain of publicity ("Dona Lota Dies in New York," the papers said) but to wait until she was stronger. Perhaps knowing that Elizabeth could not be alone successfully under such stress, Baumann also called Suzanne Bowen, told her the story, and in her imperious way suggested that Suzanne contact Elizabeth. Perhaps she could help with her most pressing problem—what to do next. By October 18, Elizabeth was considering living with Suzanne in San Francisco.

Also by mid-October, Elizabeth knew that Lota's will had been opened and that she had divided her estate just as they had agreed the year before. Mary Morse would inherit Samambaia; Elizabeth would get the Rio apartment, control of the seven offices she and Lota had owned in Rio, all the furniture and books in Rio, and what was her own at Samambaia. She intended to sell the apartment as soon as possible and use the income from rents on the offices to finish the Ouro Prêto house, which she hoped very much to keep. She planned to fly to Brazil on November 1, move all the furniture and books to Ouro Prêto, and pack all she wanted for the immediate future to ship to San Francisco. Also in the will was this quotation from Voltaire: *Si le Bon Dieu existe, il me pardonnera. C'est son metier;* this, she thought, might indicate that Lota had intended to kill herself.

But Elizabeth had not expected that Lota's sister, Marietta Nascimento, would be so angry over being excluded from her sister's will that she would challenge it, saying that Lota had been insane when she wrote it. The protracted legal struggle that ensued prevented Elizabeth from getting money out of Brazil for a long time and kept her involved, through lawyers, with the painful circumstances of Lota's illness. It also became important from a legal standpoint to convince Marietta that Lota had died accidentally.

Elizabeth's travel plans were disrupted when, having drunk too much vodka, she fell and broke her left arm and shoulder. She was staying at the Lowells' apartment on West Sixty-seventh Street at the time, and her friends had hidden their supply of alcohol for her benefit, but she had searched it out. After a week at Lenox Hill Hospital, she returned to the Lowells' to recuperate. She apologized all around for her "stupid behavior" with alcohol and endured a lecture from Anny Baumann about getting herself under control. When she did fly to Rio on November 15, her left arm was in a cast and a sling, and she carried a supply of Antabuse.

Elizabeth spent three "grisly" weeks in Rio and Petrópolis, packing, meeting with lawyers, and quarreling with both Lota's sister and Mary Morse, who for reasons of her own had turned against Elizabeth. "People are more like buzzards than I'd suspected," she said.[26] Her friends Magú Leão and Stella Periera behaved well, but the rest seemed to blame Elizabeth for Lota's death and essentially abandoned her. She accused Mary Morse of destroying her letters to Lota and said she would never go back to Petrópolis.[27] By December 9, Elizabeth had reached Ouro Prêto, where she stayed with Lilli at the Chico Rey waiting for her belongings to arrive and enjoying the company of Vinicius de Moraes, who was a great help to her spirits and her situation. Feeling somewhat restored by the town and the company, she flew to San Francisco on Christmas Eve (Vinicius had chivalrously accompanied her to the airport in Belo Horizonte and had paid her excess-baggage duty), arriving at the Hotel Canterbury very early on Christmas morning. Suzanne Bowen joined her two hours later from Seattle. They spent three days apartment hunting before Suzanne went back to Seattle to pack her things and pick up her eighteen-month-old son, whose custody she shared with her former husband. On January 8, they moved together into a four-bedroom apartment at 1559 Pacific Avenue on a six-month lease.

Sixteen

A TOTALLY WASTED STRETCH
1968–1970

ELIZABETH SAID that her English Tory blood had helped her
recover from Lota's death and survive the pain and humiliation in
Brazil and that a "built-in kind of momentum" had kept her moving
forward to San Francisco. Nonetheless, these seventeen months in
her life are a little hard to imagine. She managed to get for herself
the minimum requirements for her continued existence—caring
company, new surroundings, and diverting activity. The household
on Pacific Avenue, near Polk Street and in a neighborhood that was
mostly Chinese, might not have pleased her at another time in her
life; now it was what she needed, and she was incapable of being
alone. But even though she had had contact with the American
youth culture of the mid-1960s while in Seattle and briefly while in
Greenwich Village, she was not quite prepared for San Francisco
the winter following the Summer of Love or for the denouement of
the 1960s that took place in 1968–1969. Suzanne Bowen, at twenty-
seven, was her guide, and Elizabeth was alternately fascinated and
horrified by what that culture did to language and to the rules of
good conduct as she had known them all her life. For Elizabeth,
there was no gradual working up to a tolerance for disrespect, foul
language, bizarre art, and new standards of personal grooming; she

was simply plunged into the middle. And though she had always considered herself rebellious in a modest kind of way, nothing she could imagine herself doing in San Francisco would be considered at all out of the ordinary.

She arrived with a few connections in the Bay Area. Pat and Cass Humble, relatives of Ilse and Kit Barker whom she had met in Seattle, lived across the Golden Gate Bridge in Mill Valley; Murray and Betty McGowan Ross were connections she had made through James Merrill; she knew the poet and critic Anthony Ostroff, who in turn saw that she met the best-known of the young San Francisco poets of this era—Robert Duncan and Thom Gunn, among others—and introduced her to Josephine Miles, who was teaching at Berkeley. Mark Strand was at Hayward State in the East Bay; they had known each other briefly in the fall of 1965, when Strand had replaced Ashley Brown as the Fulbright lecturer in Rio. She had two Brazilian friends in the area as well: Hilgard Sternberg, a professor of geography at Berkeley, and his wife Carolina were reassuring contacts with her old life.

But by far the most important person in her San Francisco world was Suzanne. Immensely grateful for her company and her help, Elizabeth was defensive about forming this new attachment so soon after Lota's death, but she perceived, as Anny Baumann had, that her well-being depended on it. Suzanne was "wonderful company" and immediately took care of Elizabeth's immense need for secretarial and accounting help, set up their apartment, and shortened Elizabeth's skirts to a more "contemporary" length. "Thank God, Cal, I have such a bright, kind and funny companion right now—I don't think I could bear to live alone just yet, or in New York, and certainly not in Brazil. [Suzanne] is really a nice girl—and is typing all my business letters, will type for me, etc.—'Secretary' does sound decadent to me, but maybe I've been needing one for a long time."[1] But "this does not mean that I don't love Lota and always shall."[2] To others, she said she felt loved by Suzanne and her son; they were "nice to" her, and for the time being that was enough. At the outset,

Elizabeth seemed to observers to hold the power in the relationship; she was older, and she had the money. Little by little, however, as Elizabeth became more dependent on Suzanne's energy and labor, the younger woman became the planner and orchestrator of their lives as well as Elizabeth's much-needed caretaker.

There was a stream of visitors through San Francisco that first spring—Gold and Fizdale played a concert in January; Wesley Wehr came down from Seattle, as did Dorothee Bowie and Suzanne's mother and sister. Virginia Pfeiffer, Elizabeth's old friend now living in Los Angeles, was up in April, and Elizabeth must have been reminded of her days in Key West, the trip to Haiti in 1949, and the terrible struggles that had led up to her departure for Brazil in 1951. For public purposes, Elizabeth and Suzanne defined their relationship as employer and assistant; Elizabeth introduced Suzanne as "my secretary," and Suzanne called Elizabeth "Miss Bishop." They permitted themselves no public gestures of affection, even in front of friends, and part of Suzanne's means of holding her own in this inherently unequal relationship was the fact that this "conspiracy of silence" was designed entirely to protect Elizabeth's reputation, which she clung to rather desperately in these difficult years.[3] All her life subject to the demands that her sense of shame imposed on her psyche and her circumstances, Elizabeth would soon enough want to put this whole time far behind her.

Also included in this conspiracy of silence was any reference to Elizabeth's alcoholism. Despite mounting evidence to the contrary—visits with friends to Trader J's, the Polk Street bar and artists' hangout; Elizabeth's collapse at a party in Patrick Humble's Mill Valley studio—the pretense was that Elizabeth was a teetotaler. Cass Humble tells the story of a visit she, her husband, and her mother-in-law made to the Pacific Avenue apartment for dinner in late March 1969. Elizabeth served her guests small glasses of wine but poured none for herself. When they seated themselves on the sofa in the living room, a liquor bottle clattered through the couchsprings and rolled out onto the tile floor. The unflappably

British Monica Humble kicked the bottle back under the couch, and conversation continued as if nothing at all had happened. Elizabeth had apparently arrived at the point of absurdity in living as the "false self" she felt the United States required of her.

Her painful adjustment to this new life was interrupted when she fell on a steep wet sidewalk in San Francisco on February 1 and broke her right wrist in two places. As her left arm and shoulder were not entirely healed yet, the new injury was especially depressing and kept her from writing or typing. The work she had set herself to do—on the Brazil book; on a bilingual anthology of Brazilian poetry that she was editing with Emanuel Brasil, a friend of Ashley Brown's who worked for the United Nations; on her *Complete Poems,* as Farrar, Straus, and Giroux insisted on calling the book (Elizabeth herself preferred "collected" so that she could edit out poems she wished not to republish); and on the Phi Beta Kappa poem she had promised to Vassar—all fell by the wayside. Elizabeth said in mid-March (typing with one hand) that she had "never been so low for so long, . . . and it is very fortunate that i have [Suzanne] with me so i do have to try hard for her sake."[4] Elizabeth's alcoholism got the best of her often during this stretch, and she felt she could barely hold her head above the flood.

The financial situation was relatively difficult all spring, and when Elizabeth finally sold the Rio apartment in early April, she could not get the money out of Brazil. As a result, she was able to designate more money for the Ouro Prêto house renovations through her agent in Rio, but life in San Francisco continued under a financial cloud. An Academy of American Poets grant of three thousand dollars helped fund the preparation of the anthology and arrange for its eventual publication by Wesleyan University Press, but Elizabeth realized during this spring that she would have to teach or do a lot of readings to pay for the trips back and forth to Brazil and for the life she had been accustomed to living—not extravagant, but decidedly comfortable and free. (Elizabeth's "poverty," however, was of a very different kind than that of many of Suzanne's friends and

Elizabeth's colleagues. Cass Humble recalls their collective surprise when Elizabeth had Suzanne tear out the brand-new carpeting in the Pacific Avenue apartment and replace it with black and white tiles.) She scheduled readings—at the University of Arizona on April 15, at Berkeley on April 28, and several on the East Coast for late May, including one at Harvard, where Robert Lowell would introduce her. All this was scheduled around the June 2 commencement ceremony at Smith College, where she would receive her first honorary degree.

The Tucson reading, the first Elizabeth had done since 1966, went well enough, she thought. There she saw her old Walnut Hill School classmates Barbara Chesney Kennedy and Shirley Clark Van Cleef. At Berkeley, all her San Francisco friends gathered round, and she left to do her East Coast readings, which were much more intimidating to her, with some confidence. Never having seen the middle of the North American continent, Elizabeth and Suzanne decided to take the train across Canada to get to the East; they would go via Seattle, to leave Suzanne's son with his father (as the custody agreement required), then cross the Rockies and the plains on the Canadian Pacific Railroad to Montreal and Halifax, where Elizabeth would see her Canadian relatives, Aunt Mary and Aunt Grace, for the first time in ten years. Unfortunately, as the trip progressed, Elizabeth grew ill from an infection in her jaw caused by complications from a wisdom tooth removal done in late April. By the time she got to Montreal on May 15, she went straight to Jewish Hospital, with osteomyelitis of the jaw and an abscessed tooth. She spent a week there being fed antibiotics and having more teeth pulled (while Suzanne stayed in a convent nearby), followed by an outpatient week at Ruby Foo's Motel, a name she delighted in. A page of anecdotes, titled "MORE HOSPITAL NOTES," describes how impressed the nurses were that she could read English, and records the Yiddish conversations that went on around her. "All the signs were in Yiddish, English, French & Greek," she noted.

Her illness forced her to cancel her trip to Halifax and her East Coast readings—Harvard, Wesleyan, and the Guggenheim Museum—and she and Suzanne spent six or seven dreary weeks in the haunted studio at 61 Perry Street. (Elizabeth refused to stay there again, though it meant expensive hotel rooms in New York from then on.) They both had checkups from Anny Baumann, as Suzanne had been having migraines, and they made and hosted visits to and from friends. Robert Lowell, Margaret Miller, and Jane Dewey all turned up, and Suzanne and Elizabeth escorted Marianne Moore from her West Ninth Street apartment to the polls in Greenwich Village so she could vote in the presidential primary. "Marianne's was probably the only Republican vote cast there that day," she wrote in "Efforts of Affection." Elizabeth remarked that in her seven months' absence all her men friends seemed to have grown out their hair and beards. They looked like marmosets, she thought. She conducted a little business from New York; quarreled mildly with Farrar, Straus, and Giroux over the contract for her *Complete Poems;* and argued with Caedmon Records again over its use of recordings she had made and then changed her mind about. (She had a way of losing track of such details; after cashing royalty checks from Caedmon for eight years, she insisted suddenly that she had asked that the recordings be destroyed immediately after she made them. Caedmon was understandably confused.) She negotiated with poet friends over translations to be included in the anthology. The *New Yorker* took the one poem she managed to finish over the summer, the apparently light but painful "Trouvée," set in Greenwich Village and dedicated to Harold Leeds and Wheaton Galentine, the neighbors across Perry Street who had been so helpful with Lota's death. The "quaint / old country saying" about why the chicken crossed the road encompasses all the "why" questions of her recent stay in New York, and the trivial but sad vision of the hen smashed flat in the soft tar of West Fourth Street stands for all its sadness:

Oh, why should a *hen*
have been run over
on West 4th Street
in the middle of summer?

She was a white hen
—red-and-white now, of course.
How did she get there?
Where was she going?

Her wing feathers spread
flat, flat in the tar,
all dirtied, and thin
as tissue paper.

A pigeon, yes,
or an English sparrow,
might meet such a fate,
but not that poor fowl.

Just now I went back
to look again.
I hadn't dreamed it:
there is a hen

turned into a quaint
old country saying
scribbled in chalk
(except for the beak).

Elizabeth and Suzanne returned to San Francisco on Amtrak's
Zephyr, arriving on July 26. They visited the Art Institute in Chicago on their five-hour stopover and rode in the Vista Dome
through Utah, which looked to Elizabeth "exactly like hell." For
her, the return to San Francisco was a conscious decision to give the
city another try after her ill and weary spring. She liked it well

enough, she thought. It was beautiful (though Brazil had "spoiled" her for scenery), and the light sometimes reminded her of Key West. She was "dying to get back to work," having "done nothing but write business letters" since Lota's death.

They got back to the Pacific Avenue apartment to find that they had been robbed. The ordinary thieves took ordinary things, cameras and the like, and Elizabeth had insurance to cover the loss, but it took them that much longer to get resettled, and the strange, cold San Francisco summer passed slowly and sadly. To cheer herself at the end of July, Elizabeth bought "Jacob," a mynah bird. She was missing bird noises, she said, and though Jacob would never replace her lost Uncle Sam, mynahs were the best talkers around. Among the phrases she hoped to teach him were "Nobody knows" (from Grandmother Boomer); "I, too, dislike it," from Moore; and "awful but cheerful." "What of yours can I use?" she asked Lowell.

A few weeks later, she bought a "lotus white" Volkswagen Beetle (they had missed "toga white" by one model year) so Suzanne could drive her around the city and across the Bay Bridge to Berkeley, where Elizabeth liked to work in the university's Bancroft Library. She really engaged the idea of San Francisco and American culture in the late 1960s on this second stint in the city, and she did not especially like what she found. For a while, her curiosity kept her seeking out its more outrageous manifestations, but irony and anger seeped into her descriptions. By the spring of 1969, she was desperate to return to Brazil.

For one thing, they rented a television set to watch the political conventions of August 1968, and she was so appalled by events at the Democratic convention in Chicago that she did not know whom to blame. She confined her analysis to lamenting that for the first time in twenty years she could vote in a presidential election, and there was no one to vote for. She had caught a little of Lowell's enthusiasm for Eugene McCarthy but thought he was "too good" ever to win. Hubert Humphrey seemed a lackluster choice, and if Nixon won, she said, she would move back to Brazil permanently.

The assassinations of 1968 went virtually unremarked on in her letters; when Martin Luther King, Jr., was killed on March 10, her wrist was in a cast and she wrote almost nothing. When Robert Kennedy was shot in California on June 5, she was in New York and noted only that the following days were "awful" in the city and that Lowell had been in California with McCarthy at the time. But for Elizabeth Bishop, as for many Americans of her generation, the world seemed to be going to hell in the proverbial handbasket in 1968, and she caught the spirit of the jeremiads. "I feel it is a period of re-learning my own pop-culture & TV," she wrote to Lowell, "except I feel I've had just about enough of that, now—some of the Olympics very beautiful – 'Soul on Ice' (confused), Reagan, grape boycott (the mynah bird, Jacob, glares at me when I bring him only bananas and no seedless grapes), astronauts this morning, Jackie's wedding – filthy books, North Beach, imagine TOPLESS STEAMED CLAM LUNCH."[5]

She blamed Brigitte Bardot for the fact that "all girls" now wanted to look like "depraved little tramps" and pronounced herself "really sick of it" by the fall of 1968.[6] To James Merrill, she said, "I still haven't quite made up my mind about San Francisco, but certainly feel re-patriated now. If this is the U S A, I have been right in it for over a year and feel deafened, blinded, gassed, beat-up, and everything else that goes on constantly: newspapers, T V, conversations, everything."[7]

Suzanne saw to it that Elizabeth did not condemn this pop culture sight unseen. They went to movies, they saw the banned San Francisco Connection comedy troupe, they spent a good deal of time in Berkeley and toured Haight-Ashbury. They saw a concert by Janis Joplin and they played rock and roll music on their stereo. Suzanne's friends, the baby-sitters for her son, and people they met in the laundromat next door to their building were all entrees for Elizabeth into the dynamic counterculture of San Francisco. In other circumstances, this would not have been her milieu; but she had no such compelling introduction to the dominant culture—

even other poets seemed to her to be doing something so different from what she thought of as poetry that they had nothing in common. For eight or nine months in 1968–1969, this was her life. And she bravely set out to observe it.

Suzanne became friendly with members of a rock and roll band called The Threshold, and she and Elizabeth went a few times to hear them practice and play. Elizabeth began a prose piece about the band that, in its careful observation of detail and its pessimistic interpretation of that detail, is reminiscent of Joan Didion's essays about the 1960s. Electric guitars, amplifiers, and the insistent beat of the music suggested a "heavily orgiastic grinding sexuality," "sex without pleasure," even music without the pleasure of distinct notes and individual performances that could be listened to and applauded.

> The leader did most of the singing & one number played a harmonica along with the ugly guitar that looks like a [guitar] that has been put through a torture session and then killed and revived [by] means of gadgets and wires – everything out of place – broken bones and so on – why all those spurs and jags? – and no belly – no resonance chamber, of course, since that is taken care of artificially – like a dying man attached to all the machines in the intensive care unit – with a tracheotomy, no voice – the what was it Salazra has? re-vivifying machines? – anyway – nothing left of the . . . living instrument – the woods that make a Stradivarius, remember – the strange living things that go on in them like aging wines, etc. – all gone – Nothing but mechanics – and the voice – the most beautiful instrument of all abused into an obscenity –[8]

The piece returns several times to the perversion of sexuality that the music represents:

> All gone – the sexual quality of the human voice and all its infinite [variety] of appeals caresses even gratitudes, and so on – none of that. . . . It is hard to imagine any delicate sex-play – flirtation – a

kiss that is led up to by looks and round-about remarks, any delicately growing heightening excitement – no – just grind and bang . . . and then blank exhaustion. . . . All has been transferred to a machine – so it is so that amplification . . . has become the emotional or non-emotional part of music – it is a fucking machine.

This was not a blanket rejection of rock and roll; Elizabeth liked the Beatles and Janis Joplin, among others. When British pop singer Donovan briefly considered setting "The Burglar of Babylon" to music, she was delighted. It would be fun "and profitable."[9] She and Suzanne, a gifted musician, were thinking seriously about music; they took a clavichord lesson together in the spring of 1968.

In other prose about hippies in San Francisco, Elizabeth wondered frivolously why it was that "hippy girls" were always so short, and she sought again and again to put her finger on what seemed familiar and old about the tactics of this rebellion. Watching a young couple at the Beatles' movie *Yellow Submarine,* she indulged a fantasy:

He kept his arm around her – he turned and I had a close look at his face – both were very serious, pale, loving, wistful, sick-looking – Suddenly he looked like an illegitimate son, the Bastard Son of Edward X's – the 1st son of Louis? – one who inherited when his father was killed in the Battle of ? – at the age of 15 and reigned for seven months, dying of syphilis, or dying of a fever, or of the wasting disease, at 16 – leaving his pregnant bride of 15 behind him – Badly depicted in a portrait by – or on the clumsy coinage of – . . . Suspected murdered by his uncle the regent – his mother died at birth – known as Wenceslaus the Weak –

Perhaps the most astonishing confrontation of Elizabeth's world with the new age of the 1960s was the interview she conducted with Kathleen Cleaver, wife of the then-jailed Black Panther Party leader Eldridge Cleaver, who was staying in a house just down Pacific

Avenue from them. The Cleavers were all over the news media in 1969, and Elizabeth was fascinated by the beautiful, intelligent, young black woman who had gone underground after her husband's arrest. Twenty-four pages of transcription remain of this hard-to-imagine interview, which took place on February 1, 1969. Elizabeth's background and values—even beyond her belief that "blacks" (as she was now learning to call Negroes) deserved equal rights—were probably closer to Kathleen Cleaver's than she realized. Cleaver had grown up in an educated, middle-class family; but Elizabeth was utterly unfamiliar with the idea of middle-class or upper-middle-class black people. Her second question, "Where did you go to school?" got a mildly antagonistic answer: "I went to school everywhere I lived."

Cleaver's bodyguard stood by while the interview went on, muttering insults ("Judas, white Judas") under his breath. Suzanne controlled the flow of talk and rescued it when it foundered on reefs of hopeless cultural and generational difference. Elizabeth tried to express her assumptions about relations between races, to defend the superiority of race relations in Brazil, and to assert her own superior knowledge about that country, but Cleaver was quick to point out the limitations in Elizabeth's thinking about the meaning of tolerance and equality.

Their car was broken into while they were in the house, and later it was vandalized while parked on the street, though they never knew exactly who was responsible. Elizabeth said the interview was "not a success" and remarked dryly that it would be one-third shorter if she removed the word "shit" wherever it appeared. The interview was never published, although the *New York Review of Books* had expressed some interest in it.

. . .

Suzanne prepared the manuscript for the *Complete Poems* (she later designed the cover) and mailed it off to Farrar, Straus, and Giroux on September 22, 1968. Elizabeth had finished one old poem to include; "House Guest" is based loosely on the visit to Samambaia in 1956 of the sister of one of Lota's aristocratic friends. At Robert Giroux's insistence, the book contained all the poems she had previously published in books; at her own insistence, "The Mountain," "Exchanging Hats," and "Norther—Key West" remained uncollected. Robert Lowell's suggestion that she include her short stories received strange treatment—"In the Village" is not here, although the 1937 fable "The Hanging of the Mouse" is. That and the four monologues of "Rainy Season; Sub-Tropics" are the only prose in the book. She also included the sonnet "Some Dreams They Forgot," first published in *Con Spirito* in 1933, and "Song" ("Summer is over upon the sea") from 1937. The book also collected for the first time her translations of Brazilian poets, including Carlos Drummond de Andrade (she published "The Table" in the January 14 *New York Review of Books*) and João Cabral de Melo Neto.

As had often been the case for Elizabeth, sending off the manuscript for her book freed her to begin new poems, but so fragmented was her attention by the chaos of San Francisco and her own depression that she would finish none of them. They address not the politics of the 1960s or the amusing absurdity of life in San Francisco, but the delicate mental and emotional balance she was trying to maintain in a life that, at bottom, made little sense to her. All are very preliminary, in most cases single, drafts.

Far far away there, where i met
those strange affectionate animals
that seemed to like me too & ate the bread
but forgot me naturally the moment I left
oh that was a nice day, Rosinha, wasn't it...
one of the nicer ones. OH I hate memories
sometimes.

S F
light hexagons in tiers and tiers
honeycomb rifled by the bears

and left uneaten on the hills
all the bay windows unconnected
with the bay really, coincidence

Another draft anticipates, perhaps, "Five Flights Up":

In the dark night
when the sea shifts over
and leaves a tract
and continents of gravel
never seen
you grit your teeth in sleep

and I am grateful for
your human temperature.

Then one bird, or two?
a crowded hurried song
or two together

The light
It was the moon & not the laundromat
that woke me, love. But soon the laundromat
opens its doors and all the lonely people
will come to wash their clothes.

In December 1968, Elizabeth was awarded five thousand dollars
from the Ingram-Merrill Foundation, probably at the suggestion of
James Merrill, who knew that Elizabeth's financial life was complicated by her legal problems in Brazil. This removed some of the
pressure to make herself into a money-earning public figure. She
had flown to Cambridge for two days for an October 30 reading,
rescheduled from the previous spring, and she intended to make up
the rest of the appearances she had canceled when she went east in
the spring—on her way, she hoped, to Ouro Prêto. She read twice

in San Francisco, once at the Museum of Modern Art and once at Glide Memorial, the so-called hippy church, in a benefit for striking teachers at San Francisco State University. Elizabeth said she did the reading out of curiosity rather than political commitment; she had never seen Lawrence Ferlinghetti, Richard Brautigan, Kay Boyle, or any of the other famous San Francisco poets and wanted to know what they were like. She smoked a little marijuana at the reading and decided she liked Brautigan, but "in general, I'm afraid, I'm just a member of the eastern establishment to everyone here, and definitely passée. I don't mind. I thought that Thom [Gunn]'s poems and mine were the best!—the rest were propaganda that takes me back to my college days and the WPA theatre and so on — propaganda, or reportage of all-too-familiar events."[10] "Flow poetry," which even the most serious poets in the city seemed to write, was to her the antithesis of everything she believed about good poetry. It was at about this time, in response to a letter from Diane Wakoski enclosing poems, that Elizabeth wrote that Wakoski was writing the kind of poetry that she herself had been fighting against all her life.[11] "Heavens what sophistication and artistry and restraint & various other qualities . . . seem to be necessary to any art, to me." Wakoski displayed, in Elizabeth's eyes, precisely the lack of craft and the reliance on tawdry personal adventures and sensational sexuality she was seeing in the popular culture all around her. The poems of her own that she discarded show her continuing to resist the confessional, even as she was moved to write less "discreet" poems.

She had trouble modifying these standards even to accommodate Lowell's "sonnet habit." When he sent her a copy of the proofs for *Notebooks 1967–68* in the winter, for the first time she could not take on his poems directly:

> I've had the link-bound proof copy of your sonnets here now for a
> couple of weeks and this is the third letter I have undertaken. I
> [really] don't know what to say at all—I am overcome by their

sheer volume partly, but also by the range, the infinite fascinating detail, the richness, and everything else. I shall have to read them many more times through to get it all. . . .

As for me, I barely keep my head above water.[12]

For the next three years she watched Lowell's collections of sonnets grow increasingly personal and confessional and more and more loosely constructed, until in 1972, horrified at the revelations and excesses of an early draft of *The Dolphin,* she asked him not to publish it. Early in the spring, Lowell had solicited her contribution to a special *Harvard Advocate* issue on the poetry of John Berryman. She wrote a "paragraph," she said, but apparently discarded it. What eventually appeared were these four punning, ambivalent lines:

Mr. Berryman's songs and sonnets say:
"Gather ye berries harsh and crude while yet ye may."
Even if they pucker our mouths like choke-cherries,
Let us be grateful for these thick-bunched berries.

. . .

Three bouts of flu in February, March, and April 1969 kept both Elizabeth and Suzanne down, and Elizabeth was in the hospital for a week in February after an overdose, ambiguous in meaning, of Valium and Antabuse mixed with alcohol. She blamed San Francisco for her troubles. "Everything awful happens here," she complained. And even if San Francisco was okay, Ronald Reagan and the state of California were unbearable. The scenery was nice but not up to Brazilian standards; she had seen only a couple of hundred miles of the coast north of the city, up to the redwoods. San Francisco was not her "scene," she decided; the foul language she heard all the time around her and the "overwhelming" nature of her first U.S. Christmas in nearly twenty years got to her so much that she wished Joe and U. T. Summers a "ficky shutty" holiday.[13] She hardly had a social life, she said, though they had managed to gather thirty-five people for a New Year's party on December 29 (a great success—"rock and roll 'til 3 AM"), and had poets over in March, including Robert Duncan and Denise Levertov, who hired Suzanne to do secretarial work one day a week.[14] But she and Levertov were not friends, and even though she liked Thom Gunn and Duncan (especially his "disarming manic-ness"), she was lonely and nostalgic for Brazil.[15] She kept missing parts of these poets' conversation, she said, "because they are all so familiar with the Japanese."[16] She thought that after she returned from the summer in Ouro Prêto, she would move over to Berkeley, where she did know a few people, including the Sternbergs and Josephine Miles.

In mid-March, she decided to take Suzanne with her to Brazil for the summer, despite her uncertainty about her own long-term plans, her lack of information about the political situation in Brazil and how close to being finished her house was, and her doubts about their relationship. By April, she was dreaming in Portuguese of a Brazilian life like she and Lota had had. On May 4, having sublet the apartment, left the Volkswagen with one of Suzanne's friends, and installed Jacob at the offices of the *Good Times,* a local newspaper, they flew to Washington, D.C.

The five East Coast readings that Elizabeth had arranged for early May 1969 helped pay for the flight to Rio and then Belo Horizonte and also coincided with the appearance of her *Complete Poems.* She read to big audiences in the East, who did not find her poetry passé: at the Library of Congress on May 5; at the Guggenheim Museum on May 6 (where Lowell introduced her as "the famous eye"); at Wesleyan on May 8; at the Walnut Hill School on May 10 (to a crowd of classmates, including Rhoda Wheeler Sheehan, whom she had not seen in nearly forty years); and at Rutgers University on May 12. She and Suzanne spent a few days at the old Hotel Chelsea making frantic preparations to leave the country and then flew from New York to Rio on May 15.

. . .

Elizabeth saw no reviews of her *Complete Poems* for nearly a year; books and magazines piled up at the San Francisco apartment as her stay in Brazil kept extending itself. The book was not as widely reviewed as *Questions of Travel* had been, but it was received with universal praise. John Ashbery wrote a major piece for the *New York Times Book Review* in which he (like nearly every reviewer of the volume) expressed his hope that the title was an error, and that there would be more poems. A confessed "addict" of her work, Ashbery lamented the slimness of the volume, too—"like other addicting substances, this work creates a hunger for itself: the more one tastes it, the less of it there seems to be."[17] For Ashbery, Bishop was an "establishment poet" whose work happily proved that the establishment was not all bad. Donald Sheehan praised her "merely" descriptive poems, "nevertheless quite radiant with intelligible meaning."[18] Jerome Mazzaro puzzled over the effect of presenting Bishop's poems "complete," and remarked, as Sheehan had, on the "isolation" of each—"This sense of boundaries . . . militates against any cumulative effects and keeps her works discrete. . . . Miss Bishop does not want to create an imagined cosmos to compete with the real world. She wants her readers to return to life, not to escape into some cozy, romantic archipelago which she can create either in Maine or in Brazil."[19] *Life* magazine reviewed her warmly, and the book brought David Kalstone to write about her for the first time, in the *Partisan Review*. His essay, called "All Eye," was the most scholarly consideration the book received and an important foundation for the small industry of scholarship on Bishop that was about to develop.

It should be clear that when Miss Bishop writes about nature, about objects, about experiences, it is with a very strong sense of their intractability and challenge. Nature cannot easily be combed for moral emblems. Her poems, every bit as conservative in form as other poems of the forties and fifties, are much stranger than what in those decades we took to be poetry. What the sixties have left behind is a notion, a false reading perhaps encouraged by Eliot's criticism, of the perfect "metaphysical" poem, one in which an observed object or deed can be taken securely as an "objective correlative" for inner experience. . . . Going back to Miss Bishop's poems, one finds it all there without any fuss: the most precise psychological connections made between the needs of exact observation and the frail nightmares of the observer, between the strangeness of what is seen and the strangeness of the person seeing it.[20]

Elizabeth learned in early February that she was again a nominee for the National Book Award, and in the first week of March she learned that she had won. She had gone down to the post office in Ouro Prêto to call Bob Giroux; when she placed her call, she discovered that he was calling her at exactly the same moment with the news that William Meredith, Kenneth Rexroth, and Eugene McCarthy had awarded her the 1970 National Book Award for poetry. Elizabeth declined to go to New York for the ceremony, saying that she had no winter clothes with her in Brazil and had only twenty-four hours to prepare. Soldiers came to the house to escort her to the airport; she had to disappoint them. In fact, she was in no condition to go.

Elizabeth and Suzanne had arrived in Ouro Prêto in May 1969 to find that the house was nowhere near complete, that Elizabeth's agent in Rio had been speculating with her money rather than sending it to Lilli to put into the house, and that most of the money that had been spent had gone for supplies that had been stolen. Elizabeth was convinced that she had been robbed all around and that Lilli was responsible. This unpleasant situation ensued: Elizabeth and Suzanne lived in Lilli's house across the street for four months, while Elizabeth's house was being slowly and inefficiently completed. She and Lilli were barely on speaking terms, and without Brazilian allies in the town—without Lilli, without Lota—Elizabeth was at the mercy of workmen and suppliers who saw her as a ready and bottomless source of money. Elizabeth insisted that she had been robbed of millions of cruzeiros' worth of supplies and labor, and while her sense of justice was outraged, Suzanne's sense of order was thoroughly upset. In a town where North American efficiency was a laughable affectation, neither woman could quite find her place. The quarrel with Lilli made it imperative that the house be finished promptly; but they did not move in until August 31.

The house, however, was very beautiful. Elizabeth had decided in early August to call it "Casa Mariana" after Marianne Moore and because it stands on the road to Mariana, a small town northeast of Ouro Prêto. As the house assumed its finished form, she "fell in love" with it all over again, and as the Brazilian winter became the early spring and the garden bloomed, Elizabeth felt it would be a shame to leave just as they had moved in. Suzanne wanted to stay, with her son, for the year. She liked Brazil, had used her isolation to study Portuguese, and had proved herself indispensable in handling the complicated business aspects of Elizabeth's life. Although she and Elizabeth had had serious "personal troubles" (as Elizabeth called them) during the summer—quarrels and disagreements much complicated by the inherent inequalities in the relationship, Elizabeth's worsening alcoholism and increasing paranoia, Suzanne's quick tongue, and the tense and frustrating negotiations with lawyers, workmen, and neighbors in the town—Elizabeth could see herself neither staying on alone in Ouro Prêto nor going back to San Francisco or New York. So, somewhat by default, Suzanne flew to Seattle in late September, to see her family and to bring back her son, now three years old. She returned in late October, and the "one-month" trial period they had agreed on quickly became a commitment for the year.

By the end of August, Elizabeth was feeling that she had "no friends in this hemisphere." Only Lota's nephew Flavio was still speaking to her from that old life, and her major contacts with Brazilians were manifestly antagonistic—lawyers to help her sue other lawyers (and to threaten even Lilli), quarrels with workers, maids, and townspeople who she felt continued to steal from her. Bobby Fizdale and Arthur Gold had visited in June, and a young San Francisco friend (who traveled by a combination of riverboat and bus) had turned up in August. But otherwise Elizabeth had seen no friend and had no hope of seeing friends for months and months. Her cat, Tobias, died in early October, an event not so trivial as it might seem. Her connections to the old Brazil life were disappearing quickly; only Lota's Siamese cat, Suzuki, was now left of the Petrópolis menagerie. Shortly after Suzanne left for the United States, Elizabeth broke down and spent most of the month in the hospital in Belo Horizonte recovering from an emotional collapse and alcohol binge, which brought on an asthma attack, a pattern that had become painfully regular in her life.

After Suzanne's return, both women tried to establish a normal life in Ouro Prêto. Everything mitigated against it; the political situation in Brazil was worse than it had ever been, and the mood of the country was pessimistic and despairing. There were thousands of arrests on flimsy evidence, and numerous disappearances; when Flavio, who was in the diplomatic service of Brazil, visited them, his room in Elizabeth's house was ransacked, and Suzanne says he was convinced that he would be arrested or killed. Many Brazilians with means left the country to stay away until the situation improved. The global phenomena of the 1960s counter-culture had reached Ouro Prêto by this time—the *praça* in the town looked like the Berkeley campus, Elizabeth said—except that the students had no real ponchos and so wore pink and blue boardinghouse blankets over their heads. But the Brazilian government was even less tolerant of student demonstrations than its U.S. counterpart had been, and the gatherings had none of Berkeley's heady revolutionary atmosphere.

In early November Elizabeth was wondering if she would ever write another poem. There seemed no repose in the life in Ouro Prêto, no chunks of conflict-free time to think or write. Some of this conflict she generated herself; two uncharacteristic incidents illustrate. First, she accused Robert Bly, whom she had never liked, of plagiarizing her "Rainy Season; Sub-Tropics" in prose poems of his own (eventually collected in *The Morning Glory* [1975]). Bly was taken aback by this accusation (and defended himself against it by pointing out that his poems predated hers), and especially by its tone. She came on like the Joe McCarthy of literature, he said. Second, she wrote (or at least signed) a chilly and formal accusation to Ashley Brown that he had stolen her baby book, the treasure mentioned in the "Inventory" draft, a family album with photographs of her parents and grandparents. The book had been missing since 1965, she said (in fact, she had had it in February 1967). In the spring of 1970, Elizabeth apologized for the letter and said that Suzanne had persuaded her that Brown must have been guilty.

Some of the conflict came from her relationship with Suzanne—the age difference, Suzanne's economic dependence, Elizabeth's emotional dependence, her impatience with the inevitable disruptions in life with a three-year-old. And some came from their awkward position in the town. People shouted, "Whores!" at them when they walked down the street, Elizabeth said, and Suzanne was hit by a rock one day. She blamed the dishonesty and suspicion of her neighbors on the celebrated "Minas character," about which books had been written in Brazil. (The argument went something like this: the state of Minas Gerais had been under the thumb of the Portuguese for so long that stealing and cheating the powers-that-were became a commonplace survival strategy. This opportunism was passed down through the generations to the present.)

By December these conflicts had escalated, and Elizabeth conceded that coming back to Brazil at all had been a mistake and that coming with Suzanne had been "the worst mistake I have made in my life."[21] Brazil without Lota was nothing to her. Now she thought she should put the house in Suzanne's name and go to a rest home, which she needed not only because she had "personal troubles" but because she was drinking as she had never drunk before—no longer in binges or episodes but constantly, nearly every day. Her paranoia continued to escalate, and she suffered at times from delirium tremens and hallucinations, some of which were violent. Even though Elizabeth had won her lawsuit against the Rio agent, no amount of money could fix what was clearly a crisis in her life.

In a very real sense, Elizabeth was disintegrating psychically, emotionally, physically. She was "horribly weary," confused, drunk, or hung over most of the time; her letters are uncharacteristically vague about what day it was—"November 2 or 3"; "December, sometime"; "March 5 or 6." On "December 1st? No—FIFTH," she asked the Barkers for advice on "how to re-make one's entire life." To Lowell, on "December 15 or 16," she wrote:

> It has been a totally wasted stretch – and had been for a long time before that, too – oh maybe some of it will seem comic, sometime, but if I had stayed in N Y or SF, I think I might have worked on the Brazil book & even managed to say some nice things...now I've forgotten what they were! – I suppose I had Lota for so long to intervene for me, in Petrópolis, at least – and I really was happy there for many years. Now I feel her country really killed her – and is capable of killing anyone who is honest and has high standards and wants to do something good...and my one desire is to get out. But How to LIVE?[22]

By January, she was primarily concerned, she said, with "getting out alive."[23]

Elizabeth had been taking the amphetamine Dexamyl to cheer herself up daily for several years. Her supply had run out just as Suzanne left for the United States in the fall; the drug was then unavailable in Brazil, and the supply Suzanne was supposed to bring back with her was apparently stolen as she slept on the plane. (Elizabeth told Anny Baumann that she had given Suzanne all her drugs—tranquilizers, Nardil, cortisone, Anorexyl—to dole out to her, evidence of the dependence she had developed on her friend.) Desperate, Elizabeth planned a Christmas visit to Buenos Aires and the Iguaçu Falls, ostensibly for the Brazil book but primarily to buy Dexamyl. When she could not make the trip, she asked Baumann for some other drug, readily available anywhere, that would cheer her up enough to get through the days.[24] In the meantime, she used alcohol.

In "the worst situation I have ever had to cope with," Elizabeth found herself without options.[25] She and Suzanne fought, sometimes violently. She thought Suzanne was dismantling, rather than finishing, the house; pocketing household money; stealing or destroying manuscripts and papers; and exacerbating Elizabeth's quarrels with the townspeople. Several Ouro Prêto residents still remember Suzanne, frustrated with the town's erratic garbage service, carting the household trash a mile down the hill and depositing it on the steps of the town hall; without exception they describe her as *uma louca*, a madwoman. They also blame Suzanne for the collapse of Elizabeth's relationship with Lilli and the rest of the town, and even, indirectly, for Lota Soares's death.

Elizabeth's interpretation of these events was also that Suzanne was ill, as Lota had been, as Lowell was from time to time, as her mother had been. Powerless to address that problem, and intimately caught up in it by her own dependence on Suzanne, Elizabeth held on as best she could in Ouro Prêto and dreamed of unlikely solutions—an apartment alone in New York, the New York of 1936, "with no emotions brewing around me but my own."[26] She began to think of selling the house, though the beauty of the summer there convinced her that she would rather rent it, and she asked all her famous friends if they knew anyone who would be interested. Suzanne wanted to stay in Ouro Prêto, and to avoid further conflict, Elizabeth made her plans in secret. "Have you ever gone through caves?" she wrote to Lowell. "I did once, in Mexico, and hated it so I've never gone through the famous ones right near here. Finally, after hours of stumbling along, one sees daylight ahead – faint blue glimmer – and it never looked so wonderful before. That's what I feel as though I were waiting for now."[27]

Elizabeth settled at last into a crisis-management mode. She cut back on her drinking in the first few months of 1970; she hired a professional construction firm from Belo Horizonte to finish the house once and for all, though Suzanne continued to work constantly on it as well. Elizabeth had made two friends in Ouro Prêto; the friendly and likable painter José Alberto Nemer and his sister Linda Nemer were Lebanese-Brazilians who lived in Belo Horizonte and taught classes from time to time in Ouro Prêto. They became allies and were with her to celebrate her fifty-ninth birthday on February 8, and at the party Suzanne gave in honor of the National Book Award on March 7. Elizabeth took on José Alberto as a project, as she had Flavio Soares Regis, and asked James Merrill to help him get an Ingram-Merrill grant so he could study in the United States; Linda eventually became Elizabeth's lover. She began to sort through her books and papers with the vague notion of lightening her freight for a move back to the United States and the even vaguer notion that she might sell them. (She had heard that the Rosenbach Museum and Library had paid one hundred thousand dollars for Marianne Moore's papers the previous year.) Carnival came and went; Suzanne's blond and blue-eyed son "danced for four days" and was a sensation among the dark hair and faces of the townspeople. On one afternoon he got lost among the hundreds of dancers; over a loudspeaker in the plaza they called for his return, and someone brought him back, still dancing, to the judges' platform.

Elizabeth tried to write, but poetry would not come. She did a little translating, still working on pieces for the anthology she and Emanuel Brasil were slowly editing. Notably, she finished Vinicius de Moraes's "Sonnet of Intimacy"; its language could have come to her only after her time with Suzanne:

> Farm afternoons, there's much too much blue air.
> I go out sometimes, follow the pasture track,
> Chewing a blade of sticky grass, chest bare,
> In threadbare pajamas of three summers back,

To the little rivulets in the river-bed
For a drink of water, cold and musical,
And if I spot in the brush a glow of red,
A raspberry, spit its blood at the corral.

The smell of cow manure is delicious.
The cattle look at me unenviously
And when there comes a sudden stream and hiss

Accompanied by a look not unmalicious,
All of us, animals, unemotionally
Partake together of a pleasant piss.

One is reminded vaguely of "In the Village" and Nelly's reassuring
cow-flops. Elizabeth was also glumly rewriting the introduction for
the anthology: "It is awful to think I'll probably be regarded as some
sort of authority on Brazil the rest of my life."[28]

As she sometimes did when she was unable to write poetry, Elizabeth thought and wrote about it informally. In an entirely uncharacteristic moment, she agreed to give a talk on American poets to a
group of English-speaking professional people in Belo Horizonte
and even prepared the talk before she canceled it. Her notes survive;
in them she presents very briefly the lives and major contributions
of Wallace Stevens, Marianne Moore, and Robert Lowell, prefaced
by a short discussion of the differences between the situations of
poets in the United States and in Brazil. In the United States, she
says, poets belong to no social class (in Brazil, because they can read
and write, they are almost by definition "upper class") and suffer
from alienation and the need for money. Thus, they have to teach
in universities but are rarely supported by positions within the government. They live lives of great anxiety and uncertainty, she would
have told her audience.

Also in this uncharacteristic mood, she wrote to Howard Moss
at the *New Yorker* asking to take over Louise Bogan's position as

poetry critic for the magazine. Bogan had died recently, the job was vacant, and this, she reasoned, she could do; she would have to write only about books she liked, and she could focus in her three or so essays per year on people whose work she knew well—"commentary," not "contradictions or criticisms." Moss asked her to write a sample review of Stanley Burnshaw's *The Seamless Web;* this she was unable to do—the book seemed overwhelming, and she was having trouble concentrating. The *New Yorker* gave her the job anyway and began having review copies shipped to Ouro Prêto. The eighty or so books that eventually made it to the Casa Mariana reminded Elizabeth once again of the enormous chaos and flux of the literary world, and she retreated from the attempt to order it. A few notes remain, which complain about the failure of Denise Levertov's *Relearning the Alphabet* and of political poems in general and, conversely, about why it was that female poets wrote so often about silly domestic tasks and situations. Could they not go for walks, as male poets did? She never wrote a review for the magazine; perhaps it was in part because she found it as hard to praise honestly as to criticize.

The National Book Award ceremony went on without Elizabeth at Philharmonic Hall in New York on March 5. Robert Lowell accepted the award for her (he had also been a nominee—"you deserve it, . . . [but] I'd be delighted to have the money," Elizabeth had said).[29] He read "Visits to St. Elizabeths" and remarked that Pound's *Drafts & Fragments of Cantos CX–CXVII* should have been nominated as well. This statement incited Kenneth Rexroth, one of the judges, to announce that he wanted to disassociate himself from this "anti-Semitic and fascist propaganda." Several people rose to the defense of Lowell, Bishop, and the poem. It was the best reading Cal ever gave, Robert Giroux reported. In all, Elizabeth was glad she had not gone.

While she struggled to write, she got regular reports from Lowell on the progress of his sonnet making; fifty-six new ones were done in November, even more in February. She complained that in her frustration with Ouro Prêto and its atmosphere, "I'm not seeing things properly any more."[30] She was on the point of giving up the Brazil book (and in fear of "disappointing" the Rockefeller Foundation) and in despair about how or when she would write more poetry. When Lowell wrote explaining how he had rearranged "Water," his poem about their day in Stonington in 1948, into sonnet form, Elizabeth wrote back that she was "dumbfounded at [his] capacity for re-doing things. . . . I think I'll try to turn that damned FISH into a sonnet."[31] On the verge of another breakdown himself, Lowell was about to "redo" his life once more, as Elizabeth was trying to redo hers.

Elizabeth said she was willing to wait out Suzanne's illness because she knew Suzanne would have to go back to Seattle in early summer to take her son to his father anyway. But apparently the situation grew more desperate than that. As both women deteriorated under the strain of their position in the town and their relationship with each other, Elizabeth intervened in what she and others believed was Suzanne's nervous breakdown, as she wished she had intervened with Lota. She enlisted the help of two friends, one a doctor, to have Suzanne forcibly hospitalized in a clinic in Belo Horizonte. Elizabeth probably did not know exactly where her friends were taking Suzanne but took responsibility for her little boy, placing him temporarily with a local family. Elizabeth believed that Suzanne had been given electroshock treatments, to stabilize her so she could fly to the United States.

According to Suzanne Bowen, that is not at all what happened. She says that she was not ill; and that if she was taken to a hospital at all it was to a wing that served as some sort of detention center for political dissidents. There she claims she was beaten, forcibly sedated with morphine, and placed in an insulin coma, a form of brainwashing. "I was a prisoner; it wasn't a hospital." She managed to escape by convincing a receptionist to call the American consul in Belo Horizonte, who arranged for her release, got her son to the airport, and flew them home to Seattle. "I knew Elizabeth had arranged the whole thing as a way of getting rid of me," Bowen says.

Although the scenario that Suzanne describes is plausible in the Brazil of the late 1960s and early 1970s—a firmly entrenched system of political repression claimed many victims through incarcerations, druggings, "disappearances," and even murder—it is impossible to judge the truth of her story. If Suzanne was taken anywhere but to a hospital, it is unlikely that Elizabeth knew it; she had asked her friends to help and they had agreed. She was pleased with how she had handled the situation; she had stopped drinking. She thought she had done the right thing by both Suzanne and her son, and she had written Suzanne's mother, one of her friends, and her former husband, describing her condition and telling them that they must see that she go immediately to a hospital in Seattle.

For the first month after Suzanne left, Elizabeth relaxed considerably. She said she felt like herself again for the first time in years, and living quietly among her maids and with the occasional company of José Alberto and, increasingly, Linda Nemer, she began to write poems. One draft, called "Aubade and Elegy," suggests that in Suzanne's absence, Elizabeth was free again to think about Lota. At about this time she also wrote to Ashley Brown, asking if he had any photographs of Lota that he could copy for her.[32]

> For perhaps the tenth time the tenth time the tenth time
>   today
> and still early morning I go under . . .
> the black wave of ~~your~~ death
>
> Not there! & not there! I see only small hands in the dirt
> transplanting sweet williams, tamping them down
> Dirt on ~~your~~ hands on ~~your~~ rings, but no more than that—
>
> No coffee can wake you no coffee can wake you no coffee
> No revolution can catch your attention
> You are bored with us all. It is true we are boring.

the smell of the earth, the smell of the dark roasted coffee
black as fine black as humus—
No coffee can wake you no coffee can wake you no coffee can
wake you!

She also finished a poem and sold it to the *New Yorker,* she said, her first in almost three years, probably "In the Waiting Room." By May 20, she had four more poems going, in her "subliminal uprush" resulting from "relief."[33] It seems likely that she worked on "Poem," "The Moose," and "Crusoe in England" as well.

In this quiet interval, Elizabeth was also asked to take over Robert Lowell's part-time teaching position at Harvard for the fall of 1970. (Lowell and his family were planning to spend the year in England, and he had recommended her as his replacement.) Offered ten thousand dollars for one semester, a free apartment, and a much lighter load than she had had at Seattle, Elizabeth accepted the offer and began to make plans to move to Cambridge in the fall. In the meantime, she tried to maintain, or to make, for herself some sort of Brazilian life in the quiet aftermath of a terrible year. Recalling the similar circumstances of her childhood, she wrote to Lowell, "Probably what I am really up to is re-creating a sort of de luxe Nova Scotia all over again, in Brazil. And now I'm my own grandmother."[34]

When Suzanne's family failed to answer Elizabeth's letters, and then reported that Suzanne had not gone to a hospital and was ill only with severe dysentery, Elizabeth became alarmed. She enlisted the help of Dorothee Bowie to provide reliable communication from Seattle, to make telephone calls to inquire about Suzanne's whereabouts, and to carry medical records from Brazil to her doctor. At first, Elizabeth was most frightened for Suzanne: "Oh God, the poor poor child." Elizabeth apparently sent money—several hundred dollars—to help pay for therapy. When Suzanne seemed to be getting no treatment, Elizabeth thought about taking her to Cambridge, finding her an apartment, and "at the first sign of trouble" putting her in McLean's—where Lowell had been, where Elizabeth thought her mother had been, "where I could see [Suzanne]"—all contingent on her leaving her son with his father for at least a year.[35] Despite her belief that Suzanne had a serious mental illness, and against mounting evidence that she was angry at having been forced to leave Brazil, Elizabeth insisted that she would "save" Suzanne if possible. "My fighting blood is up & I'm going to *cure* that wretched girl if it's the last thing I do. – & teach her to tell the truth & respect her betters. I am even thinking of adopting her legally, so I can be the BOSS."[36] (Suzanne turned twenty-eight in 1970.) But two days later she changed her mind, on the information from Dorothee Bowie that Suzanne had had previous breakdowns. She got an injunction to keep Suzanne from entering the apartment in San Francisco and began actively to separate their lives.

Throughout the summer, Suzanne wrote Elizabeth letters, and eventually Elizabeth feared, with justification, that Suzanne might come to Cambridge on her own and might do or say things that would embarrass her at Harvard; her concern shifted to her own reputation. Certain that Harvard would not accept her if it knew her "real self," Elizabeth set out to make sure that Suzanne, the sole witness to her loss of control in the years since Lota's death and who saw herself as the victim of that loss, would not be believed if she decided to tell.

Elizabeth wrote long letters during this crisis to Dorothee Bowie, who was her one friend who also knew Suzanne. (Elizabeth told James Merrill, Anny Baumann, and a few others the real circumstances; most often she simply said that Suzanne had left.) In these she defended herself against the possibility that she might be construed as "the villain in this melodrama," against Suzanne's complaints about how she had been mistreated in Brazil and had had her son "stolen" from her, and against the idea that Elizabeth herself was paranoid and "insane": "Queer, drunk, and all the rest, I am sane."[37] She wrote out in great detail the "evidence" for her diagnosis of Suzanne—examples of missing money, tasks left undone, violent arguments. She also used these letters to place this latest episode—her third lover to go mad before her eyes, and the fifth or sixth person if one includes her mother, Robert Lowell, and Margaret Miller—in a context or pattern in her life. She saw similarities all around—Suzanne's son had endured what she herself had endured at about the same age ("It was awful to re-live it"); Suzanne was very much like Lota and had emotional needs like Lowell's. But Elizabeth could not see that the pattern, which had originated with her mother, might have perpetuated itself in her choice of friends and lovers or that something in that pattern might have swayed her response to Suzanne's apparent illness. She admitted to Dorothee Bowie, however, that "the only prose book I ever thought I wanted to write is a book about the life of Dorothea Dix . . . a wonderful young woman who devoted herself to the insane."[38]

Elizabeth got through the lonely and painful summer of 1970 with help from José Alberto and Linda Nemer, who stayed with Elizabeth for the month of July during the annual arts festival in Ouro Prêto. A visit from James Merrill, who was traveling in South America, was the summer's highlight. He came bearing stove polish and stove parts unavailable in Brazil, ground ginger and curry powder, and bourbon, at Elizabeth's request. She "broke down" during the week he was in Ouro Prêto—they spent the first evening drinking and talking and weeping ("Don't worry, I'm only crying in English," she told José Alberto), and she spent most of the rest of the week in bed drinking and recovering. But they made at least one memorable side trip—to the jail in Mariana to visit the prisoners. She could not have had a more sympathetic listener in this awful time. "I adore you," she wrote to Merrill afterward, and his reassurances were equally warm.

After Merrill left, Elizabeth struggled to get her personal affairs in order so that she could leave Brazil; she was still untangling legal and financial confusion caused by Suzanne's erratic behavior and her own inattention over nearly three years. And she struggled to write the first poetry review asked of her under the terms of her contract as the New Yorker poetry critic. Because of this obligation, she was unable even to take her usual solace in the arrival of each day's mail, for often that mail contained books—sometimes forty at once—for her consideration. In thanking Merrill for a gift he had sent ("Don't be alarmed; it's only me"), Elizabeth wrote, "At least, thank goodness, they apparently aren't to be reviewed."[39]

Amid these strains, Elizabeth broke down further in August and spent two long stretches in Belo Horizonte, one in the hospital and one in the spare room of the Nemer family apartment in the city, where she was attended by Mrs. Nemer, who spoke neither English nor Portuguese. Elizabeth returned to Ouro Prêto late enough so that her remaining weeks there would be filled with the frenzy of preparing to leave for the United States. Emanuel Brasil visited, and they completed the first volume of the *Anthology of Twentieth Century Brazilian Poetry*. She worked on her piles of letters and manuscripts, tried to get the house ready to rent to Donald Ramos and his family, who would stay there and in exchange for fifty dollars a month and free rent help to organize the papers. Elizabeth said she had hired Ramos to do "Suzanne's job"—that is, to get these things in sufficient order to sell. This valedictory activity was fraught with ambivalence for Elizabeth, as the baskets and boxes represented the bits of her own life she had salvaged from the ruin of Lota's. "I keep making bad discoveries as I work away here–but occasionally useful old notes and clippings turn up. & WHAT to do with valuable letters and MMS . . . ???"[40]

On her way north, Elizabeth stopped for a few days to see her old dressmaker, Esmerelda, to have some teaching and reading clothes made. She was tired and ill and dreading the stay in Rio, lonely and outcast among people she had known and cared about.

Seventeen

CRUSOE IN ENGLAND

1970–1971

ELIZABETH ARRIVED in Cambridge at about midnight on September 24, 1970, having spent ten days in Rio's Hotel Serrador across the street from her dressmaker. She had dreaded the Rio stay, fearing loneliness and the inevitable painful associations with the place. But she also needed clothes for the North and for teaching, and there were still more lawyers to see. Several canceled flights and delays had kept her from leaving for the United States until the twenty-fourth, and she arrived only four days before the start of fall semester classes.

William Alfred, the poet, playwright, and friend to writers on the Harvard English faculty, was Elizabeth's "one dear friend" in Cambridge. They had met in Boston in 1957 and were reacquainted in 1968 when Elizabeth had finally read at Harvard, at Alfred's invitation. He met her at the airport and installed her the next morning at Harvard's Cronkhite Graduate Center. She spent her first week back in the United States in a small, hot apartment before the somewhat more spacious accommodations she had been promised in the university's Kirkland House were ready. She moved in on Saturday, October 3 and joined "the boys" in the house for brunch the next morning. She was pleased to note that there were "ladies and babies" also present at the meal, though Harvard and Radcliffe had not yet merged.

She caught Cambridge just after the violent student uprisings of the spring and summer of 1970. If Harvard Square was normally chaotic, it was doubly so that fall. Elizabeth was simultaneously attracted to and put off by the "hippy" presence in the square and in her classes. She decided that her Cambridge life reminded her simultaneously of boarding school—the view from her apartment looked out on a peaceful and tree-filled quadrangle—and of the Praça Tiradentes in Ouro Prêto during the arts festival, "except here they have real 'ponchos.' "[1] Several shops in the square still had boarded-over windows left from the summer's rioting; the scene also reminded her of San Francisco State and Berkeley a couple of years earlier.

Elizabeth described herself during the first week of classes at Harvard as "a scared elderly amateur prof." One of her students, the poet Dana Gioia, has presented her similarly in his memoir "Studying with Miss Bishop":

> Teaching did not come naturally to her. She was almost sixty when she became an instructor at Harvard, and one could sense how uneasy she felt in the role. She would not lecture to us, even informally. Sessions with her were not so much classes as conversations. She would ask someone to read a poem aloud. If it were a long poem, then each of us would read a stanza in turn. (At times it reminded me of a reading class in grammar school.) Then we would talk about the poem line by line in a relaxed, unorganized way. . . . "Use the dictionary," she said once. "It's better than the critics."[2]

Others of her students remember her remarkable modesty there among the famous writers. She was "a real genius," and at Harvard and in other creative writing programs there were people with a lot less talent claiming a lot more privilege. She could not bring herself to claim a superior knowledge about poetry; and those "conversations" in her classes included some awkward silences. She never developed the student "following" that Lowell, for example, had. Nor did she particularly want it.

Elizabeth was assigned that first fall to teach "Advanced Verse Writing" ("Isn't that ridiculous?" she wrote to a friend) and English 285, which she called "Subject Matter in Modern Poetry." (The catalog says, "Studies in Modern Poetry.") Her first duties at Harvard involved selecting students for the verse-writing course, choosing from among fifty manuscripts twelve writers to admit. English 285 had fifteen students, mostly from the graduate schools, and they studied eight modern poets, "up to Lowell." Later, as she gained confidence in her ability to discuss poetry in depth with students, she cut the syllabus to as few as four poets. Both courses met in a dreary seminar room in the basement of Kirkland House, which Gioia describes as "vast," "colorless," and "full of unwanted furniture and dismembered bicycles. There were pipes on the ceiling and an endless Ping-Pong game went on behind a thin partition." Despite such handicaps, the two courses went well enough. Although she reported at midterm that she thought she had "chosen badly," her final judgment of her students was quite positive. Among them that first fall was Ezra Pound's grandson, Walter de Rachewiltz, whom Elizabeth had met when she read at Rutgers in 1969.

Her two seminars met for two hours each, one on Tuesday and one on Wednesday afternoon. She was amazed at how much lighter her load at Harvard was than it had been at Washington and crowed to Dorothee Bowie about her "five-day weekends." The first of these, however, she had to spend in San Francisco cleaning out the flat on Pacific Avenue and once again packing her worldly goods for shipping and storage. Elizabeth's San Francisco attorney, Gerald Wright, had been overseeing her affairs there, and his services included placing two staff members from his office in the apartment until Elizabeth could come to clear it out and monitoring the traffic fines (and thus the whereabouts) of the lotus white Volkswagen, which had been left in the inconsistent care of one of Suzanne's friends. Elizabeth flew to San Francisco on Wednesday, October 7, and Bowie joined her there for the weekend, offering physical help, moral support, and assurances that Suzanne Bowen did not know that Elizabeth was in San Francisco and could not interfere. The work was hard and depressing, as Elizabeth tried to decide what to do with "the American part of [her] psyche." Some things she gave to Bowie to store in Seattle, some she brought back to Cambridge, others she placed in storage to be shipped later—either to Ouro Prêto or to Cambridge when she decided where she would live. She flew back, weary and depressed, on Monday evening, October 12, to meet her class on Tuesday.

Elizabeth returned to her Kirkland House flat to find that the house's administrative assistant, Alice Methfessel, had improved its furnishings and supplies while she was gone. Alice was twenty-six years old in 1970, a warm, generous, active, and energetic person who Bill Alfred said was "the best thing about Kirkland House" and whom the young men living in the house "adored." Her efficiency as an administrator and a secretary was legendary at Harvard, and Elizabeth's tangled affairs could not have fallen into more capable hands. The only child of wealthy parents, Alice was just striking out for her independence when she met Elizabeth and in the years following worked on a master of business administration degree at Boston University and thought of pursuing a business career. From this time until the end of her life, Elizabeth depended on Alice for support of many kinds, and Alice became Elizabeth's main source of secretarial help and tax advice, her chauffeur, her traveling companion, her nurse, her rescuer from the consequences of alcoholism, her "saving grace."

The remarkable liberation that Elizabeth apparently felt in writing more intensely personal poems in the last years of her life, and her increasing frankness in discussing her intimate life with her friends, makes the passion she felt for Alice more readily available to us. Although Elizabeth still described Alice as her "young friend" or "secretary" to certain correspondents, very quickly "Elizabeth and Alice" became a recognized couple in the circle of poets and teachers in which Elizabeth moved and in her letters to faraway friends. Her descriptions of Alice in letters bubble with enthusiasm and gratitude, though she was unfailingly discreet about the sexual aspect of their relationship.

> Alice [is] a wonderful travelling companion. Since she is so athletic and big, tall, I mean – I thought I'd never keep up with her (and she is 28 or 29, too [in 1972]) – but I managed to. I think you'd like her very much – very American in the nicest way; she cheers me up a lot about my native land –. . . . Alice has had a happy life and is the only child of devoted parents – pampered, really – but nevertheless has turned out to be kind and generous and very funny. – She's good for me because she cheers me up. The boys at Kirkland House, where she works, are crazy about her. . . . Did I tell you that she almost married Michael Harrington (?—the man who wrote about Lytton Strachey) a year or so ago?[3]

But an intimate relationship between apparently unequal partners, one of whom was an alcoholic, was bound to have unruly energies, as had the relationship with Suzanne Bowen. Alice grew weary from time to time of the great demands placed on her by Elizabeth's pain and poor health; of the cycles of illness, drunkenness, and injury that often marked the last years of Elizabeth's life; and of doling out the Antabuse that helped to prevent such cycles from getting started. And Elizabeth lived in mortal fear of losing Alice and of what would happen if she were to be left alone to grow old and care for herself in her indispositions and incapacities. Alice's attempts to put distance between herself and Elizabeth's myriad problems resulted in desperate attempts on Elizabeth's part to get her back. At times, and under the influence of alcohol, the resentments natural in such a relationship showed themselves in harsh words and actions that friends were forced to witness.

Elizabeth's physical passion is documented in unpublished poems and in discarded drafts of published ones, which tend to franker and more positive eroticism than any of her earlier verse. In one remarkable fragment, entitled "Vague Poem," the color of the rock roses given to her at a reading to commemorate "Faustina, or Rock Roses" merge to the other kind of "rock roses," pale pink rose quartz and the mystery of its formation, which in turn suggests to the speaker the color of her lover's skin.

> I almost saw it: turning into a rose
> without any of the intervening
> roots, stem, buds, and so on; just
> earth to rose and back again.
> Crystalography and its laws:
> something I once wanted badly to study,
> until I learned that it would involve a lot of arithmetic,
>   that is, mathematics.
>
> Just now, when I saw you naked again,
> I thought the same words: rose-rock; rock-rose...
> Rose, trying, working, to show itself,
> forming, folding over,
> unimaginable connections, unseen, shining edges.
> Rose-rock, unformed, flesh beginning, crystal by crystal,
> clear pink breasts and darker, crystalline nipples,
> rose-rock, rose-quartz, roses, roses, roses,
> exacting roses from the body,
> and the even darker, accurate, rose of sex—

Elizabeth loved Alice and needed her and introduced her to the group of interesting and well-known friends in and around Cambridge and New York, including Octavio and Marie Jo Paz, Seamus Heaney, Robert Lowell, John Malcolm Brinnin, Alberto Lacerda, Helen Vendler, James Merrill, Robert Fitzgerald, and Robert Giroux. In return, Alice devoted most of her time for nine years to

Elizabeth's well-being, putting aside her own plans for a job and a career. Elizabeth was a compelling, needy person who did not drive and who arrived essentially alone, and Alice was not the only one drawn into that neediness. The poets Frank Bidart and later Lloyd Schwartz were also virtually on call. Together they formed a small and supportive community from which Elizabeth could face the complex politics of the American poetry scene and the Harvard academic hierarchy.

. . .

The rest of October 1970 saw Elizabeth getting used to teaching again and struggling to give her two classes shape and direction. She was awkward in the classroom and uncertain about her "right" to be there, so the work was a great drain on her emotional and physical energy. On October 18, Aunt Grace Bulmer Bowers celebrated her eighty-fifth birthday, and Elizabeth traveled to Nova Scotia alone for the celebration. On October 22, she visited Jane Dewey in Maryland. But otherwise during the term she did little traveling and almost no writing. The weekly Tuesday-Wednesday routine of classes was disrupted when Suzanne Bowen appeared outside the door of the writing class on October 28. Elizabeth brought her back to the Kirkland House apartment, very concerned that Suzanne might be observed and that there might be a "scandal." In the scene in the room, Suzanne insisted that Elizabeth had tried to get rid of her in Brazil and that Alice, who appeared to see what was the matter, was "trying to take her job." Both of these accusations were in some way true.

Elizabeth gave Suzanne one hundred dollars to help her leave town and exacted a promise that she would not return to Kirkland House. On October 30, Suzanne came to the apartment on her own, and Elizabeth refused to answer the door. She left a note asking for letters of recommendation to help her return to college. Elizabeth obliged but also wrote to the Wellesley College admissions dean that Suzanne was "disturbed." Nevertheless, she was admitted to Wellesley, and Elizabeth arranged with her lawyer to pay one half of Suzanne's tuition for the first year, then wrote bitterly, "I have [always] been a sucker."[4] Eventually, Suzanne completed her pre-med courses as a special student at Harvard, attended medical school, and became a doctor.

Elizabeth's desperation about putting that time far behind stemmed partly from a desire to keep word of her alcoholism and lesbianism from the attention of her seemingly upright and genteel employers. Suzanne was the only one of her female lovers with a grievance, a reason to break the conspiracy of silence. Elizabeth may also have feared that Suzanne's version of what happened in Ouro Prêto would not coincide with her own and that she would indeed become "the villain in this melodrama."

. . .

Elizabeth returned from a reading in Chicago to spend Thanksgiving 1970 with Bishop relatives in Salem, Massachusetts, and then traveled to New York for the rest of the weekend to see friends and in particular to see a show of Loren MacIver's paintings. She flew back to Boston on Sunday the twenty-ninth and found to her "astonishment" that Alice was waiting for her. The two returned together to Cambridge and sat up drinking and talking about "our Thanksgivings" into the night. Holidays had always depressed Elizabeth, a person without much family and certainly none to whom she was particularly close. Alice's similar skepticism was a great gift.

The Harvard calendar, which sends students home for the winter holidays at the end of classes and then has them return for "reading period" and final exams, stretches the fall term through the entire month of January. Elizabeth collected and read student papers during the month, gave a final exam in English 285, and held a party for the students in her writing class. On the twenty-fifth, she did her second reading of the year, at Bristol Community College in

Fall River, Massachusetts, for Rhoda Wheeler Sheehan. Rhoda still lived in the family house near Westport that Elizabeth had visited as a teenager. On the twenty-ninth, she set out for a week in New York to see doctors, dentists, and accountants before leaving for Ouro Prêto on February 7.

She arrived in Brazil on her sixtieth birthday, weary from the rough plane ride. After the social whirl and constant companionship of her time at Harvard, she found Ouro Prêto "too lonely" and began to think of selling or renting out her house on a long-term basis and leaving Brazil for good. Her relationship with Lilli had not survived the dispute over the house, and her connections to the town were tenuous and few. Her attempts to work were sporadic and unsuccessful, as she was unable to complete a poem during the spring or to make headway in the essays she still intended to put together in a book on Brazil, with photographs by Mariette Charlton. In March, the lonely run of days was interrupted by a visit to Ouro Prêto from the notorious Living Theater, which scandalized the town with such displays of nudity and raucous humor that the cast was eventually arrested by the local police and jailed in Belo Horizonte. (The cast stayed in Elizabeth's house after she returned to Cambridge, and her reputation in the town sank further.)

Early in February, Elizabeth learned of the suicide of Flavio Soares Regis, in whom she had taken a deep but frustrated interest and who was one of only two or three friends she still had in Brazil. His death surprised and shocked her. She wrote to James Merrill:

> I am very unhappy about Flavio. It was awful to arrive here and find his grandfather's desk, that I was sending him as a wedding present, all crated and on the porch waiting to be sent to Brasilia. I still don't know what happened or why...I have sent word to his widow, in Rio, to see if she'll write me or come to see me – and maybe that is not a good idea, but I want to learn what I can.[5]

Others speculated that Flavio might have been a victim of the increasingly oppressive political regime in Brazil. In Elizabeth's mind, Flavio, like Lota, had been killed by the country he had tried to serve.

Elizabeth's descriptions of events and people she had once found quaint or heroically simple grew more and more ironic as her stay progressed, and she looked forward anxiously to visits from friends, writing urgent pleas for communication when too much time passed between letters. She invited Frani and Curt Muser to visit for Easter, giving directions to her house as the one with "dirty words all over the front door."[6] In April, Ashley Brown visited and, with the Musers, spent Holy Week in Ouro Prêto, prompting Elizabeth to hold a party on Hallelujah Saturday. She saw them off from Belo Horizonte on the fourteenth and had them carry a carved stone Easter egg back to Alice.

Elizabeth's work in Ouro Prêto consisted of little writing and much organizing of her scattered belongings into transportable form. She burned bushels of papers and periodically expressed alarm over treasures she had lost track of, including the matched childhood portraits of her mother and Uncle Arthur. These eventually turned up. Other works of art, including paintings by Wesley Wehr, Loren MacIver, and Kit Barker, were harder to locate and disappeared in the confusion for months at a time. By May 1, Elizabeth had conceded that she was miserable in the house and that her "Brazilian world has really come to an end, and I must get out of it fast."[7] On April 30, 1971, sadly belatedly in her eyes, the Brazilian government awarded her a high civilian honor, the Order of the Rio Branco, "for the services which you have rendered to Brazil." The irony was almost too much for her. In a series of gestures indicating her approach to a final departure from the country, she canceled her plans for doing the Brazil book with Mariette Charlton (indeed "disappointing" the Rockefeller Foundation) and engaged the help of an American neighbor to do a final sorting of her papers.

Elizabeth had been feeling depressed and run down for several weeks; but, as was often the case, any specific symptoms she might have shown were masked or confused by the havoc alcohol wreaked on her body. She hoped only to hold herself together until May 15, when she was due to leave Brazil for a two-week stay with James Merrill in Greece and a trip to the International Poetry Conference at Rotterdam, scheduled to begin on June 1. The conference would pay her expenses, and Elizabeth was nearly desperate for the sympathy and understanding she knew she would get from Merrill and his friend, David Jackson. But her persistent digestive ailments and depression grew acute enough that she traveled to Belo Horizonte on May 3 to see a doctor. He diagnosed typhoid fever, and Elizabeth was both chagrined—she had stopped taking preventive shots in 1967—and almost relieved to find that her despair had a physical cause. She spent eight days in the Hospital São Lucas, which forced her first to postpone her trip to Greece until after the Rotterdam conference and then to plan the flight to Rotterdam via New York so she could see Anny Baumann.

After a hellish trip North, which ended in her being escorted off the plane in New York by the police because of irregularities in her visa, Elizabeth finally saw Anny Baumann on May 24. Dr. Baumann was alarmed at Elizabeth's condition and sent her immediately to see a specialist in tropical diseases, who diagnosed not typhoid but four persistent strains of dysentery that Elizabeth had no doubt been harboring for several months. She stayed at the Hotel Elysee in New York while undergoing treatment and still hoped to travel if the elaborate medications "took hold" in time. On the twenty-ninth, she flew to Cambridge to sign the lease on the apartment Alice had found for her at 60 Brattle Street near Harvard Square. She signed the lease, got a haircut, and then collapsed in Alice's bed and bathroom, at 16 Chauncy Street in Cambridge, with a violent attack of her illness. She remained at Alice's, more or less in bed, for a week.

For the first three days, she found herself unable to read or do much of anything. But by the weekend of June 5–6, she was up and about in the apartment while Alice was away, remarking on its myriad electrical appliances and reading Sylvia Plath's *The Bell Jar*. During the week when she slept at odd hours and awakened at others, she observed this scene out Alice's window and over the back fence:

> A man with 2 or 3 corgies (?) and 2 or 3 small puppies, also
> Corgies, I think, is down in the yard below. He has an awful scene
> with them every afternoon – training them, I gather – shouting
> "Stop!" and "Stay!" and yesterday, in a horrified, moralistic tone:
> "You should be ashamed!" I tried to make out what the puppies
> were up to, but couldn't see for all the leaves.[8]

The poem that grew from this anecdote, "Five Flights Up," was not finished until December 1973 and remained uncertain about how much shame for the past should weigh on the present.

Alice invited Elizabeth to stay with her until the end of June, when Elizabeth would return to Ouro Prêto for the annual arts festival and to complete the organizing of her belongings interrupted by her illness. By June 10, she was feeling cheerful for the first time in several months, and she and Alice began planning a trip about which Elizabeth had fantasized for years—to the west coast of South America for a cruise in the Galápagos Islands and a visit to Machu Picchu. They would meet in Quito, Ecuador, on August 2.

The two women spent the remaining weekends in June at the summer home of Alice's cousin in Rockport, Massachusetts. They also visited, among other events, the Cézanne show at the Boston Museum of Fine Arts, which, Elizabeth remarked in her newly restored sense of humor, had "nice ladies' rooms."[9] She made steady gains in strength and morale and began to exercise, swimming, walking, and (surprising even herself) playing Frisbee. She was able to leave for Ouro Prêto on June 30 fortified in body and spirit and cheerful because she knew her stay would be both lively and limited.

But this year's Ouro Prêto arts festival merely depressed Elizabeth. Although José Alberto Nemer stayed with her for most of the month and she entertained visitors to the festival in her home, which was something of a tourist attraction, she had not been there a week before she declared herself to be merely waiting for her Galápagos trip to begin. The Living Theater, by this time in jail in Belo Horizonte, provided diversions in the newspaper headlines and some anxiety for Elizabeth, who was being linked with the group's activities because she had let the cast stay in her house. Elizabeth refused to testify at the trial but almost welcomed the distraction. Her mail was being held up and censored (perhaps because of her ties to the Living Theater) and she felt very much out of touch with her world. The usual Brazil worries dogged her as well—what to do with the house when she returned to Cambridge, how to get her papers organized, how uneasy the political and economic situation of the country was; nevertheless, she said on July 20, she was feeling better than she had in several years, anticipating the Galápagos trip and a reunion with Alice. Late in the month, she was able to summon the lessons of her own experiences of pain, guilt, and loss to give encouragement to her friends Loren MacIver and Lloyd Frankenberg, who were having troubles of their own: "I've discovered . . . that when it looks as if things just couldn't get any worse—one is surprised to find how strong one really is."[10]

On July 17, the *New Yorker* printed Elizabeth Bishop's first poem in nearly three years, "In the Waiting Room." In its frankness and self-naming, the poem was so different from anything Bishop had published to that point that the three-year gap makes some sense. Elizabeth claimed that the magazine had held the poem for over a year, and she had enclosed a complete draft in a letter to Robert Lowell on August 30, 1967, so it had been with her at least that long.

The correlation, or lack thereof, between the content of this poem and the content of the actual February 1918 issue of the *National Geographic* has been much remarked. The drafts of the poem among Elizabeth's papers show that she struggled even more than usual with her credo of accuracy. The earliest drafts closely resemble the finished poem; the content of the *National Geographic* little Elizabeth reads consists of volcanoes but, more important, of "black, naked women" with "awful hanging breasts" and cannibals cooking a human being to eat. Explorers in pith helmets watch them. Elizabeth's trip to the New York Public Library, which she described to Lowell, is clearly reflected in the following drafts, as she tried to "correct" her error—there were no naked cannibals in the February 1918 issue, and Osa and Martin Johnson had not yet become famous. So she took the actual content—"The Valley of 10,000 Smokes" and an article about pork production in Canada—and tried to make it work. It did not. In a letter to Frank Bidart written shortly after the poem was published, she explained this herself:

> Well, it is almost a true story – I've combined a later thought or two, I think – and – because you might like this kind of information – I did go to the Library in N Y and look up that issue of the N G. Actually – and this is really weird, I think – I had remembered it perfectly, and it was all about Alaska, called "The Valley of Ten Thousand Smokes." I tried using that a bit but my mind kept going back to another issue of the NG that had made what seemed like a more relevant impression on me, so used it instead. Of course I was sure the New Yorker would "research" this, or "process it" or something – but apparently they are not quite as strict as they used to be – or else are sure that none of their present readers would have read N G's going back that far.[11]

Perhaps none of the *New Yorker*'s usual readers cared about the license Bishop took here, but several of her critics have fairly cackled with glee at catching her in an inconsistency. Her own apologies for the "inaccuracy" of the poem suggest that the *New Yorker*'s standards were more consistent with her own than she generally admitted.

. . .

Alice and Elizabeth did meet in Quito to begin their west coast travels. Signed on for a cruise of the "southern" Galápagos Islands, they spent five leisurely and "wonderful" days on the islands, ful-filling each woman's ambition to see a blue-footed booby before she died. Elizabeth had long been waiting to follow in Darwin's foot-steps, and she described the islands as "one's idea of Eden, really," with animals unafraid of humans and the chance to swim with sea lions in the warm southern Pacific waters.[12] From Ecuador they traveled to Peru, then up to Machu Picchu, where they were able to spend the night of August 13. Elizabeth described the ruins of the fifteenth-century Incan city as the emotional as well as the physical high point of the trip, though both she and Alice suffered from altitude sickness at Cuzco, some twelve thousand feet above sea level. They also visited the Museum of Gold in Lima before returning together to Ouro Prêto on August 23. There they caught the last entertaining days of the obscenity trial of the Living Theater, which Elizabeth could enjoy freely in Alice's competent company. After a quiet week of packing and organizing, the two women flew to Cam-bridge on September 2, where Alice was due to return to work at Kirkland House.

Elizabeth spent the first three weeks of September at Alice's Chauncy Street apartment while moving a little at a time into the new place on the second floor of the Brattle Arms ("sounds like a stage direction," Elizabeth said), a neat, square brick building with a formidable presence between the Blacksmith House and the Loeb Theater on a street of distinguished homes and apartment houses. At midmonth, she spent four days in New York at the Cosmopolitan Club; she saw her doctor and visited with Jane Dewey and her sister, who were up from Maryland. Elizabeth also delivered to Howard Moss at the *New Yorker* the corrected proofs of "Crusoe in England."

Like more than half of the poems in *Geography III*, "Crusoe in England" was begun much earlier than its publication date, and its drafts show composition over a long period of time. In August 1964, she reported to Lowell that she had been up late working on a poem about Crusoe, and in 1965 she remarked with delight that a restoration of an eighteenth-century slave church in Ouro Prêto, Santa Efigênia, had uncovered a mural of Crusoe, "umbrella, goats, and all—gilt on red lacquer panels."[13] In 1963, she had noted a newspaper account of a volcano's eruption and "an island being born." The earliest extant drafts of "Crusoe in England," entitled "Crusoe at Home," are very close to the final version, and she had been half-promising the poem to Howard Moss for three years before she finally sent it in the spring of 1971. Elizabeth reread the novel before she wrote the poem and told an interviewer that her intention had been to retell the story without Defoe's message of Christian consolation. But the poem is as close as Elizabeth came to a verse autobiography.

The initial parallels between the lives of Elizabeth and the fictional Crusoe account for her attraction to him as a speaking persona, and the changes she incorporated into her version emphasize precisely where her experience intersects with his. Hers is an older and more cynical "poor Robin" than Defoe's ever was, and he is without the madcap adventures and wild intrigue of the final chapters of the novel. But this is the Robinson Crusoe of the first two-thirds or so of Defoe's book, the at first unwitting, unwilling, despairing solitary who grows to love his position as God-appointed ruler of his domain, an island off the coast of Brazil.

Most important for Elizabeth's purposes, Defoe's Crusoe is a solitary man who has built his life and work from materials at hand, taking no more than needed but observing all. He is, by implication, a geographer, mapmaker, discoverer, and possessor of colors "subtler" than those of the time-bound historian. He has stepped out of time for the twenty-eight years of his solitude. An inveterate, if apologetic, traveler, he may share with Elizabeth the "questions of travel" and the restless search for a home—though in the end, England satisfies him. His greatest accomplishment on the island is supreme domestication, the making of a wilderness into a recognizably English household, the appropriation of birds, soil, trees, berries. Of necessity, his account is object centered; he makes the things he owns, and the things come to stand for sensations of pride and accomplishment, loneliness and loss. As Defoe presents him, however, Crusoe is a dull and pious fellow without much to say for himself. His story is luminously significant to Elizabeth's life but eminently adaptable.

Beyond the existing affinities, the changes Elizabeth makes in Crusoe's account move the story in a sharply autobiographical direction. By making his life center around the idea of home, rather than the idea of God, she brings him in line with her own habitually secular and domestic points of view. In addition, the terrain of his island reflects that of several Elizabeth visited and described in her prose. His waterspouts and blue snail shells are from her canoe trip through Florida's Ten Thousand Islands in 1939, and his goats and stubby volcanoes come from the brief visit she and Lota made to then-desolate Aruba in 1957. The giant tortoises are Brazilian. And yet the tone, the pastoral sense of Crusoe there among his animals and plants, his quasi-scientific interest in them, must come in part from Darwin, whom Elizabeth read throughout her life, and perhaps from the pleasures of her recent trip to the Galápagos Islands.

In the details of Crusoe's activities, Elizabeth also makes significant alterations. Defoe's pious Crusoe does not manufacture alcohol on his island, and Elizabeth's own alcoholism may account for this discreet confession. Having the supposedly seventeenth-century Crusoe recite Wordsworth to his "iris" beds also calls attention to his updated status: " 'They flash upon that inward eye / which is the bliss—' The bliss of what?" he asks. "Solitude" is the word he ironically forgets. (The *New Yorker* editors queried these lines: "Anachronism?") The question "Why didn't I know enough of something?" does not occur to Defoe's Crusoe, whose great island discovery is the utter sufficiency of the Bible; his books are not "full of blanks." Despite her wide reading, Elizabeth worried constantly about her lack of learning and confessed it often. These lines might well have been taken from one of her letters.

Elizabeth's account of Friday differs from Defoe's, especially in its brevity. Whereas the earlier Crusoe admires Friday's physique ("He was a comely handsome Fellow, perfectly well made") and expresses fondness for him ("I had a singular satisfaction in the fellow himself . . . and I began really to love the Creature"), the cross-cultural shock of the heathen's cannibalism keeps the two some distance apart.[14] And in no sense is Bishop's Friday like Defoe's Noble Savage, sent by God to be converted. This new Friday is redefined in the single line "(Accounts of that have everything all wrong.)" Accounts always do have it wrong; this Friday is a fellow solitary encountered in the journey who is also a sexual being, and the section may be read as a reticent account of Elizabeth's life with Lota Soares. Here both Elizabeth and her Crusoe try to portray in a few words the single most important relationship in their lives to an almost certainly uncomprehending audience; it is well to be reticent. Elizabeth's brevity where Friday is concerned also allows her to dispense with nearly a third of Defoe's plot, the silly adventure story that gets Crusoe and Friday rescued and back to England. Instead, we get the single-line stanza "And then one day they came and took us off." What Elizabeth does not say in the space created by the stanza sanctifies with respectful silence her life with Lota. The unspecified "they" recalls Elizabeth's belief that the hypocritical Brazilian government had killed Lota Soares. The final lines of the poem erase any suspicion that this Crusoe undervalued his friend: "—And Friday, my dear Friday, died of measles / seventeen years ago come March." As Elizabeth wrote of the real Friday in 1968, "I miss Lota more every day of my life."[15]

Elizabeth's most significant change in Defoe's plot is having Crusoe speak of his adventure in the past tense, from his old age. Although she had been working on the poem for several years, it began to assume a satisfactory shape only after Elizabeth's return from Brazil following Lota Soares's suicide and then again after the more permanent good-bye Elizabeth said to the country as she left for Cambridge in the fall of 1970. At nearly sixty years old, she felt that radical travel and far-ranging searches for a lover or a home were behind her.

Placing her Crusoe in the same condition reveals something of Elizabeth's own state of mind. Arriving back and finding herself legendary, or at least famous, she could lament that her "poor old island's still / un-rediscovered, un-renamable" and complain that the published details of her life were always inaccurate: "None of the books has ever got it right." She might have wondered at the sudden interest in her papers—queries about their availability for purchase had sent her to Ouro Prêto to sort and pack. These Brazilian and Nova Scotian artifacts perhaps no longer spoke to her: "How can anyone want such things?" And she could mourn the loved one she had lost.

Elizabeth's career as a poet is ironically summarized and eulogized in "Crusoe in England" as well. In details she adds to Defoe's account, we learn that Bishop/Crusoe "had time enough to play with names"—that is, time enough to play with "words," to write her kind of Adamic poetry, which names things. And we see in Crusoe's lament about his "nightmares of other islands / stretching away from mine" and in his dreamed obligation to register "their flora, their fauna, their geography" an irony for her geographer's method and her perceived responsibility to get descriptions exactly right. Elizabeth must have known that she could not at this stage use the word *geography* in a poem without evoking her whole life's work, from "The Map" to *Questions of Travel.*

Elizabeth's lifelong concerns become Crusoe's and are summarized in this central stanza, perhaps the poem's most beautiful lines:

> The sun set in the sea; the same odd sun
> rose from the sea,
> and there was one of it and one of me.
> The island had one kind of everything:
> one tree snail, a bright violet-blue

with a thin shell, crept over everything,
over the one variety of tree,
a sooty, scrub affair.
Snail shells lay under these in drifts
and, at a distance,
you'd swear that they were beds of irises.
There was one kind of berry, a dark red.
I tried it, one by one, and hours apart.
Sub-acid, and not bad, no ill effects;
and so I made home-brew. I'd drink
the awful, fizzy, stinging stuff
that went straight to my head
and play my home-made flute
(I think it had the weirdest scale on earth)
and, dizzy, whoop and dance among the goats.
Home-made, home-made! But aren't we all?
I felt a deep affection for
the smallest of my island industries.
No, not exactly, since the smallest was
a miserable philosophy.

The solitary sun, "odd" and made to seem odder by the abrupt shift to a regular iambic pentameter and the loud rhyme of "sea" and "me," stands opposite Crusoe himself, each alone. A kind of anti-ark whose climate limits its species to single examples, the island is sexually barren, its iris beds really dead shells. Into this scene comes the human, naturally paired off, but here frustrated and solitary. After prudent and scientific testing (he is, like Darwin and like Defoe's Crusoe, "Master of his Business"), Crusoe turns his one kind of berry to "home-brew" and frolics among the flocks, even playing the traditional shepherd's pipe. The mention of goats recalls the goatlike Pan, and the "whoop"-ing dance in honor of home-madeness, a pastoral value, makes Crusoe's appearance in that god's realm appropriate, yet painfully ironic: "I wanted to propagate my kind, / and so did he, I think, poor boy." At age fifty, just before

Mary Morse's Monica came to live with them, Elizabeth had called her childlessness her "worst regret in life."[16]

The flute, which Crusoe thinks "had the weirdest scale on earth," introduces both Elizabeth's love of music and her persistent concern with the rules, standards, measures, and "scales" of a society from which she had felt estranged, she said, since the age of six. Earlier, Crusoe had worried about his "actual" size among his miniature volcanoes and giant turtles. Here, without a tuning fork and no ear but his own, he cannot be sure what "scale" his flute plays relative to others "on earth." He is, alarmingly, master of musical conventions on this island as surely as he is master of goats.

The homemade flute and dance, inspired by home brew, are, Crusoe reflects from his old age, celebrations of homemadeness itself—in this case, the process of making one's home. The words to the dance—"Home-made, home-made!"—suggest not only the pleasure the castaway takes in his rustic implements and diversions, his "making do" on limited resources, but also a statement of accomplishment, as in "My home is made! My home is made!" The smallest industry is, not wine making, but homemaking, the domestication of wilderness through necessity without the help of conventional aids—family, friends, teakettles. The industry is something like recreating a "deluxe Nova Scotia" in Brazil or, as David Kalstone has written, like "re-invent[ing] the world."[17]

The pouty, recalcitrant tone of much of "Crusoe in England" makes explicit an attitude introduced by "In the Waiting Room." After describing the six-year-old Elizabeth's fall from graceful connection with the human race, the poem announces that "The War was on." Crusoe is a veteran of that war, and like an old soldier, he misses the exhilaration of combat. He looks back on his twenty-eight-year imprisonment with both horror at the loneliness and acute nostalgia for the privilege of setting his own standards (England is "another island / that doesn't seem like one, but who decides?") and for life with Friday. Crusoe's questions ("Do I deserve this? / . . . Was there a moment when I actually chose this?"

"Why didn't I know enough of something?") are Elizabeth's "questions of having traveled," which are answered, if they ever can be, by the poem itself.

. . .

By Friday, September 24, 1971, Elizabeth was in the flat on Brattle Street, but the next day she and Alice left to visit James Merrill's house in Stonington, Connecticut, for the first time. David Kalstone had arranged the visit (Merrill was still out of the country), and the day was beautiful. The Stonington house pleased Elizabeth as a refuge from the pressures and discomforts of being in Cambridge and of living away from the sea. On Tuesday, she was back in the city, beginning to prepare her two seminars for the fall. Classes began on September 29.

Elizabeth had decided to teach English 285 this fall as a course on poets and their letters, an idea that had long fascinated her. The course involved complicated arrangements with the "reserve table" in the library, but Elizabeth thoroughly enjoyed it. Students read the letters of Keats and Sydney Smith, among others, and wrote letters themselves and shared the responses. Elizabeth reported that it was all "very sociable"; it was perhaps her most positive teaching experience, at least in terms of content. The writing class she ran essentially as a course in versification ("I must leave the class for an hour today," one student quoted her as having said. "Write a sestina while I'm gone"). She had not yet gotten comfortable in the classroom, but her students remember her generosity as much as her awkwardness—and her high moral sense about language and poets. Among the books she ordered for the course were Edwin Newman's *Strictly Speaking,* and Nadezhda Mandel'shtam's *Hope Against Hope*—she wanted her students to know how easy American poets had it. The class featured one of Elizabeth's all-time favorite students, John Peech, a young pianist, physicist, and poet who died of cancer soon after her own death.

In this second fall at Harvard, Elizabeth began to see and take her place on the enormous, conservative, sexist campus. In the virtual absence of women on the faculty, she welcomed the writers who came to Cambridge under the Radcliffe Institute of Research and Study (now the Bunting Institute) fellowship program, including the poet Jane Shore, who remained at Harvard to teach until 1977 and sat in on Elizabeth's verse-writing course that fall. Elizabeth identified herself with the group of Harvard English faculty who taught writing; Robert Fitzgerald and Monroe Engel were the leaders, and it usually included three or four younger writers as well (and Lowell when he was in town). Perceived consistently as the "lower level" of the English Department, the writing group met separately and conducted its courses and programs with considerable independence. Few writers attempted to penetrate the enormous reserve of the more traditional academics on the faculty.

Money was a persistent problem during this fall of 1971 because of serious and much-postponed dental work Elizabeth said would use up more than half her take-home pay from Harvard. She began to think more seriously about doing readings, and selling papers and letters, and she began to advise her friends and correspondents to hold on to papers they had of hers until the right moment to sell. She was a bit sickly early in the fall, with two bad colds before the middle of October. But on the sixteenth, she and Alice traveled to Killington, Vermont, during the peak foliage weekend of the year; rode the ski lift to the top of the mountain; and hiked down through stunning fall colors.

During the last week of the month, Elizabeth participated in a "week of culture" at Vassar, where she was an honored guest along with Mary McCarthy and Muriel Rukeyser. The week began for her with a terrible asthma attack brought on by a sheepskin coat in the back seat of her host's car, which necessitated trips to the doctor and shots of adrenalin before she could do her reading on Wednesday the twenty-seventh. Elizabeth never really recovered from this attack, and on November 9 she collapsed and was taken by the university police to the Harvard infirmary. Transferred immediately to Peter Bent Brigham Hospital in Boston, she remained in an oxygen-deficit fog for eight days. Elizabeth complained that her treatment at Brigham had been harsh, that in haste to do a broncoscopy, the doctors had knocked out two capped upper teeth and had broken off pieces of two lower ones. She was "black and blue all over" from intravenous needles and adrenalin injections. When she was clear enough to write letters again, she was back at Stillman Infirmary at Harvard, where she remained for three more weeks, until December 6. Stillman was, she said, "heaven" compared to Peter Bent Brigham.

Elizabeth's new friends gathered round her in this illness; she herself had thought her "time had come," and the people who cared about her took this seriously. Bill Alfred pressed a rosary into her hand (Elizabeth said later, "I don't know what to do with it, I can't seem to throw it out"). Frank Bidart appeared at the hospital "as in a dream . . . carrying a toy stuffed tiger . . . life-size, for a half-grown cub, – about a yard long, anyway, with green glass eyes."[18] Later, at the infirmary, Bidart came every day to visit bearing custard cups from Sage's Market and French coffee. Alice arrived at her lunch hour every day as well, eating and staying to talk. James Merrill visited, as did many of her students. Elizabeth missed each of her two seminars four times, but her writing class continued to meet without her, under the direction of various of her colleagues, in an upstairs classroom in the infirmary building. "I love them all," she said. More alarmingly for Elizabeth, Suzanne Bowen appeared at the hospital twice. She awoke to find Suzanne standing by the bed, then had the nurse intercept her the next time and send her away.

On December 2, Elizabeth reported that she was finally able to read again, and she spent the next two weeks buried in Walker Percy and Henry James's letters. On December 6, she came home, having survived what she called "the worst asthma of my life." Anny Baumann speculated that the attack was a "trigger reaction" to a viral infection, not an allergic response, and Elizabeth resolved, once again unsuccessfully, to stop smoking. Her stay at Stillman infirmary cost her nothing, and she paid only two hundred forty-four dollars over her Blue Cross coverage for her treatment at Peter Bent Brigham. From this time forward, Elizabeth worried continually about maintaining her medical coverage and encountering the inevitable incapacities of old age. She became sensitive and easily upset about signs of degenerative illnesses and all but refused to look at contemporary photographs of herself. When Richard Howard's anthology *Preferences* appeared in 1974, she placed it on her coffee table, but only after ripping out the full-page portrait accompanying her poems. "Why all this change?" she asked Lowell, and she chided her friends for "going on and on about old age" in their poems, as if by keeping up a brave and cheerful front, as she did most of the time, they could avoid growing old at all.

Elizabeth dreaded Christmas in 1971, as she dreaded it every year. Alice had her home to go to, and Elizabeth would be alone. She traveled on the eighteenth to New York and took a room at the Cosmopolitan Club. She spent ten days there visiting with friends, including Anny Baumann, and drinking and then recovering in her room. She spent Christmas Eve and Christmas Day entirely in bed—"very dismal." She returned to Boston on the twenty-seventh just as Alice returned from her holidays. Together they rescued the season by spending the New Year's holiday in Jackson, New Hampshire.

There were classes to make up in the first two weeks of January, but as the term wound down, Elizabeth's Cambridge social life picked up. During the weekend of January 15, she went with Alice to Woodstock, Vermont, to try cross-country skiing for the first time. Taking lessons with rented equipment in fairly icy conditions, Elizabeth and the other novices took several falls, but she was enchanted. Two weeks later, she had bought her own equipment and after a weekend skiing on fresh snow in Putney, Vermont, pronounced it "heavenly." She bragged about how quickly she had recovered from her illness and wrote to James Merrill, "I was athletic in my youth & apparently am going to be in my old age...just a 40 yr slump in middle life."[19] She bought a bicycle and organized Ping-Pong competitions on the table in her apartment, on which she also served her legendary dinners.

Octavio Paz returned to Cambridge to teach for the winter of 1972, and though she claimed at first not to like his poems, Elizabeth was immediately taken by the poet and his wife, Marie Jo. Soon Elizabeth was translating Paz's poems for the *Harvard Advocate* as well. Alberto Lacerda, the Portuguese poet whom Elizabeth had met in London in 1964, was also in town, as were Robert and Sally Fitzgerald. Joe Summers paid a visit, and Maya Osser came down from Montreal. Mark Strand was teaching at Brandeis and occasionally stopped by on his New York–Boston commute. The continual amusements provided by Alice and Frank Bidart awakened in Elizabeth a maternal feeling or, as she said, in terms more familiar in her own life, the wish to be someone's good aunt. Frani Blough Muser's daughter Anne and her two children were her frequent guests, and Elizabeth reported to Frani a few days after their lunch on January 20 that she and Margaret Miller had talked about subtle and marvelous Muser family resemblances and had realized together that they were both only children and that perhaps such resemblances were commonplace to others.[20] At the end of the month, Elizabeth attended a wedding in Keene, New Hampshire, with Alice, remarkably the first she had been to in her life.

In the crush of finishing grades, of skiing, of furnishing the Brattle Street apartment, and of enjoying for the first time in several years the respectful friendship of people of her own age and experience, Elizabeth decided not to return to Brazil until summer and then only to wrap up her affairs there. She wanted to spend the spring in Cambridge working, for it began to seem to her that at last she would finish poems long under way and that she would write new ones. She continued to worry almost constantly about where she should live and whether she should become a "Cambridge old lady," echoing her friend cummings: "The Cambridge ladies who live in furnished souls / . . . they believe in Christ and Longfellow, both dead." But she settled into Brattle Street for the rest of her first New England winter in twenty-one years.

Eighteen

JOHN BERRYMAN'S SUICIDE on January 6, 1972, prompted responses from all over the community of American poets. Elizabeth said it was "an awful shock."

> I've talked to [Robert] Fitzgerald on the telephone since – he said that John had been on the wagon (AA of all things) for 11 months – until a final disastrous bout of drinking, I gathered – It is so sad & awful. "Love & Fame" made me feel badly about him – there is something so wrong about many of those poems – sick and miserable and boasting – And I never even wrote to thank him for the copy he sent, all inscribed, "with love to Elizabeth."[1]

A comparison between her own situation and Berryman's is implicit here, and his example urged her to distinguish her illness from his, if only by not "boasting" of it in her poems. His death was the first of several among Elizabeth's friends and acquaintances in these years, a series of sorrows recalling those between 1963 and 1965 and including Berryman, Marianne Moore, Ezra Pound, Edmund Wilson, and Jean Garrigue. Elizabeth clipped obituary notices of all these people, and they are among her papers.

Elizabeth expanded her interests and activities as a poet during this winter more than she had at any other time in her life. On January 2, she was buried in student papers and "17 unsolicited manuscripts" asking for her evaluation: "<u>How</u> am I going to get away?"[2] On February 3, she did, to read at the University of Pennsylvania to an audience of two hundred. She began to worry about the performance aspect of her readings, as all Boston was abuzz with Anne Sexton's reading to the accompaniment of a rock and roll band called "Her Kind." "It seems impossible just to get up and read after what's been going on lately – I shd. have a small 'combo' at least."[3] During the week, she also met Sexton for the first time, and despite a native dread of self-promotion in public, Elizabeth tried to enliven her readings, which were still rather flat and dry. Elizabeth also began to be asked more regularly and more spontaneously to speak her mind about issues of poetry and politics. In particular, in the face of the growing women's movement and the proliferation of all-women anthologies and editions of journals, she was called on to defend her refusal to appear in such anthologies. To the editors of *Little Magazine*, she wrote:

> I don't want to scold or preach – but I have never believed in segregating the sexes in any way, including the arts...It is true there are very few women poets, painters, etc., – but I feel that to print them or exhibit them apart from works by men poets, painters, etc., is just to illustrate in this century, Dr. Johnson's well-known remark – rather to seem to agree with it.[4]

On February 5, Marianne Moore died. She had been "helpless," Elizabeth said, for nearly two years, "with 2 black nurses and her old black maid," and unconscious for a week after a series of strokes—exactly the image of old age Elizabeth feared for herself. She could not feel too badly about Moore's death under those circumstances, "but nevertheless – we were friends for 38 years or so and I miss her."[5] On her sixty-first birthday, Elizabeth got up early to fly to New York for the funerals, one private and one public. She was moved by the program Moore had composed herself, which included "a morning-glory blue" cover with "Beauty is everlasting / but dust is for a time" printed in gilt letters and the hymns she had quoted in her poems. Elizabeth attended with Louise Crane, Anny Baumann, and Margaret Miller and spoke between the services with Bob Giroux, who, she said, was "still very depressed by Berryman's death."[6] Elizabeth resolved immediately to finish her "half-, or quarter-done, small piece on Marianne," which she would get into shape to read at the English Institute at Harvard on September 1, 1973, but would not publish before her own death.

The night before the funeral, Elizabeth held a party at Brattle Street in honor of Octavio and Marie Jo Paz and including James Merrill and Alberto Lacerda (it had long been planned and could not be canceled). Almost all the ten men and four women were poets (Alice was intimidated but came anyway), and the evening consisted of "sports and poetry"—Olympic figure skating on the television, Ping-Pong and then dinner on the dining room table, and lots of talk. "Well, a great deal of Scotch was drunk (usually it's bourbon) and Octavio fell down stairs, but no harm done, and a good time was had by all, I believe." Elizabeth said the party was "such a success" that she would have another, clearly enjoying her new social self.[7] She was "the best cook ever" in the estimation of her guests, and sought out opportunities to exhibit her skills.

On February 10, Elizabeth wrote to Robert Lowell her first note of caution about the poems he was planning to publish as *The Dolphin,* poems in which he revealed intimate details of his life with Elizabeth Hardwick and their daughter Harriet and in which he used bits of his wife's letters, rearranged and altered by him. Frank Bidart had returned from working with Lowell on the manuscript in England and had distributed copies of the current draft to Elizabeth and Bill Alfred, both of whom were shocked by the contents. In this first letter, Elizabeth said carefully that the poems were "lovely in spots" but that "I'm just worried about <u>all</u> of them &

hope & pray you have been reticent enough—."[8] By March 21, after weeks of trying to find the words to tell her dearest poet-friend not to publish his poems, she found them and could no longer contain her concern. She began by saying that "DOLPHIN is magnificent poetry...I have one tremendous and awful BUT." Quoting Thomas Hardy on the danger of " 'mixing fact and fiction in unknown proportions,' " Elizabeth went on:

> I'm sure my point is only too plain...Lizzie is not dead, etc.—but there is a "mixture of fact & fiction", and you have changed her letters. That is "infinite mischief", I think. The first one, page 10, is so shocking—well, I don't know what to say. And page 47...and a few after that. One can use one's life [as] material—one does, anyway—but these letters—aren't you violating a trust? IF you were given permission—IF you hadn't changed them...etc. But art just isn't worth that much. I keep remembering Hopkins' marvellous letter to Bridges about the idea of a "gentleman" being the highest thing ever conceived—higher than a "Christian" even, certainly than a poet. It is not being "gentle" to use personal, tragic, anguished letters that way—it's cruel.

The problem of the *Dolphin* poems engaged Elizabeth's deepest feelings on the subject of contemporary poetry. She alludes to the same passage in Hopkins's letter at the conclusion of "Efforts of Affection," her memoir of Marianne Moore. But she recognized Lowell as the founder, or the legitimizer, of confessional poetry:

> In general, I deplore the "confessional"—however, when you wrote LIFE STUDIES perhaps it was a necessary movement, and it helped make poetry more real, fresh and immediate. But now— ye gods—anything goes, and I am so sick of poems about the students' mothers & fathers and sex-lives and so on. All that can be done—but at the same time one surely should have a feeling that one can trust the writer—not to distort, tell lies, etc.[9]

In the March 21 letter, Elizabeth enclosed a closely typed, page and a half, poem-by-poem criticism of *The Dolphin,* that included grammatical and punctuation changes, notation of factual errors, and queries as to tone and propriety. Lowell's notes on the pages show his responses to her comments, and he wrote to Bidart that even though Elizabeth's letter was a "masterpiece of criticism," it showed "extreme paranoia" in its concern for "revelations."[10] It seemed not to have occurred to Lowell that art might not be worth such costs.

On April 10, in receipt of two letters of self-defense from Lowell, Elizabeth restated her points, then retreated slightly: "Of course, I don't know anything about your possible agreements with E. about this, etc...and so I may be exaggerating terribly–."[11] She may have been willing to retreat somewhat because Lowell had promised to make changes in the overall structure of the book and in the most objectionable poems. Those changes, however, were not enough. When the book appeared on June 20, 1973, Elizabeth Hardwick was hurt deeply, and reviewers pounced on Lowell for the publication of the book, the quality of the poems, and, oddly, the characters of Elizabeth Hardwick and Harriet Lowell as they appeared in the poems. In particular, a painful *ad feminum* attack by Marjorie Perloff shocked Elizabeth into writing a letter of sympathy to Hardwick, which was gratefully acknowledged. Lowell conceded to Elizabeth Bishop, amid the furor, that publishing the poems may have been a mistake.

Elizabeth continued to entertain during the winter and spring of 1972—a St. Patrick's Day party for Bill Alfred, an Easter egg hunt brunch for the Pazes, outings with Frani Muser's daughter Anne and her children. Elizabeth was writing poetry regularly now, and having been asked to read a poem for the Phi Beta Kappa ceremony at Harvard in June, she had decided to try finishing "The Moose," begun nearly twenty-five years before. She struggled with the poem all spring and even had Linda Nemer find among her papers in Ouro Prêto an additional draft to bring with her when she came to visit in June. Jane Shore remembers seeing one version of the long, narrow poem tacked to the bulletin board in Elizabeth's apartment, apparently awaiting inspiration. By late May, Elizabeth had nearly completed four new poems, though "The Moose" continued to develop even after the June 13 deadline of the Phi Beta Kappa ceremony. In this first sustained stretch of writing since the mid-1960s, Elizabeth often worked in Alice's Chauncy Street apartment, where the phone did not ring and there were no distractions. This arrangement served for a couple of years, until she left Cambridge for Boston's waterfront.

Elizabeth's days in Alice's apartment were astonishingly productive, and she was delighted to find herself working on "three shorter poems while working on 'The Moose' "; these were probably "Poem," "Night City," and "12 O'Clock News." She said she had not finished anything in two years (apparently dating the completion of "In the Waiting Room" and "Crusoe in England" as prior to 1970) and was gratified for the relative peace of mind. "It's strange how time has to elapse – no set time–," she wrote to the Barkers, "but then suddenly one day one thinks – well, I can write that now."[12] These most recent poems, which she now regularly distributed among her friends and asked their advice about, drew their admiring attention. James Merrill wrote to her on May 15:

> I really adore the new poems you gave me. How can you not write at least one a month, for all our sakes? . . . Strange, in retrospect, what Octavio said—I don't see the bitterness of that line, "The little that we get for free"; or if it's there, so deep within acceptance + serenity (the goose in all of us being perhaps what feels such things) that it doesn't count as bitterness at all. What you feel, the way you feel these things, is precious beyond words to me.[13]

She worked so well during this period perhaps because her non-working hours were often filled with social events and with the companionship of Alice and because she had found other ways to combat boredom and depression. She became increasingly attached to television programming, having purchased her first color set in 1971. She liked certain sporting events, the "Carol Burnett Show," Jacques Cousteau specials, and National Geographic programs about other cultures. She liked radio, particularly the Harvard University station and its music "orgies," hours of opera programming, show tunes, or the work of specific artists. She called the station to make requests and was pleased that they were almost always played immediately, though often with a comment such as "Here's a real oldie, from 1938." And as she always had, she loved live musical performances, including, in May 1972, *La Traviata* with Beverly Sills, and a concert by Ella Fitzgerald at Boston's Symphony Hall.

On April 13, Elizabeth interrupted her concentration to go to New York for what was probably the biggest literary event of her career to that time. The publication party for the *Anthology of Twentieth Century Brazilian Poetry,* which she and Emanuel Brasil had edited (and had been working on since 1968) for Wesleyan University Press, had four hundred guests, including most of Elizabeth's Brazilian and American friends. She spent the following weekend at Frani and Curt Muser's in Cornwall, New York, before returning home on April 17.

On May 21, she received her second honorary degree, from Rutgers; and on June 4, her third, from Brown. Over Memorial Day weekend in between, Frank and Alice rescued her from steady and frustrating work on "The Moose" and flew her to Bermuda for the weekend, where the three of them ate, drank, and toured the island on rented mopeds. They returned to Boston on May 31 for Elizabeth's last frantic bit of work on the poem, which she read at the joint Harvard-Radcliffe Phi Beta Kappa ceremony on June 13. Elizabeth thought the performance went well enough, though she claimed to "hate" the poem and had "almost collapsed" for fear she would not get it done in time. She found it funny that she had been introduced as reading a poem called "The Moos," and Alice heard one student say that "as poems go—it wasn't bad." The poem that Elizabeth read was a patched together draft, and after the reading, she made several major changes. Some of these the *New Yorker* version reflected, but most came too late for the July 15 publication date. The changes were made for the *Geography III* printing three years later, and it remains one of her most revised poems.

"The Moose" began with that bus ride from Nova Scotia in August 1946 or with Elizabeth's account of it in her letter to Marianne Moore. Drafts of the poem appear in the script of nearly all Elizabeth's typewriters, indicating that she worked on it from time to time for more than twenty-five years. Once a year or so between the late 1940s and early 1960s, Elizabeth wrote to Aunt Grace promising a poem "mostly about Nova Scotia and dedicated to you." In the months before the Phi Beta Kappa reading, Elizabeth showed version after version to Frank Bidart, anxious and angry that she had let herself be pressed to finish a poem for a deadline; she said several times over the following summer that she "hated" the outcome. It is nonetheless one of her masterpieces, and its development from the initial incident shows the complex workings of her gift.

The events of the poem were "all true," she claimed.[14] But they were not, or at least not according to her original account of the trip to Moore. As in her rewriting of the *National Geographic* for "In the Waiting Room," or of *Robinson Crusoe* for "Crusoe in England," what Bishop selects from the "truth" to use in her poem says a great deal about her craft and, given the poem's autobiographical content, about her interpretation of the events. Because her account to Moore was immediate and probably preceded even the earliest drafts of the poem, it is probably "truer" than the poem. In the former, we see the collie dog who "supervises" in the poem, her reluctant good-bye to relatives (though no particular number), the nighttime ride (though here Elizabeth boards the bus after dark), the lantern hailing, the cow moose in the road, and the driver's wry comment. The fog and the moose's specific behavior "really happened," but to a different group of passengers on a different trip.[15]

The changes made between the prose description and the poem are significant only because Bishop would not have made them lightly; the persuasive force of "what really happened" was her favorite rhetorical device. The demands of this rich rhyme scheme may dictate some changes—"seven relatives," for example; the resonance of the consecutive short *e*'s and the two-syllable number that fulfills the line's metrical requirements. And the local bus-route movement of the poem proceeds on a series of geographical landmarks and details that are also subject to prosodic demands.

But all the basic elements of the poem are present in the first prose account, though the nighttime hallucination of the passengers is barely suggested. And though Bishop discards no detail, she consents to borrow a part of the driver's earlier encounter—the moose who "came right up and smelled the engine"—without borrowing all of it. In fact, his tale involves a "huge bull moose," perhaps even more sensational or frightening. Her decision to take half the earlier incident but not the rest suggests that she especially likes the antlerless femaleness of the moose and develops the rest of the poem in some sense around that central idea.

The images Bishop makes of the details of the prose description seem to take in the reality of this bus ride through the countryside and of the many other rides Elizabeth had taken in this land or other lands like it. The present tense of the narration contributes to the timeless quality of its events, the feeling of scenes framed and then lost in the windows of many passing buses.

The first three stanzas of the poem set up a timeless territory not present or necessary in Elizabeth's letter to Moore. With brisk adjectives, she describes a primitive landscape of unnatural colors but home to a peaceful domesticity:

> From narrow provinces
> of fish and bread and tea,
> home of the long tides
> where the bay leaves the sea

twice a day and takes
the herrings long rides,

where if the river
enters or retreats
in a wall of brown foam
depends on if it meets
the bay coming in,
the bay not at home;

where, silted red,
sometimes the sun sets
facing a red sea,
and others, veins the flats'
lavender, rich mud
in burning rivulets;

The stanzas describe, not a particular day in this place, but sunset
on different days, when the huge Bay of Fundy tide is high or low
and the river empties into the sea or seems to flow backward. The
bus whose journey begins in the next stanza comes by at sunset also,
but we need not know which day or where the tide is. Buses, tides,
and sunsets are all activities we keep schedules on; we know exactly
when they happen—17:31, 6:54, 3:29. And even more than buses,
the sea and the sun come and go according to a plan, and their
coming and going constitute the life rhythm of people in the Maritime Provinces and of Elizabeth's family—situated as they were
under the influence of those enormous tides. This is a figure for
Bishop's lifelong ideal sense of time: the foreground rushing past
and the background remaining essentially changeless, like the horizon relative to the ship's passage or like the familiar landscape relative to the bus's movement.

Bishop traces the bus's route before it reaches her stop. She boards
the bus as the "lone traveller" in the pink sunset, not after dark, as

she had described it to Moore. This leaves Bishop time to record
the passing landscape in detail before darkness falls.

<blockquote>

        The light
grows richer; the fog,
shifting, salty, thin,
comes closing in.

Its cold, round crystals
form and slide and settle
in the white hens' feathers,
in gray glazed cabbages,
on the cabbage roses
and lupins like apostles;

the sweet peas cling
to their wet white string
on the whitewashed fences;
bumblebees creep
inside the foxgloves,
and evening commences.

</blockquote>

The details bespeak domesticity: cabbages, sweet peas, whitewashed fences. Later, after several stops, "a woman shakes a table-
cloth / out after supper." But nighttime in this landscape is neither
wholly safe nor wholly dangerous. The impressions swing back and
forth between vague alarm and familiar comfort. "An iron bridge
trembles / and a loose plank rattles / but doesn't give way." Later,
the "hairy, scratchy, splintery" New Brunswick woods are domes-
ticated, "moonlight and mist / caught in them like lamb's wool /
on bushes in a pasture." In the same way, the "ship's port lantern"
and "two rubber boots," illuminated ominously to hail the bus, turn
out to belong to a type of Gammie:

<blockquote>

A woman climbs in
with two market bags,

</blockquote>

brisk, freckled, elderly.
"A grand night. Yes, sir,
all the way to Boston."
She regards us amicably.

The conversation in the bus and the "auditory, / slow hallucination" have the same dual nature as the earlier events. The comforting voices mumble on about tragedies: " 'Life's like that. / We
know *it* (also death).' " The sound of the conversation—"Talking
the way they talked / in the old featherbed, / peacefully, on and
on"—overrides the melancholy of the subjects, just as the Boomer
grandparents' soothing talk had concerned the violence and losses
in Elizabeth's life: her mother, the insane family member they
"finally" had to "put away"; the child's uncertain future; the daily
worries of the farm. The talk does not deny or repress tragedy: not
"no," but "yes," "that peculiar / affirmative." Knowing this, feeling
this, "it's all right now / even to fall asleep / just as on all those
nights."

The moose's appearance returns the poem to its prehallucination
pattern, only more so. The jolting stop, the utter darkness, and the
looming creature not yet clearly perceived, reestablish the uncertain
terrain of earlier in the night. The moose is an "it" here: "It
approaches; it sniffs at / the bus's hot hood." Then by degrees, the
passengers register their domesticating observations, and the moose
becomes homely and safe even as she remains "grand, other-
worldly," "amicable" herself, as she is incorporated into the night's
sorrowing/comforting domestic hallucination.

Towering, antlerless,
high as a church,
homely as a house
(or, safe as houses).
A man's voice assures us
"Perfectly harmless...."

Some of the passengers
exclaim in whispers,
childishly, softly,
"Sure are big creatures."
"It's awful plain."
"Look! It's a she!"

To the blinking passengers, the moose resolves from a worrisome mystery into the idiomatic humanity of their conversation only so far. It is precisely her lingering grandeur and otherworldliness that generate the "sweet / sensation of joy." Her appearance from the depth of the woods and her return there convince Elizabeth and the passengers that despite their initial desire to fit her presence into their night-long litany of human losses, she will remain "curious" and they will drive on.[16]

On her return from Nova Scotia in October, her first trip there since the poem had been published, Elizabeth wrote to James Merrill that her relatives had liked it, but with a domesticating urge of their own: "Well, that is about the only poem of mine that branch of my family has really taken to. (One second cousin or something—not really related–had just taken out his Moose License for the season. I asked my cousin what on earth one would do with a shot moose and she replied 'Roast it!')"[17]

. . .

Elizabeth flew to Ouro Prêto ("for six weeks at the most") with Linda Nemer and Emanuel Brasil on June 22, where they arrived to three weeks of lovely weather and the beginning of the arts festival. By the end of June, Elizabeth had made firm plans to move all her books and papers to the United States and was burning baskets of trash at a time. Most of her month in Brazil was spent tangling with "lawyers, banks, taxes, tickets," and she found herself growing more and more lonely and missing Lota as well. By mid-July, she was in the *santa casa,* or rest home, in Ouro Prêto suffering from severe asthma brought on by handling her mildewed books and papers and trying to detoxify herself of the alcohol she was prone to drink when alone. Emanuel Brasil rescued her, got her on a plane in a wheelchair, and booked her through to New York first class. Alice flew down from Cambridge to meet the flight in New York and accompanied Elizabeth back to Boston. She later returned to Ouro Prêto only to collect her last belongings.

By August 6, she had recovered just enough to leave with Alice on a long-planned cruise through Scandinavia to the Soviet Union. She left Boston in a wheelchair, but by the third day out the sea air had all but cured her lingering bronchitis. The trip featured stops in Stockholm, Helsinki, Leningrad, and Bergen and a cruise aboard the SS *Harold Jarl,* a Norwegian mailboat, over Norway's North Cape. They flew home from Oslo on September 4. Highlights for Elizabeth were the ceramic plaque she bought at the Arabia Ceramic Works factory in Helsinki (entitled "Easter") and the four-day bus trip to Leningrad. She found the city thoroughly depressing, except for the architecture, but she got direct access to the top floors of the Hermitage Art Gallery—"we had our 1 1/2 hrs. alone with the collection – absolutely staggering – 4 rooms of Matisse – 2 lovely Vuillards (almost my favorite painter) – Cezannes – early Picassos – almost a room of Gauguin – oh my–." The Scandinavian landscape, she said, was like Newfoundland or Peggy's Cove, Nova Scotia, "only more of it": "There have been glaciers, snow-topped peaks, a wonderful stretch of hundreds of rock islands, flat & low, called 'Skenies' –...2 nights ago the full moon on one side (but it never rises) & a sunset, for several hours, on the other."[18]

Elizabeth was thoroughly happy, as had often been the case in her life, when at sea. She was not particular about accommodations—a Norwegian mailboat with sixty other passengers and much crated cargo served her as well as had the SS *Brasil Star* or the SS *Mormacstar.* The trip cleared her asthma and her mind and prepared her to begin teaching her third term at Harvard on September 26.

Back in Cambridge was the news that Robert Lowell would be there during the fall and that he was "all signed up" to return to teaching at Harvard the next year. Elizabeth's appointment had been as Lowell's replacement, and his unexpected return seriously jeopardized her job. She had already accepted an invitation to return to the University of Washington for the spring quarter of 1973—the salary was high and the quarter relatively short—and had assumed her Harvard job would be waiting for her on her return. When this seemed not to be the case, the controversy over the job threatened to widen the breach that had opened between Elizabeth and Lowell over *The Dolphin* and that had opened a bit wider when Elizabeth criticized Lowell's failure to dedicate the book to Frank Bidart in return for his many weeks of work on it. Lowell did come to the United States to arrange his divorce from Elizabeth Hardwick so he could marry Lady Caroline Blackwood, the mother of his new son (and Elizabeth's godson), Robert Sheridan Lowell. He arrived in Boston on October 17.

By the end of the month, Lowell had become anxious about the "tone" their relationship was taking, and when he left at the end of November, Elizabeth wrote to Anny Baumann, "The less said about Cal's visit the better."[19] Elizabeth removed herself from concern about the comparisons that might arise if she and Lowell were to teach verse writing at Harvard at the same time; her salary at Washington was high enough to permit her to take off the fall term of 1973. At the same time, she was being courted heavily by Peter Taylor and the University of Virginia to move there and become their poet in residence. Elizabeth had no interest in ending her days in a new place where she knew almost no one and was relieved when Harvard granted her a contract. It was a four-year term appointment at half-time, independent of any contract of Lowell's, beginning in the spring of 1974 and ending with her mandatory retirement in the spring of 1977. Elizabeth believed that if she "made it" and taught until 1977, she would be eligible for Harvard's excellent health coverage for the rest of her life, and this, along with the salary, was her only inspiration for continuing to teach. "I must check on this to see if it is true," she said to Anny Baumann before she signed the contract. It was not, but she had already signed by the time she found out.[20]

Elizabeth's two courses in the fall of 1972 were "both delightful," she said; the writing class was "the best yet," and the "reading class" got steadily better. She had been frightened early in the fall by a mentally ill student who disrupted the latter. The student was eventually removed, and Elizabeth later visited her in the infirmary to offer encouraging words. Margaret Holmes, daughter of poet John Holmes (a guru of sorts to Boston poets), was also in the reading class and wrote an "excellent" paper on James Merrill, which Elizabeth forwarded to her friend the poet.

She continued to write during the fall, gradually finishing both new poems and poems that had been with her for many years. She sent a final draft of the prose poem "12 O'Clock News" to Merrill on October 26; it had been with her in fragments of verse since her Vassar days. Merrill said he felt it was her "saddest poem."[21] On November 13, the *New Yorker* published "Poem." In March, Elizabeth had finally, with obvious pleasure, sent a draft of it to Aunt Grace, saying, "I'm sending you a poem. . . . It's about a tiny little painting you gave me, I think – or Mary did – no, Mary did, in Montreal. I've stuck to the facts pretty much – took a little 'poetic license' here & there. . . . You may even remember the picture, – I just made up 'Miss Gillespie' because it's a good Scotch name & went well with geese!!"[22] "Gillespie" was also the last name of Lucius, Elizabeth's first literary version of herself.

Lawrence Lipking has written in *The Life of the Poet* that a poet in need of renewal frequently looks back on his earlier work, returns "to the pages where his new life is already written and learns what his words have meant."[23] David Kalstone and others have noted this general movement in the *Geography III* poems. The clearest example of such reconsideration in Bishop's work is the way "Poem" revisits the earlier "Large Bad Picture."

In "Large Bad Picture," published in 1946, Bishop examined in quatrains a large painting done by her grandmother's brother. It begins with these words:

Remembering the Strait of Belle Isle or
some northerly harbor of Labrador,
before he became a schoolteacher
a great-uncle painted a big picture.

As the poem goes on, awkwardness in the rhythm reflects perhaps the awkwardness of the painter's style. The tone of Bishop's evaluation of his work is comic ("fretted by little arches," "perfect waves," "hanging in n's in banks"), with an occasional appreciative response. Having seen "the Strait of Belle Isle" itself, the poet can consider the scene full scale and can judge the painter's presentation. In the end, however, Bishop steps away from what she shares with her ancestor, seeing his carefully rendered pink sunset comically, "rolling, rolling, / round and round and round," and then questioning his motive for painting the picture: Had "commerce" (is this a mercenary art?) or "contemplation" brought the ships here? Communication with him is finally impossible.

Elizabeth may have dismissed Uncle George's painting this way at one time, but by the late 1950s she was trying with some energy to get Aunt Mary Ross to give or sell her some of his work, particularly one that had hung over the bookcase in the hall of her grandparents' house in Great Village. "Poem" reflects the way in which family connections, common ground across temporal and national boundaries, have allowed Uncle George's painting to transcend its enduring and endearing ineptitude.

"Poem" picks up the "commerce" idea from the last line of "Large Bad Picture":

About the size of an old-style dollar bill,
American or Canadian,
mostly the same whites, gray greens, and steel grays
—this little painting (a sketch for a larger one?)
has never earned any money in its life.

Having answered the earlier poem's question, "Poem" leaves the commercial theme and becomes an elegy for a place, a time, and a distant relative.

Like "Large Bad Picture," "Poem" first establishes a tentative place ("It must be Nova Scotia") and proceeds to a technical evaluation of the artist's style. Bishop moves in and out of the painting—"tiny cows, / two brushstrokes each" and "the air is fresh and cold"—her tone tolerant and humorous, vaguely appreciative of the artist's accuracy. Then: "Heavens, I recognize the place, I know it! / It's behind—I can almost remember the farmer's name."

Seeing the place and its representation in the painting, the poet reaches back through time and its transformations to a connection with the painter. It is no longer "hard to say what brought them there." In the "sketch done in an hour," the artist has represented what he knew and loved, "memorized" and "memorialized." The three ways "memory" appears in the final stanza differentiate between his use of the place in the painting ("art 'copying from life'") and her experience ("life itself"), even though they "coincide":

Our visions coincided—"visions" is
too serious a word—our looks, two looks:
art "copying from life" and life itself,
life and the memory of it so compressed
they've turned into each other. Which is which?
Life and the memory of it cramped,
dim, on a piece of Bristol board,
dim, but how live, how touching in detail
—the little that we get for free,

the little of our earthly trust. Not much.
About the size of our abidance
along with theirs: the munching cows,
the iris, crisp and shivering, the water
still standing from spring freshets,
the yet-to-be-dismantled elms, the geese.

The final stanza conveys the painter's sense of time frozen, of both "life and the memory of it" immobilized on the Bristol board. But the poet, having known the place at a later time than her great uncle and being the elegist still subject to the processes of time ("it must have changed a lot"), remembers the scene with a sense of its movement, its transience. The painting's features, necessarily frozen in the picture, are in motion for the poet—"munching," "shivering," even "still standing"—poised on the edge of autumn and then winter and eventual extinction: "the yet-to-be-dismantled elms." The artlessness and indigence of the painting, described in the first stanza, equal at the end "the little that we get for free" and the "size of our abidance." "Abidance" is not "bitter"; it carries the sense of both "endurance" and "lingering." "The size of our abidance" is the length of our memories and our lives or the measure of what we can keep from the past, the physical embodiment of passing time.

In contrast with the poet's rendering of her great uncle's painting in "Large Bad Picture," through which she discovers the impossibility of recovering him or the place or the motive behind his work, here the poet is surprised by her communication with him, by her sudden appreciation of his need to memorize and memorialize: "Heavens, I recognize the place, I know it!" Perhaps what we get for free is this flash of recognition, these "coincidental" visions. The unpretentious sketch should earn, not money, but a glimpse of the sufficiency of Elizabeth's "abidance," of the inseparability of life and the memory of it, and of the way memory makes art possible and necessary. Such modesty in art, in poetry, or in painting, she always valued.

On the anniversary of her mentor's birthday, November 15, 1972, Elizabeth attended the opening of the Rosenbach Museum's Marianne Moore display—the minutely accurate recreation of her West Ninth Street apartment—which Elizabeth found "sad, but a wonderful exhibition."[24] She fed Thanksgiving dinner in 1972 to Hilary Cross, who was a young friend from San Francisco days, and Frank Bidart. Then Elizabeth went off to Providence to read for a big audience at Brown on November 30. Her program for the Brown reading was identical to that of several later readings and altogether typical. She began with "The Moose," and then read "Crusoe in England," "Poem," "Large Bad Picture," "The Man-Moth," "Cirque d'Hiver," "Little Exercise," "Manuelzinho," "The Armadillo," and "Filling Station." She ended, as a memorial to Ezra Pound, who had died on November 1, with "Visits to St. Elizabeths." In advice to her poet-students, Elizabeth recommended that they never read for more than forty minutes. She was known, on occasion, to read for considerably less than that.

Elizabeth spent December improving the Brattle Street apartment with Alice's help, enjoying the two classes, and preparing to dread once again the Christmas holidays. On December 22, Adrienne Rich came to dinner, and Elizabeth expressed sympathy for Rich's busy life—writing, teaching, and raising three sons. Elizabeth and Rich moved in the same circle of readings and cocktail parties over the next several years, though they did not become friends. In 1983, Rich, in reviewing the *Complete Poems, 1927–1979*, wrote with warmth and characteristic honesty about Bishop. In the essay, Rich describes driving with Bishop from New York to Boston "in the early 1970's":

> We found ourselves talking of the recent suicides in each of our lives, telling "how it happened" as people speak who feel they will be understood. In the course of this drive I forgot to take the turnoff at Hartford, and drove as far as Springfield without noticing. This conversation was the only one approaching

intimacy I ever had with Elizabeth Bishop, and almost the only time I saw her alone.[25]

Rich's life was changing quickly at this time, as is fully recorded in her poems; Elizabeth's life was not. Elizabeth remained suspicious of dogmatic feminism and resisted any identification with "women poets," just the kind of identification that Rich has argued is central to freedom for all women. That they found this much common ground is testimony to each woman's generosity.

Emanuel Brasil joined Elizabeth and Bill Alfred for Christmas dinner at the home of Arthur Smithies, master of Kirkland House. The meal was awkward but memorable to several of the guests because of a diving midair catch Brasil made of a falling pitcher of martinis. Jean Garrigue died on December 26, so the dreary holidays were separated by a large literary funeral at Harvard's Memorial Church. Shortly afterward, Alice and Elizabeth left for a New Year's weekend of skiing in New Hampshire.

Nineteen

JANUARY'S COLD, gray, snowless weather depressed Elizabeth, and even though she executed the usual reading period duties of ending classes (her students came to a party at Brattle Street on January 18), writing exams, and grading papers, she began to feel even more hopeless than usual about the possibility of teaching writing at all and about her own false position as the teacher. She wrote to Dorothee Bowie, who was helping her prepare for the spring's courses at Washington:

> Actually I think it is all a lot of nonsense, but don't tell anyone. Anyone who wants to write poetry or read poetry should do it on his or her own, and probably will – on the side. These things shouldn't be taught – I'll be relieved and have a moral load off my mind when and if I sell my house & my papers and don't have to do this any more. . . . I simply loathe what I have learned, not much but enough, of the academic world. Maybe it isn't quite so bad at other places – but here there is an assumption of superiority that drives me wild...And the more I see of the attitude towards women (this is not nearly as bad at Wash., I think) the more amazed I am that I'm here at all.[1]

What saved her from the "moral load," she said, was that she personally knew most of the poets she taught. Teaching Moore, Lowell, and cummings as people, as friends, gave her the touchstone to the real that she always wished for in her work. At the same time, she was "so appalled" at her students' writing skills that she offered to teach expository writing in the spring of 1974, though it is equally true that she wished not to be teaching verse writing at Harvard at the same time Lowell was. Lowell had a large following among the student writers; the "cult" of Elizabeth Bishop was distinctly modest by comparison.

Her own writing during the spring focused on one old poem she had been working on since the death of Uncle Sam the toucan, in 1959 and on her memoir of Marianne Moore, which had also been with her for years in notes. The "Ode to Sammy" was among Elizabeth's papers when she died, fragmentary and nowhere near finished. In twenty years of trying, she could not transform her guilt into art: "Mea culpa / Sammy I killed you."

Even though she seemed to catch every round of flu or cold that passed through the Harvard community, Elizabeth stayed physically active with hiking and skiing and kept up her professional and personal contacts during the winter. A long night of drinks and talking with Cal Lowell healed some of the rough spots in their relationship. James Merrill came to lunch on February 6, and a birthday dinner with Alice and Frank, along with flowers from students, cheered her. Richard and Betty Eberhart visited Cambridge the following week, and though Elizabeth maintained an inexplicably strong dislike for Eberhart based on her knowledge of him at Washington in 1966, she attended the festivities in his honor. Her professional activities included a reading at Bryn Mawr, a class for Bidart at Wellesley, and a reading at the University of Oklahoma in Norman, which Elizabeth loved. She "had a wonderful time," though "the desolation of the scenery at that time of year is incredible.—I've seen 'lonely New England farmhouses' – but nothing can compare to a lonely small-sized ranch-house in Oklahoma. . . . One can see for miles—all pale tan—only pumping oil-wells lend animation to the scene—even on the "Wild Life Reservation"—pumping away like lost lunatics—."[2] She read to an audience of more than six hundred on February 28 and found her hosts warm, friendly, and unpretentious. She hosted a cocktail party for them at the Holiday Inn Club—one way around Oklahoma's no-package-sales alcohol law. A tour of the National Cowboy Hall of Fame was a highlight.

Elizabeth returned to Cambridge to finalize her four-year contract with Harvard. With that security in hand, she took the last major step toward solving her lifelong "where to live" dilemma. Her doubts about Cambridge as a place to grow old kept her from settling there, and despite her numerous and continuous trips to the beaches in Westport (near Rhoda Sheehan's house), Rockport, and Maine, she longed for a permanent ocean view. Rents on Boston Harbor were a prohibitive seven hundred dollars a month. But at ritual Sunday brunches with Alice at the Rusty Scupper in the city's North End, Elizabeth had been eyeing across Atlantic Avenue a warehouse conversion project known as Lewis Wharf. Suddenly one day, she signed an "intent to buy" agreement on a condominium in the project, scheduled to be completed in September or October 1973 (but not destined to be done until a year later). "Fearfully expensive" at sixty-five thousand dollars, the purchase mandated that Elizabeth continue teaching and that she acquire the first mortgage of her life, for forty thousand dollars. (In shocked disbelief, she asked Lowell, "Do you know it is hard for women to get mortgages?") But she did "fall in love." The "Granite Warehouse" had been built in 1838 of, according to the architect, "the finest granite-work in the world except for Machu Picchu." Exposed brick walls "with iron loops and hooks still in them," original beams—Elizabeth gushed:

> It is a marvellous old building, huge, all granite...I'll have a verandah (4th floor) looking at the harbor—the Mystic River side—

fireplace, as much room, or a bit more, than I have here –
although the ping-pong table will have to go. After years of being
spoiled by some of the world's best scenery I've really hated
looking at the Loeb Theatre and being wakened by garbage trucks
etc.[3]

From this time on, money was a continual concern, acute at times
and a factor in all Elizabeth's considerations. This worry surfaced
regularly in her letters, and she stepped up her reading schedule.
With the failure of the Ouro Prêto house to sell, suddenly the large
salary that had attracted her to the Washington job was not enough,
and she began inquiring about opportunities to read in the Northwest. She went almost directly from Oklahoma to the University of
Virginia, where she stayed with the Irvin Ehrenpreises and did a
reading. She was being courted by Virginia, and the university
showed her a good time. She had two meals there with Eleanor and
Peter Taylor and toured the campus and surrounding countryside
with them. Elizabeth loved Monticello but concluded that Jefferson
must have been "a domestic tyrant." Of the famous "Lawn" at the
university, she remarked, "The effect is so beautiful, and the details
so absurd."[4]

Despite her financial worries, Elizabeth refused when Lowell suggested that when he sold his papers to Harvard, the university should
take the irregular step of paying her five thousand dollars for her
wonderful letters to him. (The law says that the recipient owns the
letter as object; the writer owns only the content.)

Oh! No, no, a thousand times no – or five thousand times no...I
feel guilty enough living with the possible intention of selling
personal letters. And I have just read the collection of Auden's
reviews or most of it – FORWARDS & AFTERWARDS – and in
almost every piece he goes on & on about the wickedness of
printing private letters (although one can't help noticing he's a bit
ambivalent about this sometimes – he regrets – but he does love a
good bit of gossip). And now I've just finished – after reading

almost all night – the last vol. of the Edel <u>Henry James</u> – & James was even more severe on the matter – and <u>burnt</u> almost all his papers in his garden.[5]

A year later, when Harvard sent the money anyway, Elizabeth was extremely grateful and wrote warmly to Lowell that it came at a time of such financial anxiety that it alone allowed her to keep the Lewis Wharf apartment.

Elizabeth left for Seattle by train on March 21 and arrived via Glacier National Park on March 24 in time to begin teaching two days later. From the start, she hated her time at Washington. Her teaching schedule, though still only two courses, involved seven contact hours per week instead of four. That, and the long walk from her suite at the University Motel to the Washington campus, wore her down. She felt "abused and overworked" and said her teaching was "futile and frantic." On May 8, she wrote, "3 weeks to go – WHEE!" And a week later, "2 weeks to go – WHEE!" Despite side trips—to Portland, Oregon, to read at Portland State, and to Mt. Rainier—and visits with old friends, Elizabeth was miserable from the start of the term to the finish. Her usual code of not letting alcohol interfere with her teaching failed her, and Dorothee Bowie made excuses for her when she was unable to rise to the occasion of class.

A one-week reprieve was not much help. The trip to New York in April involved a National Book Award Translation Prize committee meeting and a joint reading with James Merrill at the YMHA on April 11, neither of which Elizabeth found restful. New York still frightened her as no other stop on her reading itinerary did, and committee work was an unrelenting drag. Dinner with Bob Giroux, Michael DiCapua, and Merrill; a party at John Hollander's; and a trip to the Metropolitan Opera to see *Der Rosenkavalier* helped lighten the burden, as did a two-day stop in Cambridge to visit Alice and to check on Lewis Wharf. While walking on Atlantic

Avenue near the building, Elizabeth was startled to meet Frani Muser on the street.

Alice arrived in Seattle on May 25 to see Elizabeth through the last few days of classes and to scoop her up for a driving trip to Victoria, British Columbia, and the beautiful Olympic Peninsula over the Memorial Day holiday. Alice was certainly Elizabeth's driver in their time together; one thinks of Henry James's pleasure in his friend Edith Wharton's "magical car" as they motored around Europe. Alice and Elizabeth left Seattle on the day of her last class for San Francisco, Sausalito, Palo Alto, and the beach at Watsonville, at the home of her friend Billy Abrahams. On June 4, having gathered up term papers and exams, they flew to Cambridge, where Elizabeth did her grading and mailed the results back to Bowie. She then "slept for two weeks."

Her Harvard contract did not begin until January 1974, and Elizabeth was pleased, in all ways but the financial, not to teach until then. She spent the summer in hot, sticky Cambridge, with frequent trips to swim at Rhoda's, at Rockport, at John Malcolm Brinnin's house in Duxbury, and on the beaches of Maine for relief. The summer's political and literary events were the opening of the Senate's Watergate hearings and the publication and aftermath of Lowell's *The Dolphin*. The hearings dominated television and conversation, and the poems stirred the literary world out of its summer apathy. Consoling both Lowell and Hardwick, Elizabeth felt torn, but she was too gracious to say to Lowell, "I told you so." Instead, she wrote, "We all have irreparable and awful actions on our consciences – that's really all I can say now. I do, I know. I just try to live without blaming myself for them every day, at least – every day, I should say – the nights take care of guilt sufficiently. (But for God's sake don't quote me!)"[6]

Elizabeth remained sensitive to writers' unauthorized and inevitably distorted uses of the experience of others. She had been disturbed by Lowell's use of her story in "The Scream," and in October 1973 she asked Elizabeth Hardwick not to use a mild, anonymous characterization of Lota in a memoir of Castine. Later in the same month, Elizabeth was shocked to find her own name in David Shapiro's poem "On Becoming a Person" and insisted that the poem be changed or that an errata slip be inserted in the book indicating that the subject was a different Elizabeth Bishop. The latter was done.

Elizabeth worked most days during the summer at the air-conditioned Chauncy Street apartment. She made slow progress on her memoir of Marianne Moore, which she had promised to read at the Harvard English Institute meeting on September 1. From the start, she was thinking on a much larger scale than the paper she would read at the meeting, and the work of writing and then cutting against a firm deadline was onerous to her. Although she worried about the paper constantly, she finished it in time and read it as a part of a program that featured Ted Weiss and Howard Nemerov discussing Dante and Harold Bloom discussing Emerson. Elizabeth was thoroughly intimidated by her first experience at an academic conference, though she conceded that it had gone well enough. A few days later, Octavio and Marie Jo Paz returned to Cambridge, Lowell assumed his teaching duties, and Elizabeth was glad to be once again among the few academics she found socially tolerable.

But she fell ill with viral pneumonia and pleurisy in September and spent the second half of the month recovering. Over the Columbus Day weekend, she was well enough to travel to Nova Scotia with Alice, specifically to visit childhood places. They did not get as far as Tatamagouche to see Aunt Grace but did visit Bass River, Truro, and even MacLachlan General Store in Great Village, where Muir MacLachlan was working and looking "just as he did aged 6 in 'Primer Class' – except for being bald." They brought apples, cheese, and salmon back with them on the Prince of Fundy ferry service from Halifax to Portland, Maine.

On their return, Elizabeth, Alice, and Frank Bidart gathered with the rest of East Coast sports fans to cheer on the New York Mets in the World Series. Elizabeth had "nowhere near the interest in this 'boys game' that Marianne had," but she had become an "ignorant fan."[7] She also joined the rest of the nation that fall in coping with the oil embargo and the ensuing energy crisis. Because she had no car, she was spared the various gasoline rationing strategies and perhaps thus could afford to say, as she had many times before, that the U.S. national character flaw was wastefulness and that she hoped the energy crisis would straighten it up. A wave of attacks against women in Cambridge during the fall—so serious that all female employees of the university were sent home each day before dark—convinced Elizabeth that she should never go out unaccompanied, except "directly into a taxi." In general, the situation in her native country depressed her.

Late in October, Ilse, Kit, and Thomas Barker visited Cambridge, and Elizabeth took advantage of the lift in spirits their presence inspired to celebrate Halloween with the Barkers and the Pazes. For such trick or treaters as might make their way to Brattle Street (and for Thomas's amusement), Elizabeth put on a witch's costume and filled a leather glove with ice to offer a cold handshake to any child brave enough to take one. She was noted now, as she had been as a teenager, for her spontaneous and generous creativity. In December, Dorothee Bowie came out from Seattle. Each visit lifted Elizabeth out of a trough of depression and dissatisfaction. In between, she spent several weekends in Duxbury and worked on details of the renovation at Lewis Wharf as she grew more and more anxious to move out of Cambridge. Although she entertained the Pazes often and attended a few literary parties, including a very large one given by Helen Vendler on November 17, her spirits were low, and she did almost no work.

The approach of the holiday season, as always, reminded her of her solitude and of unsatisfactory Christmases past, and she made no plans to relieve the gloom. Although scheduled to go to Ouro Prêto on December 26 to wind up her affairs there and to see again about selling the house and its contents, she canceled the trip because she was having stomach pains and needed medical tests. She was virtually alone in Cambridge for the whole of the Christmas holidays—Alice was in Vienna, Frank Bidart was away, her academic friends all had stronger ties elsewhere—and the week dragged. She apparently drank a good deal and thus constantly felt ill. On December 27, she sent the final draft of "Five Flights Up" to Bidart. The poem had originated with a dream that featured the voices of the birds and the dog, which Elizabeth combined with the words of the dog trainer who lived next door to Alice. Its messages about guilt, shame, and the burden of the past provided a theme for this "miserable season."

> The little black dog runs in his yard.
> His owner's voice arises, stern,
> "You ought to be ashamed!"
> What has he done?
> He bounces cheerfully up and down;
> he rushes in circles in the fallen leaves.
>
> Obviously, he has no sense of shame.
> He and the bird know everything is answered,
> all taken care of,
> no need to ask again.
> —Yesterday brought to today so lightly!
> (A yesterday I find almost impossible to lift.)

On January 2, Elizabeth fell as she was leaving the Casablanca Bar in Harvard Square and broke her right shoulder. She was taken by the Harvard police to Stillman Infirmary, where she remained for more than a week. In the absence of any close friends, Elizabeth called Lloyd Schwartz, a friend of Frank Bidart's whom she knew casually, and asked him to go to her apartment on Brattle Street and gather the mail and pack an overnight bag for her. Schwartz delivered these and then stayed for several hours. He came every day to her room at the infirmary to talk, did errands for her, and helped her get home at the end of her stay. He was virtually her only visitor during the week. By the time she was writing letters again at the end of January, she said simply that she had had "a nice rest" in the infirmary, which is very likely true. For one thing, she was no longer alone and responsible for taking care of herself, which she grew less and less good at as she grew older. For another, her stay at Stillman probably broke a destructive cycle of drinking, freeing her and allowing her body to recover. Only Schwartz knew the real story of her fall; to others she wrote almost no details, saying only that she fell as a result of "haste and distraction." The shoulder continued to bother her for six months and virtually prevented her from writing for more than two.

Her verse-writing and poetry-reading courses began on January 27. The two class meetings each week gave some needed structure to her schedule, and despite the committee work and thesis advising she now had to do because of her contract appointment, she spent the spring more productively than she had the fall. She met often with the group of writing teachers in the department: Robert Fitzgerald, Monroe Engel, Alexander Theroux, Robert B. Shaw, and Jane Shore. They planned courses and assignments cooperatively and bolstered one another's morale in the not-altogether-friendly atmosphere. Her personal dramas, after her shoulder healed enough so that movement was comfortable, involved continuing awkwardness in her relationship with Lowell, continuing efforts to sell the Ouro Prêto house, and continuing attempts to avoid having to take on a mortgage for Lewis Wharf. Lowell, feeling the sting of numerous literary attacks, had taken personally a blurb Elizabeth wrote for her former student Sandra McPherson that complimented her for eschewing "confession and irony" in her poems. Lowell wrote, "I suppose confession is the use or exploitation of painful experience that gets on conscience, that must out—but must it? Irony is being amusing (or worse acid about) about what we can't understand. I guess one can't write much without possibly falling in with both—."[8]

Elizabeth denied that she had been thinking of Lowell at all and insisted that she had no theoretical objection to either confession or irony. "After all—irony has always been <u>my</u> chief stock-in-trade, and how could one live without it?" As for confession, "Well, you've been blamed for starting some of that, we know—but there's all the difference in the world [between] "Life Studies" and those who now out-sex Anne Sexton."[9] Two months later, Elizabeth was sure that Alan Heimert, chair of the English Department at Harvard, was strangely angry with *her* because Lowell had not yet turned in his grades from the fall, and she passed along his anger.

Elizabeth finally flew to Ouro Prêto for the last time on March 29, hoping to secure a buyer for her house and arrange for the shipping of all the belongings she intended to keep to Boston for the Lewis Wharf apartment. She was moving, she said, "from one Avenida Atlántica to another." Stopping over in Rio, she said it was "beautiful, even if I hate it," and Ouro Prêto was, as always, lovely but sad.[10] Elizabeth spent eight frantic days in Brazil but believed by the end that she had found a buyer for the house and could at last say good-bye to the country for good. When the agreement fell through, she all but gave up trying to sell and conceded the need for the Lewis Wharf mortgage.

The spring's teaching and socializing were punctuated from time to time by more deaths among Elizabeth's friends—in March, Philip Rahv, Reuben Brower, and Lloyd Frankenberg all died, and Loren MacIver was hospitalized after a severe fall. By the end of the spring, after having chided Lowell for dwelling too much on old age in his poems and letters, Elizabeth wearily conceded, "I think I'll try to tackle Old Age now myself."[11] This was at the end of a busy schedule of professional activity, including a joint reading with James Merrill at the Library of Congress and one by herself at the New School for Social Research in New York. There Elizabeth felt she had "sagged" in the middle. The podium was too high; "I couldn't see the 1st six rows or so – & some lady kept reading along with me, out loud – sometimes a little ahead of me.. very disconcerting."[12] On May 1, she read the Marianne Moore memoir at the YMHA, along with several of Moore's poems. On May 17, she flew to New

York for an Academy lunch and then went on to Seattle for four days of festivities connected to the annual Roethke reading, which she gave, presenting her memory of meeting Roethke at the Library of Congress in 1949 (he had said she was "a quick kid in a caper," praise she delighted in), reading a few of Roethke's poems and then her own. She came to stay at Dorothee Bowie's house bearing ten fresh lobsters and pounds of steamer clams for a New England seafood supper and was the guest of honor at a "big bash" hosted by Bowie. The trip was exhausting but went well. Elizabeth spent the rest of the month grading exams and by the end was ready for several weeks at the Duxbury house, while John Malcolm Brinnin and Bill Read were away.

She spent several days alone in Duxbury, while Alice was working in Cambridge, but the two women spent the better part of a month together planting a garden of tomatoes, rhubarb, and wildflowers and watching the progress of the birds nesting in the eaves. Elizabeth did manage to write some during the month and to read from the house's well-stocked shelves. By midmonth, she had pronounced herself recovered from the stress and exhaustion of the long semester. The Duxbury house became an important retreat for Elizabeth, and she went there to find the peace and solitude of the ocean and the company of congenial souls to whom she did not need to explain the nature of her relationship with Alice, her struggle with alcohol, or her deliberate pace of composition. At the end of the month, she enclosed in a thank-you note to John and Bill an almost-finished version of "The End of March."

Although "The End of March" was a new poem in 1974, it brought together ideas Elizabeth had been contemplating for a long time. Back in New England after twenty years in the tropics, she had the ambivalence of March to contend with once again and often remarked on its leonine or ovine qualities. She had been taking long walks on Atlantic beaches for sixty years. The impossible "proto . . . crypto" dream house brings to a close the poet's lifelong preoccupation with places of refuge, shelters, and solitary retreats. This preoccupation had begun, in print anyway, with "In Prison" and "The Sea and Its Shore." The wish to "do *nothing*, / or nothing much, forever in two bare rooms" was almost as old as her need to take comfort in *grog à l'américaine*. The pain behind the poem, the loss or absence for which the sun's rays compensate in the end, is the same loss at the heart of all her poems of this period. Elizabeth said it had started out as "a sort of joke thank-you-note – John B. was so appalled when I said I wanted that ugly little green shack for my summer home! (He doesn't share my taste for the awful, I'm afraid.)"[13] The trouble, whatever it is exactly, predates the poem and seems to force the poet and her companions out onto a wintry shore:

> It was cold and windy, scarcely the day
> to take a walk on that long beach.
> Everything was withdrawn as far as possible,
> indrawn: the tide far out, the ocean shrunken,
> seabirds in ones or twos.
> The rackety, icy, offshore wind
> numbed our faces on one side;
> disrupted the formation
> of a lone flight of Canada geese;
> and blew back the low, inaudible rollers
> in upright, steely mist.

Out of the chill, forbidding atmosphere, out of this absence of sensation, rise depressing reminders, ominously unfulfilled expectations, and ambiguous circumstances. The poet notices everything and yearns naturally for resolutions. The sky was darker than the water "—*it* was the color of mutton-fat jade." The italics confuse rather than clarify the issue and call to mind that mutton-fat jade may also be the color of a corpse. The mysterious dog prints, big enough for lion prints, produce no dog, and the "lengths and lengths, endless, of wet white string" yield no kite, another March emblem. Both end instead at another corpse—"a thick white snarl, man-size, awash, / rising on every wave, a sodden ghost, / falling back, sodden, giving up the ghost." She trails off at this thought of surrender or suicide, remembering perhaps the coma and death of Lota Soares and evaluating for herself that possibility, in the figure of waves extinguishing themselves against the shore—among her earliest images of surrender.

In response to this tension, Bishop turns to her adult version of the wish for submission—she contemplates withdrawal to a house of her own, here a "proto-dream-house, / . . . crypto-dream-house." The process of remembering the house, seeing in her mind its possibilities and impossibilities as a place for safe retreat, returns her from the dangerous territory of the previous stanza. It is the process of imagining the house that brings her back; she does not see it on this walk.

> that crooked box
> set up on pilings, shingled green,
> a sort of artichoke of a house, but greener
> (boiled with bicarbonate of soda?),
> protected from spring tides by a palisade
> of—are they railroad ties?
> (Many things about this place are dubious.) . . .
> There must be a stove; there *is* a chimney,
> askew, but braced with wires,
> and electricity, possibly
> —at least, at the back another wire
> limply leashes the whole affair
> to something off behind the dunes.

When the house proves impossible—"that day the wind was much too cold / even to get that far, / and of course the house was boarded up"—she is ready to turn back. The redemption found in thoughts about the future—careful, detailed thinking that names things and places them—makes the poet receptive to a modest epiphany:

On the way back our faces froze on the other side.
The sun came out for just a minute.
For just a minute, set in their bezels of sand,
the drab, damp, scattered stones
were multi-colored,
and all those high enough threw out long shadows,
individual shadows, then pulled them in again.
They could have been teasing the lion sun,
except that now he was behind them
—a sun who'd walked the beach the last low tide,
making those big, majestic paw-prints,
who perhaps had batted a kite out of the sky to play with.

Elizabeth struggled with this ending, asking for and taking advice
from Lowell and others. The *New Yorker* published an earlier version
as she was late in getting the magazine her corrections. Between the
magazine publication and *Geography III,* "The sun came out for just
a minute / and for a minute the embedded stones / showed what
colors they were" became "The sun came out for just a minute. /
For just a minute, set in their bezels of sand, / the drab, damp,
scattered stones / were multi-colored."

Despite the qualification implied in her repetition of "for just a
minute," the triumph is real. As she walked out, the things she saw
were not themselves but stood for other, darker things; the beach
spoke to her of death and unfulfilled expectations. As she returns,
the kite string belongs to a kite, the paw prints are happily expli-
cable, and the scene bespeaks art in life, playful powers, recovery,
even the possibility of the sun's return—a March reversal—to thaw
frozen faces.

Bishop's manipulation of the first person in this poem defines the
crisis and its resolution. From the community of the shared walk
("The wind numbed *our* faces"; "Then *we* came upon lengths"),
we are suddenly privy to a private, interior voice: "I wanted to get
as far as my proto-dream-house." Her companions disappear, while

we hear her consideration of this primal, secret urge to hide. But "giving up the ghost" would in the end be "impossible." The poet seals a covenant here with the lion sun and the stones and, by implication, with the difficult world. Then we are "back in it": "On the way back *our* faces froze on the other side." The poet takes comfort in, perhaps even chooses, the community over solitude.

A year later, Elizabeth wrote to Brinnin from Duxbury, "My House is GONE!...Perhaps the owners saw my poem & looked at it with new eyes – at any rate, a flimsy, gray but 'moderne' affair is rising on the site, and the railroad ties lie in confusion all around it."[14] The houses that did serve for Elizabeth in the last few years of her life—Brinnin's Duxbury house, Rhoda Sheehan's Hurricane House at Westport, and, soon to appear, the Sabine Farm house on North Haven Island, Maine—were among the most comforting she had ever had.

Elizabeth expected to move to Lewis Wharf almost any day during the summer, and compounded delays caused by labor strikes, material shortages, and the usual inexplicable attenuations caused her considerable frustration. At the same time, she waited with more and more anxiety for the arrival of her Brazil belongings, which she also expected at any time after June 1 (and which did not arrive until February 1975). When the sale on the Ouro Prêto house fell through, she began to think that nothing would work. But on June 25, the plans made when moving to Lewis Wharf seemed imminent began to take effect, and Alice vacated her Chauncy Street apartment and moved into Brattle Street with Elizabeth, who was supposed to be gone by then. The small apartment with all their worldly goods boxed and stacked around them grew tiresome and would have grown more so had not Elizabeth already rented the North Haven farmhouse for the last two weeks of July. After a July 4 weekend in Duxbury, for which Elizabeth produced her famous strawberry shortcake for nine guests, and the following weekend at Wood's Hole on Cape Cod, Elizabeth, Alice, and Frank Bidart headed up to the island that would be, even more than Lewis Wharf, Elizabeth's spiritual home in the last five years of her life.

Elizabeth had answered a newspaper ad about a farmhouse for rent on North Haven Island and was delighted with what she found. Sabine Farm, owned by Mrs. Horace Pettit, was "a dream – peace and quiet and so beautiful."[15] While Bidart found the island a bit too far from civilization, Elizabeth and Alice were enchanted and immediately engaged the house for the whole of the following July. The island's activities were limited by isolation and geography to sailing (in an eighty-year-old dinghy belonging to the house), boating, beachcombing, bird-watching, and wildflower collecting. Elizabeth found the farm an ideal place to work. In that first summer, as in those that followed, friends visited, many on their way to or from the homes of Mary McCarthy and Elizabeth Hardwick in Castine, Maine. Rhoda Sheehan and Brinnin and Read came that first summer, and their visits prompted Scrabble and backgammon games around the fire and large pots of lobster stew—made from lobsters pulled right from the water—for supper. Mussels and blueberries were also island offerings, and Elizabeth pronounced it "paradise."

In subsequent years, Elizabeth kept a journal of her weeks on North Haven, and reading the year-to-year entries, one sees her attraction to the changelessness of the place. The journals resemble those of Gerard Manley Hopkins in their intense interest in visual effect and the poems of Marianne Moore in their curiosity as to how things work and why animals do what they do. A few poems begin to take shape in these pages, including "North Haven" as it might have been written had Robert Lowell not died; but no other poem was ever finished. Several pages of the journal contain a running list of birds and wildflowers spotted on the island, and some record day-to-day developments in Elizabeth's health. On the whole, this life resembled the early days at Samambaia in its concern with elemental matters.

Elizabeth and Alice returned to hot, muggy Cambridge on August 4 for a tedious week of waiting for Lewis Wharf to be ready.

On August 9, "the day Nixon resigned," she moved in. Alice, Frank, various students, and some professional movers were all in on the process, which was simplified by the continued nonappearance of the shipped goods from Brazil, including more than three thousand books. Nevertheless, as soon as she could, Elizabeth escaped the chaos for a weekend at Duxbury and, at the end of the month, a week at Hurricane House. She settled in for the duration on September 1.

Elizabeth liked living at Lewis Wharf and bragged after less than a month that she knew the names of all the tugboats in the harbor. But moving was "pure hell," she said. "Pray God I'll never do it again."[16] The gentrification of an old neighborhood that the Lewis Wharf project represented bothered her from time to time, as did the Jaguars and Mercedes Benzes in the parking lot. The new phenomenon of "condominium meetings" disgusted her ("How can people so rich be so stupid?"), and as businesses moved into the vacant first floor of the warehouse—a convenience store, a Japanese restaurant, a nightclub—Elizabeth said, "My one fear is it [will] turn into a sort of super-Holiday Inn." And she was aware of the compromise in watching such "polluted tides" rise and fall. The passing ships, whose names she noted in letters she wrote from her study overlooking the water, the Revolutionary War monuments visible from the window, the steeple bells from St. Stephen's and the Old North Church, and the expanse of water reflecting the lights of the city at night consoled her. But the process of moving and its attendant stock-taking dragged her down, and throughout the fall her outlook was "gloomy," and the world seemed a "vale of tears." Her only writing project was the continuing revision of the last stanza of "The End of March."

Elizabeth was not anxious for classes to begin in September 1974, but she was impatient for the arrival of the friends who would come with the new term, especially Octavio and Marie Jo Paz. Preparing for classes, working on the apartment, and giving a few parties and dinners filled the time before the university opened on September

25. Visits to Duxbury and to Aunt Grace in the nursing home in Truro where she had been placed broke up the steady round of Tuesday and Wednesday classes that fall—the poetry-writing seminar was "unusually good"; the reading class was "on the dumb side."[17] On October 15, Elizabeth received the check for five thousand dollars from the sale of Lowell's papers to Harvard. She had not wanted to take the money, but in the intervening months she had grown both more needy and more resigned to the marketing of poets' papers. She advised her relatives and friends to save her letters to them and sell to the highest bidder but was still squeamish about the revelations those letters might contain—for instance, she asked Frani Muser if perhaps the details of the 1937 accident in which Margaret Miller was injured should be destroyed.

Anne Sexton committed suicide in October, and Elizabeth attended the "well-meant, but rather awful" Boston University memorial service for her—the displays of emotion by Sexton's students and colleagues made Elizabeth uncomfortable, as such displays always had. For primarily that reason, she turned down the offer to take over Sexton's writing class at a fine salary; she felt she could not fill those particular shoes.[18] Her Harvard classes were proving difficult enough, as she commuted to Cambridge by subway and spent Tuesday nights at Brattle Street with Alice.

On December 4, Elizabeth read at the Morgan Library in New York at the invitation of the Academy of American Poets. Octavio Paz provided the introduction, which delighted her. A black tie, by-invitation-only affair attended by nearly three hundred people, the reading amused Elizabeth (she had been offended when Mrs. Hugh Bullock, the academy president, wrote to suggest that she "wear something becoming"). She still did not enjoy reading, least of all in New York; but this one had been attended by many of her closest friends, and it had yielded an unexpected benefit. When a downcast Elizabeth confessed to Louise Crane that she had no plans for the Christmas holiday, "the expleted season," Crane offered her a guesthouse at Ft. Myers Beach, Florida, near the home of Charlotte and

Red Russell, who took care of Crane's handicapped brother, Stephen. So after a Christmas Eve party with Frank Bidart and the Pazes, and Christmas dinner with a former student, Elizabeth left for Florida, her first visit back there in seventeen years.

Swimming in the warm waters rejuvenated her, and her long-depressed spirits began to improve. She tried to write, even though she could not seem to finish anything. Alice joined her on December 31, bringing champagne and sorely needed company. The last ten days were filled with sightseeing and sailing, including a three-day trip to Cabbage Key on the Russells' boat and a trip to the Corkscrew Swamp Wildlife Sanctuary, where an island covered with pure-white pelicans captured her imagination and stayed with her through several letters and journal entries. On January 11, Elizabeth returned to Boston more cheerful than when she had left. By mid-month, she was feeling positive enough to chastise Lowell again for the dark tone of his letters to her and for his fuzzy, romanticized memory of their first meeting.

> I am now going to be very impertinent and aggressive. Please, please don't talk about old age so much, my dear old friend! You are giving me the creeps. . . . In Florida, my hostess's sister . . . and her husband, also 76, went walking miles on the beach every day, hand in hand, as happy as clams, apparently, and I loved it. . . . Of course – it's different for a writer, I know – of course I know! – nevertheless, in spite of aches & pains I really don't feel much different than I did at 35 – and I certainly am a great deal happier, most of the time. . . . I just won't feel ancient – I wish Auden hadn't gone on about it so his last years, and I hope you won't.
>
> However, Cal dear, maybe your memory is failing! – Never, never was I "tall" – as you wrote remembering me. I was always 5 ft 4 and ¼ inches – now shrunk to 5 ft 4 inches – The only time I've ever felt tall was in Brazil. And I never had "long brown hair" either! – It started turning gray when I was 23 or 24 – and probably was already somewhat grizzled when I first met you. . . . I think

you must be seeing someone else! So <u>please</u> don't put me in a beautiful poem tall with long brown hair! What I remember about that meeting is your dishevelment, your lovely curly hair, and how we talked about a Picasso show then on in N.Y., and we agreed about the Antibes pictures of fishing, etc – and how much I liked you, after having been almost too scared to go. . . . You were also rather dirty, which I rather liked, too. . . . Well, I think I'll have to write <u>my</u> memoirs, just to set things straight.[19]

January was spent finishing up her Harvard courses and taking the Pazes on a farewell tour of northern New England (to "Vair-mont," she quoted Octavio as saying) before their departure for Mexico at the end of the month. Elizabeth thought of Octavio and Marie Jo as her "twin suns" in lonely Cambridge, and Harvard was an even less appealing place to her without them.

Early in February, the crates of Brazil belongings finally arrived, and daily life became a struggle among teaching, unpacking, and discovering new storage places and where to hang things. The brick walls of Lewis Wharf proved difficult to penetrate, and Elizabeth loaned a few paintings from her collection of MacIvers, Barkers, Schwitterses, and others to trustworthy friends. When she got those she could keep hung, her friend Jerry Reich came to help light them. Also in the crates were Elizabeth's favorite Brazilian antiques, including wooden carvings of Saints Sebastian and Anthony, a ship's figurehead (*carranca*) from the Rio São Francisco, an enormous Venetian mirror carved with "blackamoors," and nearly three thousand books to sort, shelve, store, sell, or give away. New appliances had left her with big boxes, which she filled with cast-off books; pieces of her library were distributed among her students and friends.

The process went on for months, and Elizabeth took to spending occasional nights at Alice's "to escape the crates" and to work on a memoir she had returned to in the fall, "Primer Class." Feeling "hopeless" about writing poetry, she tried prose. She also took up a Key West memoir from 1940, published after her death as "Mercedes Hospital." In other ways she felt alienated from her writing self, as when her high school friend Judy Flynn sent her old copies of the Walnut Hill School's literary magazine, the *Blue Pencil*, which Elizabeth had edited and in which she had published a good many poems. She despaired over how bad her "serious" poems were. She liked the comic ones but said, "I haven't the faintest recollection of having written them."[20] The magazines are among her papers, and the poems have been collected. They are hardly so awful as that.

Elizabeth prepared and taught her classes in the spring term, including her first attempt at teaching William Carlos Williams's *Paterson,* but she was set back several times by attacks of flu. She spent a gloomy spring without her best Harvard friends, the Pazes, and pronounced herself "lucky to have nice cheerful Alice" around. A trip to New York and the Metropolitan Opera in April, with Bob Giroux and Robert and Caroline Lowell, cheered her, as did a visit from Dorothee Bowie late in the month. On May 1, her university duties found her at a luncheon with the Canadian critic Northrop Frye. The two immediately took to each other, and Elizabeth considered paying him a visit in Toronto. Her only original poem of 1975, "The End of March," appeared on March 24 with the wrong version of the final stanza, Elizabeth having lost track of her changes and mailed them too late to have them included. This reminder of her own slow progress discouraged her.

Energy for teaching came primarily from her eager anticipation of another stay at North Haven and a month at the Duxbury House, which would be empty in May and June while John Brinnin and Bill Read traveled. When classes ended in early May, Elizabeth "slept for four or five days" before heading down to the beach, where she stayed for most of the month. Alice had begun business school at Boston University and commuted back and forth, so Elizabeth had some solitary days in the house; as she grew older, she grew less and less able to tolerate extended solitude. But Duxbury had friendly neighbors, and she and Alice entertained visitors to the house much as they would at North Haven. The flow of guests, including poet Anthony Hecht and Rhoda Sheehan, was steady, and Elizabeth managed some "rest," some grading, and some writing, including what she called "sonnets," though she distinguished them from Lowell's ventures in the same line.[21] She tended the house's kitchen garden of tomatoes, rhubarb, and flowers and kept Brinnin informed of its condition. Although her movements were somewhat limited by a hiatal hernia that had begun to bother her, when she left for good on June 12, she knew she would miss the house.

Less than a week later, however, she was in Mexico City for eight days filming a round-table discussion of poetry in the *Encuentro* series for Mexican television. Octavio Paz, Vasko Popa, and Joseph Brodsky joined her in the discussion, and Elizabeth felt the three men had talked a bit over her head. She had mixed feelings about her first visit to Mexico in thirty-two years as well.

> Everything has changed so much that I would never have recognized it – to coin a phrase. Mexico City has grown from about a million then to almost eleven million now. . . . It is approximately my idea of hell, I'm afraid. . . . It was my first (& I hope last) T V – and that was funny and, I suppose, interesting. . . . But the trip was all paid for and I am really glad I went. – Octavio was as sweet as ever.[22]

Alice joined her for a few days, and the trip also included visits to Cuernavaca, where the Pazes were then sharing a house with Mark Strand and his family; Puebla, Oaxaca, and Teotitlán—destinations on her 1942 trip as well.

Just a few days after returning from Mexico, Elizabeth installed herself in the North Haven farmhouse for the month of July and said that she "wish[ed] every day this was forever."[23] Between visitors, she worked on a short story at least twenty years in the making, "Memories of Uncle Neddy." She had begun the piece in the late 1950s as "Uncle Artie" and had worked on it from time to time, unwilling to finish it or have it published before Uncle Artie's widow died. Elizabeth struggled in particular with how to depict her uncle's destructive alcoholism. But she was pleased with the story and pleased with the work she had done on it through the idyllic island days. In the fall, her general depression was deepened when the story was rejected by both the *New Yorker* and *Atlantic*. It appeared in 1977 in the *Southern Review*.

But the lift in spirits North Haven always brought her lasted nearly a month after the fact, until the end of August, though she was never happy being in Boston in the summer. Her trip to Mexico had helped her finish a translation of Octavio Paz's "Primero de Enero" for the edition of *Ploughshares* being edited by Frank Bidart, a poem that shares her own fear and fascination with the passage of time. Paz liked her translation so much that he said he thought it a better poem in English than in Spanish:

> The year's doors open
> like those of language,
> toward the unknown.
> Last night you told me:
>   tomorrow
> we shall have to think up signs,
> sketch a landscape, fabricate a plan
> on the double page
> of day and paper.
> Tomorrow, we shall have to invent,
> once more,
> the reality of this world.

Elizabeth enjoyed this task, though she felt it was almost routine, so easily did the Spanish yield English equivalents.

She spent most of the month continuing to dispose of her books (there were still twenty-nine boxes left on August 25) and worrying about accusations made against her by a student in a letter to Alan

Heimert of being late, missing class, and being "cruel and contemptuous." The incident disappeared, as such incidents do, but Elizabeth found it upsetting. A weekend at Hurricane House for a huge "Quaker Clam Bake" of crabs, clams, and lobsters helped. In September, she stayed several days at Alice's working desperately on a commissioned review of Sylvia Plath's *Letters Home* that she never finished. The review cost her a good deal of anxiety over the month but remains among Elizabeth's papers, a painfully edited two pages of theorizing about writers and their letters, with "gave up on this" written at the top in Elizabeth's hand. Instead, she worked in Alice's kitchen canning corn, tomatoes, and blueberries in an attempt to bring some order to a life that seemed increasingly chaotic. She wrote to Aunt Grace that this domestic economy represented "a big saving."[24] She struggled to stay sober, asking for and receiving recipes for nonalcoholic drinks from Dorothee Bowie, and to stay reasonably cheerful, with the help of Dexamyl, against a weighty depression. When Elizabeth heard that Calvin Kentfield, an old friend from the Yaddo days, had killed himself, she said dryly, "I do wish people I know would stop committing suicide."[25] Classes began at Harvard on September 23, and Elizabeth met her first two; but by the second week she was in the Harvard infirmary for five days of rest on the advice of a Harvard psychologist. At that point, she began formal therapy with antidepressant drugs.

The fall of 1975 was the bleakest time in Elizabeth's Cambridge years because her life line, her "saving grace," as she described Alice in an unpublished poem, seemed to be abandoning her. As the demands of Elizabeth's alcoholism and illnesses began to tell on Alice's patience and interest, she attempted to pull away. Having begun a relationship with a young man she thought she might marry, Alice was reevaluating her intense involvement in Elizabeth's life. Elizabeth herself could see only that she might be left alone in her impending and increasingly enfeebling old age, that she might lose Alice, whom she loved. Terribly afraid and even less capable of staying alone successfully, Elizabeth fell apart. The fall was a nightmarish cycle of drinking and brief recovery. The drinking episodes saw painfully explicit revelations of guilt and remorse to her closest friends; the brief recoveries, embarrassed apologies. John Malcolm Brinnin recalls Elizabeth's solitary visits to Duxbury (she had always before come with Alice), her consumption of alcohol, and the alcohol-induced destruction of her usual barriers of reserve and restraint. Her middle-of-the-night litany of self-accusations included the names of people whose lives she felt she had "ruined"—Lota Soares, Suzanne Bowen, Robert Seaver. What role she did play in the troubles of these people she loved cannot be known yet cannot be great—one person does not drive another to mental illness. But throughout her life, Elizabeth was indeed attracted to men and women of charismatic instability.

Elizabeth often said that she was "born guilty"—and this is very likely true. The child of a dysfunctional mother often assumes the burden of responsibility herself, and a guilty self-hatred is also the emotional territory of the alcoholic. A nature as restrained, even as repressed, as Elizabeth's expresses little emotion except under extraordinary circumstances. In this crisis, as in others in her life, alcohol allowed her the expression. But there can be no constructive mourning under the influence of alcohol, and all too often these confessions occurred in alcohol-induced blackouts so that she did not even remember having made them. As is almost always the case when alcoholics drink, the problems incurred far outweigh the illusory benefits, and Elizabeth found herself facing awkward social situations because she could not remember if she had spoken on the phone to this friend or acquaintance in the previous evening's blackout or, if so, what she had said. But even after several binges that wreaked havoc on her new friendships and on the antidepressant therapy she was undergoing, Elizabeth insisted that alcohol was not the major problem. She quarreled with Anny Baumann, with whom she had an appointment:

I'll be there—and sober. Please don't worry about that! I am full of Antib [Antabuse]—at the moment—& couldn't possibly take a drink before Thursday, even if I wanted to. . . .

What I'm writing to ask you is this—please don't just discuss drinking with me, or scold me for any past lapses...please. There were two or three bad days about two weeks ago now—and I have talked & talked with Dr. Wacker (Head of the Harvard Med. services) about this—OF COURSE I know I shouldn't drink, and I try hard not to. I have missed only one class in five years because of this and I have NEVER taken a drink before class. . . . I feel I can't bear to be made to feel guilty one more time about the drinking. There are things that are worse, I think, and I hope you can help me with them.[26]

This statement is almost a textbook alcoholic's denial. In fact, Elizabeth did miss numerous classes for reasons certainly related to drinking—physical injuries incurred while she was drunk, for example. According to her friends, she was occasionally too hung over to teach her classes, particularly while she was in Seattle. And her careful calculation of the length of the Antabuse's effectiveness casts doubt on the phrase "even if I wanted to." The "thing that was worse" involved her desperate fear of losing Alice.

Although Elizabeth struggled through the weekly round of classes in the fall of 1975, she was barely functioning. She wrote almost nothing, not even letters, and yet the one piece she did write tells the story of her struggle more clearly and less evasively than any letter would have. The villanelle "One Art" is an exercise in the art of losing, a rehearsal of what we tell ourselves to keep going, a speech in a brave voice that cracks once in the final version and cracked even more in the early drafts. The finished poem, which may be the best modern example of a villanelle, shares with its nearest competitor, Theodore Roethke's justly famous "The Waking" ("I wake to sleep and take my waking slow"), the feeling that in the course of writing or saying the poem the poet is giving herself a lesson in

waking, in losing. Elizabeth's lines share her ironic tips for learning
to lose and to live with loss.

> The art of losing isn't hard to master;
> so many things seem filled with the intent
> to be lost that their loss is no disaster.
>
> Lose something every day. Accept the fluster
> of lost door keys, the hour badly spent.
> The art of losing isn't hard to master.
>
> Then practice losing farther, losing faster:
> places, and names, and where it was you meant
> to travel. None of these will bring disaster.
>
> I lost my mother's watch. And look! my last, or
> next-to-last, of three loved houses went.
> The art of losing isn't hard to master.
>
> I lost two cities, lovely ones. And, vaster,
> some realms I owned, two rivers, a continent.
> I miss them, but it wasn't a disaster.
>
> —Even losing you (the joking voice, a gesture
> I love) I shan't have lied. It's evident
> the art of losing's not too hard to master
> though it may look like (*Write* it!) like disaster.

More than once in the drafts of Bishop's published poems, one
finds that she came to express in the final draft nearly the opposite
of what she started out to say. As Barbara Page has pointed out, for
example, in the seven available drafts of "Questions of Travel,"
Elizabeth developed the key line of the last stanza from an early
"The choice perhaps is not great . . . but fairly free" to the final
"The choice is never wide and never free," as the poet comes to

realize restrictions that bind the traveler by articulating them in the poem.[27]

Something similar occurs within the seventeen available drafts of "One Art." Bishop conceived the poem as a villanelle from the start, and the play of "twos" within it—two rivers, two cities, the lost lover not being "two" anymore—suggests that the two-rhyme villanelle is a form appropriate to the content. Elizabeth said that after years of trying to write in that form, the poem just came to her. "I couldn't believe it—it was like writing a letter."[28] The two attempts among her papers, "Verdigris" and the "aviary" poem, do indicate that she had struggled with the form before.

The first extant draft is a series of partly worked up notes, apparently a basis for developing the rhymes and refrains of the final version. Its overall thematic shape is familiar in the final poem, with the evidence of the speaker's experience at losing followed by a somewhat strained application of that experience. In its unedited catalog of losses, the draft resembles one of the alcohol-induced outpourings of grief and guilt she experienced that fall; but it is heartbreaking to read.

The draft is tentatively titled "HOW TO LOSE THINGS," then "THE GIFT OF LOSING THINGS," and finally "THE ART OF LOSING THINGS." (The title "One Art" appears to have been arrived at very late in the process; none of the other drafts is so titled.) It begins with the suggestion that the way to acquire this art is to "begin by mislaying" several items—keys, pens, glasses. Then she says:

> – This is by way of introduction. I really
> want to introduce myself – I am such a
> fantastic lly good at losing things
> I think everyone shd. profit from my experiences.

She then lists her qualifications: "You may find it hard to believe, but I have actually lost / I mean lost, and forever, two whole houses."

Among her other losses are "a third house," "one peninsula and one island," "a small-sized town . . . and many smaller bits of geography or scenery," "a splendid beach," "a good-sized bay," "a good piece of one continent," "another continent"—indeed, "the whole damned thing!" In the end, she writes:

> One might think this would have prepared me
> for losing one average-sized not ~~especially~~ exceptionally
> beautiful or dazzlingly intelligent person
> except for blue eyes)   (only the eyes <u>were</u> exceptionally
>   beautiful and the hands <u>looked</u>
>   intelligent)   the fine hands
> But it doesn't seem to have, at all...

The draft trails off with "He who loseth his life, etc. – but he who / loses his love – neever [*sic*], no never never never again –."

In Elizabeth's handwriting in the margins of this typed draft are notations about possible rhymes for the villanelle, including "ever/ never/forever," "geography/scenery," and a version of her final choice involving "intelligent," "continent," "sent," "spent," and "lent." This catalog served to set the terms for working into the form. By the second draft, the poem is an incomplete villanelle with "The art of losing isn't hard to master" as the first line and the "no disaster" play in the third line. The final stanza is crossed out, though legible under the scoring is "But your loss spelt disaster." The words "evident" and "false" are set to one side, ready to be worked in.

The subsequent drafts work mostly on the first four stanzas, whittling the catalog of losses into a discreet and resonant form and setting the rhyme scheme firmly. It is not until the fifth draft, which consists otherwise of a simple list of end-rhymes, that Bishop once again breaks her controlled tone in the final stanza. Here the original refrain is dutifully repeated, but the poetic frame, for a moment, will not bear the emotional weight:

> The art of losing's not so hard to master
> ~~But won't help in~~ think of that disaster
> No – I am lying—

This transformation of the "false"/"evident" play into "lying" is Elizabeth's first major change aimed at solving to her logical, emotional, and aesthetic satisfaction the problem of how the experience of losing car keys, houses, and continents could apply in handling this truly, as she perceived it now, disastrous loss. In the sixth draft, the final stanza reads, "The art of losing's not so hard to master / until that point & then it / fails & is disaster–." The poem bogs down here; the seventh draft stops short of the final stanza, and the eighth is sketchy, with such lines as "losses nobody can master" and "the art of losing's not impossible to master / It won't work"—most of which are crossed out.

Apparently some time passed between the eighth and ninth drafts, for all the later attempts are typed and contain completed versions of all six stanzas. In the ninth, Elizabeth develops in the last stanza a more complete version of the "lying" theme: "All that I write is false, it's evident / The art of losing isn't hard to master. / oh no. / [anything] at all anything but one's love. (Say it: disaster.)" The formalized spontaneity of "(Say it: disaster.)" enables the poem to accommodate the overflow of emotion that to this point had disarrayed the final stanza and made the villanelle's ritual repetitions inadequate to manage the emotional content.

The next version of the final stanza begins with the first real exploration of possible code words that might stand for "you," a phrase or aspect that would bring Alice wholly into the poem. The line is "But, losing you (eyes of the Azure Aster)" and recalls the "remarkable" blue eyes of the first draft. This awkward and self-consciously poetic phrase hung in through several drafts until both its awkwardness and Bishop's need to generalize caused her to discard it for the more discreet and more melodious "gesture," which had been haunting the edges of the final stanza in the previous few drafts. Here, in the tenth, the idea is still that "I've written lies above" (which she has crossed out in pencil, with "above's all lies" written in) and that "the art of losing isn't hard to master / with one exception. (Say it.) That's disaster."

In draft eleven, the final stanza is reworked five times, and the last line becomes, as Bishop had written and crossed out in the previous draft, "with one exception. (Write it.) Write 'disaster.' " Here both words in the phrase "write it" are to be italicized, as they would be until the poem was collected in *Geography III*—a slight but significant alteration of tone. The change in her means of affirmation or validation from "say it" to "write it" is the crux that, once solved, lets the poem speak its curiously independent truth.

For midway through the twelfth draft, quite abruptly, "above's all lies" becomes "above's not lies" and then "I haven't lied above." And yet, still, "The art of losing wasn't hard to master / with this exception (Write it!) this disaster." This draft reworks the last stanza four tortured times and clearly wavers on "above's all lies" and on the status of the crisis at hand. "Wasn't hard to master" vies with "isn't." Versions of both feelings are tried and crossed out, and even the parenthetical outburst "write it" alternates with "oh isn't it?" What remains is the idea that whatever the brave speech, or the possibilities for mastery, this loss still looks like disaster.

The thirteenth draft is the last that thoroughly reworks the final stanza, and it is at this point that the "gesture" becomes a "special voice," then a "funny voice," and finally the "joking voice." There are two tentative versions of the ending.

> And losing you ~~now (a special voice, a gesture)~~
> doesn't mean I've lied. It's evident
> the loss of love is possible to master,
> even if this looks like (Write it!) like disaster.

> In losing you I haven't lied above. It's evident . . .
> The loss ~~of love is something one must master~~
> even if it looks like (Write it!) like disaster.

Firmly in place is the idea that this apparent disaster does not mean that losing cannot after all be mastered, even though when Elizabeth sat down to write the poem the first time, the disaster must have seemed to preclude any such mastery. In the fourteenth draft, the words "not too hard to master" indicate Bishop's approach to the final version—the colloquial tone is a trademark of her polished style. The Vassar-numbered fifteenth draft makes few changes in the poem, notably in line two: "So many things seem really to be meant" to be lost becomes "so many things seem filled with the intent to be lost." The draft is typed and has an almost-finished version of the final stanza. But handwritten notes show her still struggling with how to express the "above's not lies" idea—"these were not lies" is the typed version; the handwritten notes offer "I ~~still do~~ can't lie" and "I still won't lie."

Another draft, which Elizabeth sent to Frank Bidart, seems to be a cleanly typed carbon version of draft fifteen, with changes dictated to Bidart over the telephone. The two major changes are the "filled with the intent to be lost" change, and in the second line of the final stanza, "these were not lies" becomes the now seemingly inevitable "I shan't have lied." What is odd about this late change is that "I shan't have lied" is technically in the future perfect tense. The phrase retains the past-tense sense of "I haven't lied above" (referring to the list of mastered losses in the rest of the poem) and of "wasn't hard to master" and yet also poses a possible resolution in the future: "After I come to terms with this loss, then I won't have lied, but right now I don't know." The most significant ramification of the change to "I shan't have lied" is that it reminds us forcefully that this poem is a crisis lyric in the truest sense—"Even losing you" comes to mean "Even if I lose you"—and we know that this is not emotion recollected in tranquility but is a live moment of awful fear, with relief only a hoped-for possibility.

One way to read Elizabeth's modulation from "the loss of you is impossible to master" to something like "I am still the master of losing even though losing you looks like disaster" is that in the writing of such a disciplined, demanding poem lies the mastery of the loss. Working through each of her losses—from the bold, painful catalog of the first draft to the finely honed and privately meaningful final version—is the way to overcome them or, if not to overcome them, then to see the way in which she might possibly master herself in the face of loss. This is all, perhaps, "one art"— writing elegies, mastering loss, mastering grief, self-mastery. The losses in the poem are lifelong and real: time, in the form of the "hour badly spent" and, more tellingly for the orphaned Elizabeth, "my mother's watch"; the lost houses, in Key West, Petrópolis, and, the one still in doubt, Ouro Prêto. The city of Rio de Janeiro and the whole South American continent were lost to her with Lota Soares's suicide. And currently, in the fall of 1975, she seemed to have lost Alice, her dearest friend and lover, she of the blue eyes and fine hands. But each version of the poem distanced the pain a little more, depersonalized it, moved it away from the tawdry self-pity and "confession" that Elizabeth disliked in many of her contemporaries.

Yet Elizabeth's letters to Anny Baumann describe the despair of the fall of 1975. Elizabeth was sure she had lost the last person on earth who loved her. As in the dissolution of any close relationship, the entanglements of objects and activities seemed impossible to sort out. The letters agonize over her prospect of a lonely old age crowded with fans, students, and hangers-on but empty of love and of trips and retreats with Alice. Out of this despair, apparently, came "One Art." But the poem is also Elizabeth's elegy for her whole life. She apologized for the poem, saying, "I'm afraid it's a sort of tear-jerker"—clearly she was somewhat uncomfortable with even this careful approach to the confessional.

For a long time, Elizabeth's friends remained protective of her personal reputation and unwilling to have her grouped among lesbian poets or even among the other great poets of her generation— Lowell, Roethke, Berryman—as they self-destructed before their readers' eyes. Elizabeth herself taught them this reticence by keeping her private life very private indeed, for better or for worse, and by investing what "confession" there was in her poems deeply in objects and places, thus deflecting biographical inquiry. In the development of this poem, discretion is a poetic method and part of a process of self-understanding, the seeing of a pattern in her own life.

Elizabeth lamented all her life her tendency to lose things, and the joking voice, which people who knew both women say evokes Alice as surely as blue eyes would have done, recurred in Elizabeth's relationships. As she had written to Anne Stevenson in 1964:

> I have been very lucky in having had, most of my life, some witty friends, – and I mean real wit, quickness, wild fancies, remarks that make one cry with laughing. . . . The aunt I liked best was a very funny woman: most of my close friends have been funny people; Lota de Macedo Soares is funny. Pauline Hemingway (the 2nd Mrs. H.) a good friend until her death in 1951 was the wittiest person, man or woman, I've ever known. Marianne [Moore] was very funny – [E. E.] Cummings, too, of course. Perhaps I need such people to cheer me up.[29]

The "joking voice," the gesture Elizabeth loved (and employed even in writing this painful poem) in Alice, in Lota Soares, in these other friends dead and gone—the phrase brings them all into the poem. In Elizabeth's distillation of immediate crisis into enduring art, the lesson in losing becomes even more a lesson one keeps learning throughout one's life.

The tentative resolution offered in the poem was not, alas, a real one; Elizabeth struggled terribly with this loss for months afterward. Only Alice's return solved it. The poem is a wish for resolution or a resolution in the sense of a determination to survive—"I *will* master this loss; I *will*." It is also a means of assessing the true magnitude of the present disaster in the middle of the crisis, a kind of "How bad is it?" question.

It was very bad. Elizabeth missed several classes in late November and early December, as, in addition to her depression and alcohol abuse, she developed a recurrence of dysentery and began to suffer discomfort from the hiatal hernia. She felt physically and emotionally miserable enough that she asked for and was granted a paid medical leave of absence from Harvard for the spring term on the pretext that she would be hospitalized for at least four weeks at the outset. She wrote frankly about her physical troubles during December but said nothing about Alice, whom she still saw occasionally. Alice delivered Elizabeth to the airport on December 21 as she dragged herself through a major snowstorm to Ft. Myers, the Russells, and Louise Crane's guesthouse for the Christmas holidays.

Elizabeth stayed alone at Ft. Myers "in a black depression," drinking and talking to friends on the phone, then writing to apologize the following morning, until Rhoda Sheehan arrived on December 29 for a ten-day stay. Two days later, Elizabeth claimed to have "pulled herself out of it," and she and Rhoda enjoyed some travels around Florida, including a visit to the Ringling Brothers Circus Museum in Sarasota. Elizabeth also came out of her isolation to talk with her culture-starved neighbors about literature and poetry and even wrote to friends asking them to send books down for her to distribute.

But Rhoda Sheehan had to return to her own family on January 11, not sure herself that her friend was really okay. Elizabeth was desperately afraid to be left alone, and the Russells arranged for a nurse to stay with her. Nevertheless, she panicked. On January 13, she miscalculated the risky combination of tranquilizers and alcohol she was using and overdosed. Back from the hospital on January 16, she wrote to Anny Baumann, "I hope you believe I am careful about drugs – and I don't think such a thing will happen again. – I can't believe I'd do any such thing to others – it has now happened to me eight times in all – four close friends – & I know what it does to those who love one. . . . Forgive me if you can for having behaved so stupidly."[30]

The ambivalence of this language suggests that Elizabeth herself was unclear about whether this overdose was a suicide attempt and whether it might happen again. If she had not set out to end her life—and such action would have been uncharacteristic of her—then she had let down her guard; under the influence of alcohol and narcotic drugs, her remarkable self-preserving instinct had collapsed, long enough for her to risk irreparable harm to herself, but not long enough for her to die.

Both Anny Baumann and Alice sent packages of Antabuse to Florida to help Elizabeth resist the urge to drink, but it was soon clear that she could not remain in Florida by herself. Her attempts to work were fruitless, and she could not be alone. On January 19, three days earlier than she had intended, she flew back to Boston.

Elizabeth does not resurface in letters or in the recollections of her friends until February 21, when she flew from Boston to New York to see her tropical disease specialist and Anny Baumann, which Elizabeth said she should have done long before. On the twenty-third, she wrote to Lowell enclosing "One Art," letting the poem tell all the story she was willing to tell. In a shaky hand, she wrote to Brinnin, who more than anyone else had been her confidant in this awful time, "Well, please pray for me, or something...I rec'd your kind letter 2 days ago. I do have some nice friends; that's a mercy."[31] In that long stay in New York, she attended the premiere of Elliot Carter's song settings for six of her poems ("Anaphora," "Argument," "Sandpiper," "Insomnia," "View of the Capitol from the Library of Congress," and "O Breath"), performed by the Speculum Musicae at Hunter College on February 24. *A Mirror on Which to Dwell* was well received, and the premiere was followed by a large and festive party given by Frani and Curt Muser. The next day, Elizabeth saw an exhibition of Joseph Cornell's boxes and collages and Tom Stoppard's play *Travesties*. The day after, just as she was leaving to return to Boston, she fell on the sidewalk and tore ligaments in her ankle. Back at the Harvard infirmary, she was x-rayed and fitted with crutches and a wheelchair and began another long period of rehabilitation.

But waiting for Elizabeth on her return was notification from Ivar Ivask, editor of *Books Abroad,* that she had won the 1976 Books Abroad / Neustadt International Prize for Literature over other finalists Robert Lowell and Czeslaw Milosz. The jury, which included her friends John Ashbery of the United States and Marie-Claire Blais of Canada, among others, voted ten to two to award the ten-thousand-dollar prize to Elizabeth Bishop and requested her presence at the award ceremony in Norman, Oklahoma, on April 9. Among her papers is a much-worked-over draft of her brief acceptance speech, which ran in its final version barely three hundred words and reflected a characteristic emphasis on the modestly personal:

> The night before I left Boston to come here, I had dinner at a Chinese restaurant. I thought you might be interested in hearing the fortune I found in my fortune cookie. Here it is. It says: YOUR FINANCIAL CONDITION WILL IMPROVE CONSIDERABLY.
>
> However, I don't want to express my gratitude *only* for the "improvement" in my "financial condition," grateful as I am for that. Of course there is a great deal more to it than that. Mr. Ivask has selected a poem called "Sandpiper" to be printed in the program today, and when I saw that poem, rather old now, I began to think: Yes, all my life I have lived and behaved very much like that sandpiper—just running along the edges of different countries and continents, "looking for something." I have always felt I couldn't *possibly* live very far inland, away from the ocean; and I *have* always lived near it, frequently in sight of it. Naturally I know, and it has been pointed out to me, that most of my poems are geographical, or about coasts, beaches and rivers running to the sea, and most of the titles of my books are geographical, too: *North & South, Questions of Travel,* and one to be published this year, *Geography III.*
>
> The first time I came to Norman, Oklahoma—in 1973—it was the farthest I had ever been inland in my life. I enjoyed myself

very much on that first visit, and of course I am enjoying myself on this second, and very special, visit. I find it extremely gratifying that, after having spent most of my life timorously pecking for subsistence along coastlines of the world, I have been given this recognition from so many different countries, but also from Norman, Oklahoma, a place so far inland.[32]

A film clip documents the speech, one of only two moving pictures of Elizabeth Bishop extant. It shows her looking overweight and unwell but sounding like her warm and humorous self. To honor the occasion, *World Literature Today (Books Abroad,* newly renamed) assembled a special issue devoted to Elizabeth Bishop's work and containing tributes to her from friends such as Octavio Paz, Celia Bertin, Penelope Mortimer, Frank Bidart, Lloyd Schwartz, Eleanor Taylor, and Howard Moss as well as scholarly appreciations by Helen Vendler, Jerome Mazzaro, Candace Slater, and Anne Newman. It was the first such collection published on her work.

These warming events helped lift Elizabeth's spirits, and for the rest of her life she was a major literary figure in a way she had never imagined she would be. But Alice's reappearance on the scene, to cook and run errands while Elizabeth was still getting about awkwardly on her damaged ankle, did more to cheer her. On March 4, she read before Boston's St. Botolph Club in her wheelchair and enjoyed the occasion, stripped as it was of some of its pretense of formality. The next day, she wrote to Aunt Grace that she was feeling like herself again for the first time in two months, and indeed things seemed to have returned to an uneasy normalcy. Threats to the relative peace and health erupted whenever Alice's attention was focused elsewhere, as it was when Penelope Mortimer came to teach at Boston University and Alice helped her find an apartment and settle into the city. Elizabeth feared a possible defection, and, once again upset, she asked Mortimer to let Alice alone. In those dark times, Elizabeth drank, her asthma returned, her hernia flared up, and old injuries representing other troubled times—her shoulder, her ankle—began to ache.

Farrar, Straus, and Giroux planned a September publication date for *Geography III,* but having only nine poems in hand, including "One Art," the editors hoped for more to fill the volume out. Elizabeth struggled through the spring and summer to finish "two or three" more, including the ode to Uncle Sam, but could not. The book was postponed until December and then appeared with the nine original poems and Elizabeth's translation of Octavio Paz's poem to Joseph Cornell, "Objects and Apparitions." The book was warmly reviewed and won the 1977 Book Critics' Circle Award for poetry, but it was clear that Elizabeth was at a terrible impasse in writing poetry. She did not finish "Santarém" (begun in 1960) or "Pink Dog" (1963) for two more years. The only new poems she finished between 1975 and her death were the enigmatic "Sonnet" and her elegy for Robert Lowell, "North Haven." Although among the handful of unfinished poems dated or traceable to this period are several remarkable beginnings, Elizabeth was clearly not writing with any energy or direction.

Yet the festivities in Oklahoma from April 8 to 11 were warm and affirming of her vocation, if a bit ridiculous:

> Although I knew I'd been nominated I never dreamed for a moment I'd actually get it. It is "International" – & what sort of pleases me is that I was the 1st woman and the 1st American to get it – the lovely money and a 2' by 3' diploma, AND a "silver eagle's feather" – solid silver, over a pound of it, a foot long – in a velvet-lined walnut coffin-like box. I carried this back in a brown paper market bag –[33]

In her notebook is an extended, "awful but cheerful" description of the Holiday Inn "Executive Suite" where she stayed. Its carpet "looks exactly like chopped-up red cabbage," and its chairs are "deep-bile green," but it is "all so very well-meant." The ten thousand dollars were "horrible, ill-gotten dollars"; she could not escape the irony of her arrival as a major figure coinciding with her conviction that her poems were all written.

But the money made suddenly possible a dream she had had of travel with Alice after a rescheduled (from 1971) appearance at the International Poetry Conference in Rotterdam in June. Elizabeth would visit England before the conference, and together they would tour Portugal for two weeks after.

She returned home from Oklahoma to find waiting for her notification from Sybil Estess that two sessions at the 1976 Modern Language Association Convention in New York would be devoted to her work, including a reading, a performance of *A Mirror on Which to Dwell,* and a panel of scholars giving papers. Elizabeth agreed to appear, read, and attend the musical performance, but she refused to hear the papers. Her inclusion in the MLA program signified to the academic world, if not to Elizabeth herself, that her work, despite her lifetime of refusals to play the academic game, had been effectively canonized. The convention was scheduled for December 27–30, 1976.

Preparations for the trip to Rotterdam and Portugal occupied much of May, though Elizabeth gave a party on the fourteenth for John Ashbery, who had graciously accompanied her to Oklahoma for the Neustadt ceremony, in honor of his Pulitzer Prize and National Book Award for *Self-Portrait in a Convex Mirror.* A week later, she was in New York to see Lowell's plays then being produced, attend an Academy of American Poets luncheon (for the first time since 1957), and see Anny Baumann. Alice had left to join her parents in Switzerland on May 15, and on June 2, struggling with asthma and uncomfortable in her solitude, Elizabeth went ahead and flew to London.

In four days there, she visited friends, including Robert Heilman, who had been her department chair at the University of Washington, and Henry Reed and Bea Roethke, also Washington friends. At a party at the Heilmans', "One Art" was passed around and praised, and Elizabeth felt warmly appreciated. On June 7, she traveled to Bexley Hill, Sussex, to stay with Kit and Ilse Barker. There she rested and recovered some from persistent asthma and also visited Stonehenge, for the first time, at dawn. On June 12, she left for Kent and Milgate Park for an intense weekend with Robert, Caroline, and Sheridan Lowell. After her stay, she reported that Cal had looked better and Caroline worse but confessed wearily that "being so fearfully, automatically 'observant' can be a 'calvary.' "[34] On her return to London two days later, her resources for traveling alone expired, Elizabeth began to struggle with her solitude and the consequent depression. Going to the theater by herself to see a "disappointing play" left her "very low," and she called Frank Bidart in Cambridge for consolation, then wrote to apologize the next morning. Needing to meet with her editor at Chatto and Windus, Elizabeth had to stay in London a dreary extra day before leaving for Rotterdam on the sixteenth.

The International Poetry Conference was a "confusion" and a "torture" to Elizabeth, though individual poets impressed her. Zbigniew Herbert and Reiner Kunze set her thinking again about poets in the Eastern bloc, as she was astonished to discover Kunze holed up in a makeshift office for most of the conference, writing and mailing letters he would not be allowed to send from his native East Germany. She genuinely enjoyed Judith Herzberg, her assigned translator, and had dinner with Judith and her Brazilian (born in Petrópolis) husband, Leon, in Amsterdam. In the way such conferences bring together poets of dissimilar styles and tastes, Elizabeth was paired for a while with "the other American," Diane Di Prima, and the differences fascinated her:

[Her poetry] is "hippy" stuff – very Ginsberg-ish, etc. – . . . She has five children – all with different fathers, I gathered – (she refers to her "husbands" but has never married any of them). She thinks that at nineteen the female body wants to have a child (odd – mine never seemed to) and should, and is delighted that her eldest, a 19 yr. old girl, is about to have a baby – she didn't seem to know who had fathered that one...Well, rather to my surprise we got along very well! . . . I'd think I wd. have represented all the worst of the "establishment" to her – but perhaps I'm so old it doesn't matter any more! . . . I felt sorry for Diane – all these ideas of love, peace, vegetarianism, babies, and so on – and underneath it all a really frightening hostility.[35]

She toured the Dutch countryside and visited the famous port at Rotterdam and several art museums in Amsterdam. Her reading on the eighteenth went off very well, though she was astonished to hear that the next day's newspaper account had remarked on her "Texas accent."

Elizabeth met up with Alice in Lisbon, Portugal, on June 21, and the two began a tour that she had dreamed about since her brief visit after Lota's departure for Brazil in 1964. Their travels by car— to Lisbon, Évora (where they were arrested and detained briefly for parking illegally), Tomar, Obidos, Sagres, and Madeira—were beautiful but increasingly painful and stressful because of Elizabeth's persistent asthma. By the end of the first week, she was having acute attacks nearly every night and was trying to convince Alice that everything was okay. When they left for Boston on June 3, Elizabeth was in severe oxygen deficit. The plane made a scheduled stop at Santa Maria in the Azores, and Alice had two doctors "in white jackets" waiting at the airport with shots of aminophelyn. Frank Bidart met the plane in Boston with an ambulance, and Elizabeth was taken to the Harvard infirmary and then on to Cambridge Hospital, where she remained for twelve days. In contrast to how she had found Peter Bent Brigham in 1972, Elizabeth loved Cambridge Hospital, with its informal, "hippy" ways. "I found it really wonderful – 12 days of it – I've never had so much attention in my life. . . . My opinion of mankind has gone up a lot in the last 12 days or so."[36] Her doctor was a young female intern also named Bishop, and she and Elizabeth shared the same birthday. Dr. Bishop spent two nights at the hospital monitoring her patient's condition, and the hospital's gentler ways enabled Elizabeth to recover from the attack relatively quickly. When she got home from the hospital on June 17, she was frail and weak, but she tried to write a poem about her impressions of a ward at the hospital, full of Portuguese charity cases of mental illness and senility, and the care the staff gave them.

Elizabeth and Alice had been returning to Boston on a tight schedule to see the arrival of the Tall Ships in Boston Harbor, just beyond the balcony at Lewis Wharf. In Elizabeth's absence, Alice and other friends held a party in Elizabeth's apartment and reported to her via telephone when a particularly interesting ship sailed in.

In the confusion of transportation from airport to hospital on the return from Portugal, Elizabeth's writing case—containing all the unfinished poems and stories she had been working on and thinking about working on for several years—disappeared. ("Oh why did I write that cursed villanelle?" she asked the Barkers.)[37] As she convalesced and packed and prepared to leave for North Haven on August 5, she was in genuine despair about whether she would write again. "Alas it had all the better things I was working on in it. (Plus all 3 address books, Lota's photograph, my birth certificate – notebooks, oh well – you can imagine – it's like starting life all over again."[38] When the writing case was found—in the trunk of a taxicab, hidden under a blanket, seven weeks after it was left there—and returned to her late in August, Elizabeth resumed her struggle to finish "one more poem" for *Geography III,* but she could not. The poem, "Florida Revisited," remains among her papers. It revisits both the state—her gloomy stays at Ft. Myers—and her early poems, including "Florida," "The Bight," and "A Drunkard":

> Just at the water's edge
> a dead, black bird, or the breast of one,
> coal-black, glistening, each wet [feather] distinct
> that turned out to be a piece of charred wood,

feather-light, feather marked
but not a bird at all – dead, delicately graven, dead
   wood
light as the breast of a bird in the hand –
feathers ///

The coconut palms still clatter;
the pelicans still waddle, soar, and dive,
sickly-looking willets pick at their food.
The sunset doesn't color the sea; it stains
the water-glaze of the receding waves instead.
At night the "giant dews" drip on the roof
and the grass grows wet and the hibiscus drops blossoms
folded, sad and wet, in the morning
It still goes on and on, more or less the same.
It has, now, apparently, for over half my life-time –
It's gone on after, or over, how many deaths,
how many deaths by now, friendship and love lost, lost
   forever. . . .

Change is what hurts worst; change alone can kill.
Change kills us, finally – not these earthly things.
Finally one hates all the immutability,
Finally one hates the Florida one knows,
the Florida one knew.

    Rhoda Sheehan spent the first week at North Haven with Eliz-
abeth, while Alice commuted from Boston, spending weekdays in
class and weekends at the farm. Celia Bertin Reich was also resident,
and visitors included her husband, Jerry, and Ricardo and Chrissy
Sternberg and their new son, Miguel, son and daughter-in-law of
the Brazilian Sternbergs Elizabeth had known in Rio and in Berkeley
in 1968. The five-week stay passed in the way Elizabeth loved, with
friends around and exchanges with Mrs. Pettit and her family, boat
rides in the bay, occasional swimming in "water so cold it <u>burns</u>,"

long walks around the island, toying with the idea of buying a house there—the more secluded and abandoned looking, the more attractive. She passed the evenings drinking bourbon and making conversation, playing backgammon and Scrabble, watching the season change from summer to fall and the flowers from Queen Anne's Lace to goldenrod, watching the fog come and go, patiently recording in her journal the sensation of being there:

> Celia has gone down for a swim—although the tide won't be high until 9, & she'll probably swim in seaweed the way A. & I did this morning. Yesterday evening we went about this time. It was almost cloudless & the sun sank, bigger & bigger, redder & redder. The surface of the water—deep & black below—was lit with gentle pink and blue ripples, & warm. If you put your hand on the surface, on the sun's path—the illusion was perfect that there the water was warmer. It was delicious, after a stifling day.

Elizabeth spent a difficult week alone in the farmhouse late in August, but Alice arrived for the last three weeks of the summer, bringing Penelope Mortimer with her. By the time they returned to Boston on September 12, Elizabeth had just two weeks to prepare her courses and begin her final year of teaching at Harvard. Lowell was also planning residence, and Elizabeth bowed out of pitting her verse-writing class against his once again and offered the intermediate expository writing course instead. At the last moment, Lowell had another breakdown and entered a hospital in London and did not come to teach after all. Elizabeth learned three days before the term began that she would be teaching verse writing.

The fall passed as semesters do. Elizabeth began unpleasant periodontal treatment in October and had trouble with asthma in November and missed three classes. Injections of Prednisone, a cortisone derivative, brought her out of the attack. She theorized that her autumn attacks had to do with fallen leaves growing moldy on the ground, and she saw an allergist who started her once again on desensitization therapy—weekly injections of "DOG, CAT, HOUSE DUST & MILDEW," Elizabeth said. Nevertheless, the fall was relatively smooth and healthy. She did readings in North and South Carolina in late October and made several trips to New York for committee meetings and the like. She and Alice spent Thanksgiving in Woodstock, Vermont, eating a cheese sandwich in the car in honor of the day. In December, Lowell appeared, "thin and gloomy" after his breakdown, though at a dinner Elizabeth gave for him on December 4 he seemed like his old self, "wonderful," she said.

The Christmas season was better in 1976 than it had been in several years. Elizabeth enjoyed a performance of the *Messiah* at Symphony Hall on December 10 and on Christmas Eve served dinner for a few stray friends. She skipped over the dreaded day itself, then traveled to New York on the twenty-seventh for the MLA convention. Staying at the Cosmopolitan Club and dropping in and out of the convention as she chose, Elizabeth still found it a "crazy affair." But copies of *Geography III* were on sale at the conference exhibit hall, and Elizabeth was delighted with its looks, if not its contents. She had envisioned a book about the size and shape of her old primer class reader, and Cynthia Krupat designed it beautifully. The book is thin, its poems stretched across pages to the point that page turning interferes with reading. But among the nine poems there is hardly a weakness. "Night City" perhaps recalls the quirkiest *North & South* poems in its obscure analogy, circular structure, and unnamed "creature"; and "12 O'Clock News" is more clever than profound. But the rest show Bishop at her strongest, if not her most prolific. Her new, more directly personal style dominates: "In the Waiting Room"—"You are an *I*, / you are an *Elizabeth*"—opens the book; and "Five Flights Up" ends it: "Yesterday brought to today so lightly! / (A yesterday I find almost impossible to lift.)"

Twenty

NORTH HAVEN

1977–1979

Reviewers loved *Geography III*. Distinguished scholar followed well-known poet in lamenting the book's brevity and in praising its contents. "Crusoe in England" was universally named a
"masterpiece": "A poet who has written this poem really needs to
write nothing else," Helen Vendler wrote in the *Yale Review*.[1] "The
End of March" was equally acclaimed. The much-worked-over ending was singled out: "How can one praise this stanza enough?" wrote
Harold Bloom.[2] Others had more general tributes to give:

> The special qualities of this new book include a perfected
> transparence of expression, warmth of tone, and a singular blend
> of sadness and good humor, of pain and acceptance—a radiant
> patience few people ever achieve and few writers ever successfully
> render. The poems are works of philosophic beauty and calm,
> illuminated by that "laughter in the soul" that belongs to the best
> part of the comic genius.[3]

> "Geography III" defines that kind of survival which neither blurs
> nor romanticizes its cost. It maps the regions we live in and the
> journeys we make—country to country, childhood to adulthood,
> imagination to fact, art to life—with the greatest care for

topographical truth. As always, it is the accumulation of familiar, seemingly minor details and events that illuminates the intense experiences—pain, joy, loss.[4]

Several reviewers, notably J. D. McClatchy, saw the poet returning in these late poems to earlier preoccupations: "Bishop is here deliberately struggling with her past—her self and her sense of self—in such a way, and with such disturbing and deceptive success, that we are now in a position to see what she has been about all along."[5]

Throughout the spring, Elizabeth fit her teaching of expository writing and modern poetry in among command performances to read from and to receive numerous accolades for *Geography III*, committee meetings, and social events. She read at the Boston Public Library, at Sarah Lawrence College, at Bryn Mawr (for the annual Marianne Moore memorial), in Washington, D.C., and at Yale. Together with Ricardo Sternberg, she did a lecture on Brazilian music and poetry, including sambas, for Rhoda Sheehan's classes at Bristol Community College. Elizabeth read the "embarrassingly good reviews" of her book but was exhausted by the hoopla surrounding its publication. "On the whole," she wrote to Anny Baumann, "I am very glad I was out of the country every time a book was published before."[6] In late February, Ecco Press announced that it would reissue *The Diary of Helena Morley* in a paperback edition and that Cynthia Krupat would do the cover. Elizabeth was delighted that her old infatuation with Helena's book was finally being shared.

She wanted very much to retire from teaching for good at the end of her Harvard contract in May 1977 but felt that with the Ouro Prêto house still unsold and the Lewis Wharf mortgage to be paid she could not. She accepted for the fall of 1977 a two-course load at New York University, which offered an apartment in the city in the bargain. Elizabeth planned to commute between Boston and New York by bus and said at first that she thought it would be fun. Accepting the job, at least, gave her a measure of security.

Visiting Aunt Grace in her Nova Scotia nursing home had renewed Elizabeth's persistent worries about what she would do if she became old and helpless, with no family to care for her and no national health insurance, as Grace had. Elizabeth grew even more sensitive about discussions of old age, especially her own.

Elizabeth wrote only a brief preface to the new edition of *Helena Morley* in the spring of 1977 and barely had time to worry about not writing. In Washington, D.C., for a mid-March reading, she visited galleries and wrote to the Barkers. "How I wish I'd been a paintr...that must really be the best profession–none of this fiddling around with words–there are a couple of Daumiers at the Phillips [Collection] that make me feel my whole life has been wasted."[7] The spring presented her with a paradox she had felt at other times in her life—as the poetry consultant at the Library of Congress, as the Pulitzer Prize winner in 1956, as the Neustadt Prize winner the previous year—her life was full of the activity, accolades, and "hoopla," as she called it, of the business of poetry, but she had finished no poem in more than two years. Once again, she felt like a "poet by default."

But the whirl of activity continued, and Elizabeth blamed this for the fact that she began to feel more and more tired, depressed, and run-down: "I–born guilty–just thought I was being lazier than usual, growing old awfully fast, etc." Once she began to grow pale and then "green" in early April, she made a doctor's appointment but could not get one for six weeks. As she dragged herself through the last few class meetings of her last term at Harvard, she began to suspect that she might be seriously ill. She made the last session of her writing course on Tuesday, May 3, but when she set out the next day to finish up the reading course, she could not do it. "I sat down on someone's steps, and gave up." At the doctor's office the next day, Elizabeth discovered that her hiatal hernia had reacted to the cortisone by beginning to bleed. (She had also been taking as many as sixteen aspirin a day for arthritis over the past several years; the effect of these on either the asthma or the hernia is unknown.)

The doctor told her he had never seen someone so anemic come into his office under "her own steam"—her red blood cell count was down sixty percent from normal. She was hospitalized at Phillips House in Massachusetts General Hospital ("where I had my appendix out on my 12th birthday") for ten days, received numerous blood transfusions and large doses of iron supplements, and sat back again to recuperate.[8]

Elizabeth Bishop's retirement from Harvard was thus unceremonious, and the early summer, without readings or many social events, was quiet. Her iron pills made her ill, and she felt feeble. When Loren MacIver asked her to write a catalog note for MacIver's new show, she balked, saying that her weakness made her "cross" and sensitive about "extra writing." After several weeks of negotiations—down from ten pages to two—Elizabeth dropped the project.[9]

She gathered herself and her belongings—along with Alice and hers—and headed on June 30 for two months at North Haven. The slow pace and relative peace of island life were their usual tonic for her; after about three weeks she felt "much better." She wrote often in her journal—careful descriptions of the natural phenomena of the island and very thorough lists of birds and flowers:

> (as usual)
> (Barn-swallows; Cliff Swallows; White-throated sparrow; Warblers–
> Tennessee (?) – others; Red-winged Blackbird; Goldfinches (very
> close to the house); Ducks (?) – some Eider ducks; Cormorants [?];
> Black-beaked gulls; Jays; Cow-birds; song-sparrow – & others –
> came, went away, back again – bobolinks; pine siskin; cedar wax
> wings.

There are pages of description of the flight of these birds, their migratory patterns, and their development with the seasons. "Oh, for a tenth of the energy of one barn-swallow–," she wished, "these babies, flying for the 1st time 2 days ago – all over the sky now, &

presently to fly to Mexico, or <u>Brazil</u>." In among these and her reading notes is the beginning of a new poem, her first in many months:

THIS IS NOT A BILL

There are 2 or 3 sets of clouds at different heights
The highest look like milk-weed silk
blown out, thin & sheer, vast—
Did I say that, or did someone else?
—after all, it doesn't really matter
because that's what they <u>do</u> look like
(& the truth can't be repeated too often)—

She wrote many letters during the month, and they were full of her usual delight with North Haven, her pleasure at being able to stay for two months, the great round of harvests (mussels, berries, mushrooms, lobsters), and the modest socializing that the little island community offered her. She allowed only her favorite guests to come—Alice, Rhoda, Frani—and wrote asking Cal Lowell not to come, knowing that a visit from him would upset her. Her notebook shows she was working on two old poems—"Pink Dog" and "Santarém"—and wished to be disturbed as little as possible.

The summer passed, and Elizabeth and Alice packed and returned to Boston at the end of August, where Elizabeth began preparing her New York University classes for the fall. For a delicious break, they drove back up to North Haven on the second weekend in September to bring the last load of belongings down to the city. But as they got to the farmhouse on the afternoon of September 12, Frank Bidart called with the news that Robert Lowell was dead. Elizabeth was dimly aware of the miseries of Lowell's present life— his indecision about his relationships with Caroline Blackwood Lowell and Elizabeth Hardwick, his conviction that he, like his parents, would die at age sixty—but his death in a taxicab on the way from the airport in New York was a terrible shock. The many memorial services and tributes to Lowell necessitated public appearances for Elizabeth; among all these mourners she was uncomfortable and unwilling to show the depth of her loss. After the funeral on September 16, Elizabeth hosted a hastily arranged party at Lewis Wharf; crowds of Lowell admirers and hangers-on filled the apartment and the balcony, but Elizabeth suffered privately and long.

Perhaps because she felt guilty at her refusal to allow Lowell to visit North Haven that summer—she did not see him again; because she had heard about his death on the island; and because the great and telling moment of their relationship had taken place at Stonington, Elizabeth's reaction to Lowell's death allowed her at last to crystallize her years of impressions of the Maine coast. In her elegy for him, "North Haven," finished on the island in July, Elizabeth composes her notebook lists of birds and flowers, her paradoxical view of the place as both timeless and ceaselessly changing, and her sensation of living by the water, into a natural metaphor for the pathos of Lowell's last years. The riggings of a schooner, new cones on the spruce, bay, clouds, islands, carefully identified flowers and birds—all recall the place they shared (or did not share, as in 1977) at intervals of time, one summer to the next, stormy and passionate youth to contemplative or regretful old age.

Elizabeth works with an idea of mutability different from the one she expressed in "Poem." Here, change is both inevitable and good; we see the stage beyond the "dismantled" elms. These are not the same flowers but the same kinds of flowers; not the same sparrows but "others like them." Each of nature's repetitions is a slight revision, even though the island itself, "North Haven, anchored in its rock," has not "shifted since last summer." This positive image of the passage of time, which Elizabeth first glimpsed for herself watching her freighter move across the still horizon on its way to Brazil, helps her make peace with Lowell's frantic life. Even though she had structured her poem around the fact that Lowell had compulsively revised his poems and had made periodic dramatic changes in his life, and even though she had disapproved of that ("You can't derange, or re-arrange, / your poems again"), she had come to understand that the ability to change and to look forward to change is what kept the troubled Lowell living. Elizabeth understood the strength of Lowell's conviction that a new writing style, a new place to live, or a new lover would somehow restore him to himself, and she understood the pathos of Lowell's failure to understand for himself the example he might have taken from nature's version of change.

Elizabeth did fly to New York on September 18, and she began teaching the next day. The semester began with a huge New York memorial service for Lowell on the twenty-fifth. She spent the rest of the fall executing an increasingly awkward and tiring commute between New York and Boston—leaving for Boston after her Tuesday seminar and returning in time for the Monday class. The fall was almost a blank in Elizabeth's life—a discouraging teaching experience, an awkward schedule, struggles with depression and alcohol. She wrote few letters and no poems. She did manage three readings, all in New York and in November—one celebrating Marianne Moore's birthday on the fifteenth and another at the Guggenheim Museum on the twenty-ninth. But she ended the semester sick again, in Lenox Hill Hospital (where Anny Baumann practiced) with a recurrence of anemia caused by internal bleeding from her hiatal hernia, "exactly like last spring."[10] The doctors would not operate on the hernia; her asthmatic condition made nonessential surgery unwise. She was miserable with a variety of complaints, including recurring dysentery and a head wound from a fall in her Lewis Wharf kitchen over the Christmas holidays. Nearly everything bothered her except asthma, from which she was free for once, and after her stay in the hospital she was sober for several weeks. Nevertheless, the state of her health frightened her; she pleaded with Anny Baumann to tell her the "truth" about her condition.[11] A special diet, the end of her chaotic commute, and the freedom of not teaching soon restored her to relative health. By February 1, she was well enough for a two-day trip to Pittsburgh for a reading before the Pittsburgh Poetry Forum. By the end of the month, she could report feeling better than she had in a long time, and having a "perfect" blood count, and "a few ideas" in her head for "the 1st time in a yr. or 2." "I wish I could have a cat or a dog!" she lamented. "Not even a canary, the dr. says."[12]

Just after her return from Pittsburgh, the blizzard of 1978 hit, dropping thirty inches of snow on Boston and bringing the city and much of the rest of New England to a virtual standstill for more than a week. Mail service stopped, public transportation failed, and Elizabeth cheerfully settled in for a week with Alice at 60 Brattle Street, where she had been when the storm hit. She managed to get out to New York on the twelfth to see the doctor and down to Duxbury with Alice a few days later, but like those of most people, her movements were limited. In her last batch of mail before the storm hit were the *New Yorker*'s proofs for "Santarém"—her first poem since "One Art" had appeared in April 1976. She managed to get the proofs back to the magazine in time for the poem to appear in the February 20 issue.

"Santarém" is another of Elizabeth's late poems with very early origins, and the drafts among her papers chronicle its development almost comically—the first two lines move from "Of course I may be remembering it all wrong / after two years" to "after five years" to "after eight years," until she abandons the count for "after, after—how many years?" And the central idea of the poem had been with her from the moment she saw the isolated town on her Amazon River trip in February 1960. The poem's quite prosy description of the river town is governed by its backward-glance perspective, which Bishop had discounted in the first line: "Of course I may be remembering it all wrong." The disclaimer serves her devotion to accuracy and announces that the enchanted place of her memory may not have been quite this "golden." That responsibility relieved, the description is free to take on what aura of precious metal it might—

"everything gilded, burnished along one side, / and everything bright, cheerful, casual—or so it looked."

Elizabeth's own voice is wonderfully apparent in this poem, insisting more than usual on its subjectivity and correcting itself with some energy: "or so it looked" and "the church, the Cathedral, rather" twice. Strategic repetition—a device she had used to great effect elsewhere—reinforces the feeling that the response of the "scents, colors and sounds" to her particular needs is the point: "I liked the place; I liked the idea of the place." The scene comes to stand for a state of mind, as other objects and places have been memory emblems for her. "The idea of the place" recalls an atmosphere of feeling, a golden mood described in her characteristically sorrowful and slightly ironic voice.

This is another poem of lifetime concerns for Elizabeth, as one might suspect given the poem's eighteen-year retrospective. The two flowing rivers recall those in "One Art" and the other streams of knowledge and memory in her poetry. The early "Quai d'Orleans" is one of the first:

> Each barge on the river easily tows
>   a mighty wake,
> a giant oak-leaf of gray lights
>   on duller gray;
> and behind it real leaves are floating by,
>   down to the sea. . . .
>
> "If what we see could forget us half as easily,"
>   I want to tell you,
> "as it does itself—but for life we'll not be rid
>   of the leaves' fossils."

The two rivers, "grandly, silently flowing, flowing east," recall directly the ending of "At the Fishhouses." Then, the sea was,

like what we imagine knowledge to be:
dark, salt, clear, moving, utterly free,
drawn from the cold hard mouth
of the world, derived from the rocky breasts
forever, flowing and drawn, and since
our knowledge is historical, flowing, and flown.

The confluence of "two great rivers" is balm to a mind habitually in conflict with itself, "a creature divided," as Elizabeth suggests she was in the tiny "Sonnet," which dates from this period. The "coming together" will not heal the breech but does postpone the need for analysis:

Even if one were tempted
to literary interpretations
such as: life/death, right/wrong, male/female
—such notions would have resolved, dissolved, straight off
in that watery, dazzling dialectic.

The poem also resembles "One Art" and "Questions of Travel" because it ends up saying nearly the opposite of what Elizabeth started out to say. In the final version, Bishop describes the confluence of the Tapajós and the Amazon, and remembers that she was enchanted by this coming together. But the earliest drafts show that in trying to articulate the emotion she felt in seeing the conflux of two great rivers, she was at first concerned with choosing between them, between the literary interpretations she dismisses in the final version. The poem originally evaluated, as "Questions of Travel" had, the traveler's possibility for "choice"; the resolution the conflux first offered was the chance to decide: "Choice – a choice! That evening one might choose." In the final draft, even the idea of choice has disappeared, and the place offers only resolution.

The truth distilled from this consideration of opposites sprawled on the riverbanks is an urn painting, a silent procession of people and zebus moving through muffling sand, a painter's landscape in painter's colors, blue and white and black and buttercup yellow; a sense of things repeated ("ritual afternoon rain"); a timeless, quaint acting out of the archetypes behind those "literary interpretations." We see male and female in the "marriage" of cows and bulls; life and death in a miraculous delivery from a bolt of lightning, *graças a deus;* right and wrong in the extension of American slavery into Brazil. A potential refuge for a divided soul, this true place is another Elizabeth considered for her withdrawal from the conflict: "That golden evening I really wanted to go no farther." But as surely as "the house was boarded up," "my ship's whistle blew. I couldn't stay." Innocent Mr. Swan must stand for the uncomprehending world that forces the division. With the laudable aim of wanting "to see the Amazon before he died," he can only look at Bishop's prize, a "small, exquisite, clean matte white" wasp's nest, and ask, " 'What's that ugly thing?' " The "ugly thing" is, of course, an emblem of the poet's "difference" and alienation, a tangible symbol of why she might have stayed in the town where no answer would ever be necessary. The poem has a valedictory air and resembles "Crusoe in England" most among these late poems.

. . .

On March 1, Robert Lowell's birthday, Elizabeth participated in a reading at Harvard's Boylston Hall, which was followed the next day by the huge Harvard memorial service for him, which Elizabeth Hardwick attended. Caroline Blackwood Lowell and Frank Bidart sat and talked in her apartment afterward; Elizabeth did not take sides with either of Lowell's wives. A few days later, thinking about what her public response to his death would be, she left for Washington for a reunion of Library of Congress poetry consultants, which she said was "awful." Still somewhat enfeebled by her illness and convinced that taking the NYU job had been "a terrible mistake," Elizabeth lay low for a couple of weeks, gathering strength for an early-spring car trip she and Alice had planned. At midmonth, she received notification that she had been awarded a Guggenheim Fellowship for twenty-one thousand dollars running from September 1978 to September 1979. The relief from teaching for the year was a great gift—she wrote immediately to Brandeis University, where she had been engaged to teach, to say she would not be coming—and she announced herself as "dying to recuperate and get to work."

Elizabeth had indicated on her Guggenheim application, submitted on October 1, 1977, that her project would be a new volume of poems entitled *Grandmother's Glass Eye* (an old title) and a book-length poem called *Elegy*, which she indicated was "partly written." Robert Fitzgerald, Helen Vendler, Harold Bloom, and Robert Giroux wrote letters of recommendation for her application, and Alice Methfessel was listed as her "next of kin." Four poems toward the projected volume were finished before Elizabeth died—"Santarém," "North Haven," "Pink Dog," and "Sonnet." The last poem she said she was working on, called "The Foggy Summer"—presumably after her stay on North Haven in 1979 when she and Alice scarcely saw the sun—was apparently destroyed. Only the barest outline of "Elegy" is left among Elizabeth's papers. It indicates that she planned to write the poem "in sections, some anecdotal, some lyrical, different [lengths] – never more than two short pages–." The poem was to be an elegy for Lota Soares; her "reticence and pride"; her "heroism, brave & young"; her "beautiful colored skin"; "the gestures (which [you] said you didn't have)." The poem was also to investigate specific memories: "the [door] slamming, plaster-falling – the [cook] and I laughing helplessly"; Lota's "courage to the last, or almost to the last–"; "regret and guilt, the nighttime horrors"; "WASTE."

Elizabeth and Alice flew to Raleigh, North Carolina, on March 27, rented a car, and headed to the Outer Banks. "A wonderful bird sanctuary [was] the best part of that trip–snow geese, Canada geese, swans, otters, turtles, almost every kind of marsh bird one can think of – marvellous beaches," Elizabeth wrote.[13] After this brief vacation, Elizabeth read to a small group at Duke University on March 30. By luck she was housed with Roma Blackburn, the widow of a Duke professor who became one of her dearest friends. She and Roma sat up talking that night until half past four in the morning. Blackburn's summer home at Lake Memphremagog, Quebec, became a favorite destination and gave Elizabeth occasion to compare inland lake flora and fauna with the Atlantic varieties. After the reading, she and Alice flew from Raleigh to St. Louis, rented another car, and drove to Fayetteville, Arkansas, where Elizabeth read to a huge audience and taught a graduate seminar at the university. As she had been on her first visit to Oklahoma, she was surprised at the levels of interest and sophistication among the Arkansas students, there in what seemed to her "the end of the world."

After the Arkansas seminar, they drove back to St. Louis via the Ozark Mountains, lovely in the early spring but also full of the trappings of the tourist industry: motels, souvenir shops, arts and crafts ("I wish we'd go back to machine-made products," Elizabeth said.)[14] "Seven motels" later, and after a visit with former Lewis Wharf neighbors who had moved to Missouri, they flew from St. Louis back to Boston—running into Stephen Spender on the plane—just in time for Elizabeth to read at a Wallace Stevens event in Storrs, Connecticut. It was an itinerary to make almost anyone tired.

The spring passed with Elizabeth on a more modest schedule of readings and social events as she continued to recover from her persistent anemia. Aunt Grace died in May; Elizabeth knew it was "time," but her lack of relatives and virtually absent direct connection to the future also saddened her. She read at Bennington College in Vermont on May 4 and received an honorary degree from Brandeis on May 28, but her activities were otherwise few. She wrote very little and, thinking about mortality, spent her time arranging her papers and her affairs. She again revised her will, making Alice her sole heir and literary executor and former student Anne Hussey the substitute executor. Having sorted her papers one last time, Elizabeth asked Harvard to hold them for safekeeping until they could be appraised and sold. Elizabeth felt that Harvard would not be willing to pay enough for them, and eventually, after her death, they were sold to Vassar College.

At mid-June, she and Alice began their summer travels with a wide circuit of New England, beginning with a stop at North Haven to drop off part of the summer's larder. From there they went to Skowhegan, where a couple of moose surprised them by appearing in the road, and then up to Lake Memphremagog to visit Roma Blackburn. The trip wound down to Cummington, Massachusetts, where they visited with their friend Helen Muchnic, and then back to Lewis Wharf on June 24, just a week before they were to leave for two months on North Haven Island. Elizabeth promised Anny Baumann that after drinking on the trip and gaining several pounds, she would lead "a life of blameless purity and hard work" on the island to keep her blood count up.[15]

In the first month in Maine, Elizabeth was preoccupied with completing "North Haven," which she was sure was overly sentimental, "pure corn." She finished the poem the first week in August and read it over the telephone to Frank Bidart on the fifth before mailing it off to him the following day. She also worked on two stories—"Primer Class" was certainly one—and undertook what she considered to be a more serious reading agenda, beginning with Samuel Johnson and St. Augustine's *City of God.* She continued work on the "Sammy" poem and on one about Carlyle, and wrote to her cousin Phyllis Sutherland in Tatamagouche, Nova Scotia, and to Roma Blackburn, asking for details about education in Nova Scotia in the early twentieth century—gathering details for the story she never finished. Rhoda Sheehan visited, and later John Brinnin and Frank Bidart did, but Elizabeth allowed few others to interrupt what she hoped would be a happy mix of writing, beachcombing, berry picking, boating, and swimming. She wanted badly to finish the two stories and sell them; her single-minded goal was to use her Guggenheim year to generate enough money so that she would not have to return to teaching when the year was over. But "writer's block about everything" frustrated her for most of the summer.

In early August, Ilse, Kit, and Thomas Barker arrived from England, and Elizabeth was able to share the wonders of the relatively primitive village life on the island with a fresh audience of appreciative artists she had long entertained with her best letters. Kit Barker painted island seascapes on this visit, one of which a year later illustrated Herb Yellin's broadside printing of "North Haven," and Ilse Barker wrote about the place as well. Watching schooners pass, taking lobster-boat rides, exploring the island's empty houses, and dreaming of buying them were activities all made new by the chance to share them. It was a hot, dry summer in Maine, and along with worries about the water level in the well came "hellish sunsets" and persistent fog. So absorbed was Elizabeth by the timeless rhythms of life on the island that she apparently missed the turn of the month and misdated most of her August letters "July."

Elizabeth toyed over the summer with ideas of where to spend her Guggenheim year. John Malcolm Brinnin, living a consoling social existence in Venice (Bill Read had died of cancer in the spring), recommended it to Elizabeth. She thought for a while she might go to Italy and stay for several months in the winter and asked Brinnin to scout for a *pension* for her. When she left North Haven on August 27, in tears because it was so beautiful, she returned to Lewis Wharf with mixed feelings not just about the city (she was "horrified to be back" there), but also about the building itself, with its wealthy and transient tenants. As if to address this discomfort, she traveled with Alice to all their favorite oceanside houses during September, beginning with Labor Day at Duxbury and several more visits there, a three-day stay at Hurricane House, and at the end of the month a "foliage trip" to Down East, Maine—Machias, Harrington, Cape Split—and to North Haven to retrieve possessions they had left behind. The schedule of retreats from Boston and Lewis Wharf continued into October, with lots of weekend stays at Duxbury while John Brinnin was away.

She began to think again of "becoming a recluse," she said, as her wish for money to prevent her from having to teach interfered with her desire not to read or make other public appearances. Her fellowship did not insulate her from the many requests for letters of recommendation, advice ("Would you read these poems of mine and tell me if you think they're any good?"), and, most onerous to her, interviews. Elizabeth was horrified at the plans of one young female scholar to travel to Brazil to research a dissertation on her and wrote to Joe Summers in a panic that the woman's intentions were "biographical – and gossipy." How did this woman know she had lived in Brazil? Elizabeth wondered, still thoroughly uncomfortable with her almost-celebrity status, with the idea that her life had become public property.[16]

On October 20, Elizabeth gave a party, her first in several years, in honor of Howard Moss. "Seven men and 6 ladies," she said, and "all but 1 a poet." Shortly afterward, she embarked on her busy schedule of fall readings with a stop at the University of Rochester, where she stayed with the Summerses and had a couple of meals with Tony Hecht. She loved the Eastman Museum but was disappointed in her reading (a hoarse voice, trouble with the microphone) and all but furious when U. T. Summers reported that one of her students had said that Elizabeth Bishop looked, not like a poet, but like "somebody's grandmother." "Oh dear. This was unkind, I think – so I wrote her and said that anyone, male or female, at 67, would look like somebody's grandfather or grandmother, & we can't all look like Lord Byron."[17] The incident and a similar comment in a newspaper account of a reading she did in January in New Jersey brought Elizabeth's "feminist facet uppermost"—surely no one had ever said that T. S. Eliot looked like somebody's great uncle![18]

The string of readings went on, including a wonderful return visit to the University of Virginia on November 6. "The Dome of the

University building has been restored exactly as Jefferson designed it (it burned years ago & Stanford White had changed it a lot) – and I read in the Dome – rather like the Pantheon, only pure white – beautiful, and wonderful acoustics and a wonderful audience."[19] Peter and Eleanor Taylor gave her a party, she had a dinner with John Ciardi, and she stayed with Irvin Ehrenpreis, whose wife had died in the previous year and who wrote Elizabeth shortly after she left, thanking her for her sympathy and kindness to him. They were both masters of the art of losing, he said.

A reading at Boston College followed, as did a trip with Alice to Dallas, Texas, for another on November 11. They flew down with Amram Shapiro and Rosalind Wright, friends from Cambridge who went to attend the reading and see relatives, and Elizabeth looked up an old high school friend, Elizabeth Bell Higgenbotham, and was delighted to have done so. Her impressions of Dallas, however, were among her most incisive and dismissive:

> It is vast, depressing, yellow-brown, no white people in sight, just cars – and then groups of miserable-looking Negroes waiting for the busses that don't seem to run...We spent 2 days seeing "East Texas"... – that was better than Dallas, at least. Did you know that state is bigger than France? And that ALL the lakes – except the one we saw, half in Louisiana – are artificial?[20]

Dorothee Bowie and her son, Taylor, visited during Thanksgiving week, and Elizabeth offered a few books from her collection for Taylor's used and rare bookstore in Seattle. The visit was fun but tiring; when icy weather gave her a chance to skip a reading she was scheduled to give at Vassar on November 28, she took it.

December's round of typical Boston weather—rain followed by ice followed by snow, or the reverse—would have depressed Elizabeth had the Duxbury house not been so constantly available. She and Alice spent most of the month there, where they did a good deal of socializing and not much "work." On December 11, "North

Haven" appeared in the *New Yorker,* and though most of Elizabeth's friends had seen the poem in manuscript, those who had not wrote or called their appreciation for the poem, and Elizabeth was once again more or less in the public eye.

Holiday celebrations in 1978 consisted of a Christmas Eve "Maine supper"—lobsters and blueberry pudding—for eight friends. (Elizabeth was by now confirmed in her determination to ignore Christmas Day altogether.) Alice gave Elizabeth a world atlas for Christmas, the first she had ever owned. A New Year's Eve party at Celia Bertin and Jerry Reich's, with Frank, Amram, Rosalind, and Alice, saw Elizabeth into the last year of her life.

The winter was quiet, with Elizabeth spending as much time as possible at Duxbury; she found it impossible to work at Lewis Wharf. She continued to revise "Primer Class," but without consistency or much satisfaction, and she found herself turning increasingly back to older things. "Everything I'm working on now was begun long ago," she wrote from Duxbury.[21] "I'm here to try to finish an endless story – and a couple of poems. – I'm digging up a lot of old Brasilian things I couldn't use while there – like a dog digging up old bones."[22] As she struggled with where and how and what to write, she speculated that perhaps such questions did not much matter: "In fact, when I think about it, it seems to me I've rarely written anything of any value at the desk or in the room where I was supposed to be doing it – it's always in someone else's house, or in a bar, or standing up in the kitchen in the middle of the night."[23]

In the middle of this struggle, Elizabeth and Alice decided suddenly that they would go to Greece in the spring on a Swan's cruise, reputed to be both physically strenuous and intellectually challenging. The trip gave the spring some focus—plans and details for visiting the Barkers in England and James Merrill's friend David Jackson in Athens. To get in shape for the trip, Elizabeth rented a stationary bicycle to strengthen her weak knees.

She spent the days before and after her sixty-eighth birthday at Alice's, beginning with a dinner on the seventh at which she, Seamus Heaney, and Amram Shapiro were guests of honor. She said that she "almost enjoyed this" birthday but that it was "AWFUL to be so old–it seems all of a sudden."[24] But she wrote with enthusiasm to Octavio Paz in response to his news that he planned to translate "North Haven" into Spanish:

> I'd love to see your translation of my poem for Cal. "daisies pied" is from the same Shakespeare song as "paint the meadows with delight"–as you probably know! Perhaps there is an equally archaic phrase (or quote) in Spanish for daisies, and wild flowers etc. that you could use. The rhymes aren't very important–mostly off-rhymes, I think–& a goldfinch seems to be either a cardelina or a pintacilgo!...Heaven knows what kind of a pardal (the one word I do know) a "white-throated sparrow" is!–but it's the only one that has that particularly plaintive and characteristic song. A Maine neighbor calls it the Bartok bird.[25]

And on February 26, "Pink Dog"—one of the "old Brazilian things"—appeared in the *New Yorker*. The earliest drafts of the poem date from 1963. At the time of its publication, the magazine already had what would be Elizabeth's last published poem, "Sonnet," which it held for more than a year before publishing it on October 29, 1979, three weeks after her death. Why the magazine held the poem perhaps only Howard Moss knew, but one suspects that he, at least, had doubts about the kind of veiled confession it contains. The poem is as stunning an example of verse autobiography as one sees. Uncharacteristic of Elizabeth's poetry after *North & South* (bearing superficial resemblance only to "Night City" among her recent poems), it seems without a speaker or definable perspective. Liberated by indirection, it can be unusually frank:

Caught—the bubble
in the spirit-level,
a creature divided;
and the compass needle
wobbling and wavering,
undecided.
Freed—the broken
thermometer's mercury
running away;
and the rainbow-bird
from the narrow bevel
of the empty mirror,
flying wherever
it feels like, gay!

In the first half of the poem, the "creature divided" is "caught"—
like the alcohol-suspended bubble in a carpenter's level—compelled
to move only as the level moves, seeking equilibrium but always
falling left or right. The compass needle, a geographer's tool, struggles to register the direction the creature faces, but wavers. The
second half is a tiny anthology of Elizabeth Bishop's early poems.
"The broken / thermometer's mercury" recalls the moonlight in
"The Man-Moth," which shines at "a temperature impossible to
record in thermometers." The "rainbow-bird" evokes Bishop's most
anthologized poem, "The Fish," and its "rainbow, rainbow, rainbow" epiphany. "The narrow bevel / of the empty mirror" echoes
"Insomnia"—"she'd find a body of water, / or a mirror, on which
to dwell"—and the ironically reversed world of that poem. And
"flying wherever it feels like" recalls "Seascape"—"white herons got
up as angels, / flying as high as they want and as far as they want."[26]
This little poem, in its synopsis of a life and a career, is as valedictory in spirit as "Crusoe in England" or "Santarém." Its mis-
chievously disguised confessions of alcoholism and homosexuality
are nonetheless terribly serious. The poem is an agony of identity

writ small. The "freedom" of a unified soul comes with being able to face one direction finally, with confessing, which Elizabeth did only cautiously, cryptically, and belatedly, as it turned out, from beyond the grave. One wonders why, of course. The gesture has a measure of perversity, in Poe's sense of the word—the urge to reveal to a wide audience what one has struggled to conceal—that we do not find in Bishop's poetry. Its playfulness may be desperate; certainly the dramas it enacts were the major ones in her life.

Over the spring, Elizabeth read and then reread Flannery O'Connor's letters, edited by Sally Fitzgerald in the volume called *The Habit of Being*. When Elizabeth finished, she said she felt as if she had "been through a lot," the letters were so moving. The drama of O'Connor's tragic death played in Elizabeth's mind alongside the current illness and slow dying of John Peech of cancer. Elizabeth admired Peech's poems and his range of interests (he held a graduate degree in physics), and she frequently hired him to work on the Lewis Wharf apartment. Although he did not die until after Elizabeth herself had, his decline saddened her.

There were a few readings in the spring, a trip to Bryn Mawr for the annual Marianne Moore reading (given by James Merrill that year), days in New York for National Book Award committee meetings (Elizabeth was on the poetry board), a reading/teaching stint at Vassar in early May, social gatherings with Seamus Heaney and his family, and teaching at Harvard for the spring semester. With special delight, she traveled to Nova Scotia on May 11 to receive an honorary degree from Dalhousie University, with the remainder of her Canadian relatives and friends in attendance. But the ceremony was an unexpected trial: from her seat on the platform she looked across the way to Dartmouth Hospital, where her mother had been kept for eighteen years. Elizabeth was thoroughly upset. A week later, she and Alice left for Greece, but not before Elizabeth, with a sigh, had signed on to teach a course at MIT in the fall.

The trip began with a flight to London, where the two planned to spend a few days. But the days of sightseeing and theatergoing were interrupted when Alice was hospitalized with what seemed to be appendicitis but later turned out not to be. After a few days of recuperation, they left London with the Swan's Hellenic Cruise No. 169 on May 24. Aside from there being "too many English" on the tour, Elizabeth and Alice enjoyed their strenuous travels through the Greek Isles, including stops at Delphi, Mykonos, Delos, Piraeus, Athens, and Santorini—where Elizabeth stayed behind while Alice climbed the famous five hundred eighty-eight steps. The trip fulfilled a lifetime ambition for Elizabeth and, she said, brought back her Vassar education, which had included three years of Greek. The trip ended with a return to London on June 8 and then a visit to the Barkers in Sussex before a flight to New York on the eleventh. On the twelfth, Elizabeth went to Princeton, New Jersey, where she received her fifth honorary degree. She fulfilled one more lifelong dream before heading to North Haven on July 1 and bought for herself the full thirteen-volume edition of the *Oxford English Dictionary*.

The summer of 1979 on North Haven Island was dominated in its first half by national speculation about where the remains of Sky Lab would fall. (Elizabeth reported that her landlady, Mrs. Pettit, "says she isn't conceited enough to think it's going to land on her.")[27] When the pieces had finally fallen and everyone could turn back to more usual preoccupations, Elizabeth considered a request by David R. Godine that she edit a new edition of Sarah Orne Jewett's fiction. She pondered the idea seriously for several weeks, rereading Jewett and locating her papers at Colby College, before deciding that Willa Cather had done a good enough job with the earlier edition and that there was not enough good Sarah Orne Jewett to justify the effort. Elizabeth had long admired *The Country of the Pointed Firs* and continually recommended it to friends, but nothing else of Jewett's moved her as much. Amidst these negotiations, the little community at North Haven muttered about the hot and foggy summer, entertained guests—old friends Harold Leeds, Wheaton Galentine, Amram Shapiro, and Rosalind Wright, among others—and read books. When Alice and Elizabeth returned to Boston on August 29, they hated it so much they left right away to visit Roma Blackburn at Lake Memphremagog for five days, before it was really time to settle in at Lewis Wharf and begin preparing the verse-writing class at MIT, set to begin on September 11, just as the Guggenheim ended.

Elizabeth felt ill when she began the class—the long process of reading submissions and choosing students tired her—and by September 21 she was again in the hospital with anemia caused by renewed bleeding from the hiatal hernia. On September 10, Alice's mother had died suddenly, and she had left to be with her father for six days. Elizabeth was thoroughly discouraged—with her health, with the class ("Why would they want to write poetry, anyway?"), and with Alice's absence. Elizabeth came home from the hospital on September 26, and ten days later she was dead.

Among Elizabeth's papers is a draft of a letter written to John Nims on the morning of October 6, 1979, the day she died. Always one to disrupt routine procedures with her insistence on absolute accuracy and pleasing forms, she took Nims to task on this autumn morning for his plan to footnote her poems in the anthology he was editing. With undiminished moral energy, she wrote:

> Now I'm going to take issue with you – rather violently – about the idea of foot-notes...With one or two exceptions (I'll mention them later) I don't think there should be ANY footnotes. You say the book is for college students. and I think anyone who gets as far as college should be able to use a dictionary...If a poems catches a student's interest at all, he or she should damned well be able to look up an unfamiliar word in the dictionary.

"Damned well" is a little more energetic than Elizabeth was likely to be in a business letter; the phrase would probably have been edited out of the final draft. She continued in this vein for a single-spaced page and a half.

At about six o'clock on that Saturday afternoon, Elizabeth Bishop died quickly and painlessly in her Lewis Wharf study of a cerebral aneurysm. Alice found her there, the telephone off the hook beside her, when she arrived to take her to dinner at Helen Vendler's. Elizabeth had been scheduled to read with Irish poet Mary Lavin the following evening at Harvard's Sanders Theater, and in her absence her Boston friends gathered there in her memory, for an audience of seven hundred fifty, and read her poems for her.

. . .

Elizabeth Bishop was remembered in numerous obituaries and at many memorial services in terms she would have liked: the greatness of her poems and the modesty of her self-presentation. She was not "famous" when she died, except in the Boston and New York literary circles she had feared so much as a young poet. James Merrill remarked on her "instinctive, modest, life-long impersonations of an ordinary woman." Lloyd Schwartz remembered that her favorite example of iambic pentameter had been "I hate to see that evenin' sun go down."

She has become more famous since her death, defying the more typical inverted arc of the American poet's reputation by refusing to disappear immediately after dying, only to reappear twenty or thirty years later. As critical judgments of her poetry have developed, the early comments on her "objectivity" and "impersonality" have yielded to the gentle insistence of the personal voice in her poems, as her readers have come to see that she, like most other poets, told the story of her life in her work. She told it with sorrow, humor, and almost perfect understanding of her own strengths and failures. "Awful, but cheerful," she asked Alice Methfessel to inscribe on her tombstone in the Bishop family plot in Worcester.

NOTES

PREFACE

1. "Elizabeth Bishop's New Book," *Shenandoah* 17, no. 1 (Winter 1966): 89.

1. THE SCREAM

1. Elizabeth Bishop, letter to Robert Lowell, 27 July [1960], Houghton Library, Harvard University, Cambridge, Massachusetts.

2. Bishop, letter to Anne Stevenson, 18 March 1963, Washington University Library Special Collections, St. Louis, Missouri.

3. William Thomas Bishop, letter to Elizabeth Hutchinson Boomer, 12 February [1911], Vassar College Library Special Collections, Poughkeepsie, New York.

4. N.d. [1911], Vassar College Library, p. 643.

5. Elizabeth Bishop, *Collected Prose* (New York: Farrar, Straus, and Giroux, 1984) pp. 251–274.

6. *Poetry* 79 (January 1952): 213.

7. In a letter to Robert Lowell (11 December 1957, Houghton Library), Bishop describes her own experience directly in similar terms: "I don't remember any direct threats, except the usual maternal ones – her danger for me was just implied in the things I overheard the grown-ups say before and after

her disappearance. Poor thing, I don't want to have it any worse than it was."

8. Elizabeth Spires, "The Art of Poetry XXVII," *Paris Review* 23 (Summer 1981): 74.

9. *Collected Prose,* pp. 3–12.

10. "Gwendolyn," ibid., pp. 213–226.

11. Ibid., pp. 13–33.

12. Bishop, letter to Joan Keefe, 8 June 1977, Vassar College Library.

13. Bishop, interview by Alexandra Johnson, *Christian Science Monitor,* 23 March 1978, p. 20; interview by Ashley Brown, in *Elizabeth Bishop and Her Art,* ed. Lloyd Schwarz and Sybil P. Estess (Ann Arbor: University of Michigan Press, 1983), p. 292.

14. *Owl* (North Shore Country Day School, 1926–1927), p. 65.

15. *Collected Prose,* pp. xii–xiii.

16. A letter from Eleanor Prentiss to Bishop is enclosed in a letter from Bishop to Frani Blough (Muser), 31 December 1928, Vassar College Library.

17. *Blue Pencil* (Walnut Hill School) 13, no. 1 (December 1929): 18.

18. *Blue Pencil* 12, no. 1 (December 1928): 30.

19. Ibid., p. 28.

20. *Blue Pencil* 12, no. 2 (April 1929): 18.

21. Bishop, letter to Frani Blough (Muser), 30 August 1929, Vassar College Library.

22. 4 September 1929, Vassar College Library.

23. Bishop to Blough (Muser), 20 April 1930, Vassar College Library.

24. Bishop to Stevenson [March 1964], Washington University Library.

25. Bishop to Blough (Muser), [March 1930], Vassar College Library.

26. Bishop to Blough (Muser), 20 April 1930, Vassar College Library.

2. "THE HIGHER TYPES"

1. Julia Bacon, letter to Anne Stevenson, 21 January 1963, Washington University Library.

2. Barbara Swain, letter to Stevenson, 19 January 1963, Washington University Library.

3. Helen Sandison, letter to Stevenson, 19 January 1963, Washington University Library.

4. *Vassar Journal of Undergraduate Studies* 7 (1933): 102–103.

5. *Assault on Mount Helicon* (Berkeley and Los Angeles: University of California Press, 1984), p. 98.

6. Bishop to Blough (Muser), 17 July 1933, Vassar College Library.

7. 9 August 1932, Vassar College Library.

8. Bishop to Blough (Muser), 5 September 1929, Vassar College Library.

9. 8 July 1932, Vassar College Library.

10. Harriet Tompkins Thomas, "Travels with a Young Poet: Elizabeth Bishop," *Vassar Quarterly* (Winter 1986): 20.

11. Elizabeth Spires, "An Afternoon with Elizabeth Bishop," *Vassar Quarterly* (Winter 1979): 7–8.

12. "The Art of Poetry XXVII," pp. 77–78.

13. Bishop to Blough (Muser), 12 December 1933, Vassar College Library.

14. 5 March 1934, quoted in Donald Stanford, "From the Letters of Elizabeth Bishop, 1933–1934," *Verse* 4, no. 3 (November 1987): 25.

15. 23 (February 1934): 5.

16. Ibid., p. 7.

17. Schwartz and Estess, *Elizabeth Bishop and Her Art,* pp. 297–298.

18. *Vassar Review* 19 (Spring 1933): 8.

19. 18 February 1934, quoted in Stanford, "From the Letters of Elizabeth Bishop," p. 19.

20. 1 April 1924, Vassar College Library.

21. "The Art of Poetry XXVII," p. 75.

22. 22 October 1933, Vassar College Library.

23. Bishop's letters to Margaret Miller are still in Miller's possession.

24. Bishop to Lowell, 11 October 1963, Houghton Library.

25. Bishop to Lowell, 26 August 1963, Houghton Library.

26. 1 April 1934, Vassar College Library.

27. 19 March 1934, Rosenbach Museum and Library, Philadelphia, Pennsylvania.

28. 2 March 1934, Vassar College Library.

29. 4 June 1934, Vassar College Library.

3. THE U.S.A. SCHOOL OF WRITING

1. 30 June 1934, Vassar College Library.

2. R. P. Blackmur, "The Method of Marianne Moore," in *Marianne Moore: A Collection of Critical Essays,* ed. Charles Tomlinson (Englewood Cliffs, N. J.: Prentice-Hall, 1969), p. 67.

3. 6 September 1954, Vassar College Library.

4. 24 October 1954, Rosenbach Museum and Library.

5. *Collected Prose,* pp. 121–156.

6. "As We Like It," *Quarterly Review of Literature* 4 (1948): 134.

7. "A Sentimental Tribute," *Bryn Mawr Alumnae Bulletin* (Spring 1962): 3.

8. The story of the relationship between Marianne Moore and Elizabeth Bishop has been well told several times. See Lynn Keller, "Words Worth a Thousand Postcards: The Bishop/Moore Correspondence," *American Literature* 55, no. 3 (October 1983): 405–429; and David Kalstone, *Becoming a Poet* (New York: Farrar, Straus, and Giroux, 1989), pp. 3–106.

9. *Collected Prose,* pp. 35–49.

10. Bishop to Blough (Muser), 1 November 1934, Vassar College Library.

11. Bishop to Blough (Muser), 1 January 1935, Vassar College Library.

12. Bishop, draft of letter to "Leo," 26 April 1948, Vassar College Library.

13. 25 January 1935, Rosenbach Museum and Library.

14. 2 April 1935, Rosenbach Museum and Library.

15. 30 January 1935, Vassar College Library.

4. "EVERYTHING CONNECTED ONLY BY 'AND' AND 'AND'"

1. 21 August 1935, Rosenbach Museum and Library.

2. 17 September 1935, quoted in Thomas, "Travels with a Young Poet," p. 23.

3. Bishop to Blough (Muser), 20 October 1935, Vassar College Library.

4. Thomas, "Travels with a Young Poet," p. 24.

5. Bishop to Moore, 10 November 1935, Rosenbach Museum and Library.

6. Draft, 29 October 1935, Rosenbach Museum and Library.

7. Bishop to Blough (Muser), 20 October 1935, Vassar College Library.

8. Bishop to Moore, 4 February 1936, Rosenbach Museum and Library.

9. 14 February 1936, Vassar College Library.

10. 6 March 1936, Vassar College Library.

11. Bishop to Blough (Muser), 14 February 1936, Vassar College Library.

12. Bishop to Blough (Muser), 12 May 1936, Vassar College Library.

13. Thomas, "Travels with a Young Poet," p. 25.

14. 11 April 1936, quoted in ibid.

15. Bishop, letter to Martha Millet, 15 June 1956, Vassar College Library.

16. Robert Dale Parker, *The Unbeliever* (Urbana: University of Illinois Press, 1988), writes extensively on this idea in Bishop's early poetry.

17. Bishop to Blough (Muser), 12 May 1936, Vassar College Library.

18. Ibid.

19. 21 May 1936, Rosenbach Museum and Library.

20. 2 June 1936, Vassar College Library.

21. Bishop to Blough (Muser), [June 1936], Vassar College Library.

22. Bishop to Blough (Muser), 9 July 1936, Vassar College Library.

23. Bishop to Blough (Muser), 27 July 1936, Vassar College Library.

24. Bishop to Moore, 5 May 1938, Rosenbach Museum and Library.

25. Rosenbach Museum and Library.

26. 28 August 1936, Vassar College Library.

27. 29 September 1936, Rosenbach Museum and Library.

28. Bishop to Moore, n.d. [October 1936], Rosenbach Museum and Library.

29. Bishop to Moore, 5 December 1936, Rosenbach Museum and Library.

30. Ibid.

31. *Collected Prose,* pp. 171–180.

5. PITY SUCH SORROW

1. For obvious reasons, there are few witnesses available to verify this story. The postcard does not survive. Seaver's parents maintained to their deaths that their son was not a suicide, indicating that they had not been aware of any note he might have left. Seaver's sister, Elizabeth Helfman, believes that her brother did kill himself but knows nothing about the postcard. Barbara Chesney Kennedy remembers Elizabeth telling her about the postcard in 1937, and Frank Bidart says that Elizabeth told him about it.

2. 17 December 1936, Rosenbach Museum and Library.

3. Bishop to Moore, 5 January 1937, Rosenbach Museum and Library.

4. Bishop to Blough (Muser), 4 January 1937, Vassar College Library.

5. 5 January 1937, Rosenbach Museum and Library.

6. Bishop to Blough (Muser), 1 January 1937, Vassar College Library.

7. Bishop to Blough (Muser), 4 January 1937, Vassar College Library.

8. 4 February 1937, Rosenbach Museum and Library.

9. Draft, 9 February 1937, Rosenbach Museum and Library.

10. Bishop to Moore, 4 February 1937, Rosenbach Museum and Library.

11. 25 February 1937, Rosenbach Museum and Library.

12. 12 March 1937, Vassar College Library.

13. Bishop to Moore, 26 May 1937, Rosenbach Museum and Library.

14. Bishop to Blough (Muser), 8 June 1937, Vassar College Library.

15. Bishop to Blough (Muser), 28 July 1937, Vassar College Library.

16. Bishop to Blough (Muser), 9 August 1937, Vassar College Library.

17. Rosenbach Museum and Library.

18. Draft, n.d. [August 1937], Rosenbach Museum and Library.

19. Bishop to Blough (Muser), 9 August 1937, Vassar College Library.

20. 2 September 1937, Rosenbach Museum and Library.

21. 7 October 1937, Vassar College Library.

6. "WELL, WE HAVE COME THIS FAR."

1. *Collected Prose,* pp. 181–191.

2. 31 January 1938, Rosenbach Museum and Library.

3. Draft, 10 February 1938, Rosenbach Museum and Library.

4. Draft, 1 May 1938, Rosenbach Museum and Library.

5. Bishop to Moore, 5 May 1938, Rosenbach Museum and Library.

6. Bishop to Blough (Muser), 7 February 1938, Vassar College Library.

7. *Collected Prose,* pp. 51–59.

8. 3 June 1938, Vassar College Library.

9. Bishop to Moore, 10 [21] September 1938, Rosenbach Museum and Library.

10. 31 January 1938, Rosenbach Museum and Library.

11. 20 November 1939, Rosenbach Museum and Library.

12. 19 February 1939, Rosenbach Museum and Library.

13. Draft, 16 January 1940, Rosenbach Museum and Library.

14. Bishop to Moore, 20 March 1939, Rosenbach Museum and Library.

15. Bishop to Anny Baumann, [November 1950], Vassar College Library.

16. Thomas Dardis, *The Thirsty Muse: Alcohol and the American Writer* (New York: Ticknor and Fields, 1988), p. 20.

17. 27 July [1960], Houghton Library.

18. Dardis, *The Thirsty Muse,* p. 45.

19. Bishop to Blough (Muser), "Sunday afternoon" [November 1939], Vassar College Library.

20. 1940, Rosenbach Museum and Library.

21. "Monday Morning" [February 1940], Rosenbach Museum and Library.

22. *Poetry and the Age* (New York: Knopf, 1953), p. 235.

23. Bishop to Stevenson, 8 January 1964, Washington University Library.

24. 8 June 1940, Rosenbach Museum and Library.

25. Bishop to Moore, 10 July 1940, Rosenbach Museum and Library.

26. Bishop to Moore, 11 September 1940, Rosenbach Museum and Library.

27. Bishop to Swenson, 18 February 1956, Washington University Library.

28. 17 October 1940, and addendum, "Sunday Morning," Rosenbach Museum and Library.

7. *NORTH & SOUTH*

1. 11 March 1941, Vassar College Library.

2. Bishop to Moore, 28 December 1941, Rosenbach Museum and Library.

3. 14 May 1942, Rosenbach Museum and Library.

4. 25 June 1925 [1942], Vassar College Library.

5. 15 July 1943, Rosenbach Museum and Library.

6. Bishop to Moore, 1 September 1943, Rosenbach Museum and Library.

7. Bishop to Moore, 25 October 1943, Rosenbach Museum and Library.

8. The drafts of "Faustina, or Rock Roses" are in the collection at Harvard's Houghton Library.

9. 4 August 1944, Vassar College Library.

10. Bishop to Moore, 8 December 1944, Rosenbach Museum and Library.

11. Lorrie Goldensohn discovered this poem in the "Key West notebooks" she found in the possession of Linda Nemer, in Belo Horizonte, Brazil, in 1987. See her "Elizabeth Bishop: An Unpublished, Untitled Poem," *American Poetry Review* (January-February 1988): 35–46. This material is now in the collection at Vassar.

12. Marjorie Stevens, letter to Bishop, 9 March 1946, Vassar College Library.

13. Moore to Bishop, 14 August 1946, Vassar College Library.

14. 29 August 1946, Rosenbach Museum and Library.

15. "Prize Poet," *Atlantic* (August 1946): 148.

16. Bishop, letter to Ferris Greenslet, 8 September 1946, Houghton Library.

17. "A Just Vision," *Poetry* 69 (January 1947): 230.

18. "A Meritorious Prize Winner," *Saturday Review,* 12 October 1946, p. 46.

19. "Carefully Revealed," *New York Times Book Review,* 27 October 1946, p. 18.

20. *Poetry and the Age,* p. 235.

21. "Thomas, Bishop and Williams," *Sewanee Review* 55 (July-September 1947): 498.

8. "PLOUGHING THROUGH LIFE ALONE"

1. Bishop to Greenslet, 28 November 1946, Houghton Library.

2. Houghton Library.

3. Bishop, letter to Dr. Anny Baumann, 22 July 1947, Vassar College Library.

4. 10 August 1947, Vassar College Library.

5. Bishop, letter to Joseph Summers, 24 August 1947, Vassar College Library.

6. Lowell, letter to Bishop, 25 September 1947, Vassar College Library.

7. Bishop to Lowell, 18 November 1947, Houghton Library.

8. Bishop to Lowell, 3 December 1947, Houghton Library.

9. Bishop to Lowell, 14 February 1948, Houghton Library.

10. Bishop to Lowell, [15] January 1948, Houghton Library.

11. Quoted in Wesley Wehr, "Elizabeth Bishop: Conversations and Class Notes," *Antioch Review* 39 (Summer 1981): 324.

12. Bishop to Lowell, 3 December 1947, Houghton Library.

13. Bishop to Lowell, [15] January 1948, Houghton Library.

14. Bishop to Lowell, 8 April 1948, Houghton Library.

15. Bishop to Lowell, 18 March 1948, Houghton Library.

16. Lowell to Bishop, 9 June [1948], Vassar College Library.

17. Vassar College Library. The reference may also be to Robert Lowell, of course. But Elizabeth said very little to others about her friendship with Lowell, whereas Wanning was a familiar character in the Key West circle.

18. Bishop to Lowell, 30 June [1948], Houghton Library.

19. Bishop to Baumann, 5 August 1948, Vassar College Library.

20. Bishop to Lowell, 11 July [1948], Houghton Library.

21. Ian Hamilton, *Robert Lowell* (New York: Random House, 1982), p. 135.

22. Lowell to Bishop, 15 August 1957, Vassar College Library.

23. *Selected Poems* (New York: Farrar, Straus, and Giroux, 1976), pp. 99–100.

24. Moore to Bishop, 15 October 1947, Vassar College Library.

25. 24 September 1948, and 25 September 1948, Vassar College Library.

26. 29 August 1956, Vassar College Library.

27. Bishop to Lowell, "Late August, 1948," Houghton Library.

28. Bishop to Lowell, 8 September 1948, Houghton Library.

29. "Late August, 1948," Houghton Library.

30. Bishop to Summers, "Monday Morning" [13 November 1948], Vassar College Library.

31. Bishop, letter to Loren MacIver / Lloyd Frankenberg, 21 December 1948, Vassar College Library.

32. Bishop to Lowell, 21 December 1948, Houghton Library.

33. Bishop to Lowell, 11 January 1949, Houghton Library.

34. Bishop to Lowell, 21 January 1949, Houghton Library.

35. Bishop to Lowell, 21 February 1949, Houghton Library.

36. Bishop, letter to Carley Dawson, 3 March 1949, University of Oregon Library, Eugene, Oregon.

37. 22 March 1949, Vassar College Library.

38. Bishop to Dawson, "Tuesday Morning" [26 April 1949], University of Oregon Library.

39. Hamilton, *Robert Lowell*, pp. 144–156.

40. Lowell to Bishop, [29 April 1949], Vassar College Library.

41. 26 April 1949, University of Oregon Library.

42. Bishop to Dawson, 17 July 1949, University of Oregon Library.

9. THE INDRAWN YES

1. Bishop, letter to Loren MacIver/Lloyd Frankenberg, 26 July 1949, Vassar College Library.

2. Bishop to MacIver/Frankenberg, 31 July 1949, Vassar College Library.

3. 2 August 1949, University of Oregon Library.

4. 31 July 1949, Vassar College Library.

5. 12 August 1949, Vassar College Library.

6. Vassar College Library.

7. Enclosed in Bishop to MacIver/Frankenberg, 2 August 1949, Vassar College Library.

8. "It All Depends," in *Mid-Century American Poets,* ed. John Ciardi (New York: Twayne, 1950), p. 267.

9. Kees, letter to Norris Gerry, 18 March 1950, quoted in Robert Knoll, ed., "The New York Intellectuals, 1941–50: Some Letters by Weldon Kees," *Hudson Review* 38, no. 1 (Spring 1985): 51–52.

10. Bishop to Lowell, "Late August, 1950," Houghton Library.

11. Bishop to Stevenson, 20 March 1963, Washington University Library.

12. *United States Quarterly Book Review* 6 (June 1950): 160–161.

13. Bishop to MacIver/Frankenberg, "Wednesday" [21 August 1950], Vassar College Library.

14. Bishop to Baumann, 10 November 1950, Vassar College Library.

15. "The day after the hurricane" [26 November 1950], Vassar College Library.

16. 17 January 1951, Vassar College Library.

17. Bishop to Lowell, 23 November 1955, Houghton Library.

18. Bishop to Summers, 19 October 1967, Vassar College Library.

19. From David Wagoner, *Through the Forest: New and Selected Poems* (New York: Atlantic Monthly, 1987). Used here with the permission of Atlantic Monthly Press.

20. Bishop to Lowell, 31 March 1951, Houghton Library.

21. Bishop to Summers, 30 April 1951, Vassar College Library.

22. Bishop to Lowell, 11 July 1951, Houghton Library.

10. BRAZIL

1. *New Republic* 127, no. 7 (18 August 1952): 20.

2. Bishop to Lowell, n.d., Houghton Library.

3. 8 January 1952, Vassar College Library.

4. 7 August 1952, Vassar College Library.

5. Bishop to Summers, 17 September 1952, Vassar College Library.

6. Bishop to Swenson, 19 September 1953, Washington University Library.

7. Bishop to Lowell, 8 January 1963, Houghton Library.

8. 9 December 1953, Vassar College Library.

9. 3 March 1952, Rosenbach Museum and Library.

10. 21 March 1952, Houghton Library.

11. 28 July 1953, Houghton Library.

12. 16 September 1952, Vassar College Library.

11. "A DELUXE NOVA SCOTIA"

1. Spires, "An Afternoon with Elizabeth Bishop," p. 7.

2. 5 December 1953, Houghton Library.

3. 10 May 1956, Washington University Library.

4. Bishop, letter to Ilse and Kit Barker, 5 [7] June 1956, Princeton University Library, Princeton, New Jersey.

5. "Introduction," in *The Diary of Helena Morley,* by Alice Brant (New York: Farrar, Straus, and Giroux, 1957), pp. xxx, xxvi.

6. Bishop to Barkers, 29 August [5 September] 1953, Princeton University Library.

7. Bishop to Barkers, 24 May 1953, Princeton University Library.

8. Bishop to Barkers, 28 February 1955, Princeton University Library.

9. Bishop to Barkers, "Good Friday, 1953," Princeton University Library.

10. Bishop to Barkers, 19 January [26 February] 1955, Princeton University Library.

11. Bishop to MacIver/Frankenberg, 1 May 1959, Vassar College Library.

12. Bishop to Barkers, 22 April 1958, Princeton University Library.

13. *Poetry* 93 (October 1958): 50–54.

14. Bishop to Barkers, 26 January 1956, Princeton University Library.

15. Bishop to Swenson, 2 February 1962, Washington University Library.

16. 5 June 1956, Rosenbach Museum and Library.

17. Bishop to Baumann, 24 June 1955, Vassar College Library.

18. Swenson to Bishop, 20 May 1956, Washington University Library.

19. Bishop to Lowell, 8 May 1958 and 5 December 1953, Houghton Library.

12. "SOBRIETY & GAYETY & PATIENCE & TOUGHNESS"

1. Bishop to Barkers, 5 [7] June 1956, Princeton University Library.

2. Bishop to Summers, 2 October 1956; and Bishop, letter to Grace Bulmer Bowers, 2 December 1956, Vassar College Library.

3. Bishop to Barkers, 14 October 1956, Princeton University Library.

4. Lowell to Bishop, 15 August 1957, Vassar College Library.

5. 11 [August 1957], Houghton Library.

6. Bishop to Lowell, 10 July 1957, Houghton Library.

7. Bishop to Lowell, 28 August 1957, Houghton Library.

8. Lota Soares, letter to Loren MacIver, n.d., Vassar College Library.

9. Bishop to Lowell, 11 December 1957, Houghton Library.

10. 14 December 1957, Houghton Library.

11. Bishop to Lowell, 29 January 1958, Houghton Library.

12. Bishop to Barkers, 24 March 1958, Princeton University Library.

13. 26 November 1957, Vassar College Library.

14. Bishop to Lowell, 1 April 1958, Houghton Library.

15. Bishop to Barkers, [January 1959], Princeton University Library.

16. Bishop to Moore, 2 February 1960, Rosenbach Museum and Library.

17. Bishop to Barkers, 19 December 1963, Princeton University Library.

18. Bishop to Barkers, 23 March 1956, Princeton University Library.

19. Bishop to Bowers, 12 November 1959, Vassar College Library.

20. 12 March 1960, Princeton University Library.

21. 28 February 1960, Vassar College Library.

22. *Collected Prose,* pp. 111–120.

23. 21 February 1960, Vassar College Library.

24. 28 February 1960, Vassar College Library.

25. 22 April 1960, Houghton Library.

26. Lowell, *Selected Poems,* p. 116.

27. 27 July 1960, Houghton Library.

28. 12 July 1960, Vassar College Library.

29. 27 July 1960, Houghton Library.

30. Bishop, letter to Howard Moss, 10 May 1960, Berg Collection, New York Public Library, New York, New York.

31. Bishop to Bowers, 23 September 1960, Vassar College Library.

32. Bishop to Barkers, 28 [29] December 1960, Princeton University Library.

13. AT WHAT . . . COST IN NERVOUS ENERGY?

1. Bishop to MacIver/Frankenberg, 31 January 1963, Vassar College Library.

2. Bishop to Barkers, 4 March 1961, Princeton University Library.

3. 6 August 1960, Princeton University Library.

4. "Mid-March, 1961," Houghton Library.

5. 25 June 1961, Houghton Library.

6. 15 February 1961, Vassar College Library.

7. Bishop to MacIver/Frankenberg, 23 April [1961], Vassar College Library.

8. Bishop to Lowell, 25 June 1961, Houghton Library.

9. Bishop to Bowers, 3 August 1963, Vassar College Library.

10. Bishop to Barkers, 4 September 1961, Princeton University Library.

11. Bishop to Bowers, 22 September 1962, Vassar College Library.

12. 19 January 1962, Vassar College Library.

13. Bishop to Swenson, 10 April 1962, Washington University Library.

14. *New Republic* 146, no. 18 (30 April 1962): 22.

15. 4 April 1962, Houghton Library.

16. 19 May 1960, Houghton Library.

17. Bishop to Lowell, 27 July 1960, Houghton Library.

18. Moore to Bishop, 12 July 1961, Vassar College Library.

19. "Poetry in English, 1945–1962," *Time* 79, no. 10 (9 March 1962): 93.

20. Bishop to Stevenson, 5 December 1964, Washington University Library.

21. Bishop to Baumann, 18 June 1965, Vassar College Library.

22. See Hamilton, *Robert Lowell,* pp. 300–303.

23. 8 October 1962, Houghton Library.

24. 7 January 1963, Washington University Library.

25. 1 March 1961, Houghton Library.

26. *Kenyon Review* 26 (Summer 1964): 507–508.

27. Ibid., p. 506.

28. 7 November 1962, Houghton Library.

29. Bishop to Barkers, 25 April 1963, Princeton University Library.

30. Bishop to Barkers, 1 March 1963, Princeton University Library.

31. Bishop to Lowell, 2 [12] July 1963, Houghton Library.

32. Bishop to Lowell, 26 May 1963, Houghton Library.

33. Bishop to Lowell, 5 March 1963, Houghton Library.

34. Bishop to Lowell, 17 June 1963, Houghton Library.

35. Moore, *A Collection of Critical Essays,* pp. 44, 23.

36. 8 January 1964, Washington University Library.

37. Bishop to Barkers, 14 October 1963, Princeton University Library.

38. 10 June 1963, Vassar College Library.

39. 3 August 1963, Vassar College Library.

40. Bishop to Bowers, 28 October 1963, Vassar College Library.

41. Bishop to Lowell, 27 August 1964, Houghton Library.

42. Bishop to Barkers, 10 August 1963, Princeton University Library.

43. Bishop to Bowers, 25 September 1963, Vassar College Library.

44. Bishop to Barkers, 27 October 1963, Princeton University Library.

45. Bishop to Muser, 5 December 1963, Vassar College Library.

14. "THERE *IS* NO RAILROAD NAMED DELIGHT."

1. 30 December 1963 [3 January 1964], Washington University Library.

2. Washington University Library.

3. Bishop to Barkers, 13 April 1964, Princeton University Library.

4. Bishop to Lowell, 13 June 1964, Houghton Library.

5. "No Jokes in Portuguese," *Times* (London), 26 July 1964, p. 36.

6. Bishop to MacIver/Frankenberg, 19 June 1964, Vassar College Library; Bishop to Swenson, 26 July 1964, Washington University Library.

7. Bishop to Lowell, 30 July 1964 [#2], Houghton Library.

8. Bishop to Barkers, 27 July 1964, Princeton University Library.

9. Bishop to Lowell, 1 October 1964, Houghton Library.

10. Bishop to Stevenson, 27 October 1964, Washington University Library.

11. *New York Times Magazine,* 7 March 1965, p. 86.

12. 13 March 1965, Vassar College Library.

13. Bishop to Barkers, 13 March 1966, Princeton University Library.

14. An English draft of her response to Castro is among Bishop's papers at the Vassar College Library.

15. Bishop to Summers, 28 April 1965, Vassar College Library.

16. Lilli Correia de Araújo allowed me to copy out this poem. It remains in her possession but has since been published in Lloyd Schwartz, "Annals of Poetry (Elizabeth Bishop and Brazil)," *New Yorker* 67, no. 32 (30 September 1991): 85–97, and is copyrighted by Alice H. Methfessel.

17. Bishop to Swenson, 21 May 1965, Washington University Library.

18. Bishop, letter to Ashley Brown, 2 September 1965, Princeton University Library.

19. Bishop to Barkers, 24 November 1965, Princeton University Library.

20. A photocopy of this poem was given to me by Lilli Correia de Araújo. It was also printed in Schwartz, "Annals of Poetry," and is now copyrighted by Alice H. Methfessel. Lilli has the original.

21. 23 November 1965, Princeton University Library.

22. "New Books of Poems," *Harper's* 233 (August 1966): 90.

23. "Recent Poetry: Looking for a Home," *Yale Review* 55 (Spring 1966): 459.

24. "Books," *Michigan Quarterly Review* 6 (Fall 1967): 297.

25. "Elizabeth Bishop's School," *New Leader* 48 (6 December 1965): 22.

26. "The Gilt Edge of Reputation," *Atlantic* (January 1966): 85.

27. "A Poet of Landscape," *New York Review of Books,* no. 27 (12 October 1967): 4, 6.

28. "The Sun the Other Way Around," *Poetry* 108 (August 1966): 337.

29. "The Poet as Voyager," *Christian Science Monitor*, 6 January 1966, p. 10.

30. 28 (March 1966): 255–262.

15. THE ART OF LOSING

1. Bishop to Summers, 22 November 1965, Vassar College Library; Bishop to Lowell, 18 November 1965, Houghton Library.

2. Bishop to Brown, 23 November 1965, Princeton University Library.

3. Bishop, letter to Lilli Correia de Araújo, 1 January 1966, still in Araújo's possession.

4. Bishop to Barkers, 8 February 1966, Princeton University Library.

5. "Suzanne Bowen" is a pseudonym.

6. Lilli Correia de Araújo, personal interview, August 1990.

7. 19 March 1966, Vassar College Library.

8. Wehr, "Elizabeth Bishop," p. 321.

9. Bishop to Barkers, 8 February 1966, Princeton University Library.

10. *Randall Jarrell: 1914–1965*, ed. Robert Lowell, Peter Taylor, and Robert Penn Warren (New York: Farrar, Straus, and Giroux, 1967), p. 20.

11. Bishop to Brown, 23 November 1965, and 3 October 1966, Princeton University Library.

12. 1 September 1966, Vassar College Library.

13. Bishop to Brown, 3 October 1966, Princeton University Library.

14. Bishop to Barkers, 13 January 1967, Princeton University Library.

15. Houghton Library.

16. Bishop to Baumann, 19 February 1967, Houghton Library.

17. Bishop to Brown, 20 June 1967, Princeton University Library.

18. "Giant Weather," *Blue Pencil* 13, no. 1 (December 1928): 4–5.

19. 1 March 1955, Vassar College Library.

20. Bishop to Lowell, 23 April 1967, Houghton Library.

21. "Pink Dog" and "Santarém" are entirely successful as well, but both were substantially written before 1965.

22. Bishop to Baumann, 3 July 1967, Vassar College Library.

23. 10 July 1967, Houghton Library.

24. Houghton Library.

25. Bishop to Baumann, 11 October 1967, Vassar College Library.

26. Bishop, letter to Dorothee Bowie, 20 December 1967, Vassar College Library.

27. Bishop to Baumann, 6 January 1968, Vassar College Library. Bishop included especially in this accusation the letters she had written Lota from the Amazon in 1960. Those, of course, survived into the archive at Vassar. Mary Morse denies the charge of having burned the letters.

16. A TOTALLY WASTED STRETCH

1. 9 January 1968, Houghton Library.

2. Bishop to Baumann, 6 January 1968, Vassar College Library.

3. An interview with Cass Humble in June 1991 was especially helpful to me in my thinking about the relationship between Elizabeth and Suzanne.

4. Bishop to Barkers, 16 March 1968, Princeton University Library.

5. Bishop to Lowell, 22 October 1968, Houghton Library.

6. Bishop to Summers, 18 December 1968, Vassar College Library.

7. 27 February 1969, Vassar College Library.

8. The drafts of these prose pieces about San Francisco are extremely rough, much rougher than was typical of Bishop. For purposes of readability, I have corrected the many typographical errors.

9. Bishop to Muser, 24 February 1969, Vassar College Library.

10. Bishop to Merrill, 27 February 1969, Vassar College Library.

11. Diane Wakoski, letter to Bishop, 30 April 1975, Vassar College Library.

12. Bishop to Lowell, 20 April 1969, Houghton Library.

13. 18 December 1968, Vassar College Library.

14. Bishop to Brown, 4 January 1969, Princeton University Library.

15. Bishop to Barkers, 31 March 1969, Princeton University Library.

16. Bishop to Lowell, 28 August 1969 [1968], Houghton Library.

17. "Throughout is this quality of thingness," *New York Times Book Review,* 1 June 1969, p. 8.

18. "The Silver Sensibility," *Contemporary Literature* 12, no. 1 (1971): 107.

19. "Elizabeth Bishop's Poems," *Shenandoah* 20, no. 4 (Summer 1969): 100.

20. *Partisan Review* 37 (Spring 1970): 313.

21. Bishop to Baumann, "December sometime" 1969, Vassar College Library.

22. Houghton Library.

23. Bishop to Barkers, 2 January 1970, Princeton University Library.

24. "December sometime" 1969, Vassar College Library.

25. Bishop to Lowell, 27 February 1970, Houghton Library.

26. Bishop to Merrill, 18 January 1970, Vassar College Library.

27. 27 February 1970, Houghton Library.

28. Bishop to Lowell, "December 9 or 10," 1969, Houghton Library.

29. 27 February 1970, Houghton Library.

30. Bishop, letter to Mariette Charlton, 24 February 1970, Houghton Library.

31. 27 February 1970, Houghton Library.

32. 20 May 1970, Princeton University Library.

33. Bishop to Brown, 20 May 1970, Princeton University Library; Bishop to Baumann, 10 June 1970, Vassar College Library.

34. 15 June 1970, Harry Ransom Humanities Research Center, University of Texas, Austin, Texas.

35. Bishop to Bowie, 14 June 1970, and 17 June 1970, Vassar College Library.

36. Bishop to Bowie, 15 June 1970, Vassar College Library.

37. Bishop to Bowie, 10 August 1970, and 14 June 1970, Vassar College Library.

38. 14 June 1970, Vassar College Library.

39. Merrill to Bishop, 29 August 1970; Bishop to Merrill, 30 August 1970, Vassar College Library.

40. Bishop to Barkers, 28 August 1970, Princeton University Library.

17. CRUSOE IN ENGLAND

1. Bishop to Barkers, 6 October 1970, Princeton University Library.

2. *New Yorker* 62, no. 30 (15 September 1986): 90–91.

3. Bishop to Barkers, 12 February 1972, Princeton University Library.

4. Bishop to Bowie, 2 January 1971, Vassar College Library.

5. Bishop to Merrill, 31 March 1971, Vassar College Library.

6. 11 February 1971, Vassar College Library.

7. Bishop to Lowell, 3 May 1971, Harry Ransom Humanities Research Center.

8. Bishop to Lowell, 7 June 1971, Harry Ransom Humanities Research Center.

9. Bishop to Bowers, "Tuesday morning" [14 June 1971], Vassar College Library.

10. 31 July 1971, Vassar College Library.

11. Bishop, letter to Frank Bidart, 27 July 1971, Houghton Library.

12. Bishop to Bowers, 15 September 1971, Vassar College Library.

13. Bishop to Lowell, 27 August 1964, Houghton Library; Bishop to Stevenson, 15 August 1965, Washington University Library.

14. Daniel Defoe, *Robinson Crusoe* (Oxford: Oxford University Press, 1981), pp. 205, 213.

15. Bishop to Lowell, 28 August 1969 [1968], Houghton Library.

16. Bishop to Lowell, 6 October 1960, Houghton Library.

17. *Five Temperaments* (New York: Oxford University Press, 1977), p. 36.

18. Bishop to Barkers, 29 January 1972, Princeton University Library.

19. Bishop to Merrill, 1 February 1972, Vassar College Library.

20. 27 January 1972, Vassar College Library.

18. "HALF GROAN, HALF ACCEPTANCE"

1. Bishop to Lowell, 19 January 1972, Harry Ransom Humanities Research Center.

2. Bishop to Bowie, 2 January 1972, Vassar College Library.

3. Bishop to Bowie, 1 February 1972, Vassar College Library.

4. 5 (Fall-Winter 1971): 79.

5. Bishop to Barkers, 12 February 1972, Princeton University Library.

6. Bishop to Lowell, 10 February 1972, Harry Ransom Humanities Research Center.

7. Bishop to Barkers, 12 February 1972, Princeton University Library.

8. 10 February 1972, Harry Ransom Humanities Research Center.

9. 21 March 1972, Harry Ransom Humanities Research Center.

10. Lowell to Bidart, 10 April 1972, Houghton Library.

11. Harry Ransom Humanities Research Center.

12. 8 September 1972, Princeton University Library.

13. Vassar College Library.

14. "The Art of Poetry," p. 62.

15. The letter to Moore (29 August 1946, Rosenbach Museum and Library) is quoted in chapter 7, pp. 182–183.

16. This reading, as any of this poem must be, is indebted to Helen Vendler, "Domestication, Domesticity, and the Other Worldly," in Schwartz and Estess, *Elizabeth Bishop and Her Art,* pp. 32–48.

17. 26 October 1972, Vassar College Library.

18. Bishop to Barkers, 26 August 1972, Princeton University Library.

19. 6 December 1972, Vassar College Library.

20. Bishop to Baumann, 19 March 1973, Vassar College Library.

21. 30 November 1972, Vassar College Library.

22. 24 March [1972], Vassar College Library.

23. (Chicago: University of Chicago Press, 1981), p. 64.

24. Bishop to Bowers, 17 November 1972, Vassar College Library.

25. *Boston Review* (April 1983): 15.

19. ON THE WAY BACK

1. 15 January 1973, Vassar College Library.

2. Bishop to Lowell, 20 March 1973, Harry Ransom Humanities Research Center.

3. Ibid.

4. Ibid.

5. Bishop to Lowell, 29 April 1973, Harry Ransom Humanities Research Center.

6. Bishop to Lowell, 22 July 1973, Harry Ransom Humanities Research Center.

7. Bishop to MacIver/Frankenberg, "Thursday morning" [18 October 1973], Vassar College Library.

8. Lowell to Bishop, 18 January 1974, Vassar College Library.

9. 22 January 1974, Harry Ransom Humanities Research Center.

10. Bishop, letters to John Malcolm Brinnin, 29 March 1974, and 2 April 1974, University of Delaware Library, Newark, Delaware.

11. Bishop to Lowell, 30 May 1974, Harry Ransom Humanities Research Center.

12. Bishop to Swenson, 22 May [April] 1974, Washington University Library.

13. Bishop to Lowell, 3 September 1974, Harry Ransom Humanities Research Center.

14. 26 May [1975], University of Delaware Library.

15. Bishop to Lowell, 3 September 1974, Harry Ransom Humanities Research Center.

16. Ibid.

17. Bishop to Lowell, 18 October 1974, Harry Ransom Humanities Research Center.

18. Bishop to Lowell, 1 November 1974, Harry Ransom Humanities Research Center.

19. 16 January 1975, Harry Ransom Humanities Research Center.

20. Bishop to Muser, 22 January 1975, Vassar College Library.

21. No poems fitting this description are among Bishop's papers at Vassar.

22. Bishop to Lowell, 1 August 1975, Harry Ransom Humanities Research Center.

23. Bishop to Charlton, 12 July 1975, Houghton Library.

24. 10 September 1975, Vassar College Library.

25. Bishop to Barkers, 22 September 1975, Princeton University Library.

26. 29 November 1975, Vassar College Library.

27. "Shifting Islands: Elizabeth Bishop's Manuscripts," *Shenandoah* 33, no. 1 (1982): 55–57.

28. "The Art of Poetry," p. 64.

29. 8 January 1964, Washington University Library.

30. 16 January 1976, Vassar College Library.

31. [February 1976], University of Delaware Library.

32. "Laureate's Words of Acceptance," p. 12.

33. Bishop to Barkers, 19 April 1976, Princeton University Library.

34. Bishop to Bidart, 14 June 1976, Houghton Library.

35. Bishop to Barkers, 18 July 1976, Princeton University Library.

36. Ibid.

37. Bishop to Barkers, 28 August 1976, Princeton University Library.

38. Bishop to Lowell, 21 August 1976, Harry Ransom Humanities Research Center.

20. NORTH HAVEN

1. "New Books in Review," *Yale Review* 66 (Spring 1977): 419.
2. "Books Considered: Geography III by Elizabeth Bishop," *New Republic* 176, no. 6 (5 February 1977): 29.
3. Alfred Corn, *Georgia Review* 31 (1977): 533.
4. Margo Jefferson, "The Map Maker," *Newsweek* 89 (31 January 1977): 73.
5. "The Other Bishop," *Canto* 1 (Winter 1977): 168.
6. Bishop to Baumann, 10 February 1977, Vassar College Library.
7. Bishop to Barkers, 8 March 1977, Princeton University Library.
8. Bishop to Barkers, 8 July 1977, Princeton University Library.
9. Bishop to MacIver, 21 June 1977, Vassar College Library.
10. Bishop to Bowie, 26 January 1978, Vassar College Library.
11. Bishop to Baumann, 7 January 1978, Vassar College Library.
12. Bishop to Barkers, 21 February 1978, Princeton University Library.
13. Bishop to Barkers, 19 April 1978, Princeton University Library.
14. Ibid.
15. Bishop to Baumann, 30 June 1978, Vassar College Library.
16. 11 September 1978, Vassar College Library.
17. Bishop to Barkers, 4 December 1978, Princeton University Library.
18. Bishop to Summers, 1 March 1979, Vassar College Library.
19. Bishop to Barkers, 4 December 1978, Princeton University Library.
20. Bishop to Brinnin, 16 November 1978, University of Delaware Library.
21. Bishop to Barkers, 1 February 1979, Princeton University Library.
22. Bishop to Muser, 22 January 1979, Vassar College Library.
23. Bishop to Merrill, 23 January 1979, Vassar College Library.
24. Bishop to Bowie, 9 February 1979, Vassar College Library.
25. Bishop, letter to Octavio Paz, 8 February 1979, Vassar College Library.
26. This reading was first suggested by Charles Sanders, "Bishop's 'Sonnet,' " *Explicator* 40, no. 3 (Spring 1982): 63–64.
27. Bishop to Barkers, 11 July 1979, Princeton University Library.

BIBLIOGRAPHY

COLLECTIONS IN LIBRARIES

Berg, Henry W. and Albert A., Collection. New York Public Library; Astor, Lenox, and Tilden Foundations, New York, New York. Quotations from materials in this collection are used with permission from Wayne Furman of the library and from Alice Methfessel, executor of Elizabeth Bishop's literary estate.

Bishop, Elizabeth. Letters to Ilse and Kit Barker and letters to Ashley Brown. Princeton University Library, Princeton, New Jersey. Quotations from materials in this collection are used with permission from Don C. Skemer of the library and from Alice Methfessel.

———. Letters to John Malcolm Brinnin. John Malcolm Brinnin Papers, University of Delaware Library, Newark, Delaware. Quotations from materials in this collection are used with permission from Timothy Murray of the library and from Alice Methfessel.

———. Letters to Carley Dawson. University of Oregon Library, Eugene, Oregon. Quotations from materials in this collection are used with permission from J. Fraser Cocks of the library and from Alice Methfessel.

———. Letters to Robert Lowell, 1970–1977. Harry Ransom Humanities Research Center, University of Texas, Austin, Texas. Quotations from materials in this collection are used with permission from Alice Methfessel.

———. Letters to Marianne Moore. Marianne Moore Papers, Rosenbach Museum and Library, Philadelphia, Pennsylvania. Quotations from materials in this collection are used with permission from Natania Rosenfeld of the library and from Alice Methfessel.

———. Letters to May Swenson; and May Swenson, letters to Elizabeth Bishop. Washington University Library Special Collections, St. Louis, Missouri. Quotations from materials in this collection are used with permission from Kevin Ray of the library, from Alice Methfessel, and from Rozanne Knudson, executor of May Swenson's literary estate.

———. Papers. Houghton Library, Harvard University, Cambridge, Massachusetts. Quotations from materials in this collection are used with permission from Elizabeth A. Falsey of the library and from Alice Methfessel.

———. Papers. Vassar College Library Special Collections, Poughkeepsie, New York. Quotations from materials in this collection are used with permission from Nancy McKechnie of the library; from Alice Methfessel; from James Merrill; from Frank Bidart, executor of Robert Lowell's literary estate; and from Marianne C. Moore, literary executor of the estate of Marianne Moore.

An Anthology of Twentieth Century Brazilian Poetry, edited by Elizabeth Bishop and Emanuel Brasil. Introduction by Elizabeth Bishop. Middletown, Conn.: Wesleyan University Press, 1972.

The Battle of the Burglar of Babylon. New York: Farrar, Straus, and Giroux, 1968.

Brazil (with the editors of *Life*). New York: Time-Life Books, 1962.

"A Brief Reminiscence and a Brief Tribute." *Harvard Advocate* 108 (1974): 47–48.

"Chimney Sweepers." *Vassar Review* 19 (Spring 1933): 8–10, 36.

The Collected Prose. New York: Farrar, Straus, and Giroux, 1984. Copyright © Alice Helen Methfessel. Introduction copyright © 1984 by Robert Giroux. Reprinted by permission of Farrar, Straus, & Giroux, Inc.

Complete Poems. New York: Farrar, Straus, and Giroux, 1969.

The Complete Poems, 1927–1979. New York: Farrar, Straus, and Giroux. 1983. Quotations from Bishop's published poems are from this edition unless otherwise noted. Copyright © 1979, 1983 by Alice Helen Methfessel. Reprinted by permission of Farrar, Straus & Giroux, Inc.

"Dimensions for a Novel." *Vassar Journal of Undergraduate Studies* 8 (May 1934): 95–103.

"Flannery O'Connor, 1925–1964." *New York Review of Books* 3 (8 October 1964): 21.

Geography III. New York: Farrar, Straus, and Giroux, 1976.

"Gerard Manley Hopkins: Notes on Timing in His Poetry." *Vassar Review* 23 (February 1934): 5–7.

"An Inadequate Tribute." In *Randall Jarrell: 1914–1965,* edited by Robert Lowell, Peter Taylor, and Robert Penn Warren. New York: Farrar, Straus, and Giroux, 1967, p. 20.

"It All Depends." In *Mid-Century American Poets,* edited by John Ciardi. New York: Twayne, 1950, p. 267.

" 'I Was But Just Awake.' " Review of *Come Hither: A Collection of Rhymes and Poems for the Young of All Ages,* by Walter de la Mare. *Poetry* 93 (October 1958): 50–54.

"Laureate's Words of Acceptance." *World Literature Today* 51, no. 1 (Winter 1977): 12.

Letter to the Editor. *Little Magazine* 5 (Fall-Winter 1971): 79.

Letter to the Editor. *New Republic* 146, no. 18 (30 April 1962): 22.

North & South. Boston: Houghton Mifflin, 1946.

"On the Railroad Named Delight." *New York Times Magazine,* 7 March 1965, pp. 30–31, 84–86.

Poems: North & South—A Cold Spring. Boston: Houghton Mifflin, 1955.

Questions of Travel. New York: Farrar, Straus, and Giroux, 1965.

Review of *XIAPE: 71 Poems,* by e. e. cummings. *United States Quarterly Book Review* 6 (June 1950): 160–161.

"A Sentimental Tribute." Review of *The Marianne Moore Reader. Bryn Mawr Alumnae Bulletin* (Spring 1962): 3.

"Time's Andromedas." *Vassar Journal of Undergraduate Studies* 7 (1933): 102–103.

"Unseemly Deductions." *New Republic* 127, no. 7 (18 August 1950): 20.

"What the Young Man Said to the Psalmist." *Poetry* 79 (January 1952): 213.

Trans. *The Diary of Helena Morley,* by Alice Brant. New York: Farrar, Straus, and Giroux, 1957.

Trans. "Three Stories by Clarice Lispector." *Kenyon Review* 26 (Summer 1964): 500–511.

WORKS ABOUT ELIZABETH BISHOP AND
OTHER WORKS OF INTEREST

Anon. "Poetry in English, 1945–1962." *Time* 79, no. 10 (9 March 1962): 92–95.

Ashbery, John. "Throughout is this quality of thingness." Review of *Complete Poems* (1969), by Elizabeth Bishop. *New York Times Book Review*, 1 June 1969, pp. 8, 25.

Baker, Sheridan. "Books." Review of *Questions of Travel*, by Elizabeth Bishop. *Michigan Quarterly Review* 6 (Fall 1967): 296–298.

Barnard, Mary. *Assault on Mount Helicon*. Berkeley and Los Angeles: University of California Press, 1984.

Blasing, Motlu Konuk. "Mont D'Espoir or Mount Despair: The Re-Verses of Elizabeth Bishop." *Contemporary Literature* 25, no. 3 (Fall 1984): 341–353.

Bloom, Harold. "Books Considered: *Geography III* by Elizabeth Bishop." *New Republic* 176, no. 6 (5 February 1977): 29.

Booth, Phillip. "The Poet as Voyager." Review of *Questions of Travel*, by Elizabeth Bishop. *Christian Science Monitor*, 6 January 1966, p. 10.

Bromwich, David. "Elizabeth Bishop's Dream Houses." *Raritan* 4, no. 1 (Summer 1984): 77–94.

Corn, Alfred. Review of *Geography III*, by Elizabeth Bishop. *Georgia Review* 31 (1977): 533–537.

Costello, Bonnie. *Elizabeth Bishop: Questions of Mastery*. Cambridge, Mass.: Harvard University Press, 1991.

Dardis, Thomas. *The Thirsty Muse: Alcohol and the American Writer*. New York: Ticknor and Fields, 1988.

Davison, Peter. "The Gilt Edge of Reputation." Review of *Questions of Travel*, by Elizabeth Bishop. *Atlantic* (June 1966): 36.

Edelman, Lee. "The Geography of Gender: Elizabeth Bishop's 'In the Waiting Room.' " *Wisconsin Studies in Contemporary Literature* 26, no. 2 (Summer 1985): 179–196.

Ellman, Richard, and Robert O'Clair, eds. *The Norton Anthology of Modern Poetry.* New York: Norton, 1988.

Frankenberg, Lloyd. "A Meritorious Prize Winner." Review of *North & South,* by Elizabeth Bishop. *Saturday Review,* 12 October 1946, p. 46.

Garrigue, Jean. "Elizabeth Bishop's School." Review of *Questions of Travel,* by Elizabeth Bishop. *New Leader* 48 (6 December 1965): 22–23.

Gibbs, Barbara. "A Just Vision." *Poetry* 69 (January 1947): 230.

Gioia, Dana. "Studying With Miss Bishop." *New Yorker* 62, no. 30 (15 September 1986): 90–91.

Goldensohn, Lorrie. "Elizabeth Bishop: An Unpublished, Untitled Poem." *American Poetry Review* (January-February 1988): 35–46.

————. *Elizabeth Bishop: The Biography of a Poetry.* New York: Columbia University Press, 1991.

Greenhalgh, Anne Merrill. *A Concordance to Elizabeth Bishop's Poetry.* New York: Garland, 1985.

Hamilton, Ian. *Robert Lowell.* New York: Random House, 1982.

Jarrell, Randall. *Poetry and the Age.* New York: Knopf, 1953.

Jefferson, Margo. "The Map Maker." Review of *Geography III,* by Elizabeth Bishop. *Newsweek* 89 (31 January 1977): 73–74.

Johnson, Alexandra. "Artists and Their Inspiration: Poet Elizabeth Bishop: Geography of the Imagination." *Christian Science Monitor,* 23 March 1977, pp. 20–21.

Kalstone, David. "All Eye." Review of *Complete Poems* (1969), by Elizabeth Bishop. *Partisan Review* 37 (Spring 1970): 310–315.

————. *Becoming a Poet.* New York: Farrar, Straus, and Giroux, 1989.

————. *Five Temperaments.* New York: Oxford University Press, 1977.

Kees, Weldon. Letter to Norris Gerry, 18 March 1950. Quoted in "The New York Intellectuals, 1941–50: Some Letters by Weldon Kees." *Hudson Review* 38, no. 1 (Spring 1985): 15–55.

Keller, Lynn. "Words Worth a Thousand Postcards: The Bishop/Moore Correspondence." *American Literature* 55, no. 3 (October 1983): 405–429.

Lipking, Lawrence. *The Life of the Poet.* Chicago: University of Chicago Press, 1981.

Lowell, Robert. "Thomas, Bishop, and Williams." Review of *North & South*, by Elizabeth Bishop. *Sewanee Review* 55 (July-September 1947): 498.

Lucie-Smith, Edward. "No Jokes in Portuguese." *Times* (London), 26 July 1964, p. 36.

McClatchy, J. D. "The Other Bishop." Review of *Geography III*, by Elizabeth Bishop. *Canto* 1 (Winter 1977): 165–174.

McMahon, Candace. *Elizabeth Bishop: A Bibliography, 1927–1979.* Charlottesville: University Press of Virginia, 1980.

Martz, Louis. "Recent Poetry: Looking for a Home." Review of *Questions of Travel*, by Elizabeth Bishop. *Yale Review* 55 (Spring 1966): 458–460.

Mazzaro, Jerome. "Elizabeth Bishop's Poems." Review of *Complete Poems* (1969), by Elizabeth Bishop. *Shenandoah* 20, no. 4 (Summer 1969): 99–101.

Mazzocco, Robert. "A Poet of Landscape." Review of *Questions of Travel*, by Elizabeth Bishop. *New York Review of Books*, no. 9 (12 October 1967): 4–6.

Merrin, Jeredith. *An Enabling Humility: Marianne Moore, Elizabeth Bishop, and the Uses of Tradition.* New Brunswick, N.J.: Rutgers University Press, 1990.

Moss, Howard. "All Praise." Review of *Questions of Travel,* by Elizabeth Bishop. *Kenyon Review* 28 (March 1966): 255–262.

Mueller, Lisel. "The Sun the Other Way Around." Review of *Questions of Travel,* by Elizabeth Bishop. *Poetry* 108 (August 1966): 335–337.

Page, Barbara. "Shifting Islands: Elizabeth Bishop's Manuscripts." *Shenandoah* 33, no. 1 (1982): 51–62.

Parker, Robert Dale. *The Unbeliever.* Urbana: University of Illinois Press, 1988.

Rich, Adrienne. "The Eye of the Outsider: The Poetry of Elizabeth Bishop." *Boston Review* (April 1983): 15–17.

Rodman, Seldon. "Carefully Revealed." Review of *North & South,* by Elizabeth Bishop. *New York Times Book Review,* 27 October 1946, p. 18.

Sanders, Charles. "Bishop's 'Sonnet.' " *Explicator* 40, no. 3 (Spring 1982): 63–64.

Schwartz, Lloyd. "Annals of Poetry (Elizabeth Bishop and Brazil)." *New Yorker* 67, no. 32 (30 September 1991): 85–97.

Schwartz, Lloyd, and Sybil Estess, eds. *Elizabeth Bishop and Her Art.* Ann Arbor: University of Michigan Press, 1983.

Scott, Nathan A., Jr. "Elizabeth Bishop: Poet Without Myth." *Virginia Quarterly Review* 60 (Spring 1984): 255–275.

Sheehan, Donald. "The Silver Sensibility: Five Recent Books of American Poetry." Review of *Complete Poems* (1969), by Elizabeth Bishop. *Contemporary Literature* 12, no. 1 (Winter 1971): 106–110.

Shore, Jane. "Elizabeth Bishop: The Art of Changing Your Mind." *Ploughshares* 5 (1979): 178–191.

Smith, William Jay. "New Books of Poems." Review of *Questions of Travel,* by Elizabeth Bishop. *Harper's* 233 (August 1966): 89–91.

Spires, Elizabeth. "An Afternoon with Elizabeth Bishop." *Vassar Quarterly* (Winter 1979): 7–8.

———. "The Art of Poetry XXVII" (interview with Elizabeth Bishop). *Paris Review* 23 (Summer 1981): 57–83.

Stanford, Donald. "From the Letters of Elizabeth Bishop, 1933–1934." *Verse* 4, no. 3 (November 1987): 19–27.

Stevenson, Anne. *Elizabeth Bishop.* New York: Twayne, 1966.

Thomas, Harriet Tompkins. "Travels with a Young Poet: Elizabeth Bishop." *Vassar Quarterly* (Winter 1986): 20.

Tomlinson, Charles, ed. *Marianne Moore: A Collection of Critical Essays.* Englewood Cliffs, N.J.: Prentice-Hall, 1969.

Travisano, Thomas. *Elizabeth Bishop: Her Artistic Development.* Charlottesville: University Press of Virginia, 1988.

Weeks, Edward. "The Atlantic Bookshelf." Review of *North & South,* by Elizabeth Bishop. *Atlantic* (August 1946): 148.

Wehr, Wesley. "Elizabeth Bishop: Conversations and Class Notes." *Antioch Review* 39 (Summer 1981): 319–328.

INDEX

Abrahams, Billy, 485
Academy of American Poets, 402, 491, 498, 520
Adams, Leonie, 209, 210, 212, 219
Aguirre, Isa, 343, 385
Aiken, Conrad, 227
Alberto and Maria (servants at Samambaia), 316
Alcohol, 105, 111, 123, 185, 191
Alcoholism, 28. *See also* Bishop, Elizabeth: alcoholism
Aleijadinho (Antônio Francisco Lisbôa), 359
Alfred, William, 292, 432, 435, 455, 461, 463, 479
Alice in Wonderland, 220, 279
Alisette Mara (child of Maria, servant at Samambaia), 297
Allen, Oliver E., 327
Allen, Ross, 114
Alliance Française, 93
Almyda, Hannah, 144, 162–64, 171, 173
Amado, Jorge, 366
Amazon River, 304, 306–10, 312, 313, 316, 534–37. *See also* Bishop, Elizabeth: travels
American Academy of Arts and Letters, 187, 233

Ames, Elizabeth, 209, 213, 215, 227
Amsterdam, 250, 382, 521, 522
Anderson, Hans Christian, 30, 108
Antabuse, 212. *See also* Bishop, Elizabeth: alcoholism
Anthon, Catherine Scott, 238
Antwerp, Belgium, 88
Aristophanes, 44
Arizona, University of, 403
Arkansas, University of, 539
Arles, France, 127
Armstrong, Phyllis, 220
Aruba, 293, 448
Ashbery, John, 416, 517, 520
Asthma, 126, 305, 339. *See also* Bishop, Elizabeth: illnesses: asthma
Aswell, Edward, 92, 93
Atlantic Monthly, 183, 503
Auden, W. H., 50–51, 67, 78, 118, 121, 384–85, 483, 499; death of, 341

Bach, Johann Sebastian, 74
Baker, Sheridan, 372
Baptist Church, 2, 14, 16, 17, 90
Barata, Ruy, 310
Bard College, 203, 208
Bardot, Brigitte, 407

Barker, Ilse, 339, 393, 400, 541; correspondence with EB, 258, 307, 340, 523, 529; EB visits to, 355, 356, 382, 521, 544, 548; visits to EB, 487, 541; at Yaddo, 1950, 228

Barker, Kit, 339, 393, 400; correspondence with EB, 258, 307, 523, 529; EB visits to, 355, 356, 382, 521, 544, 548; paintings, 441, 500, 541; visits to EB, 487, 541; at Yaddo, 1950, 228

Barker, Thomas Crispin, 340, 355, 487, 541

Barnard, Mary, 46, 146

Baro, Gene, 356

Baudelaire, Charles, 196, 263

Baumann, Dr. Anny, 235, 246, 297, 392, 456, 461; EB correspondence with, 191, 201, 211, 222, 228, 229, 245, 251, 258, 374, 378, 382, 429, 473, 474, 513, 515, 516, 528; EB visits to, 200, 212, 234, 289, 326, 520; as EB's physician, 191, 216, 219, 220, 233, 244, 245, 249, 397, 404, 422, 442, 455, 504, 505, 516, 533, 540; and Lota Soares's death, 395, 396, 400; visits to EB, 358–59

Baumgarten, Bernice, 257

Beach, Sylvia, 92; death of, 341

Beatles, The, 409

Bell, Pearl (Kazin), 215, 218, 235, 243, 289

Belo Horizonte, Brazil, 286, 431

Bennett, Peggy, 228

Bennington College, 539

Beppo (dog), 20, 28

Berkeley (University of California), 400, 403, 406, 407, 415, 419, 433, 524

Berryman, John, 146, 150, 343, 360, 361, 390, 513; death of, 459, 461; as subject in EB's work, 414

Bidart, Frank, 461, 463, 473, 481, 488, 499, 518, 531, 537, 540, 544, 555n.1; correspondence with EB, 445; and EB's poems, 466, 488, 494, 503, 512, 540; friendship with EB, 438, 455, 457, 478, 486, 495, 497, 521, 522

Bishop, Elizabeth: alcoholism, 93, 147–53, 162, 173, 191, 198, 200, 201, 211–12, 217, 223, 227–29, 251, 262, 370, 375, 381, 397, 401–2, 414, 418, 420–21, 430, 436, 484, 488–89, 504, 505–6, 508, 514–16; Antabuse, 152, 249, 262, 382, 397, 414, 436, 506, 516; hospitalizations, 213–14, 227–28, 262, 350; origins, 4, 5–6, 41, 43, 148–49; as subject in EB's work, 152, 230–31, 384, 448, 546; treatments, 180, 194, 249

—as teacher, 374, 378–79, 433–34, 438, 439, 453, 474, 489, 525, 533; philosophy, 343, 480–81

—attitudes about race, 144, 363–65, 409–10

—childhood, 1–30, 60, 252–53, 256–57, 266–71, 329, 357

—college writing, 44–46, 49–55, 58

—comments on poetry: her own, 73, 106, 137, 157, 170, 195, 313–14, 324, 340, 352, 394, 413, 544; in general, 72–73, 218, 322–23, 341, 346, 390, 394, 413, 424, 461–63; other people's, 105, 165, 197, 294–95, 323, 331–33, 342–43, 356–57, 361, 379, 413–14, 415, 425, 461–63, 485–86, 489–90, 521

—correspondence, 37–39, 258–61, 321, 341, 342, 375, 381, 444

—death of, 549–50

—early writing, 33–37

—education: college, 41–60; elementary school, 30; high school, 30–40; Primer Class, 15

—employment, 71, 171–72, 219, 227, 352–53, 361, 374–80, 433–34, 472–74, 484–85, 528, 533–34, 538, 547, 549

—family history, 2–3

—financial circumstances, 41–42, 71, 174, 296, 311, 316, 402, 454, 456, 482, 490

—on gender issues 23, 26–27, 331–33, 334, 343, 460, 479, 542

—honorary degrees, Brandeis, 539; Brown, 465; Dalhousie University, 547; Princeton, 548; Rutgers, 465; Smith College, 403

—honors and awards: Academy of American Poets (1964), 359, 370; Book Critics' Circle Award (1977), 519; Books Abroad/Neustadt International Prize for Literature (1976), 517–18, 519–20, 529; Chapelbrook Foundation Fellowship (1960),

Prodigal," 149, 211, 230–31; "Quai d'Orleans," 125–26, 134, 141, 175, 184, 535; "Questions of Travel," 240, 260, 273–75 (drafts), 507, 536; *Questions of Travel*, 13, 253, 300, 323, 328, 337, 340, 347, 360, 392, 416, 450, 517, (publication of) 366–67, 372, (reviews) 372–73, 380; "Rain Towards Morning," 176; "Rainy Season; Sub-Tropics," 315, 386–88, 411, 420; "The Reprimand," 51, 76, 92; "The Riverman," 273, 304, 306, 313; "Roosters," 67, 107, 131, 155, 158–60, 165, 166, 179, 184; "Sandpiper," 116, 334–35, 516, 517; "Santarém," 308, 309–10, 519, 531, 534–37, 538, 546 (drafts), 536; "Seascape," 84, 131, 165, 546; "Sestina," 13, 14, 267–68, 329, 330; "The Shampoo," 247–48, 252, 254, 265; "Sleeping on the Ceiling," 84, 89, 90, 92, 134, 144, 152; "Sleeping Standing Up," 84, 92, 134, 144; "Some Dreams They Forgot," 55, 411; "Song for the Rainy Season," 304–6, 313; "Song," 109, 122, 411; "Songs for a Colored Singer," 81, 172, 173, 174, 273, 365; "Sonnet" (1928), 34; "Sonnet" (1979), 100–101, 519, 536, 538, 545–47; "Squatter's Children," 268–70; "A Summer's Dream," 191; "Sunday at Key West," 138; "Thank-You Note," 414; "The Colder the Air," 93, 101–2; "Three Sonnets for the Eyes," 50; "Three Valentines," 55, 76, 92; "Thunder," 33; "Trouvée," 404–5; "Twelfth Morning or What You Will," 299–300, 351; "12 O'Clock News," 121, 464, 474, 526; "The Unbeliever," 84, 109, 116, 141; "Under the Window: Ouro Prêto," 369, 380, 384, 392; "Varick Street," 56, 188, 189; "View of the Capitol from the Library of Congress," 223, 230, 516; "Visits to St. Elizabeths," 143, 222, 280–84, 425, 478; "Wading at Wellfleet," 67, 178; "The Wave," 34; "The Weed," 84, 90, 107, 108, 118–20, 166; "While Someone Telephones," 217; "A Word with You," 50

—unpublished poetry: "Prince 'Winsome' Mannerly," 91; "A mother made of dress-goods," 12–13; "After the Rain," 254; "Apartment in Leme," 344, 366; "Aubade and Elegy," 427; "aviary villanelle," 346, 508; "Baby's Grave," 178; "Bone Key," 178; "Brasil, 1959," 300–301; "Crossing the Equator," 236, 254; "Dear Dr. Foster," 180; "A Drunkard," 4–6, 43, 148, 150, 313, 523; "Edgar Allan Poe," 178; *Elegy*, 538; "Far far away there, where i met," 411; "First Syllables," 30; "Florida Revisited," 523–24; "The Foggy Summer," 538; "Geographical Mirror," 182, 192; *Grandmother's Glass Eye*, 538; "Hannah A.," 163; "In the dark night," 412; "INVENTORY," 385, 420; "It is marvellous to wake up together," 176, 177–78; "Juke-Box," 178; "Key West," 178; "A Letter to Two Friends," 314–15; "Monica, falling asleep," 346; "Ode to Sammy," 481, 519, 540; "On the Amazon," 308–9; "The Owl's Journey," 217; "Poem from 1935," 78; "Poem: For M.B.S., buried in Nova Scotia," 158; "The Proper Tears," 91; "Salem Willows," 29; "The Salesman's Evening," 178; "THIS IS NOT A BILL," 531; "The Trip to the Interior," 346; "Vague Poem," 437; "Verdigris," 224, 239, 508; "We are God's angels, we are, we are," 104; "We lived in a pocket of Time," 16, 19; "Where are the dolls who loved me so," 22

—prose: "The Baptism," 19, 36, 90, 108, 265; *Brazil*, Life World Library, 324–26, 327–29; "Chimney Sweepers," 54; "The Country Mouse," 19–23, 27–28, 253; "Dimensions for a Novel," 44; "Efforts of Affection," 58, 68, 108, 333–34, 404, 462; "The Farmer's Children," 19, 36; "Gerard Manley Hopkins: Notes on Timing in his Poetry," 52–54; "Giant Weather," 35, 386; "Gregorio Valdes," 139, 147, 156; "Gwendolyn," 14, 18, 19, 37, 252, 262;

Bishop, Elizabeth: prose (*continued*),
"The Hanging of the Mouse," 109,
117, 118, 411; "I Was But Just Awake"
(review), 270–71; "In Prison," 134–37,
315, 425, 492; "In the Village," 3, 6,
8–11, 13, 14, 16, 19, 24, 27, 148, 214,
252–53, 257, 262, 267, 330, 360, 366,
373, 411, 424, 485; "An Inadequate
Tribute," 380; "Introduction" to *The
Diary of Helena Morley*, 257, 286; "It
All Depends," 218; "The Last Animal," 54; "Love From Emily"
(review), 225; "Memories of Uncle
Neddy," 14, 18, 19, 149, 253, 294, 329,
330, 502; "Mercedes Hospital," 156,
501; "Mr. Pope's Garden," 55; "On
Being Alone," 35; "On the Railroad
Named Delight," 362–65; "Picking
Mushrooms," 37; "Primer Class," 15,
19, 28, 253, 500, 540, 544; review of
Brooks, *Annie Allen*, 224; review of
cummings, *XAIPE*, 224; "The Sea and
Its Shore," 66, 71, 92, 109–11, 116,
492; "A Sentimental Tribute," 333;
"Seven Days Monologue," 50; "Then
Came the Poor," 49, 50, 58; "The
Three Wells," 36; "Time's Androme-
das," 44, 45, 53, 239; "A Trip to
Vigia," 287, 310–11; "The U.S.A.
School of Writing," 71–73;
"Unseemly Deductions" (review), 238;
"What the Young Man Said to the
Psalmist" (review), 3
—unpublished prose: "Americanism,"
21, 29; "At Mrs. Pindar's," 137; *Black
Beans and Diamonds*, 367, 402, 440,
441; "Embarrassment and Tact," 134;
"Grandmother's Glass EYE—an Essay
on Style," 118; "Homesickness," 201;
"The Labors of Hannibal," 118, 121;
"Lucius" stories, 6–8, 10–11, 14, 17–18,
19, 20, 60, 148, 214, 474; "May Day,"
358; "Mrs. Sullivan Downstairs," 28–
29; "The Sandpiper's Revenge," 116,
334; "A Trip on the Rio São Francisco," 391–92; "W. H. Auden: The
Mechanics of Pretense," 121;
—translations: 225, 287, 411, 423–24,
503, 519; *Anthology of Twentieth Cen-*

tury Brazilian Poetry, 402, 404, 423,
424, 431, 465; *The Diary of Helena
Morley*, 256–58, 263, 285–86, 288, 289,
292, 321, 528, 529, (publication of)
296, (reviews) 296; Clarice Lispector
stories, 337–38
Bishop, Florence, 20, 25, 46, 289, 326
Bishop, Gertrude May (Boomer), 2, 3, 8,
21, 173, 252, 321, 329, 422, 429, 430,
470, 505, 547; death of, 6, 60; por-
trait, 17–18, 293
Bishop, John W., 2, 19
Bishop, John W., Jr., 20
Bishop, Sarah Anne (Foster), 2, 19
Bishop, William Thomas, 2, 21, 173
Bissier, Julius, 390
Black Panther Party, 409
Blackburn, Roma, 539, 540, 549
Blackwood, Lady Caroline, 473
Blais, Marie-Claire, 517
Blake, William, 334
Bloom, Harold, 486, 527, 538
Blue Pencil, The, 33, 35, 501
Blum, Harry, 326
Bly, Robert, 356, 420
Blythewood (Conn.), 213–14, 216
Bogan, Louise, 290, 424
Books Abroad/World Literature Today,
517–18
Boomer, Arthur, 14, 294; portrait, 17–18,
293–94
Boomer, Elizabeth (Hutchinson), 2, 8,
14, 18, 19, 29, 36, 257, 295, 321, 406,
469, 470, 475
Boomer, Frank, 4, 17
Boomer, William Brown, 2, 14, 19, 29,
267, 295, 470, 475
Booth, Phillip, 373
Borden, Fannie, 58, 59
Boston, Mass., 2, 3, 21, 39, 57, 60, 290,
335, 454, 460, 465, 473, 533, 550; EB
visits to, 32, 46, 47, 121, 132–33, 143,
182, 208, 289, 432, 443, 456; EB's residence there, 497–550; Lewis Wharf,
82, 464, 482, 490, 497–550; as subject
in EB's work, 3
Boston College, 543
Boston University, 435, 498, 501, 518

Casa Mariana (Ouro Prêto, Brazil), 391, 393, 397, 402, 417, 418, 425, 483, 489, 495, 513, 528; EB's purchase of, 370–71, 374
Casson, Jean, 89
Castelo Branco, Humberto de Alencar, 354, 381
Castine, Maine, 202, 290, 292, 394, 486, 496
Castro, Fernando de, 362, 365, 367
Cather, Willa, 548
Catholicism, 130, 167, 211, 242, 273, 300, 357, 363, 366, 393
Caudwell, Christopher, 127
Cezanne, Paul, 443, 472
Chambrun, Comte and Comtesse de, 90
Charlton, Mariette, 326, 440, 441
Chatto and Windus, 382, 521
Chekhov, Anton, 352
Chicago, Ill., 405, 406, 439
Ciardi, John, 217, 543
Clark, Eleanor, 46, 220, 289
Clark, Eunice, 46
Clavichord, 81–82, 93, 95, 103, 113, 153, 165, 226, 245, 409
Cleaver, Eldridge, 407, 409
Cleaver, Kathleen, 409–10
Coe, Priscilla, 326
Coelho, Joaquim-Francisco, 310
Colby College (Maine), 548
Coleridge, Samuel Taylor, 64, 110, 259, 288
Colt Press, 165
Columbia University, 82
Communism, 98, 327, 353–55, 364
Con Spirito (Vassar), 49–50, 54, 411
Confessional poetry, 255, 323, 331, 361, 394, 413–14, 462, 489–90, 513
Congress for Cultural Freedom, 326, 335
Contemporary Poetry and Prose, 108
Cootchie, 138, 273
Corn, Alfred, 527
Cornell, Joseph, 339, 516, 519
Cornell Medical School, 106
Correia de Araújo, Lilli, 264, 316, 359, 362, 370, 371, 565n.16 and 20; EB correspondence with, 375–76; relationship with EB, 368–70
Correia de Araújo, Pedro, 264

Correio da Manha (Rio de Janeiro), 362
Cousteau, Jacques, 465
Crane, Hart, 216
Crane, Louise, 46, 57, 97, 117, 210, 461, 498, 515; car accident (1937), 124, 129; letters to her mother, 91; relationship with EB, 38, 60, 103, 107, 143, 153, 156; and 624 White Street, Key West, 139; travels with EB, 89, 90–98, 102–3, 112, 121–32, 139, 153
Crashaw, Richard, 45, 52, 141, 159, 271
Croll, M. W., 54
Cross, Hilary, 478
cummings, e. e., 135, 170, 224, 289, 310, 361, 458, 481, 514; death of, 341
Cuttyhunk Island, Mass., 62–63, 104, 263

Dalhousie University, 234
Dante Alighieri, 486
Dartmouth, Nova Scotia, 11, 60, 180, 547
Darwin, Charles, 89, 259, 346, 351, 356, 357, 367, 446, 448, 451
Daumier, Honoré, 219, 529
Davison, Peter, 373
Dawson, Carley, 199, 201, 202, 211, 213, 214, 216
De Kooning, Willem, 326
de la Mare, Walter, 270–71
DeBrisay, Elsie, 180
Defoe, Daniel, 447–51, 466. See also Robinson Crusoe
Delacroix, Eugène, 265
Delaney, Beauford, 228
Dewey, Jane, 295; EB visits to, 208, 219, 289, 326, 404, 438, 446; farm in Havre de Grace, Maryland, 223, 227, 233, 394; friendship with EB, 146
Dewey, John, 146, 174, 180, 187, 195
Di Prima, Diane, 521–22
Diamantina, Brazil, 256–57, 285–86, 296
DiCapua, Michael, 484
Dickinson, Emily, 63, 225, 237–38, 314, 331
Didion, Joan, 408
Directions: A Quarterly Review of Literature, 83
Dolmetsch, Arnold, 81, 93

Giroux, Robert; as EB's editor, 286, 289, 292, 366, 411, 417, 425, 538; friendship with EB, 380, 395, 437, 461, 484, 501
Glacier National Park, 484
Glide Memorial Church (San Francisco), 413
Godine, David R., 548
Gold, Arthur, 289, 394, 401, 419
Goldensohn, Lorrie, 558n.11
Good Times (San Francisco), 415
Goulart, João, 317, 327, 352, 353, 354
Goya, Francisco José, 102
Grace Church, 2, 173
Great Depression, 73
Great Village, Nova Scotia, 3, 15–16, 19, 32, 133, 157, 180, 293, 347; EB visits to 180–83, 486; EB's residence there, 13–19, 243; as setting for EB's work, 6, 13, 19, 36; as subject in EB's work, 158, 475
Greece, 442, 544, 547–48. *See also* Bishop, Elizabeth: travels
Greenberg, Clement, 289
Greenslet, Ferris, 174, 179, 183, 187
Greenwich Village, New York City, 170, 224
Gregory, Horace, 174, 188
Grifalconi, Anne, 393
Grimm, Jacob and Wilhelm, 30
Guggenheim Fellowship, 187. *See also* Bishop, Elizabeth: honors and awards
Guggenheim Museum, 404, 415, 533
Gunn, Thom, 400, 413, 415

Haiti, 130, 211, 242, 258
Halifax, Nova Scotia, 403, 404
Hall, Donald, 255, 341, 356
Hamilton, Ian, 202, 291
Hansen, Polly, 227, 228, 289
Harcourt Brace, 156, 157, 165, 174
Hardwick, Elizabeth, 226, 485, 496; and *The Dolphin,* 461, 463, 485; EB correspondence with, 212, 225, 290; EB visits to, 326; marriage to Robert Lowell, 203, 215, 473, 531; and *New York Review of Books,* 340, 351, 360; visit to Brazil (1962), 335
Harper and Brothers, 92

Harvard University, 51, 183, 208, 292, 310, 547; and Alice Methfessel, 435; and the EB papers, 540; EB readings at, 403, 404, 412, 465, 518, 537, 550; EB's teaching job, 428, 429, 432–530 (discussed), 472, 474, 481, 482, 485, 515; and Flavio Soares Regis, 349; Poetry Room, 194; and the Robert Lowell papers, 483, 484, 498; and Suzanne Bowen, 439
Harvard Advocate, 414, 457
Harvard English Institute, 486
Harwichport, Mass., 32, 38, 62
Hasecher, Nora, 157, 162
Havre de Grace, Maryland, 147, 219, 223, 233, 234, 235, 326, 394. *See also* Dewey, Jane
Heaney, Seamus, 437, 545, 547
Hecht, Anthony, 255, 502, 542
Heilman, Robert, 520
Heimert, Alan, 490, 503
Heiss, Cordie, 161, 273
Helfman, Elizabeth, 555n.1
Helzel, Mr. and Mrs., 168
Hemingway, Ernest, 89, 102–3, 116, 150, 151, 156, 352; death of, 341
Hemingway, Pauline (Pfeiffer), 156, 180, 195, 201, 210, 236, 514
Herbert, George, 45, 52–53, 83, 118–19, 144, 192, 290
Herbert, Zbigniew, 521
Herzberg, Judith, 521
Herzberg, Leon, 521
Hiaff, Alexy, 289
Higgenbotham, Elizabeth Bell, 543
Higginson, Harriet, 211, 216
Holiday, Billie, 81, 364
Hollander, John, 484
Homosexuality, 187. *See also* Bishop, Elizabeth: sexuality
Honig, Edward, 255
Hooper, Mrs. (EB's Paris friend), 93, 94
Hopkins, Gerard Manley, 6, 35, 59, 64, 65, 314, 361, 462; influence on EB, 30, 44, 45, 50, 51, 52–54, 55, 76, 81, 92, 122, 496
Houghton Mifflin Co., 187, 287, 289, 316, 321, 331; and *The Diary of Helena Morley,* 257; and EB's short stories,

253; and *North & South*, 174, 178, 179, 180, 184, 188; and *Poems: North & South—A Cold Spring*, 226, 233, 253–54
Hound & Horn, 51
"House that Jack Built, The," 143, 280–81
Howard, Richard, 373, 456
Hudson River, 43
Hudson, W. H., 36
Humble, Cass, 400, 401, 403
Humble, Monica, 402
Humble, Patrick, 400, 401
Humel, Mrs. (EB's neighbor in Rio), 339
Humphrey, Hubert, 406
Huntington, Evelyn, 47
Hussey, Anne, 539
Hutchinson, George, 302, 475
Hutchinson, William, 17

Iguaçu Falls, Brazil 422
Ingram-Merrill Foundation, 423
International Poetry Conference, Rotterdam, 442, 520, 521–22
Ireland, 121, 122, 216. *See also* Bishop, Elizabeth: travels
Italy, 130–33, 210, 226, 233, 349, 355, 359, 541. *See also* Bishop, Elizabeth: travels
Ivask, Ivar, 517

J. W. Bishop Company, 2
Jackson, David, 442, 544
Jacob (mynah bird), 406, 407, 415
Jacob, Max, 225
James, Henry, 43, 49, 74, 89, 341, 455, 484, 485
Jameson, Dr. (EB's psychiatrist), 174
Jarrell, Mackie, 186, 190, 235
Jarrell, Randall, 146, 190, 255; death of, 341, 380; EB visits to, 235, 289; friendship with EB, 186, 292; on Marianne Moore, 70; on *North & South*, 155, 184, 185; as subject in EB's work, 380;
Jefferson, Margo, 527
Jefferson, Thomas, 483, 543
Jewett, Sarah Orne, 548
Joanna (Lota Soares's maid), 351
Johnson, Lyndon, 363

Johnson, Osa and Martin, 26, 80, 445
Johnson, Samuel, 460, 540
Johnson, Thomas H., 237
Jonson, Ben, 80, 91
Jonsrud, Harold, 57, 62
Joplin, Janis, 407, 409

Kafka, Franz, 295
Kalstone, David, 27, 416–17, 452, 453, 474
Kazin, Alfred, 227, 228
Keats, John, 130, 259, 453
Kees, Weldon, 221
Keewaydin (Naples, Florida), 112–16, 118, 139
Kelly, Richard, 361
Kennedy, Barbara (Chesney), 46, 56, 170, 243, 335, 403, 555n.1
Kennedy, Jacqueline, 324, 407
Kennedy, John F., 273, 324, 350, 363
Kennedy, Robert, 407
Kentfield, Calvin, 228, 504
Kenyon Review, 331, 337, 373
Key West, Florida, 62, 116, 134, 135, 173, 174, 182, 194, 200, 201, 203, 401, 406, 513; EB residence there, 138–40, 143–47, 153–60, 161, 162–65, 170–72, 174, 179, 195, 208, 212; EB visits to, 116, 245, 289; as subject in EB's work, 137–39, 141, 155, 158, 159, 165, 175–77, 188, 230, 501
King, Martin Luther, 363; assassination, 407
King, Mrs. (EB's friend in Key West), 153
Kirkland House, 432, 434, 435, 436, 438, 446, 479
Kirkpatrick, Ralph, 81, 82, 165
Kirstein, Lincoln, 51
Kizer, Carolyn, 378
Klee, Paul, 295, 323, 390
Klein, Melanie, 267
Kokoschka, Oskar, 208, 295
Königstein (ship), 86
Kraft, Victor, 235
Krupat, Cynthia (Muser), 164, 372, 526, 528
Kunze, Reiner, 521

466, 474, 494, 534, 544, 545; and EB's prose, 234, 253, 265, 503; first read contracts with EB, 188, 322, 323, 390; EB as poetry critic for, 136, 424, 425, 431

Newfoundland, 62, 472. *See also* Bishop, Elizabeth: travels

Newman, Anne, 518

Newman, Edwin, 453

Newton, David, 234

Nimes, France, 127

Nims, John F., 342, 549

Ninita (friend of Lilli Correia de Araújo), 362

Nixon, Richard M., 406

Norman, Oklahoma, 517

Normandy (ship), 103

North Haven, Maine, 495, 501, 502, 523; EB visits, 62, 495, 496, 502–3, 524–25, 530–31, 540–41, 548–49; as subject in EB's work, 532–33, 538

North Shore Country Day School (Mass.), 30, 31

Nova Scotia, 2, 36, 63, 82, 156, 210, 289, EB visits, 180, 182, 191–94, 230, 438, 466, 471, 498, 529, 547; 472; EB's adult interest in, 1, 252, 315, 316, 348, 357, 540; EB's residence there, 13–19, 24, 28, 29, 62, 263, 428, 452; Indrawn Yes, 234–35, 470; as setting for EB's work, 6–11, 13, 16–19, 36, 60, 90, 149, 194, 235, 258, 264, 267, 287–88, 294, 302, 328, 476; as subject in EB's work, 450, 466, 471

O'Connor, Flannery, 293, 341, 547; death of, 359, 360

O'Donnell, George William, 146

O'Hara, Frank, 310, 341, 380

O'Neill, Eugene, 150

Odets, Clifford, 85; death of, 341

Oklahoma, 519–20, 539

Oklahoma, University of, 481, 482

Olimpio, Seu, 370

Orr, Jack, 62

Orr, Kay, 38, 326

Orr, Nancy, 326

Orr, Ruby, 38

Osser, Maya, 312, 457

Ostroff, Anthony, 400

Ouro Prêto, Brazil, 362, 391, 397, 412, 415, 417, 433, 435, 439, 443, 447, 450, 463, 487; EB visits, 264, 316, 359, 361, 365, 366, 367, 368, 371, 381, 383, 386, 398, 440–42, 443–45, 446, 471–72, 490; EB's residence there, 162, 417–31

Ouro Prêto Arts Festival, 443, 471

Oxford English Dictionary, 548

Page, Barbara, 507

Paratí, Brazil, 316

Paris, France, 81, 89, 130, 198, 220, 243; EB visits, 80, 88–90, 95, 97, 103, 123–27, 128; as setting for EB's works, 125. *See also* Bishop, Elizabeth: travels

Paris Review, 8, 323, 346

Partisan Review, 134; and EB, 136; and EB's poems, 134, 141, 144, 153, 155, 165, 173, 175, 188, 198, 255, 280, 416; and EB's prose, 137, 139, 147

Pascal, Blaise, 118

Patrimonio (Brazilian Historical Preservation Agency), 368

Patterson, Rebecca, 238

Pavese, Cesare, 384

Paz, Marie Jo, 437, 486, 497, 501, 502; friendship with EB, 457, 461, 463, 487, 499, 500

Paz, Octavio, 437, 486, 497, 498, 501, 502, 518; EB correspondence with, 545; friendship with EB, 457, 461, 463, 487, 499, 500; judgments of EB's poetry, 464; "Objects and Apparitions," 519; "Primero Enero," 503

Peace Corps, 273

Pedrick, Jean, 174

Peebles, Rose, 43, 44, 332

Peech, John, 453, 547

PEN Conference, Rio de Janeiro (1960), 315

Penteado, Darcy, 372

Pentecost, Mary, 214, 216, 217

Percy, Walker, 455

Periera, Stella, 398

Perloff, Marjorie, 463

Peru, 316. *See also* Bishop, Elizabeth: travels

Peter Bent Brigham Hospital (Boston), 454–56, 522

Petrópolis, Brazil, 320, 325, 335, 337, 340, 384, 386, 398, 513, 521; EB visits, 243, 397; EB's residence there, 8, 16, 245, 247, 249–320, 419, 421; as setting for EB's work, 304, 306

Pettit, Mrs. Horace, 496, 524, 548

Pfeiffer, Evelyn, 156, 195, 216

Pfeiffer, Virginia, 195, 210, 211, 213, 216, 217, 401

Phi Beta Kappa, 183, 386, 391, 402, 463, 464, 465, 466

Phillips Collection (Washington, D.C.), 219, 227, 529

Picasso, Pablo, 472

Piero della Francesca, 355

Pindar, Mrs. (EB's Key West landlady), 138, 139

Pittsburgh, Penn., 534

Plath, Sylvia, 443, 504; death of, 341

Ploughshares, 503

Poe, Edgar Allan, 37, 208, 547

Poetry (magazine), 108, 109, 122, 184, 207, 225, 248, 270, 322, 337

Poetry Consultant to the Library of Congress, 191, 209, 219, 227, 529

Popa, Vasko, 502

Pope, Alexander, 94

Porter, Katherine Anne, 332

Portugal, 520. *See also* Bishop, Elizabeth: travels

Potter, Beatrix, 356

Pound, Ezra, 81, 105, 194, 199–200, 352, 361, 367, 434; death of, 459, 478; EB visits, 199–200, 220–22, 226; influence on EB, 81, 143; as subject, 143, 280–84, 425

Powers, James, 218

Prentiss, Eleanor, 33, 39, 208

Presbyterian Church, 14, 16

Prohibition, 49, 149, 150

Provence, France, 128

Provincetown, Mass., 140–43

Psychoanalysis, 126

Puerto Rico, 383

Pulitzer Prize, 187, 360, 520. *See also* Bishop, Elizabeth: honors and awards

Quadros, Jânio, 317, 324, 325

Quarterly Review of Literature, 69, 205

Rachewiltz, Walter de, 434

Radcliffe College, 433, 454, 465

Rahv, Philip, 134, 138, 188; death of, 490

Ramos, Donald, 431

Random House, 121, 146

Ransom, John Crowe, 288

Read, Bill, 491, 496, 501; death of, 541

Reagan, Ronald, 407, 414

Reed, Henry, 377, 383, 520

Reich, Celia Bertin, 518, 524, 525, 544

Reich, Jerry, 500, 524, 544

Renoir, Pierre Auguste, 219, 279

Revere, Mass., 28

Rexroth, Kenneth, 208, 417, 425

Rice, Elmer, 315

Rich, Adrienne, 333, 478, 479

Rimbaud, Arthur, 89, 337

Rio de Janeiro, Brazil, 170, 235, 240, 242, 262, 293, 298, 312, 513, 524; EB visits, 243–44, 397, 415, 432, 490; EB's residence there, 319–84; as subject in EB's work, 362–65, 388

Rio São Francisco, Brazil, 385, 500. *See also* Bishop, Elizabeth: travels

Rizzardi, Alfredo, 280

Robbins, Tom, 380

Robinson Crusoe, 62, 447–51, 466

Rochester, University of, 542

Rockefeller Foundation Grant, 441

Rodman, Seldon, 184, 210

Roethke, Bea, 520

Roethke, Theodore, 150, 353, 360, 361, 375, 379, 491, 506, 513; death of, 341

Rome, Italy, 130–31, 132. *See also* Bishop, Elizabeth: travels

Rorem, Ned, 81

Rosenbach Museum and Library (Philadelphia), 423, 478

Rosenberg, Julius and Ethel, 98

Ross, Betty McGowan, 400

Ross, Elizabeth, 321

Ross, Mary (Boomer), 14, 19, 321, 403, 474

Ross, Murray, 400

Rotterdam, 442, 520. *See also* Bishop, Elizabeth: travels

Roughton, Roger, 108

Designer: Steve Renick
Compositor: Impressions, a division
of Edwards Bros.
Text: Adobe Garamond 12/14½
Display: Adobe Garamond
Printer: Edwards Bros.
Binder: Edwards Bros.